NICHOLAS KALDOR

NICHOLAS KALDOR

THE ECONOMICS AND POLITICS
OF CAPITALISM AS A
DYNAMIC SYSTEM

Ferdinando Targetti

CLARENDON PRESS · OXFORD
1992

Oxford University Press, Walton Street, Oxford OX2 6DP
Oxford New York Toronto
Delhi Bombay Calcutta Madras Karachi
Petaling Jaya Singapore Hong Kong Tokyo
Nairobi Dar es Salaam Cape Town
Melbourne Auckland
and associated companies in
Berlin Ibadan

Oxford is a trade mark of Oxford University Press

Published in the United States
by Oxford University Press, New York

Original title: Nicholas Kaldor: Teoria e politica economica diun capitalismo in mutamento
© 1989 Società Editrice Il Mulino, Bologna
© This edn.: Oxford University Press 1992

British Library Cataloguing in Publication Data
Data available

Library of Congress Cataloging in Publication Data
Targetti, Ferdinando.
[Nicholas Kaldor. English]
Nicholas Kaldor : the economics and politics of capitalism as a
dynamic system / Ferdinando Targetti.
p. cm.
Translation of: Nicholas Kaldor.
Includes bibliographical references and index.
1. Kaldor, Nicholas, 1908-1986. 2. Capitalism.
3. Economic policy. I.Title.
HB103. K36T3713 1992 330.12'2—dc20 91- 44582
ISBN 0-19-828348-2

Typeset by Pure Tech Corporation, Pondicherry, India
Printed in Great Britain by
Bookcraft (Bath) Ltd,
Midsomer Norton,
Avon

To Bogna

Foreword

I FIRST became acquainted with Nicholas Kaldor in 1937 when I was spending the year in the dense Keynesian atmosphere of Cambridge University. On frequent occasions, however, I attended classes at the London School of Economics where we met and began a life-long friendship. At the end of the Second World War he served with me in Germany on the staff of the United States Strategic Bombing Survey assessing the effect of the air attacks and reconstructing the performance of the German war economy. In later years we discovered India together, met for many other exercises in mutual instruction, agreement and, more rarely, disagreement. I once suggested that I relied on him to convey my views to the House of Lords of which he was in later years, without close rival, the most distinguished economic voice. I have no doubt that he preferred to offer his own.

This he did to a great and influential circle both in Britain and around the globe (we once made a lecture tour together in Japan). No economist of his generation was in better command of the basic literature of economics and the requisite statistical and theoretical tools of the trade. But that in the case of Kaldor was only the beginning. He saw economic and political life not alone as something to be understood but as something to be improved, made more humane. He was never content with the *status quo* and certainly not the *status quo ante*. He, it must be said, deeply suspected both the motives and the intelligence of those who were. Very often he was right.

I am delighted to offer this brief word of reminiscence and welcome to this volume. It has often been said too casually of others. It can be said truthfully of Nicholas Kaldor: we will not see his like again.

J. K. GALBRAITH

Preface

FROM 1972 to 1974 I was a student at Cambridge and attended the lectures of Nicky Kaldor: economic analysis closely interwove with economic history, as did classical theory with new models and fresh theoretical insights. It was only in 1979 that I came to know him personally when I proposed to him a three-volume Italian edition of his eight books of collected essays. It was then, as I deepened my knowledge of Kaldor's work and during my many conversations with him, that the idea of writing this book began to grow.

The present volume is not a textbook on Kaldorian economics nor the intellectual biography of an economist. It is not a textbook because, although it arranges its subject matter more logically than chronologically, the contents of its individual chapters are organized so as to trace the various stages in the evolution of Kaldor's thought. A biography it is certainly not, nor did I ever intend it to be. Indeed, as I commenced my labours, Kaldor said to me, "I can't see why one wants to write about my life, because there is nothing in it of any great importance. It's my ideas that are interesting." I took him at his word: my book is almost entirely devoted to his ideas, while only the introductory chapter deals with his life.

One of my chief aims in writing this book has been to show the reader how Kaldor "did" economics: his method was the same as Keynes's. Kaldor incorporated the phenomena he was investigating into a theoretical framework; but this he constantly altered to accommodate new facts, novel situations, further problems. He learned his lesson well from Keynes, who, although a connoisseur of the beautiful, never indulged in pure aesthetics when he wrote on economics. Theory is abstraction and theory is indeed important, but raw facts should never be sacrificed on the altar of elegant abstraction. Facts change, they press for attention, they compel new patternings of reality for their interpretation. This, the method of Keynes, was also the method of his great pupil.

In each chapter I have sought not only to expound Kaldor's ideas and to trace their development, but also to describe the debate that invariably followed their publication. On this some chapters go into greater detail than others.

A further aim has been to show that Kaldor was not solely a specialist in restricted areas of his discipline; he had a general vision of the world which led him to investigate almost all aspects of political economy, and in each of these to formulate original and often controversial theories.

As the reader will have noted, two of this book's chapters were not written by myself, although I have discussed their contents at length with their authors to ensure their smooth integration. Chapter 6 describes the debate that followed Pasinetti's extension to Kaldor's theory of distribution. The literature on this subject is now so vast that only an expert can guide us through it. Apart from Professor Pasinetti himself, few others could perform this task so well as Professor Baranzini—who indeed, for many years, has been one of the leading protagonists of the debate itself.

The other chapter not written by myself is Chapter 10. Kaldor's work on taxation ranged from the economics of welfare to the structure of taxation. His selective employment tax, his expenditure tax, his capital-gains tax—to name only the best- known of his proposals—were each given such detailed analysis as to fill an entire book. This mass of material would have proved too much for me, in practicable terms, to provide a thorough exposition of Kaldor's ideas and of the reaction to them by specialists in the field. I therefore again called in an expert, Aldo Chiancone, who, apart from being an outstanding scholar of the subject, was, more than twenty years ago, one of the first to introduce Kaldor's ideas into Italy.

I dedicate this book to my wife Bogna, for her support during my years of work, for her discussions with me on much of its content, for her patient rereading of the manuscript, for having so patiently borne my ill humour in the last four years as I veered so frequently from one field of study to another (Kaldor wrote about everything); and for dealing with so many problems that should have concerned us both, coping on her own because I could think of nothing but 'Kaldor'. I should mention, though, that she also endured these sacrifices because of her great (and reciprocated) liking for Nicky, whose smile and sense of humour reminded her so much of her father.

I must thank two people in particular: Professors Pasinetti and Thirlwall. It was Professor Pasinetti who first gave me the crucial moral support I needed to start off on a road that at the time seemed endless. When the Italian version of this book was almost finished in August 1987 (I only had the conclusions to write), Professor Thirlwall was our guest for a week and let me read the proofs of his book on Kaldor—which I had heard about but never seen. With great generosity he allowed me to supplement my introduction on Kaldor's life with details taken from his book, which, in this respect, is much richer than my own. I thus rewrote the introduction and amplified it considerably. I am further indebted to Professor Thirlwall for having carefully and patiently read the first English draft of my book. Almost all his acute and valuable suggestions for improvements, corrections, and changes have been incorporated into the text.

I wish also to thank Wilfred Beckerman, Robert Boyer, Daniele Checchi, Francis Cripps, Elisabetta de Antoni, Massimo Egidi, Jorge Fodor, Alessandro Foti, Roman Frydman, John Kenneth Galbraith, Richard Goodwin, Augusto Graziani, Geoff Harcourt, Lady Kaldor, Michael Kuczinski, Giorgio Lunghini, Maria Cristina Marcuzzo, Robin Marris, Gianni Nardozzi, Edward Nell, Robert Neild, Carlo Panico, Pascal Petit, Riccardo Parboni, Maurizio Pugno, Alberto Quadrio-Curzio, Lorenzo Rampa, Fabio Ranchetti, Alessandro Roncaglia, Robert Rowthorn, Michele Salvati, Tibor Scitovsky, Ajit Singh, Robert Skidelsky, Paolo Sylos-Labini, Roberto Tamborini, David Vines, Enrico Wolleb, and Maurizio Zenezini for their stimulations, suggestions, and discussions during the years I have dedicated to writing this book. Last but not least, my thanks go to the Department of Economics of the University of Trento for generously providing funds for its publication; and to Adrian Belton for his careful translation into English of the Italian version and of the various changes I made to the text for the English edition.

Note

TRANSLATIONS of works published only in Italian are the author's own unless otherwise stated.

Contents

List of Figures

List of Abbreviations

ACC	*Accountant*
AER	*American Economic Review*
AS	*Asian Studies*
BAN	*Bancaria*
BID	*Bulletin d'Information et de Documentation National* (Bank of Belgium)
BK	The *Banker*
BNLMC	*Banca Nazionale del Lavoro, Moneta e Credito*
BNLQR	*Banca Nazionale del Lavoro, Quarterly Review*
BOIES	*Bulletin of Oxford Institute of Economics and Statistics*
CBI	Confederation of British Industry
CE	*Cuadernos de Economia*
CEMLA	Centro de Estudios Monetarios Latinoamericanos
CEX	*Comercio Exterior*
CH	*Challenge*
CJE	*Cambridge Journal of Economics*
CP	Kaldor, Collected Papers (London, Duckworth, 1960–89), 9 vols.
CR	*Cambridge Review*
DAE	Department of Applied Economics
EA	*Économie Appliquée*
EB	*Econômica Brasileira, Clube de Economistas*
EBLA	*Economic Bulletin for Latin America, Exclusive Secretariat of the Economic Commission for Latin America, United Nations*
EC	*Economica*
ECLA	Economic Commission for Latin America
ECTR	*Econometrica*
EJ	*Economic Journal*
EL	*Eco di Locarno*
EN	*Economic Notes*
ENR	*Energia*
EPW	*Economic and Political Weekly*
ER	*Economic Record*
EWA	*Economic Weekly Annual*
FA	*Foreign Affairs*
FAO	Food and Agricultural Organization
FeD	*Finance and Development*
G	*Guardian*
HBR	*Harvard Business Review*
HMSO	Her Majesty's Stationery Office
ICE	*Información Comercial Española, Revista de Economia, Ministerio de Comercio*
IE	*Investigación Económica*
IEAB	*International Economic Association Bulletin*
ILO	International Labour Office

IMF	International Monetary Fund
IS	*Informazione Svimez*
ISAB	*International Science Association Bulletin*
IST	*Ifo-Studien, Zeitschrift des Ifo Instituts für Wirtschaftsforschung* (Berlin)
It. edn. i	Kaldor, *Equilibrio, distribuzione e crescita*, ed. F. Targetti (Twin, Einaudi, 1984)
It. edn. ii	Kaldor, *Inflazione, moneta e tassazione*, ed. F. Targetti (Twin, Einaudi, 1986)
ITO	International Trade Organization
JES	*Journal of the Economic Society, Hong Kong University*
JMAS	*Journal of Modern African Studies*
JPE	*Journal of Political Economy*
JPKE	*Journal of Post Keynesian Economics*
KCAR	*King's College Annual Report*
LLBR	*Lloyds Bank Review*
LSE	London School of Economics
MA	*Mondo Aperto*
MLR	*Monthly Labor Review, US Dept. of Labor, Bureau of Labor Statistics*
MO	*Mondoperaio*
MS	*Manchester school*
NeN	*New Statesman and Nation*
NIESR	National Institute for Economic and Social Research
NS	*New Statesman*
OEP	*Oxford Economic Papers*
PaE	*Parorama Económico*
PE	*Problèmes Économiques*
PEE	*Politica ed Economia*
QJE	*Quarterly Journal of Economics*
QREB	*Quarterly Review of Economics and Business*
RBE	*Revista Brasileira de Econômia*
RCE	*Revista de Ciencias Económicas*
REA	*Rivista di Economia Agraria*
RES	*Review of Economic Studies*
REST	*Review of Economics and Statistics*
RI	*Rinascita*
RPE	*Rivista di Politica Economica*
SAN	*Sankhya* (The Indian Journal of Statistics)
SJPE	*Scottish Journal of Political Economy*
ST	*The Sunday Times*
TE	*Trimestre Económico* (Fondo de Cultura Económica)
TT	*The Times*
UNCTAD	United Nations Committee on Trade and Development
WG	*Wirtschaft und Gesellschaft, Kammer für Arbeiter und Angestellte für Wien*
ZN	*Zeitschrift für National ökonomie*

Introduction

The Life of Nicholas Kaldor

> Those wonderful words by Poussin at the end of his life:
> 'Je n'ai rien negligé'.
>
> H. von Hofmannsthal, *Il libro degli amici*

1. Childhood

Nicholas Kaldor—throughout his life 'Nicky' to his family, friends, and students—was born in Budapest, one of the great capitals of mid-European culture, on 12 May 1908 and a few years before the end of the Austro-Hungarian Empire.

His father Julius Kaldor was born in 1870 into a Jewish family of humble circumstances. From his small village of Kereny 250 kilometres south of Budapest, he moved to the capital in order to study law. On completing his studies, he worked as a criminal lawyer and then also as a legal consultant to the German Delegation. He thus ensured a comfortable lifestyle for his family and was able to send Nicholas to further his studies abroad, first in Berlin and then in London. He just had time before he died in 1932 to see his son receive his degree at the LSE and join the teaching staff of that prestigious university. Kaldor's mother Joan came from a wealthy Jewish family of businessmen and bankers in Budapest, although just before she married in 1901, her family suffered a series of financial misfortunes.

Nicholas was the youngest of four children. Tragically, his two elder brothers died before he was born, one of fever at the age of 6 months and the other of scarlet fever at the age of 2. The little Nicholas was therefore the only male child in the family and, as the centre of love and attention, enjoyed an extremely happy childhood. His greatest pupil and friend Luigi Pasinetti would write: 'This privileged childhood affected Kaldor's attitudes through his life and may help explain his exuberant, egocentric and undisciplined character.'[1]

Nicholas showed himself to have a lively and enterprising turn of mind even as a child: at 10 years old he published his own children's magazine and at 15 was already giving his parents advice on how to invest on the stock exchange.

---

[1] L. L. Pasinetti, 'Nicholas Kaldor', *International Encyclopedia of the Social Sciences*, biographical suppl. (London, Macmillan, 1979).

2. School and University Studies

Kaldor started school in Budapest when he was 6 years old. Between the ages of 12 and 16 he attended the *mintagynnasium* (model gymnasium), a high school famous for the quality of its teaching and, among its several virtues, was the fact that it was open to children of every class and social background. Many of its pupils went on to illustrious careers: the historian Michael Polanyi, the economist Thomas Balogh, the mathematician Theodor Von Karman, the physicist Eugene Wigner (Nobel Prize in 1963), the atomic scientists Nicholas Kurti (who later emigrated to Oxford), Leo Szillard, and Edward Teller, father of the H-bomb, were all ex-pupils.

When Kaldor passed his high-school examinations a year early in 1924, his father wanted him to enrol in the law faculty at Budapest. The young Nicholas agreed, but then in 1925 persuaded his father to allow him also to study economics at the Humboldt University of Berlin; not only because of the university's reputation as one of the finest in Europe but also because, since childhood, he had been a fluent German speaker. Another factor in Kaldor's decision to go to Berlin was his interest in political economy; an interest, as he would recall many years later, first aroused in him when at the age of 15 he had spent a family holiday at Garmisch-Patenkirchen in the Bavarian Alps and had witnessed at first hand the German hyperinflation of the 1920s.[2]

Although the teaching staff at Humboldt included such distinguished economists as Werner Sombart and Hermann Schumacher (the father of E. F. Schumacher), Kaldor was dissatisfied with the university. He preferred instead to pursue his new activity as the Berlin correspondent of a Hungarian newspaper, with access to the Reichstag and to the Foreign Ministry. It was at this time that his curiosity in England was kindled by his contacts with German students returning from London and with the British citizens he met in the homes of friends. Since lectures were not compulsory at the University of Berlin, in the spring of 1927 he left for London. His original intention was to spend a term at the LSE; in fact, he stayed there for more than twenty years.

In London, too, he devoted more time to journalism than to his studies. Apart fom his work for Hungarian newspapers like the *Magyar Hirlap*, he was now also writing for the British press. He specialized in interviews with well-known British and European personalities, especially literary figures (he interviewed Sir Arthur Conan Doyle). Thanks to his journalism he was able to travel around Europe and to supplement the allowance sent to him from Budapest by his father. In October he decided to enrol for a B.Sc. degree course at the LSE. But he continued to take his examinations at the University of Berlin and in 1929 was awarded his degree there.

The relatively few courses in political economy at the LSE were taught by Hugh Dalton and Allyn Young (John Hicks was a young teaching assistant at

---

[2] N. Kaldor, 'Recollections of an Economist' (1986), repr. in CP ix. 13.

the time). Young was the best-known economist at the LSE, having served as head of the US Treasury delegation to the Versailles Peace Conference in 1919. He came to London from Harvard in 1927 on the invitation of the LSE director, William Beveridge, to succeed Professor Edward Cannan, who had retired the year before. Young was Kaldor's first real teacher of economics, although their relationship was unfortunately a brief one because Young died unexpectedly of pneumonia in the winter of 1928–9 aged 53. Nevertheless Young's teaching and his 1928 article for the British Association for the Advancement of Science[3] had an extraordinary intellectual impact on Kaldor which lasted the rest of his life.

The LSE needed to revitalize its department of economics, something which Young had been unable to do. Dalton's candidate for the job was the young Lionel Robbins from New College, Oxford, where he had taught in 1925–7 after graduating from the LSE in 1923. Despite the opposition of Harold Laski, professor of political science and leader of the left wing at the LSE, Robbins was appointed to the chair when he was only 30. He would stay at LSE for the next fifty years.

Kaldor described Robbins as young and flamboyant, with an enthusiasm that inevitably gathered disciples around him. He was deeply influenced by Von Mises and was a zealous advocate of Continental neo-classical theory, mainly of the Vienna circle. His lectures concentrated on the general equilibrium theory of Walras, the theory of distribution of Wicksell and Wicksteed, and the Austrian theory of capital as set out by Knight in the first half of *Risk, Uncertainty and Profit*. After 1929 Robbins considerably strengthened the teaching staff at the LSE. Among those he appointed were Maurice Allen, Abba Lerner and Ursula Webb (the future Mrs Hicks), Richard Sayers and Evan Durbin, and subsequently Kaldor. In 1931 a professorship was offered to Friedrich von Hayek. At the 1987 Conference on Kaldor at the New school of New York, Tibor Scitovsky told me that it was Kaldor who persuaded Robbins to invite Hayek to deliver the LSE lecture following which Robbins offered him the chair. Visiting professors to LSE in those years were Haberler and Machlup from Vienna; Bresciani-Turroni from Rome; Lindhal, Ohlin, and Frish from Scandinavia; Rothbarth and Emminger from Germany; Kalecki from Poland; Knight and Viner from the United States.

As a student, Kaldor largely neglected his work in his first year but then made rapid progress until he passed his finals with first class honours—a degree awarded that year to only two students. The LSE external examiner at the time was Maurice Dobb—later Kaldor's colleague at Cambridge—who was much impressed by the brilliance of the young candidate.

---

[3] A. A. Young, 'Increasing Returns and Economic Progress', *EJ* (Dec. 1928).

3. The Friendship with von Neumann

After graduating, Kaldor spent various summer vacations in Budapest, where he became a close friend of John von Neumann, the great mathematician. von Neumann had attended a different school (the so-called 'evangelical gymnasium') from Kaldor's and was five years older. Although von Neumann was already well known as one of the most brilliant pupils of the famous Professor Polya of Budapest University, while Kaldor was only a young research student at the LSE, they took a liking to each other and went on long walks together in the Buda hills talking about economics, and in particular about the causes of economic recession. von Neumann was also interested in the theory of capital and growth and asked Kaldor for some basic texts: Kaldor suggested Walras and Wicksell's *Uber Wert, Kapital und Rente*. von Neumann's reading of these texts and his conversations with his young economist-friend had an extraordinary outcome.

In 1935 the great mathematician attended a seminar in Vienna led by Professor Menger (son of the famous economist) and gave a paper, later published in German in 1937, entitled 'About a System of Economic Equations and a Generalization of Brouwer's Fix-Point Theorem'. When translated into English, this paper was massively influential on economic theory and is now regarded as the most formidable paper on mathematical economics ever written. In 1939 Kaldor asked von Neumann—then at Princeton—for his authorization to have the paper translated into English. Von Neumann agreed and Kaldor found a translator: a Czechoslovakian refugee whose mother-tongue was German, with a degree in mathematics and a good knowledge of English. In his spare hours left over from his research in development of the computer, von Neumann revised the text and made relatively few corrections. Kaldor then handed the article to D. Champernowne (the most mathematically minded of the economists he knew), who rewrote it to make it more accessible for less numerate economists.

During the war the two friends saw little of each other. In 1944 von Neumann told Kaldor that he was spending a lot of time at Los Alamos, but without mentioning the purpose of his research. Their last meeting took place at the Walter Reed Hospital in Washington.

Kaldor said of his mathematician friend that he came nearest to genius than any person he had ever met.[4]

4. Lecturer at the LSE

Kaldor's brilliant examination results at the LSE persuaded Robbins and Beveridge to offer him the only research scholarship awarded for the academic

---

[4] N. Kaldor, 'John von Neumann (1903–1957)', (July 1985), pub. in CP ix. 306.

year 1931–2. Kaldor's duties included supervising Robbins's second- and third-year students, while his research concentrated on the problems of the Danubian states (Hungary, Romania, Czechoslovakia, and Yugoslavia) that had arisen from the dissolution of the old Habsburg Empire. This research provided him with the material for his first article in an economics journal,[5] four articles in *The Economist*, and his first letter to *The Times*. (I mention this letter because writing to *The Times* became a passion of Kaldor's: in his lifetime he wrote more than two hundred and sixty!) In these various publications he declared himself in favour of the devaluation of the exchange rate as a remedy for the trade-balance problems of the Danubian countries, instead of the policy of customs protection that they had adopted. In the last years of his life, however, in suggesting a cure for Britain's commercial ills he would take exactly the opposite line.

In 1932 he joined the teaching staff of the LSE, where he would stay until 1947, first as assistant lecturer, then as lecturer and finally as reader. In the early 1930s he was much influenced by Hayek, and in 1931 and 1933 translated two of the Austrian economist's works into English. However, as he pointed out many years later, while working on the translation of Hayek's 1931 article for *Economica*, he began to have serious misgivings about the validity of the Austrian theory, which Hayek's argument did nothing to dispel. This realization of the flaws in the Austrian doctrine prepared the ground for his subsequent easy conversion to Keynesianism.

Among his young colleagues who had either been his fellow-students or his teaching assistants, he was particularly friendly with Thomas Balogh, Tibor Scitovsky, Paul Rosestein Rodan, John Hicks, and Maurice Allen. He had attended high school in Budapest with Balogh and for a short while shared a flat with him in Bloomsbury. Scitovsky was also Hungarian, while Rosestein Rodan was Polish. However, it was Hicks and Allen who exerted the greatest intellectual influence over him in those years.

Hicks had come to the LSE from Oxford in 1926 to take up an assistant lectureship. He was a student and in part a disciple of the Lausanne school, and it was he who first introduced Kaldor to the Swedish economists, in particular to Myrdal's *Monetary Equilibrium* published in German in a collection of articles edited by Hayek. It was this reading of Myrdal that Kaldor later remembered as the second decisive factor in his Keynesian conversion—a conversion that placed him in a difficult position at the LSE, where Keynes, Hawtrey, and Robertson were little taught and the intellectual leadership of Robbins was inimical to Keynes, both ideologically and over economic policy.[6] Hicks and Kaldor lived in neighbouring flats and saw much of each other:

---

[5] Id., 'The Economic Situation of Austria', *HBS* (Oct. 1932).

[6] The group of economic consultants set up by Ramsey MacDonald in 1930 included Keynes, Pigou, and Robertson. Keynes was in favour of customs protection, whereas Robertson was a staunch supporter of free trade and of the 'Treasury view' that public works were useless as a cure for unemployment.

before Kaldor married they even spent their summer holidays together. However, their close friendship did not survive Hicks's departure from the LSE, first to Cambridge, then to Manchester, and finally to Oxford. Yet, as Kaldor later pointed out, their intellectual interests often unexpectedly converged during their subsequent careers.[7]

Kaldor also greatly enjoyed his discussions with Maurice Allen, who had graduated the year before Kaldor at the LSE and was then appointed to a lectureship there. In 1931 Allen moved to Balliol College, Oxford, where on his friend's invitation Kaldor spent numerous weekends. At that time Allen was influenced by the ideas of Robertson and Harrod. His views on employment were therefore to the left of Kaldor's, who was still a follower of Hayek. In later years, however, their positions were reversed: Allen, as consultant to the Bank of England, became a hard-line economic conservative, while Kaldor became one of the most radical of Keynesians.

Kaldor's first important article, 'A Classificatory Note on the Determinateness of Stable Equilibrium', was entirely in the mainstream of neo-classical tradition—although it was precisely over Walrasian equilibrium that his ideas would undergo their most radical evolution in the course of his lifetime. His article was published in the first issue of the *Review of Economic Studies*, the new journal founded by the younger generation of economists at the LSE. Contrary to the pessimism expressed both by Hayek and by Keynes over its chances of success, the *Review* became one of the most prestigious journals of economics in the world. From 1934 to 1940 it was edited by A. Lerner, P. Sweezy, and Ursula Webb. In 1941 Kaldor became chairman of the editorial board, with Ursula Hicks and M. E. A. Bowley as secretaries and Lerner, Sweezy, and O. Lange also on the board. Kaldor remained as chairman until 1960, from which date until 1979 he was editorial consultant.

During his first years at the LSE Kaldor lectured on the problems of the Danubian countries and on 'costs theory', expounding the ideas that Clapham, Sraffa, and Young had set out in the *Economic Journal* during the 1920s. It was in this area that he wrote his first important articles of 1934 and 1935 criticising the long-term increasing supply curve and the theory of imperfect competition (see Chapter 1).

5. Marriage and the Trip to the United States

In 1934 the young Hungarian economist obtained his British citizenship. In December of the same year he married Clarissa Goldschmidt, who was a year younger than him and a brilliant history graduate from Somerville College, Oxford. Clarissa was then working in London at an association for German Jewish refugees founded by her uncle Sir Osmond d'Avidgor-Goldsmid.

---

[7] Id., 'Recollections of an Economist', 17 n. 8.

In the next academic year (1935–6) Kaldor was awarded a Rockerfeller scholarship to study the 'theory of production in relation to the problem of equilibrium of market demand' (the other two scholarship winners were Oskar Lange and Georgescu-Roegen). This gave him the chance to spend his honeymoon in the United States. At Harvard Kaldor met Schumpeter, Chamberlin, Samuelson, Solow, and Sweezy, and he also visited the universities of Columbia, California, and Chicago—where he met Milton Friedman and Jacob Viner. In December 1935 he gave a paper to a conference of the Econometric Society entitled 'Wages Subsidies as a Remedy for Unemployment' which Viner published in the *Journal of Political Economy* (see Chapter 1.6). He also met Henry Simons and Irving Fisher at two other conferences, and from them acquired ideas on taxation which he would later develop in the 1950s.

When Kaldor died, Samuelson wrote a warm letter of sympathy to Clarissa (which she gave me permission to read and part of which I quote from memory) in which he recalled their first meeting at a party given by Schumpeter at the Harvard Faculty Club:

Nicky showed himself to be brilliant on the theory of capital. Until he left this stage behind, Kaldor was the best neo-classical of us all, and we grew up on his great articles in the *Review of Economic Studies, Economica, Economic Journal* and *Econometrica.*

6. The Years of Conversion to Keynesianism

In 1936 Kaldor was back from America for the beginning of the autumn term at the LSE. His teaching duties were increased in 1936–9 and now included not only courses on subjects where his ideas were largely in line with LSE doctrine—equilibrium theory and the theory of capital—but also on more innovative subjects such as Harrod's dynamic theory, Swedish monetary theory, the Keynesian theory of liquidity preference, and the theory of the cycle.

The great economic crisis of those years placed economists under considerable pressure, and Kaldor's reading of the Swedish school's theory of money, his realization of the weaknesses in Hayek's theory of savings, and his discussions with Hicks, Allen, and Abba Lerner (the leading Keynesian at the LSE), mentally prepared him for the impact of Keynes's ideas (he had met Keynes at numerous seminars at the LSE) almost as soon as the *General Theory* was published.

In 1937 Kaldor's ideas on the theory of capital were still very orthodox (see Chapter 1.4): they would only change in 1939 when he had sharpened their critical focus on Hayek (see Chapter 3.1). However, on the relation between money-wages and employment his position now became openly Keynesian following his critical review of Pigou's 1937 article (see Chapter 2.2). As a result of Kaldor's review, the 'Prof.' (as the Cambridge Keynesians had nicknamed Pigou) became a convert to the 'Keynes effect', which he first attributed to Kaldor himself. Kaldor would go on to subject much of Pigou's subsequent work to close and critical scrutiny. Yet, despite this radical on-slaught against Pigou by himself and other young Keynesians, Kaldor always had great personal liking and respect for the old Cambridge professor; a sentiment which he did not feel for Robbins and Hayek, the anti-Keynesians at the LSE—probably (as Scitovsky has suggested to me) because of their differences in social philosophy. Compared with the *laissez-faire* rationalism that ruled at the LSE, Kaldor felt much closer to the egalitarian utilitaranism of the Cambridge professor. And Pigou, for his part, had a sincere admiration for the young and brilliant economist. Many years later, when the old professor had been dead for some time, Kaldor was the first to spring to Pigou's defence (in a letter to *The Times* of 6 June 1979) when he was accused in Richard Deacon's *The British Connection* of being a Soviet spy at Cambridge. Kaldor's sarcastic rejoinder was that it was more probable that he himself had been a Communist infiltrator at the Treasury.

In the period 1937–40 Kaldor's work was now unmistakably Keynesian in other fields: speculation and interest rates (Chapter 2, sections 3–5) and the economic cycle (Chapter 3, sections 4–7). In both these areas his ideas were easily the most lucid and innovative of the time.

7. War Years

In 1938 Kaldor was offered a professorship at Lausanne on Hicks's recom-mendation. He turned it down. At the beginning of the war similar offers were made by various Australian universities, but these too he refused. He was ready to serve in some important capacity in Britain as a civil servant, but in the climate of those years his Hungarian origins excluded him from positions of responsibility and prestige.

He therefore moved with the LSE to Cambridge when it was evacuated to Peterhouse at the beginning of the war. Many members of the LSE took leave to join the war effort in various capacities, including Robertson—who had recently been awarded a professorship—and Robbins—who departed to Whitehall. Apart from his normal teaching duties, which now also included a course on public finance, Kaldor also gave lectures on the problems of the economic management of the war.

As soon as the LSE arrived in Cambridge, Keynes used his influence on the economics faculty for an invitation to be extended to Kaldor to teach a course on the theory of income distribution, for a fee of a hundred pounds. Robbins—probably because his relations with Kaldor had cooled considerably since his ex-pupil's conversion to the ideas of his rival—flew into a rage and objected that Kaldor had been the only member of the LSE to be offered such a privilege, and that it was contrary to the agreement between the two faculties. Once Robbins had left Cambridge for the Army, however, an understanding was reached: the fee would be paid to the director of the LSE, who would then hand it over to Kaldor.

It was thus that Kaldor's name first appeared on the list of the teaching staff at Cambridge. He gave the course from 1941 to 1943 under the title 'Value and Distribution', and his lecture notes provided the material for his entry in the 1948 *Chambers Encyclopedia* on 'Theory of Distribution'—which first sketched out the ideas that he would later develop in his famous articles of the late 1950s (see Chapter 5). Apart from his course on distribution theory, he gave three others on the international economy, on the theory of employment, and on the war economy.

In those years Kaldor's research interests focused mainly on problems of applied economics. Apart from issues concerning taxation and advertising, he was chiefly interested in various aspects of the economic management of the war: war finance; national income accounting; and the problems of post-war reconstruction, particularly social security and full employment (see Chapter 4). On these latter two subjects he wrote two articles with Erwin Rothbarth, who had been one of Kaldor's first students at the LSE and was now a close friend. Rothbarth had graduated with brilliant honours from the LSE in 1936 and had then gone on to Cambridge as a research assistant. When in 1944 he was killed in action in Holland, Kaldor and Champernowne wrote his obituary in the *Economic Journal*. Another of Kaldor's pupils to join the Cambridge faculty (in 1951) was Lazslo Rostas. He too died prematurely, in 1959, and this time it was Kaldor who wrote his obituary in *The Times*.

Kaldor was now not only on the editorial board of the *Review of Economic Studies* but was also a frequent referee for the *Economic Journal* edited by Keynes. Keynes and Kaldor also corresponded voluminously over war finance and national accounting. On several occasions during the war years Keynes and his wife Lydia invited the Kaldors to the Cambridge Arts Theatre, which Keynes had helped to found. Keynes had great personal and intellectual admiration for the young LSE graduate—an admiration already evident in his letters to Kaldor about publication of his critical review of Pigou in the *Economic Journal* in 1937. Further proof of Keynes's esteem is provided by the letter in which he invited Jesus College to consider Kaldor for a fellowship in economics:

I put him very high among the younger economists in the country. Only his alien origin has prevented him from having a government job. I should expect . . . that the Economics Faculty would gladly co-operate with the College in making joint arrangements for him to leave the London school to join us. He is of the calibre which would justify the immediate election to a Readership.[8]

In 1943 Kaldor worked with Beveridge on the writing of his famous report on *Full Employment in a Free Society* (see Chapter 4.3). Kaldor's contribution was an econometric model (of the kind that after the war would enjoy consid-

---

[8] This letter has been brought to my attention by Prof. Thirlwall.

erable popularity) which enabled comparison among the various fiscal policies that could be pursued to achieve full employment. Kaldor's model attracted considerable attention and earned him the reputation of an economist outstandingly able to combine theory with practice. Thus, when John Kenneth Galbraith was placed in charge of the US Strategic Bombing Survey with the task of recruiting economists who—for their professional skill and knowledge of German—could analyse the military and economic effects of the allied bombing campaign against Germany, he appointed Kaldor as head of the planning division. Other gifted economists recruited by Galbraith for the survey included P. Baran, E. Denison, Griffith Johnson, E. F. Schumacher, T. Scitovsky, and P. Sweezy. The research team was installed a few miles outside Frankfurt and each member was given a military rank corresponding to his civilian status and a uniform (without stripes); Kaldor was given the rank of colonel.

In June 1945, while Kaldor was working for the Allied Intelligence Agency in Bavaria, he interviewed General Halder, ex-Chief-of-Staff of the German Army in 1938. Halder told Kaldor that before the war the most important German generals had organized a *putsch* against Hitler because they believed that their army was unready to invade Czechoslovakia and, in general, unready to go to war. The idea was to have Hitler arrested in Berlin. But on the very same day as the planned arrest, Chamberlain announced his trip to Munich and Hitler stayed at Berchtesgaden to receive the British premier. The *putsch* was postponed, and thus perhaps the last chance of averting the Second World War was lost. Kaldor would later have an exchange of opinions on this subject with Dr Otto John and Lord Boothby in the correspondence columns of *The Times* (letters of 10 and 12 August and of 4 and 8 September 1970).

8. Post-War Years

With the end of the war the LSE returned to London. Kaldor, however, continued to live in Cambridge and, despite his heavy teaching load at the LSE, preferred to commute. His relations with the LSE were now in fact deteriorating fast: his promotion to reader was only thanks to Laski's support (whom Kaldor would later say was the only 'left-winger' at the LSE at the time) and in the face of Robbins's campaign against him.

Because of this unhappy atmosphere he undertook a great deal of work outside the LSE. In 1946 he was adviser to the Air Ministry and to the Ministry of Supplies (with the rank of brigadier-general): his brief was to assist the British Bombing Survey Unit in the construction and comparison of the output series of the British and German armaments industries. He was a regular contributor to the *Manchester Guardian* on problems of the war economy, as well as on the problems of the Danubian countries and of Hungarian hyperinflation. In the same year he was invited by the Hungarian Social Democrats—

who were members of their country's coalition government—to help them draw up an economic plan as a counter-proposal to the plan devised by the Communists under Eugene Varga. In little more than a month Kaldor and his team of researchers elaborated a detailed three-year plan that aroused general interest, including that of the Hungarian Communists.

Back in Britain he waged a campaign for the introduction of economic planning and criticized the Labour government, in a series of letters to *The Times* during the first three months of 1947, for their lack of a plan. In the same year, Sir Stafford Cripps became Chancellor of the Exchequer but, despite the government's increased commitment to planning, Kaldor still admonished them for neglecting the external balance and for not targeting exports as an important component in their national plan.

In 1947 he was invited to France by the director of the 'Commissariat Général au Plan' Robert Marjolin, Jean Monnet's chief adviser, to prepare a plan for financial stabilization. The French government wanted to achieve the objective of monetary stability without affecting the country's high level of investment. Kaldor recommended substantial tax reforms which increased revenues in ratio to income by means of duties which both streamlined the system and treated taxpayers fairly. He was helped in the writing of his report by Pierre Uri—with whom he would collaborate in the future on other research studies for the United Nations.

At the beginning of the same year Gunnar Myrdal, Minister of Commerce in the Swedish government and director of the Economic Commission for Europe—a branch of the newly created Economic and Social Council of the United Nations—invited Kaldor to become head of its Planning and Research Division in Geneva. Robbins refused to give Kaldor leave of absence, although this was normally granted in such circumstances. This was the last straw. The LSE's right-wing atmosphere and Robbins's hostility towards him persuaded Kaldor to resign, almost twenty years after he had first joined the LSE as a student, and move to Geneva.

In Geneva his task was to recruit a research group to prepare a report on the economic conditions and prospects of Europe. Kaldor created a first-rate team of economists, outstanding among them being Tibor Barna, Robert Neild, and P. J. Verdoorn. Barna—Hungarian like Kaldor—was an ex-pupil who had helped Kaldor to collect the data for his appendix to Beveridge's book. Neild would become a lifelong friend of Kaldor's, and soon after their work together in Geneva they wrote an article together on the economic aspects of advertising. In 1949 Verdoorn published his well-known article on the factors governing productivity growth. His theory, which was revived and developed by Kaldor in the 1970s, achieved fame as the 'Kaldor–Verdoorn law' (see Chapter 7). The annual reports by the Geneva research group appeared as *A Survey of the Economic Situation and Prospects of Europe*: those relating to 1947 and 1948 were written by Kaldor on his own, at the expense of considerable time and effort.

During his stay in Geneva, Kaldor was invited to join two other committees. At the end of 1948 he acted as 'counsel' to a committee of six non-aligned countries at the UN Security Council meeting in Paris on the restoration of a common currency to Berlin (the Russian condition for lifting the blockade on the city). After listening to the opinions of the four great powers, Kaldor wrote a report in which he recommended that only the 'Eastern mark' should circulate in Berlin, while the 'Western mark' should be withdrawn. The plan fell through, however, because the Soviet blockade was broken by the Berlin airlift—which enabled the Western powers to take over a sector of Berlin (where only the 'Western mark' now circulated) and forced Stalin to lift the blockade unconditionally.

In 1949 Kaldor played a role in the government's decision to devalue the pound. The Chancellor, Sir Stafford Cripps, was in hospital in Zurich, but the situation had deteriorated to such an extent that a decision had to be taken without him. Kaldor left Zurich and travelled to London to advise Hugh Gaitskell and Douglas Jay (on 13 July): they decided that devaluation was the best course of action. In 1950 he continued working with the Labour government and wrote a memorandum on income policy for Cripps (see Chapter 12.5).

In October 1949 Kaldor was invited to serve on a committee of experts appointed by the Secretary-General of the UN, Trigve Lie, and was assigned the task of drawing up a plan that would enable member states to follow full-employment policies. Apart from Kaldor—who alone was appointed on merit—the committee comprised the Americans J. M. Clark from Columbia University and A. Smithies from Harvard; the Australian E. R. Walker, councillor of the Foreign Ministries; and P. Uri from France, economic councillor to the Commissariat Général du Plan. The committee produced a unanimous report ('Report on National and International Measures for Full Employment') written in large part by Kaldor, which, largely thanks to Kaldor's powers of persuasion, was adopted by the United Nations. However, it did not find favour with Washington, and after extensive but futile discussion was shelved. Kaldor continued to collaborate with the United Nations in following years: he was consultant to the FAO in 1952 and to the ECLA in 1956 and 1963.

9. Cambridge

In the years immediately after the war the Cambridge economics faculty lost two of its great masters: Keynes in 1946 and Shove in 1947. The faculty's depleted ranks had to be replenished. King's College (Keynes's college) was also looking for an economist; and a Fellow, Richard Kahn, on Joan Robinson's advice, persuaded the members of the college to offer a fellowship to Kaldor. During his first year in Geneva, Kaldor had already been approached by the provost of King's about a teaching fellowship in the college. He accepted on the condition that his teaching duties did not begin before September 1949, so that he could fulfil his commitments with the United Nations. The provost accepted, the fellowship was awarded in July 1949, and at the beginning of the following year Kaldor returned to academic life in Cambridge.

Meanwhile, the economics faculty (which was still directed by Pigou) appointed him to a lectureship. After only two years Kaldor became reader, but had to wait until 1966 to obtain a chair. This had to be *ad personam* because the two available chairs of economics had in the meantime been assigned to James Meade in 1957 and to Joan Robinson in 1965. Kaldor stayed at Cambridge as professor until 1975 when, having reached retirement age, he was awarded the title of emeritus professor. From 1952 to 1975 he lectured on 'the economics of growth'. Perhaps in recognition of Joan Robinson's advocacy of him for a fellowship, many years later Kaldor would be in turn one of her most zealous supporters for an honorary fellowship at King's, when the college opened its doors to women lecturers and students.

Cambridge is the place where, especially since Keynes, originality and anti-conformism have found their most congenial habitat. It was only to be expected, therefore, that Kaldor would establish a happy and fruitful relationship with the university—a relationship that lasted for the rest of his life and enriched both the man and the institution. When he died, his daughter Mary declared: 'My father felt much more English than Hungarian. He loved Cambridge and he loved King's College.'

At Cambridge Kaldor formed extremely close and long-lasting friendships with Joan Robinson, Richard Kahn, and especially Piero Sraffa. With Joan Robinson and Richard Kahn he created the nucleus of what came to be called the post-Keynesian school (see Chapter 5) and with them dominated the economics faculty for many years. Kaldor's friendship with his three celebrated fellow-economists began in the early 1930s and blossomed during the war years when the Kaldors were evacuated to Cambridge. The intellectual brotherhood among them was sealed when the three Cambridge economists invited Kaldor to join their 'war circus'. Here discussion centred on such topics as the war economy, technical progress, and the reasons for America's greater prosperity compared with Europe. After the war the 'circus' survived for another twenty-five years, during which debate ranged across the theory of capital and the problems of Keynesian macro-economics. It would be called the 'secret seminar' because, with more than a whiff of sectarianism, invitations to join were only extended to select members of the faculty.

For many years the Kaldors, Sraffa, Robinson, and Kahn spent their summer holidays together in the Alps and the Scandinavian mountains: with long walks for the Kaldors and adventurous climbs for the others. At home, for nigh on forty years, their regular Sunday walks from Cambridge to Granchester were part of university folklore.

10. The Friendship with Piero Sraffa

Of his three friends it was to Piero Sraffa that Kaldor felt the closest. 'Piero and I were twin souls', he wrote in the last year of his life.[9] He was tied to the Italian economist not only by bonds of friendship but also by great respect: 'Piero Sraffa was one of the most remarkable personalities in Cambridge during the years (1927–1983) that he spent there.'[10]

Kaldor could not recall when he had first met his friend, only that their first encounter had taken place before the war. Sraffa invited Kaldor to Cambridge for several weekends, during which they would spend entire nights deep in conversation. The friendship grew when the Kaldors transferred to Cambridge during the war. It was then that Sraffa acquired the habit—which would persist until he died—of going every afternoon to Kaldor's house to spend long hours in his friend's company. Their discussions very rarely dealt with economic topics, but concentrated almost entirely on national and international politics. At Kaldor's house, it was said, the two friends spent hours, sometimes whole days, trying to discover what was really hidden behind official declarations on the political and military matters in the news.

An important exception to their rule not to talk about economics occurred during the years of the LSE evacuation to Cambridge. Pigou, then director of the Cambridge faculty, organized a series of lectures on 'The Great Economists'. Each great economist of the past was to be the subject of a public lecture delivered by a scholar especially associated with him. Adam Smith was assigned to C. R. Fay (author of a book on the great Scotsman), Marx of course to Maurice Dobb, Marshall to Guillebaud (his nephew and editor of his works), John Stuart Mill to Gerald Shove, Jevons—a less happy choice—to Joan Robinson and, obviously, David Ricardo to Piero Sraffa, who was editing the collected works of the great British classical economist for the Royal Economic Society. Sraffa, however, suffered from an incurable shyness at speaking in public and tried doggedly to be let off the unwelcome task until, the day before the lecture, Pigou told him that he would be exonerated only if he could find someone to take his place. Sraffa appealed to Kaldor to give the lecture for him, promising that he would help him in its preparation. Thus, Kaldor wrote, 'I went to his room and listened to him for three hours, accumulating enough material for a fully-fledged course on Ricardo, not just one lecture. I took notes and naturally made good use of them. This was one of the rare occasions when Piero talked to me about economics.'[11]

At Cambridge a great number of students from all over the world, but Italians in particular, were taught by Sraffa and Kaldor. Their most outstanding pupil was Luigi Pasinetti, who did more than anyone else—with his teaching at Cambridge and with his research in the field of the theory of

---

[9] N. Kaldor, *Ricordi di un economista*, ed. M. C. Marcuzzo (Milan, Garzanti, 1986), 48.
[10] Id., 'Piero Sraffa (1898–1983)' (1985), repr. in CP ix. 277.
[11] Id., *Ricordi di un economista*, 50.

production and distribution (see Chapter 6)—to conserve and develop the ideas of his two masters.

When Sraffa died in 1983, Kaldor delivered an address in memory of his friend at Trinity College on 12 November.

11. First Assignments as a Tax-Adviser

The report on full employment written by Kaldor (and others) for the United Nations was well received by Hugh Gaitskell, who (in 1950) had succeeded Sir Stafford Cripps as Chancellor of the Exchequer in Attlee's Labour government. In 1951 Gaitskell asked Kaldor to join the Royal Commission on Taxation of Profits and Income. This marked the beginning of a period of Kaldor's life that saw his intense world-wide travel as a tax specialist, his appointment as adviser to Wilson's Labour government, and the culmination of his career with his elevation to the House of Lords.

The Royal Commission—consisting of businessmen; trade-unionists; and two academic economists, Kaldor and John Hicks—first met on 2 January 1951 under the chairmanship of Sir Lionel Cohen and from April 1952 of Lord Radcliffe. During its four years of unstinting work Kaldor acquired a deep knowledge of the British tax system and an unshakeable conviction that it was absurd and unjust—above all because the tax burden varied from person to person according to the type of income earned. He came to believe that the fairest and most efficient system of taxation was a tax on expenditure, i.e. one levied on income when it was spent rather than when it was earned, and also that the cornerstone to fiscal reform should be a tax on capital gains. The commission agreed to consider the latter tax, but rejected the former.

Kaldor admired the personality and working methods of the chairman of the commission; an admiration that was renewed when in 1959 he was asked to submit a memorandum to a committee, again chaired by Lord Radcliffe, on the working of Britain's monetary and financial system (see Chapter 11). However, within the commission, his progressive stance, especially on capital gains, increasingly isolated him from its other members. After two provisional reports which were unanimously approved, the commission produced two further, final reports—one signed by the majority, the other by the minority and called 'Memorandum of Dissent'. This latter was drafted by Kaldor on behalf of himself and two trade-union members of the commission, George Woodcock (who later became general secretary of the Trades Union Congress) and H. L. Bullock.

When published, the minority memorandum provoked the ire of Labour MPs because many of its proposals went beyond the official party programme: British socialism's spiritual leaders on matters fiscal, the Webbs and Hugh Dalton, were opposed to a capital-gains tax. However, Kaldor's ideas were shared by Hugh Gaitskell—himself an economist of note—who after serving as Chancellor of the Exchequer in Attlee's government became leader of the Labour Party in opposition. Thus during the election campaign of 1959 the memorandum's proposals for a capital-gains tax and a distinction between personal and company taxation were written on to the Labour manifesto. After Gaitskell's death, the new Chancellor in the Wilson cabinet, James Callaghan, asked Kaldor to become his special adviser in the drawing up of a general scheme for tax reform.

12. World-Wide Travels as a Tax-Adviser

When the Royal Commission disbanded in 1954, Kaldor devoted his energies to writing a book, *An Expenditure Tax*, published in 1955, in which he developed at length the idea of the expenditure tax that he had unsuccessfully advocated. Professor Thirlwall reminds us that 'the book received wide acclaim. Alan Peacock in the *Manchester Guardian* (23 December 1955) described the book as "one of the most stimulating post-war books on Public Finance". Arnold Haberger, the American public-finance expert praised the book as "one of the best books of the decade in public finance ranking with the classic works of Edgeworth, Pigou, Simons and Vickrey" (*Journal of Political Economy*, February 1958), and Richard Musgrave remarked "the book excels in the high idea-to-page ratio. It makes a splendid contribution to rethinking of the traditional principles of taxation. Like the tracts of old, it may even have an effect on the actual course of legislation" (*American Economic Review*, March 1957).'[12] Kaldor's fame as a tax-adviser spread rapidly throughout both the academic and the political world, and his advice was soon sought by several (mainly developing) countries. As fitting for a great British economist, his first assignment took him to India. In 1956 he was on sabbatical, and this and the following year were among the most fruitful of Kaldor's career: for his ideas not only on the theory of distribution and growth, but also on development and taxation. During the first three months of 1956 he worked in the offices of the Department of Economic Affairs in New Delhi. With the help of department officials he produced a report[13] which contained many of the ideas that he had been elaborating in recent years, as well as new insights developed in those months and which would recur in his subsequent studies of the tax systems of other developing countries.

His premiss was that personal taxation should be based on a tax capability defined by various indicators: not only income, but also capital gains, gifts, and personal expenditure. The definition of tax capability was to be drawn up in a single tax declaration, so that cross-referenced checks could be used to combat

[12] A. P. Thirlwall, 'Kaldor as a Policy Adviser', *CJE* (Mar. 1989).
[13] N. Kaldor, *Indian Tax Reform: Report of a Survey*, (1956), repr. in CP viii; summarized in 'Tax Reform in India' (1958), repr. in CP iii.

tax evasion. Another principle (one that still inspires projects for tax reform today) was that of a broad tax base to which modest tax-rates could be applied.

The year following Kaldor's departure, the Indian Finance Minister Krishnamachari tried to put the English economist's proposals into practice. However, they were subjected to numerous and substantial amendments in the Indian parliament, and when after fierce debate the new tax law was finally passed it bore very little resemblance to Kaldor's original recommendations.

While he was in India, Kaldor was invited to China. He thus had a rare chance to visit a country that at that time was almost entirely inpenetrable to Western visitors. In China he met Mao Tse tung and delivered a lecture at Peking University comparing Marxist and Keynesian theory of growth and development (see Chapter 5.6). He also lectured in several Japanese universities. In June he left for the United States, where he was expected by Tibor Scitovsky at Stanford University. After brief stops in Mexico and Peru, at the end of the month he arrived in Chile. On the invitation of Raul Prebisch, he spent three months in Santiago at the headquarters of the ECLA working on fiscal policy in relation to economic development. During his first weeks he gave a course of about twenty lectures as part of a training programme organized for Latin American economists by the ECLA and the Chilean economist Jorge Ahumada. He delivered further lectures at the end of the year in Brazil, where he attended a meeting of the International Economic Association. The ever-growing interest among Latin American economists in Kaldor's work began in this period. While in Santiago, he wrote a paper on Chile's economic problems which set out a number of ideas that would subsequently move to the centre of Kaldor's thinking on development (on taxation and income distribution, on the relation between agriculture and industry, etc.). They were, however, too unconventional and left wing (e.g. his proposal for increasing domestic saving by taxing the consumption of capitalists) for the ECLA's *Bulletin* to publish, and the paper only appeared three years later in the Mexican journal the *Trimestre Economico*, despite its very high quality. Indeed, Palma and Marcel have recently written: 'It requires a particular quality of genius for a person to be able to visit briefly a country, which has never previously been a subject of his/her investigation, and write in a few weeks one of the most insightful papers about its economic problems that has ever been written.'[14]

When the Indian Prime Minister Pandit Nehru paid an official visit to Ceylon (now Sri Lanka) he described the Kaldor plan to Prime Minister Solomon Bandaranaike. Thus in 1958 Kaldor was invited by the Ceylon government to prepare a report on the reform of the country's system of direct taxation.[15] He went twice to Ceylon and, as in India, worked closely with the

---

[14] J. G. Palma and M. Marcel, 'Kaldor on the "Discreet Charm" of the Chilean Bourgeoisie', *CJE* (Mar. 1989), 265.
[15] N. Kaldor, *Suggestions for a Comprehensive Reform of Direct Taxation in Ceylon* (1958), repr. in CP viii.

committee entrusted with the task of drafting the law. Once again an expenditure tax was a central feature of his proposed reform; but once again the law lapsed soon after it came into effect. In Kaldor's view, the reform's failure in both India and Ceylon was due to the corruption of officials and connivance between the ministries and the minority of the population who would have to bear the brunt of the tax.

In 1959–60 Kaldor was Ford Visiting Research Professor at Berkeley. While in California he received an invitation to Mexico by the country's Minister of Finance, who had read his report on the Indian tax system. The corruption of the Mexican administration left Kaldor undecided as to whether to accept; but, on receiving assurances that he would receive all the assistance he required, and that he could freely publish the results of his work, he decided to go. Nevertheless in Mexico, too, his recommendations for fiscal reform[16] were quietly shelved by the government, although his report had considerable impact on the country's economists.

In 1961 he received urgent requests for his advice from two countries suffering serious crises in their economies and balances of payments: Ghana and British Guiana. Ghana was the first country in Africa, and the second in the British Empire after India, to achieve independence. Kaldor was so fascinated by the personality of Nkrumah, who had led Ghana to independence, that after May 1961 he returned to Accra several times to work closely with the Ministry of Finance on the country's economic problems, although on this occasion he did not write a report. In British Guiana, however, where he was invited by the Ministry of Finance, he did publish his proposals for tax reform in the form of a special report.[17] Both countries needed to re-equilibrate their balance of payments by means of higher taxation both on the incomes of those members of the population who were lucky enough to have a job, and on the profits of the multinational companies, which were using the device of transfer prices among their subsidiaries to hide their profits in 'fiscal havens'. Although the economic problems of the two countries were similar, the differences in their styles of government were enormous. For Kaldor, despite his fascination with Nkrumah, the Ghana government was like a medieval court, 'flamboyant, extravagant and corrupt', whereas the cabinet of Jagan, the Prime Minister of Guiana, reminded him of the elders of a Scottish Presbyterian chapel, honest and puritan, although almost entirely bereft of economic wisdom and experience.

In Ghana, Kaldor's proposals for taxing the multinationals, for compulsory savings, and for administrative reforms to stamp out corruption led to strikes, outbreaks of violence, and such hostility from the ministries that Nkrumah was obliged to abandon Kaldor's consultancy. Ghana's legislation nevertheless still retained some elements of Kaldor's proposed reform, and these would bring benefits to the country's economy in the future. In British Guiana, the January 1962 budget incorporating Kaldor's recommendations provoked

---

[16] Id., 'Report on Mexican Tax Reform' (1960), repr. in CP viii.
[17] Id., 'Proposals for a Reform of Taxation in British Guiana' (1961), pub. in CP viii.

strikes and riots. As in Ghana, the strikes were fomented by the trade unions in order to overthrow a government guilty, according to them, of seeking to tax employed workers; the violence was serious enough to require the intervention of the British Army. Approval of the budget was delayed, but the main reforms came into effect and brought some improvement to the country's financial situation.

In 1962 The Turkish government—taking advantage of an English programme for technical assistance—asked for Kaldor as a tax-consultant (his fame was now rapidly spreading in the Third World). The British Conservative government made no secret of the fact that it would have preferred to send a less controversial economist, but the Turks insisted and obtained Kaldor's services. Turkey was now governed by the Republicans—a relatively progressive party—after a military coup had ousted Menderes's Justice Party two years previously. Turkey's greatest problem was agricultural stagnation, which Kaldor saw as chiefly responsible for its inflation and trade deficit. His proposals[18] hinged on a progressive land tax (see Chapter 9.6): the idea, however, was rejected by the government, despite the support of Prime Minister Ismet Inönü, and despite the mass resignation in protest by the State planning office (the resignations were accepted). This spelt the end to Kaldor's proposed reform and indeed to any kind of agricultural reform in Turkey.

Kaldor was still consultant to the ECLA (headed by Raul Prebisch): this time his paper for the commission on the stabilization of the terms of trades was accepted for publication by its *Bulletin*. Finally, in 1963 Kaldor travelled to Sydney as economic consultant to the Australian Central Bank.

His disillusioning experience in Turkey and after 1964 his intense activity as special adviser to the Chancellor of the Exchequer of the new Labour government in Great Britain kept Kaldor away from the developing countries—with the exceptions of Iran and Venezuela. He was invited to Iran by Prime Minister Hoveyda and, having obtained permission from his superiors (the ministers James Callaghan and Sir William Armstrong), travelled to Tehran in the summer of 1966 to produce, extremely rapidly, a report on the country's economic and fiscal problems.[19] The interesting aspect of his Iranian experience was his discovery of the function in that country performed by corruption. Whereas in India bribery was a vice confined to the administration, in Iran it was the only instrument available to functionaries if they were to levy some sort of tax on the incomes of the well-to-do.

Kaldor's last report on the financial system of a country was written ten years later in Caracas, on the invitation of the Minister of Economic Planning and Co-ordination, Gunesal do Rodriguez.[20] His task was to design a fiscal system which would equip Venezuela to cope with the foreseeable future situation when its fiscal revenues were no longer sufficient to cover its current

---

[18] Id., 'Report on the Turkish Tax System' (1962), pub. in CP viii.
[19] Id., 'Economic and Taxation Problems in Iran' (1966), pub. in CP viii.
[20] Id., 'Observations on Fiscal Reform in Venezuela' (1976), pub. in CP viii.

and capital outlays. The Finance Minister, Hurtado, used Kaldor's suggestions to lay the basis for fiscal reforms that went a good way towards achieving this objective.

13. Economic Adviser to Labour governments: 1964–1976

For many years Kaldor acted as adviser to the National Executive Committee of the Labour Party, and from the 1950s onwards he was a close friend of Hugh Gaitskell—who intended to appoint Kaldor as his adviser should the Labour Party return to power. Gaitskell died in 1963, however, and it was Wilson who won the election of the following year. Nevertheless the new economic leaders of the party, Callaghan and Healey—who had known Kaldor for some time and were aware of their predecessor's wishes—asked him to work with the new government. This was the beginning of the period in which Kaldor served as 'Special Adviser' to three Chancellors of the Exchequer: James Callaghan in 1964–7, Roy Jenkins in 1967–8, and Denis Healey in 1974–6.

The influence of the Cambridge economist on the British government, especially in the early years, was of major importance. After Kaldor's death, his friend and colleague Robert Neild wrote: 'He probably had more influence on policy making than any British political economist since Keynes.'[21]

His appointment as special adviser meant that Kaldor had to give up his seat on the boards of several finance companies.[22] His government duties (at first part time and then full time from 1965) engaged his energies in London for half the week; but he kept his fellowship at King's College and continued to teach at Cambridge.

His work as economic adviser concentrated on two areas: balance of payments and taxation. His advice on the former would be heeded much less than his advice on the latter, however. Wilson's Labour government had inherited a country in full employment but with a balance-of-payments deficit. Ever since the 1950s (see Chapter 4.5), Kaldor had argued that external equilibrium with full employment could only be maintained by fluctuating exchange rates. In the spring of 1963 he again stressed, in an article in *The Times*, that devaluation of the pound was necessary. Although the Treasury was in two minds on the matter, the Bank of England came out strongly against such a move. What is more, even the Labour Party disagreed with Kaldor: the cabinet members who opposed devaluation were Callaghan, Chancellor of the Exchequer, and George Brown, Minister of Economic Affairs. But it was Wilson himself who was most tenaciously hostile to the idea that the new Labour government should be associated with the loss of value of the country's currency. Also Balogh, Wilson's adviser, was against devalu-

---

[21] *Guardian* (2 Oct. 1986).
[22] These were: Investing in Success Equities, Investing in Foreign Growth Stocks, Anglo-Nippon Trust, and Acorn Securities.

ation, and instead recommended the introduction of quantitative import control measures. (Balogh used to accuse Kaldor of being a 'free-trader': because of Kaldor's faith, which he did not share, in exchange-rate adjustment. Kaldor, however, was in favour of both an active policy on the exchange rate and of tighter controls on direct investment overseas.) Pressing for devaluation, though, was the new 'Chief Economic Adviser' to the Treasury, Robert Neild, and as time passed he and Kaldor were joined by an increasing number of those who agreed that devaluation was necessary. In the Labour Party its leading advocates were Roy Jenkins and Kaldor's two best friends in the party, Tony Crosland and Richard Crossman.

Between 1964 and 1967, mainly because of speculative pressure on the pound, Britain's balance-of-payments situation worsened. The government now realized that it could delay devaluation no longer and in November 1967 the decision was taken. Although Kaldor believed that the extent of the devaluation was not enough to revive the country's flagging exports, he was nevertheless optimistic for the future now that the step that he had been urging for years had been taken. The Chancellor of the Exchequer—who had always given his assurances that the government would not devalue—resigned, and his place was taken by Roy Jenkins, the second Chancellor to have Kaldor as his special adviser.

Kaldor's advice was more favourably received in his second area of competence: tax reform. His official title was in fact 'Special Adviser to the Chancellor of the Exchequer on Social and Economic Aspects of Fiscal Policy'. His appointment caused alarm in the City and in sections of the Conservative press, where he was remembered as the writer of the 'Memorandum of Dissent'. It was feared that the new government would act on his advice and use every possible means to harass capitalists. Because Kaldor's Hungarian compatriot Balogh had now been appointed by Harold Wilson as Adviser on Economic Affairs to the cabinet, jokes (sometimes caustic) now began to circulate about the two fearsome Hungarians.[23]

His activities as adviser brought him into frequent contact with the Director-General of the Treasury, William Armstrong, and he worked closely with the same officials with whom he had enjoyed a fruitful relationship during the years of the Royal Commission on Taxation. The civil servants from the Ministry also felt at their ease with Kaldor, both because he treated them with the same attention as he would research students and because every proposal of his, however original, was always amply endowed with the technical instruments necessary to put it into practice.

The 1964 and (especially) 1965 budgets—which Kaldor regarded as the closest approach ever made to a fair tax system in Great Britain—contained a

---

[23] The press dubbed them the 'Hungarian Mafia', 'Terrible Twins', 'B and K' (after Bulganin and Khrushchev). Of the many cartoons lampooning him and Balogh, Kaldor once showed me one from the *Financial Times* which depicted two Treasury officials queuing for lunch in the canteen and complaining that 'goulash' was on the menu again.

number of his proposals, although not all of them would become law. His recommendations for a capital-gains tax and a company tax levied uniformly on profits were, however, taken up. These two measures were a first step towards a more radical reform which Kaldor believed should aim at creating a regular source of revenue from a wealth tax. But, because of opposition from the Treasury and from Callaghan himself (and also from his successor Healey in the next and last Labour government of 1974–9) this was never introduced; and neither was the most innovative part of Kaldor's overall scheme, an expenditure tax. Nevertheless, even in its truncated form, his proposed reform, with its taxes on company profits and on capital gains, reached Parliament. Here, however, the Opposition with the help of some members of the Labour majority managed to blunt the reform's impact; and it was further weakened when the Conservatives returned to power in 1970.

Another absolutely innovative tax, one patently Kaldorian in origin, was the selective employment tax (SET) introduced in September 1966. In his Cambridge inaugural lecture of the same year, delivered when he received his professorship, he had argued that the limit on the economic growth of Great Britain was the shortage of labour supply to the manufacturing sector (see Chapter 7). He recommended that this labour constraint should be relaxed by levying a tax on the services sector and by paying the manufacturing sector a subsidy of an equivalent amount to be divided among firms in proportion to their employment within the sector.

The classification of the types of firms qualifying for subsidies and of those that would pay the tax was drawn up by Wynne Godley, a Treasury official who became a close friend of Kaldor and who, on his recommendation, succeeded Brian Reddaway as director of the DAE at Cambridge. There was no lack of opposition to the tax, on the ground that it was pointless because it would be shifted on to prices. In 1967 Kaldor asked the Treasury to investigate, and the research work was officially assigned to Reddaway, still director of the DAE. Kaldor, however, decided to carry out his own study with the assistance of Christopher Allsopp, Francis Cripps, and Roger Tarling. Although Kaldor criticized Reddaway for having misunderstood the rationale of the tax, the DAE's results did in fact prove Kaldor right: the tax was only shifted to a minor extent. It was therefore not inflationary, significantly increased productivity in the services sector, and also considerably raised government revenue with low administrative costs. For these various reasons Kaldor continued to defend the tax even after its abolition in the 1970s (see Chapter 10).

On Kaldor's suggestion, a year after its introduction, the SET was adopted in modified form as part of regional policy. As Kaldor explained to the Scottish Economic Society in 1970, differentiated subsidies to regions—the so-called Regional Employment Premiums—had the same effect on the regional economy as a devaluation on the national economy.

As already said, after the devaluation of 1967 Roy Jenkins replaced Callaghan at the Treasury. Kaldor stayed on as a special adviser and worked with

Jenkins on the 1968 budget. However, there was a certain amount of friction between the two, and Kaldor decided to leave his post in London and return to full-time teaching in Cambridge, where he was now professor.

In his years of work as a government adviser Kaldor had never given up his research, nor had he abandoned his role as a globe-trotting international lecturer. In 1967 alone he gave lectures in four countries: the Soviet Union, Japan, India, and Israel. He and his team at the Treasury had begun a number of research projects which he now continued at the DAE; summoning several of his ex-Treasury colleagues (including Godley, Cripps, and Tarling) to Cambridge for the purpose. He was now principally interested in the relation between output and productivity, the effect of the SET on the economy, and the relation between the national budget and the trade balance.

However, he only partially reduced his engagements as government economic adviser: in 1969 he became special adviser to Richard Crossman at the Department of Health and Social Security—giving advice and making recommendations on delayed retirement, negative income tax, a guaranteed minimum wage, and pension reform.

From 1970 to 1974 the Conservatives were back in power with Edward Heath, and Kaldor now gave free rein to his passion for writing numerous, pithy letters to *The Times* on the government's performance. But his opposition to Heath was never as radical as his later assault on Mrs Thatcher: his criticisms of the Heath government's anti-inflationary measures were aimed at their method not at their morality. Kaldor had always been a proponent of an incomes policy as the chief weapon against inflation, but in his view such a policy had to be more long lasting and incisive than that proposed by Heath (see Chapter 12).

It was in these years that Kaldor developed his thesis that the balance-of-payments deficit could never be eliminated as long as the national budget was in deficit. This theory, which in fact Kaldor only gave in outline form, took the name of the 'New Cambridge school'—to be attacked by a number of Cambridge economists like Richard Kahn and Michael Posner, and embraced, developed, and publicized by Robert Neild and a good part of the DAE, notably Wynne Godley and Francis Cripps (see Chapter 13.4). This period also saw the beginning of Kaldor's virulent polemic against Britain's membership of the Common Market (see Chapter 13.6).

In 1974 Wilson and the Labour Party won the general election and Kaldor returned to his post of special adviser, this time with Denis Healey, the new Chancellor of the Exchequer. Healey was now Labour's spokesman on economic affairs—after Roy Jenkins had defied party policy and come out in favour of Britain's joining the Common Market. Kaldor continued to enjoy a good working relationship with the Treasury staff and with the Director-General, Sir Douglas Wass, although his relations were not so happy with the Chief Economic Advisers, first Sir Kenneth Berrill and then Sir Bryan Hopkin. He also clashed with the other advisers to the Chancellor—Michael Posner, Andrew Britton, and Hans Leisner—on how to deal with the country's severe

economic problems. Apart from Kaldor's continuing emphasis on re-equilibrating the public sector as a pre-condition for dealing with the problem of
the trade balance, he was now also calling for exchange controls and import
restrictions. His advocacy of import controls would become a new battle-
ground; one which would increasingly engage his energies over the years to
come—with the help, once again, of the DAE (see Chapter 13.5). And, in this
same period, he became more and more critical of the policy of flexible
exchange rates because of their frequently inflationary effects.

Kaldor's proposals on matters of taxation were granted a better hearing than
his recommendations for re-equilibrating the trade balance; even so, his ideas
had less impact on the government's economic policy than they had achieved
in the period 1964–7. Nevertheless, his 1975 proposal for tax exemption on
the revalutions of certain equity assets extended a lifeline to the many firms
which, in years of high inflation, had gone deeply into debt. He also pressed
for the introduction of a capital-transfer tax to replace death duties, and in
1975 the government adopted a scheme of family allowances which he had
been advocating since 1967. Finally, he also recommended reform of the
system of company taxation; a recommendation in line with Treasury thinking
but rejected because of opposition by the CBI. Kaldor's ideas on tax reform,
especially at the macro-economic level, were too radical for Chancellor Healey, who was more inclined to heed the advice of the Bank of England, and
to their mutual relief in August 1976 Kaldor left his last government post.

Two years previously he had received a life peerage, with the title of Baron
of Newnham in the city of Cambridge. I was in Cambridge the day that the
news of his honour arrived, and I remember as he walked through the faculty
that he made no secret of his pleasure. Kaldor was anything but a snob; indeed
he always and unashamedly gave vent to his feelings, and his behaviour was
invariably natural and spontaneous. But one can understand the enormous
satisfaction of the Hungarian emigré on becoming a peer of the realm! His
wife, however—still a Labour Party activist—let it be known in no uncertain
terms that Lady Kaldor would continue to be 'comrade Clarissa' as before.
Thomas Balogh had been awarded a peerage by Harold Wilson shortly before,
and for several years the joke went the rounds that to receive a peerage you
had to be an economist, left wing, and Hungarian.

14. The Last Decade

In the last ten years of his life Kaldor continued to work unceasingly, but he
also found the time to go to the House of Lords to deliver speeches vehemently
critical of the Thatcher governments (see Chapter 13.7). Pure theory still
engaged his intellectual energies, especially in the fields of monetary theory,
the theory of growth, and of equilibrium. His writings on monetarism from
1970 to 1984 were the most radical onslaught on the Chicago school yet

unleashed by the Keynesians (see Chapter 11, sections 3–8). On the theory of growth and equilibrium his critical writings of the early 1970s on the Walrasian equilibrium school opened new avenues for research into the dynamics of the economy (see Chapter 14); an example of which he provided himself with his two-sector model (see Chapter 8), first elaborated in the early 1970s and expounded in his last lectures at Cambridge.

During the very last years of his life he continued to accept invitations to lecture on a wide variety of subjects. Even in 1986, the year of his death, he was still working relentlessly, despite recurrent circulatory problems: he delivered two lectures in Italy, one in Rome and the other in Perugia; two in Finland; one at Oxford; and two in Budapest. Just a few days before he was taken to Papworth Hospital, Cambridge, where he died on 30 September, he was at work on a lecture on Keynes's *General Theory* to be delivered at the University of Freiburg on November 14.

15. Honours

Kaldor was elected honorary member of the Société Économique Royale of Belgium in 1955, member of the British Academy in 1963, chairman of Section F of the British Association for the Advancement of Science in 1970, and in the same year honorary fellow of LSE, president of the Royal Economic Society in 1974, honorary member of the American Economic Association in 1975, and honorary external member of the American Academy of Arts and Sciences. He was also awarded honorary doctorates by the University of Dijon in 1962 and by the University of Frankfurt in 1982. One honour that always eluded Kaldor—despite the fact that few economists of this century have made such a prolific and original contribution to their science—was the Nobel Prize. This, though, is not particularly surprising: all the great economists of Cambridge and of the British Keynesian school (from Sraffa to Kalecki, from Harrod to Lord Kahn and Joan Robinson) have died without recognition from a dull and biased Nobel jury.

16. His Family and his Personality

Nicky, as his daughter Frances remembered during his Memorial Service in King's College Chapel, was a man who 'had a number of unusual characteristics. It was not any one of them singly which made him unique, but rather the combination of brains, self-confidence, honesty, lack of respect for authority, persistence, persuasiveness and charm, which made him a brilliant teacher and a lovely father'.

His family was always very close. His first daughter Catherine was born in 1937, Frances in 1940, Penelope in 1942, and Mary in 1946. Each of his daughters had three children, except for Mary who had two. Kaldor both adored and was extremely proud of his wife, his four daughters, his sons-in-law, and his eleven grandchildren; and he was deeply loved in return. His daughter Frances said of him that he was for all of them 'everything-of-last-resort, always ready to give all kinds of support and advice when asked (and sometimes when not asked)'. At Christmas, and at many other times of the year, the whole family gathered in the large house at 2 Adams Road.

He was an extraordinary teacher, an enthusiast for his work and his subject, ready to listen to the ideas of others but also to defend his own convictions to the utmost, conceding little to his adversaries but ready to write long letters of reply to those who asked for his opinion on economic matters or on his own theories. But he was never so wrapped up in his economics or politics that he did not find time for other interests.

He was throughout his life an *enfant gaté*, first by his family in Budapest and then by his wife and daughters. He was, however, extremely generous: for example (and this I personally can vouch for), he had no hesitation over lending his house in Cambridge to visiting scholars or to a young foreign colleague while he and his family were away for the summer. He had a sharp sense of humour, although he was not always good-tempered: if something annoyed him he said so in no uncertain terms. He was blessed with great vitality, and he knew how to savour the intellectual joys of life as well as those pleasures, like female beauty, good food and drink, not purely of the mind.

His fertility of ideas, his political commitment, and the vigour of his personality came finally, ineluctably, to an end on 30 September 1986.

Chapter 1

Equilibrium, Competition, and Capital Theory

When I was green in judgment.
Shakespeare, *Antony and Cleopatra*

1.1. The First Articles and the Equilibrium Method

After Kaldor's early experiences in journalism his first publications on economics appeared in 1932; and here he revealed his whole-hearted commitment to the doctrines of the Austrian school. These first writings of his were two reviews of German books, each of which dealt with technical progress.

Lederer, professor at the University of Berlin, had argued in his *Technischer Fertschrift und Arbeitslosigkeit* against the prevailing opinion of the time: that technical progress reduced employment in machine-using industries, while it increased employment in equal proportion in industries that produced machines. Lederer believed that the effect of technical progress was to reduce total employment, especially in the presence of rigid wages. In 'A Case against Technical Progress',[1] his first publication on economics, Kaldor criticized Lederer's position on a number of counts—thus showing himself already fully in command of his subject, even though he was at the beginning of his economic studies and only 24 years old at the time. Kaldor based his argument on the distinction between neutral, labour-saving, and capital-saving technical progress, and in doing so quite clearly showed his allegiance to the Austrian school. This distinction, an innovative one for the time, would later become part of the theoretical apparatus of neo-classical economics—precisely the apparatus that Kaldor would try, for the rest of his life, to dismantle.

His next article, a critique of Landauer's book *Planwirtschaft und Verkehrswirtschaft*[2] also dealt with the subject of technical progress. Although Kaldor agreed with Landauer that technical progress reduced the 'social dividend' by accelerating the monopolization of the market economies, he maintained that Landauer's criticisms of capitalism in terms of its allocation of resources were equally applicable to a system of centralized planning. Kaldor's arguments reflected the debate on socialism that was in progress

---

[1] N. Kaldor, 'A Case against Technical Progress', *EC* (May 1932).
[2] Id., Review of C. Landauer, *Planwirtschaft und Verkehrswirtschaft*, *EJ* (June 1932).

during those years—a debate to which the economists of the Austrian school made a major contribution.

The young economist declared his allegiance to the Austrian school in further articles on applied economics. In 1931 he was awarded a scholarship by the LSE and then spent a term at the University of Vienna where he researched the problems of the Danubian states of Austria, Hungary, Czechoslovakia, Romania, and Yugoslavia. Kaldor published four anonymous articles on the subject in *The Economist* (14, 21, 18 May, and 4 June 1932), his first letter in *The Times* (31 March 1932) on the predominance of agriculture in the Danubian states, and an article on the Austrian economy.[3] In this latter article he argued that Austria's economic difficulties of the period 1925–9 stemmed from excessive investment by firms, at a time when the country was unable to reduce its living standards. Kaldor's allegiance to the Austrian school was equally evident in economic policy, where he was a convinced advocate of the *laissez-faire* theories of Hayek and Robbins. In his articles on the Danubian economies he called for the abolition of trade and currency restrictions and proposed the devaluation of the currencies of the states that had arisen out of the dissolution of the old Austro-Hungarian Empire. He also emerged as a free-trader in his polemic against Keynes, who in 'National Self-Sufficiency'[4] had argued that in the twentieth century the advantages deriving from the international division of labour had been largely outweighed by the disadvantages of free trade—and that it was above all because of the free movement of capital that interest rates had risen to levels incompatible with the well-being of countries. Kaldor, in a commentary published in the same periodical as Keynes's article,[5] took the side of free trade. He based his argument on Allyn Young's idea of the advantages, in terms of increasing returns, that an expanding market brought to the national industry. In the last years of his life, however, Kaldor would become a proponent of the protectionist ideas that he was now criticizing, basing his arguments once again on Young's principle.

The first article to bring Kaldor to the forefront among the young economists at the LSE was written in 1933 and published the following year in the *Review of Economic Studies*—the LSE's new journal. I shall not go into details of this article here: it was mainly didactic in purpose and described the conditions for the existence, uniqueness, and stability of equilibrium; an analysis that is today to be found in any text book on micro-economics. Kaldor handled his subject-matter with considerable skill and gave an outstandingly clear exposition of the various definitions of the concept of equilibrium elaborated by the great economists of the past: Walras, Edgeworth, Marshall, and the Austrian school.[6] The article is noteworthy for its lucid exposition of the condi-

---

[3] Id., 'The Economic Situation of Austria', *HBR* (Oct. 1932).

[4] J. M. Keynes, 'National Self-Sufficiency', *NeN* (8 and 15 July 1933).

[5] N. Kaldor, 2 letters to *NeN* (22 July and 5 Aug.).

[6] In this article, Kaldor argued that Edgeworth's method of 'recontracting' and Walras's method of 'tatonnement' were two different ways of achieving the same purpose: preventing exchanges from taking place outside equilibrium values. Detailed examination reveals, however, that ex-

tions of the stability of equilibrium (the greater elasticity of the demand curve compared with the supply curve), and because it was in this article that he first labelled these conditions the 'cobweb theorem'[7]—a term that had first occurred to Kaldor when he was describing the theorem to a seminar at the LSE. The article is also significant for certain methodological aspects which should be commented on, since they and the theory of capital would later undergo radical evolution in Kaldor's thought.

Kaldor was aware that the theory of equilibrium rested on a variety of hypotheses—the invariance of fundamental data (endowments and tastes) and the absence of expectations, for example. However, it was the *method* of equilibrium that he sought to defend; a method which consisted in the construction of a framework of hypotheses from which causal relations could be derived on strictly deductive principles. It was these hypotheses that rendered static equilibrium *determinate*. Research then uncovered further elements which gave renewed indeterminateness to the previous model. The causes of this indeterminateness disappeared when these forces were incorporated into the model by increasing the number of hypotheses. This process was the engine of scientific progress.

As the years passed, however, Kaldor gradually retreated from this position. From the mid-1960s onwards, in fact, he maintained that the Walrasian equilibrium was sterile. Rather than eliminating those hypotheses furthest from reality, it called for new hypotheses which were even more nebulous, purely for the purpose of making the theory more rigorous. The method only led to the discovery of new hypotheses to be incorporated into the theory; hypotheses that were accepted as valid regardless of how well or badly they matched the facts.[8]

Kaldor would always argue that the neo-classical creed obliged its adherents to suppose that, apart from the abstractness of its basic postulates, research proceeded step by step until it freed itself from its scaffolding of unrealistic hypotheses, leaving its basic structure intact. Moreover, as this process unfolds, when the neo-classical economist was asked for his opinion as a political economist on subjects such as unemployment, foreign trade, the effect of taxes or exchange-rate changes, he behaved as if the scaffolding had already been dismantled and as if the theory of general economic equilibrium is now a free-standing structure. Thus conclusions and economic policies taken whole-

changes outside equilibrium are only excluded by Walras's method, and that the two methods only give the same results in special cases. F. Ranchetti, 'Tatonnement, recontracting, mercato ideale e mercato reale: la discussione fra Walras, Bertrand, Edgeworth and Bortkievicz', *Annali della fondazione Luigi Einaudi*, 14 (1980).

[7] The theorem as such had already been formulated a few years previously by H. Schultz, *Der Sinn der Statistischen Nackfragekurven* (Bonn, Schroeder, 1930); U. Ricci, 'Die synthetische Okönomie von Henry Ludwell Moore', *Zeitschrift für Nationalokönomie* (Apr. 1930).

[8] N. Kaldor, 'Marginal Productivity and the Macro-Economic Theories of Distribution: Comment on Samuelson and Modigliari' (1966), repr. in CP v.

sale from the theory were applied to the real world, without any thought as to their adequacy.[9]

The method that Kaldor would instead try conscientiously to follow for the rest of his life was one that drew 'meaningful generalizations about the real world . . . as a result of empirical hypotheses, and not by *a priori* reasoning'.[10]

1.2. Costs and Returns: The Criticism of the Long-Run Competitive Supply Curve

Kaldor began his studies at the LSE in 1927, a year after publication of Sraffa's famous article[11] in the *Economic Journal*. Kaldor did not read Sraffa's article immediately, however, since his first years of study were devoted to the classics of economics (in the broad sense of the term). As a student, Kaldor was greatly impressed by the lectures of Allyn Young, the notes from which he would keep for the rest of his life. He later said that he had known the main outlines of Chamberlin's 1933 book[12] based on his Ph.D. thesis (supervised by Young at Harvard in 1927) even before they were published, because Young had incorporated them into his LSE lectures. Kaldor's first readings as a postgraduate student centred around the proceedings of the symposium on 'Increasing Returns and the Representative Firm' and the articles on this topic published in the *Economic Journal*. He was particularly impressed by the articles by A. Young (December 1928), R. F. Harrod (June 1930 and December 1931), and G. F. Shove (March 1933).

Sraffa had argued in his 1925 article in *Giornale degli economisti*[13] that in the case of partial equilibrium each market must be assumed to be separate from all others; in the sense that any change occurring in one market has no influence on the price of the output sold in other markets. However, this feature is generally incompatible with an industry that produces at increasing or decreasing costs: an increase in the production of an industry producing at increasing or decreasing costs raises or lowers the price of its inputs, and for this phenomenon to be limited to the industry's market, it must totally and exclusively use up its inputs. In Sraffa's words, the Marshallian construct was therefore valid, 'only for the study of that minute class of commodities in the production of which the whole of a factor of production is employed'.[14] But not only must these economies and diseconomies created by the variation in the price of a factor consequent on its greater use be internal to the industry;

---

[9] Id., general introd. to CP, vol. i (2nd edn., 1980), p. x.

[10] Id., introd. to CP i (1st edn., 1960), 3.

[11] P. Sraffa, 'The Laws of Return under Competitive Conditions', *EJ* (Dec. 1926).

[12] E. Chamberlin, *The Theory of Monopolistic Competition* (Cambridge, Mass., Harvard University Press, 1933).

[13] P. Sraffa, 'Sulle relazioni tra costo e quantità prodotta', *Giornale degli economisti e annali di economia*, 2 (1925), repr. in *La rivista trimestrale*, 9 (1964), 177–213.

[14] Id., 'Laws of Return', 539.

they must also be external to the firms that make up that industry. If increasing returns are effectively internal to the firm, this latter may become monopolistic and thus undermine the hypothesis of the competitive market.

In the light of Sraffa's next work,[15] it has been argued[16] that the purpose of his two articles was more to provide a critique of the Marshallian theory of value than to lay the foundations of a new branch of economic theory: imperfect competition. Towards the end of his life, Kaldor wrote:

This paper anticipated many of the important 'discoveries' in economic theory over the next fifty years—though in a somewhat oblique way, so that its true significance was sometimes only appreciated when one arrived at the same conclusions independently after an interval of many years.[17]

And it was thus almost half a century later that Kaldor confessed in a lecture given at Harvard in 1974[18] that when he had argued that constant returns to scale were the fundamental axiom of the Walrasian theory of general equilibrium, he had merely repeated Sraffa's original, long-forgotten, criticism.

Although Kaldor's thought moved independently of the Sraffian objective of laying a new foundation for the theory of value, in his 1934 and early 1935 articles on the equilibrium of the firm[19] and on imperfect competition,[20] he showed rare skill in his critical examination of the subject—without, however, ever relaxing his insistence that what matters is seeking for what is important in practical terms.

In 'The Equilibrium of the Firm' Kaldor employed arguments different from Sraffa's to demonstrate that long-term static equilibrium and the hypothesis of perfect competition are incompatible. In Kaldor's view, the vast literature of those years on the equilibrium of the firm—with contributions by Pigou, Shove, Harrod, Austin, and Joan Robinson in England; Viner, Yntema, and Chamberlin in the United States; Schneider and von Stackelburg in Germany; and Amoroso in Italy—had never correctly interpreted the compatibility between the long-run supply curve and the static analysis of competitive equilibrium. The 'supply curve' (the relation between price and rate of supply in various *industries*), as a counterpart to the demand curve, is an integral part of the Marshallian system. However, this symmetry is not easily proved. The assumption that buyers respond to price stimuli in a certain manner derives from the subjective theory of value. The assumption that sellers do the same must presuppose perfect competition and a definite cost function for each *firm*. Hence, 'it is necessary to analyse the conditions of equilibrium for the indi-

[15] Id., *Production of Commodities by Means of Commodities* (Cambridge, CUP, 1960).

[16] A. Roncaglia, *Sraffa e la teoria dei prezzi* (Bari, Laterza, 1975).

[17] N. Kaldor, 'Recollections of an Economist' (1986), repr. in CP ix. 18.

[18] Id., 'What is Wrong with Economic Theory' (1974), repr. in CP v.

[19] Id., 'The Equilibrium of the Firm' (1934), repr. in CP i.

[20] Id., 'Mrs Robinson's Economics of Imperfect Competition' (1934), repr. in CP i; id., 'Market Imperfections and Excess Capacity' (1935), repr. in CP i; id., 'Professor Chamberlin on Monopolistic and Imperfect Competition' (1938), repr. in CP i.

vidual firms *before* any postulates are made about the supply function of an industry'.[21]

Marshall's solution of the representative firm was rejected by Kaldor as an example of circular thinking: Marshall created the representative firm as a replica of the supply curve and then deduced the supply curve from the representative firm—instead of analysing first the equilibrium conditions for each individual firm and then deriving the equilibrium conditions for an industry: '[e]xplicitly or implicitly the equilibrium of the firm is made dependent upon the equilibrium of the industry rather than the other way round'.[22]

Kaldor's procedure was first to determine the factors that could explain the rise in the costs curve and then to see if these are compatible with the hypothesis of stationary equilibrium and perfect competition. In the short run, certain reproducible factors are assumed to be fixed for a firm; they therefore explain the upward slope of the supply curve. But in the long run, under the hypothesis of perfect competition, all the factors must be freely available to the firm at the given market price. Diseconomies external to the firm and internal to the industry are no use, because they affect all firms to an equal extent. If the market provides the firm with the price of the factors, the optimum combination of factors can be determined, but not the optimum size of the firm. To do this, there must exist one factor that is fixed for the firm (in order to determine its optimum size) and flexible for the industry (under the hypothesis of perfect competition). Marshall identified this factor in entrepreneurship.

Having examined the three functions of the entrepreneur—risk-bearing, supervision, and co-ordination—Kaldor demonstrates that of these only co-ordination has the characteristic of being both fixed and flexible at different levels. Risk-taking can be shared out among a number of people, as witness the growth of the joint-stock company. There is no reason why the supervisor should be a fixed factor, since production and the number of supervisors can be doubled. The co-ordinator, however, is indeed a fixed factor because everything that must by its nature be co-ordinated necessarily passes through a single head or a single team. The thesis that co-ordination sets a limit on firm size was elaborated by E. A. G. Robinson in 1934 and Coase in 1937.[23] Kaldor, however, argued that it is only within the context of firm dynamics that co-ordination problems constitute a genuine limit to firm size. Under truly static conditions the problem of co-ordination vanishes: in the Marshallian conditions of steady state, the manager's only function is supervision, the function of co-ordination becomes a free good, and the size of the firm is once again indeterminate.

---

[21] Id., 'Equilibrium of the Firm', 35.   [22] Ibid. 37.
[23] E. A. G. Robinson, 'The Problem of Management and the Size of the Firm', *EJ* (June 1934); R. H. Coase, 'The Nature of the Firm', *EC* (Nov. 1937), repr. in G. J. Stigler and K. E. Building (eds.), *Readings in Price Theory* (Homewood, Ill., Irwin, 1952).

The scarcity of the entrepreneurial factor might limit the growth of the economy as a whole, but it cannot determine the size of the firm, which, under long-term stationary conditions and in perfect competition, remains indeterminate.

The debate continued for several decades. In the late 1950s a survey of the literature by E. T. Penrose concluded that the task of identifying the fixed factor as the managerial function of co-ordination 'has never been satisfactorily accomplished',[24] thus agreeing with Kaldor that it is only dynamics that set limits on firm size. In the 1960s Williamson attempted to resolve the dilemma by applying his concept of 'bounded rationality'. He maintained that the Kaldor–Robinson controversy could be stated in terms of deterministic versus stochastic equilibrium. 'A steady state is reached in each. But whereas in the former the data are unchanging, in the latter the firm is required to adapt to circumstances which are predictable in the sense that although they occur with stochastic regularity, precise advance knowledge of them is unavailable . . . Coordination in these circumstances is thus essential.' Williamson concluded 'that bounded rationality imposes a quasi-static limitation to firm size through the mechanism of control loss and that growth considerations act mainly to intensify the underlying conditions.'[25]

One notes with interest that although Kaldor was dealing with extremely abstract issues, and although he owed allegiance to a school that was more concerned with pure theory than with empirical matters, he finished his article by asking a wholly practical question: whether the theoretical problem of the indeterminateness of the equilibrium of the firm might not have some relevance to the real problem of the 'instability of capitalism'. He concluded:

When compared with the instabilities due to the monetary system, the rigidities of certain prices and the uncertainty of international trading conditions, the instability caused by the vagaries of the factor 'coordinating ability' must appear insignificant.[26]

1.3. Costs and Returns: Imperfect Competition and Excess Capacity

The theory of imperfect competition was trapped in a blind alley: it was unable to keep analysis at the level of an individual enterprise and unable to extend such analysis to the market as a whole. In a monopoly situation the market of the firm is the same, by definition, as that of the entire industry. In conditions of perfect competition, however, matters are not so simple, and the discussion of the previous section has illustrated the problems involved.

The theory of monopolistic competition was intended to show the way out of the impasse into which Sraffa's criticisms had driven the Marshallian theory

[24] E. T. Penrose, *The Theory of the Growth of the Firm* (Oxford, Basil Blackwell, 1959), 12.

[25] O. E. Williamson, 'Hierarchical Control and Optimum Firm Size', *JPE* (Apr. 1967), repr. in B. S. Yamey (ed.), *Economics of Industrial Structure* (Harmondsworth, Penguin Books Ltd., 1973).

[26] Kaldor, 'Equilibrium of the Firm', 50.

of value. But, in certain respects, the theory complicated the problem rather than simplify it. In a situation of static and long-term perfect competition, the hypothesis of perfect knowledge of the future is a heroic but legitimate one. Here the market-demand curve for a product (which Kaldor called the 'real-demand curve') is very similar to the demand curve imagined by the individual producer. In other words, the price is established by the market. But this hypothesis no longer holds when it is the firm that makes the price. In this circumstance, when the producer makes his price, he must also imagine the reaction to his behaviour by other producers in terms of variations in price and/or product quality. Not only this, he may also find that the price mechanism fails to provide him with all the information he needs to plot the curve. Hence the market-demand curve will be indeterminate—but the indeterminateness of the real-demand curve is not compatible with the equilibrium position if there is no point at which the imaginary-demand curve and the real-demand curve meet.

This state of affairs gives rise to the theoretical possibility that, under conditions of imperfect competition, ignorance can persist through time 'with impunity'. It was because Joan Robinson's book on imperfect competition[27] overlooked the fact that subjective conjecture was one of the independent determinants of equilibrium that Kaldor judged it more a treatise on monopoly than a book about the subject cited on its title-page. In spite of his assertion that this was not to be taken as criticism of the Cambridge economist's work, Kaldor nevertheless declared: 'one almost has the impression that Mrs. Robinson would have written much the same book if Mr. Sraffa's path-breaking article (to which she acknowledges so much debt) had never been written'.[28] And in one of his last published works, Kaldor made the point again when he claimed: 'in five pages Sraffa develops the theory of imperfect competition, which contains much the same reasoning and conclusions as are found (developed of course in much greater detail) in Joan Robinson's book published seven years later, and E. H. Chamberlin's book published at the same time.'[29]

It was for these reasons that Kaldor rejected Chamberlin's hypothesis that every producer had perfect knowledge of the reactions of other producers. Even so, he believed that the Harvard economist's book made an important contribution, specifically because it elaborated the doctrinaire basis of the theory of 'excess capacity'. For Kaldor, this doctrine was valid only in certain circumstances; Chamberlin's opinion, of course, was very different.

I shall now, for simplicity's sake, make use of a diagram to illustrate Chamberlin's theory of monopolistic competition. This will be of help in setting out Kaldor's position and in explaining why he disagreed with Chamberlin.

[27] J. Robinson, *The Economic of Imperfect Competition* (London, Macmillan, 1933).
[28] N. Kaldor, 'Mrs Robinson's Economics', 54.
[29] Id., 'Piero Sraffa (1898–1983)' (1985), repr. in CP ix. 286.

The principal feature of monopolistic competition lies in 'the absence of indifference on the part of the buyers of goods as between the different producers'.[30] This means that a firm has its own customers, tied to it by geographical location, the qualitative characteristics of the product, or its image, or by the sales terms that they receive. Such customers show 'a willingness to pay, if necessary, something extra in order to obtain the goods from a particular firm rather than from any other'.[31] When the firm raises its price, only some of its customers will abandon it for its competitors. These latter produce goods that are not homogeneous with those offered by the firm in question (if they were homogeneous, competition would be perfect), but which have a comparatively higher price elasticity and cross-elasticity (the lesser these elasticities are for the firm, the closer monopoly is approached).

Product differentiation enables each firm to be a price maker and to have its own downward-sloping demand curve (Figure 1.1, curve d_s). The more elastic this curve, the more the situation approaches perfect competition. If the demand curve (and therefore average revenue) is not flat (as it would be in perfect competition) but slopes downwards, then the marginal-revenue curve will also slope downwards and more steeply than the demand curve (curve MR_s). The firm's average- and marginal-cost curves (which Chamberlin hypothesized as equal to those of all other competing firms) are represented by curves AC and MC. The principle of profit maximization induces the firm to produce that output q_s at which the marginal revenue is equal to the marginal cost (at ES). In the short run, there is no reason why—given the demand curve—the firm should not sell this output at a price p_s higher than average costs AC_s and therefore at a profit.

This situation tends to change, however, because opportunities for profit encourage other firms to enter the market until the profit is eliminated. The entry of new firms on the one hand pushes the firm's demand curve to the left (from d_s to d_l) and, on the other, increases the average costs for every firm (a shift upwards to the left along AC), in a continuous process until the demand curve becomes a tangent to the average-cost curve. In this equilibrium situation, not only does marginal revenue equal marginal cost (at point E_l), but also price p_l is equal to average cost (at point E_l'); the profit therefore disappears. However, this long-run equilibrium differs from long-run competitive equilibrium in that the average cost, and therefore the price, stays higher than the marginal cost ($MR = MC < AC = p_l$) while in the case of long-run competitive equilibrium (E_C) all four values are equal ($MR = MC = AC = p_l$).

Compared with perfect competition, therefore, a situation of monopolistic competition is characterized by a higher equilibrium price and lower output. This is because there are too many firms of too small a size: the very same process that led towards long-run equilibrium has induced the entry of new firms and increased the average costs per unit of all firms. Each firm therefore

[30] Sraffa, 'Laws of Return under Competitive Conditions', 544.   [31] Ibid. 545.

FIG. 1.1 Prices and output equilibrium of a firm in monopolistic competition

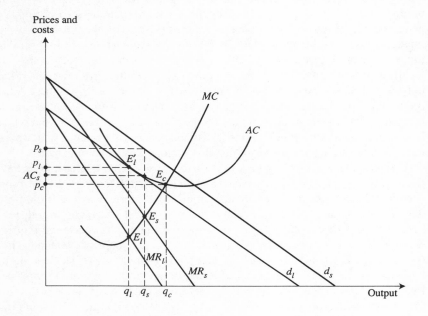

operates at a sub-optimum level with an 'excess capacity' $(q_c - q_l)$ measured by the difference between the potential output of competitive equilibrium and the effective equilibrium output of monopolistic competition.

The theory of 'excess capacity' had social implications that became a matter of considerable controversy. Its principal consequence was the 'conflict'—excluded by *laissez-faire* orthodoxy—arising between the goal of *freedom*, which is the freedom of firms to enter the market and of consumers to be able to choose among a wider range of alternative goods, and the goal of *allocative efficiency*, which would instead be achieved by a smaller number of firms (and therefore with a narrower range of alternative goods) producing at lower unitary costs. Kaldor put it as follows:

It is a highly ingenious and one might almost say revolutionary doctrine: it shows up 'free competition' (i.e. the freedom of entry into any trade or industry) not in the traditional and respectable role as the eliminator of the unfit but in the much more dubious role as the creator of excess capacity. It affords an excellent theoretical background for the age-old cry of business-men about the 'wastes of competition'—so far completely neglected by economists.[32]

---

[32] Kaldor, 'Market Imperfection and Excess Capacity', 65.

Although Kaldor disputed neither the doctrine's reasoning[33] nor the unorthodoxy of its consequences, he detected several weaknesses in the assumptions on which it was based. First, he extended to Chamberlin the criticisms he had made of Joan Robinson's book three years before: it is arbitrary to suppose that an individual producer can know the demand curve for his product (constructed on the hypothesis that other firms produce partially substitutable goods) if he is unaware of the reaction of his (existing and potential) competitors whenever he adjusts his price. Second, the outcome of the theory depended on a certain number of restrictive hypotheses—the absence of joint production, for example. But Kaldor's chief criticism turned on the notion of indivisibility.

Kaldor argued, and Chamberlin[34] denied, that in the case of perfect divisibility, and therefore in the absence of economies of scale, the free forces of the market will necessarily lead to perfect competition. With perfect divisibility the marginal-costs curve and the average-costs curve (curves MC and AC in Figure 1.2) would flatten and coincide. In addition, according to Kaldor, the entry of new firms would not only shift the demand curve to the left; it would also make it flatter (from d_0 to d_1 in Figure 1.2).[35] In fact, although on the one hand it is possible to have intense competition even with lower elasticity of the demand curve (should the competition operate in an area other than that of prices), on the other, a greater number of firms entering the market and bringing more competitive prices would undoubtedly make the demand curve more elastic for each firm.

It is therefore clear that if perfect divisibility and free entry exist, firms will become increasingly smaller in size and increasingly larger in number. However, unlike the case of monopolistic competition, the forces pushing towards long-run equilibrium tend to reduce the difference between price and marginal cost to zero, thus bringing the system to a situation of perfect competition.

With indivisibility and economies of scale, however, the inflow of new firms on to the market will stop before the point where the demand elasticities of individual firms become infinite, because of the movement along the average-costs curve due to the entry of the new firms. But there is no reason to suppose that this process will stop at exactly that point where the demand and cost curves are tangential: indeed, the indivisibility hypothesized of costs can be easily extended to the size of the firms entering the market. Hence, for example, one may have a market where price is consistently above the average cost of the two existing producers, the interpolation of a third producer being

[33] There is one point in Kaldor's exposition of this doctrine that strikes me as mistaken. He states that 'The effect of the entry of new competitors will not necessarily reduce the *price* of existing products; it may even raise them' (ibid., italics mine). In point of fact, in Fig. 1.1. the shift to the left of the demand curve raises *costs*; it cannot raise prices.

[34] E. Chamberlin, 'Monopolistic or Imperfect Competition', *QJE* (Aug. 1937).

[35] Chamberlin disputed this assertion in 'Monopolistic or Imperfect Competition', on the basis of three arguments which Kaldor then criticized in 'Professor Chamberlin on Monopolistic and Imperfect Competition', 84–7.

precluded by the fact that average costs will rise above the price and bring losses for all those concerned. In this case, anybody already in the market enjoys an advantage purely by virtue of being first.

FIG. 1.2 The equilibrium of the firm with perfect divisibility

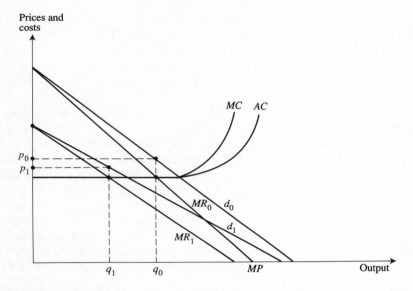

Kaldor maintained that the only difference between these two doctrines—Joan Robinson's 'imperfect competition' and Chamberlin's 'monopolistic competition'—was the side of the Atlantic on which they were born (Chamberlin, of course, did not agree). One possible justification for the difference in terminology might be that the former expression refers to the economic factors that set limits on competition and therefore the presence of indivisibility, while the latter refers to those institutional factors that limit the entry of new firms on to the market. Each of these phenomena is individually responsible for a reduction in the amount of competition. The restriction or limitation of competition in the real world is the outcome of the joint operation of these two limiting cases.

I have dwelt at some length on Kaldor's ideas concerning imperfect competition—not so much because of their importance in his immediately subsequent work, but because of the significance they would acquire much later on in his intellectual career. Kaldor himself once told me that, accustomed as he was to the separation between theories of value (i.e. of relative prices) and of the price level, in the years following these writings he kept the theories of imperfect competition and of effective demand distinct. As we shall see in the next chapter, Kaldor did *not* connect his theory of indivisibility as the cause of excess capacity with the Keynesian theory of wages and employment. If he had done so, he would have realized then and not many years later (see

Chapter 14) that not only is there no inverse relation—in a closed market—between money-wages and employment, but also that there is none between real wages and employment.

1.4. On the Austrian Theory of Capital

In this century there have been three periods, at thirty-year intervals, in which the theory of capital has been at the centre of violent controversy. The first decade of the century witnessed the clash between J. B. Clark and E. Böhm-Bawerk. The 1930s saw the dispute between the opponents of the Austrian theory of capital, F. H. Knight, R. Nurske, and many others, and the defenders of the theory, led by F. Machlup and F. A. von Hayek. Then in the 1960s the controversy erupted again, this time ranging the Cambridge (England) post-Keynesians, opponents of the neo-classical theory of capital and distribution, against the Cambridge (Massachusetts) neo-Keynesians, defenders of the neo-classical orthodoxy.

Kaldor joined the second and third rounds of the controversy, but on completely different sides. It was in this area, in fact, that his ideas underwent their most marked metamorphosis. In truth, Kaldor only intervened in the debate on the theory of capital in the strict sense of the term and as a defender of the Austrian position in 1937. After that he radically changed his mind on the relation between the distribution of income and choice of techniques (or degree of indirectness of the productive process), and seriously doubted whether economic theory could move any further along a road which he came increasingly to believe was a blind alley.

The instability of capitalism during the 1930s prompted many economists to make careful re-examination of not a few of their basic assumptions, prominent among which was the notion of 'average period of production'. Knight, in numerous articles published between 1933 and 1936, contested the view that this concept was a relevant tool for analysis of industrial fluctuations. In contrast with the Austrian school, Knight's theory treated the capital factor as indistinguishable from the primary factors of labour and land. Moreover, the accumulation of capital did not lead to more indirectly capitalist methods; the quantity of capital and the average period of production were therefore not necessarily correlated. This, however, did not entail rejection of the more general of the neo-classical theses, which held that the returns on a factor decreased as the utilized quantity of it increased. In Knight's opinion, there was no need to resort to the average period of production as a means for measuring capital, since the interest rate could be calculated as the discount rate that equalizes the actual value of future returns on an investment with the cost of production of the investment itself. The returns on capital with increasing accumulation do not decrease because of the substitutability effect among factors accomplished by the producer, as required by the Austrian school, but because of the effect of substitutability among products accomplished by the consumer. As investment grows, the supply of the products increases, and therefore—the demand function remaining equal—their prices, the profit on the flow of sales, and the discount rate on the future yield of the capital good all fall.[36]

In his criticism of Knight[37] and in his rejoinder[38] to Knight's reply,[39] Kaldor was aware of the difficulties involved in measuring capital as a productive factor. He also acknowledged that it was difficult to apply the Austrian concept of the average period of production if there existed more than one original productive factor (land or labour) and/or if there existed more than one good produced. However, he did not endorse Knight's criticism of the Austrian theory: in his view, the average period of production was the only analytical tool by which, through the homogenizing of physically heterogeneous capital goods, it was possible to express the production function in just two variables—labour and waiting period—and have the rate of interest (which is the price of waiting) reflect the intensity of the use of the capital factor. Kaldor maintained that the inevitable conclusion to be drawn from the Austrian theory was the principle that

So long as the quantity of annual labour service remains constant with variations in the quantity of capital . . . there will be a unique correlation between the rate of interest and the amount of labour input by unit of final output,[40]

i.e. between the rate of return on capital and labour productivity.

Twenty-three years later Kaldor declared that he no longer believed in the existence of this 'unique correlation'; and that labour productivity and the capital/labour ratio had nothing to say about the rate of return on capital—which can only be deduced once one knows the rate of growth in labour productivity and the propensities to consume of profit- and wage-earners.[41]

Despite Kaldor's subsequent disowning of the ideas that he had expressed in this article, its final section is nevertheless of some interest for its development of the idea of the particular case of a 'capitalist-slave' economy, where

---

[36] The Cambridge critique of the 1960s of the neo-classical theory of capital would be much more radical than the criticisms set out here—and aimed against them as well. In fact, for Knight, the cost of production of an investment was given by the remuneration of the 'productive agents' employed in different periods of time for production of the investment. Since these productive agents comprised not only original factors, but other capital goods as well, it followed that Knight's theory for determining the rate of interest on capital was caught in an insoluble dilemma: either the interest rate was calculated in relation to the *value* of the capital productive agent, and thus the argument was circular, or the capital goods were physically specified, in which case there was no guarantee of the necessary uniformity of the interest rate on heterogeneous capital goods. See, for criticism of Knight, P. A. Garegnani, *Il capitale nelle teorie della distribuzione* (Milan, Giuffrè, 1960), app. F.

[37] N. Kaldor, 'The Recent Controversy on the Theory of Capital' (1937), repr. in CP i.

[38] Id., 'Addendum: A Rejoinder to Professor Knight', *ECTA* (Apr. 1938).

[39] F. H. Knight, 'On the Theory of Capital: In Reply to Mr Kaldor', *ECTA* (Jan. 1938).

[40] Kaldor, 'Recent Controversy on the Theory of Capital', 184–5.

[41] Id., introd. to CP i (1st edn.), 7.

all the goods produced are capital goods, and wages and consumption are zero. In the general case in which labour is an independent variable, the distribution of income is determinable—according to the theory of Böhm-Bawerk and Wicksell—in terms of marginal substitutability among factors. But in the particular case of a slave economy, the rate of interest is equivalent, within a particular unit of time, to the rate of capital accumulation, which, on the model's assumptions, is equal to the system's maximum rate of growth. This theory was very similar to the one expounded by von Neumann in his celebrated article published the year after Kaldor's. The great mathematician arrived at his conclusions by a route very different from his economist-friend's although Kaldor did not exclude (in a private conversation with the present writer, but only with vague recollection) that they may have influenced each other in their discussions of economics in Budapest during the early 1930s.

1.5. On Interpersonal Comparisions of Utility

Even though it places chronological sequence under a certain amount of strain, we may say that this phase of Kaldor's not strictly 'Keynesian' studies also comprises his work on welfare economics and on a wages policy for full employment.

In the 1920s welfare economics were dominated by Pigou's utilitarian theories, a central strut of which was the egalitarian principle that

Any cause which increases the absolute share of real income in the hands of the poor, provided that it does not lead to a contraction in the size of the national dividend from any point of view, will, in general, increase economic welfare.[42]

Under this principle it was not necessary to suppose that utility was open to cardinal measurement, only to accept the postulate of diminishing marginal utility, on the presupposition that human beings have equal capacities for satisfaction. At the end of the 1930s this essential component in Pigou's theory came under attack from Robbins. Briefly, Robbins argued that economists were unable to pronounce on value-judgements, in that economics has no inherent set of obligatory principles that it can apply in practice. For example, one may agree that economic subjects in similar conditions have equal capacities for satisfaction on equal incomes, but one cannot prove that this assumption is based on any scientifically verifiable fact. The inevitable conclusion, therefore, is that no interpersonal comparison of utility can be scientifically justified.[43] Such scepticism ruled out not only Pigouvian utilitarian precepts, but also all the chief principles held by economists at the time—for example, the superiority of competition over monopoly or of free trade over monopoly.

---

[42] A. C. Pigou, *The Economics of Welfare* (London, Macmillan, 1921), 91.

[43] L. Robbins, *An Essay on the Nature and Significance of Economic Science* (London, Macmillan, 1932).

This outcome also troubled Harrod, who wrote: 'If the incomparability of utility to different individuals is strictly pressed, not only are the prescriptions of the welfare school ruled out, but all prescriptions whatever. The economist as an adviser is completely stultified . . .'.[44]

Kaldor regarded Robbins's argument both as arid and as implicitly supporting the most extreme form of *laissez-faire*. He countered with his 'compensation test' described in the celebrated article of 1939.[45] This short work represents one of the earliest attempts to solve the problem of interpersonal comparisons of utility: how to assess policy measures which improve the economic conditions of some but worsen the conditions of others. Kaldor's proposal, which was substantially based on common sense, had a famous precedent in a similar device used by Barone at the beginning of the century to define the situation of the 'maximum' (one would nowadays say 'optimality') of perfect competition. Barone wrote:

'Maximum' signifies . . . that one cannot . . . improve the conditions of all by substituting one or more conditions; indeed if anyone gains an advantage by this substitution, his advantage is less than the loss of anyone who suffers because of it.[46]

Kaldor's argument ran as follows:

In all cases, therefore, where a certain policy leads to an increase in physical productivity, and thus of aggregate real income, the economist's case for the policy is quite unaffected by the question of the comparability of individual satisfactions; since in all such cases it is *possible* to make everybody better off than before, or at any rate to make some people better off without making anybody worse off. There is no need for the economist to prove—as indeed he never could prove—that as a result of the adoption of a certain measure nobody in the community is going to suffer. In order to establish his case, it is quite sufficient for him to show that even if all those who suffer as a result are compensated for their loss, the rest of the community will be better off than before.[47]

But Kaldor was quick to caution that the economist lacks criteria with which to judge different schemes for the distribution of incomes and, consequently, assess the enrichment or impoverishment of different individuals and social groups. The crucial point in his argument is that when the production of wealth increases, some distribution of incomes can certainly be found which improves the situation of some without significantly worsening the situation of anybody. If the increase in wealth brought by a particular measure is sufficient to compensate any loss and to ensure a residual advantage, this measure when implemented will be unanimously agreed to.

[44] R. Harrod, 'Scope and Methods of Economics', *EJ* (Nov. 1938), 397.

[45] N. Kaldor, 'Welfare Propositions in Economics and Interpersonal Comparisons of Utility' (1939), repr. in CP i.

[46] E. Barone, 'The Ministry of Production in a Collectivist State', in F. Hayek (ed.), *Collectivist Economic Planning* (London, Routledge & Kegan Paul, 1936).

[47] Kaldor, 'Welfare Propositions in Economics', 144–5 (Kaldor's emphasis).

The prolific literature that followed Kaldor's brief article took the title of 'New Welfare Economics'. Not only was it of considerable theoretical importance, but its close relevance to post-war cost-benefit analysis gave it great practical impact. Here I can only deal with the main developments in the ten-year debate that followed its publication.

As we have seen, Kaldor did not argue that those who suffered a loss because of a certain policy measure should be *effectively* compensated. J. R. Hicks, in an article also published in 1939,[48] after restating Kaldor's general position, maintained that the economist *qua* scientist cannot decide whether compensation should *always* be made: decisions on such matters involve distribution—over which no identity of interests can exist and to which, therefore, no generally accepted principle can apply. This was also Kaldor's view. In general, however, Hicks was in favour of policy measures that increase aggregate income to the extent that he regarded distributive problems as being of strictly secondary importance, especially considering the practical difficulties involved in paying compensation.

In an essay of 1941,[49] also on the topic of potential compensation, Scitovsky pointed out an asymmetry in Kaldor's and Hicks's criterion. Once a certain measure has been introduced, he noted, and after gains have been calculated as largely outweighing losses, it might be the case that those worse off could compensate those better off with a residual gain. This outcome, which took the name of 'Scitovsky's paradox'—i.e. that both the situation before the introduction of the measure and the situation after it are equally preferable and for the same reasons—follows from the unilaterality of the Kaldor–Hicks criterion, which, according to Scitovsky, 'attributes undue importance to the particular distribution of welfare obtaining before the contemplated change'.[50] To overcome the problem, therefore, it was necessary first to ensure that a measure increased productive efficiency to the extent that those who gained could compensate those who suffered; and, second, that those who suffered could not compensate those who gained in a way that made the initial status quo preferable. In other words, the new situation should be better than the old one when the test was applied to the previous distribution of incomes; and the old situation should be worse than the new one when the test was applied to the present distribution of incomes.

The next major contribution to the debate was Baumol's article of 1946,[51] which argued that Kaldor's criterion was inadequate to define an optimal situation if in the context altered by the new welfare measure, the community, although now more efficient according to the Kaldor–Scitovsky principle, found itself with a distribution of incomes that made it worse off than before

---

[48] J. R. Hicks, 'The Foundations of Welfare Economics', *EJ* (Dec. 1939).
[49] T. Scitovsky, 'A Note on Welfare Propositions in Economics', *RES* (Nov. 1941).
[50] Ibid. 88.
[51] W. Baumol, 'Community Indifference', *RES* 1 (1946).

in terms of some general precept—such as, for example, the principle of equality. Baumol's criticism was followed by Little's[52] similarly argued but more general attack on the whole of New Welfare Economics. Little showed that it was not enough to ensure the potential superiority of one situation rather than another when it came to taking concrete action. In this event, the separation between efficiency, represented by the increase in wealth, and distribution was unacceptable: they were, in fact, inseparable.

In his reply to Baumol,[53] Kaldor agreed that the case might arise where, although a measure fulfilled the compensation test by securing the different distribution of incomes, it was only preferable to other arrangements on the basis of value-judgements.[54] In other words, different distributive situations could be classified in order of preference only when the social-welfare function was known. Modern welfare economics, which addresses the problem of this function's definability, has its roots in the debate of the 1930s and 1940s.

I shall go no further in my reconstruction.[55] Kaldor himself—perhaps aware that the level of abstraction at which the debate was conducted was about to lead it into a cul-de-sac—had only this brief further comment to add:

In the light of this subsequent work I feel, however, that it would have been wiser to have protected the 'scientific status' of Ricardo, Cobden and the many other opponents of the Corn Laws by suggesting that in their capacity as 'economists *qua* economists' they should have recommended that actual compensation be paid to the landlords . . . For none of the strictures of Scitovsky, Samuelson, Arrow, Little et al. against the validity or sufficiency of compensation tests alters the fact that repealing the Corn Laws *and* compensating the landlords was in every way a preferable alternative to leaving the Corn Laws 'in being'.[56]

I must, however, make brief mention of another contribution to welfare economics made by Kaldor during the 1940s, this time on the optimum tariff and the terms of trade. At issue was whether an improvement in a country's terms of trade consequent on the imposition of a tariff could compensate for the smaller volume of trade that resulted from it; a problem that Edgeworth and Bickerdike had examined at the beginning of the century. Kaldor showed that a system of import duties improved the position of the country imposing

[52] I. M. D. Little, *A Critique of Welfare Economics* (London, OUP, 1950).

[53] N. Kaldor, 'A Note on W. J. Baumol's Community Indifference', *RES* 14:1 (1946–7).

[54] Kaldor's compensation test has recently been revived as a test used only to assess economic efficiency, which should be valid '*without* the act itself of compensation'. J. V. de Graaf, 'Kaldor on Welfare', *CJE* (Mar. 1989), 22.

[55] For a review of economic thought on this subject from Kaldor until the present day, see U. Krause, 'Interpersonal and Intrapersonal Comparison of Utility', paper given at a conference at New school for Social Research and Bard College, New York, 29–31 Oct. 1987, proceedings pub. under the conference title: E. J. Nell and W. Semmler (eds.), *Nicholas Kaldor and Mainstream Economics: Confrontation or Convergence?* (New York, St Martin's Press, 1991); J. S. Chipman, 'Compensation Principle', in id., *The New Palgrave* (London, Macmillan, 1987).

[56] Kaldor, introd. to CP; (1st edn.), 5–6.

it, provided that the tariff was below a certain critical level and provided that competitor countries did not retaliate with higher duties of their own. Kaldor also showed that

the introduction of import duties can reproduce exactly the same effects as the introduction of monopoly. The extent to which it is possible to exploit the foreigner in this way depends on the country's monopoly power; i.e. the elasticity of foreign demand for its products, and the extent to which the foreign power desires, or is able, to retaliate.[57]

The debate was taken up again after the Second World War in the literature produced on the 'optimum tariff' by Scitovsky, Kahn, Johnson, Gorman, Graaff, Pollak, and others under pressure from the balance-of-payments problems of post-war Europe. A non-discriminatory method of dealing with the problem through devaluation would have brought additional losses consequent on a deterioration in the terms of trade; losses which could instead have been avoided by imposition of the tariff.

1.6. A Policy of Wage Subsidies for Full Employment

I shall now consider Kaldor's final pre-Keynesian contribution: his scheme of wage subsidies as a policy for full employment, a scheme that has recently become topical again,[58] couched in arguments not unlike those adopted in the mid-1930s by the young economist.

Kaldor had already been at work on this project for a year before he left for America in October 1935, and had discussed his plan with a number of his economist friends—Hugh Gaitskell of University College London, Piero Sraffa, and Joan Robinson. In December he presented his article in New York to the conference of the Econometric Society. Although the *analysis* on which his proposal rested was strongly neo-classical in its treatment of the relation between the yield and employment of a factor, the *spirit* of the project was Keynesian in its opposition to wage cuts.

The first step of analysis consisted in uncovering the causes of unemployment:

When unemployment is *general* [it] must be the result of either a reduction in the marginal productivity of labour relatively to other factors or an increase in the cost of labour; and whatever the cause, the remedy will always involve either an increase in marginal productivity or a reduction in labour cost.[59]

Hence it follows that an increase in employment can be the result of policies designed either to increase labour productivity or to decrease the cost of

---

[57] Id., 'A Note on Tariffs and the Terms of Trade' (1940), repr. in CP i.

[58] F. Cugno and M. Ferrero, 'Partecipazione ai profitti e sussidi all'occupazione', *PEE* (Dec. 1986).

[59] N. Kaldor, 'Wage Subsidies as a Remedy for Unemployment' (1935), repr. in CP iii. 3.

labour. The first group comprises policies involving the employment of labour in public works, tariffs, or subsidies differentiated by industry, or a reduction in the rates of interest. Policies of the second kind seek to reduce the wage level or provide a general subsidy on wages. Kaldor was very much in favour of this latter solution. Among the leading economists of the time, only Pigou had seriously considered an economic policy measure of this sort[60] and, among politicians, only Von Papen. About thirty years later, in the introduction to *Essays on Economic Policy* (the third volume of his Collected Papers), Kaldor declared that although his argument in support of the proposal was faulty, the idea itself was sound—and the German example was proof of its validity. In fact, the adoption in 1932 of the Papen Plan had considerably reduced unemployment and led to an unexpected drop in the Nazi Party's popularity. However, the experiment was too short-lived to prevent Hitler from seizing power in January 1934.

Kaldor carefully weighed the merits of a policy of a general subsidy on wages against the advantages of alternative policies. But at no point did he take account of the effects that a subsidies policy might have on the level of income by modifying the propensity to spend—this being the objection raised by Joan Robinson when she first discussed Kaldor's plan with him. Although at the beginning he found it difficult to accept this criticism, Kaldor would later use it as material in defence of his policy.

Compared with the alternative measure of reducing wages, Kaldor's arguments in favour of subsidies were markedly Keynesian in spirit. A reduction in money-wages, he argued, reduces consumption and prices so that the final effect on unemployment is either zero or negative, while a subsidy on wages (and here Kaldor used a Keynesian instrument) brings about a shift in the aggregate-supply curve which, given aggregate demand, leads to an increase in employment.

The form that the subsidy might take in practice was a reduction in social charges. Kaldor's assessment of the policy fully accounted for the tax burden that it might entail. He showed that the cost of the subsidies was negative for the State if the elasticity of demand for labour was equal to, or greater than, the ratio of wages to unemployment benefits. Since a number of research studies had suggested that the elasticity of the demand for labour was around two, and that in many countries the ratio of wages to subsidies was a value lying between two and three, it followed that the cost of the scheme to the State would be zero. Nor would the policy be a burden on the taxpayer: both because unemployed workers, even if 'extra-marginal', must—unlike land or machines—be maintained by deductions from taxpayers' incomes, and also because the cost of the wage-subsidy scheme was even negative to the extent that it increased employment and therefore the national product.

[60] A. C. Pigou, *The Economics of Welfare* (London, Macmillan, 1932), pt. IV, ch. 7, id., *The Theory of Unemployment* (London, Macmillan, 1933), pt. III, ch. 4.

The increase in employment generated by wage subsidies and financed out of taxation was the same—if investment was constant—as the increase that would result from a reduction in real wages. But a side-effect of the reduction in the cost of labour consequent on the introduction of the subsidy was an increase in investment opportunities at given rates of interest.

The 'scheme' had an effect on employment if the wage rate remained constant, otherwise 'the wage subsidy ceases to be an unemployment-relief measure and becomes a measure of socialist income redistribution, for then the subsidy will not benefit employers but only workers'.[61] The wage subsidy as a stable policy for full employment was therefore feasible only if the State had the authority to make the payment of subsidies conditional on a curbing of wage-rate increases.

Kaldor defended his scheme for labour-cost reduction against various counter-claims for measures aimed at increasing labour productivity, among which he included the employment of labour on public works. The policy of financing public works out of taxation was a measure designed to increase labour productivity, in so far as one unit of State spending created an extra demand for labour greater than the private spending that it replaced. It should be clear that we are here very far from the provocative Keynesian idea of public works financed at a deficit and with no direct social usefulness. Kaldor's opposition to the policy of public works centred on the government's technical difficulty in adjusting the intensity and duration of such works, compared with the greater technical ease with which it could implement a scheme of wage subsidies. Subsidies on wages were also preferable to subsidies on output because the former, unlike the latter, would not affect the competitive equilibrium.

Kaldor finally compared the advantages of his scheme against those of a policy of increasing investments via a reduction in the long-term rates of interest. He was sceptical whether, with the monetary and credit instruments available at the time, the authorities could effectively regulate long-term interest rates by changing the short-term rate. However, on this subject he showed himself already on Keynes's side when he stated:

The present writer is not one of those who believe that the maintenance of a lower level of interest rates necessarily involves a process of 'cumulative inflation' . . . so long as there is unemployed labour to draw upon at a given level of wages.[62]

On this his ideas would remain unchanged—ideas which paved the way for his subsequent wholesale conversion to Keynesianism.

---

[61] Kaldor, 'Wage Subsidies', 17.   [62] Ibid. 21–2.

Chapter 2

Wages, Speculation, and Interest

Nature, and Nature's Laws lay hid in the night: God said, 'Let
Newton be!' and all was light.

A. Pope, *Epitaphs*

2.1. The Conversion to Keynesianism

It is difficult to say who the founders of modern macro-economics were. There
is no doubt, however, that a starting-point for much of the subject's subsequent
development was Wicksell and his monetary theory, 'which Lindhal clarified,
and to which Myrdal gave the vital spark with his distinction between the two
temporal viewpoints of ex-ante and ex-post'.[1] An extraordinary contribution
to the development of the Swedish theory of monetary equilibrium was
Myrdal's essay *Monetary Equilibrium*. This was 'in its original Swedish and
German versions equally as remarkable and in certain respects equally as
successful as Keynes's own contribution in explanation of variations in the
general level of output'.[2] Myrdal's essay broke new ground in strictly monetary matters as well, with its pioneering ideas on the variability of the velocity
of circulation and, to a certain extent, its thesis of the endogeneity of the
money supply.

Kaldor's enthusiasm for the Austrian doctrine had already begun to wane,
however, in his first year as a research student at the LSE, when he translated
Gibt es einen Widersinn des Sparens into English[3] and noticed the gaps and
flaws in Hayek's reasoning. And his misgivings increased as he followed up
the bibliographical suggestions of John Hicks, his friend and colleague at the
LSE.

Hicks (unlike me) was an indefatigable reader of books in at least three foreign
languages, and it was through him that I was put on the track . . . of the younger
Swedish economists, particularly Myrdal, who first made me realize the shortcomings
of the 'monetarist' approach of the Austrian school of von Mises and von Hayek and
made me such an easy convert to Keynes after the appearance of the *General Theory*
three years later.[4]

[1] G. L. S. Shackle, *The Years of High Theory* (Cambridge, CUP, 1967), 91.
[2] Ibid. 89.   [3] 'The Paradox of Savings', *EC* (May 1931).
[4] N. Kaldor, 'Recollections of an Economist' (1986), repr. in CP ix. 17.

As we saw in the previous chapter, although in 1937 Kaldor was still solidly 'Austrian' on the theory of capital, he was already showing manifest signs of Keynesianism in other areas, especially in his views on money-wages and level of employment. For the time being, though, Kaldor's thinking was (as we shall see) closely aligned with Hicks's and in the mainstream of what would later come to be called the neo-classical synthesis of Keynes.

Opinions differed between Keynes and the economists of his time over the relation between *money-wages* and employment, although their views concerning the relation between *real wages* and employment broadly coincided. Even in his more mature works, Keynes accepted the neo-classical postulate of the decreasing marginal productivity of labour, which had been the analytical core of Pigou's book *Theory of Unemployment*[5] published three years before the *General Theory*. Many years later Kaldor would write:

> Keynes's acceptance of this neo-classical postulate enabled his conservative critics (from Pigou, Robertson, Viner, Robbins right up to Friedman) to confute him on empirical grounds, arguing that there was no evidence that workers would be more willing to accept lower real wages, and since a higher level of employment would cause real wages to be lower, there is no reason to suppose that any stimulus to demand could increase employment more than temporarily.[6]

At that time, however, few economists—and Kaldor was not among them—contested the inverse relation between *real wages* and employment. And even though Keynes was persuaded by some of these critics, such as Dunlop, Tarshis, and Kalecki, to review his initial position,[7]

> his position remained a guarded one, and he never produced a theoretical explanation of why his original argument of diminishing returns being a necessary consequence of non-homogeneity was wrong. To do so would have required an analysis of monopolistic competition, which renders the traditional rules of resource allocation inapplicable.[8]

Since those years a great deal of empirical research has been conducted in this area—research which mostly contradicts the neo-classical assumption of an inverse relation between real wages and employment.[9] At the time, how-

[5] A. C. Pigou, *Theory of Unemployment* (London, Macmillan, 1933).

[6] Kaldor, 'Recollections of an Economist', 20.

[7] J. T. Dunlop, 'The Movement of Real and Money Wage Rates', *EJ* (Sept. 1938); L. Tarshis, 'Changes in Real and Money Wages', *EJ* (Mar. 1939); J. M. Keynes, 'Relative Movements of Real Wages and Output', *EJ* (Mar. 1939). The statistical significance of Dunlop and Tarshis's data was disputed by R. Ruggles, 'The Relative Movements of Real and Money Wage Rates', *QJE* (Nov. 1940); and by J. Tobin, 'Money Wage Rates and Employment', in E. H. Seymour (ed.), *The New Economics: Keynes's Influence on Theory and Public Policy* (London, Dobson, 1948).

[8] Kaldor, 'Recollections of an Economist', 21.

[9] R. R. Neild, 'Pricing and Employment in the Trade Cycle' (NIESR, Occasional Paper, 21; Cambridge, CUP, 1963); E. Kuh, 'Unemployment, Production Function and Effective Demand', *JPE* (June 1966); G. R. Bodkin, 'Real Wages and Cyclical Variations in Employment: A Re-Examination of the Evidence', *Canadian Journal of Economics* (Aug. 1969); K. Coutts *et al.*, 'Industrial Pricing in the U.K.' (University of Cambridge, DAE monograph 26; Cambridge, CUP, 1978); M. J. Bils, 'Real Wages over the Business Cycle: Evidence from Panel Data', *JPE* 93: 4 (1985);

ever, debate centred almost exclusively on the relation between *money-wages* and employment, and it was to this argument that Kaldor made the first of his contributions to show a markedly Keynesian frame of mind.

2.2. Wages and Employment

After publication of the *General Theory*, the pages of the *Economic Journal* carried two of the most heated debates to be provoked by Keynes's controversial book—the first on the interest rate and liquidity preference, the second on the relationship between money-wages and unemployment. In the latter, Pigou rose to the defence of orthodoxy to argue that a fall in money-wages led to greater employment.

In an article submitted to the *Economic Journal* in his capacity as president of the Royal Economic Society,[10] Pigou had money income depend on banking policy—the banking money supply depending positively on the interest rate. The interest rate balanced money demand and supply, and also the rate of time preference à la Ramsey.[11] A reduction in money-wages, with output and time preferences remaining equal, therefore led neither to a fall in the interest rate, nor to a reduction of the supply of money and of money income, nor to a drop in the level of prices. With equality of prices, a fall in wages and therefore of costs raised profits and this led to an increase in the labour demand; an outcome, Pigou believed, that could not be achieved by lowering the interest rate.

Keynes read the proofs of Pigou's article in August 1937 while he was convalescing from the first of the heart attacks that would afflict him until his death. E. A. G. Robinson had accepted the article for publication in Keynes's absence as editor of the *Economic Journal*. Keynes, however, declared the article to be 'the work of a sick man, which no one who was in his right mind would print',[12] and unsuccessfully attempted to halt its publication—in a sincere attempt to save an economist of Pigou's reputation (he was, like Keynes, a Fellow of King's College) from making a fool of himself. Keynes also wrote to Robinson: 'The Prof's article I have recently considered thoroughly; and I think you have committed an unforgivable sin in letting him print it. It's outrageous rubbish beyond all possibility of redemption.'[13]

The article was extensively discussed in Cambridge by Keynes and his pupils, but the only criticisms of it to appear in the *Economic Journal*—both

M. L. Mitchel *et al.*, 'Real Wages over the Business Cycle: Some Further Evidence', *Southern Economic Journal* (Apr. 1985).

[10] A. C. Pigou, 'Real and Money Wages in Relation to Unemployment', *EJ* (Sept. 1937).

[11] F. P. Ramsey, 'A Mathematical Theory of Saving', *EJ* (Sept. 1937).

[12] J. M. Keynes, letter to E. A. G. Robinson, 7 Aug. 1937, pub. in *The Collected Writings of John Maynard Keynes*, ed. D. Moggridge, xiv (London, Macmillan for the Royal Economic Society, 1973), 234.

[13] Ibid. 250.

in December 1937—were a short article by Keynes[14] and a long one by Kaldor.[15] On 27 September Kaldor submitted his article to Keynes with a view to publication, accompanying it with a note saying, 'I'm sure there must be several people in Cambridge who could point out the same thing, yet I'm sending it along in the hope of getting in first.'[16] In fact, R. Kahn wrote to Keynes on 18 October that Gerald Shove had told him that Pigou's article was the worst that he had ever read, and that Piero Sraffa agreed with his verdict. Kahn wrote again on 20 October: 'I have not seen Kaldor's article but I am sure that publication of it will darken counsel. After all, we could all of us write replies to Pigou if you wanted them and I do not see why Kaldor should be thus favoured;'[17] and in another letter of the same day: 'Piero confirms that Kaldor is thoroughly muddled and merely fogs the issue.'[18] Three days later Keynes answered Kahn by saying: 'I must print Kaldor's article and I cannot possibly use my editorial discretion to suppress it. In fact, no one else has sent me any comment on Pigou.'[19]

On 30 September Keynes returned Kaldor's manuscript and asked him to shorten it. On 1 October Kaldor replied to Keynes justifying the length of his article because 'he was anxious to meet Pigou on his own ground; and explore the implications of the framework he has set up'.[20] Moreover, in this and in a later letter, he contested a number of Keynes's own criticisms of Pigou. It was Robinson who showed Kaldor's article to Pigou, and Pigou wrote to Keynes when he had read it, saying: 'Your note is based on a misunderstanding of what I was trying to say . . . Kaldor's article, on the other hand, interprets me, I think, correctly . . . I think it would be best for Kaldor's article to be published, but not yours.'[21]

In Kaldor's brief review of Pigou's theory he distinguished two separate cases, depending on whether the savings–investment equilibrium comes about at a nil or positive level of savings. In the former case, Kaldor agreed (like Keynes but unlike Kahn or Sraffa) that savings are determined by the inter-temporal preference rate (long-term equilibrium with zero saving). He accepted Pigou's model in its entirety; his only modification being that he had savings depend not only on the interest rate but also directly on the level of activity.[22] Thus a fall in money-wages brought prices down and increased the

---

[14] J. M. Keynes, 'Professor Pigou on Money Wages in Relation to Unemployment', *EJ* (Dec. 1937).

[15] N. Kaldor, 'Professor Pigou on Money Wages in Relation to Unemployment' *EJ* (1937), repr. as an app. to CP ii (2nd edn., 1980).

[16] *Collected Writings of John Maynard Keynes*, xiv. 240.

[17] Ibid. 260.   [18] Ibid.   [19] Ibid. 262.   [20] Ibid. 241.   [21] Ibid. 256.

[22] It was Kaldor's opinion that '[t]he assumption that savings are largely a function of real income has not been questioned by any of Mr Keynes's critics. Yet, in the present writer's view, it is this assumption, more than any other, which is responsible for the "revolutionary" innovation of Mr Keynes's system', 'Professor Pigou on Money Wages', 304 n. 2. Having expressed this view in a letter to Keynes, he received the following reply: 'I agree with you that the assumption of saving varying with income is one of the most essential differences between my system and the classical,' *Collected Writings of John Maynard Keynes*, xiv. 242.

value of liquid assets. This led to a drop in the interest rate and if—but only if—this led to a decline in savings and therefore to an increase in consumption, employment would rise. There was no other way to increase employment apart from operating through a change in the interest rate.

In the other case—where investment has positive value—we can express the hypotheses required to support Pigou's conclusions in the terms that Hicks had used in his famous article 'Mr Keynes and the Classics: A Suggested Interpretation', published a few months previously.[23] In terms of *IS–LM*,[24] Kaldor argued, a reduction in money-wages did not move the *IS* curve—which would, however, move if the government adopted the scheme for money-wage subsidies that he had proposed a few years previously (see chapter 1.6)—but shifted the *LM* curve to the right as a result of a decline in the 'working balances' for a given level of income. If the policy of the 'banking system' was *not* to keep the interest rate invariant (if, that is, the *LM* curve was not infinitely elastic), the effect on employment was a positive one. However 'It will still be true . . . that the result on employment and on the rate of interest will be exactly the same as if the real value of these (idle) balances had been increased by the same amount in some other way.'[25] The underlying cause of rising employment was therefore not wage cuts as such, but an increase in the magnitude of 'idle balances'.

Kaldor had therefore identified a process—known today as the 'Keynes effect'—by which a reduction in wages is equivalent to an increase in the quantity of money or to a reduction in the liquidity preference. Kaldor reached this conclusion independently of Keynes (though it was to be found in the appendix to chapter 19 of the *General Theory*), and it was he who convinced Pigou of its validity. Thus Kahn wrote to Keynes on 19 December saying: '[U]nless he changes his mind again, the Prof. will merely publish a note to the effect that he entirely agrees with Kaldor!'[26] And ten days later: 'The Prof.'s article has now arrived . . . This article is in effect a complete and frank withdrawal of the whole of his previous argument.'[27] In the same letter, however, Kahn disagreed with Pigou that the 'theory of the relation between money-wages and employment, via the rate of interest was invented by Kaldor'.[28] And Keynes finally wrote to Pigou on 3 January 1938 explaining that

Kaldor is mainly a restatement of my *General Theory* with references to your special assumptions . . . I wish very much that you would now, in the light of this more recent discussion, read over again chapter 19 of my book together with its Appendix. This is the source of the theory that the effect of changes in money-wages on employment in a closed system is through the rate of interest, though in the general case it can also work in other ways.[29]

[23] J. Hicks, 'Mr Keynes and the Classics: A Suggested Interpretation', *ECTA* (Apr. 1937).
[24] Kaldor used Hicks's *IS–LM* scheme in 'Professor Pigou on Money Wages', 309 n. 1.
[25] Ibid. 309–10.   [26] *Collected Writings of John Maynard Keynes*, xiv. 265.
[27] Ibid. 266.   [28] Ibid. 267.   [29] Ibid.

Although, in an article in the *Economic Journal*, Pigou had declared himself convinced by Kaldor's explanation,[30] he nevertheless continued to reject the idea that a change in the interest rate could be brought about by a change in the liquidity preference—even if he did accept that it might be the result of a variation in the intertemporal preference rate. This connection between interest rate and employment could therefore be handled both by the Keynesian theory of liquidity preference and by the non-Keynesian theory of intertemporal preference. The co-presence of two theses in explanation of a single phenomenon provoked the debate between Kaldor and Somers of 1939–40:[31] Kaldor managed to persuade his critic that since there was no liquidity-preference function in Pigou's model, investments and savings were directly governed by intertemporal preference. Hence a decline in the intertemporal preference rate automatically reduced savings and increased employment. Liquidity preference, on the other hand, was needed for explanation of why a reduction in intertemporal preference might *fail* to have an effect on the reduction in the interest rate and therefore on employment.

As the echoes of the controversy over Pigou's article died away in the months that followed, he published a book[32] which now revealed him as a partial convert to Keynesian ideas, although he expressed them in a macro-economic model using neo-classical terminology and tools. Kaldor admired Pigou's new book, and even as late as 1960 would write that 'Pigou's book *Employment and Equilibrium*, published at an inauspicious moment, did not receive the attention it deserved.'[33] However, he raised a number of objections against the hypotheses and method of Pigou's model and made a number of substantial changes to it; changes indicative of the research into the trade cycle and speculation with which he was occupied in those years.[34]

Pigou's basic model consisted of three equations. The first of these expressed the equality of saving decision—which depends on the interest rate and the level of activity (which in turn depends on the output of consumption goods)—and investment decision, which is a function of the interest rate. Pigou's second equation stated the equality between savings as thus defined and the output of investment goods; his third equation stated the equality between the level of money income (money supply by velocity of circulation) as a direct function of the interest rate and money demand, as determined by

[30] A. C. Pigou, 'Real and Money Wages in Relation to Unemployment: A Rejoinder', *EJ* (Mar. 1938).

[31] H. M. Somers, 'Money Wages Cuts in Relation to Unemployment', *RES* (Feb. 1939); N. Kaldor, 'Money Wages Cuts in Relation to Unemployment: A Reply to Mr Somers', *RES* (June 1939); H. M. Somers, 'Money Wage Cuts in Relation to Unemployment: A Rejoinder to Mr Kaldor', *RES* (Feb. 1940); N. Kaldor, 'A Comment to a Rejoinder of Mr Somers', *RES* (Feb. 1940).

[32] A. C. Pigou, *Employment and Equilibrium: A Theoretical Discussion* (London, Macmillan, 1941).

[33] N. Kaldor, introd. to CP ii (1st edn., 1960).

[34] Id., 'Employment and Equilibrium: A Theoretical Discussion' (1941), repr. in CP ii as 'Pigou on Employment and Equilibrium'.

money-wages and marginal labour productivity in the two sectors. Since there were four unknowns in these equations—the levels of activity in the two sectors, wages, and the interest rate—Pigou had to 'close' the system with a further equation derived from one or other of the following two hypotheses: (1) that total output could be taken as given (a 'classical' hypothesis that Pigou regarded as valid for the nineteenth century), or (2) that wages could be taken as given (a Keynesian hypothesis valid for the twentieth century). If the model was closed by this latter hypothesis, it bore out Pigou's contention that every money-wage was matched by an equilibrium level of activity.

Kaldor made three changes to Pigou's 'twentieth-century' model. First, he modified the investment function. This depended not only on the interest rate but also on the level of activity, and therefore gave stability to the model only under certain conditions. When these conditions were violated, the system showed no tendency towards even short-period equilibrium, but was subject to persistent disequilibria: it was these disequilibria that would be later analysed by Kaldor's theory of the cycle (see Chapter 3.4). Kaldor's second modification was to draw a distinction between the long-term rate of interest—on which (besides the level of activity) savings and the interest rate depended—and the short-term rate of interest, which determined the money supply (always assuming that of the various policies available to the banks, they would opt for the only one considered by Pigou as tying the money supply directly to the rate of interest).

However, now that a fifth variable—the short-term rate of interest—had been introduced, a fifth equation was required. This Kaldor took to be the long-term rate of interest determined, as in Keynes, by the 'state of expectations'. These modifications altered the shape of the model. The level of activity could be deduced only from the first two equations of savings and investments and from the fifth equation on the state of expectations. The level of activity and the money-wage equation together determined the short-term interest rate. On the basis of the model's hypotheses, these modifications meant that a reduction in money-wages did not affect the level of activity or of employment.[35]

Kaldor's third modification to Pigou's model concerned the time period handled by analysis. For Kaldor, the model should make it possible to examine the effects of a variation in the stock of capital. If this variation was a small one, the techniques of production could be taken as given, and the effects of the variation in the stock of capital on the investment function could be measured. In this way he obtained a picture of a 'moving equilibrium' consisting of a series of stationary equilibria.

This makes it possible to deal with movement (admittedly not *all* kinds of movement) within the framework of equilibrium analysis; to rescue it from the bleak houses of

[35] The situation would be different, Kaldor observed, if the assumption of a closed economy was modified, or if short-term investments sensitive to the short-term interest rate were incorporated into the model.

'disequilibria' and 'transitional periods' to which processes of change would otherwise all be relegated.[36]

It was Kaldor's belief that the model should demonstrate that the long-period equilibrium position—where net investment is zero—could be approached gradually through successive reductions in the amount of unemployment. However, this long-period equilibrium would never be achieved by an unstable system with multiple equilibria and in permanent oscillation.[37]

2.3. Speculation and Level of Income

Kaldor's outstanding contribution of this period was undoubtedly his 1939 article 'Speculation and Economic Stability'.[38] This, when read again nearly half a century later, preserves all its freshness and capacity for intellectual stimulation, even and especially in an era dominated by the theory of 'rational expectations' (although this may already be in decline). When Hicks reread the article in 1986, he wrote to Kaldor: 'I think that your paper was the culmination of the Keynesian revolution in *theory*. You ought to have had more honour for it.'[39] Highly influential at the time, the article is perhaps even more important today, despite its comparative neglect. It sets out a general theoretical framework for classifying the speculative behaviour of various markets. Its merits are twofold. First it identifies all the features that goods and capital markets must possess to give validity to the Keynesian theory of the determination of income. In doing so, the article reassesses the role of expectations—given such prominence in the *General Theory* and so widely forgotten in its 'vulgarized' version (as developed through *IS–LM* models)— and provides a robust overview of the Keynesian theory of income determination, without basing it on such limiting hypotheses as the rigidity of the money-wage and the 'liquidity trap'. Second it demonstrates that the premisses which must hold if markets are to behave as hypothesized by the modern theory of rational expectations are highly restrictive compared with the multiplicity of features that these markets assume.

In Kaldor's own words, the aim of the long article was to attempt 'to generalize Keynes's theory of money, interest and employment on the basis of a general theory of speculation'.[40] Many of its ideas, Kaldor wrote, were inspired by the *Treatise on Money*. The article therefore had the further merit of building a theoretical bridge between Keynes's two major works.

[36] Ibid. 95.

[37] Note that Kaldor made these criticisms of Pigou only a year after his analysis of the trade cycle, as discussed in Ch. 3.4.

[38] N. Kaldor, 'Speculation and Economic Stability', *RES* (Oct. 1939), repr. with alterations to para. 4 in CP ii.

[39] This letter was originally brought to my notice by Prof. Thirlwall. Now see A. P. Thirlwall, *Nicholas Kaldor* (Brighton, Wheatsheaf Books, 1987), 75 n. 46.

[40] Kaldor, introd. to CP ii (1st edn.), 3.

If the central argument of the *General Theory* was that savings adjust to exogenous investment through a change in income rather than in the interest rate, then one has to identify the conditions under which this mechanism is able to operate. Post-Keynesian theory—especially in Cambridge and as developed by Kaldor in his later years—has tended to identify these conditions in two distinctive features of modern economic systems: (1) a goods-supply curve which is infinitely elastic because of imperfect competition in the manufacturing sector (see Chapter 14); (2) a money-supply curve which is infinitely elastic because of the principle of the endogeneity of money in a financial system based on credit money (see Chapter 11).

In his 1939 article, however, Kaldor set off in a different direction. He specified the conditions that, irrespective of the structure of supply, make it possible for the Keynesian multiplier to operate through the various forms of speculative behaviour to be found in different markets. One notes, however, that if hypotheses (1) and (2) above are sound, Kaldor's theory of speculative behaviour as elaborated in this article is redundant as a condition for the validity of Keynes's thesis.[41] Many years later Kaldor declared:

One of the purposes of the article was to show that Keynes's theory of interest contains two separate propositions. The first regards interest as the price to be paid for parting with liquidity, and it arises on account of the *uncertainty* of the future prices of non-liquid assets. The second concerns the dependence of the current rate of interest on the interest rates expected in the future. While the first proposition provides an explanation of why long-dated bonds should normally command a higher yield than short-term paper it is the second which explains why the traditional theory of the working of the capital market was inappropriate—why, in other words, savings and investment are brought into equality by movements in the level of incomes far more than by movements in interest rates[42]

Although Kaldor's argument operates as a unified whole, I shall deal with the latter problem first and then move on to the relation between short- and long-term interest rates in the next section.

Traditional theory had argued that speculation—that is, the purchase (or sale) of securities with the sole purpose of reselling (or repurchasing) them at a later date at a higher (or lower) price—only existed in markets with imperfect foresight. In these circumstances, speculators were those who possessed better than average powers of prediction. Their actions (intervening when

[41] Kaldor was aware of this. In a letter to the present writer dated 17. 3. 1986 he wrote: 'I . . . agree with you that if a Central Bank follows a policy of keeping interest rates constant irrespective of changes in the levels of activity, this makes the theory of speculative behaviour redundant in explaining why an increase in investment demand should be followed by an increase in income and not an increase in the rate of interest.'

[42] Id., 'Recollections of an Economist', 22–3. In a note to this article Kaldor describes how he met Keynes at a Cambridge tea party a few weeks after the article appeared (Oct. 1939) and was astonished to hear that Keynes had already read the article and was intrigued by Kaldor's idea that it is the behaviour of speculators, rather than the premium that the public requires for parting with liquidity, that explains the inability of an increase in the propensity to save to increase investment. However, Kaldor never again had a chance to discuss the point with Keynes.

prices fell and backing out when they rose) stabilized prices, improved the predictive capacity of the system, and contributed towards a better allocation of resources. This was why, in a free market, the speculator's earnings were justified.

Kaldor disputed this theory by returning to Keynes's thesis that these conditions hold only if speculation concerns a small proportion of overall demand and supply. Speculation involving a large share of the market destabilizes it. In this situation, the market cannot expel the destabilizing speculator through bankruptcy, because he will continue to reap profits as long as he is able to make better forecasts than anyone else concerning the predictions of the majority of his fellow speculators. Traditional theory, moreover, also implicitly assumed that, by stabilizing prices, speculation also stabilized the level of activity. This Kaldor saw as a serious flaw in the theory because, in certain markets, if speculation stabilizes prices it must destabilize the level of activity, and if it stabilizes incomes it must destabilize prices.

The first step in Kaldor's analysis was to explore the conditions under which speculation stabilizes prices. Goods that can serve as the objects of speculation have to be highly standardized, with a large market, durable, and with a high value relative to their size. In practice, speculative markets are those of raw materials for the manufacturing and food industries and the bond and share markets—the four markets examined by Kaldor.

Kaldor used two analytical tools: the 'elasticity of speculative stocks' and 'the elasticity of expectations'. The former, denoted by e, 'may be defined as the proportionate change in the amount of speculative stocks held as a result of a given percentage change in the *ratio* of the expected price to the current price'.[43] The greater this elasticity, the more the current price depends on the expected one. Its value ranges from zero to infinity: at zero, the current price is unaffected by speculation—that is, the expected price—and is determined solely by the flow of demand and supply. At infinity, the current price is wholly determined by the expected price, and changes in non-speculative demand and supply have no influence over current price because they are offset by variations in current stocks moving in the opposite direction.

Kaldor's second concept—'the elasticity of expectations'—he took from Hicks.[44] This elasticity, denoted by η, is defined as the percentage change in the expected price relative to the percentage change in the current price. This elasticity is unity when a change in current price causes an equiproportionate change in the expected price. If this elasticity is zero the speculation has a stabilizing influence; if it is between zero and one the influence is weaker but still stabilizing; if it is higher than one its influence is destabilizing.

[43] This formulation is taken from the version of the article that appeared in CP ii. It differs from his original position set out in the 1939 article and takes account of P. Streeten's remarks in 'A Note on Kaldor's "Speculation and Stability" ', *RES* (Oct. 1958), 67.

[44] J. Hicks, *Value and Capital* (Oxford, Clarendon Press, 1939). The two economists were very close friends at the time, and Hicks had given the manuscript version of his book to Kaldor to read before publication.

These two elasticities, η and *e*, together determine the degree of price-stabilizing influence of speculation. They stand in the following relation:

(2.1) $\sigma = -e(\eta - 1)$.

Since *e* cannot be negative, σ will be negative or positive according to whether η is greater or lesser than one. Thus speculation is destabilizing and amplifies price variations if the elasticity of expectations is greater than one. Since the elasticity of expectations is greater (1) the shorter the time-horizon, and (2) the smaller the range of price oscillation, it follows that it is under these two conditions that speculation destabilizes prices. This signifies that if the idea forms that the 'normal price' refers to a distant future, and if in the short period speculators do not behave according to the long-term price, but instead seek to anticipate the reactions of other speculators, the market is subject to destabilizing speculation. In every speculative market, however, there will be a point—which may be a time-span or a range of price oscillation, and which differs from market to market and is not knowable a priori—beyond which the elasticity of expectations becomes zero and speculation becomes stabilizing. If within the market there is a firm belief in a normal price which will not alter in the future, speculation stabilizes prices. Indeed,

in all circumstances, speculation must have the effect of narrowing the range of fluctuations of the current price *relatively to the expected price*. Hence, if the expected price is taken as given, speculation must necessarily exert a stabilizing influence.[45]

This theory has an important Keynesian corollary. Since the belief that the future normal supply price will not differ greatly from what it has been in the past grows stronger the greater the confidence in money-wages stability, it follows that 'it is in this way that the rigidity of money-wages contributes to the stability of the economic system, by inducing the forces of speculation to operate in a much more stabilizing fashion than they would do if money-wages were flexible'.[46]

From formula (2.1) it follows that if the elasticity of expectations is zero (i.e. the expected price does not vary with changes in the current price) and if the elasticity of speculative stocks tends towards infinity (i.e. the current price is wholly determined by the expected price), the price stabilizing influence of speculation will tend towards infinity. If, in addition, the expected price is actually the same as the future price would be if future flow factors operated (in stock exchange terms, if only the 'fundamentals' operated), we have the situation envisaged by the modern theory of 'rational expectations'.[47] However, for Kaldor, in some markets, adjustment between demand for and supply of the *flows* of output and consumption works through prices; in others, a different mechanism operates because the demand for and supply of stocks of these goods are governed by the expectations of future prices relative to

[45] Kaldor, 'Speculation and Economic Stability', 31.   [46] Ibid. 35.
[47] This point was made to me by Dr Tamborini.

current ones. In these markets 'it is not possible, however, to express the behaviour of expectations at any given moment in terms of a single elasticity'.[48] Even more so, a situation where σ is infinite may arise in some markets but not in others. It does not occur, for instance, in the market for agricultural raw materials, because unpredictable changes in the weather cause the supply curve to fluctuate. Nor does it occur on the shares market, where there is no normal level of long-term profits—both because profits in the more distant future are discounted with great uncertainty and because speculators gamble more on increases in capital value than on dividends. Speculation does, however, stabilize prices on the industrial-raw-materials market. If prices fluctuate in this market, therefore, it is not because of speculation but because of the instability of demand.

There remains the market for long-term bonds. Although there is no 'normal price' on this market—and this is crucial, for the reasons given in the following section—the elasticity of expectations is low and speculation stabilizes prices, as one would expect from the observed stability of the long-term interest rate.

In his second stage of analysis, Kaldor explores the effects of speculation on the level of activity through variations in the amount of speculative stocks held. The more speculation stabilizes prices on a particular market, the more the level of activity fluctuates. This is because an increase (reduction) in supply or a reduction (increase) in demand leads to an increase (reduction) in stocks rather than a reduction (increase) in price. Hence the price-stabilizing variation in stocks destabilizes the level of activity and of incomes. This, however, only concerns a single market. In the case of several interconnected markets, the mechanism equalizing supply and demand through variations in stocks and level of activity in one market becomes much weaker. This is because the income utilized to increase stocks on one market is—other conditions being equal—subtracted from the income utilized on others. Keynes's revolutionary innovation lay in his demonstration that capital markets do not adjust investments to savings through variations in the interest rate. On the contrary, it is savings that adjust to investments through a variation in income. In Kaldor's view, Keynes's argument entailed that, on the capital market, speculation stabilizes prices. Let us assume an increase in the propensity to save: demand for producible goods declines; the demand for long-term, low-risk securities increases; the price of bonds tends to rise; and the percentage yield tends to fall. Given the low elasticity of expectations on this market, a slight increase in price induces speculators to sell securities and to demand money. By doing so, they prevent security-prices from rising and the interest rate from falling. If the interest rate remains steady, the effect of the initial increase in saving on investments is nil. The price-stabilizing influence of speculation on the long-term securities market nullifies its mechanism of

[48] Kaldor, 'Speculation and Economic Stability', 33.

demand–supply (investments and savings) adjustment through prices (interest rate).

Vice versa, in the capital-goods market an increase in demand is not followed by a reduction in stocks, but by an increase in prices and output. Nor does it lead to a change in demand in the reverse direction. In this market, σ is zero; there is therefore no speculation, and an increase in demand raises incomes. If σ were positive, an increase in demand would be accompained by a reduction in stocks—and this would depress the Keynesian multiplier.

In Kaldor's view, therefore, in the *General Theory* Keynes was dealing with the case where the degree of price-stabilizing influence by speculation is infinite on the long-term capital market and zero on the market for other goods. Since this is indeed a feature of these markets, Keynes's 'special case' thus 'gives, nevertheless, a fair approximation to reality'.[49]

2.4. Structure of Interest Rates and the Liquidity Preference

Kaldor's 1939 article 'Speculation and Economic Stability' contained two paragraphs which provoked a great deal of discussion: one dealing with the forward market (paragraph 4), the other examining the relation between short- and long-term interest rates (paragraph 10).[50] The criticisms brought against the article over the next fifteen years obliged Kaldor to reformulate his theory of the forward market. Regarding his second argument, however, despite its hostile reception, Kaldor never substantially changed his mind; and his article 'Keynes' Theory of the Own-Rates of Interest', written in the same year (1939) but only published in 1960, merely provided a reworking of his earlier version of the theory.[51]

Here I shall dwell on Kaldor's theory of forward markets only to enunciate the proposition underpinning his thesis of the relation between short- and long-term interest rates.

Having defined 'arbitrage' as simultaneously buying spot and selling forward while holding stock until the date of delivery, Kaldor argued that when

[49] Ibid. 52.

[50] Para. 4 of the article appearing in CP ii (1st edn.) is a rewriting of the para. in the original 1939 article and incorporates elements from Kaldor's contribution to the June 1940 symposium on forward markets. The rewriting was also necessary because of criticisms of the original version by esp. J. C. R. Dow, 'A Theoretical Account of Future Markets', *RES* (June 1940). Contributors to the symposium in the June 1940 issue of *RES* were: N. Kaldor, 'A Note on the Theory of Forward Market'; J. C. R. Dow, 'Addenda to Mr Kaldor's "Note" '; R. G. Hawtrey, 'Mr Kaldor on the Forward Market'. Para. 10 Kaldor never altered, even though his theory of the relations between long-term and short-term interest rates was the object of much discussion and criticism. Note esp. the critiques by S. C. Tsiang, 'A Note on Speculation and Income Stability', *EC*, (Nov. 1943), and by C. Kennedy, 'Period Analysis and the Demand for Money', *RES*, 16 (I): 39 (1949–50); see also D. H. Robertson, 'Some Notes on the Theory of Interest', repr. in id., *Utility and All That and Other Essays* (London, Allen & Unwin, 1952); and R. F. Kahn, 'Some Notes on Liquidity Preference', *Manchester school* (Sept. 1954).

[51] Kaldor, 'Keynes's Theory of the Own-Rates of Interest' (1939), Pub. in CP ii.

the relationship between the future price and the current price of a good ensures a risk-free profit, the forward price of a good is given by the current price plus the cost of arbitrage. This latter arises from the marginal cost of maintenance plus the difference between the marginal cost represented by interest and the marginal return generated by the good (which is positive in the case of a security and zero in the case of a good). In a world of uncertain expectations, the expected price is given by these same elements plus a marginal-risk premium, which is higher, the greater the amount committed.[52] From this one may state the proposition that the future price is equal to the expected price minus the marginal-risk premium; it cannot be more than this amount because of the effect of arbitrage, and it cannot be less because of the effect of speculation.

As we saw in the previous section, there is a particular feature of the bonds market that is difficult to account for: in general, it possesses no element that can be used to determine a 'normal price'. Nevertheless a conviction of this sort must in fact exist, since it provides the only possible explanation for the stability of the long-term interest rate relative to the short-term one.

In the long-term bonds market, the elasticity of stocks is high: current price thus depends closely on expected price. The problem is therefore one of identifying the value of the expected price, to which a possible solution might be that the expected price is determined by past current prices. This explanation, though, is faulty, because if the current price depends on past prices, one has then to explain how these past prices were determined. The long-term rate of interest is therefore—to use Robertson's famous phrase—'left hanging in the air by its own boot-straps'.

Kaldor's solution (one also adopted by Hicks and Pigou[53]) is that the *current long-term* rate of interest depends on the *expected short-term* rates of interest. Thus a long-term loan (e.g. for two years) can be regarded as a short-term spot loan (e.g. for three months) plus a series of successive (e.g. seven) short-term loans. Since, as we have seen, the future price is lower—if uncertainty exists—than the expected price of the marginal-risk premium, it follows that the current long-term rate of interest is higher than the average of expected future short-term rates for the same duration of time. It also follows that the risk premium is given by the difference between the long-term rate and the expected average of short-term rates. On the other hand, the current short-term rate depends neither on the long-term interest rate nor on expected short-term interest rates—otherwise the argument would be circular—but only on money supply and demand. 'And since the elasticity of supply of cash with respect

---

[52] For Kaldor, the risk premium varies not only with the size of commitments but also with the individual psychological propensity to bear risks and with the standard deviation of the probability distribution of the future market values of the asset. Consequently, he anticipated some features of the analysis by H. M. Markowitz ('Portfolio Selection', *Journal of Finance* (Mar. 1952)) and by J. Tobin ('Liquidity Preference as Behaviour toward Risk', *RES*, (Feb. 1958)).

[53] J. R. Hicks, *Value and Capital*, (London, OUP, 1939), 145–6; A. C. Pigou, *Industrial Fluctuations* (London, Macmillan, 1929), 230–2.

to the short-term rate is normally much larger than the elasticity of demand, the current short-term rate of interest can be treated simply as a datum, determined by the policy of the Central Bank'.[54]

Kaldor's treatment of the relation between short- and long-term shows both resemblances and differences with respect to the Keynesian thesis of 'liquidity preference'. In both theories, the short-term rate of interest is determined, not by savings or investment, but by money supply and demand.

However, over the long-term rate of interest Keynes and Kaldor's positions diverged. For Keynes, the long-term rate of interest was insensitive to the demand and the supply of savings because of the 'liquidity premium' available, in situations of uncertainty, to short-term bonds and money. Kaldor argued instead that a distinction should be drawn between two cases. The first of these concerned the equalizing process of savings to investments that takes place outside the capital market through a variation in the long-period rate of interest. His explanation for this (as we saw in the previous section) was that, given the behaviour of speculators operating on the fixed-yield bonds market, a variation in the supply or demand for savings does not induce a change in price (interest rate); rather, it induces a compensatory variation in speculative stocks. Kaldor's second case concerned the liquidity preference, which is none other than (the negative of) the marginal-risk premium paid to holders of long-term bonds. This premium, as has been said, is given by the difference between the current long-term rate of interest and the average of expected short-term rates of interest.

Keynes and Kaldor drew different conclusions from their respective premises. For Kaldor, although a variation in the quantity of money directly affects the short-term rate of interest, it does not have a direct influence on the long-term rate of interest. An upward (or downward) variation in the quantity of money does not have an immediate bearing on the willingness of speculators to hold more or fewer long-term assets; it only does so, indirectly and slowly, as expectations are progressively influenced by the reduction (or increase) of the current short-term rate of interest below (or above) the expected short-term rate. By contrast,

changes in the 'liquidity preference' (i.e. in the preference for holding short-term as against long-term assets) or in expectations as to future interest rates, can only induce changes in the yield of long-term paper and cannot affect the short-term rate.[55]

We have already met this extremely tenuous link—almost a division—between short- and long-term rates in Kaldor's critique of Pigou (Chapter 2.2). Nevertheless, under certain circumstances, a connection between the two rates does exist, although it is not unique and determined a priori.

---

[54] Kaldor, 'Speculation and Economic Stability', 39. Note that here and in Kaldor's diagram reproduced in the footnote we have a first outline of the theory that Kaldor would subsequently call 'the endogeneity of money supply': see Ch. 11.

[55] Id., 'Keynes's Theory of the Own-Rates of Interest', 64.

If in Figure 2.1 the horizontal axis measures the maturity of bonds and the vertical axis measures interest rates, the rates of interest at any particular moment can be represented by a series of curves. What Kaldor called the 'normal yield curve'[56] (curve *A* in Figure 2.1) intersects the vertical axis at a certain value judged to be the 'normal' short-term rate of interest—that is, around the average level of the short rates of interest prevailing in the past. The curve slopes positively because, as a bond's maturity lengthens, the marginal-risk premium increases and is added to the future short-term rates of interest expected to be the same as the current 'normal' rate. Note, however, that the risk premium has a ceiling level at a certain date beyond which the marginal-risk premium is zero; consequently, the bond bearing that redemption date determines the perpetual annuities of irredeemable bonds. The short-term rate can be abnormally high or abnormally low. In these two cases (curves *B* and *C* respectively), the interest-rate curve changes shape accordingly. If the short-term rate is abnormally high, it may even overtake the rate on long-term bonds. This reflects the expectation that the short-term rate, and therefore the yield on bonds with any maturity, will fall in the future, while their prices will rise regardless of the nearness of the redemption date. The nominal yield of long-term bonds therefore appears to approach or even to dip below the short-term rate, although in fact the *expected* yield of these bonds is judged to be higher than their apparent yield.

The normal-yield curve slopes positively, Kaldor argues, because the expected price is given by the future price plus a (growing) marginal-risk premium; an argument that is valid provided that the hypothesis of uniform expectations—or at least of a prevalent expectation among speculators—holds true. If, however, there is a divergence of expectations in a market such that speculators enter in large numbers both as sellers and buyers, then the 'future price' will not necessarily be lower than the 'expected price' (or lower than the current price, in that it can be assumed to reflect the average of prices expected by bull and bear speculators) and the theory therefore no longer holds true. In the case of the bonds market

[i]f there is sufficient divergence of opinions concerning future interest rates there is no longer any necessary reason to suppose that the long-term rate will be above the average of past short-term rates; and the theory underlying our 'normal yield curve' . . . will break down.[57]

2.5. The 'Dominant' Rate of Interest

In chapter 17 of the *General Theory* Keynes explored the peculiar nature of money compared with other goods. Why, he asked, should the money rate of interest be dominant, and why should it set the standard to which the yields

---

[56] Ibid. 66.   [57] Ibid. 68.

FIG. 2.1 The structure of interest rates

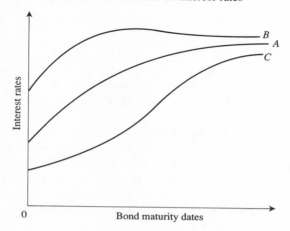

on other goods adjust? Keynes's search for an answer employed two special concepts. The first was the 'own-rate of own-interest' (henceforth 'oroi') of a commodity or activity (henceforth 'good')—that is, a rate of interest in terms of itself, or the return in terms of a good deriving from the loan of that good. For example, if 100 kilos of corn for spot delivery buys 98 kilos for future delivery, the oroi is − 2 per cent.[58]

Keynes's second concept was the 'own-rate of money-interest' (henceforth 'ormi') of a good, which is the oroi corrected for the expected increase in the price of that good. The ormi is the income earned by buying a good at spot and then selling it forward.

Since the difference between these two rates is given by the variation in the *money* price of a particular good, it follows that if there exist *n* goods, the two rates can only *ever* coincide for the good used as the unit of account, i.e. only for money. This does not hold for other goods because they may have temporarily different orois and the same ormi. This equality between the two rates in money terms is ensured in the short period by a variation in the spot price relative to expected price. Over the longer period, the orois also equalize through variations in production relative to consumption.

Given *n* goods, each with its oroi and its ormi, and given that all these 2*n* rates tend to equality over the long period, there arises the Keynesian problem of singling out that specific good whose own-rate rules the roost. If we accept Kaldor's argument outlined in the previous section, and according to which the long-term rate of money-interest is determined by the risk premium on long-term as against short-term loans, the question becomes:

---

[58] Keynes acknowledged Sraffa as having first formulated this concept: J. M. Keynes, 'Doctor Hayek on Money and Capital', *EJ* (Mar. 1932), 50.

How do we know whether it [this premium] sets the standard for the general level of own-rates of own-interest of houses, factories, plant and equipment, land, commodity stocks, etc., and not the other way round?[59]

Keynes had argued that the good whose oroi 'declines most slowly as the stock of assets in general increases, [is the one] which eventually knocks out the profitable production of each of the others',[60] adding that, generally, this good was money. However, he did not believe this to be always the case, since in certain periods other goods such as land[61] might possess this property, or gold in a country that had gone over to a non-Gold Standard.

Kaldor's criticism of Keynes focused on the assumption of inelastic expectations implicit in his thesis of the 'dominance' of the money-interest rate. Kaldor argued that the limit on the level of employment created by the liquidity preference can in practice be attributed *only* to those assets that function as numéraire; it cannot be attributed to any asset other than money, like land or non-monetary gold.

Let us suppose that a state of equilibrium is affected by a fall of X per cent in the oroi of a good a. The ormi of good a will be adjusted to the same value of the ormis of other goods through the expectation that the asset will appreciate in money terms because of a short-term fall of X per cent in its market price relative to its expected price. This adjustment mechanism presupposes that the expected price of the goodwill not change as a result of the change in the current price, and that the expected price is formed by reference to a normal long-term supply price. Only if current prices are higher than or equal to their normal supply prices will goods be reproduced. Assets with orois below their own ormis will not induce the production of goods.

In conditions of inelastic expectations

all assets other than money can adjust their own-rates of money-interest to that of money by a variation of their current price in terms of money; while the money-rate of money-interest can only be changed by varying money's own-rate of own-interest.[62]

Thus it is necessarily the oroi of money that rules the roost.

One notes that this conclusion depends closely on the assumption of the inelasticity of expectations (an assumption appropriate to reproducible goods). If, however, expectations are elastic, every change in the current price brings with it a change, in the same direction, in the expected price; the change in the market price does not arouse the expectation of plus or minus variation that equalizes the differences among the various orois. Only with elastic expectations, therefore, is it possible for the oroi of a good other than money

---

[59] Kaldor, 'Keynes' Theory of the Own-Rates of Interest', 69. Note the similarity with Sraffa's solution of 'closing' his model of prices and distribution with the money-rate of interest. P. Sraffa, *Production of Commodities by Means of Commodities* (Cambridge, CUP, 1960), 33.

[60] J. M. Keynes, *The General Theory of Employment, Interest and Money* (London, Macmillan, 1936), 279.

[61] Ibid.   [62] Ibid. 70.

to rule the roost. It is very unlikely that these conditions could exist in anything more than the short period, because a continued increase in the price of one good relative to others must, sooner or later, render expectations inelastic.

For this reason, Kaldor concludes, Keynes had no reason to fear that the desire to possess land or to hoard gold might prove an insurmountable obstacle to the production of other goods. Of course, as long as elastic expectations predominate, an increase in the price of hoarded gold and/or land will bring with it a further increase in the expected price of gold and/or land relative to reproducible goods like houses or machines. But a cumulative increase in the current price cannot last indefinitely, and sooner or later people will have increasing misgivings that the price of gold and/or land is too high relative to that of other goods and growing expectations that their price is bound to fall.

Thus, for Kaldor, the only liquidity preference that can set a limit to employment is that associated with money. 'It is because the *money*-rate of interest cannot become negative . . . that the risk premium associated with investment in factories, houses, etc., can set a limit to their profitable production.'[63] However, in these circumstances, full employment can also be achieved by other means: the inflation of prices or wages, for instance, has the same effect as a negative money rate of interest (we shall return to this topic in Chapter 12.2).

2.6. Interest and Investment

Many elements in Hawtrey's theory anticipated Keynes's by a number of years. Despite these similarities, however, there is one difference between the two theories that has never been resolved, namely, Hawtrey's distinction between short- and long-term investment. Even after publication of the *General Theory*, Hawtrey continued to argue[64] that there was a substantial difference between the behaviour of the money market, which determines the short-term rate of interest, and the capital market, where the long-term rate is determined.

In Hawtrey's theory, the economic cycle depends on variations in the stocks of goods held by 'traders', i.e. entrepreneurs. The average holding of stocks in relation to turnover is determined by borrowing conditions and by the rate of interest, which is determined by monetary policy. By contrast, investment in fixed capital is influenced by variations in the long-term interest rate. When the system achieves full employment, investments pass from a 'widening process' to a 'deepening process'—hence there is an increase in the capital/output ratio. When this happens, the equilibrium rate of interest equalizes savings and investment and corresponds to the marginal productivity of capital.

---

[63] Ibid. 73–4.

[64] R. G. Hawtrey, *Capital and Employment* (London, Longmans Green & Co., 1937).

In his review of Hawtrey's book,[65] Kaldor brought a number of criticisms against the above theory; criticisms which taken as whole provide a first outline of his own ideas on the trade cycle. First, the causes of depression are only to be found in the behaviour of long-term investment, any change in which depends on expectations of fluctuations in aggregate demand and not on the long-term rate of interest. Further, the long-term rate cannot be the cause of the investment-deepening process and simultaneously remain stable over the long period. The diverse nature of Kaldor's explanation of the cycle (based on expectations of demand rather than on monetary policy) is also reflected in his treatment of the savings–investment relation: large fluctuations in savings during the cycle cannot come about on their own. They can only be the result of strong fluctuations in investment and are, therefore, an *effect* not a *cause* of the cycle.

As early as 1938 Kaldor was already arguing that the *General Theory* was not a theory of the stagnation of capitalism à la Hansen or Steindl, nor was it a demonstration of the *stability* of a state of unemployment: it was a demonstration of the cyclical *instability* of economic activity and of employment. In his 1939 article 'Stability and Full Employment'[66] Kaldor discussed possible reasons why the system seemed destined to depart from full employment once it had achieved it; and he identified a number of obstacles that, in the short and long period, stood in the way of investment stability.

The first of these obstacles—the raising of interest rates by the banking system (the Kaleckian principle of increasing risk)—operated in the short period. But it was Kaldor's analysis of medium-period obstacles that gives a first inkling of the ideas that he would go on to develop, both in his theory of the cycle and then twenty years later in his theory of the distribution of income and economic growth. In a situation of full employment, the share of savings tends to adjust to the share of investments through the price mechanism in the presence of rigid money-wages (this idea will be explored in Chapter 5.6). However, the process is impeded by a series of major obstacles, which threaten the system with the constant risk of inflation or deflation. In the longer period, the first impediment to full employment is the scarcity of labour. If new machinery cannot find the workers to operate it, there ensues an excess of productive capacity which depresses investment. It is true, of course, that new plant tends to be labour-saving, but this is not enough: new machinery should be labour-saving, but only to the extent that no more labour is employed on it than is left idle by the replacement of the old machinery. This depends not only on technical progress, but also on the intensity of the investment process by which such technical progress is introduced. The greater the investment, in fact, the more new machinery saves labour. Hence it follows that, with the passage of time, the labour-saving capacity of new machinery is bound to

---

[65] N. Kaldor, 'Mr Hawtrey on Short- and Long-Term Investment' (1938), repr. in CP ii.
[66] Id., 'Stability and Full Employment' (1938), repr. in CP ii.

increase. And for this reason, whenever investment activity rises to a high level, sooner or later an excess of productive capacity will appear.

Economic policies must therefore be sufficiently diversified to deal with each of these obstacles separately. The first obstacle can be overcome by an accommodating monetary policy, although this will still be inadequate if the obstacle is an excess or insufficiency of saving (of full employment). In this latter case, policies must act on the propensity to save. In Kaldor's opinion, 'government can increase earnings by altering the distribution of income in favour of profit':[67] higher taxes or lower subsidies on wages increase the share of profit and hence the propensity to save. Similarly, the levying of turnover taxes or taxes on consumption goods will have a similar outcome. But this policy is not enough to deal with the final obstacle: the maladjustment between 'machines' and 'labour'. The transfer of workers from investment-goods industries to consumption-goods industries would be an effective remedy, although a difficult one to put into practice. A less effective but more feasible measure might be a policy of anticyclical public investments. Full-employment activity, Kaldor concluded,

is like a peculiar steeplechase, where the horse is bound to fall at one of four obstacles. If it survives the first, it might be checked on the second, the third or the fourth. It is probably a rare horse which survives until the last hurdle.[68]

Two years after publication of his early works on investment, Kaldor expounded a theory of the trade cycle as a phenomenon of dynamic adjustment of saving to investment, the pioneering nature of which was universally acknowledged in a field where Keynesian-derived theory would rule unopposed for thirty years.

---

[67] Ibid. 112.   [68] Ibid. 119.

Chapter 3

The Trade Cycle

Why is it that economic development does not proceed
smoothly as a tree grows, but as it were jerkily; why does it
show these characteristic up and downs?

J. A. Schumpeter, *The Theory of Economic Development*

3.1. The Criticism of the Austrian Theory of the Trade Cycle

Before Keynesian theory rose to pre-eminence, explanations of the trade cycle
were based on monetary, technological, and entrepreneurial factors. In Schumpeterian theory growth took place through innovation; but innovation by entrepreneurs and their followers forced the economy first into an upswing and
then into a downward movement until a new innovation set off another business cycle. Explanations of the business cycle were advanced in monetary
terms by the 'pre-Keynes Keynesians' like Hawtrey, and by the economists of
the Wicksellian school, for whom the cycle originated in the discrepancies
between monetary and real magnitudes. The Austrian school held the trade
cycle to be principally the outcome of a change in the relative prices of
consumption goods and capital goods. (This extremely simplified taxonomy
should not obscure the fact that many interpretations of the cycle belonged to
more than one of these various lines of thought; they therefore must not be
taken to be mutually exclusive.)

The leading exponent of the Austrian theory was undoubtedly Hayek, who
produced two accounts of his theory: the first in 1931,[1] and the second eight
years later.[2] Despite considerable differences between the two versions, they
are substantially similar in their underlying concept of insufficient savings as
the ultimate cause of crisis and unemployment. The effects of the shortage of
savings become apparent in changes in production techniques consequent on
alterations both in the money market and in the real market where the demand
for and the supply of savings meet.

The notion of the shortage of savings enjoyed considerable support in the
early 1930s because of the theoretical rationale it provided for an opinion then
widespread among the statesmen of the major Western countries. The idea that

---

[1] F. Hayek, *Prices and Production* (London, Routledge & Kegan Paul, 1931).

[2] Id., *Profits, Interest and Investment* (London, Routledge & Kegan Paul, 1939); id., *The Pure
Theory of Capital* (London, Routledge & Kegan Paul, 1941), pt. IV; id., 'The Ricardo Effect', *EC*
(May 1942).

the only cure for deflation is increased saving can be found in Snowden's budgetary policies of 1937, Roosevelt's electoral speeches of 1932, and the financial policies of Dr Bruning. The theory declined in importance between the mid-1930s and the end of the 1970s; but since then it has enjoyed a certain revival.

In *Prices and Production*, Hayek argued that a policy of excessive monetary expansion brings the rate of interest below its 'natural' level (i.e. the level that equalizes the demand for, and the supply of, 'voluntary savings'). A low interest rate induces both 'forced savings' and the adoption of more capital-intensive techniques of production.[3] As long as the interest rate stays low, it generates increasing consumption and therefore a rise in the prices of consumption goods. The resulting inflation contracts the real supply of money and raises the interest rate. Planned investments at a high capital/output ratio are not realized, and this provokes depression and unemployment. Hence, depression is caused by the shortage of voluntary saving in relation to the 'round-aboutness' of methods of production.

Hayek's book aroused heated discussion; and its most penetrating criticism was written by Kaldor himself—even though in the past he had been one of Hayek's disciples.[4] In 'Capital Intensity and the Trade Cycle', Kaldor still attached great importance to changes in production techniques during the progress of the trade cycle. However, he now argued, as did Knight, that capital intensity in a boom period moves in the opposite direction to that suggested by Hayek. I shall not follow Kaldor in what he described as his 'rather intricate reasoning',[5] because in a further article[6] criticizing Hayek's second version of his theory—an article that represents Kaldor's more developed thinking on the matter—he took up a more generally critical position towards the thesis of the importance of changes in production techniques in the trade cycle. Despite the differences in the arguments advanced by these two articles, they both rejected the doctrine that he had learnt during his formative years at the LSE, and they both moved in a direction that was increasingly and unequivocally Keynesian.

In 1939, no more than a year after Kaldor's first critical review, Hayek published a second version of his theory. In *Profits, Interest and Investment*, the Austrian economist still asserted that depression was caused by a shortage of saving and that it manifested itself in a change in production techniques. But he now maintained that capital intensity diminished in the upward phase

[3] In several previous articles Kaldor had argued that the Austrian school's concept of the 'investment period' or 'amount of waiting' should be replaced by the notion of 'capital intensity', defined as the ratio between the initial cost and the annual cost involved in producing a given quantity of goods ('The Recent Controversy on the Theory of Capital', *ECTR* (July 1937); 'Addendum: A Rejoinder to Professor Knight', *ECTR* (Apr. 1938)). The dependence of the ratio's numerator and denominator on the prices of goods makes this concept, too, unsuitable for measuring capital. See P. Garegnani, *Il capitale nelle teorie della distribuzione* (Milan, Giuffrè, 1960).
[4] N. Kaldor, 'Capital Intensity and the Trade Cycle' (1939), repr. in CP ii.
[5] Id., introd. to CP ii. 11.
[6] Id., 'Professor Hayek and the Concertina Effect' (1942), repr. in CP ii.

of the cycle, as Kaldor had argued in his review of *Prices and Production*. Hayek's second version of his theory was again attacked by his ex-pupil, with an analytical energy so disproportionate to its object that Keynes told Kaldor that he was 'using a sledge-hammer to crack a nut'.[7]

This second version of Hayek's theory assumed the constancy of interest rates and of money-wages. An excessive increase in the demand for consumption goods (compared with 'voluntary saving') due to monetary factors or some other reason, raises the prices and the profit rate in the sector producing consumption goods; this causes real wages to fall and investments to increase. Lower real wages encourage entrepreneurs to adopt less capital-intensive techniques—the 'Ricardo effect' as Hayek called it. The increase in investment demand, coupled with the decline in capital intensity, leads to falling demand in the capital-goods sector and hence to depression, which is greater, the longer the rate of profit in the consumption-goods sector continues to be high.

According to Kaldor, in Hayek's first version of his theory, depression was caused because

during the boom the capitalist system engaged in the building of superior capital goods, for the completion of which the available resources were insufficient.

In his second version

[w]hen the demand for their products goes up, entrepreneurs make higher profits. They then discover that by turning over their capital more quickly they can make still higher profits. They therefore proceed to do so, and this ultimately involves a fall in investment.[8]

In both cases depression was caused neither by falling rates of profit nor by a lack of opportunities for investment (which would be the Keynesian cause of the cyclical downturn), but by what Kaldor called the 'concertina effect'—i.e. the wrong choice, in one way or the other, of production techniques.

Kaldor contested Hayek's use of the 'Ricardo effect': a principle from Ricardo's chapter 'On Machines'[9] first used by Jevons and then later rediscovered by Hayek in *Prices and Production* which stated that a variation (up or down) in capital intensity is determined by a variation in the relative prices of goods consequent on a variation (up or down) in the *rate of interest* and not in the *rate of profit* of the consumption-goods industries. In Ricardo, the rate of interest and the rate of profit coincide; not so, however, in Hayek's second version, where the rate of interest is assumed to be fixed (if it were not, it would belong to the first version with a pro-cyclical change in capital intensity). But if the rate of interest is fixed, Kaldor objected, investment will

---

[7] Id., introd. to CP ii. (1st edn., 1960), 11.
[8] Id., Professor Hayek and the Concertina Effect', 152.
[9] D. Ricardo, *Principles of Political Economy*, ed., Sraffa (Cambridge, CUP for the Royal Economic Society, 1970), ch. 1, pp. 42–3.

increase because of the higher rate of profit, but with capital intensity remaining unchanged.

Aside from the arbitrariness of Hayek's assumptions and from his inaccurate references to the history of economic analysis, Kaldor declared that he had simply got it wrong: his 'Ricardo effect' was unable to explain the cyclical behaviour of investment demand. Firms could in fact find themselves faced with capital-supply curves with zero, infinite, or intermediate elasticity. The extreme case of the curve of rigid supply had been hypothesized by Wicksell as a purely theoretical device to solve the problem of the size of a firm under conditions of perfect competition: entrepreneurs can only hire the factors that they do not own, and hence firms cannot borrow investment funds, although it is precisely this phenomenon that characterizes the cycle. If instead the supply curve is infinitely elastic, the Ricardo effect—as Hayek himself admitted—is inoperative. The curves must therefore be upwardly sloping but not rigid: in this case investment spending is variable and the Ricardo effect comes into operation. Here one may imagine that capital intensity and therefore investment spending are reduced by the increase in the interest rate; but since this latter only rises because the investment rate has increased, one may end up with less investment spending than before. The reduction in capital intensity due to the operation of the Ricardo effect would make investment spending less than it would have been if there had been no change in capital intensity, but it could not make such spending equal to zero because capital intensity would not have fallen if investment spending had not increased.

Such was Kaldor's criticism of Hayek's theory on logical grounds; but he also contested its empirical validity. On examining statistical evidence relating to the period 1929–41, he found a close correlation between the cycle and gross profit margins, changes in the share of investments in income *and* in per-capita output (a phenomenon that Kaldor would subject to close theoretical scrutiny for the next twenty years). Kaldor asked:

Does this mean that we should go back to Professor Hayek's original position and assume that the concertina-effect works the other way? I think the evidence rather suggests that the concertina, whichever way it goes, makes a relatively small noise—it is drowned by the cymbals of technical progress. Innovations are constantly occurring, inducing a continued increase in both capital and output per head (quite independently of interest rates or profit margins) which goes to swamp any cyclical fluctuation between deepening and enshallowing that might otherwise have occurred. The investment cycle, as Mr Hawtrey has said, is essentially a matter of widening and not of deepening.[10]

It is to the analysis of this latter phenomenon of the widening and narrowing of investment, the core of the Keynesian theory of the trade cycle, that we now turn.

---

[10] Kaldor, 'Professor Hayek and the Concertina Effect', 175.

3.2. The First 'Keynesian' Theories of the Trade Cycle

In the same year as the *General Theory* was published two outstanding economists—Harrod and Kalecki—showed that the major flaw in the new theory
was its treatment of the investment function.[11] Because of their emphasis on
the endogenous nature of investment, Harrod and Kalecki became the founders
of the post-Keynesian theory of the trade cycle and the main inspirers of
Kaldor's pioneering work on the subject.

Richard Goodwin has written recently:

With great acumen, Harrod had realised that the missing link in the *General Theory*
was a dynamic theory of investment. Consequently, in his brilliant but largely neglected book on the *Trade Cycle*[12] he combined the multiplier and the accelerator to
explain the contradictory behaviour of capitalism.[13]

According to Goodwin, Tinbergen's critical review of Harrod's book[14]—
where he argued that the combination of the accelerator and the multiplier
gave a first order difference equation and therefore could only give rise to
exponential growth and not to economic cycles—persuaded Harrod ('unfortunately', in Goodwin's opinion) to devote himself to the theory of growth: two
years later Harrod published his well-known article that generated the massive
post-war literature on the subject.

In 1939 an article published by Samuelson[15] developed a linear model based
on the interaction between an accelerator in the consumption-goods sector and
a multiplier. Here the accelerator, with constant parameters, gives rise to either
a differential equation or a first order difference equation. If the accelerator
parameter is linear, for the equation to be able to explain cyclical behaviour
in the economy it must be of second order, and for this purpose time-lags are
introduced into the working of the multiplier or of the accelerator. Cyclical
behaviour can be, in turn, either damped, explosive, or regular, depending on
the values of the parameters. It can be shown, however, that an endogenous
cycle is only deducible from very specific values for the parameters.[16]

[11] In Kalecki's review of the *General Theory* one reads: 'it is difficult to consider Keynes's
solution of the investment problem to be satisfactory. The reason for this failure lies in an approach
which is basically static to a matter which is by its nature dynamic. Keynes takes as given the
state of expectations of returns and from this he deduces a certain determined level of investment,
overlooking the effects that investment will have in turn on expectations'. M. Kalecki, 'Pare urvag
o teorii keynesa', *Ekonomista*, 3 (1936), trans. F. Targetti and B. Kinda-Hass as 'Kalecki's Review
of Keynes's *General Theory*', *Australian Economic Papers* (Dec. 1982), 252.

[12] R. Harrod, *The Trade Cycle* (Oxford, Clarendon Press, 1936).

[13] R. Goodwin, *Essays in Economic Dynamics* (London, Macmillan, 1982), quotation translated
from the Italian edn.

[14] J. C. Tinbergen, 'Über die Sekundarwirkungen Zusatzlicher Investionen', *Wertwirtscha-
fliches Archiv*, 45:1 (1937).

[15] P. Samuelson, 'Interaction between the Multiplier Analysis and the Principle of Acceleration', *REST* (May 1939).

[16] Samuelson's expression was the following second order difference equation:
$Y_t = \alpha(1 + \beta)Y_{t-1} + \alpha\beta Y_{t-2} - G = 0$ where Y is income, G is an exogenous variable, the suffixes
stand for the reference years, β is the accelerator coefficient, and α the propensity to consume. If

The two best-known of these time-lags took the names of 'Lundberg's lag',[17] where supply adjusts to demand after a period of delay (and the multiplier is instantaneous), and 'Robertson's lag', used by Samuelson, where consumption adjusts to the level of income after a period of delay. The model could be further complicated by introducing a time-lag between investment decisions and investment spending. Generally speaking, in all models generating second order different equations, a regular cycle can be obtained only in the particular case where the roots of the equation are complex and the modulus is unity.[18]

It was clear that if the subject of analysis was to be a persistent cycle, models of this sort were unsuitable. Either they did not account for a stable cycle or they did so only so long as the parameters had very specific values theoretically difficult to be justified.

In the field of post-Keynesian theory of the trade cycle, a book with even less initial impact than Harrod's *Trade Cycle* (among other things because it was written in Polish), but even more pioneering in its arguments (it was written in fact three years before Keynes's *General Theory*), was Kalecki's *Próba teorii Koniunktury*.[19] The Polish economist read a shortened version of his monograph to the International Conference on Econometrics at Leyden in October 1933. This version was published two years later in English and in French.[20]

Kalecki's first version of his model gave a zero value to the sum of certain parameters in order to obtain a persistent trade cycle—a device which provoked the criticisms of Frisch, Holme, and Tinbergen.[21] Frisch argued that, whereas in the theoretical model the value of these parameters must be *exactly* zero, in the empirical world (as the ancient Greeks knew very well), the value of a certain magnitude cannot be measured with absolute precision. One need only have, though, values of the parameters adding up to minus or plus epsilon for the theoretical model to be unable to explain a persistent cycle.

Unlike Harrod, however, Kalecki did not feel impelled to change his field of study as a result of this criticism; instead he produced two further versions

---

the roots of the equation are real, the trend of income is monotonic—towards equilibrium if $\alpha\beta < 1$ or away from it if $\alpha\beta > 1$. If the roots are complex, the movement of income is cyclical; the cycle will be either explosive or damped according to whether $\alpha\beta$ is greater or less than unity; the cycle will be regular only if $\alpha\beta = 1$ and hence the modulus is unity.

[17] F. Lundberg, *Studies in the Theory of Economic Expansion* (London, Macmillan, 1937).

[18] For exhaustive treatment of these models, see G. Gandolfo, *Mathematical Methods and Models in Economic Dynamics* (Amsterdam, North Holland Publishing Co., 1971).

[19] M. Kalecki, *Proba teorii Koniunktury* (Warsaw, 1933).

[20] Id., 'A Macrodynamic Theory of Business Cycle', *ECTR* (July 1935); 'Essai d'une théorie du mouvement cyclique des affaires', *Revue d'économie politique* (Mar.–Apr. 1935). Kalecki's model can be summarized by this equation: $\Delta^2 Y_t + (\alpha + \beta)\Delta Y_t + \gamma Y_t = 0$. The model gives a cycle which is damped, persistent or explosive if $(\alpha + \beta)$ x 0. Because Kalecki had statistical information on α and γ, but not on β, he imposed $(\alpha + \beta) = 0$.

[21] R. Frisch and H. Holme, 'The Characteristic Solutions of a Mixed Difference and Differential Equation Occurring in Economic Dynamics', *ECTR* (1935), 225–39, and J. Tinbergen, 'Suggestion on Quantitative Business Cycle Theory', *ECTR* (1935), 241–308.

of his model,[22] the second of which had certain features in common with a path-breaking work by Frisch[23]—who had been influenced in turn by a 1907 article by Wicksell.[24] Kalecki's theory of the trade cycle was based on two functions: one linking savings with profits, and the other linking investment decisions positively with profits and with their rate of change and negatively with investments effectively undertaken during the period of investment decision. The model based on these two functions had a structure[25] such that its dynamic behaviour could generate a trend of investments and therefore of income that was either explosive or damped, with or without oscillations. To counter Frisch's criticisms and to obtain persistent cycles, Kalecki first supposed that the parameters of his function were able to generate a damped fluctuating movement, and then that this movement was kept going by exogenous erratic shocks. Although this 'erratic shocks theory' was revived at the end of the 1950s and the 1960s,[26] it has not generally been taken to be an endogenous theory of the cycle, in that it treats economic fluctuations as largely the result of the interaction between certain lags and random shocks.

3.3 Non-Linear Models of the Trade Cycle

All the models discussed so far were based on difference equations in which the coefficients of the equations are constants. In economic terms, this entailed the assumption that the decisions taken by economic agents over the amount of income to save or over the capital/output ratio do not change with variations in the *level* of income or as time passes. Moroever, these models, as we have seen, could not give an endogenous account of undamped fluctuations unless

---

[22] The first of these versions—the one that Kaldor said came closest to his own thinking—is set out in M. Kalecki, 'A Theory of the Business Cycle', *RES* (Feb. 1937), rep. as ch. 6 in *Essays in the Theory of Economic Fluctuations* (London, Allen & Unwin, 1939). The model described in these works assumes a time-lag between investment decisions and the corresponding change in income to obtain a cyclical trend. Kalecki published his second version in *Studies in Economic Dynamics* (London, Allen & Unwin, 1943); subsequently revised in *Theory of Economic Dynamics* (London, Allen & Unwin, 1954). These models were stochastic based on linear difference equations of the second order.

[23] R. Frisch, 'Propagation Problems and Impulse Problems in Dynamic Economics', *Economic Essays in Honour of Gustav Cassel* (London, Allen & Unwin, 1933).

[24] K. Wicksell, 'The Enigma of Business Cycles' (1907), in *International Economic Papers* (1953).

[25] The function that summarizes the model's hypotheses is of the type: $I_t - \alpha I_{t-1} + \beta I_{t-2} = 0$ where α and β are parameters combining four coefficients—namely, the coefficient of reinvestment, the propensity to consume of profit-earners, the coefficient of acceleration, the coefficient of the investment decision induced by capital accumulation—in various relations. See A. Medio, 'Ciclo', in G. Lunghini and M. D'Antonio, (eds.), *Dizionario di economia politica* (Turin, Boringhieri, 1985), 52.

[26] I. and F. Adelman, 'The Dynamic Properties of the Klein-Goldberg Model', *ECTR* 27: 4, (1959). G. C. Chow and R. E. Leviatan, 'The Nature of Busines Cycles Implicit in a Linear Economic Model', *OEP* (Aug. 1969).

they dealt with very particular cases indeed.[27] They were therefore susceptible to the kind of criticism that Kaldor made of them:

[T]he existence of the cycle was explained as a result of the operation of certain time-lags which prevented the new equilibrium from being reached, once the old equilibrium, for some external cause, had been disturbed. In this sense all these theories may be regarded as being derived from the 'cobweb theorem'. The drawback of such explanations is that the existence of an undamped cycle can be shown only as a result of a happy coincidence, of a particular constellation of the various time-lags and parameters assumed.[28]

The solution to the problem lay in the construction of non-linear models. The idea that economic fluctuations could be captured by such models had been first advanced in a brief note to *Econometrica* by the French physicist Le Corbellier.[29] The simplest way of introducing non-linearity into analysis of the trade cycle was to set 'ceilings' or 'floors' on the rate of change in the variables described by a linear model of accelerator–multiplier interaction (Samuelson called it the non-linearity of the 'billiard ball'). This was the approach adopted by Hicks in his celebrated book of 1950:[30] the system expands until it is blocked by the full utilization of productive capacity or of labour (a full-employment ceiling); it then contracts until it reaches a limit represented by positive gross investment equal to the level of depreciation (i.e. a depreciation floor).

The most thorough analysis along Hicksian lines was Goodwin's.[31] In an article published in 1953 he had already obtained—by incorporating a non-linear accelerator into the multiplier—a Rayleigh-type mathematical relation[32] (thus named for the nineteenth-century English physicist who had discovered it).

Two Russian scientists, Andronow and Chaikin, had found that a Van der Pol equation (similar to Goodwin's) generated a single stable periodic solution, and that every solution tended towards the periodic solution. The equation's solution led to a stable *movement* as opposed to a stable *equilibrium*. Goodwin thus detected the presence of 'limit cycles': a kind of cyclical trajectory of gravity, in the sense that the system approached it with the passage of time. The solution took the form of a graphic description showing that the variables suddenly change velocity in time (so-called 'relaxing oscil-

---

[27] See n. 16, above. These models also entail that phases of expansion must be identical with phases of recession—which contradicts the evidence of the real world.

[28] N. Kaldor, 'A Model of the Trade Cycle' (1940), repr. in CP ii. 191–2.

[29] P. Le Corbellier, 'Les systèmes autoentretenus et les oscillations de relaxation', *ECTR* (1933). Non-linear analysis attracted the attention of physicists and engineers during the 1920s, when they realized that linear models were unable to handle certain mechanisms such as the electronic amplifier or the electronic oscillator correctly.

[30] J. R. Hicks, *A Contribution to the Theory of the Trade Cycle* (Oxford, Clarendon Press, 1950).

[31] R. Goodwin, 'A Non-linear Theory of the Cycle', *RES* 32: 4 (1950); id., 'The Non-Linear Accelerator and the Persistence of Business Cycles', *ECTR*, 19: 1 (1951); id., 'A Model of Cyclical Growth', *The Business Cycles in Post-War World*, ed. E. Lundberg (London, Macmillan, 1955).

[32] This took the following general form: $\ddot{x} + X(\dot{x}) + x = 0$, where the dots represent the degree of the derivative relative to time.

lations').[33] The general features of persistent oscillations achieved by means of non-linear equations are the following: (1) the final result is independent of the initial conditions; (2) the oscillations are self-perpetuating and do not need external intervention; (3) the mechanism is triggered automatically by the smallest disturbance; (4) there is no need to introduce arbitrary time-lags. Further, although the cycle obtained by non-linear functions repeats itself, it does not have to be regular: it may have phases of expansion and contraction of varying duration.[34]

However, ten years before the Hicks–Goodwin[35] model appeared, Kaldor had already presented, in the *Economic Journal*,[36] a cyclical model based on non-linear functions of saving and investment.[37] Although this model was illustrated in graphic terms, and although it required further analytical development by mathematical economists, it was nevertheless the first cyclical model based on non-linear functions to appear in the literature. And even recently a review of the theories of the trade cycle has declared that 'apart from Goodwin's model, perhaps the most influential model of the trade cycle was Kaldor's'.[38]

3.4. Kaldor's Model of the Trade Cycle

According to Kaldor himself, the two works that exerted the greatest influence over his theory of the trade cycle were Harrod's book of 1936 and Kalecki's articles of 1935. Both Kalecki and Kaldor held that investment depended positively on the *level* of profit and therefore on the level of activity, and negatively on the stock of capital. Unlike Kalecki, however, Kaldor asserted that the slope of the investment function relative to output changes as output (which he measured in terms of employment) rises and falls. The investment curve is flatter than normal when the level of activity is either very low or very high. In the former case, because of the large amount of unutilized

[33] After publication of his 1951 article, Goodwin realized that of the two limits that made income oscillate, only full employment was an exogenous constraint, while the lower limit was endogenous to the dynamic structure of the system. He therefore came to the conclusion that the multiplier–accelerator mechanism, which was unstable, required only one non-linearity to obtain a cyclical trend. He described his idea of the economy as an example of a unilateral oscillator to Le Corbellier—who was sceptical because an oscillator of this kind was not to be found in the literature on cyclical movements of any other discipline. However, with time, Le Corbellier became convinced of the validity of Goodwin's intuition and gave it formal exposition.

[34] In Goodwin's 1952 model the system spent more time in depression than it did in expansion.

[35] It should be pointed out that prior to Hicks an Italian economist had already formulated a cyclical model based on non-linear functions. A. Marrama 'Short Notes on a Model of the Trade Cycle', *RES* 14 (I): 35 (1946–7), 34–40.

[36] Kaldor, 'A Model of the Trade Cycle'.

[37] Richard Goodwin has told me that the idea of an S-shaped investment curve came to Kaldor in 1939 when he was examining war finance and noticed that the curve of investment relative to output flattened near full employment and at very low levels of income.

[38] A. W. Mullineux, *The Business Cycle after Keynes: A Comparative Analysis* (Totowa, NJ, Barnes & Noble Books, and Brighton, Wheatstreay Books Ltd., 1984), 21.

productive capacity, an increase in production will not lead to more investment—the level of which never drops to zero, however, because of autonomous investment; in the latter case, investment is inevitably low because of
the increase in production costs (full utilization in the sector producing capital
goods) due either to a shortage of funds or to the high cost of borrowing them
(Kalecki's increasing risk[39]).

The slope of the saving curve (propensity to save) also alters according to the
level of income. But here things are the other way round: the propensity to save
(the inverse of the multiplier) is high with abnormally low levels of income and
low with abnormally high levels. When income is low, consumers reduce their
savings to keep as close as possible to their customary levels of consumption;
when incomes are high, they save proportionately more. One notes that this
hypothesis anticipated Duesenberry's theory of relative income, which became a
popular account of consumption behaviour in the years that followed.[40] Kaldor's
hypothesis, however, was based not so much on psychological as on social
arguments: when income levels are low, unemployment is high and a larger
proportion of income derives from unemployment benefits; when income levels
are high, profits rise and there is accordingly a greater propensity to save. (This
idea will be discussed in more detail in Chapters 5 and 6.)

In Kaldor's model the two curves of savings (S) and investment (I) are
therefore curvilinear in relation to income (Y): the investment curve is S-
shaped and the saving curve is an inverted S. If the two curves meet in the
first quadrant of the Cartesian plane, the situation is one of two stable saving–
investment equilibria (A and B) and one unstable equilibrium (C) (Figure
3.1(a) continuous curves). To the right of both equilibrium points A and B,
saving is greater than investment and hence the level of activity, and then
income, tends to contract; to the left of them, investment is greater than saving
and hence the level of activity tends to increase. By the same principle, point
C represents a situation of unstable equilibrium, because if the system stands
at a point to the right or left of it, activity tends to leave equilibrium. (Note
that in order for this to occur, only one curve need be non-linear.)

If no other forces are at work, the system tends towards stable equilibrium
with very high (A) or very low (B) levels of activity. That this does not happen
in reality is because these are only short-period equilibria. If the system stays
for any prolonged period of time at the equilibrium point of maximum activity
(Figure 3.1(a) stage I, point B), the accumulation of capital—by restricting the
range of available investment opportunities—causes the investment curve to
shift downwards.[41] At the same time the saving curve shifts upwards[42] (Figure

[39] M. Kalecki, 'The Principle of Increasing Risk', *ECTR* (Nov. 1937).

[40] J. Duesenberry, *Income, Saving and the Theory of Consumer Behaviour* (Cambridge, Mass.,
Harvard University Press, 1949).

[41] This hypothesis—an extremely old one in economic theory—was associated in the 19th cent.
with Ricardo, Marx, and J. S. Mill and in the 20th cent. with Keynes, Robertson, and Kalecki.

[42] Kaldor gave no convincing explanation as to why this should happen. In the years that
followed, a contrary hypothesis bearing the name of the 'Pigou effect' gained ground, i.e. that

FIG. 3.1 The shifts of the curvilinear savings and investment curves
    (*a*) Stages I and II   (*b*) Stages III and IV
    (*c*) Stage V   (*d*) Stages VI and VII = Stage I

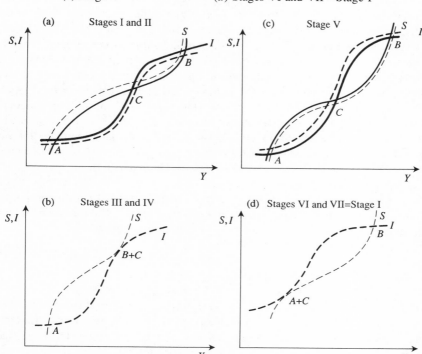

3.1(*a*), stage II, dotted line). This process lasts until the equilibrium of maximum activity becomes unstable (Figure 3.1(*b*), stage III, point *B* + *C*). This
new equilibrium is unstable in a downward direction, and the level of activity
therefore falls to the lower level of activity (Figure 3.1(*b*), stage IV, point *A*).
However, the stable equilibrium of low activity is also short-lived because
gross investment is not enough to cover the replacement of equipment; the net
investment is therefore negative. Opportunities for investment gradually accumulate, and this tendency is reinforced by new inventions. The investment
curve therefore shifts upwards (Figure 3.1(*c*), stage V, dotted curve). This
process will continue until the point of equilibrium at a low level of activity
becomes unstable (Figure 3.1(*a*), stage VI, point *A* + *C*) and the level of
activity is pushed up to maximum levels again (Figures 3.1(*d*) and (*a*), stages
VII and I, point *B*). The cycle has now returned to the point at which it started,
and the cyclical movement begins once again.[43]

$\delta S/\delta K < 0$. However, even if the Pigou effect is valid, Kaldor's conclusions still hold as long as
$\delta I/\delta K < \delta S/\delta K$.

[43] The route leading from *B* + *C* to *A* or from *A* + *C* to *B* follows either the *I* = *f*(*X*) curve or the

Kaldor maintained that there are three assumptions that are necessary and sufficient to explain why cyclical fluctuations should be persistent in time: (1) for normal values, the slope of the investment curve must be steeper than the saving curve, otherwise there will be one single stable value of the equilibrium activity level $S = I$; (2) for extreme values of the level of activity, the slope of investment function must be shallower than the slope of the saving function, otherwise the system becomes explosive; (3) with high (or low) levels of activity, the investment function must fall (rise) over time relative to the saving function, otherwise the cycle comes to a halt at one of the two points of stable equilibrium. Thirty years after the publication of Kaldor's theory, Chang and Smyth showed that these three conditions were, in fact, neither necessary nor sufficient to obtain a limit cycle.[44] In his final contribution on the subject, Kaldor accepted this criticism but pointed out that his conclusions were still valid if a fourth condition was added; a condition that he had neglected to specify since it was implicit in all the Keynesian models of 'short-period equilibrium': namely, that the time required to adjust output to changes in investment must be less than the time required to alter investment (at a given level of activity) because of a change in capital stock.[45]

3.5. The Phases of the Cycle

Kaldor's theory of the trade cycle was much more powerful than its predecessors because it was based only on factors endogenous to the model. Kalecki and Samuelson's theory required time-lags in order to explain the existence of the cycle, while for Kaldor time-lags[46] were important only as regards the cycle's *period*. For Kalecki and Frisch the amplitude of the cycle depended on the size of the initial shock. In Kaldor's model the amplitude was determined by endogenous factors; the hypothesis of 'initial shocks' was therefore entirely redundant to it.

If the cycle is divided into four phases—recovery, boom, recession, and depression—it was Kaldor's opinion in 1940 (in keeping with the generally pessimistic mood of the time) that a depression phase would last much longer than a boom phase; the reason being that it took more time for capital goods to wear out than it did to build them.[47] Fifteen years later (perhaps because of the renewed optimism of the post-war years) he changed his mind.

$S = f(X)$ curve according to whether ex-post I is adjusted to ex-post X or vice versa.

[44] W. W. Chang and D. J. Smyth, 'The Existence and Persistence of Cycles in a Non-Linear Model: Kaldor's 1940 Model Re-Examined', *RES* (Jan. 1971).

[45] N. Kaldor, 'The Existence and Persistence of Cycles in a Non-Linear Model: Kaldor's 1940 Model Re-Examined: A Comment', *RES* (Jan. 1971).

[46] The two time-lags explaining the period of the cycle were (1) the rate at which the I and S curves shifted at any particular level of investment; (2) the time required for the system to move from $B + C$ to A or from $A + C$ to B.

[47] Goodwin came to a similar conclusion with his 1951 model in its simple version: 'A striking

Contrary to the general belief (including my own previous views) . . . I now believe that the relative duration of the boom phase and the depression phase is simply a matter of the relationship of the output capacity of the investment goods industries to the normal annual depreciation of the capital stock.[48]

FIG. 3.2 Different phases of Kaldor's model of the cycle

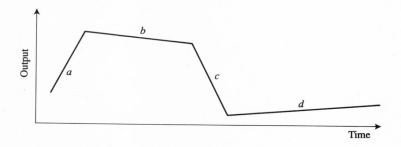

The greater the capacity of the capital-goods industries, the greater the rate of capital accumulation in boom periods, the shorter the boom phase itself is and the greater the amplitude of the cyclical movement. The relationship between the capital-goods industries and the consumption-goods industries depends in turn on the proportion of income saved at full employment. In conclusion, the amplitude and the duration of the phases of the cyclical movement are simply determined by the nature of the short-term savings function.

A point first raised by Chang and Smyth and recently made again by Goodwin[49] should be mentioned here. In Kaldor's model the phases have different spans depending on whether the system moves along the fixed curves or whether the curves themselves move. In the former case the phase lasts approximately one year (Figure 3.2, phases *a* and *c*); in the latter case it lasts approximately ten years (Figure 3.2, phases *b* and *d*)—and this, especially as regards the depression phase, is unrealistic.

---

consequence of the mechanism is its tendency to spend more time in situations of depression than of boom' (*Essays in Economic Dynamics*, 147). However, he obtained the opposite result when he introduced, in his 1957 model, a trend factor (ibid. 151) or the assumption of a time-lag between a production decision and the installation of new capital goods. In this latter case, 'the model will have a contraction phase much shorter than the expansion phase and thus accommodates one of the most widely-held generalizations on economic cycles' (ibid. 240).

[48] N. Kaldor, 'The Relation of Economic Growth and Cyclical Fluctuations' (1954), repr. in CP ii. 217.

[49] Chang and Smyth, 'Kaldor's 1940 Model Re-Examined'; M. Pugno, *Teorie del ciclo economico: appunti dalle lezioni di R. M. Goodwin all' Università di Trento* (Trento, Università degli Studi, 1990), 19. See also G. Gabish and H. Lorenz, *Business Cycle Theory* (Berlin, Springer, 1990).

3.6. The Ensuing Debate

As we have seen, Kaldor's investment function depended, like Kalecki's, on the level of activity and not, as in Hicks and Goodwin's accelerator, on the rate of change in output. The accelerator principle had been subject to various criticisms,[50] which were renewed by Kaldor's review of Hicks's book.[51] The main difference between the two economists was that, whereas Kaldor took account in his theory of the depressive effect of the level of the capital stock on investment, Hicks did not give it any explicit consideration.

For Hicks–Goodwin the cycle turned downwards because of the depressive effect of real shortages at high levels of production. It was a theory that was in some respects similar to the theories of 'hyperinvestment' of Tugan Baranowski, Spiethoff, Wicksell, and Hayek, all of whom agreed that when output increases at high rates, the shortage of productive factors changes relative prices and the composition of output. (However, the differences between Hicks–Goodwin's models and Hayek's are much greater than their similarities: in Hicks–Goodwin, for example, the ceiling constraint is shortage of labour, while in Hayek it is 'investable funds'.) Kaldor's theory came closer to the theories of 'underconsumption' elaborated by economists such as Aftalion, Schumpeter, Foster, and Catchings, and also by Robertson and Pigou—for whom the downswing began when incremental output, obtained from greater accumulation during the upward phase, came on to the markets and generated an excessive supply of consumption goods relative to demand.

Kaldor's first criticism of Hicks's model was that its ceiling of full employment was only one of a number of factors that could account for the upper turning-point of the cycle.[52] For example, 'the rate of expansion of firms is confined by their financial resources (quite independently of market rates of interest)';[53] an area of analysis that would be profitably explored by H. Minsky in subsequent years.[54] Moreover, if the boom was immediately broken by colliding with the full-employment ceiling—unlike the case where a free cycle changes direction because of a fall-off in investment—its downward movement would, in Kaldor's opinion, be too violent to be realistic.

Finally, in a note to his review of Hicks's book, Kaldor was apparently aware of the intuition that Goodwin had confided to Le Corbellier (see note 33, above), when he stated:

It is not even necessary for the initial movement to bump against *both* barriers to become streamlined into a constant cycle. Provided the cycle is inherently explosive,

---

[50] A criticism similar to Kaldor's is to be found in M. Kalecki, *Essays in the Theory of Economic Fluctuations*, 64–6, and in Tinbergen, 'Critical Remarks on Some Business Cycle Theories', *ECTR* (Apr. 1942).

[51] N. Kaldor, 'Hicks on the Trade Cycle' (1951), repr. in CP ii.

[52] Ibid. 202.   [53] Ibid. 200.

[54] H. P. Minsky, 'A Linear Model of Cyclical Growth', *RES* (May 1959).

it is enough if it hits one of the two barriers in the course of an initial swing for the subsequent oscillations to become reproductions of each other.[55]

In the early 1950s two Japanese economists examined Kaldor's model and compared it with those of Hicks and Goodwin. Yasui transposed the model into the terms of the Van der Pol theory of relaxing oscillations and, by using the so-called Poincaré-Liénard method, demonstrated the existence of a limit cycle and therefore of persistent fluctuations in the system.[56] Ichimura then identified the conditions necessary for the existence and uniqueness of a limit cycle in the Kaldor and Hicks–Goodwin models, using theorems taken from Levinson and Smith.[57] Fifteen years later the stability of the limit cycle was verified within a stochastic framework.[58] Finally, mention should be made of the recent application to Kaldor's model of catastrophe theory.[59]

The theory of the economic cycle broadly coincided with the development of the Keynesian theories on the trade cycle from the early 1930s until the mid-1970s.[60] However, during the 1950s interest waned in the use of cycle theory as a tool in analysis of the capitalist phenomena of those years, and it was only the technical aspects of the problem that continued to interest mathematical economists. The attention of most economists (although Kalecki and Goodwin were two important exceptions), after publication of Harrod's pioneering work, shifted towards theories of growth.

Nevertheless, the beginning of the 1970s, with the end of the great boom in post-war capitalism, saw a revival of theoretical interest in the trade cycle. Three main schools of thought now emerged. The first, which concentrated on long waves, divided among various sub-schools—depending on whether the fifty-year cycle was attributed to Schumpeterian technological innovations, Marxian distributive conflict, or other causes.[61] The second school began with the publication in 1975 of Lucas's article on the 'equilibrium cycle'; and the third with the article published in the same year by Nordhaus on the 'electoral cycle'.[62] These two articles broke with the Keynesian conception of the cycle,

---

[55] Kaldor, 'Hicks on the Trade Cycle', 196 n. 3.

[56] T. Yasui, 'Non-Linear Self-Excited Oscillations and Business Cycles' (Cowles Commission, Discussion Papers in Economics, 2065; 1953).

[57] S. Ichimura, 'Towards a General Nonlinear Macrodynamic Theory of Economic Fluctuations', in K. K. Kurihara (ed.), *Post-Keynesian Economics* (London, Allen & Unwin, 1955).

[58] L. R. Klein and R. S. Preston, 'Stochastic Non-Linear Models', *ECTR* (1969). R. F. Kosobud and W. D. O'Neill, 'Stochastic Implications of Orbital Asymptotic Stability of a Non-Linear Trade Cycle Model', *ECTR* (Jan. 1972).

[59] H. Varian, 'Catastrophe Theory and the Business Cycle', *Economic Inquiry* (Jan. 1979). D. George, 'Equilibrium and Catastrophes in Economics', *SJPE* (Feb. 1981).

[60] The only other area to be profitably explored was the idea of the Marxian cycle of the reserve army, to which Goodwin gave a more robust analytical foundation. R. Goodwin, 'A Growth Cycle', in C. H. Feinstein (ed.), *Socialism, Capitalism and Economic Growth* (Cambridge, CUP, 1967).

[61] See: International Workshop, 'Technical and Social Factors in Long Term Fluctuations', conference held at Università degli Studi di Siena, 15–17 Dec. 1986.

[62] R. E. Lucas, 'An Equilibrium Model of the Business Cycle, *JPE* 84: 6 (1975); W. D. Nordhaus, 'The Political Business Cycle', *RES* (Apr. 1975). The basic ideas of these two articles can, however, be traced much further back, respectively to F. A. Hayek, *Monetary Theory and the*

according to which the capitalist system is marked by endogenous instability explainable in strictly economic terms. However, there is still lively interest in the Kaldorian explanation of the trade cycle today, as witness the numerous papers on the subject given at a recent symposium on Kaldor held the year after his death.[63]

Trade Cycle (London, Jonathan Cape, 1933) and M. Kalecki, 'Political Aspects of Full Employment', *Political Quarterly*, 14 (1943).

  [63] R. Day, 'A Keynesian Business Cycle', and R. Franke and W. Semmler, 'Debt Financing of Firms, Stability and Cycles in a Dynamic Macroeconomic Growth Model': papers given at a conference at New school for Social Research and Bard College, New York, 29–31 Oct. 1987, proceedings pub. under the conference title: E. J. Nell and W. Semmler (eds.), *Nicholas Kaldor and Mainstream Economics: Confrontation or Convergence?* (New York, St Martin's Press, 1991).

Chapter 4

War Economy, Welfare State, and Full Employment

They still say that great poverty makes men vile, astute,
thieving, sly, outlaws, liars, bearers of false witness; and that
wealth makes them insolent, haughty, ignorant, traitorous,
loveless, presumptuous of what they do not know.

T. Campanella, *La città del sole*

4.1. The Effects of the Second World War on English Economic Thought

The government's management of the economy during the Second World War had a major impact on the economic-policy ideas of both Kaldor and the English Keynesians in general. The British government, in fact, implemented a number of planning policies that enabled the country to bear the economic brunt of the war: the mobilizing of idle resources; the easing of the State's financial burden through low interest rates on government securities; the containment of inflation by means of a strict policy of prices and incomes control; the levying of taxes on all forms of income (taxes which were generally regarded as fair). One might say that these principles would henceforth become 'Holy Writ' for the economic policies of the English Keynesians.

Keynes and the Second World War had demonstrated the baselessness of Chamberlain's notorious statement when, as Chancellor of the Exchequer, he had replied to a question in the House of Commons by declaring that the government had as much chance of regulating the level of employment as it had of regulating the weather. The change in opinions and socio-political conditions brought about by Keynes and the war persuaded the coalition government that employment policy was very much indeed its responsibility.

As Kaldor wrote in 1955, ten years after the end of the war:

The assumption of a formal obligation to maintain 'high and stable levels of employment' (as the famous declaration by the wartime coalition government in 1944 put it) was probably the most revolutionary innovation of the century in the sphere of government. It emerged as the result of the joint impact of the Keynesian revolution in economic thought and the Second World War—neither of which could have brought it about in the absence of the other.[1]

[1] N. Kaldor, 'The Lessons of the British Experiment since the War: Full Employment and the Welfare State' (1955), pub. in CP iii. 96.

The coalition government's commitment to high levels of employment, together with its undertaking to extend the social services after publication of the Beveridge Report in 1942, 'laid the foundations of the British New Deal which has come to be known as the Welfare State'.[2]

Confirmation that this change of policy was not merely governmental but part of a new cultural and social climate was provided by the Conservatives when they returned to power in 1951. Contrary to the expectations of many, they pursued the same policies as their predecessors, and sometimes with equal vigour.

However, in the early 1950s it became clear that if the objective of full employment was pursued by a single country, it would clash with external balance. What was required, therefore, was a concerted effort on an international scale to implement full-employment policies.

In each of these fields—war economy, financing of the public insurance system, fiscal and exchange-rate policies to achieve full employment, the international transmission of economic cycles—Kaldor's work was so outstanding that, after his path-breaking writings on pure economics, he now established his reputation as an applied economist as well.

4.2. The War Economy

Minimizing the real burden of the war effort on the economy, and its equitable distribution among taxpayers, were principles that Kaldor had already set out in a 1939 article in The *Banker*.[3] As long as unemployment existed, he wrote, expenditure should be financed by borrowing. Although this policy ran contrary to majority opinion, its adoption would ease the real burden of indebtedness on the economy. As regards taxation, he argued for a levy on labour incomes and a tax—similar to the one that had been introduced during the First World War—to be imposed on overall profits, not just on war profits.

Throughout the war years, Kaldor constantly exchanged opinions with Keynes over the war economy and the principles on which national accounting should be based. An example is provided by an exchange of letters between them in 1940,[4] where the two economists debated the relation between net and gross income. Although Keynes expressed his dislike of the idea of gross income, he was grateful to Kaldor for his clarification. Kaldor favoured the introduction of the gross income into the national accounting for two reasons: first because of the arbitrariness of the principles by which amortization was calculated; second because net income underestimated the resources available for war use.

---

[2] Ibid. 97.
[3] Id., 'Principles of Emergency Finance', *BK* (Aug.1939).
[4] This exchange of letters has been brought to my notice by Prof. Thirlwall. Now see A. P. Thirlwall, *Nicholas Kaldor* (Brighton, Wheatsheaf Books, 1987).

In 1941 Kaldor's article on cost-of-living indices in an economy with rationing[5] made a further contribution to war-economy statistics. In the same year he wrote a comment on the first White Paper on national income and war finance published by the Treasury.[6] Kaldor regularly commented on each of the White Papers of 1940, 1941, and 1942 in the pages of the following June–September's *Economic Journal*.[7] These comments swiftly turned him into a recognized expert on the war economy—both at home and internationally. When the first of Kaldor's comments appeared, his former fellow student at the LSE, Tibor Scitovsky, wrote to him from the United States: 'Your articles on the two British White Papers on War Finance are regarded as classic in this country . . . everybody regards them as a model on which the corresponding estimates in this country are being based'.[8] Kaldor's third comment (written jointly with T. Barna, an ex-student of his) was also translated into French.

I shall not go into details of these comments here, except to provide the following brief outline of the conclusions of the third and last one. According to Kaldor's calculations, the real source of war finance in the three years 1940–2 was principally a rise in output due to an increase in both employment and labour productivity per hour. Between 1940 and 1942 the country's annual expenditure on goods and services was 50 per cent higher than it had been in 1938. But this increase was almost entirely covered by increased production, and to a much lesser extent by a squeeze on consumption and private investment, or by the deterioration of the trade balance. If one also remembers that the inflation rate between 1938 and 1942 was only slightly above 7 per cent, one understands the optimistic tone with which the two authors spoke of the British war economy:

[T]he performance greatly exceeded the promise: there are few economists (if any) who would have dared to predict in 1939 that the wartime increase in the national income could be so large, or that the wartime capital consumption or the degree of price inflation could be kept so small.[9]

Kaldor and Barna concluded their article with a forecast of the post-war situation:

Given reasonably full employment, therefore, post-war home produced output can be expected to be about a quarter above the pre-war level; and this expectation should provide the framework in which plans for post-war reconstruction are to be fitted.[10]

[5] N. Kaldor, 'Rationing and the Cost of Living Index', *RES* (June 1941).

[6] *An Analysis of the Sources of War Finance and an Estimate of the National Income and Expenditure in 1938, 1940, 1941 and 1942*, Cmnd 6438 (London, HMSO).

[7] N.Kaldor, 'The White Paper on National Income and Expenditure', *EJ* (June–Sept. 1941); id., 'The 1941 White Paper on National Income and Expenditure', *EJ* (June–Sept. 1942); id. and T. Barna, 'The 1943 White Paper on National Income and Expenditure', *EJ* (June–Sept. 1943).

[8] This letter has been brought to my notice by Prof. Thirlwall. See now Thirlwall, *Nicholas Kaldor*, 81.

[9] Kaldor and Barna, '1943 White Paper', 263.   [10] Ibid. 274.

Such optimism was not unjustified, as the figures on the British economy of the immediate post-war years would later demonstrate.

In another article written in 1946 Kaldor reiterated his extremely positive view of the ability of the British political and economic system to cope with the economic requirements of war. In the summer of 1945 he found himself in Germany as a member of the US Strategic Bombing Survey. He was working with a team of economists and statisticians headed by Galbraith and brought together to write the survey's report 'The Effects of Strategic Bombing on the German War Economy', published in October of that year. The American Air Force had claimed that it was their bombing campaign that won the war for the Allies: the survey's report instead concluded that victory should be credited to the ground troops, because the damage caused by aerial bombing had been slight and German war production had grown steadily until 1944.[11]

Kaldor used the data collected by the report to write an article on the German war economy,[12] in which he declared:

The waging of 'total war'—the utmost concentration of resources and effort on the single objective of military victory—has alway been regarded as a peculiarly German doctrine, ever since the days of Clausewitz. The proclaimed political philosophy of the Nazis was the total subordination of individual interest to the interests of the State; and State interest was conceived in terms of aggrandisement of power to be achieved by war. The 'totalitarian' system of Nazi Germany was thus generally regarded—by its supporters, as well as its opponents—as one whose main purpose and *raison d'être* was the translation of Clausewitz's ideas into practice.[13]

After minute examination of the resources mobilized in Germany's war economy, Kaldor came to the conclusion that the country, despite its propaganda, had not fought a 'total war' (apart from a brief period in the summer of 1944). And nor had Germany asked its citizens to make economic sacrifices comparable with those borne by the English or by the Russians. The cause of Germany's failure to achieve total mobilization of its economy was, in his view, the initial clash between Hitler and the Army over how the country should rearm itself. The generals were in favour of 'rearmament in depth',

---

[11] The report argued that the first air raids had had little effect because they had not been selective. Matters improved with the advent of radar, but even then the bombers failed to strike the nerve centres of the enemy economy because of Germany's skill in decentralizing its productive apparatus. The only damage inflicted by aerial bombing was its disruption of the German transport system, whose heavy reliance on the railways was due the shortage of petrol for road transport. The report, however, had no influence over future American war strategy—either in Japan, where the war ended with the bombing of Hiroshima and Nagasaki, or later in Vietnam, where it was again ignored. The Vietnamese, too, were able to decentralize their industrial production, saving it from destruction by the American bombers. Robert Neild has told me that when Kaldor, in his polemic with Rostow during the Vietnam War, criticized the American intervention he did so not only on moral and political grounds, but also because he remembered the report of the Strategic Bombing Survey and knew that the strategy of saturation bombing was useless.

[12] N. Kaldor, 'The German War Economy' (1946), repr. in CP iv.   [13] Ibid. 203.

which would have safeguarded the country against any eventuality. Hitler wanted 'rearmament in width' which concentrated efforts on munitions. The 1936 four-year plan, a compromise between the two positions, enabled Germany to wage a successful *blitzkrieg* in a few short weeks against Poland, Norway, and France; but even then no real attempt was made to mobilize the German economy. Consequently, after the defeat in the Soviet Union and after the United States entered the war in December 1941, the German leaders found themselves faced with the prospect of fighting a prolonged campaign for which they were not equipped.

In February 1942 Speer was appointed Minister of Armaments. According to Kaldor, his administration was the only success story of the German war economy; although early on his powers were relatively limited, they increased in 1943 and 1944, but were still modest (for example, Speer never had control over labour mobilization). German war production now increased significantly, but the process had started too late to overcome the country's inertia against the full mobilization of its economy. Hence the principal fault of the German war economy was its consistent failure to plan for a total expansion and mobilization of the economic system in any way comparable with what the United Kingdom's economy was able to accomplish.

The final paragraph of Kaldor's analysis of the German war economy gives us one of the best summaries of his political views:

It would be a mistake to conclude from this analysis that the German war economy provides any evidence of the inefficiency of 'planned' or 'controlled' economies. Its failures were due to the absence of planning and co-ordinated control, and not to any abandonment of a *laissez faire* system. But it will stand as a monument to the inefficiency of a system of personal dictatorship. Those of us who are fortunate enough to live in a free society will take comfort from the fact that even in the matter of efficiency of administrative control and co-ordination, the 'cumbrous' methods of democratic government should prove so superior to systems based on the ruthless exercise of personal power.[14]

4.3. Welfare State: The Financing of Social Insurance

In 1941 the Government appointed Sir William Beveridge as head of an Interdepartmental Committee on Social Security and Connected Services. The committee's report published in 1942 only ran to 172 pages—it was therefore much shorter than the report its predecessor, the Royal Commission on the Poor Laws, published in 1909—but it and the following Report on Full Employment had an extraordinary impact on European social democratic thinking and attitudes towards the Welfare State. As chairman of the committee (which, apart from himself, comprised only civil servants), Beveridge took the report

[14] Ibid. 232.

well beyond its original brief and showed how society could virtually eliminate involuntary poverty by the courageous use of existing institutions.

According to the report's findings, three-quarters of urban poverty was
attributable to loss of earnings, and the other quarter to incomes insufficient
to support a family. The report therefore recommended: (1) that the system of
social insurance should be strengthened so that 'a minimum national income'
could be guaranteed to all unemployed workers, pensioners, and those unable
to work; and (2) family allowances should be paid according to the number
of children in the family and its circumstances, and benefits paid to the
widowed and the separated. The report also called for measures against mass
unemployment and against the prolonged unemployment of individual workers. Finally, it provided for a national health service.[15]

An important feature of the scheme was that social security should be
available to *all* citizens irrespective of their incomes, and that equal benefits
should be offered to everyone in the same circumstances (unemployed workers, pensioners, etc.) regardless of their economic situation. It was this recommendation that distinguished the Beveridge Report from the odious and
discriminatory Poor Laws.

Administration of the plan was to be the responsibility of a new Ministry of
Social Security set up to rationalize, centralize, and reduce the costs of the
various bodies already in existence. Welfare services would be financed out
of a social-insurance fund created from contributions paid by dependent workers, employers, and the self-employed. These contributions should vary from
group to group but be standardized within the group itself.

The report was greeted with instant acclaim, although there was some
scepticism over the effects that a guaranteed minimum wage would have on
labour mobility, and minor misgivings over two specific recommendations:
that contributions were not to be proportionate to the level of income, and that
benefits were not to be proportionate to the cost of living. There was, by
contrast, serious anxiety over the financial repercussions of the plan. And it
was this aspect that Kaldor first analysed in a pamphlet written jointly with
Joan Robinson, A. A. Evans, E. F. Schumacher, and P. Lamartine Yates for
the National Peace Council on policies for reconstruction,[16] and then in an
article for the *Economic Journal*, in which he sought to show that

contrary to a widely held opinion, the financial burden which the Plan imposes on the
various classes of the community (even if one leaves the benefits entirely out of
consideration) is extremely small and cannot affect post-war levels of taxation or
disposable real income to any significant extent.[17]

Kaldor divided his analysis into two stages. In the first he examined the
burden of the plan on the taxpayer, in the second its burden on industry and

[15] A. D. K. Owen, 'The Beveridge Report: I. Its Proposal', *EJ* (Apr. 1943), 1.

[16] N. Kaldor *et al.*, *Planning for Abundance* (London; Peace Aims Pamphlet, 21, National Peace
Council, 1943).

[17] Id., 'The Beveridge Report: II. The Financial Burden', *EJ*, (Apr. 1943), 10.

the trade balance. His results obviously depended on assumptions concerning a series of magnitudes: the level of national income, public expenditure, and the level of post-war taxation. On the hypothesis that, compared with 1938, hourly productivity would increase after the war by 12 per cent (in real terms), public expenditure by 100 per cent (in nominal terms), and that the terms of trade would stay the same, Kaldor concluded that

We could afford to keep about one million in the army, another 1.5 million in unemployment, restore aggregate real consumption to its pre-war level, spend on capital improvements about double the pre-war amounts (in real terms), export a sufficient amount to pay for our imports, adopt the Beveridge scheme in full all at the same time, and with income tax only 6/6d in the pound.[18]

Each of Kaldor's articles stressed that the feasibility of the plan did not depend on the amount of resources available: rather than being reduced, these were shared out more equally. The working class did not suffer because—according to Kaldor's calculations—the cost of the plan to the average worker was less than the amount he had been paying voluntarily before the war for the same kind of insurance.

With regard to the social class distribution of the financial burden of the plan, distinctions had to be drawn between the ways in which employers could be required to contribute. If employers paid contributions in the form of a tax on wages, they would offset this by increasing their final prices. Thus, directly or indirectly, it would be the workers, as consumers, who bore the cost. This would still be so even if a proportion of goods were bought abroad. If contributions were paid on wages, but by employers who offloaded them on to final prices, the financing of the plan would harm the trade balance only if Britain kept to the Gold Standard. But, if the country remained off the Gold Standard after the war (Britain had abandoned the Gold Standard in 1931), exchange rates could be fixed according to the price levels of various countries; and the sterling exchange rate could be adjusted to compensate for the increase in domestic prices caused by employers shifting contributions on to them. However, there was no reason why the burden should not fall on employers, although in this case it would have to take the form of a tax on profits.

For the whole of 1943 Kaldor actively campaigned to have the Beveridge Plan approved. He wrote numerous letters to the press and also gave a talk on the radio entitled 'The Cost of Social Assistance' as part of the BBC series *The World We Want* edited by Joan Robinson—to which Keynes also contributed with a talk on 'Will the War Make Us Poorer?'.

[18] Ibid. 21.

4.4. Welfare State: Fiscal Policies for Full Employment

At Nuffield College, G. D. H. Cole had organized a series of seminars on full employment to which industrialists, trade-unionists, and economists were invited. These latter included Thomas Balogh, Joan Robinson, Evan Durbin, and Kaldor. It was on this occasion that Beveridge asked Kaldor to write an appendix to his new report on full employment.[19]

Unlike his 1942 report on social insurance, Beveridge's report on full employment, published in 1944,[20] had not been commissioned by the government. Nevertheless, he believed that its writing was a natural extension to his previous report.

The aim of Beveridge's first report had been 'Freedom from Want', the aim of his second, accordingly, became 'Freedom from Idleness'. It set three objectives: (1) that the economy should achieve a minimum level of frictional unemployment (around 3 per cent), and no unemployed worker should remain idle for longer than the time required for him or her to find another job; (2) that the work on offer should pay a fair wage; (3) that labour mobility should be organized so that the geographical location of work meant real job opportunities for the unemployed.

While drafting his report, Beveridge drew on the expertise of economists working at Oxford and in the Institute of Statistics of that university. Kaldor was responsible for appendix C, which analysed the fiscal policies available to the State in ensuring full employment. The importance of the appendix lay much more in its analytical method than in its forecasts. It referred, in fact, to the immediate post-war period, and although its forecast that hostilities would end in mid-1945 was absolutely correct, its predictions concerning the post-war economic situation turned out to be over-optimistic. Hence Kaldor's remark that 'military forecasts are easier to make than economic ones'.[21]

Nevertheless, as regards method, although analysis of full-employment budgetary policies had already been carried out by Hansen in 1941,[22] Kaldor's 1944 approach was 'the first attempt to build up comprehensive estimates from a large number of separate forecasts (and assumptions) within the framework of a consistent econometric model'.[23]

Kaldor had already written on fiscal policies in two articles published as part of a series in *The Times* on full employment.[24] He suggested the use of the budget as a non-inflationary instrument for full employment. The Treasury

[19] Id., 'The Quantitative Aspects of the Full Employment Problem in Britain' (1943), repr. in CP iii.

[20] W. H. Beveridge, *Full Employment in a Free Society* (London, 1944).

[21] N. Kaldor, introd. to CP. vol. iii, p. xi.

[22] A. H. Hansen, *Fiscal Policy and Business Cycle* (New York, W. W. Norton & Company Inc., 1941).

[23] Kaldor, introd. to CP, vol. iii (1st edn., 1964), p. x.

[24] Id., 'Budgeting for Employment, National Income and State Finance, Closing the Deflationary Gap', in *Full Employment* (London, The Times Publishing Company, 1943).

should have two budgets: the first indicating current outlay covered by tax revenues; the second indicating capital outlay covered by loans. This, one notes, was also an idea advanced by Keynes.

Kaldor's appendix to the Beveridge Report went into greater detail and singled out four budgetary policies for full employment: an increase in public expenditure covered by loans; an increase in public expenditure covered by higher taxation; an increase in private spending brought about by reduced taxation; a change in the ratio between direct and indirect taxes. The first two policies brought major resources under the State's control, the third and fourth policies placed them under the control of private citizens.

Kaldor's analysis of the first policy demonstrated that its net effect depended: (1) on the induced increase in income (which depended on the public's marginal propensity to consume out of its available income); (2) on the accelerator; (3) on the propensity to import. In his analysis of the second policy, Kaldor expressed an idea that Haavelmo later made famous under the name of the 'balanced budget theorem':[25]

Full employment could be secured, however, by means of increased public outlay, even if the State expenditure is fully covered by taxation—for the reason that an increase in taxation is not likely to reduce private outlay by the full amount of the taxes paid.[26]

This was because the taxpayer would cover the cost of additional taxes not only by reducing consumption but by reducing saving. In his discussion of the third route to full employment, Kaldor pointed out that the deficit created by reducing taxation would be larger than the deficit created by a policy of increasing public expenditure because some part of the additional income provided by lower taxes would be saved. Kaldor's fourth route to full employment was an increase in direct taxation and a reduction in indirect taxation. This latter, he believed, was the least efficient method of the four because the British system of taxation was already sufficiently progressive. If, however, the objective was to change the distribution of income, it was better to tackle the problem head-on by forcing producers to reduce their prices relative to costs.

Of the four policies, the first and the third implied deficit budgets, the second and the fourth did not. From retrospective analysis, and on the basis of forecasts of the future state of the British economy, Kaldor argued that only the deficit budget policies would have worked before the war. After the war, however, this was no longer the case: in the changed circumstances of those years balanced budget policies would also have been effective.

The appendix closed with careful examination of the long-term effects of a growing national debt. Contrary to the popular conception of the national debt—as either a net loss of real wealth or a way of shifting the burden of financing public expenditure on to future generations—Kaldor asserted that the

[25] T. Haavelmo, 'Multiplier Effect of a Balanced Budget', *ECTR* 13: 4 (1945), 311–18.
[26] Kaldor, 'Quantitative Aspects of Full Employment', 25.

national debt did not reduce the real income of the community: all its servicing required was a transfer of income among different members of society (and even this transfer could be ameliorated by an appropriate tax system). This process could, however, adversely affect incentives to produce if all citizens received the same net income, but with a higher proportion of rent and fewer rewards for current effort. This outcome depended, not on the absolute size of the debt, but on the ratio between spending on interest and the national income. An increase in indebtedness, however, could even reduce this ratio if the expenditure financed by the debt led to an increase in tax revenues that was greater than the increase in the interest charge.

Kaldor's work was welcomed with enthusiasm, to say the least. He received letters of congratulation from Alvin Hansen in the United States and Colin Clark in Australia. Minsky—who was at Chicago at the time—has recently said of Simons that, although he was severely critical of the Beveridge Report, he singled out Kaldor's appendix for praise. Appendix C received excellent reviews in the British press, including one in the *Manchester Guardian* of 17 November 1944 written by John Hicks, and was followed by specialist studies of its arguments in both the United States[27] and Great Britain.[28]

4.5. Instruments for Full Employment

More than ten years later Kaldor issued the following verdict on the effects of policies for full employment and on the instruments used to achieve it.[29] The main benefit of full employment was the accelerated rate of productivity due to the adoption of labour-saving innovations. Its two principal disadvantages were inflation and Britain's balance-of-payments deficit. In an economy with full employment, inflation was caused, not by the pressure of demand, but by the general rise in money-wages due to the adjustment in the relative wages paid to workers of different grades and in different occupations (see Chapter 12.3). Full employment's second disadvantage was its effects on the country's balance of payments—as discussed below.

As regards the instruments adopted in those years, Kaldor was critical of the Labour Government's wholesale reliance on fiscal policy in the second half of the 1940s. In fact, although the great advantage of the budgetary instrument was that it acted directly on expenditure and adjusted the structure of demand to that of the distribution of resources, it was nevertheless unable to control speculative fluctuations in inventories. Kaldor was even more critical of the policies of the Conservative Government of the early 1950s, which relied entirely on monetary policies. This insistence on the monetary instru-

---

[27] A. G. Hart, 'Model Building and Fiscal Policy', *AER* (Sept. 1945).

[28] R. Stone and E. F. Jackson, 'Economic Models with Special Reference to Mr Kaldor's System', *EJ* (Dec. 1946).

[29] Kaldor, 'Lessons of the British Experiment since the War'.

ment led to high interest rates in the long period, and to a steady reduction of the share of investment in income (see Chapter 11.2). Kaldor was in favour of an approach which used both instruments, although this was still not enough: in an open economy the maintenance of full employment also required an exchange-rate policy (see Chapter 13.3).

Kaldor criticized the Labour Government on two counts: first, in articles in the *Manchester Guardian* (in 1946) and letters to *The Times* (in 1947), he admonished the government for its failure to provide industry with a plan which established the production targets needed to overcome bottlenecks created by shortages of raw materials and of certain industrial products; second, he censured Sir Stafford Cripps for paying too little attention to the trade balance, even after the devaluation of September 1949—which Kaldor himself had helped to bring about by persuading Hugh Gaitskell,[30] against the opinion of several ministers, that it was necessary.

Kaldor expounded his ideas on full-employment policies in an open economy at the 1950 conference of the International Economic Association.[31] It was on this occasion that he first set out the problem—widely debated until the end of the 1960s—of the incompatibility between a country's pursuit of a full-employment policy and the maintenance of fixed exchange rates among countries.

4.6 Full-Employment Policies in an Open Economy

From the latter half of the 1940s onwards, Kaldor became increasingly aware that the greatest impediment to achieving full employment was the problem of the balance of payments; and that one of the main tasks of post-war governments was therefore to render the objective of full employment and the balance-of-payments constraint compatible. This conviction stayed with him for the rest of his life.

Harrod, in his 1939 revision of his *International Economics* published six years previously, had, to use his own words, 'provided a systematic account of the relation between the Keynesian theory of unemployment and balance-of-trade theory'.[32] However, it was not until the 1940s that any precise definition of the conditions of adjustment of the trade balance through induced changes in income was forthcoming.[33] Kaldor, too, believed that

[u]nder a régime of stable exchanges, such fluctuations represented the major automatic mechanism for restoring balance of payments equilibrium when the balance was, for any reason, disturbed.[34]

[30] The Chancellor of the Exchequer at the time was Cripps, but in summer 1949 he was ill in hospital. Gaitskell became Chancellor in 1950.
[31] N. Kaldor, 'Employment Policies and the Problem of International Balance' (1950), repr. in CP iii.
[32] A. Harrod, *Towards a Dynamic Economics* (London, Macmillan, 1948), 101.
[33] L. H. Metzler, 'Underemployment Equilibrium in International Trade', *ECTR* (Apr. 1942).
[34] Kaldor, 'Employment Policies and the Problem of International Balance', 85.

And he was also aware that

the 'multiplier' effect of the fall of exports will not normally proceed far enough to reduce imports by the full extent of the fall in exports, but will leave a residual deficit in the balance of payments on current account.[35]

If, therefore, policies designed to restore equilibrium to the balance of payments were necessary in the presence of fluctuations in income, they were even more necessary when a country intended to maintain high and stable levels of internal employment.

In a world in which each country kept to these high and stable levels of internal employment, there were three possible policies for securing international payments equilibrium: (1) more frequent recourse to exchange-rate adjustments; (2) allowing deficit countries to restrict imports; (3) the co-ordination of economic policies by international organizations.

In the absence of this third policy, a country had to rely on one of the first two. Of these Kaldor was in favour of the former—until the end of the 1960s after which he preferred the latter. Thus, although he initially favoured a policy of exchange-rate adjustments, he was nevertheless aware of its limitations—which were, principally, three in number. First, under a regime of adjustable exchange rates a rise in employment would be matched by a loss in the terms of trade. Second, exchange-rate adjustments could be used for the purpose of 'exporting unemployment rather than for the purpose of restoring the international balance'[36] and thus generating competitive devaluations. Third, 'too frequent use of exchange-rate adjustments (or a regime of freely fluctuating exchange rates) in itself renders the preservation of stable conditions in international transactions far more difficult'.[37]

A country could also resort to a policy of import restriction in order to 'export unemployment'. In this case, other countries would be forced to adopt protectionist policies in retaliation, which would eventually lead to a general reduction in international consumption. In fact, it was during this period that Kaldor was arguing that the provisions of the ITO Charter should allow for free-trade exceptions to be made of those countries 'suffering from balance of payments difficulties'. He put his case in the following words, which give an excellent summary of the policy that a quarter of a century later he would prescribe so forcefully as a remedy for Britain's economic ills (see Chapter 13.5):

If the effects of a relatively high internal level of employment on the (potential) equilibrium rate of exchange, and thus on the terms of trade, are large, the country may be justified in imposing additional import restrictions (in the form of higher tariffs, etc.) in order to reduce its propensity to import and thus render any given volume of imports consistent with a higher level of internal employment. Such import restrictions need not invite retaliation in so far as the . . . imposition of restrictions does not effectively reduce the volume of international trade (since the volume of

[35] Ibid. 88.   [36] Ibid. 86.   [37] Ibid.

imports of the country imposing restrictions will be no smaller than they would have been in the absence of full employment and without restrictions); nor does it compromise the ability of other countries in maintaining successful employment-stabilization policies.[38]

However, this policy would not be cost-free either, because 'the economic welfare generated at the given level of economic activity will certainly be less, as a result of the lower degree of international specialization and exchange'.[39]

Therefore both of these policies for full employment in an open economy entailed costs. Hence 'a more adequate solution of the problem would presuppose new international arrangements whereby each country would undertake to maintain the normal supply of its own currency to the rest of the world, irrespective of fluctuations in its internal level of activity'.[40] This was the idea that provided the basis for the United Nations' 'Report on National and International Measures for Full Employment'[41]—in the drafting of which Kaldor was actively engaged between October and December 1949.

4.7. International Co-operation for Full Employment

The 1949 United Nations' plan for an international full-employment policy was heavily influenced by Kaldor. Indeed, on the occasion of the New York conference in Kaldor's honour held a year after his death, Stephen Rousseas—who in the late 1940s had been a member of the United Nations' research group headed by Kaldor in Geneva—declared that his personality had 'dominated' the group of experts who drew it up. At the same conference, Sidney Dell, for many years a senior official of the United Nations, insisted that 97 per cent of the report had been Kaldor's work. (Even if one takes account of a possible overestimation due to the long-standing friendship between Dell and the Kaldor family—a friendship that began in those years—this percentage would still be high.)

According to Dell, Kaldor was always a 'U.N. man' and always placed his trust and hopes in the United Nations Organization. It is no surprise, therefore, to find that Kaldor saw the United Nations as the ideal body for the planning and implementation of an international programme for full employment. Indeed, the report begins with the following words:

The commitment to full employment contained in the charter of the United Nations marks a historic stage in the evolution of the modern conception of the functions and responsibilities of the democratic State.[42]

---

[38] Ibid. 84–5.   [39] Ibid. 90.   [40] Ibid. 94.

[41] N. Kaldor *et al.*, *Report on National and International Measures for Full Employment* (Geneva, UN, 1950).

[42] Ibid. 29. Kaldor is here referring to article 5 of the UN Constitution. All page repr. to this report are to the Italian edn., *Politiche della piena occupazione* (Milan, Instituto per gli studi di economia, 1950).

The report is the first example of an international co-operation project aimed at the general target of full employment. It provides a detailed exposition of the principle of the international propagation of the variations in effective demand originating in one particular country. Because the effects of the contraction in income and international trade consequent on a drop in one country's income are cumulative, the report argues that achievement of the full-employment target depends on three conditions. First that the governments concerned should unite under the auspices of the Economic and Social Council, so that each country harmonizes its external re-equilibration measures with those of the others, 'avoiding every policy that leads to a persistent surplus or deficit in the balance of payments'.[43] The writers of the report were aware that this phenomenon was not necessarily cyclical, and recommended that 'governments should also be prepared, if necessary and with mutual cooperation, to change the *productive structures* of their economies'.[44]

Moreover, since 'the prosperity of both the backward countries and the world as a whole depends in large part on the existence of an abundant and constant flow of investments from the chief industrial countries',[45] the second condition for providing a solid basis for international economic relationships 'is the creation of the conditions so that the flow of international investments can be stabilized for long periods of time'.[46] But, since 'foreign investments, if left to private initiative, tend to be extraordinarily unstable . . . it is difficult to see how to deal with this fact without direct intervention by governments'.[47] The International Bank for Reconstruction and Development should serve as the instrument for this purpose, provided that it is given increased funding 'so that it can grant funds to backward countries not only for specific development projects, but also for the implementation of plans for general economic development'.[48]

Finally, the third condition for full employment is the adoption of provisions that ensure the stability of international trade. The instability of international exchanges can arise from at least three sources: instability of a first kind caused by protectionist policies; instability of a second kind caused by the deflationary or inflationary trend of the national economies; instability of a third kind caused by phenomena like crop failures. If it was not possible to eliminate this latter fluctuation (even though suitable international policies would mitigate its effects) the first two could be greatly reduced if individual countries adopted economic policies to liberalize trade *together with* full-employment policies. In doing so, they should be encouraged and helped by the ITO and the IMF. According to the writers of the report, this latter organization should perform a very different function from what it had hitherto. Since the Second World War the IMF had been the international institution that had obliged each country to re-equilibrate its balance of payments through

---

[43] Ibid. 75.   [44] Ibid. 116 (my italics).   [45] Ibid. 81.
[46] Ibid. 80.   [47] Ibid. 81.   [48] Ibid. 118.

the reduction of its domestic demand, and it had limited the growth of currencies by means of pre-fixed quantitative targets: an objective and an instrument
that Kaldor had always harshly criticized. The report recommended instead
that the IMF should be the international institution holding the international
currency reserve and, as such, should 'give temporary aid to a country whose
currency reserves have been depleted by a depression in other countries'.[49] On
the other hand (and this is the plan's crucial proposal), each country should
assume responsibility 'for replenishing the currency reserves of other countries to the extent that these reserves have been depleted because of an increase
in the currency reserves of a government consequent on a fall in its demand
for imported goods and services',[50] caused in turn by a fall in effective internal
demand.

The report aroused wide discussion and general consensus both in European
social democratic circles and in Britain. However, Washington disapproved,
condemning it as too interventionist; and it therefore never reached the implementation stage. On rereading the report forty years later, one gains the
impression that it undervalued, even if it did not ignore, the problem of
different inflationary dynamics among countries. Its major shortcoming, however, was that it failed to realize that the co-presence of surplus and deficit
countries is not just the outcome of cyclical lags between domestic income
changes, but the effect of different dynamic changes in their productive structures. The two situations generate substantially different attitudes towards
international collaboration. For the writers of the report, in fact, since it was
the *reduction* of internal demand and employment in the surplus countries that
was responsible for the diffusion of international deflation, it followed that
the countries with balance-of-payments surpluses would also see the plan as
being in their interests.

In the years that followed, however, it became evident that the problem was
more complex. Changes in productive structures differ among countries. Some
countries in fact have 'export-led' growth, and in their economies the balance-
of-payments surplus is tied not to unemployment, but to increasing employment. This is so the more the growth of income of these countries fails to
activate imports from the rest of the world. Since this pattern of growth cannot
be followed by all countries individually, for the obvious reason that the sum
of the trade balances of all countries cannot be anything but zero, the trade
deficit in some countries is not caused by the persistence of a deflationary
situation in some of their trading partner countries, but, on the contrary, by
their growth of income and employment (and ownership of foreign assets).
Co-operation thus becomes more difficult: instead of the immediate interests
of one group of countries coinciding with those of the others, they conflict
with them. This is not to imply that there is no need today for a plan along
the lines of the one described here—indeed one is required that is even more

---

[49] Ibid. 89.   [50] Ibid. 123.

interventionist in character, in so far as it would have to consider measures for the structural harmonization of the various economies in greater detail. And today, as forty years ago, one shares the opinion of the 1949 report that 'in the absence of such a plan, we believe that there is no real hope that the world will manage to extricate itself from its present economic difficulties even in the long period'.[51]

[51] Ibid. 117.

Chapter 5

Cambridge and the Theories of Growth and the Distribution of Income

Accumulation for accumulation, production for production, with
this formula classical economists expressed the historical
mission of the bourgeois period.

K. Marx, *Das Kapital*

5.1. The Cambridge Debates

Joan Robinson began her studies of economics five years before Kaldor.

When I came up to Cambridge, in 1922, and started reading economics, Marshall's
Principles was the Bible, and we knew very little beyond it. Jevons, Cournot, even
Ricardo were figures in the footnotes. We heard of 'Pareto's Law' but nothing of the
general equilibrium system. Sweden was represented by Cassel, America by Irving
Fisher, Austria and Germany were scarcely known.[1]

At that time Cambridge enjoyed the fortunate position of being both one of
the most important cultural centres in the world and having a relatively small
amount of inherited doctrinal baggage to contend with. Thus, during the forty
years that followed, the university became the centre from which would emanate three innovative periods of high theory. The first of these seasons saw
the development during the mid-1920s of the theory of imperfect competition;
the second saw the theory of income and employment as originally formulated
during the early 1930s; and then the third, during the early 1950s, the theories
of capital, growth, and distribution.

The first of these Cambridge periods began with Sraffa's famous article of
1926, although Kaldor would only participate after an interval of ten years
(see Chapter 1). The starting-point of the second can be located in the months
between October 1930, when Keynes's *A Treatise on Money* was published,
and June 1931, the month in which Kahn's article on the multiplier appeared
(although he had already been working on it for almost a year).[2] During the
academic year 1930–1 on Sraffa's suggestion a 'circus' was organized in
Cambridge to hold informal discussion on Keynes's ideas (the 'circus' was
attended, apart from Sraffa, by Richard Kahn, James Meade, Joan and Austin

[1] J. Robinson, *Collected Economic Papers*, vol. i (Oxford, Basil Blackwell, 1951), P.
[2] R. F. Kahn, *The Making of the General Theory* (Cambridge, CUP, 1984).

Robinson). Joan Robinson wrote: 'In the summer of 1934 the fundamental features of *The General Theory* became clear, although the book was not published until 1936.'[3] Kaldor himself was not a member of the 'circus'; but he did make an extremely important contribution (as we saw in Chapter 2) to the climate of euphoria and the profusion of ideas that followed publication of Keynes's great work. He was, finally, a major protagonist in the third period of theory, when he became one of the leading exponents (together with Joan Robinson, Richard Kahn, and Piero Sraffa) of the Cambridge school.

The theoretical link between the second and third of the Cambridge periods was the relation between the theories of the cycle and growth; while the central concerns of the third period were—as has been said—the theories of capital, growth, and distribution. Although Kaldor never directly addressed the theory of capital during the 1950s, his publications on growth and distribution were outstanding. Nevertheless, during those years between the early 1950s and 1960s (when his attention began to move elsewhere), his position was never a static one: his opinions changed on both the specification of the chief subject for analysis and the assumptions underlying its analytical models. Since neither of these shifts of opinion was evident or explicit, the reconstruction of Kaldor's theories in the pages that follow is organized so that each section deals with a specific topic and shows the development of his thought in that particular area.

5.2. Kaldor's Critique of Previous Theories of Distribution

Whereas in the Cambridge of the 1920s Marshall had been 'the Bible', official doctrine during the 1950s and 1960s was, apart from Keynes, Ricardo and Marx. In fact, Adam Smith was the classical economist who had probably the greatest influence on Kaldor—an influence, though, that would only become apparent during the last twenty years of Kaldor's life, when the importance he attributed to increasing returns in industry emerged more clearly. Nevertheless, during the 1950s Kaldor was second only to Sraffa in being responsible for the revival of interest in Ricardo. And from the early years of that decade—on the invitation of Keynes—he gave courses of lectures in the Cambridge economics faculty on the theory of distribution; lectures which would provide the material for his entry on the topic in the 1948 *Chambers Encyclopedia*.[4] Eight years later Kaldor wrote his best-known article on the subject: 'Alternative Theories of Distribution'.[5] Both his encyclopedia entry and the article begin with a critical review of the major distribution theories of the past, using an admirable summary of Ricardo's theory as their point of departure.

---

[3] J. Robinson, *Collected Economic Papers* (Oxford, Basil Blackwell, 1973), 175.
[4] N. Kaldor, 'The Theory of Distribution', in *Chambers Encyclopedia* (1948).
[5] Id., 'Alternative Theories of Distribution' (1955), repr. in CP i.

The Ricardian model as set out by Kaldor posits three social classes—wage-earners, capitalists, and landowners—and two goods—corn and iron. These latter are synthesized into a single good on the hypothesis that workers spend the whole of their income on corn and on the hypothesis that all workers are endowed with the same iron capital good in equal measure. In agriculture, past accumulation determines the number of workers employed on the land and therefore the acreage of cultivated land producing wage goods. Given these assumptions, it follows that rent derives from the difference between the output of labour on land of average fertility and the output of labour on marginal land. The output of labour on marginal land is equal to the sum of wages and profits; by deducting wages (the unitary value of which is given by purchasing power in terms of subsistence goods) from this output, one obtains profit as the residual magnitude. The ratio between this magnitude and capital (as the sum of the wages paid over the year) determines the rate of profit in the agricultural sector. This is also the average rate of the whole system because of the hypothesis of competition and hence of profit uniformity in the two sectors. As more land is brought under cultivation, the share of rent in the national product increases, the share of wages remains constant, and the residual share of profits therefore falls.

Kaldor saw two principles at work in Ricardo's model—namely, the marginal principle in its explanation of rent, and the surplus principle in its explanation of the distribution of income between profits and wages. Ricardo was the starting-point for two lines of theoretical thought: Marxian theory based entirely on surplus, and marginalist theory based entirely on the principle of diminishing returns.

Although Kaldor's interest in Marx was never as constant and penetrating as Joan Robinson's, one may justifiably claim that he too contributed to Cambridge's rediscovery of the classical economists. This was a revival that moved in two directions: one purely Sraffian, which reviewed and recast the classical theory of value; the other, more Kaleckian and Keynesian in spirit, which re-examined classical analyses of accumulation and crises. This latter was the reading that Kaldor gave to Marx.

Kaldor always acknowledged Marx as having given the first and most detailed treatment of the idea that accumulation is not the fruit of free individual *choice*, but of the *necessity* that competition imposes on individual capitalists—who risk 'falling by the wayside' if in a dynamic context of economies of scale they do not reinvest their profits and do not increase the size of their firms. In the Marxian scheme of things, when the stage has been reached at which the concentration of capital into a few hands eliminates the obligation to accumulate, the conditions are ripe for the realization crisis—which has analogies with the Keynesian crisis of lack of effective demand. However, Kaldor regarded two other Marxian principles—generally known as the 'law of the falling rate of profit' (because of increasing organic composition of capital) and the 'law of the increasing immiseration of the proletariat'—as logically and factually false.

Kaldor pointed out numerous shortcomings in the marginalist theory of distribution. Here I shall only single out those several instances where the theory is flawed or inadequate. If one excludes the hypothesis of constant returns to scale, one cannot claim that output 'exhausts' itself in the sum of the distributive shares obtained on the basis of the marginal productivity of the factors; the very concept of 'factor of production' is indefinable if, like the capital 'factor', it is given by an aggregate of heterogeneous goods which are themselves produced, in that the value of the production factor depends on the cost of producing the goods of which it consists, a cost that depends in turn on the way in which the product is divided between the factors themselves. It is impossible, moreover, to define a marginal product if the factors are indivisible. Further, the marginal product cannot be attributed to a single factor if the factors enter productive conditions in fixed proportions. Finally, the price of the service of the production factor cannot be equal—as the theory requires—to its marginal product in any situation other than perfect competition.

Kaldor also argued for the inadequacy of theories that, like Kalecki's, determined the distributive shares in terms of the degree of monopoly. For Kalecki, the share of profits depends only on the elasticity of demand. Under the hypothesis that, in the short period, the prime-cost curve has a reverse L-shape because prime costs are constant up to full capacity output, marginal costs are equal to average prime costs. As a consequence the elasticity of the firm's demand curve explains the ratio of price to prime costs and, in a closed economy, the ratio of gross profit to wages. For Kaldor, however, the concept of demand elasticity is legitimate only if it refers to a single firm, not to the economy as a whole, since the prices of individual firms are not independent of each other. In a second version of his theory, Kalecki simply defined the degree of monopoly as the ratio of price to prime costs; and here, according to Kaldor, the theory lapses into tautology.

Kaldor was also critical of 'full cost' theories of the kind developed by Hall and Hitch (although he would be more receptive to similar theories later in his scientific career: see Chapter 14). These theories, by asserting 'that prices are determined quite independently of demand, in effect destroy existing price theory without putting anything else in its place.'[6]

Despite Kaldor's dissatisfaction with Kalecki's theory of the degree of monopoly, he always acknowledged the Polish economist as the inspirer, together with Keynes, of his own theory of distribution. After Kalecki and Keynes, Roy Harrod was the third economist whose work led Kaldor to the idea that the theory of distribution should be closely connected with the theory of growth.

[6] Ibid. 226.

5.3. The Inspirers of Kaldor's Theory of Growth and Distribution

It is widely known that the problem of the distribution of income was not a central component of Keynes's *General Theory*—probably because Keynes did not see the question as having any significant bearing on his treatment of the level of activity and employment, which was the principal subject of his book. This, however, was not the case in the *Treatise*, where Keynes's main purpose was to specify measures for monetary stabilization and to identify the determinants of the level of prices that arise from the distribution of the national income between profits and wages.

Keynes's two major works share a number of features, as well as having a number of elements in contrast. The principal similarities between the two books—apart from their common assumption of given techniques and their modelling in terms of macro-economic magnitudes—are two: the idea that wage bargaining determines money-wages not real wages, and the idea that it is the investment decision that takes priority over other economic variables. However—and this is the chief difference between the two books—whereas in the *General Theory* the level of investment determines the level of output, in the *Treatise* it determines the division of output between available goods (consumption goods) and non-available goods (investment goods).

In the *Treatise* the difference between expenditure on consumption goods and the costs involved in producing them determines the profit of the sector producing consumption goods. The real wage is defined as the money-wage (exogenous) divided by the price of consumption goods, the level of which equalizes aggregate demand and supply. The distribution of income is therefore determined—in the *Treatise*'s 'fundamental equation'—by the level of investment and by the propensity to consume among income-earners. The level of prices remains constant when investment is compatible with that share of income not spent on consumption. If consumption exceeds the residual income as represented by savings, the price level increases. Thus, money-wages remaining the same, there is a drop in real wages and excess profit with respect to the 'normal profit' arising from the previous equilibrium. This 'windfall profit' establishes the new savings–investment equilibrium. If profit-receivers decide to spend a greater proportion of their incomes on consumption, the effect is to increase aggregate demand, prices, and hence profits themselves. For this paradoxical reason, Keynes compared profits with the contents of the 'widow's cruse, which remain undepleted however much of them may be devoted to riotous living', and compound losses (with the induced increase in savings) with a 'Danaid jar which can never be filled up; for the effect of this reduced expenditure is to inflict on the producers of consumption goods a loss of an equal amount'.[7]

---

[7] J. M. Keynes, *The Treatise on Money* (1930; Cambridge, Macmillan for Royal Economic Society, 1971), i. 125.

Whereas in the *Treatise* the positive or negative excess of investment over savings changed the level of prices and the (ex-ante) distribution of income, in the *General Theory* it changed the level of income. Note that in his booklet *How to Pay for the War*, which was written after the *General Theory*, Keynes presented a theory of demand inflation in which prices change according to a mechanism very similar to the one he described in the *Treatise*. One can therefore argue that it was Keynes who first suggested that exogenous investments determine either the level of income in conditions of underemployment or the distribution of income at full employment.

No less important than the fundamental equation of the *Treatise on Money* in the development of Kaldor's thinking on the distribution of income was Kalecki's paper on the determinants of profit.[8] Unlike Keynes, Kalecki treated the level of activity and the distribution of income as merged together into a single theoretical whole. Thus, for both Kalecki and Keynes, wage bargaining determines monetary values, and investment is the exogenous variable determining the macro-economic equilibrium. But Kalecki hypothesized a different kind of behaviour among income-earners: in particular, he posited a classical propensity to spend—i.e. that wage-earners spend the whole of their income. Hence, under the simplifying hypothesis that the national income consists solely of wages and profits, one obtains a condition of ex-post equality:

Profits = Investment + Capitalist Consumption.

This equation becomes a condition of ex-ante equilibrium if a right to left order of causality is assumed. Bearing in mind that consumption by capitalists is a proportion c_p of their income P, we therefore have:

(5.1) $P = I/(1 - c_p).$

This condition of macro-economic equilibrium states that the level of investment determines the *level* of profits by means of a mechanism very similar to the Keynesian multiplier. One notes that, with an increase in the propensity of capitalists to spend, or with an increase in investment, the level of profits rises: hence Kalecki's aphorism that 'workers spend what they earn, and capitalists earn what they spend' (which expresses a similar idea to Keynes's 'widow's cruse' analogy).

Kalecki linked this first part of his analysis to his theory of price formation. A price is determined by a mark-up on prime costs. Since prime costs consist mainly of wages per unit of output, the degree of monopoly, i.e. the ratio of price to prime costs, is equal to the ratio between the share of profits and the share of wages. On the one hand, therefore, given propensities to spend, the level of investment determines the level of profits; on the other, the degree of

[8] M. Kalecki, 'A Theory of Profit', *EJ* (June–Sept. 1942). Kaldor had occasional meetings with Kalecki in London during the 1930s until, with the outbreak of war, Kalecki moved to Oxford. Despite his criticisms of Kalecki's theories of distribution and of the business cycle, Kaldor always admired the Polish economist (though not to the same extent as Joan Robinson), and he wrote his obituary in *The Times* (21 Apr. 1970).

monopoly determines the share of profits.[9] Given the level of profit and the share of profits, the national income may therefore be calculated as the ratio between the two magnitudes.[10]

Before we move on to Harrod as the third inspirational source of Kaldorian theory, we will briefly consider the work of the German economist Hans-Joaquim Rüstow. Although Rüstow never enjoyed the fame of the other two economists, Kaldor believed that 'together with John Maynard Keynes and Michael Kalecki (Rüstow) should be classed as one of the three inventors of modern macro-economics, which I consider to be the most important and the most distinctive contribution that our century has made to the body of knowledge of socio-economic processes'.[11] Indeed, according to Kaldor, the dynamic post-Keynesian theories developed in Cambridge came much closer to Rüstow's 1926 doctoral thesis *Akkumulation und Krisen* than they did to Keynes's *General Theory*, which was written ten years later. However, we should bear in mind that Rüstow's work had no influence whatsoever over the thought of Keynes's pupils, because they were totally unaware of it. It was in fact not until the early 1960s, after the publication of all Kaldor's growth models, that he received from Rüstow a copy of his work and honestly admitted that there was a very close similarity indeed between their two theories. Henceforth Kaldor would repeatedly cite Rüstow as one of the precursors of post-Keynesian theory and conduct a voluminous scientific correspondence with him.

There are important similarities among the theories of Rüstow, Keynes, and Kalecki, although there are also significant differences. The similarities centre on the conviction shared by the three economists that the role of savings is a passive one, and that changes in money-wages do not ensure equilibrium between demand and supply in the labour market, a function which is instead performed by the interest rate—since, on account of the sensitivity of investment to the rate of interest, this latter regulates the level of effective demand.

---

[9] Let P denote profits, w unitary wage, X output, L work hours, π mark-up, p price level, and $Y \equiv pX$. From the price equation we obtain $p = (1 + \pi)wL/X$ and hence, by appropriate simplifications and defining $wL = W$, we obtain: $\pi = (P/Y)/(W/Y)$. Thus, bearing in mind that $W/Y + P/Y = 1$ the share of profits is stated by:
$$P/Y = \pi/(1 + \pi).$$
Note that this is an accounting expression. It represents no law, nor is it deduced from behavioural assumptions (it is subject only to the hypothesis that costs are made up solely of wages). Thus, if no part of the theory explains the value of π, this confirms Kaldor's assertion that the share of profits in Kalecki 'are what they are because the forces of competition prevent them from being higher than they are and are not powerful enough to make them lower than they are' (Kaldor, 'Alternative Theories of Distribution', 226).

[10] For an outline survey of Kalecki's thought and a guide to his 1933–70 writings on the capitalist economy, see F. Targetti and B. Kinda-Hass, 'Kalecki's Review of Keynes's General Theory', *Australian Economic Papers* (Dec. 1982). See also M. C. Sawyer, *The Economics of Michal Kalecki*, (London, Macmillan, 1985).

[11] N. Kaldor, 'Gemeinsamkeiten und Unterschiede in den Theorien von Keynes, Kalecki und Rüstow' (1980), pub. in IST 29:1, (1983), 1 (German trans.). Rüstow's doctoral thesis is published in H. J. Rüstow, *Theorie der Volbeschäftigung in der Freien Marktwirtschaft* (Tubingen, Möhr, 1951).

For Kaldor, the superiority of Rüstow's theory (according to which, the level of profit was determined by the excess of investment over saving out of wages and salaries) with respect to Keynes's *General Theory* lay in its recognition that 'savings out of profit is not the same kind of thing as savings obtained from "cost-incomes" ' (i.e. incomes which stand as the counterpart to the 'production costs' incurred by entrepreneurs): hence they could not be integrated into a single savings function. Moreover, although Keynes recognized the importance of profits as a source of finance for investment, he gave no importance to the share of profits as a determinant of the level of employment. Kalecki, by contrast, attributed major significance to the relation between the share of profit and the level of activity. But he regarded it as an inverse relation, whereas Rüstow saw it as a positive one. For Kalecki, an increase in the degree of monopoly was one of the principal causes of lack of effective demand. Therefore both Keynes and Kalecki held that a reduction in the share of profit brought the system closer to full employment. Rüstow's theory of the 'differential share of profit' (which Kaldor considered superior to Kalecki's) had things operating the other way round. According to the German economist, for every industrial structure there exist firms or establishments with differing levels of output per worker. Since the labour cost per worker varies relatively little between the most efficient and the least efficient firm, the differences in the value of output per worker are reflected in corresponding differences in the share of profits in value added. There therefore exists a single value for the average share of profits that allows the last worker to be absorbed by the least efficient firm. As demand increases, the price level must increase relative to wages so that the extra-marginal firm can produce while covering its costs—as a consequence the overall amount of profit increases. An increase in the amount of profit is therefore associated with higher not lower employment.[12]

After the publication of Harrod's *Toward a Dynamic Economics*,[13] the attention of many economists, especially in Cambridge and with Kaldor among them, shifted away from the theory of the trade cycle to concentrate on the issues raised by Harrod's theory of growth. 'The problem of reconciling the two growth potentials—the "warranted" rate of capital accumulation and the "natural" rate of growth in the effective labour force—appeared as the basic "dynamic" problem.'[14] Since I shall repeatedly refer to this topic later, a brief outline of the problem now follows.

Let G_a denote the 'rate of effective growth', tautologously defined as the ratio between the ex-post propensity to save s and the ex-post marginal capital/output ratio v. Thus:

---

[12] Thus, for Rüstow, on the one hand profits derive from the costs mark-up and their amount can therefore only be measured ex-post; on the other hand, however, firms can only operate ex-ante if their earnings are no lower than their costs. Note the similarity with the theory of profits developed by P. Sylos Labini, *Le forze dello sviluppo e del declino* (Bari, Laterza, 1984).

[13] R. Harrod, *Toward a Dynamic Economics* (London, Macmillan, 1948).

[14] N. Kaldor, 'Recollections of an Economist' (1986), rep. in CP ix., 28.

(5.2) $$G_a = s/v.$$

This rate of growth (which is the rate that actually exists) has to be compared with two other potential rates of growth. The first, G_w, which Harrod called the 'warranted growth rate', is the rate of growth in output compatible with the ex-ante saving decisions of households s_d and which generates an increase in effective demand coherent with the expectations of entrepreneurs, i.e. it matches the desire to invest given the required capital/output ratio v_d. Thus:

(5.3) $$G_w = s_d/v_d.$$

The second potential rate is the 'natural rate of growth', G_n, given by the sum of the rate of growth of the population, n, and the rate of growth in per-capita output due to technical progress, t. This is the maximum and socially optimal rate achievable by the system should it make full use of its resources:

(5.4) $$G_n = n + t.$$

Since each of the three pairs of parameters (s and v; s_d and v_d; n and t) is independent of the other two, all three growth rates may be equal, or two of them, or none. This raises two problems: the existence of steady-state equilibrium, i.e. the convergence of G_w and G_n, and the stability of equilibrium, i.e. the convergence of G_a and G_w (Harrod's so-called 'knife-edge' problem).

Such was the 'state of the art' in the theory of dynamic economics at the beginning of the 1950s. The solutions proposed for Harrod's problem moved in two different directions: there was (1) the neo-classical explanation based on the variability of the parameter v; and (2) the Kaldorian approach—also adopted by Richard Kahn and Joan Robinson—based on the variability of the distribution of income and of the parameter s.[15]

Before beginning detailed treatment of Kaldor's theory of distribution and growth, there is an important aspect to the development of his ideas that should be clarified; an aspect, I believe, that was never properly elucidated by the copious subsequent literature on the subject. At a first stage in the development of his theory, between 1940 and 1956, Kaldor took the capitalist economy to be a system that was unstable by its very nature. At the same time,

[15] A clear exposition of the existence and stability conditions in the neo-classical model and in Kaldor's model can be found in F. H. Hahn and R. C. O. Matthews, 'The Theory of Economic Growth: A Survey', in *Survey of Economic Theory, Growth and Development* (London, Macmillan for the Royal Economic Society, and New York, St Martin's Press for the American Economic Association, 1969). As early as 1951 Hahn had also described, in his Ph.D. thesis, a mechanism for bringing the natural and warranted rates to equality through change in the distribution of income (see F. Hahn, *The Share of Wages in National Income* (London, Weidenfeld & Nicolson, 1972)); but, whereas Kaldor's work contained substantial elements of a non-neo-classical theory of distribution, in Hahn this mechanism was not clearly distinguished from the marginal theory of distribution because 'I . . . did not argue from this that the steady state real wage of labour was divorced from its marginal product' (id., 'Kaldor on Growth', *Cambridge Journal of Economics* (Mar. 1989)). Kaldor would agree that the equilibrium wage rate cannot be *higher* than its marginal product; but this does not entail that it must be *equal*—which is the necessary, if not sufficient, condition for it to be *determined* by its marginal product. See, for a similar point to Hahn's, H. Atsumi, 'Mr Kaldor's Theory of Income Distribution', *RES* (Feb. 1960), 109–18; and for a critique of Atsumi, N. Kaldor, 'A Rejoinder to Mr Atsumi and Professor Tobin', *RES* (Feb. 1960).

however, he came increasingly to believe that, in the long run, there is much to recommend the hypothesis of a growing economy with fully utilized productive capacity. His theory of distribution may be set out in these latter terms. Nowhere in his writings, though, did Kaldor tackle the problem of the distribution of income during the cycle and of the connection between the forces that render the economy cyclical and those that explain the distribution of income in the long run.

At a later stage Kaldor's view became more 'optimistic'. This was between 1957 and 1962, the years in which he developed his models of steady-state growth. In these models the distribution of income had the task of adjusting the warranted growth rate to the natural rate of growth deduced from his technical-progress function. Using Harrodian symbols as above, we may say that the articles Kaldor wrote between 1954 and 1956 on the relation between cycle and growth analysed the relation between G_a and G_n, while his later articles dealt with the relation between G_w and G_n, which, in the long run, is taken to be equal to G_a.

5.4. Trade Cycle and Growth

Kaldor himself declared[16] that his 1940 model of the trade cycle was 'static'—in the sense that the cyclical movement was regular in amplitude and period, constant, and without trend:[17] the dynamic of the system was not an element necessary for explanation of the phenomenon. In the 1950s, however, the connection between cycle and trend increasingly pressed for attention, and the solution then generally put forward was one that Kaldor also subscribed to: the 'superimposition of a linear trend introduced from the outside on an otherwise trendless model without altering, in any way, its basic character'.[18] The simplest approach—one that was adopted by all the dynamic models of those years[19]—was Kalecki's[20] superimposition of an exogenous percentage increase in the population and labour productivity on the static model.

---

[16] N. Kaldor, 'The Relation of Economic Growth and Cyclical Fluctuations' (1953), repr. in CP ii. 216.

[17] In Goodwin's view (in a private conversation with the author on the occasion of the presentation in May 1986 of Kaldor's book *Ricordi di un economista* in Bologna), Kaldor's 1940 cycle was—though Kaldor denied it—a cycle with a trend. Its upper turning-point *had to be* full employment, and the trend was disguised by this 'ceiling'. When I pointed this out to Kaldor he replied that his hypothesis did not require full employment, but full utilization in the capital-goods sector. When this sector had reached full utilization of its productive capacity, demand outstripped output, profit overtook investment, and this had a deflationary effect on production and employment. This therefore entails that capital grows disproportionately between the two sectors, because, according to Kaldor, of the capital-goods sector's relatively greater fear of over-expanding its productive capacity.

[18] Kaldor, 'Relation of Economic Growth and Cyclical Fluctuations', 225.

[19] See the bibliographical references to Hicks, Goodwin, and Marrama in Ch. 3.2.

[20] M. Kalecki, *Studies in Economic Dynamics* (London, Allen & Unwin, 1943).

Kaldor disagreed with Hicks's view (largely shared by Goodwin[21]) that 'it is on the trend rate of growth that the whole cyclical mechanism depends'[22]—since in the absence of autonomous investment the cycle could not get off the ground—and argued that the assumption of a positive trend was not necessary for the oscillation of the economy. The pure cycle 'can be looked upon as a special case of the "dynamic equilibrium" where the equilibrium rate of growth happens to be zero'.[23] The 'centrifugal forces' that surround Harrod's 'equilibrium of steady advance' are the same centrifugal forces that surround the stationary equilibrium of a trendless economy.[24]

Kaldor gave the most complete account of his ideas on the dynamic instability of the capitalist system in his Peking lecture of 1956. This instability, he argued, stemmed from the difference between the natural growth rate G_n and the rate of 'market expansion'—and therefore of output capacity—expected by entrepreneurs.[25] If the two rates G_a and G_n diverge, the system reacts in two ways: in the short run with an oscillation of G_a around G_n; in the long run through adjustment of G_a to G_n, and also through adjustment of G_n to G_a.

When entrepreneurs expect a rate of growth in output capacity higher than the natural rate of growth of the system, although this is a condition of a successfully developing economy, the economy grows in 'fits and starts'—as shown by Figure 5.1. Investment will tend to be excessive, in the sense that productive capacity expands faster than output, leading to excess capacity and a consequent interruption in the investment process until new investment becomes necessary in order to replace old machinery. The duration of the recession is longer, the higher the rate of growth predicted by entrepreneurs. And this is on account of the fact that the more rapid the increase in productive capacity, the more time is required in a recession to replace part of productive capacity itself.

In the opposite case, where entrepreneurs predict a rate of output expansion—and therefore of productive capacity—steadily below the natural growth rate, the economy stagnates with a surplus of manpower.

[21] R. Goodwin, 'The Problem of Trend and Cycle', *Yorkshire Bulletin of Economic and Social Research* (1953).

[22] J. Hicks, *A Contribution to the Theory of the Trade Cycle* (Oxford, Clarendon Press, 1950), 108.

[23] Kaldor, 'Relation of Economic Growth and Cyclical Fluctuations', 226.

[24] Ibid. Kaldor realized that the same forces could explain either the cycle or the trend but not both of them. One of the best demonstrations that the multiplier and the accelerator can, according to the parameters, give rise either to balanced growth or to cycles of various kinds has been given by L. L. Pasinetti, 'Cyclical Fluctuations and Economic Growth', *OEP* (June, 1960) repr. in *Growth and Income Distribution: Essays in Economic Theory* (Cambridge, CUP, 1974).

[25] By the 'rate of market expansion expected by entrepreneurs' Kaldor sometimes seems to have in mind Harrod's warranted rate (see Kaldor, 'Relation of Economic Growth and Cyclical Fluctuations', 230–1). But, given that G_w is the only rate of growth at which expectations are fulfilled and which therefore cannot fluctuate, we must conclude that the rate of growth fluctuating around G_n must be G_a. I have been convinced on this point by M. Pugno, *R. F. Harrod: Dall' equilibrio dinamico alla instabilitá ciclica* (Bologna, Il Mulino, forthcoming), n. 127.

FIG. 5.1 Capitalist instability: the divergence between the natural rate of growth
and the rate of market expansion

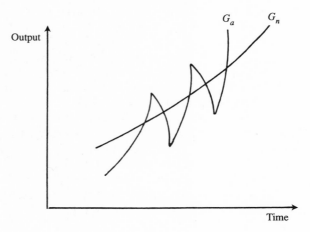

But Kaldor complicates matters even further. If the two growth rates
diverge, over the short period the growth rate predicted by entrepreneurs G_a
adjusts itself to the natural rate G_n, which is exogenous; over the long period
the natural rate G_n becomes endogenous. Indeed, the more the rate of expected
growth of output capacity tends to exceed the natural rate, the more it will
bend the natural rate in its own direction—through the introduction of labour-
saving techniques and the stimulus to population growth provided by the rapid
growth of the supply of consumer goods. Over the long period, therefore, both
technical progress and population growth are either accelerated[26] or slowed
down by the endogenous forces of the economic system.

Consequently a capitalist economy is intrinsically unstable because it is
exposed to two different hazards. If G_a exceeds G_n, the economy will be
subject to violent booms and slumps; if, on the other hand, G_a falls short of
G_n, the economy will stagnate, and this will slow down population growth, the
growth of per-capita output, and therefore G_n itself. 'There is therefore no
inevitability about economic progress in a capitalist economy (or for that
matter, in a socialist economy):[27] it all depends on whether those in charge of

[26] The scarcity of labour induces the introduction of labour-saving techniques and stimulates
population growth because of the rapid growth in the supply of consumer goods. Note that the
increase of labour is never explained in neo-classical terms of a movement *along* the labour-supply
curve because of an increase in real wages. It is explained in different ways at different stages of
Kaldor's thought, but always in terms of a shift *of* the labour-supply curve: in 1956 because of the
operation of a Ricardian–Malthusian mechanism whereby an increase in consumption goods
stimulates population growth; in 1968 (see Ch. 7.5) because of the migration of the population
among sectors or among countries in response to greater labour demand.

[27] However, Kaldor also pointed out that the argument stating that, in a capitalist economy,
growth is greater the more powerful the forces of the cycle does not imply that progress must
necessarily proceed in fits and starts, whatever the institutional framework of society. 'If invest-

production have the incentives and the will to pursue a vigorous expansion of output capacity.'[28]

Kaldor reiterated his view that although the capitalist system showed no intrinsic tendency towards stable development, it could be brought to it by wise economic policy:

There is no inherent necessity in a capitalist economy or any other economy of sustained evolution. There may be stagnation rather than development; progress may take the form of violent ups and downs, and not of a smooth or steady process; progress may be attended by a growing concentration of wealth and economic power in the hands of a few individuals. But none of these tendencies, if they arise, are either inevitable or unavoidable. They are all subject to social control once we understand the manner of operation of economic and social forces. It is my belief that in a progressive social democracy they could all be avoided.[29]

In the same year as his Peking lecture (in which he was still concentrating on the relation between cycle and trend) Kaldor published the article in which he gave the definitive version of his theory—already outlined in preliminary form in 1948—of the distribution of income in the long run.

5.5. Distribution and Growth

Kaldor's theory of distribution arose, as we have seen, from a fusion of the theories of Keynes, Kalecki, and Harrod. From the Keynesian theory of the *Treatise* he took the idea of the adjustment of savings to investment in conditions of full employment through variation in the price level and the attendant variation in distribution; from Kalecki the concept of saving propensities; from Harrod the problem of the adjustment of the effective, warranted, and natural growth rate.

Kaldor's crucial insight lay in his perception of the dual role played by the Keynesian multiplier: in conditions of underemployment the multiplier determines the level of income and employment; in conditions of full employment it determines the distribution of income between profits and wages. As a principle, therefore, it has two different applications: 'the one is used in the framework of a static model and the other in the framework of a dynamic growth model'.[30]

Kaldorian distribution theory therefore rests on the hypothesis of full utilization; a hypothesis that will be given more detailed treatment in the next

ments were centrally planned and the consumption function continually adjusted to secure full employment, (given the planned rate of investment) there is no reason, in theory, why progress could not take place at an even rate' ('Relation of Economic Growth and Cyclical Fluctuations', 232 n. 1).

[28] Kaldor, 'Capitalist Evolution in the Light of Keynesian Economics' (1957), repr. in CP ii. 255.

[29] Ibid. 258.   [30] Kaldor, 'Alternative Theories of Distribution', 228.

section (for the moment let us assume that full utilization means, in Keynesian terms, full employment of labour associated with the full utilization of productive capacity). In its simplest formulation, the theory treats investment as an exogenous datum; although Kaldor would subsequently abandon this hypothesis (and this too will be discussed below).

The innovative feature of Kaldor's theory is the savings function. The share of savings S in income Y is given by the average propensity to save out of wages s_W and out of profits s_P weighted with the respective amounts of income. Since the model comprises only two classes of income-earners, the share of wages equals 1 minus the share of profits. Thus:

(5.5) $$S/Y = s_P P/Y + s_W(1 - P/Y) = (s_P - s_W)P/Y + s_W.$$

By imposing the condition of savings–investment equilibrium, we have:

(5.6) $$P/Y = [1/(s_P - s_W)]I/Y - [s_W/(s_P - s_W)].$$

This expression, as a representation of a distributive theory, entails two assumptions: the first that the dynamic behaviour of prices (or of profit margins over costs) is the same as that described by Keynes in his *Treatise on Money*; the second that the propensity to save among profit-receivers is greater than that of wage-earners. Hence, let:

(5.7) $$s_P > s_W \geqslant 0.$$

If this expression is valid, expression (5.6) may be read as follows: an increase in the rate of investment creates an excess of demand in the consumption-goods sector which pushes up the level of prices. Since money-wages are fixed, or at any rate since they adjust more slowly than prices, the share of wages in income will fall. Hence the share of profits will rise, and with it the share of savings in the national income until this equals the share of investment. The reverse happens in the case of a reduction of the share of investment in full-employment income. The distribution of income therefore varies in such a way that any desired investment ratio is possible in a full-employment economy. This adjustment mechanism works within limits of variation in the share of profit that will be explained in the next section.

The model set out here is, in certain respects, the exact opposite of the classical Ricardian–Marxian model: wages rather than profits are residual: profits are determined by the expenditure of profit-receivers and therefore represent a sort of 'prior charge' on the national income.

Hypothesis (5.7), which as we have seen is crucial to Kaldor's argument, is assumed for two reasons. First because otherwise the model would be unstable: a fall in demand and the resultant drop in prices would in fact lead to a further fall in demand and hence in prices—and vice versa in the case of a rise in demand;[31] secondly because profits arise inside the firm and are held

---

[31] Ibid. 230. In the introd. to CP, vol. ii (2nd edn.), p. xxiv, Kaldor argues in favour of the second inequality (5.7) in different terms. Workers' savings have a negative effect on the profits of firms in aggregate because they reduce their earnings (a smaller quantity of goods sold to

within it as reserves for possible future financing of investments (this point will be discussed further in Chapters 6 and 14).

Under the extreme classical hypothesis (advanced by both Kalecki and von Neumann) that workers consume the whole of their income, and therefore $s_W = 0$, we have:

(5.8) $$P/Y = (I/Y)(1/s_P).$$

This expression, which closely resembles Kalecki's expression (5.1), states that the share of profits depends on the percentage of investment in income and on the propensity to spend out of profits: it is the distributive result generated by the fundamental equation of Keynes's *Treatise on Money*. One deduces from this expression that the greater the amount of profits devoted by capitalists to consumption, the higher the profits that derive from a certain level of investment: hence Keynes's analogy of the widow's cruse and Kalecki's dictum that 'capitalists earn what they spend and workers spend what they earn'.

The distribution of income is therefore governed by the independent variable given by the investment/output ratio. This is determined in turn (given the capital/output ratio v_d by G_w the rate of growth in productive capacity predicted by business: $I/Y = G_w v_d$. On the other hand, G_w must be equal to the rate of growth G_n if the system is to achieve long-run full-employment equilibrium. Hence it follows that:

(5.9) $$G_n v_d = I/Y = S/Y = (s_P - s_W)I/Y + s_W.$$

The conclusion to be drawn from this equation is the following: given the natural growth rate G_n (which is still exogenous at this point) and the required capital/output ratio v_d, the flexibility of the distributive shares (P/Y) will guarantee that the warranted rate of growth adjusts to the natural rate—that is to say, a dynamic savings equilibrium at full employment—as long as $s_P > s_W$. The flexibility of the distributive shares guarantees the existence and stability of steady-state growth (as regards stability, however, one must suppose that the increase in the share of profit induces an increase in the share of savings in income and a smaller or nil increase in the share of investment in output).

---

households) compared with their costs (wages are incomes for worker-consumers, but costs for firms). Hence for earnings to be greater than costs, and therefore aggregate profits higher than zero, capital expenditure (investment and therefore earnings for firms producing these goods) must be higher than personal savings. But since savings must be equal to investment Kaldor derives the two inequalities (1) $s_P > s_W > 0$; (2) $s_P > I/Y > s_W$. These he takes to be necessary for there to be a positive profit, and hence for private firms to be able to exist. I believe that this argument is incorrect. One can plausibly argue that to obtain $P > 0$ it must be the case that $I > S_W$ (amount of savings made out of wages). In fact, if P is given by the difference between earnings and costs, and if earnings are given only as investments I plus workers' consumption C_W (and not by consumption out of profits, because profits are still to come), while costs are given by wages, we have: $P = C_W + I - W = I - (W - C_W) = I - S_W$. Whence $P > 0$ if $I > S_W$. Nevertheless it is not legitimate to *deduce* $I/Y > s_W$, because s_W is not S_W/Y but S_W/W, which is a higher value than S_W/Y. It is clear, however, that if $I/Y > s_W$ and if $S_W + S_P = I$ we would obtain inequality (5.7).

5.6. Full Employment, Stylized Facts, and Historical Stages

In his entry for the 1948 *Chambers Encyclopedia* Kaldor argued that

[h]istorical evidence of the more advanced capitalist economies suggests, however, that large-scale involuntary unemployment only occurs in periods of economic stagnation; in the majority of periods in which the level of production and the stock of capital of the community are growing year by year, the pressure of demand is sufficient to secure full employment, and thus maximum production in the short run.[32]

In his 1956 article 'Alternative Theories of Distribution', Kaldor reiterated his view that total income or output should be taken as given. In 1957 he endeavoured again to justify the very un-Kaldorian hypothesis 'that in a growing economy the general level of output is at any one time limited by the available resources and not by effective demand'.[33] Finally, at the Corfu Conference of 1958 and in his 1959 lectures at the LSE,[34] he provided more thorough justification for the assumption of full employment in a model of growth.

In the latter two works he assumed that there exists a representative firm whose supply curve (see Figure 5.2) takes the form of a reverse L-shape ($SS'S''$). The greater the difference between price and marginal cost (this too represented by a flat marginal-cost (MC) curve until full employment), the greater profits and savings will be and the shallower the aggregate demand curve, which will slope negatively in relation to prices (section $D'D''$). There is a level of output (corresponding to P_1 on the demand curve) of Keynesian underemployment equilibrium. However, there exists a higher level of production (N) beyond which (and this is the crucial element in the argument) investment is induced by profit margins higher than total costs. Greater induced investments can be financed if savings are greater, but savings increase if profit margins increase: thus the aggregate demand curve will change direction and will begin its upward positive slope with respect to prices ($D'D''$). This section of the curve contains two equilibrium points of aggregate supply and demand (P_2 and P_3), of which only the latter is a point of stable equilibrium. This equilibrium is also one of full capacity utilization, since it lies in section $S'S''$ (note that full utilization also signifies full employment of labour only in a developed economy amply endowed with capital). There therefore exists only one point of stable-growth equilibrium (P_3), while the other two represent unstable equilibrium (P_2) and Keynesian underemployment equilibrium (P_1). This latter equilibrium may persist in the short term but is incompatible with a growing economy, whose driving force is induced investment.

Kaldor developed his growth models in order to provide an explanation of certain fundamental tendencies in capitalist economies. These 'stylized facts', as he called them, were the outcome of forces operating within the system.

[32] Kaldor, 'Theory of Distribution', 561.

[33] Id., 'A Model of Economic Growth' (1957), repr. in CP ii. 262.

[34] Id., 'Capital Accumulation and Economic Growth' (1958), repr. in CP v; id., 'Economic Growth and the Problem of Inflation' (1959), repr. in CP iii.

FIG. 5.2 Short- and long-run employment equilibrium: the long run is full
employment

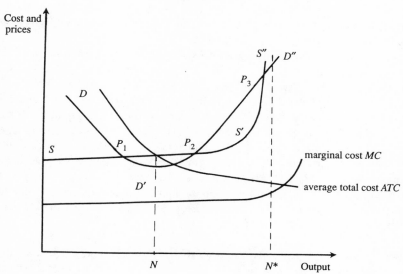

They arose from the simultaneous presence of: (1) a fairly constant trend of
output and labour productivity growth; (2) a growing trend in the capital/la-
bour ratio; (3) a steady rate of profit on capital; (4) a long-term equivalence
between the growth of capital and output and therefore a steady capital/output
ratio; (5) a high correlation between the share of investment in output and the
share of profits in income and, therefore, during periods when the coefficient
of investment is invariant, a high level of stability in distributive shares and,
thus, a change in real wages equal to the change in labour productivity; (6) a
marked difference between the rate of growth of labour productivity in various
countries associated with variations in the investment coefficient and in the
profit share.

None of these facts could be explained by the neo-classical theory of marginal productivity, according to which (and also according to the classical
economists and to Keynes) in circumstances of constant capital accumulation
the profit rate must fall—and not, therefore, remain constant. Moreover, since
the return on capital falls as accumulation proceeds, one deduces that as the
capital/labour ratio increases, the capital/output ratio should increase rather
than remain constant, and that there should be a fall rather than a rise in the
rate of growth in labour productivity. Finally, according to neo-classical theory, the shares of profits and wages are uniquely determined by the marginal
rates of distribution between capital and labour only in the special case of a
production function which is not only linear and homogeneous, but has unitary
elasticity of substitution as well. This latter assumption, which implies that

the capital/output ratio is smaller in faster-growing economies, conflicts with the empirical evidence. But if the elasticity of substitution is, in realistic terms, appreciably smaller than one, the share of profit will depend primarily on the rate of economic growth and only to a minor extent on the marginal rates of substitution between capital and labour.

Nor could Marxian theory give an explanation for these tendencies in developed economies, despite its ability to account for the early stages of capitalist development. According to Kaldor, the three main features of the Marxian theory of capitalism were the following: (1) that wages are determined by the cost of reproduction of labour and therefore stay at the subsistence level, while profit is a residue derived from the difference between output per head and cost per head; (2) that there exists a difference between labour demand and supply constituting what, in Marx's expression, was the 'reserve army of labour'; (3) that competition requires profits to be reinvested. The share of profits in total output is given by the ratio between surplus value (SV) and the sum of surplus value and subsistence cost (C) for all workers (L):

$$(5.10) \qquad\qquad P/Y = SV/(SV + CL).$$

As accumulation proceeds, the reserve army shrinks and wages rise above the subsistence level. Little by little this process leads to the disappearance of profits and hence of accumulation unless the capitalists, by increasing the 'organic composition of capital', adopt labour-saving production methods. The existence of a reserve army is a necessary condition for the safeguarding of profits and, as a consequence, of capital accumulation and economic growth. It is precisely this point that marks the principal difference between Marx's and Kaldor's theories of distribution. In Kaldor's view, one of the greatest merits of Keynes's analysis was that it showed that money-wages and real wages are determined by different forces. The condition of the labour market only influences money-wages. Real wages are determined, in periods of full employment, by the change of the price level which equilibrates the total supply of goods and total demand. The latter is induced by that expenditure which is not constrained by current income, i.e. capitalist expenditure.

We can thus compare the Kaldorian and Marxian positions by contrasting expression (5.8) with expression (5.10). At any moment, (5.8) indicates an upper limit to the wage rate beyond which workers cannot appropriate output without incurring an excess of demand over the supply of full employment; (5.10) sets a lower limit beneath which capitalists cannot appropriate output, since this would signify wages below the minimum necessary for the survival of their workers. At every moment of history either the Marxian or the Kaldorian mechanism is in operation (and the formula which yields the higher per-capita wage will apply).

In the early stages of capitalism, per-capita productivity was low; the surplus value was below the value required to satisfy equation (5.8); and wages remained at the subsistence level, despite increasing productivity per worker.

Given the constancy of the subsistence wage due to the existence of the reserve army of labour, the rate of growth of productivity determined the maximum share of profits in the national product. At this stage the only constraint on growth was the availability of savings flowing to capitalists in the form of profits; it was therefore the amount of surplus that determined the rate of accumulation. The latter, in a situation characterized by a low rate of change in productivity, led to the absorption of an increasing amount of manpower and to the disappearance of the industrial reserve army. Henceforth growth was constrained by the availability of manpower.

Here Marxian theory left the field to make way for what Kaldor called the 'Keynesian' theory of growth at full employment: the share of profits can increase no further because real wages are no longer held constant at the subsistence level; their change is now governed by the rate at which the productivity of the system increases, and this will in turn be governed by investment decisions.

In order to trace the route followed by Kaldor in reaching these conclusions, the next section will examine his theory of growth in greater detail.

5.7. The Growth Model: Savings, Investment, and Technical Progress

In the years between 1957 and 1962 Kaldor developed his three models of growth in a period of such fertility and inventiveness that Robert Solow compared him with a satellite which, on each orbit around the earth, drops a different model.

1957 therefore marked the beginning of a second stage in Kaldor's exploration of the subject of distribution and growth. Prior to that year his models had omitted the investment function: investment was exogenous; it was whatever was necessary to keep the the system on the natural growth path. The innovative feature of this second stage is Kaldor's introduction of an investment function and a technical-progress function. From the joint action of these two functions it is possible to derive the long-run equilibrium rate of growth, the basic idea being that 'the prime mover in the process of economic growth is the readiness to absorb technical changes combined with the willingness to invest capital in business ventures'.[35]

The logical structure of these models turns on three main functions. The first is the savings function, which was analysed in Chapter 5.5. The flexibility of the distributive shares equalizes the propensity to save to the share of investment in income. The second is the investment function. Investment is a function of the rate of profit, but since this latter, in conditions of long-run equilibrium growth, is a function of the rate of growth of income, it follows that the accumulation rate is also a function of the rate of growth of income. The third function is the technical-progress function. Since technical progress,

[35] Id., 'Model of Economic Growth', 270.

measured by the growth of per-capita output, is introduced into the economic system by new investments, the dynamic of technical progress is a function of the accumulation rate. These two latter functions therefore state that if there is to be continued growth: (1) the accumulation rate must be a function of the rate of growth of output (psychological investment function); (2) the rate of growth of output must be a function of the accumulation rate (technical-progress function).

The first two functions of the model can both be expressed in relation to the share of profits, as follows. The savings function is none other than equation (5.5), in which s_P and s_W are labelled α and β. The suffixes on variables I, P, Y, and K indicate the moment of time referred to by the variables:

$$(5.11) \qquad\qquad S_t/Y_t = \beta + (\alpha - \beta)P_t/Y_t.$$

The investment function derives from a set of behavioural hypotheses: (1) given the (expected) rate of profit on capital, entrepreneurs wish to maintain a constant relationship between the amount of capital invested and their turnover; (2) this relationship is an increasing function of the expected rate of profit; (3) investment decisions for each 'period' are governed by the adjustment of actual capital to desired capital;[36] (4) entrepreneurs expect the same increase in turnover for the following period as attained in the previous one; (5) they expect a margin of profit on turnover equal to that obtained in the previous period. That is to say, the ratio between capital at time t and output at time $t - 1$, must be a positive function of the actual rate of profit:

$$K_t/Y_{t-1} = \text{constant} + \beta' P_t/K_t.$$

The above hypotheses can be synthesized into one investment function (where $I_t = K_{t+1} - K_t$) by two variables: the change in output in the previous period, and the change in the rate of profit in the current period[37]. Thus we may write:

$$I_t/Y_t = \alpha'[(Y_t - Y_{t-1})/Y_{t-1}] + \beta'[(P_t/K_t) - (P_{t-1}/K_{t-1})]$$

which (since α' is the capital/output ratio at time t) is equivalent to:

$$(5.12) \quad I_t/Y_t = [\alpha'(Y_t - Y_{t-1})/Y_{t-1}] - [\beta'(P_{t-1}/K_{t-1})] + [\beta'(1/\alpha')(P_t/Y_t)].$$

---

[36] Kaldor himself pointed out that, in his articles on the trade cycle (Mar. 1940 and Dec. 1950), he criticized the use of the accelerator principle in connection with trade cycle because the cyclical mechanism must be explained by a changing relationship between output and output capacity (or capital). However, in his work on long-run models of economic growth he defended the accelerator principle by arguing that time can be divided into periods long enough for the capital stock in any one period to be fully adjusted to the output expected for that period at the beginning of the same period ('Model of Economic Growth', 271 n. 3).

[37] In Kaldor's view, rather than translating Keynes's principle of declining marginal efficiency of capital and Kalecki's principle of increasing marginal risk (M. Kalecki, 'The Principle of Increasing Risk', (1937), 440) into an investment function where $\Delta K/K$ is an increasing function of the rate of profit, they should instead be reinterpreted in an investment function where the desired stock of capital *in relation to turnover* is treated as an increasing function of the rate of profit. This latter is a more reasonable assumption because there is little empirical justification for the belief that a faster rate of growth of capital entails a higher subjective marginal risk to entrepreneurs so long as the growth of capital merely keeps pace with the growth of turnover ('Model of Economic Growth', 272 n. 1).

FIG. 5.3 The share of profit in a growing economy

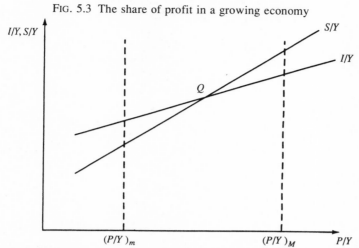

Figure 5.3 shows the two equations of savings and investment. The point of intersection Q determines the distribution of short-period income which guarantees that the share of savings equals the share of investment. Equilibrium is stable if the savings curve is steeper than the investments curve.

The model is subject to further restrictions. The first of these is that the share of profits (P/Y) must not exceed a certain maximum value $(P/Y)_M$ given by the minimum subsistence wage level. The second restriction is that the share of profits must be higher than a minimum value $(P/Y)_m$ which generates a flow of earnings sufficient to cover fixed costs and to obtain a profit margin which, multiplied by the inverse of the capital/output ratio, makes it possible to obtain a rate of return on capital that is not less than the risk premium.

The third function represents technical progress. This should be examined in detail, since it represents the major innovation in Kaldor's models of growth with respect to his simple theory of distribution, where he took the natural growth rate to be exogenous.

Kaldor maintained that it is not possible to distinguish—as neo-classical theory implicitly does with its assumption of neutral technical progress—between technical changes induced by the dynamic of factors supply (movements *along* a production function) and changes due to inventions and innovations (*shift* of the production function itself). It is therefore impossible to specify which production factor has been saved by technical progress. An increase in capital per worker always leads—according to Kaldor—to the introduction of techniques that are more productive than previous ones. Therefore a movement *along* the function entails a *shift* of the function itself. On the other hand, many, although not all, innovations require more capital per worker.[38] Thus the speed at which a society is able to accumulate capital

---

[38] It could be objected that organizational innovations are an exception to this rule. And product innovations do not seem a priori to comply with the rule either, in so far as it seems to apply

FIG. 5.4(*a*) The technical-progress function

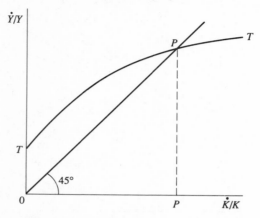

depends on its technological dynamism and, vice versa, the degree of absorption of new technology depends on the ability of a society to accumulate capital. Technical progress and accumulation of capital are two phenomena so intimately connected that they are impossible to separate. The process may be more or less rapid, but it takes place in historical not logical time and is therefore irreversible. The ability to absorb technical progress decreases as accumulation grows. These considerations can be expressed by having the technical-progress function link the rate of growth of output per worker with the rate of growth of capital per worker (Figure 5.4(*a*)). Assuming a linear relation among the variables, and assuming that certain increases in productivity (α'') occur independently of the dynamic of accumulation, the technical-progress function can be expressed by the following equation:

(5.13)　　　　　　$(Y_{t+1} - Y_t)/Y_t = \alpha'' + \beta''(I_t/K_t)$

where the rates of growth of output per worker and capital per worker have been multiplied by the rate of growth of employment. Since the rate of change of autonomous technical progress is positive, it follows that:

$$\alpha'' > 0.$$

Moreover:

mostly to process innovations. But it is also true that in almost all cases these two types of innovation appear together. The problem is further complicated if 'capital' is also taken to mean 'human capital'. The difficulty of measuring 'capital'—a snag that Kaldor always skirted around—is discussed in the next section. For a survey of theories of technical progress see C. Kennedy and A. P. Thirlwall, 'Technical Progress: A Survey', *EJ* (Mar. 1972). See also M. Amendola, *Macchine, produttività e progresso tecnico* (Milan, Isedi, 1976). On more recent theories of technological innovation see R. R. Nelson and S. G. Winter, 'In Search of a Useful Theory of Technological Change', *Research Policy*, 6 (1977); J. S. Metcalfe, 'Impulse and Diffusion in the Study of Techological Change', *Futures*, 13: 5 (1981); G. Dosi, 'Technical Paradigms and Technological Trajectories—A Suggested Interpretation of the Determinants and Directions of Technical Change', *Research Policy*, 2: 3 (1982); C. Freeman *et al.*, *Unemployment and Technical Innovation: A Study of Long Waves in Economic Development* (London, Pinter, 1982).

$$0 < \beta'' < 1.$$

The position of the technical-progress curve reflects both the ability of the system to generate new ideas and the speed with which they are adopted. A system with a low flow of innovations, or one which is unable to convey them into the economy, will be represented by a lower, flatter curve, while important new discoveries (new technological waves over the long period) will shift the curve upwards.

The intersection of the technical-progress function with the 45-degree line drawn from the origin determines the value of G_n, which represents the long-run equilibrium point of the rate of growth of the economy. The tendency towards G_n is ensured by the investment function. Let us suppose that the short-run equilibrium rate of accumulation I_1/K_1 derived from equations (5.11) and (5.12) lies to the left of G_n. This means that, for every increase in the accumulation rate, the gain in terms of productivity is, by comparison, greater, and, given the investment function (5.12), this accelerates the process itself of accumulation until $G = G_n$. It can be shown in similar fashion that, if the accumulation rate is higher than G_n, it will be reduced to the value of G_n. Hence G_n is a long-run equilibrium and represents the rate of growth of productivity that equalizes the rates of capital accumulation and of output growth (Figure 5.4(*b*)).

When capital and output increase at the same rate, and when therefore both the capital/output ratio and the rate of profit remain constant, technical progress is apparently both Hicks and Harrod 'neutral'. An upward shift in the function—because of a burst of new inventions—will reduce the capital/out-

FIG. 5.4(*b*) A linear technical-progress function

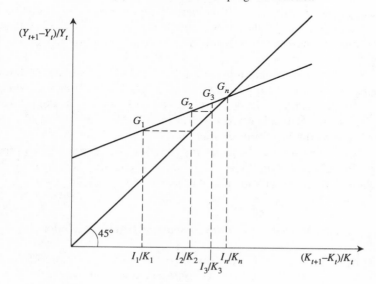

put ratio for a certain period of time and suggests that technical progress saves capital; vice versa, a drying up of new ideas and a downward shift in the function suggests that technical progress saves labour.

In short: If the system grows at full employment, it will display a number of forces that tend to push it towards a state where the rates of growth in output per worker and of capital per worker are equal. Thus the capital/output ratio remains constant, and with it the ratio between investment and income and, therefore, also the distribution of income between profits and wages. The constancy of the profits share and of the capital/output ratio entails the constancy of the rate of profit. These are the 'stylized facts' that Kaldor set out to explain.

At the point of equilibrium G_n it will be the case that:

$$\Delta Y_t / Y_t = I_t / K_t.$$

By including this equivalence in the technical-progress function (linearized), we obtain the following equation:

(5.14) $$G_n = \alpha'' / (1 - \beta'')$$

which in Kaldor's theory constitutes what Harrod's took to be the natural growth rate. The equilibrium growth rate is therefore independent of the functions of saving and investment and depends only on the technical-progress function. The share of investment in equilibrium is given by:

(5.15) $$I/Y = G_n K / Y.$$

Since, in equilibrium, the share of investment will be equal to the share of savings, on the hypothesis that the propensity to save among workers is zero, we can obtain the following expression from (5.8) and (5.14):

(5.16) $$P/K = G_n / \alpha.$$

This expression has been of great theoretical importance. It states that the rate of profit on capital depends on the growth rate G_n—which in turn depends only on the parameters of the technical-progress function—and on the propensity to save out of profits (α).

It is thus possible to determine the rate of profit irrespective of both the parameters of the production function (and in particular of the capital/output ratio) and without having to measure the stock of capital. This expression—which was also independently arrived at by von Neumann in 1937—would achieve fame as the 'Cambridge equation'.

This section has set out the theoretical framework common to all three of Kaldor's models of growth. In later versions of his theory, though, he modified the technical-progress function and the investment function.

5.8. Subsequent Developments of Kaldor's Model

Kalecki hypothesized that the subjective risks taken on by entrepreneurs are an increasing function of the rate of capital accumulation. Under this assump-

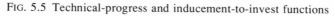

FIG. 5.5 Technical-progress and inducement-to-invest functions

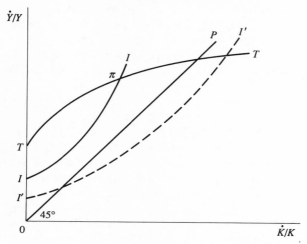

tion, the rate of capital accumulation is a single-valued function of the rate of profit and, in a steady-state growth equilibrium, a single-valued function of the rate of growth. This 'inducement to invest' function is represented by the *II* curve plotted on the same axis as the technical-progress function (see Figure 5.5). The slope of the curve represents increasing marginal risk and the point at which it cuts the vertical axes reflects the market rate of interest. This investment function, however, could cut the technical-progress function at any point; but only by pure coincidence will it coincide with the equilibrium point given by the intersection of the technical-progress function with the 45-degree line from the origin. Hence, if the matching point is to the left (*II*) or right (*I'I'*) of G_n the rate of growth will entail a constant falling or rising capital/output ratio.

However, after 1957 (see note 37, above) Kaldor gave a different interpretation to the principle of 'increasing risk', now arguing that there is no greater risk involved in a higher rate of growth of employed capital if it proceeds *pari passu* with a higher rate of growth of turnover. His investment function—which, it will be remembered, assumed a positive relation between the desired stock of capital in relation to turnover and the current rate of profit—was criticized by Champernowne for failing to guarantee that a long-run equilibrium rate of growth would be secured.

In his essay of 1958 Kaldor made a number of modifications to the investment function.[39] He made the inducement to invest depend first of all on the 'acceleration principle' (which states that growth in output induces sufficient investment to enable that rate of growth of production to be maintained) and then on the *expected* rate of profit (rather than on the *current* rate of profit, as he posited in 1957). This change gives the model more stability. In fact, if

[39] Kaldor, 'Capital Accumulation and Economic Growth', 39–44.

capital accumulation takes place at a rate which is below G_n, the trend observed by entrepreneurs is a fall in the amount of capital per unit of output: consequently, they *expect* a higher rate of profit, which will induce them to invest. A higher share of investment, on the other hand, will *realize* a higher rate of profit. The realization of expectations induces continuous accumulation up to the equilibrium point G_n. The reverse happens when the rate of accumulation is higher than G_n. Only at G_n will the capital/output ratio be constant and not induce an accumulation of capital greater or less than the rate of growth of output.

One notes that Kaldor (in keeping with his 1939 article on speculation) does not assume 'perfect foresight' of entrepreneurs, but 'static foresight'—i.e. he assumes that expectations are formed on the basis of past experience. If expectations are based on a long period, they are said to be inelastic. The less movement has followed a trend, the more expectations are inelastic. Therefore business expectations are more elastic with respect to the volume of sales than they are to the margin of profit on turnover. It was for this reason that, in his 1958 article, Kaldor assumed that entrepreneurs make investment decisions according to sales undertaken in the recent past and according to the rates of profit prevailing in a rather longer past period.

David Champernowne has shown that the substitution of an average of past rates of profit for the rate of current profit gives further stability to the equilibrium solution of Kaldor's model.[40] An investment function placed in relation to the rate of current profit may not lead to a convergence of the system to G_n (unless a value close to zero is given to the parameter), whereas the hypothesis that investment depends on moving averages of the values of the profit rate over a long period renders the investment function compatible with the stability of the model for a broad range of values of the parameters of the sensitivity of investment to the rate of profit.

Kaldor's 1962 article written with Mirrlees[41] represents a further development in his ideas on the relation between investment and technical progress. The technical-progress function now expresses a relation between the rate of growth in output per worker employed on newly-built machinery and the rate of growth of gross investment per worker. This formulation reflects the idea that in every time interval (year) new machinery is introduced that is more productive than the machinery it replaces, in the sense that the worker who uses it achieves greater output than was possible with the older plant. However, the old machinery still stays in operation. This is a so-called 'vintage model'.

A symposium organized by the *Review of Economic Studies* in 1962 showed the widespread impact of Kaldor's idea: namely that although the flow of ideas is exogenous and depends on the passage of time, this is not so in the case with technical changes, which are introduced into the economic system by

[40] D. Champernowne, 'The Stability of Kaldor's 1957 Model', *RES* (Jan. 1971).
[41] N. Kaldor and N. Mirrlees, 'A New Model of Economic Growth' (1962), repr. in CP v.

investment. At the same symposium, Arrow presented his famous paper 'The Economic Implications of Learning by Doing'.[42] According to Arrow, the extent to which new ideas are exploited is measured by the amount of gross investment made in the past: by building machines one learns how to build them more efficiently. For Kaldor, however,[43] as we have seen, the intensity of technical progress depends, not on the amount of past investment, but on the speed of the accumulation process. The difference between the two models should not be underestimated, since, whereas Arrow's vintage model still used a neo-classical production function,[44] Kaldor's was developed in antithesis to a conceptual device of this sort (although the scrapping rule in the Kaldor–Mirrlees model makes it very similar to the neo-classical one).

A consequence of the vintage model is that one is forced to tackle the problem of measuring the stock of capital—a problem that Kaldor always tried to avoid. If technical progress is embodied in new capital goods, these will differ from those that they have superseded but which still remain in operation. This makes any aggregate measurement of capital in physical terms, such as Kaldor had himself adopted in previous models,[45] even more unacceptable. The vintage model also modified the investment function. 'We shall assume that entrepreneurs will only invest in their own business in so far as this is consistent with maintaining the earning power of their fixed assets above a certain minimum, a minimum which, in their view, represents the earning power of fixed assets in the economy in general.'[46] In fact if earnings increase at a lower rate than the book value of fixed assets, the financial position of the firm weakens, and this will increase the risks of bankruptcy or take-over bids. The decision is therefore not taken on the basis of the existing rate of profit, but according to the expected rate of profit on the new investment. The fact that new capital goods embody technical progress modifies the investment function in a further respect. An entrepreneur has to make his investment choice in a period in which uncertainty increases the more the temporal horizon extends into the future. He therefore has to apply the criterion of the 'pay-off period' in order to amortize the initial costs of his investment in the

---

[42] K. J. Arrow, 'The Economic Implications of Learning by Doing', *RES* (June 1962).

[43] In his article commenting on Arrow's paper *RES* (June 1962), Kaldor pointed out close resemblances between Arrow's arguments and the ones that he himself had expressed in 'Capital Accumulation and Economic Growth' (1958), and in 'Increasing Returns and Technical Progress: A Comment on Professor Hicks's Article', *OEP*, (Feb. 1961).

[44] Since then a large number of 'vintage models' have been produced, mainly by economists of the neo-classical school. Among the best-known are: R. M. Solow *et al.*, 'Neoclassical Growth with Fixed Factor Proportions', *RES* (Apr. 1966); C. J. Bliss, 'On Putty-Clay', *RES* (Apr. 1968).

[45] In his first article on growth, Kaldor wrote: 'the measurement of the stock of *real* capital must therefore necessarily be based on some more or less arbitrary convention. One such convention would measure the stock of real capital in terms of mechanical power . . . Another such convention (which appears rather less arbitrary) measures it in terms of the total weight of steel embodied in the capital equipment. For the purposes of this model we shall adopt the latter convention' ('Model of Economic Growth', 269).

[46] Kaldor and Mirrlees, 'New Model of Economic Growth', 59.

first years of operation. And this provided Kaldor with the route by which he could introduce risk and uncertainty into his model.

The process of technical progress therefore still had the task—*a fortiori*—of explaining the principal observed phenomena:

The model shows technical progress . . . as the main engine of economic growth, determining not only the rate of growth of productivity but—together with other parameters—also the rate of obsolescence, the average lifetime of equipment, the proportion of investment in income, the share of profit and . . . the capital/output ratio on new capital goods.[47]

By way of summary, we may list the essentially new features of Kaldor's model of growth and distribution as follows:

1. technical progress is the engine of growth;
2. technical progress and the accumulation of capital are inextricably intertwined;
3. in its mature stages capitalism has a long-period tendency to grow at full employment;
4. investment decisions do not depend on the interest rate but on expectations of profit from capital and, in the long period, on the rate of growth of the system itself;
5. the distribution of income in the long period is flexible and subject to forces that depend on the rate of growth of the system;
6. in certain cases it is not necessary to measure capital in order to determine the rate of profit;
7. the 'laws of movement' listed above explain why, over the long period, the system displays the statistical constancies that Kaldor called 'stylized facts'.

5.9. A Comparison with Joan Robinson and Piero Sraffa

In view of the importance that Kaldor's models of growth and distribution attribute to the long period, it is inevitable that his analysis should differ significantly from Keynes's.

Keynes's dictum that 'in the long run we are all dead' has been interpreted in various ways. In Modigliani's neo-classical view, given that Keynesian analysis makes *ad hoc* hypotheses concerning the rigidity of wages and of interest rates, it only represents a special, though important, case of the configurations that economic systems may assume. According to counter-interpretations such as Vicarelli's, however, Keynesian analysis is genuinely general; its reference to the short period only means that it isolates the theoretically analysable elements of an unstable system like capitalism: 'Uncertainty, expectations, the transient nature of "convention" are not imperfections

[47] Ibid. 74.

and frictions that obstruct investments and employment in their progress to-wards long-period levels. Rather, they are structural phenomena of capitalism: they are capitalism.'[48] And Shackle summarized the message of the *General Theory* as 'the existence of an uncertain, an unknown future. Every step is a step into the void. It is this which makes investment hazardous and therefore often insufficient to fill the saving gap.'[49]

Kaldor's position was different from both these theoretical points of view. On the one hand he recognized that the *General Theory* taught the genuinely *general* lesson that investment decisions are the engine that drives the system;[50] on the other, he believed that Keynes's great work dealt with a *particular* case, in the sense that it could not be applied to an expanding economy. In his opinion, therefore, Keynes's theory suffered from certain restrictions and therefore needed supplementing; and on this, I believe, Joan Robinson was in agreement.

In 1954 Kaldor published his article on the relation between growth and cycle, and at the same time Joan Robinson's famous article criticizing the production function appeared.[51] In 1956 Robinson's book *The Accumulation of Capital*[52] was published, while the same year saw Kaldor's article on the theory of distribution. In the following two years Kaldor published his articles on the theory of growth, Robinson her *Exercises in Economic Analysis*,[53] and Sraffa his *Production of Commodities by Means of Commodities*.[54] The controversy raged inside and outside Cambridge for several years.[55] Even though the various arguments involved were closely related, the Cambridge school gradually took up two identifiably distinct positions. There was the Sraffian line which investigated the pure theory of capital and distribution, and where analysis dealt mainly with the 'structure' of a static system; and there was the Kaldorian theory of growth and distribution which principally addressed the 'dynamics' of the system. Although there was no overt conflict between the two approaches, one cannot say that there was any evident convergence between them either. Hence, I believe, there is a great deal of truth in the verdict on Kaldor that:

---

[48] Vicarelli, *Keynes: l'instabilità del capitalismo* (Milan, Etas Libri, 1977), 242.

[49] G. L. S. Shackle, *The Years of High Theory* (Cambridge, CUP, 1967), 135.

[50] In Kaldor's theory of growth, investment decisions become risk-taking decisions of expansion and innovation. He writes: 'Schumpeter's hero, the "innovating entrepreneur" . . . is found, after all, to have an honourable place, or even a key role, in the drama—even though we prefer to endow him with a rather more variegated character. He is a promoter, a speculator, a gambler, the purveyor of economic expansion generally, and not just of "new" techniques of production' ('Relation of Economic Growth and Cyclical Fluctuations', 232).

[51] J. Robinson, 'The Production Function and the Theory of Capital', *RES* 21 (1953–4).

[52] Ead., *The Accumulation of Capital* (London, Macmillan, 1956).

[53] Ead., *Exercises in Economic Analysis* (London, Macmillan, 1960).

[54] P. Sraffa, *Production of Commodities by Means of Commodities* (Cambridge, CUP, 1960).

[55] An overview of the 20 years of debate on the theory of capital and of economic growth is provided by G. C. Harcourt, *Some Cambridge Controversies in the Theories of Capital* (Cambridge, CUP, 1972).

because it was impossible to enter into analysis and understanding of the effective problems of growth if the formal canons required by the models that now dominated the theory were to be respected, [Kaldor] was forced to remain on the sidelines of the debate, which discussed issues that were not directly connected with the study of the mechanisms of accumulation where, for example, it was variations in the expected rate of profit that counted and not the relation between the rate of profit and alternative techniques.[56]

Despite his close friendship with Sraffa, Kaldor took no direct interest in the Italian economist's work—which he considered to be a superb example of the critical analysis of neo-classical theory (and to a lesser extent of classical theory), but not as providing the basis for a theory of the laws of movement of the capitalist system. And, in fact, Kaldor's most detailed analysis of Sraffa's book *Production of Commodities by Means of Commodities* was written a quarter of a century after it was published.[57] Kaldor believed that Sraffa's theoretical point of departure—the description of the economic system as a system using commodities to produce commodities—was very similar to von Neumann's, although the objectives of the two economists were different.

In particular, Sraffa sought to solve Ricardo's problem of finding a way to distinguish changes in relative prices due to variations in the cost of production from changes due to variations in the distribution of income between wages and profits. As we know, Sraffa's solution was to invent the logical device of the 'standard commodity' (a composite product of various commodities which stand in the same ratio to one another as the inputs that were absorbed in producing them), the value of which is not affected by the distribution of income, and to demonstrate that in one economic system with a given technique there is a unique standard commodity.

Kaldor believed that this hypothetical construct was problem-free only in the case of simple production. In the case of joint production, and hence also in the case of production with fixed capital, the manufacture of the standard commodity might require certain processes to have negative levels of activity. A solution comprising wholly positive prices and wholly positive levels of activity was proposed by von Neumann, but here wages were fixed and determined only by the technological factors affecting the reproduction of the labour force. However, problems arise if one admits—as Sraffa did—to the possibility of changes in the distribution of income, i.e. in that component of the theory which, for Kaldor, made it superior to von Neumann's. In this case, if wage-earners and profit-earners have different kinds of spending behaviour, one can always, by means of a suitable change in the multipliers, obtain a standard commodity (and a standard ratio given by the ratio in standard

[56] G. Nardozzi, 'Crescita', in G. Lunghini and M. D'Antonio (eds.), *Dizionario di Economia Politica* (Turin, Boringhieri, 1983), 184.

[57] N. Kaldor, 'Sraffa come critico della teoria economica' (1984), pub. in R. Bellofiore (ed.), *Teoria economica e grande cultura europea: Piero Sraffa* (Milan, Franco Angeli, 1986).

commodity between net output and the means of production), the value of which will be invariant relative to changes in income. But this presupposes, as Sraffa himself pointed out, that there is only one production technique for each good produced. If this condition is not satisfied, a change in the rate of profit or in the share of wages will change the value of the standard commodity. These considerations led Kaldor to conclude that in Sraffa's work

the criteria required for isolating changes in production from changes in distribution are no more definite than they were in Ricardo. Hence . . . Sraffa has not succeeded in producing a theory along classical lines that is free from the defects of already existing theories. It is questionable, however, whether this was his objective. Considered as a critique of economic theory rather than as the construction of a new theory . . . his book is a unique achievement in showing up the fallacies of existing theories.[58]

This is especially true as regards the theory of marginal productivity, which lies at the core of neo-classical economics. Sraffa's proof that the solution to the system of production equations was compatible with different distributions of income between profits and wages contradicted the theory that factor endowments determine their price.

Overall, however, the general thrust of Sraffa's work was largely irrelevant to Kaldor's principal interests.

In my opinion, price theory and distribution theory occupy a disproportionate place in both classical and contemporary economics; economics ought not to concentrate on equilibrium conditions which are never attained (or even approached), but on the forces which produce change and which themselves are subject to constant changes of direction. The rate of profit does not tend to equality easily and quickly . . . while changes in technology . . . are central to an understanding of how competition operates in a world of imperfect, quasi-monopolistic markets.[59]

By assuming uniform wages and rates of profit, Sraffa presupposed perfect competition and, by limiting output to the annual availability of manpower—according to Kaldor—he left no room for the operation of Keynes's principle of effective demand; a principle that was crucial to explanation of the level and distribution of income in modern industrial economies. Nevertheless, in the conclusion to his obituary essay on Sraffa written for the British Academy, Kaldor confessed that 'the exciting thing about Sraffa's book is that it "grows on one" with the passing of time. It appears from a distance of twenty-five years as a unique achievement of post-war theoretical literature.'[60]

When we consider the fields of research investigated by Kaldor and Sraffa, one might say that Joan Robinson's work straddles the two. Various comparative studies have been made of Kaldor and Joan Robinson as the two economists (together with Kalecki) are generally considered to be the founders of the post-Keynesian school. Although differences have often been pointed out in their theoretical objectives and methods, to give adequate treatment of

[58] Ibid. 184.   [59] Ibid. 185–6.
[60] Id., 'Piero Sraffa (1898–1983)' (1985), repr. in CP ix. 300.

the topic would require much more detailed exposition of Joan Robinson's thought than is possible here. I shall therefore restrict myself to a number of general remarks.

Robinson declared with much greater insistence than Kaldor that 'the essence of Keynes's method, which is also to be found in Marx, lies in his thinking in terms of history rather than of equilibrium'.[61] At first, Kaldor was less explicit on this point—although, as we shall see in Chapter 14, he too would come to subscribe to Robinson's view and develop it in his later critical works on equilibrium theory.

The positions of the two economists also differed in their criticisms of neo-classical theory, though not to any radical extent. Robinson's critique of the neo-classical theory of capital focused on the impossibility of finding a satisfactory theoretical measure for capital stock if one abandons fallacious reasoning in terms of logical time. When one begins to think in terms of historical time and therefore to recognize that the past is different from the future and that the present is determined by the constraints imposed by the past and by expectations of the future—if, in other words, one considers a choice once taken to be a legacy of the past that cannot be changed—it is no longer possible to rely either on a production function in which a single rate of profit corresponds to every technique or on the parables derivable from it. Robinson, like Kaldor, instead set herself the theoretical objective of applying Keynes's theory also to the long period, by extending it to encompass the area of the theory of capital, growth, and distribution. To do this, however, her analysis of the links between accumulation, capital, and distribution could only be conducted through comparison of different economies, all assumed to be in a state of tranquillity. Such assumptions were made, not because they reflected reality but because they were entailed by the technique of analysis. The theory thus lapsed into 'exercises' in comparative dynamics and a listing of hypothetical cases (various 'golden ages', 'leaden ages', and so forth).

Kaldor's approach was more 'pragmatic': he sought to 'bend theoretical exercises to understanding of the facts'; that is, he tried to provide an abstract explanation (in the sense that it concentrated on the salient facts) for the process of economic change that takes place in the real environment of the capitalist system, and to find a non-random reason for the set of stylized facts that appear in this system over the long period. He had a further practical objective: even when engaged in high theory, his aim was always to find an interpretation of the system's most essential operating mechanisms which would enable him to refine economic policy instruments for dealing with deficiencies in the operation of the system itself.

Kaldor and Robinson also took up different positions on the valuation of capital and of the rate of profit. Robinson believed that one of the chief purposes of economic analysis is to determine of the rate of profit, and that

---

[61] Nardozzi, 'Crescita', 165.

'it is only when all the prior theoretical problems have been worked out that the analysis is carried to the explanation of actual changes in actual economies, and then only with the greatest care'.[62] Kaldor, instead, in attempting to construct a behavioural model, 'works solely with the *expected* rate of profit (as symbolised in the pay off period) on the value of new gross investment calculated at existing demand prices' and rejects the necessity of deriving concepts such as the rate of profit and the value of capital, on the ground that the entrepreneurs (1) cannot know what they are, and (2) do not use them in practice.[63]

On the other hand, the distance narrows between Kaldor and Robinson when one considers that the Cambridge equation was the most concise expression of the ideas of both of them concerning the forces governing the rate of profit—though Joan Robinson left the theory 'open' to the possibility of many rates of growth, while Kaldor 'closed' it with the technical-progress function.

Again: for Robinson stability was a myth, while for Kaldor it was a property of the system over the long period. I remind the reader here of a celebrated graph drawn by Robinson (Figure 5.6) which gives a good synthesis of her ideas on growth theory and stability. If we plot the rate of growth of output and capital, g, on the vertical axis and the rate of profit, r, on the horizontal axis, we can draw two functions: an accumulation-saving function (A) which states that the rate of profit is—via the saving function and the Cambridge equation— what is required to ensure that the rate of capital accumulation is neither constrained by a shortage of savings nor affected by a change in the capital/output ratio; and an investment function (I) that states that the decision to accumulate capital is a positive function of the rate of profit, although it is a non-linear function with negative second derivative to take into account the 'increasing risk' entailed by a higher rate of capital accumulation (Kaldor disagreed on this point). In this case, two equilibrium points, E_1 and E_2, are determined by the model. Only the former is a stable equilibrium (at a high level of growth), however, because to the left of E_1 for a given rate of growth the expected profit is lower than that realized, and this induces entrepreneurs to invest, while to the right of E_1 the reverse happens. For the same reasons, point E_2 is an unstable equilibrium, and if the economy stands to the left of E_1 it is pushed into a state of continuous depression. (see the arrows of Figure 5.6).

Here too, however, the divergence between the two economists was less pronounced than it might seem. One should avoid the common misconception that Kaldor, with his models of 'equilibrium' growth, renounced his Keynesian inheritance and his own ideas on the instability of capitalism. First of all, as we saw in Chapter 5.4., he reiterated these ideas at the Peking Conference only a year before he developed his first growth model. Secondly, in conclusion to his first article on the theory of growth, he warned against misuse of the model and pointed out the restrictions that apply to it in the shorter

[62] J. A. Kregel, *The Reconstruction of Political Economy* (London, Macmillan, 1973), 192.
[63] Ibid. 190.

FIG. 5.6 Robinson's model of growth and distribution

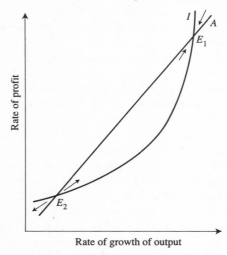

period—without, however, offering almost any satisfactory explanation as to how one passes from the short to the long period. In the short period, for example, it may well be the case that a fall in investment is not attended by a downward movement in margins of profit. The level of income will not be maintained by an increase in the share of wages and therefore of consumption; instead, according to Keynesian multiplier theory, it will fall. Similarly, while in the long period the *share* of wages is flexible both upwards and downwards because of productivity change, in the short period a large increase in investment may instead be accompanied by inflation, given the downward rigidity of the *absolute level* of real wages. In this case, too, Robinson's thesis of the 'inflation barrier' did not greatly differ from Kaldor's.

5.10. Subsequent Debate and Criticisms

The interest aroused by Kaldor's models was immediate, major, and prolonged. His theory quickly found its way into the principal textbooks on macro-economics—whether advanced like Allen's or more elementary like Lipsey and Samuelson's.[64] His articles appeared in numerous collections of essays.[65] His model was given detailed treatment in the famous article by Hahn and Matthews,[66] who judged his hypothesis on technical progress to be 'ready

[64] R. G. D. Allen, *Macro-Economic Theory* (London, Macmillan, 1967); R. G. Lipsey, *An Introduction to Positive Economics* (London, Weidenfeld and Nicolson, 1963). P. A. Samuelson, *Economics, An Introductory Analysis* (7th edn. New York, McGraw-Hill, 1957).
[65] See Bibliography of Works by Kaldor, below, for the numerous republications of his articles.
[66] F. H. Hahn and R. C. O. Matthews, 'The Theory of Economic Growth: A Survey', *EJ* (Dec. 1964).

for empirical testing'. Scitovsky even went so far as to declare that Kaldor's theory of distribution 'is the most satisfying, or perhaps the only, macroeconomic theory of the distribution of income',[67] and Reder subjected it to empirical verification.[68]

Interest in Kaldor's theories spread throughout the world. Even after an interval of more than two decades, the journal *Kyklos* devoted a special issue in 1981 to the influence of his thought in Germany.[69] Italy was the country where the Cambridge school, and with it the theories of Kaldor, had its most enthusiastic reception—mainly through the work of Luigi Pasinetti and his followers (discussed in the next chapter).

Kaldor's savings, investment, and technical-progress functions are by now an integral component of the modern theory of growth, although the field still continues to be occupied by rival theories[70]—which have raised objections and advanced counter-claims for their own validity ever since Kaldor's model made its first appearance. This, however, comes as no surprise when one remembers that the more innovative a theory and the sharper its criticism of orthodoxy, the more passionately its opponents rally to the defence of tradition.

Kaldor's opponents have followed various lines of argument. The most important of these concerns the saving function and the associated Cambridge theory of distribution: Chapter 6 will be devoted to this. Other criticisms have concentrated on the micro-foundations of Kaldor's macro-model: the behaviour of firms in a non-competitive dynamic setting; the investment function and the stability of long-run equilibrium; the technical-progress function (as such, and in relation to the investment function); and the demonstrated or alleged necessity of the full-employment hypothesis.

The micro-foundation of Kaldor's model, in particular its price-profit adjustment mechanism, has been critically examined by Robin Marris on various occasions since 1964.[71] P. Skott has followed a similar line of reasoning by observing that, under imperfect competition, firms can fix their profit margins and prices and allow stock to adjust, or else they can fix their production levels and let prices and profit margins adjust and clear the market. Kaldor's reliance on a Marshallian distribution mechanism with short-run output given and

---

[67] T. Scitovsky, 'A Survey of Some Theories of Income Distribution', in NBER, *The Behaviour of Income Shares* (Studies in Income and Wealth, 27; Princeton, NJ, Princeton University Press, 1964).

[68] M. W. Reder, 'Alternative Theories of Labour Share', in M. Abramovitz (ed.), *The Allocation of Economic Resources* (Stanford, Stanford University Press, 1959).

[69] *Kyklos*, 34: 4 (1981).

[70] For detailed treatment of modern theories of dynamic macro-economics, among which Kaldor's theory is still included, see Pierre-Yves Hénin, *Macrodynamics Fluctuations and Growth: A Study of the Economy in Equilibrium and Disequilibrium* (London, Routledge & Kegan Paul, 1986).

[71] R. Marris, *The Economic Theory of 'Managerial Capitalism'* (London, Macmillan, 1964); id., *Reconstructing Keynesian Economics with Imperfect Competition* (Aldershot, Elgar, 1991), sect. 5.3.3. An attempt to streamline the model by making adjustments to the distribution of income can be found in A. M. Moore, 'A Reformulation of the Kaldor Effect', *EJ* (Mar. 1967).

profit adjusting to clear the market entails that he cannot 'assume that firms estimate future demand conditions on the basis of the past real "sales" (output levels) without any reference to realized profit margins'.[72] In other words, why should a firm—one expecting an increase in the demand for its product—increase its productive capacity when it knows that a higher demand will lead to an increase in its profit margin? In my view, this problem is similar to the objection raised by Marris: the Cambridge equation holds in so far as the propensity to save of capitalists is independent of the rate of growth; but this conflicts with the idea that in imperfect competition firms have, within certain limits, the power to set the profit margin and the retention ratio—i.e. the share of corporate profit retained by the firm to finance new investment. How Kaldor countered these criticisms will be discussed in Chapter 6.4.

Nuti[73] also examined on Kaldor's micro-foundations and contended that the Kaldor–Mirrlees hypothesis of imperfect competition contradicts the relation between wages and the marginal productivity of labour that derives from the obsolescence criterion of the model itself: that at time t, real wages are determined by labour productivity on marginal equipment installed T periods before, according to the formula

$$(5.17) \qquad\qquad w_t = p_t - T.$$

Imperfect competition, Nuti argued, presupposes underutilization of productive capacity; the price should therefore be higher than prime costs and hence

$$(5.18) \qquad\qquad w_t = p_t - T(1 - \mu).$$

But this runs counter to the model's principle of obsolescence, according to which machinery is scrapped when the margin of profit on it is zero. Attached to Nuti's article is a brief comment by Joan Robinson to the effect that 'the level of employment is not explained', since the model assumes that labour demand grows at the same rate as supply despite imperfect competition and despite the fact that excess capacity prevails.

Kaldor published an answer to his critics[74] in which he accepted Nuti's point as 'perfectly valid'. He agreed that a typical profit-maximizing firm will abandon equipment before the quasi-rent on it is zero, and he acknowledged the validity of (5.18), where μ is the degree of monopoly or the minimum profit required for continued operation of any particular vintage of equipment. What is required, Kaldor suggested on the basis of empirical considerations, is either a further equation relating to μ, or the positing of μ as a constant.

Nuti's article served the useful purpose of forcing Kaldor to specify that the theory he was working on was of the oligopoly-cum-price-leadership type. Accordingly, the full cost on the most efficient 'vintages' sets prices; firms possessing older vintages are faced with a kinked demand curve—i.e. they

[72] P. Skott, *Kaldor's Growth and Distribution Theory* (Frankfurt-on-Main, Peter Lang, 1989).

[73] D. M. Nuti, 'The Degree of Monopoly in the Kaldor–Mirrlees Growth Model', *RES* (Apr. 1969).

[74] N. Kaldor, 'Some Fallacies in the Interpretation of Kaldor', *RES* (Jan. 1970).

must meet the prices set by the market, although this does *not* imply that they can sell any amount at that price. Differences in efficiency ranking and profit ranking are not explained by the vintage of the equipment that firms use, but by other factors that the theory does not make sufficiently explicit. Thus Kaldor's 'hunch' (to use his own term) that the least efficient firms tend also to be those that use the least efficient equipment is plausible; and hence Nuti's point is minor one.[75] Concerning Joan Robinson's objection, Kaldor pointed out that excess capacity must be related to imperfect competition; it is not a symptom of 'insufficiency of demand'. In the long run—discounting the case that full employment will push wages up relative to output so that less efficient plant becomes unprofitable and is therefore scrapped, thus reducing capital redundancy—it is perfectly plausible to assume that both output and output capacity grow at the same rate, without this implying that the two are equal. Consequently, output can grow in full employment despite prevailing excess capacity.

Kubota found the treatment of stability properties in Kaldor's 1957 model unsatisfactory.[76] Kaldor's reply was that if Kubota considered the full set of parameter restrictions (which Kubota did not), he would realize that the effect of profit rates on investment was in the direction of equilibrium. In demonstration that Kaldor's model was unstable, McCallum transformed a 'Kaldor-type model' into continuous time.[77] However, his version of Kaldor's model differed from the appropriate continuous time version of Kaldor's 1957 model, which, as Champernowne has shown,[78] produces a stable equilibrium path provided that the elasticity of expectations of the rate of profit on new investment in the investment function is not equal to one (as in the original 1957 Kaldor model), but less than one (as in the Corfu model).

Kaldor's technical-progress function has been no less controversial. When the function is linear (see 5.13), it can be integrated into a Wicksell–Cobb–Douglas function of the traditional type $Y = A e^{\alpha'' t} K^{\beta''}$ (where Y and K are output per worker and capital per worker respectively and A is a constant of integration).[79] When the model is in equilibrium of steady growth with a constant

---

[75] More than one commentator found it difficult to reconcile the Kaldor–Mirrlees's 'New Model of Growth' with Kaldor's theory of distribution. According to Skott, equation (5.17) stating that the wage rate is equal to (and not equal to *or* less than) the marginal productivity of labour negates (following Kaldor's reply to Atsumi, see n. 15, above) Kaldor's theory of distribution (see Skott, *Kaldor's Growth and Distribution Theory*, 25). This opinion is shared by F. Hahn: 'by adopting the pay-off period approach . . . the "New Model" has a soft neo-classical underbelly.' Hahn, 'Kaldor on Growth', 55.

[76] K. Kubota, 'A Re-Examination of the Existence and Stability Propositions in Kaldor's Growth Models', *RES* (July 1968) 353–60; Kaldor, 'Some Fallacies in the Interpretation of Kaldor'.

[77] B. T. McCallum, 'The Instability of Kaldorian Models', *OEP* (Mar. 1969). McCallum's 'Kaldor type models' follow Allen's exposition of Kaldor's theory (see R. G. D. Allen, *Macro-Economic Theories*).

[78] Champernowne, 'Stability of Kaldor's 1957 Model'.

[79] On the relationship between a technical-progress function and a production function, see J. Black, 'The Technical Progress Function and the Production Function', *EC* (May 1962).

capital/output ratio (5.14), the equilibrium growth rate is compatible with a production function of the kind displaying a constant rate of Harrod's neutral technical progress.[80] Another interpretation of Kaldor's technical-progress function assumed a short-run production function of the fixed coefficient type and Harrod's neutral technical progress.[81] Kaldor rejected all these arguments. First of all he insisted that the correct formulation of his technical-progress function should be non-linear. In a private conversation with the present writer he argued that it was as if there existed, at any moment, a stock of available projects leading to labour saving per unit of output. These projects are only implemented through investment: the best of them first, and then the rest of them in order of their effectiveness. At a certain point, however much capital is accumulated, no new project will be implemented. Secondly, Kaldor was seeking to make a theoretical point which, although it may not have been fully expressed by his technical-progress function, was certainly missed entirely by any sort of production function: namely, that a change from one technique to another involves learning, even if the technique is in some way already available.[82] As Hahn has pointed out, 'Neoclassical theory takes the production set as an objective entity and that is almost certainly the wrong way in which to take it. General Equilibrium Theory is very silent on new knowledge, new goods and on innovation generally.'[83]

Kregel has also criticized the technical-progress function on the grounds that its status as a continuous function has not been demonstrated. If this function represents the order of profitability of innovations

it is possible that the first technique will be available to more than one productive unit or industry. If all investment in a particular period goes into just one innovation, there will be no move along the curve to the point (of long-run equilibrium) . . . For Kaldor's constant point to be reached, the whole range of techniques up to (that) point itself must be either adopted or passed over.[84]

In more general terms, one may validly object that a necessary condition for the identification of an equilibrium point as the intersection of two curves (the technical-progress function and the investment function) is that the two curves are continuous: if the investment function has a lag, or if the technical-progress function is discontinuous, 'overshooting' may occur and a sort of cobweb equilibrium process ensue. Again on the problem of stability, Skott has argued that 'Kaldor [s] 1961 model [s] and the Kaldor–Mirrlees model are deeply flawed, and the prototype model in Kaldor (1957) thus gives the best representation of Kaldor's theory.'[85] It is the stability properties of Kaldor's subsequent models that Skott rejects: on the ground that they lack the auton-

[80] Thirlwall, *Nicholas Kaldor*, 183 n. 28.
[81] Skott, *Kaldor's Growth and Distribution Theory*, 75.
[82] A. B. Atkinson and J. E. Stiglitz, 'A New View of Technological Change', *EJ* (1989), 573–8.
[83] Hahn, 'Kaldor on Growth', 48.
[84] Kregel, *Rate of Profit, Distribution and Growth*, 139.
[85] Skott, 'Kaldor's Growth and Distribution Theories', 107.

omous investment function essential to a Keynesian model. The warranted path that results from them must be unstable, and growth issues cannot be analysed separately from cyclical fluctuations—as has been repeatedly pointed out by Goodwin.[86] Skott's reformulation of Kaldor's growth models leads him to produce an exact replica of Joan Robinson's growth model (see Figure 5.6), where the equilibrium point of high and stable growth is obtained by giving very unrealistic values to parameters, and more realistic ones to the unstable equilibrium point, with the associated representation of an economy in growing depression.

However, Kaldor would argue, this is not what actually happened in the two decades after the war. His model did not possess the perpetual validity of a pure deductive model; instead, it set out to provide an interpretation of stylized facts. He used the same argument when replying to criticism of his full-employment hypothesis.

When Kaldor's works on growth appeared, there was a certain amount of scepticism over his idea that the most advanced example of a Keynesian model of growth *must* be a full employment one. Moreover, Kaldor never made it clear whether full employment was postulated (as it was in his 1957 paper) or whether it was deduced from other assumptions (as it apparently was in his Corfu paper). A further cause for dissatisfaction was his vagueness over full employment: was it a stylized fact that must be reconciled with a Keynesian model of growth or was it a *necessary* condition for one? In Kaldor's papers comparing Marxian and Keynesian models of growth and distribution, the latter interpretation seems to prevail.

Harcourt and Riach[87] have been the two severest critics of Kaldor's theoretical *demonstration* of full-employment growth based on the inverse L-shaped supply curve of the 'representative firm' (see section 6, above). Harcourt uses a two-sector model to show the illegitimacy of this micro-economic instrument when used to justify a macro-economic assumption. Further, the short-run cost curve must be taken to be constant up to full employment *or* to full utilization of capital capacity, depending on which constraint hits output first. But Kaldor's premiss that 'I shall further *assume*, as is appropriate for a "developed" economy . . . that the effective bottleneck setting an upper limit to production is labour rather than physical capacity'[88] renders the whole of his *demonstration* of the full-employment assumption redundant.

Amartya Sen has shown that the assumption is also unnecessary. The results of the Keynesian (and neo-classical) theory of distribution based on full employment can be derived equally well from a Keynesian model without full

[86] An integration between Kaldor and Goodwin can be found in id., *Conflicts and Effective Demand in Economic Growth* (Cambridge, CUP, 1989).

[87] G. C. Harcourt, 'A Critique of Mr Kaldor's Model of Income Distribution and Economic Growth', *Australian Economic Papers* (June 1963); P. A. Riach, 'A Framework for Macro-Distribution Analysis', *Kyklos* (1969), 542–65.

[88] Kaldor, 'Capital Accumulation and Economic Growth', 24. My emphasis.

employment.[89] Subsequently, in fact, Kaldor-type models would dispense with full employment as non-essential.[90]

The rationale for Kaldor's assumption lies in his more general approach to theory-building: 'Any theory must necessarily be based on abstractions; but the type of abstraction chosen cannot be decided in a vacuum: it must be appropriate to the characteristic features of the economic process as recorded by experience.'[91] During the 1970s, in a situation of widespread and stable unemployment in all the OECD countries, Kaldor himself came to reject the hypothesis of full employment in the final version of his growth model (see Chapter 8, below).

[89] A. Sen, 'Neo-Classical and Neo-Keynesian Theories of Distribution', *ER* (Mar. 1963).

[90] R. Rowthorn, 'Demand, Real Wages and Economic Growth', *Studi Economici*, 18; K. Vellupilai, 'A Neo-Cambridge Model of Income Distribution', *JPKE* (spring 1983).

[91] Kaldor, 'Capital Accumulation and Economic Growth', 2.

Chapter 6

The Debate on Kaldor's Theory of Distribution[*]

Political economy you think is an enquiry into the nature and
causes of wealth—I think it should rather be called an enquiry
into the laws that determine the division of the produce of
industry among the classes who concur in its formation.

D. Ricardo, *Letter to Malthus*

6.1. The Work of Luigi Pasinetti

Kaldor's contribution to the post-Keynesian theory of distribution can be
summed up in the following two relations, valid in situations of balanced
steady growth:

(6.1) $$P/K = [1/(s_P - s_W)](I/K) - [s_W/(s_P - s_W)](Y/K),$$

(6.2) $$P/Y = [1/(s_P - s_W)](I/K)(K/P) - [s_W/(s_P - s_W)],$$

where P/K represents the steady-state rate of profit, P/Y the share of profits
in the national income, s_P and s_W the (constant) propensities to save out of
profits and wages, K/Y the (constant in post-Keynesian models) capital/output
ratio, and $n = I/K$ the system's steady-state rate of growth. Drawing on the
classical hypothesis that the propensity to save of workers is zero ($s_W = 0$),
Kaldor obtained these two relations:

(6.3) $$P/K = n/s_P,$$

(6.4) $$P/Y = (K/Y)(n/s_P),$$

which show the steady-state rate of profits and the share of profits in the
national income, always under the assumption that the propensity of workers
to save is zero. It is here that Luigi Pasinetti intervenes, stating his case in
similar terms to Kaldor's:

There is a logical slip, in the theory reported above [i.e. Kaldor's model], which has
so far passed unnoticed. The authors have neglected the important fact that, in any type
of society, when any individual saves a part of his income, he must be allowed to own
it, otherwise he would not save at all. This means that the stock of capital which exists
in the system is owned by those people (capitalists or workers) who in the past made
the corresponding savings. And since ownership of capital entitles the owner to a rate

[*] Apart from section 4, this Ch. has been written by Mauro Baranzini.

of interest, if workers have saved—and thus own a part of the stock of capital (directly or through loans to the capitalists)—then they will also receive a share of the total profits. Therefore total profits themselves must be divided into two categories: profits which accrue to the capitalists and profits which accrue to the workers[1]

If the two classes both possess a positive share of overall capital K, their incomes become respectively:

(6.5) $$Y_W = W + (P/K)K_W,$$

(6.6) $$Y_C = (P/K)K_C,$$

where K_C represents the income of capitalists and K_W the income of workers. If the propensity of workers to save out of wages and out of the return on capital are the same, the capital held by each class of savers becomes proportional to that class's saving. Using s_C and s_W to denote the propensities to save of capitalists and workers, in the case in which $1 > s_C > s_W > 0$, and under long-term steady-state conditions where the profit rate equals the interest rate, every year the savings by workers out of wages will equal the interest-profit earned by workers on the capital loaned to capitalists. The two flows will cancel each other out, and the only significant propensity to save will be that of capitalists, s_C —i.e. the category of savers who save only out of profits. Pasinetti obtains the following equilibrium values for the profit rate and for the share of profits in the national income:[2]

(6.7) $$P/K = n/s_C,$$

(6.8) $$P/Y = n(K/Y)/s_C,$$

which are identical to Kaldor's (6.3) and (6.4), where s_P is replaced by s_C, but with more general validity in that they are not based on the somewhat restrictive condition of a propensity to save of the working class equal to zero ($s_W = 0$). The main conclusions to be drawn from the Kaldor–Pasinetti model are the following:

1. The system's steady-state rate of profit is independent of the production function (of the marginalist kind) and of the behavioural parameters of the working class. It is wholly a function of the system's steady-state rate of growth and of the propensity to save of entrepreneurs, both given exogenously.

2. The share of profits in the national income depends on the system's technology (the K/Y ratio), on the growth rate of output, and on the propensity to save of capitalists.

3. Consequently, the propensity to save of workers, who earn income from their work and interest on their accumulated savings, cannot influence, under

---

[1] L. L. Pasinetti, 'The Rate of Profit and Income Distribution in Relation to the Rate of Economic Growth', *RES* (1962), 106–7, repr. in id., *Growth and Income Distribution: Essays in Economic Theory* (Cambridge, CUP, 1974), 106–7.

[2] Equation (6.7), known as the 'new Cambridge equation', can be derived in various, but basically equivalent, ways. The simplest is to fix, under equilibrium, $s_C \cdot P/K \cdot K_C = nK_C$ (savings of capitalists = balanced growth of their capital), from which one immediately obtains $P/K = n/s_C$. See also M. Baranzini, 'The Pasinetti and the Anti-Pasinetti Theorems: A Reconciliation', *OEP* (1975), 470–3.

equilibrium, either the level of the profit rate or the functional distribution of income between profits and wages. By contrast, the propensity of workers to save *is* important in determining, together with the model's other parameters, (*a*) the working class's share of capital, which corresponds to savings accumulated in the past, and (*b*) the distribution of income among social classes.

These are the most important conclusions of the Kaldor–Pasinetti theory of distribution. We can treat them as only 'preliminary' findings, because the model was later refined and extended to study other aspects of the distribution of income—both by Kaldor and Pasinetti[3] themselves and by a large number of other analysts.

6.2. The Marginalist Reaction: 'The Dual Theorem'

The rather unexpected results of the Kaldor–Pasinetti distribution model soon attracted the attention of such leading marginalist economists as Meade, Samuelson, Modigliani, Tobin, and Hahn,[4] who regarded the Kaldor–Pasinetti theorem (i.e. the 'Cambridge equation' $P/K = n/s_C$) as 'paradoxical'. The reaction of the marginalists was not surprising, in view of the fact that the Cambridge theory, and the Kaldor–Pasinetti theorem in particular, determined the distribution of income on the basis of parameters of social-class behaviour and the rate of growth of the economic system—independently, that is, of the marginal productivity of the production factors, which was the central strut of marginalist theory.

The marginalists accordingly tried to find a 'short cut' which would enable them to 'neutralize' the Cambridge equation and reinstate their own position.

For Meade, Hahn, Samuelson, and Modigliani the Kaldor–Pasinetti solution depended on the values of the propensity to save of workers. The Cambridge equation was valid if $s_W < n(K/Y)$ (which Samuelson and Modigliani labelled the 'primary' range à la Pasinetti). When $s_W > n(K/Y)$ (which was called 'dual' range or 'anti-Pasinetti'), marginalist theory applied. Note that the 'dual' range implies $s_W > I/Y$, an eventuality ruled out by Kaldor. The hypothesized disequality would mean that workers have such a high propensity to save that they would accumulate at a rate faster than capitalists; the share of capital owned by workers in total capital would approach unity, thus giving rise to a

---

[3] On this see Pasinetti, *Growth and Income Distribution*, ch. 6.

[4] See H. Atsumi, 'Mr Kaldor's Theory of Income Distribution', *RES* (1960), 109–18; J. E. Meade, 'The Rate of Profits in a Growing Economy', *EJ* (1963), 665–74; id., 'The Outcome of the Pasinetti Process: A Note', *EJ* (1966), 161–5; P. A. Samuelson and F. Modigliani, 'The Pasinetti Paradox in Neo-Classical and More General Models', *RES* (1966), 269–31; id., 'Reply to Pasinetti and Robinson', *RES* (1966), 321–30; J. Tobin, 'Towards a "General" Kaldorian Theory of Distribution', *RES* (1960), 11–12; K. Sato, 'The Neoclassical Theorem and Distribution of Income and Wealth', *RES* (1966), 331–5. See also J. E. Meade and F. H. Hahn, 'The Rate of Profit in a Growing Economy', *EJ* (1965), 445–58; F. H. Hahn and R. C. Matthews, 'The Theory of Economic Growth: A Survey', *EJ* (1964), 779–902.

society in which there was only one propensity to save. Harrod's model of dynamic equilibrium would have to be reformulated as follows:

(6.9) $n = s_W/(K/Y)$

where adjustment of the rate of growth to the natural rate of growth would be brought about (given a single s_W) by the flexibility of the capital/output ratio. In the neo-classical account, the solution $P/K = n/s_C$ would be dropped to be replaced by the following expression:

(6.10) $P/K = (P/Y)n/s_W$

where the rate of profit is determined by the rate of growth of the economy, by the propensity of workers to save—both exogenously given—and by the share of profits in the national income, which is the endogenous variable. In this case, post-Keynesian theory would be unable to define the distribution of income and the way was open for the reintroduction of marginalist analysis.

However, close examination[5] of the dual theorem of Meade, Samuelson, and Modigliani reveals that it is valid only as long as workers have a propensity to save so high as to secure the *totality* of the savings necessary to cover steady-state and full-employment investment. In this setting, which entails a propensity to save among workers much greater than ever recorded in the capitalist economies, there is no room for another class with a positive propensity to save—capitalists in particular, since they live only on the income accruing from capital accumulated on the basis of past savings. 'There *is* therefore a way of preventing the Cambridge equation from operating, and that is by eliminating the capitalists from the system!'[6] If capitalists disappeared from the system (by some kind of 'euthenasia', as post-Keynesians have frequently stressed), the model would reduce to one single class, the working class, as in the Harrod–Solow–Swan model.

Even if one admits that the value of s_W may be as high as required by neo-classical critics, Pasinetti shows that, if the capital/output ratio has very little flexibility relative to the rate of profit, this stays indeterminate and the economy moves on to Harrod's 'knife-edge'. If, instead, a high s_W is associated with a very flexible capital/output ratio, an equilibrium rate of growth is not definable a priori, because a univocal and inverse relation between the rate of profit and the capital/output ratio is not definable a priori. Here too, however, the rate of profit given by the Cambridge equation represents the maximum

[5] On this see L. L. Pasinetti, 'A Comment on Professor Meade's Rate of Profit in a Growing Economy', *EJ* (1964), 488–9; id., 'The Rate of Profit in a Growing Economy: A Reply', *EJ* (1966), 158–60; id., 'New Results in an Old Framework', *RES* (1966), 303–6; id., 'A Reply to Professor Chang, *RES* (1964), 106; id., *Growth and Income Distribution* ch. 6; N. Kaldor, 'Marginal Productivity and the Macro-Economic Theories of Distribution: Comment on Samuelson and Modigliani'; (1966), repr. in CP v; J. V. Robinson, 'Comment on Samuelson and Modigliani', *RES* (1966), 307–8; G. C. Harcourt, 'Some Cambridge Controversies in the Theory of Capital', *Journal of Economic Literature* (1969), 369–405; id., *Some Cambridge Controversies in the Theory of Capital* (Cambridge, CUP, 1972); M. Baranzini, 'Income Distribution in the Pasinetti Model: Comment on Woodfield and McDonald, *Australian Economic Papers* (1982), 200–6.

[6] Pasinetti, *Growth and Income Distribution*, 130.

limit to variability of the rate of profit. The marginalists, in conclusion, resorted to their own 'knife-edge' in their search for an answer to Harrod–Domar's dilemma, and it was this that provoked the controversy on the distribution of income and the determination of the rate of profit.

6.3. Developments of the Kaldor–Pasinetti Distribution Model

The controversy between the two Cambridges on the distribution of income and the determination of the rate of profit—a controversy provoked in large part by the Kaldor–Pasinetti model—generated a remarkable number of models and analyses. Between 1962 and 1987 the leading economic journals published at least 150 articles on the subject, and an ever-growing number of textbooks and specialized works devote at least one chapter to the Kaldor–Pasinetti distribution model and the ensuing debate. In discussion of these various lines of analysis, I shall group them under six main headings.[7]

1. Stability analysis and the long-term properties of the model. A large number of studies[8] have examined the process of adjustment, and its timing, required in the event of deviation from steady-state equilibrium. In other words, should there be an external shock to the system (which may be a variation in the propensity to save, or in the K/Y ratio), then answers are required for the following questions: (*a*) What will the system's new steady-state values be? (*b*) In what way will the power relations among social classes be altered? (*c*) How much time will have to elapse before the economy returns to a new steady-state situation? (*d*) Under what circumstances will the system become 'explosive', with the progressive disappearance from the economic system of a given social class?

One notes immediately that the time taken by the (two-class) model to adjust to external shocks is quite long. This, however, is understandable in a long-term steady-state model such as Kaldor–Pasinetti's, where changes in the distribution of income must be attended by changes in the distribution of the wealth from which capital income is earned. Above all, the Kaldor–Pasinetti model displays good local and global stability. One should also bear in mind

---

[7] A more complete biblio. is given in M. Baranzini, *A Theory of Wealth Accumulation and Distribution* (Oxford, OUP, 1990).

[8] I give bibliographical references for only the most important studies: R. Britto, 'A Study in Equilibrium Dynamics in Two Types of Growing Economies', *EJ* (1968), 624–40; K. Kubota, 'A Re-Examination of the Existence and Stability Propositions in Kaldor's Growth Models', *RES* (1968), 353–60; W. W. Chang, 'The Theory of Saving and the Stability of Growth Equilibrium', *QJE* (1969), 491–503; J. Conlisk and R. Ramanathan, 'Expedient Choice of Transforms in Phase Diagramming', *RES* (1970), 441–5; Y. Furono, 'Convergence Time in the Samuelson–Modigliani Model', *RES* (1970), 221–32; A. Guha, 'The Global Stability of the Two-Class Neoclassical Growth', *OJE* (1972), 687–90; W. J. Mückl, 'On the Existence of a Two-Class Economy in the Cambridge Models of Growth and Distribution', *Jahrbücher für Nationalökonomie und Statistik* (1978), 508–17; K. Taniguchi, 'The Existence of Traverse in Pasinetti's Model of Growth and Distribution' (University of Osaka, Discussion Paper, 11, School of Economics; Osaka, 1987).

that its chief aim was not to determine the rapidity of convergence towards steady state, but rather to study the mechanisms that, under general conditions of long-term equilibrium, determine the distribution of income and capital.

Given an external shock, Mückl has shown that, as the economy converges towards long-term equilibrium, the distribution of income will still be determined by the behavioural parameters of both classes. Taniguchi, moreover, has shown that in the case of the Kaldor–Pasinetti model, there always exists a 'traverse' that ensures the passage from one steady-state equilibrium to a new one, and that this holds even in quite general conditions. This, therefore, confirms the stability of the model and its ability to adapt to external shocks.

2. *The hypothesis of a differentiated interest rate for the two socio-economic classes.* The Kaldor–Pasinetti model is explicitly based on the assumption that the rate of interest earned on accumulated savings is the same for the two classes of savers. In Pasinetti's view, any statement concerning the share and rate of profit must be grounded on a theory of the interest rate. An obvious hypothesis in a long-term model is that the rate of interest is equal to the rate of profit.

The hypothesis of a rate of interest differentiated for the two classes has repeatedly appeared in the literature, despite Pasinetti's frequent statements of his position:

[A]nalysis can be conducted at various levels of abstraction; hence what is essential, when comparing alternative theories, is to keep to levels of abstraction that are homogeneous. Here discussion has centred on the theoretical foundations of the rate of profits. And the alternative theories proposed (neo-classical and Keynesian) have all kept to the level of abstraction of long-term dynamic equilibrium (so-called 'steady state'). Now, at this level of abstraction all the economic literature on the topic has argued (correctly, in my view) that the most appropriate hypothesis is that the rate of interest and the rate of profit are *equal*, given that, in conditions of dynamic equilibrium, almost all forms of uncertainty are absent.[9]

None the less, many economists have set out to explore the hypothesis of a differentiated rate of interest within a variety of theoretical frameworks.[10]

[9] L. L. Pasinetti, 'Determinatezza del saggio di profitto nella teoria post-keynesiana: risposta a Professor Campa', *Giornale degli economisti e annali di economia* (1975), 645–6; see also id., *Growth and Income Distribution*, 139–41; and id., 'Conditions of Existence of a Two-Class Economy in the Kaldor and More General Models of Growth and Income Distribution', *Kyklos* (1983), 91–102.

[10] See esp. N. F. Laing, 'Two Notes on Pasinetti's Theorem', *ER* (1969), 373–85; P. Balestra and M. Baranzini, 'Some Optimal Aspects in a Two-Growth Model with a Differentiated Interest Rate', *Kyklos* (1971), 240–56; G. Campa, 'Indeterminatezza del saggio di profitto e rilevanza della propensione a risparmiare dei lavoratori e della tecnologia nel modello di Pasinetti, *Giornale degli economisti e annali di economia* (1975), 16–55; Pasinetti, 'Determinatezza del saggio di profitto nella teoria post-keynesiana'; B. J. Moore, 'The Pasinetti Paradox Revisited, *RES* (1974), 297–9; K. L. Gupta, 'Differentiated Interest Rate and Kaldor–Pasinetti Paradoxes', *Kyklos* (1976), 31–4; E. Fazi and N. Salvadori, 'The Existence of a Two-Class Economy in the Kaldor Model of Growth and Distribution, *Kyklos* (1981), 582–92; and the reply by Pasinetti, 'Conditions of Existence of a Two Class Economy'; H. Riese, 'Theorie der Produktion und Einkommensverteilung', *Kyklos* (1981), 540–62; and K. Miyazaki, 'The Differentiated Rate of Interest and Income Distribution in

Marginalist analysis (like Balestra's and Baranzini's) has tended to stress that fact that, with a differentiated interest rate, the Cambridge (or Kaldor–Pasinetti) equation loses its validity, and should be replaced by another stating that the equilibrium rate of profit also depends on the behavioural parameters of the working class. In post-Keynesian analysis, however (like that conducted by Gupta), the assumption that the rate of interest earned by workers is proportional to the system's overall rate of profit ($r = \alpha(P/K)$) gives a steady-state value for the profit rate that strengthens the validity of the Cambridge equation.

Pasinetti, too, in reply to a critic, has agreed that exploration of the hypothesis of an interest rate different from the profit rate might be of some interest. Nevertheless, in his view, this kind of analysis 'will become (interesting) if and when it is possible to move, entirely homogenously, to a degree of abstraction less 'abstract' than that of steady state'.[11]

If the working class receives a rate of interest on its savings lower than the profit rate, it must (assuming that the system stays in equilibrium) press for a corresponding increase in the share of wages in the national income, or else for an increase in its share of capital. If these changes do not come about, or while they are doing so (which can take a very long period of time), the system may suffer deflation and a decline in economic activity stemming from the excess saving consequent on the transfer of income from workers to capitalists generated by the differentiation of the interest rate.

3. The introduction of a monetary sector and of portfolio choice. From the early 1970s onwards a number of studies[12] have sought to introduce the monetary component into the Kaldor–Pasinetti model. The aim has been (*a*) to assess the neutrality or non-neutrality of money in models of distribution and accumulation; (*b*) to determine how equilibrium values of money differed from real ones (especially in relation to the rate of profit); (*c*) to assess the effect of money on the growth and accumulation of capital; (*d*) to verify the extent to which the presence of uncertainty influences the process of saving and accumulation by classes. As Ramanathan has argued:

the Pasinetti Model of Growth and Income Distribution' (Dept. of Economics, Hosei University, Tokyo, 1986). Conceptual and empirical reasons for postulating a differentiated interest rate are set out in Balestra and Baranzini, 'Some Optimal Aspects', 242–3.

[11] Pasinetti, 'Determinatezza del saggio di profitto teoria post-keynesiana', 646.

[12] See P. Davidson, 'The Demand and Supply of Securities and Economic Growth and its Implications for the Kaldor–Pasinetti versus Samuelson–Modigliani Controversy', *AER Papers and Proceedings* (1968), 252–69; M. Baranzini, 'A Two-Class Monetary Growth Model', *Revue suisse d'économie politique et de statistique* (1975), 177–89; Sheng Cheng Hu, 'On Optimal Capital Accumulation in a Two Class Model of Economic Growth', *Metroeconomia* (1973), 229–49; R. Ramanathan, 'The Pasinetti Paradox in a Two-Class Monetary Growth Model', *Journal of Monetary Economics* (1976), 389–97; P. Skott, 'On the Kaldorian Saving Function', *Kyklos* (1981), 563–81; W. A. Darity, 'The Simple Analytics of Neo-Ricardian Growth and Distribution', *AER* (1981), 978–93; M. Kano, 'Money, Financial Assets and Pasinetti's Theory of Profit', *Economic Studies Quarterly* (1985), 169–77.

The introduction of a monetary asset that competes with a capital asset substantially alters not only the behavioural characteristics of an economic system but the long-run implications as well. For instance, in the standard two-class model with capitalists (or firms) and workers (or households), the proportion of capital held by each group is endogenously determined. If a monetary asset exists, then firms and households will not only save different proportions of their respective incomes and earn dividend income on capital assets but also have different demands for money.[13]

The way in which the demand for money is introduced into the two-class model therefore becomes crucial to the determination of the income, wealth, and socio-economic characteristics of the two classes. Indeed

The two groups will thus respond differently in terms of money demand to changes in the inflation rate or rate of return to capital. This in turn alters the portfolio composition in a dissimilar way with substantial impacts on capital accumulation and the balanced growth path of real and monetary variables.[14]

Analyses in this area show that it is only in specific cases that money does not alter the equilibrium values of the system; on the other hand, it is only when the demand for money by the classes is proportional to their economic weight that the Cambridge equation preserves its validity intact. But, once again, the attention of economists has concentrated, not on the value of the equilibrium rate of profit or on the share of profits in the national income (P/Y), but on the process of saving accumulation and the distribution of capital.

Some of their results confirm, in a certain sense, what Tobin, Patinkin, Levhari, and Sidrauski[15] demonstrated with a one-class growth model—even though the two-class analysis gives additional information on the economic system's mechanisms of growth, accumulation, and distribution. The principal finding has been that the introduction of money helps, other variables remaining the same, to slow down the process of physical capital accumulation and induces the maximization of consumption corresponding to an overall saving propensity larger than the share of profits in the national income.

   4. The introduction of the public sector and international trade. Extension of the post-Keynesian model to include the public sector has shown that the Kaldor–Pasinetti theorem preserves its validity if the government budget is balanced. This probably derives from the fact that a variation in the public debt gives rise to a redistribution of income among social classes. Steedman has proposed a model that gives lesser importance to the Meade–Samuelson–Modigliani dual theorem. Fleck and Domenghino have tried to extend analysis

[13] Ramanathan, 'Pasinetti Paradox', 389.   [14] Ibid.
[15] J. Tobin, 'The Neutrality of Money in Growth Models: A Comment', *EC* (1967), 69–72; M. Sidrauski, 'Inflation and Economic Growth', *JPE* (1967), 796–81; D. Patinkin and D. Levhari, 'The Role of Money in a Simple Growth Economy', *AER* (1968), 713–53.

to the case where the government budget is in deficit. Discussion on this issue still continues, and Pasinetti has reconsidered it in its entirety.[16]

The Kaldor–Pasinetti model has also been extended to embrace the case of two countries with not necessarily equal rates of growth and profit, in a regime of free movements of capital—the aim being to define both the power relations among the countries' various classes and the way in which the equilibrium rate of profit for the whole system is defined.[17]

5. *The long-term distribution of income and capital among classes and the inclusion of other socio-economic classes.* One of the most controversial aspects of the Cambridge model of distribution is its assumption of a society rigidly divided into classes, each with a single, fixed propensity to save. Why not, it was suggested from various quarters, postulate the existence of a larger number of social classes (perhaps on the basis of their level of income, or of their wealth, etc.), perhaps with a propensity to save determined by the nature of their income (from capital, from work, or from rent)? One of the first to venture into this area was J. Tobin, who generalized the model to include various classes of workers and capitalists, each with its specific propensity to save.[18] Tobin was followed by a conspicuous number of other economists,[19] who set out to generalize the Kaldor–Pasinetti model and to identify the profit rate and the shares of income in the national product, under the following hypotheses:

(a) the differentiation of propensities to save by classes according to the type of income earned;[20]

---

[16] I. Steedman, 'The State and the Outcome of the Pasinetti Process', *EJ* 82 (1972), 1387–95; C.-M. Domenghino, *Die Weiterentwicklung der post-keynesianischen Verteilungstheorie* (Frankfurt, P. Lang, 1982); F. H. Fleck and C.-M. Domenghino, 'Cambridge (U.K.) vs. Cambridge (Mass.): A Keynesian Solution of "Pasinetti's Paradox" ', *JPKE* (1987), 22–36; L. L. Pasinetti, 'Ricardian Debt-Taxation Equivalence in the Kaldor Theory of Profits and Income Distribution', *CJE* 13: 1 (1989), 25–36.

[17] L. Mainwaring, 'International Investment and the Pasinetti Process, *OEP* (1980), 99–101; see also C. R. S. Dougherty, *Interest and Profit* (London, Methuen & Co., 1980), 158–9.

[18] Tobin, 'Toward a "General" Kaldorian Theory of Distribution'.

[19] See P. Pettenati, 'Il teorema di Pasinetti in un diverso quadro di riferimento', *Studi economici* (1967), 581–8; R. N. Vaughan, 'The Pasinetti Paradox in Neoclassical and More General Models: A Correction', *RES* (1971), 271; A. C. Chiang, 'A Simple Generalization of the Kaldor–Pasinetti Theory of Profit Rate and Income Distribution', *EC*, (1973), 311–13; A. Maneschi, 'The Existence of a Two-Class Economy in the Kaldor and Pasinetti Models of Growth and Distribution', *RES* (1974), 149–50; Y. Hattori, 'A Note on Pasinetti's Theorem', *Bulletin of University of Osaka Prefecture* (1975), 13–15; B. J. Moore, 'The Pasinetti Paradox Revisited', *RES* (1974), 297–9; N. Blattner, 'Corporate Finance and Income Distribution in a Growing Economy', *Zeitschrift für Wirtschafts-und Sozialwissenschaft* (1976), 223–38; S. J. Moss, 'The Post-Keynesian Theory of Income Distribution in a Corporate Economy', *Australian Economic Papers* (1978), 303–22; H. Riese, 'Theorie der Produktion und Einkommensverteilung', *Kyklos* (1981), 540–62; P. Skott, 'On the "Kaldorian" Saving Function', *Kyklos* (1981), 563–81; E. Fazi and N. Salvadori, 'The Existence of a Two Class Economy in the Kaldor Model of Growth and Distribution', *Kyklos* (1981), 582–92; G. Chiodi and K. Velupillai, 'A Note on Lindahl's Theory of Distribution', *Kyklos* (1983), 103–311; J. O'Connell, 'Undistributed Profits and the Pasinetti and Dual Theorems', *Journal of Macroeconomics* (1985), 115–19. See also Pasinetti, *Growth and Income Distribution*, 141–2.

[20] See e.g., Meade, 'Rate of Profits in a Growing Economy'; id., 'Outcome of the Pasinetti Process: A Note'; Pasinetti, 'Professor Meade's "Rate of Profit in a Growing Economy" '; id.,

(b) the differentiation between pure capitalists and capitalists earning other types of income;

(c) the introduction of new kinds of income, rent in particular, and of new classes with specific propensities to save and consume.[21]

It was shown that the Kaldor–Pasinetti equation is wholly valid as long as there exists a class of 'pure capitalists'—that is, a class whose income derives solely from capital. It was also found that, when propensities to save are related to type of income and not to a specific class, the past accumulation process should be related to the historical distribution of income and not to the historical division of society into classes. In this sense, study of capital accumulation has lacked a socio-economic component. Finally, when rent and rentiers were considered, three long-term solutions were discovered: the first two coincided with those of Kaldor–Pasinetti and of Meade, Samuelson, and Modigliani, the third arose when only workers and rentiers held a positive share of the system's overall capital. In this case the profit rate (and indirectly the distribution between wages, profits, and rents) is independent of the propensities to save of the working class and of the capital/output ratio.

This latter outcome, in a certain sense, confirms the validity of the Cambridge theory—which is able to determine distribution without resorting to the criterion of marginal productivity.

6. *The introduction of micro-economic elements.* In spite of its division of the system into classes, the post-Keynesian distribution model has essentially macro-economic foundations. This absence of micro-foundations has attracted the attention of those, like Jan Kregel, who believe it to be the weakest point in post-Keynesian theory. Pasinetti, however, in a recent lecture to an Italo-Soviet conference, has stressed that there is no necessary incompatibility between a macro- and micro-economic framework, as long as the macro-economic framework and constraints are given priority:

Once the conditions of satisfactory growth (structural efficiency) have been fulfilled, a second stage follows in which the way becomes opened to the investigation and solution of so to speak 'local' problems of efficiency at the level of the single production units and of the single individuals. To these 'local' problems, the procedures and

'Rate of Growth in a Growing Economy: A Reply'; id., 'New Results in an Old Framework'; id., *Growth and Income Distribution*, ch. 6; P. P. Chang, 'Rate of Profit and Income Distribution in Relation to the Rate of Economic Growth: A Comment', *RES* (1964), 103–6; J. Craven, *The Distribution of the Product* (London, Allen & Unwin, 1979) (ch. on the Cambridge distribution theory); A. Woodfield and J. McDonald, 'On Relative Income Shares in the Pasinetti and Samuelson–Modigliani Systems', (1979), 329–35; id., 'Income Distribution in the Pasinetti Model: Reply to Baranzini', *Australian Economic Papers* (1982), 27–13; M. Baranzini, 'The Pasinetti and Anti-Pasinetti Theorems: A Reconciliation'; id., 'Income Distribution in the Pasinetti Model: A Comment on Woodfield and McDonald', *Australian Economic Papers* (1982), 200–6.

[21] See L. L. Pasinetti, 'Reply to Professor Stiglitz', in M. Morishima, 'Pasinetti's *Growth and Income Distribution* Revisited', *Journal of Economic Literature* (1977), 57–8; A. Schianchi, 'Crescita e distribuzione in un modello a tre classi: una nota', *Ricerche economiche* (1978), 103–6; M. Baranzini and R. Scazzieri, 'Profit and Rent in a Three-Class Model of Capital Accumulation', mimeo, Universities of Oxford and Bologna, 1985.

methods of maximization under constraints may well be appropriate in many circumstances; even though never in an exclusive way. We may talk in this respect of 'local' or *micro-economic efficiency*.[22]

This means that if the distributive macro-economic framework is preserved in its entirety (with its causality), the model can be extended to include a certain micro-structure—for example, in order to give more exhaustive explanation of the propensities to save and consume of social classes and of the mechanisms responsible for the intergenerational transmission of capital.

The first moves in this direction came from neo-classical and marginalist economists. In the case of the marginalists this is not surprising, since they handle distribution primarily in micro-economic terms; but several non-neo-classical economists also entered the field.[23] One extremely interesting analytical exercise involved the introduction into the consumption function of the life-cycle hypothesis: namely, that individuals seek to allocate their resources (in terms of income and inheritance) so as to maximize the utility of consumption and intergenerational legacies.

The results achieved by these models show (as does the Kaldor–Pasinetti model) that the system's rate of interest is positively correlated with its rate of growth and inversely related to the propensity to save of capitalists. Other important components emerge, however, such as legacies to the future generation or the proportion of intergenerational capital in the overall capital of classes. More complicated results are obtained in the case where all classes in the system hold not only life-cycle savings but also a part of the intergenerational stock.

Over the last twenty-five years numerous contributions, so far unmentioned in my discussion, have appeared in the specialist journals and in the many books on growth and distribution. A large number of these examine the relevance or otherwise of Meade, Samuelson, and Modigliani's[24] dual theo-

[22] L. L. Pasinetti,' ' "Satisfactory" versus Optimal Economic Growth', *Rivista internazionale di scienze economiche e commerciali* (1987), 991.

[23] See e.g., R. Britto, 'On Differential Saving Propensities in Two-Class Growth Models', *RES* (1972), 491–4; id., 'The Life-Cycle Savings in a Two-Class Growth Model', New York, Econometric Society Meeting, 1969; F. H. Hahn and R. C. O. Matthews, *Postscript to the Theory of Economic Growth: A Survey* (Paris, Éditions Economica, 1971); A. B. Atkinson, 'A Model of Distribution of Wealth', mimeo, University of Essex, 1974; D. L. Bevan, 'Savings, Inheritance and Economic Growth in the Presence of Earning Inequality', mimeo, University of Oxford, 1974; H. Bortis, 'Dr Wood on Profits and Growth', in M. Baranzini (ed.), *Advances in Economic Theory* (Oxford, Basil Blackwell, 1982), 262–70; M. Baranzini, 'On the Distribution of Income in Two-Class Growth Models', Ph.D. thesis, (Oxford, 1976); id., 'Taux d'intérêt, distribution du revenu, théorie des cycles vitaux et choix du portefeuille', *Kyklos* (1981), 593–610; id., 'Can the Life-Cycle Theory Help in Explaining Income Distribution and Capital Accumulation?', in *Advances in Economic Theory*, 243–61.

[24] See e.g., R. Findlay, 'Economic Growth and Distributive Shares', *RES* (1959–60), 167–78; B. S. Frey, 'Probleme von Heute und die Theorie des optimalen Wirtschaftswachstum', *Revue suisse d'économie politique et statistique* (1970), 149–65; N. Rau, 'Two-Class Neoclassical Growth: A Conjecture Proved', *QJE* (1972), 344–5; A. Guha, 'The Global Stability of Two-Class Neoclassical Growth', *QJE* (1972), 687–90; B. Naslund, 'Labour Power and Income Distribution', *Swedish Journal of Economics* (1973), 128–42; D. L. Bevan, 'Savings, Inheritance and Economic

rem, demonstrating once again the vast interest aroused by Kaldor's initial theory.

6.4. Kaldor's Neo-Pasinetti Theorem

In 1966 Kaldor joined the debate by both rejecting the neo-classical critique and declaring his dissatisfaction with Pasinetti's extension of his model. In Kaldor's view, distinction between kinds of spending should be less concerned with capitalists and workers (whereby the former save proportionately more because they are wealthier) than with the distinct spending decisions of workers and firms. His riposte to his neo-classical critics was that they were unable to show that firms in aggregate could be profitable if their spending for investment was lower than saving by workers. In a system without a government and a foreign sector, firms can be profitable only if their earnings are greater than costs, and this can only come about if investments are greater than workers' savings. Kaldor's further counter-criticism of his neo-classical opponents centred on the firms in the Samuelson–Modigliani model, which finance their growth just as much through internal (self-financing) as through external (loans or share issues) finance. In fact, it is characteristic of managerial capitalism that firms hold back profits, irrespective of the psychology of their shareholders, so that they may preserve or increase their market share.

In his 1955 article 'Alternative Theories of Distribution' Kaldor gave a clear explanation as to why the propensity to save of wage-earners is lower than that of capitalists:

This may be assumed independently of any skewness in the distribution of property, simply as a consequence of the fact that the bulk of profits accrues in the form of

Growth in the Presence of Earning Inequality', mimeo, St. John's College, Oxford, 1974; H. J. Ramser, 'Zur Verteilungstheoretischen Relevanz der Kaldor—Formel', *Kyklos* (1969), 585–8; H. J. Ramser, 'Keyenessche Inflations—und Kaldorsche Verteilungstheorie', *Kyklos* (1979), 205–18; Y. Hattori, 'A Note on Pasinetti's Theorem', *Bulletin of University of Osaka Prefecture* (1975), 13–15; M. Morishima, 'Pasinetti's *Growth and Income Distribution* Revisited', *Journal of Economic Literature* (1977), 56–61; H. Bortis, 'On the Determination of the Level of Employment in a Growing Economy', *Revue suisse d'économie politique et de statistique* (1976), 67–93; id., 'An Essay on Post-Keynesian Economics', University of Fribourg, 1979; H. Brems, 'Alternative Theories of Pricing, Distribution, Saving and Investment', *AER* (1979), 161–5; C. R. S. Dougherty, *Interest and Profit* (London, Methuen & Co., 1980); W. A. Darity, 'The Simple Analytics of Neo-Ricardian Growth and Distribution', *AER* (1981), 978–93; G. Bombach, 'Ein Model und sein Echo', *Kyklos* (1981), 517–39; P. Skott, 'An Examination of Kaldor's Growth and Distribution Models 1956–1966', mimeo, University of Aarhus, 1981; id., 'On the "Kaldorian" Saving Function', *Kyklos* (1981), 563–81; S. Ahmad, 'A Pasinetti Theory of Relative Profit Share for the Anti-Pasinetti Case', *JPKE* (1986), 149–58; K. Miyazaki, 'A Note on Income Distribution in the Pasinetti Growth Model' and 'Income Distribution in the Pasinetti Growth Model: The Case of Two Types of Workers with Different Propensities to Save', mimeo, Hosei University, Tokyo, 1987.

company profits and a high proportion of companies' marginal profits is put to reserve.[25]

However, this induced Marris's criticism of the Kaldor–Pasinetti model of income distribution, which rests on three premisses.[26] First, he argues, the thesis of differential saving propensities is based on evidence that the profit share retained by firms, s_c, is greater than the propensity of households to save out of dividends. Secondly, the rate of growth of the economy must be taken to be largely dependent on the rate of growth of (managerial) corporations: in an economy with a fixed number of firms, the economy's growth rate can then be approximated by the growth rate of a representative firm. The former is thus not fixed by some exogenous natural rate à la Pasinetti, but endogenous to the growth efforts of the representative firm à la Odagiri.[27] Thirdly, the retention ratio of the representative corporation, s_c, is a decision variable of its directors, which will be determined as a result of maximizing their growth aspirations traded off against financial-market constraints exercised by shareholders or take-over raiders.

Marris's conclusion is that the rate of profit can no longer be deduced from equation (6.7), where n, the rate of growth of the economy, and s_c, the propensity to save of capitalists, were both exogenously given. In his view, the profit rate must be determined by other means (his preference is for the Kaleckian theory of imperfect competition, which has the share of profit depend on the elasticity of demand), while the rate of growth is endogenously dependent on the parameter s_c, which must also be determined by corporate finance policy.

This, however, is not the only available solution to the problem. In the article in which Kaldor set out his rebuttal of the Samuelson–Modigliani critique, he developed an extremely fruitful idea into what he called a 'neo-Pasinetti theorem'.[28] This model of Kaldor's comprises three agents—corporate firms, workers, and household-shareholders—and only one asset: corporate shares. Firms finance their current investment expenditure ΔK with a fraction s_c of their profits P and by issuing new securities equal to some fraction i of their investment expenditure, given by the stock of capital K multiplied by its growth rate g.

The equation for firms' behaviour is thus:

$$\Delta K = s_c P + igK.$$

Bearing in mind that $\Delta K/K$ is g, and using ρ to denote the ratio P/K, we may derive from the previous equation Kaldor's new formula for the profit rate:

[25] N. Kaldor, 'Alternative Theories of Distribution' (1955), repr. in CP i. 229 n. 1.

[26] R. Marris, *Reconstructing Keynesian Economics with Imperfect Competition: A Desk-Top Simulation* (Aldershot, Elgar, 1991), 148.

[27] H. Odagiri, *The Theory of Growth in A Corporate Economy* (Cambridge, CUP, 1981).

[28] Kaldor, 'A Neo-Pasinetti Theorem', app. to 'Marginal Productivity and the Macro-Economic Theories of Distribution'.

(6.11) $\rho = g(1 - i)/s_C.$

For this equation to hold, one must assume that the new securities issued by corporations are absorbed by the personal sector divided between workers and household-shareholders. Workers are divided in turn between active workers, who save a certain fraction of their income for when they retire, and retired workers, who consume their accumulated savings. With a growing population, the savings of active workers exceed the dissavings of retired workers by a percentage s_W of their wages and salaries income W. Let us further suppose that household-shareholders consume a fraction c of their capital gains G (which includes dividends per share and the difference between the market value of the shares and the book value of the assets).

Equilibrium in the securities market requires that the supply of securities issued by firms should be equalized by demand for them from the net savings of household-shareholders:

(6.12) $igK = s_WW - cG.$

The capital gain G is the change in the overall market values of the securities, which is given by the market appreciation of the old shares relative to the book value of the new investment less the value of the new shares issued to finance the new investment, i.e.:

(6.13) $G = (v - i)\Delta K$

where v is the 'valuation ratio'—that is, the ratio between the market value of the shares and the 'book value' of the capital employed by the corporations.[29]

Substituting (6.13) in (6.12) gives:

$$igK = s_WW - c(v - i)\Delta K.$$

Considering that $W = Y - P$, and that P/K is given by equation (6.11), we obtain:

(6.14) $v = 1/c[(s_W/g)(Y/K) - (s_W/s_C)(1 - i) - i(1 - c)].$

Equations (6.11) and (6.14) are the outcome of the model. The latter states that the equilibrium of the stock-market is given by the change of the valuation ratio, which depends on the propensities of workers to save (s_W) and shareholders (c) and on the financial policy of firms (given by s_C and i). In steady-state equilibrium, when the rate of growth of the economy (g) and the capital/output ratio (Y/K) are constant, v will be constant and > 1 or < 1, depending on s_C, s_W, c, and i. In a steady growth state with a constant valuation ratio, household capital (which is Pasinetti's 'workers' capital') and the book value of firms' assets (Pasinetti's 'capitalists' capital') grow at the same rate as they do in Pasinetti's model. According to equation (6.11), the profit rate will depend only on g, s_C and i, and will be independent of 'personal' saving propensities

[29] This concept was used for the first time in R. Marris, *The Economic Theory of Managerial Capitalism* (London, Macmillan, 1964). It was also later developed independently by James Tobin, who gave it the name 'q': J. Tobin, 'A General Equilibrium Approach to Monetary Theory', *Journal of Money Credit and Banking* (Feb. 1969).

s_W and c. One strong assumption of the model is that corporate policy on the issue of new shares (i) is unconstrained by the valuation ratio (v); an assumption that is acceptable when the valuation ratio does not change as the economy grows. Kaldor's formula (6.11) is similar to Pasinetti's, but is reached by a different route: 'it will hold in any steady growth state, and not only in a "long-run" Golden Age; it does not postulate a class of hereditary capitalists with a special high-saving propensity. In the special case $i = 0$, it reduces to the simple Pasinetti formula $\rho = g/s_C$'.[30]

Kaldor's model thus acquires a generality that is not to be found in the early post-Keynesian models of distribution. Post-Keynesian economists who have sought to integrate financial aspects into the model of growth and distribution, like Eichner, Wood, Kregel, Harcourt, and Harris,[31] have clearly been influenced by Kaldor's thinking. As Kregel has stressed,[32] the post-Keynesian model not only lends itself to further development which takes account of the different features of modern economic systems, it also gives convincing demonstration that in a growing economy, where investment decisions are independent of the amount of saving generated, the equilibrium profit rate, and therefore distribution, depends solely on the rate of growth and on the behavioural parameters of the entrepreneurial class.

6.5. On Method

For more than thirty years Kaldor's distribution theory has been central post-Keynesian theory; and the Kaldor–Pasinetti model has generated numerous lines of research seeking to extend the boundaries of distribution and accumulation analysis.[33] Its major contribution has been not so much at the level of 'predictive' analysis seeking to forecast future events as at the level of 'inter-

[30] Kaldor, 'Neo-Pasinetti Theorem', 98.

[31] A. S. Eichner, 'A Theory of the Determination of the Mark-up under Oligopoly', *EJ* (Dec. 1975); A. Wood, *A Theory of Profit* (Cambridge, CUP, 1975); A. S. Eichner and J. A. Kregel, 'An Essay on Post-Keyensian Theory: A New Paradigm in Economics', *Journal of Economic Literature* (Dec. 1975); G. C. Harcourt and P. Kenyon, 'Pricing and Investment Decision', *Kyklos*, 3 (1976); D. J. Harris, 'The Price Policy of Firms, the Level of Employment and Distribution of Income in the Short Run', *Australian Economic Papers* (June 1974); C. Dougherty, *Interest and Profit* (London, Methuen & Co., 1980); S. A. Marglin, *Growth, Distribution and Prices* (Cambridge, Mass., Harvard University Press, 1984); S. C. Dow, *Macroeconomic Thought: A Methodological Approach* (Oxford, Basil Blackwell, 1985), 185–95.

[32] J. A. Kregel, *Rate of Profit, Distribution and Growth: Two Views* (London, Macmillan, 1971).

[33] Among the books, textbooks, and review articles giving detailed examination of the Cambridge debate on income distribution see the following chronological list, which is certainly not exhaustive of all the publications that have devoted at least a sect. or a para. to the controversy on income and wealth distribution theory postulating specific socio-economic groups with constant propensities to save: J. E. Stiglitz and H. Uzawa (eds.), *Readings in the Modern Theory of Economic Growth* (Cambridge, Mass., MIT Press, 1969); R. M. Solow, *Growth Theory: An Exposition* (Oxford, OUP, 1970); M. Bronfenbrenner, *Income Distribution Theory* (London, Macmillan, 1971); T. F. Dernburg and J. D. Dernburg, *Macroeconomic Analysis* (Reading, Mass., Addison-Wesley, 1971); D. Hamberg, *Models of Economic Growth* (New York, Harper Row,

pretative' analysis of historical phenomena and of the mechanisms of distribution and accumulation. The distinction between 'predictive' and 'interpretative' theory is commonly drawn between marginalist or neo-classical theories and classical, post-Keynesian or neo-Ricardian ones.[34] The 'predictive' nature of marginalist analysis is more suited to the mechanistic features of the functions of production; the institutional reference to the economic behaviour of social classes by classical and post-Keynesian theory gives it a 'more interpretative' character.

It has been repeatedly claimed that Kaldor's distribution theory in particular (and post-Keynesian theory in general) acts as a bridge between classical and 'modern' theory, while accentuating the break with marginalist theory. In a certain sense Kaldor is the most orthodox of the Keynesians, in that his original model closely, indeed exclusively, associates socio-economic classes with ownership of one particular factor of production. Pasinetti, on the other hand, tends to eliminate this correspondence, at least in part, by considering the case where the working class can earn income from both work and capital. For Pasinetti, the classes can be divided into various subclasses, without this altering the most important significance of the distributive process. This is not so for Kaldor.

Whereas the marginalist model takes the technological parameters of the function (or functions) of production to be important, indeed crucial, in determination of the distribution of income among factors, the post-Keynesian model gives priority to the 'behavioural parameters' of social classes and to economic growth, which, together with the autonomous investment decisions of entrepreneurs, requires a certain amount of saving. This can only be achieved through a specific distribution of income among the various social classes, in so far as they have different propensities to save and consume. An

1971); G. C. Harcourt, *Some Cambridge Controversies in the Theory of Capital* (Cambridge, CUP, 1972); S. Lombardini and A. Quadrio Curzio (eds.), *La distribuzione del reddito nella teoria economica* (Milan, Franco Angeli, 1972); W. Krelle, *Wachstumstheorie* (Berlin, Springer, 1972); M. Dobb, *Theories of Value and Distribution since Adam Smith* (Cambridge, CUP, 1973); W. A. Eltis, *Growth and Distribution* (London, Macmillan, 1973); M. Blaug, *The Cambridge Revolution* (Institute of Economic Affairs, Hobart Paperback, 1974); A. B. Atkinson, *The Economics of Inequality* (Oxford, OUP, 1975); C. J. Bliss, *Capital Theory and the Distribution of Income* (Amsterdam, North Holland Publishing Co., 1975); H. G. Jones, *An Introduction to Modern Theories of Economic Growth* (London, Nelson, 1975); D. J. Harris, *Capital Accumulation and Income Distribution* (Stanford, Stanford University Press, and London, Routledge & Kegan Paul, 1978); M. C. Howard, *Modern Theories of Income Distribution* (London, Macmillan, 1979); J. Craven, *The Distribution of the Product* (London, Allen & Unwin, 1979); C. R. S. Dougherty, *Interest and Profit* (London, Methuen & Co., 1980); J. R. Crotty, 'Post-Keynesian Economic Theory: An Overview and Evaluation', *AER Papers and Proceedings* (1980); S. A. Marglin, *Growth, Distribution and Prices* (Cambridge, Mass., Harvard University Press, 1984); P. Arestis and T. Skouras (eds.), *Post-Keynesian Economic Theory* (Brighton, Wheatsheaf Books, 1985); Baranzini, 'Distribution Theories: Keynesian', *The New Palgrave Dictionary* (London, Macmillan, 1987); H. Bortis, 'An Essay on Post-Keynesian Economics', mimeo, University of Fribourg, 1988.

[34] On the distinctive features of the various currents of economic thought, see M. Baranzini and R. Scazzieri, 'Knowledge in Economics: A Framework', in id., (eds.), *Foundations of Economics, Structures of Enquiry and Economic Theory* (Oxford, Basil Blackwell, 1986), 1–87.

excess of saving would slow down economic activity; in the opposite case a situation of chromic inflation would ensue.

Thus in post-Keynesian theory (and this applies both to Kaldor's and Pasinetti's model), profits come first—precisely because of the entrepreneurial class's need for capital growth—followed, residually, by wages and other incomes such as rent. This overt chain of cause and effect should be compared with the distributive simultaneity of the marginalists (where all the factors are rewarded according to their marginal productivity and the quantity employed—without any possible residue), and also with the differing causality relation of the Ricardian classical model, where it is the wages of the workforce that are determined first (on demographic criteria), then the rents of landowners (according to technical factors) and finally, residually, the profits of entrepreneurs.

Research since the appearance of the original Kaldor–Pasinetti model has not only blunted the criticisms brought against post-Keynesian theory; it has also demonstrated the vitality of the theory and its capacity for extension to a much broader field of enquiry than that defined by the original model.

Chapter 7

Growth at Different Rates and Kaldor's 'Laws'

The greatest improvement in the productive power of labour, and the greater part of the skill, dexterity, and judgment with which it is anywhere directed, or applied, seem to have been the effects of the division of labour.

As it is the power of exchanging that gives occasion to the division of labour, so the extent of this division must always be limited by the extent of that power, in other words, by the extent of the market.

A. Smith, *The Wealth of Nations*

7.1. Origins and Evolution of his Research Method

Before the 1960s Kaldor was engaged as an applied economist on several occasions: during the Second World War and the immediate post-war period, during the years when he acted as a tax-consultant to numerous developing countries, and also when he worked as adviser to the Labour Party.

This experience in applied economics had already influenced his thinking as he developed his growth models of the 1950s—models that he regarded as giving theoretical explanations for empirically verifiable regularities within historically determined stages of capitalist development. It was as early as the 1950s, therefore, that Kaldor's interest was first aroused by a phenomenon of extraordinary importance for the study of capitalist evolution: the differences among the rates of economic growth of industrialized countries. His models of those years were, however, still firmly rooted in the theory from which they grew: a Keynesian model of income–expenditure equilibrium, where investment was treated not only as a component of aggregate demand, but as an increase in productive capacity as well. These models disregarded changes in the structure of production because the object of their analysis lay elsewhere and because they assumed full employment—for reasons that have been already discussed in Chapter 5. However, in the 1960s and 1970s Kaldor developed a theory of growth that addressed precisely those structural changes in the productive system that he had previously ignored. The investment function and the distribution of income consequently lost the centrality as-

cribed to them by previous models, and the hypothesis of full employment was
jettisoned because it was no longer necessary.

These years also saw a change in Kaldor's research method: he moved from
the pure deductivism of the early 1930s to the 'stylized facts' of the 1950s
and 1960s, and thence to his empirically verifiable theories of the 1960s and
1970s. He became increasingly convinced that an economist should proceed
'from facts to theory and not the other way round'. This, however, is not to
imply that he surrendered to pure empiricism—that is, that he applied his
analytical energies exclusively to statistical inference—nor that he was ever
interested in designing econometric models that were not anchored in economic theories of broad generality. Kaldor continued to be an economist in
search of simple and widely applicable laws—though in economics as in all
social and historical sciences (embracing as they do numerous phenomena
which vary in time and space and which interact among themselves), the more
general a principle seeks to be, the more it eludes empirical verification.

Kaldor's empiricism buttressed his general views on the economic system.
His work was principally a Darwinian investigation into the process of growth
and evolution of the capitalist economies, and he was convinced that out-
wardly complex phenomena are governed by relatively simple and general
laws. A theory, he believed, should encompass all of such laws; and he was
uninterested in criticisms that addressed only certain aspects of such a theory.
He concluded one of his articles in reply to a critic with the following lines
from Pope's *Essay on Criticism*:

> A perfect judge will read each Work of Wit
> With the same Spirit that its Author writ,
> Survey the whole, nor seek slight Faults to find
> Where Nature moves, and Rapture warms the Mind;
> In Wit, as Nature, what affects our Hearts
> Is not th' Exactness of peculiar Parts;
> 'Tis not a Lip, or Eye, we Beauty call,
> But the joint Force and full Result of all.[1]

From the early 1960s until his death, Kaldor concentrated on two central
themes (apart from developing his theory of the endogeneity of money supply
and waging his assault on monetarism): namely, the complementarity of sectors (agriculture and industry), which is the subject of Chapter 8, and the
increasing returns of manufacturing industry, the linking argument of the
present one.

In his years as a student Kaldor had perhaps been most influenced by the
'Austrians' at the LSE; then during the 1940s and 1950s he was entirely taken
up with the Keynesian revolution. But with the early 1960s, and then increas-

---

[1] Kaldor used this quotation in 'Productivity and Growth in Manufacturing Industry:', A Reply
EC (Nov. 1968). He loved Pope's poetry ever since he was first introduced to it by Joan Robinson.
When I showed this poem to Kaldor's wife and daughters after his death, they felt that it reflected
his research method so closely that they used it as the pref. to the literary and religious passages
read to the congregation at Kaldor's Memorial Service, in King's College Chapel on 17 Jan. 1987.

ingly more so in the years that followed, he rediscovered Allyn Young, his first tutor at the LSE, and Young's insistence on the importance of increasing returns. Kaldor felt this influence so strongly that in the 1980s he set out the principles of a 'general' theory embracing the teachings of both Keynes and Young.[2]

In truth, Kaldor's interest in increasing returns had already been kindled in the early 1960s, the years in which he conducted his polemic against the use of the neo-classical production function as the basis for the theory of growth and distribution (see Chapter 5, sections 2 and 7), and as a tool of applied economics. In an article criticizing Svennilson, he wrote:

There is no reason for supposing that this function is homogeneous in the first degree, let alone of constant unity elasticity, nor that it shifts in time in a neutral manner. All the empirical evidence is to the contrary—in most industries there are increasing returns to scale, on account of both internal and external economies, and the assumption of constant unity elasticities is simply a figment of imagination unsupported by any evidence.[3]

Referring to the work of Robert Solow—who had used the production function to identify the contribution of factors of production to output growth of the United States' non-farm sector—Kaldor asked: 'What do the curves of Cambridge Massachusetts mean?' He dismissed as futile any method of estimating the parameters of a function which, in order to keep faith with the hypotheses of constant returns and all the rest, considered seven-eighths of empirically observed changes to be the result of a shift in the curve and only the residual eighth to be indicative of the slope of the curve itself.

As we saw in Chapter 5.7, Kaldor replaced the method of the neo-classical production function (with constant returns to scale and a shift in the function due to exogenous technical progress) with a function which represented technical progress as a continuous process. In reply to Hicks's criticism of this latter notion, he pointed out that his idea of continuous technical progress entailed rejection of the hypothesis of constant returns (which Hicks also rejected) and, instead, acceptance of the hypothesis of increasing returns to scale.[4]

---

[2] Research in these areas can be found in id., 'Keynesian Economics after Fifty Years', in D. Worswick and J. Trevithick (eds.), *Keynes and the Modern World* (Cambridge, CUP, 1983).

[3] Id., 'Comment on I. Svennilson's paper on "Economic Growth and Technical Progress"', OECD Conference on Residual Factor and Economic Growth, held at Château de la Muette, 20–2 May 1963, p. 5. If there is no empirical support for the hypothesis of constant returns, the only other reason for holding it is 'mathematical convenience'. Kaldor cited Edgeworth's famous criticism of Wicksteed, who had been the first to put forward the proposition that the technological relation between input and output is a 'homogeneous function of the first degree': 'There is a magnificence in this generalization which recalls the youth of the philosophy. Justice is a perfect cube, said the ancient sage; and rational conduct is a homogeneous function, adds the modern *savant*. A theory which points to conclusions so paradoxical ought surely to be enunciated with caution.' (F. Y. Edgeworth, 'The Theory of Distribution', *QJE* (Feb. 1904)).

[4] N. Kaldor, 'Increasing Returns and Technical Progress: A Comment on Professor Hicks's Article', *OEP* (Feb. 1961).

At this stage, however, Kaldor had still not settled on a single, overriding cause of the technical progress that generates increasing labour productivity. In 1964 he wrote:

We do not know how far what appears to be 'technical progress' is the result of the flow of the new inventions—of an advancement of scientific and technological knowledge—or of a dynamic spirit of entrepreneurs and managers who encourage the continuous 'knowledge'; or how far it is just the result of 'learning by doing'—the superior skill and ability which accrues automatically with more experience. Nor can we distinguish the growth of productivity associated with higher rates of production from the increasing output which results from higher productivity—how far is what we treat as 'technical progress' really the reflection of increasing returns to scale, or *viceversa*?[5]

Two years later, however, Kaldor had very definite ideas on the subject.

In 1965 the Cambridge chair of economics previously held by Austin Robinson fell vacant, and the electoral committee's choice divided between Kaldor and Joan Robinson. Although Joan Robinson was eventually appointed, such was Kaldor's reputation that a year later the faculty was obliged to award him a chair *ad personam*. Kaldor's inaugural lecture delivered in 1966[6] demonstrated that the professorship had gone to a thinker whose ideas constantly provoked lengthy controversy—not only because of their importance, but also because of the simple, general, and provocative way in which they were expressed. This was especially true of the debate that followed Kaldor's 1966 lecture, the echoes of which still reverberate today.

Over the next five years, amid proposals, criticisms, revisions and reformulations, Kaldor drew up a set of theses, each expressed in such a way as to be verifiable, and all, when taken together, constituting the central component of his final and more general view of the growth of economic systems; a component which links with his two-sector model (see Chapter 8). These propositions, four in number, came to acquire the status of 'laws'. The first has been labelled the 'law of the manufacturing sector as the engine of growth'; the second the 'Kaldor–Verdoorn law'; the third 'the law of labour migration'; the fourth we can call 'the law of external constraint' or the 'Kaldor–Thirlwall law'. The final form of these four growth laws was the outcome of a lengthy dialectic between Kaldor, his followers, and his critics: it will become clearer if we retrace the various stages of the debate.[7]

[5] Id., 'Comment on I. Svennilson's Paper', 8.

[6] Id., *Causes of the Slow Rate of Economic Growth in the United Kingdom* (Cambridge, CUP, 1966).

[7] A summary of Kaldor's laws, and of the controversy they provoked until the early 1980s, can be found in A. P. Thirlwall, 'A Plain Man's Guide to Kaldor's Growth Laws', *JPKE* (spring 1983), 345–58.

7.2. The Law of Manufacturing Sector as the Engine of Growth

How can we account for the fact—Kaldor asked in a series of three lectures delivered at the University of Cornell (New York)—that although before 1700–50 there were no great differences in income or in per-capita income among regions and countries, after that period a group of countries in western Europe experienced annual or decennial rates of economic growth thirty or forty times higher than they had achieved in the previous seventeen centuries? And why did this happen in just one particular part of the world? Kaldor was not only asking why certain countries had profited from this process whereas others had not, or not yet (a problem that will be examined in Chapter 9); he was also and chiefly concerned with the reasons for such widely differing rates of growth among highly developed countries.

Kaldor's inaugural lecture at Cambridge raised the more specific issue of the slow growth of the British economy compared with those of other countries. His explanation was that rapid rates of economic development are associated with rapid rates of development of the manufacturing sector: because this latter had gone into relative decline in Great Britain, the country's economy had reached a stage of 'premature maturity' before high levels of productivity and per-capita income could be achieved.

Kaldor's argument moved through various stages. The first was his demonstration that manufacturing industry is the 'engine' of growth (first law). From analysis of the performance figures between 1954 and 1964 of twelve leading industrialized countries,[8] he showed the existence of a high correlation between the rate of growth of GDP and the rate of growth of manufacturing production.[9] However, a theoretical explanation for the chain of cause and effect giving rise to this statistical relation was needed: for Kaldor the causal relationship went from growth in the manufacturing sector to the growth of GDP.

The high correlation between the two variables did not stem from the fact that the share of manufacturing output in total output was large. Kaldor rejected this explanation, since, if correct, it would mean that Great Britain— where the manufacturing sector accounted for a large share of total output— would grow at a rate faster than the average among countries, and this contradicted the evidence. The explanation therefore had to be looked for elsewhere. He noted that the higher the rate of growth of the GDP the greater

[8] Austria, Belgium, Canada, Denmark, France, Germany, Japan, Italy, Holland, Norway, UK, USA. The regression equations setting out Kaldor's argument are taken from his lectures at the University of Cornell, *Strategic Factors in Economic Development* (Ithaca, Cornell University Press, 1967) and from the app. to the inaugural lecture at Cambridge, *Causes of the Slow Rate of Economic Growth in the United Kingdom.*

[9] $g\text{GDP} = 1.153 + 0.614gm$, $R^2 = 0.959$, where g stands for annual rate of growth, GPD for gross domestic product, m for manufacturing sector. The reader is reminded that R^2 is called the 'coefficient of determination': it provides a measure of casual association between the two variables of the econometric regression. It can vary between 0 and 1. Hence the correlation between the two variables is more significant, the closer R^2 approaches 1.

the excess of growth of manufacturing output over production in non-manu-facturing sectors.[10] Hence the more the manufacturing sector *grows*, the greater the increase in the productivity of the system as a whole. The reasons for this relationship are both internal and external to the sector. They are external in so far as the rate of growth of manufacturing production increases the rate of growth of *other sectors*—for various reasons: first because indus-trialization accelerates the rate of technological change in the economy as a whole; second because an increase in output and employment in the industrial sector reduces employment in agriculture, but not its output; third because greater activity in the industrial sector produces greater turnover per man in the distribution sector. The internal reason for the relationship between growth of manufacturing and growth of productivity of the whole system is the operation within the manufacturing sector, and in no other sector,[11] of increas-ing returns of scale.

Increasing returns are a phenomenon, at the firm or plant level, which is less micro-economic than macro-economic. They should not be limited to the static economies of scale—which are also reversible—created, for instance, by indivisibilities or other factors (the typical example being the oil pipeline: if the radius increases by n, the volume of oil flow increases by n^2). The economies of scale generating the increasing returns to which Kaldor referred are produced by endogenous technical progress and by the process of 'learning by doing'—which are not reversible. These economies of scale stem from the discovery of new processes, from increasing differentiation, from new subsi-diary industries—that is, from general industrial expansion, not just from the expansion of a particular firm or industry.[12] It was these economies limited by size of the market that Young examined in his article of 1928.[13] He regarded them to be so important in the industrialized countries that they became the premiss for his critique of the then dominant theory of value,[14] on the ground

[10] $gGDP = 3.351 + 0.954 \, (gm - gnm)$, $R^2 = 0.562$, where nm indicates the non-manufacturing sector. The significance of this regression is that in order to have a rate of growth of GDP higher than 3.3%, the rate of growth of the manufacturing sector must be higher than that of the rest of the system.

[11] There is, however, no correlation between the growth rate of the GDP and agricultural and mining production, while in the services sector it is the rate of growth of the GDP that determines the rate of growth of the sector—and not the other way round as in the manufacturing sector. The following regressions, where serv indicates the services sector, are both significant relations: $gGDP = -0.188 + 1.060 \, gserv$, $R^2 = 0.930$; $gserv = 1.283 + 0.597 \, gm$, $R^2 = 0.846$.

[12] A case in point is the car industry: only a growing market could have induced the birth of the carburettor sector or the car-parts sector in general.

[13] A. Young, 'Increasing Returns and Economic Progress', *EJ* (Dec. 1928).

[14] Marshall, and before him Cournot and Walras, had shown that perfect competition was not compatible with decreasing marginal costs (and therefore with increasing returns). The theories of market imperfections developed during the years following Sraffa's article of 1926—of which the theory set out by Young was an example—argued that decreasing costs and some form of compe-tition were compatible, although this avenue was not explored by economists as far as the extreme consequence of discarding the static theory of value. In the real economy, firms do not stand still: most of the time, if they manage to increase their share of the market, they increase in strength; if their market share diminishes, they weaken. The only 19th-cent. economist to have recognized

that, with the extension of the division of labour, 'the representative firm, like the industry of which it is part, loses its identity'.[15]

7.3. The Kaldor–Verdoorn Law

In 1949 P. J. Verdoorn[16] (among others) demonstrated that the operation of increasing returns constitutes the theoretical foundation of the empirical relationship between the growth of productivity and the growth of production. Despite the similarities between Verdoorn's and Kaldor's empirical relations, both their analyses and their subject-matter differ. One finds it difficult to understand, therefore, why Kaldor should have felt obliged to refer to Verdoorn's work in his own theory—unless it was because Verdoorn had been a member of his United Nations' research group after the Second World War. In fact, Verdoorn deduced the coefficients of his equation from a static production function,[17] while for Kaldor the phenomenon of increasing returns was an intrinsically dynamic one. Moreover, they used different frames of reference: Kaldor, unlike Verdoorn and later authors,[18] related these regularities only to activities in the secondary sector of the economy, not to activities in its primary or tertiary sectors.[19] Finally, Verdoorn applied the relation to

the importance of this fact was Karl Marx. In neo-classical theory, every firm has an 'optimal' size: when an industry's output increases, it is the number of firms that grows, not the size of each firm.

[15] Ibid. 538–9.

[16] P. J. Verdoorn, 'Fattori che regolano lo sviluppo della produttività del lavoro', *L'industria* (Mar. 1949). In fact, even before Verdoorn, the relationship had been demonstrated by S. Fabricant, *Employment in Manufacturing 1899–1939* (New York, National Bureau of Economic Research, 1942).

[17] In 'Verdoorn's Law in Retrospect: A Comment', *EJ* (June 1980), Verdoorn wrote that he had taken his neo-classical production function from an article by Tinbergen published in German and subsequently translated into English: 'On the Theory of Trend Movements', in J. Tinbergen Selected Papers (Amsterdam, North Holland Publishing Co., 1959).

[18] W. E. G. Salter, *Productivity and Technical Change* (Cambridge, CUP, 1960); W. Beckerman and associates, *The British Economy in 1975* (Cambridge, CUP, 1965).

[19] For the countries and the time period considered, Kaldor demonstrated a significant correlation in manufacturing industry, in construction and in public utilities. Correlations proved to be significant both between productivity (p) and the growth rate (g) and between employment (e) and the growth rate (g)—something which is obvious if one remembers that $g = p + e$. The following relations held in the manufacturing sector: $pm = 1.035 + 0.484\,gm$, $R^2 = 0.826$; $em = -1.028 + 0.516\,gm$, $R^2 = 0.844$. The relations were significant and suggested that, in the manufacturing sector, with every growth of output of 1% productivity grew by roughly 0.5%, while the rate of autonomous increase in productivity was only 1%. In the case of public utilities, the autonomous element had a much higher value of about 2.7% (and the function had a lower degree of significance). In agriculture and in mining, the high value of the trend-rate and the low value of elasticity meant that productivity change depended primarily on factors that were independent of economies of scale. In transport there was no correlation between productivity growth and production growth. Finally, in commerce there was a very high correlation between productivity growth and production growth, and a very low correlation between the increase in employment and production growth. Unlike agriculture, which had the same coefficients, in commerce the constant had a negative value (while, as we have seen, the autonomous trend of productivity in agriculture was highly positive). For Kaldor, this was a reflection of the manner in which competition operated in the sector, tending

individual industries, whereas Kaldor treated the phenomenon as macro-economic. He, like Young, believed that economies of scale derive less from the expansion of each individual industry as from the expansion of the manufacturing system as a whole.

Although one can deduce, as Verdoorn does, the relationship between growth of output and growth of productivity from the production function, an explanation in these terms lacks the dynamic basis of Kaldor's theory. A number of economists have accepted this dynamic relationship, but nevertheless give an interpretation to the cause and effect relationship that is the reverse of Kaldor's. They assert that an exogenous increase in technical progress and therefore in productivity induces, through its effects on relative costs and prices, a more rapid rate of increase in demand. To this Kaldor objected that if an increase in productivity can be explained by the development of technical and scientific knowledge, this still does not account for the major differences within the same industry over the same period in different countries.[20]

Although Kaldor's second law has always been stated in econometric terms, it can also be given algebraic formulation as the outcome of three functions.[21] The first is Kaldor's technical-progress function which, as it relates to the manufacturing sector, may be written as follows:

(7.1) $pm = \beta' + \alpha' km$

where pm is the rate of growth of productivity of the manufacturing sector, km the rate of growth of capital per man in the manufacturing sector, and β' autonomous technical progress. The latter may be seen partly as true autonomous technical progress α'', and partly as the result of Arrow's learning-by-doing effect. Accordingly, we may write the second function as:

(7.2) $\beta' = \alpha'' + \beta''(gm).$

Finally, if we accept—as Kaldor did—the acceleration principle, we can write the third function as:

(7.3) $km = \alpha''' + \beta'''(gm).$

If we substitute (7.2) and (7.3) in (7.1), and if we call:

$$\alpha'' + \alpha'\alpha''' = \alpha,$$

and

$$\beta'' + \beta'''\alpha' = \beta,$$

to eliminate abnormal profits through a multiplication of units, rather than through a reduction of prices or of distributive margins. Hence, although on the one hand an increase in the turnover of the sector raised productivity per employee, on the other, the inflow of labour into these sectors was not directly connected with the rise in turnover.

[20] Comparing the British and German car industries in the 1950s—where a large proportion of the industry in both countries was owned by the same American firms—he noted that in Britain productivity in the car industry increased by less than 3%, but in Germany by 7% a year. The same industry, with the same technological knowledge, and with the same ownership, achieved different levels of performance according to the overall dynamism of the economy of which it was part.

[21] R. J. Dixon and A. P. Thirlwall, 'A Model of Regional Growth Rate Differences on Kaldorian Lines', *OEP* (July 1975).

we obtain:

(7.4) $$pm = \alpha + \beta\, gm,$$

which is the algebraic formula for the econometric Kaldor's second law.

7.4 The 'Maturity' of the British Economy

Having explored the first two of Kaldor's laws, I shall now turn to Kaldor's explanation of the growth of the manufacturing sector, and to the constraints that he regarded as restricting such growth. Initially (in 1966 and 1967), he put forward a Youngian interpretation:

[I]n order that there should be self-sustained growth, two conditions must be present: *returns* must increase, and the demand for commodities must be *elastic*.[22]

Young defined this second condition

in the special sense that a small increase in its supply will be attended by an increase in the amounts of other commodities which can be had in exchange for it. Under such conditions an increase in the supply of one commodity *is* an increase in the demand for other commodities, and it must be supposed that every increase in demand will evoke an increase in supply.[23]

Growth was therefore the result of an interactive process between stimulating factors induced by demand and restraining factors stemming from supply constraints. Supply-side constraints may derive from commodities or labour. Constraints in the form of commodities may in turn derive from diminishing returns in the primary sector—a constraint operating in the early stages of industrialization (see Chapter 9, sections 2 and 3) or at the level of the world economy as a whole (see Chapter 8, sections 2 and 3). Another constraint on the individual country may be its balance of payments. This acts as a supply-side constraint if it limits the flow of imports, and as a demand-side one if it is due to poor export performance or if it induces 'stop-go' policies. Both before and after his inaugural lecture, Kaldor stressed the importance of this factor, although in the lecture itself he blamed labour shortages in the manufacturing sector for the slower growth of the British economy.[24]

---

[22] Kaldor, *Strategic Factors in Economic Development*, 27.

[23] Young, 'Increasing Returns and Economic Progress', 534.

[24] Since the early 1950s Kaldor had been aware that the trade balance could act as a constraint on full employment (see Ch. 4.6), and was therefore in favour of a flexible exchange-rate policy. However, even before his inaugural lecture, export-led models left him unconvinced. Prof. Beckerman has told me that at a meeting of NIESR in 1964 or 1965 Kaldor was very 'scornful' of his model of export-led growth (W. Beckerman, 'Projecting Europe's Growth', *EJ* (Dec. 1962)). As we shall see in the next sect., Kaldor changed his mind at the end of the 1960s and became one of the fiercest advocates of export-led models, both on analytical (N. Kaldor, 'The Case for Regional Policies', *SJPE* (Nov. 1970)) and economic-policy grounds (id., 'Conflicts in National Economic Objectives', *EJ* (Mar. 1971)).

Kaldor pointed out that a high rate of industrial growth was, in the medium–long term, invariably associated with a rapid increase in employment in the secondary (and tertiary) sectors, which obtained most of their labour from disguised unemployment in agriculture, not from immigration or population growth. It was the differences between the earnings to be made in the second-ary sector and the other two sectors that gave labour its incentive to migrate. All countries experienced a progressive slow-down in their rates of develop-ment as their reservoirs of agricultural labour diminished.[25] However, as long as a high proportion of the working population continued to be employed in the agricultural sector—or even if this proportion was low but, as in the United States, high in the services sector *and* with wages in the services sector lower than those in the manufacturing sector[26]—the supply of labour to the second-ary sector would be sufficiently elastic. When, however, these two conditions were not fulfilled, the supply of labour to the industrial sector became inelas-tic; and it was precisely this inelasticity that was the major limitation on the British economy's potential for growth,[27] a limitation which the other indus-trialized countries had not yet encountered.

As the first country to begin the process of industrialization, Great Britain was therefore the first to reach the stage of 'maturity'. Labour income was the same in all sectors, and the consequent drying up of the domestic transfer of labour restricted the growth of the manufacturing sector and therefore the growth of the whole economy. This 'maturity' was 'premature' because it had been reached when national income and per-capita income were being out-stripped by those countries which, compared with the United Kingdom, were late-comers in the process of industrialization.

7.5. Criticism of Maturity, Dualism, and the Law of Labour Migration

In the year following Kaldor's lectures at Cornell University, his thesis that the British economy was affected by premature maturity and that the growth of output in the manufacturing sector had been hampered by labour shortages was widely criticized.[28] Kaldor responded by altering his views on the labour-supply constraint and by formulating what came to be his third law of growth.

---

[25] Other authors of these years give similar explanations along the lines of Lewis's model for the growth of European economies. As representative of these we may take C. P. Kindleberger, *Europe's Postwar Growth: The Role of Labour Supply* (Cambridge, Mass., Harvard University Press, 1967).

[26] The reason for this was that work sharing (the dividing up of a given volume of work into small activities) was widespread in the tertiary sector but not in industry. See n. 20, above.

[27] The share of exports in British manufacturing industry remained steady over the medium period. This led Kaldor to believe, although he changed his mind in later years, that it was 'the rate of growth of production of exportable goods' that determined the rate of growth of British exports, *Strategic Factors in Economic Development*, 44.

[28] It was pointed out by N. Wolfe ('Productivity and Growth in Manufacturing Industry: Some Reflections on Professor Kaldor's Inaugural Lecture', *EC* (Feb. 1968)) that in the period that

Neo-classical theory has no room for concepts such as 'disguised unemployment', 'pre-capitalist firm', or 'dual economy'. It would be a mistake, however, to assume that these terms are meaningless when applied to industrialized economies. In these economies, too, albeit to a different extent, there coexist low- and high-productivity sectors—and since there is 'disguised unemployment' in the low-productivity sectors, labour can be withdrawn from them without reducing their output. The amount of labour in the non-industrial sector is a residual magnitude given by the total supply of labour and by the demand for labour in the industrial sector. In keeping with the Keynesian concept of 'involuntary unemployment', Kaldor defined 'labour surplus' as the situation where

a faster rate of increase in the demand for labour in the high-productivity sectors induces a faster rate of labour-transference even when it is attended by *a reduction, and not an increase, in the earnings-differential between the different sectors.*[29]

The process of intrasectorial labour transfer increases the average productivity of the system for two reasons: first because the sector absorbing labour (industry) is the one in which returns increase with the growth of output; secondly because the sector losing labour (agriculture and some segments of the services sector)[30] is the one in which the productivity of those employees remaining rises with the drop in employment.

In his article in reply to Wolfe, Kaldor gave a twofold demonstration of his thesis that growth rates of output, even in the developed countries, depend on the rate of labour transfer to the manufacturing sector from other sectors. He first showed that *there is* a highly significant positive correlation between the rate of growth of output and the rate of growth of employment in the manufacturing sector, whereas *there is no* correlation between the rate of growth of output and the rate of growth of total employment.[31] These two findings were mutually compatible and confirmed Kaldor's view that the growth rates of

Kaldor considered a series of phenomena tended to disprove his thesis of the shortage of labour in the manufacturing sector. Wolfe noted that: (1) employment in services had grown more than it had in the manufacturing sector; (2) that certain growing manufacturing sectors, esp. the mechanical and electrical industries, had increased their levels of employment—and to a considerable extent; (3) if there had been a shortage of labour in the manufacturing sector, there would have been lower unemployment, whereas in fact there had been high rates of unemployment in the mechanical and building industries, which registered a high rate of growth of output; (4) there was no difference in the unemployment rate net of unfilled vacancies between the secondary and the tertiary sectors; (5) wage rates had not risen more in the manufacturing sector than in other sectors; indeed the reverse was probably the case.

[29] N. Kaldor, 'Productivity and Growth in Manufacturing Industry: A Reply', *EC* (Nov. 1968), 386.

[30] Two forces are simultaneously at work in the services sector: on the one hand industrialization absorbs surplus labour; on the other, the growth of industry induces growth in demand for various kinds of services. Thus total employment in services rises with industrialization, although it rises *less* when the overall growth of output is faster.

[31] In his rejoinder to Wolfe, Kaldor referred to the same period and to the same countries as he had done in his inaugural lecture. He gave the following two equations: $g\text{GDP} = 2.665 + 1.066\,em$, $R^2 = 0.828$; $g\text{GDP} = 4.421 + 0.431\,e$, $R^2 = 0.018$; ibid. 387.

overall productivity correlate positively with the rates of growth of employment in the manufacturing sector and negatively with those of the non-manu-
facturing sector.[32]

An economy reaches its maturity when the dual economy disappears—that
is, when the labour surplus is exhausted and when wages are at the same level
in all sectors. When this stage is reached, one would say that there is an
effective labour-supply constraint. The closer an economy approaches it, the
greater the general increase in wages throughout the economy and the lower
the level of unemployment in all sectors, not just in manufacturing. Indeed the
level of unemployment in manufacturing will tend to be greater than elsewhere
because a mature economy is more prone to stop-go policies, which exert a
greater influence on demand and employment in manufacturing than they do
in other sectors.

There has never been a long-run labour-supply constraint on the development of the manufacturing sectors of capitalist economies. Open or disguised
unemployment, foreign migration, or the entry of new social groups (women)
into the labour-market have always provided the necessary supply of manpower.[33] We may therefore conclude our treatment of Kaldor's third law by
saying that it plays a secondary role in explanation of the differences in rates
of economic growth (a task performed now by Kaldor's fourth law). Instead,
it provides support for his first law by giving one further reason (apart from
the Kaldor–Verdoorn law) for the positive correlation between the overall rate
of growth and output per worker and the growth of output in the manufacturing
sector.

Kaldor's third law—the law of labour migration—we may therefore summarize as follows: (1) 'surplus labour' is also to be found in the industrialized
economies; (2) the supply of labour to the manufacturing sector is elastic and
may stem from the migration of workers from lower-productivity sectors;
(3) the withdrawal of labour from other sectors increases overall productivity;
(4) an economy is mature when the labour surplus disappears and wages are
the same in all sectors of the economy.

Before this final stage is reached—and Britain had not yet reached it by the
end of the 1960s—other constraints on the demand side come into operation.

7.6. The Law of the Foreign-Trade Multiplier

We can now sum up as follows: (1) Kaldor's central idea is expressed by his
first law: it is the growth of industrial output that determines the overall
growth rate of the economy, and this is because industrial growth is a net

---

[32] This was confirmed by the following 3 equations: $p\text{GDP} = 1.868 + 0.991\,em$, $R^2 = 0.677$;
$p\text{GDP} = 4.924 - 1.800\,enm$, $R^2 = 0.427$; $p\text{GDP} = 2.899 + 0.821\,em - 1.183\,enm$, $R^2 = 0.842$.

[33] J. Cornwall, 'Diffusion, Convergence and Kaldor's Laws', *EJ* (June 1976). id., *Modern
Capitalism* (London, Martin Robinson, 1977).

increment in resources, not just the shifting of resources from one use to another; (2) the second law—which states that increasing returns operate in the manufacturing sector—supports these conclusions but is not in itself necessary; (3) the first law entails that capital accumulation is self-generating as output increases; (4) the first law presupposes the operation of a third law, according to which industrial labour has no real opportunity cost outside the sector itself because of surplus labour in agriculture and in services.

The existence of surplus labour and the crucial role played by expectations of profit in the process of capital accumulation constitute the principle differences between the neo-classical economists, for whom economic growth is the outcome of exogenous growth in the endowment of capital and labour factors combined with exogenous technical progress, and the post-Keynesians, for whom economic growth is 'induced by demand and not limited by resources'.[34] However, 'industrial activities, unlike agricultural activities, are not "self-sustaining"—they are dependent on the demand for their goods coming from *outside* the industrial sector'.[35]

This implies, not that 'outside demand' absorbs all or most of industrial activity, but that it is the ultimate causal factor that accounts for all other activities. Every additional sale outside the sector initiates a 'multiplier' effect whereby domestic activity amounts to $1/(1-k)$ times the original sale, where k is the proportion of the income spent in the sector itself.

Therefore, if growth is constrained by demand, rather than basing analysis on differences in factor endowments—the approach adopted by much of the literature on the subject[36]—we should examine differences in growth rates in the light of the different dynamic of this demand component, which behaves as an exogenous or autonomous factor.

Kaldor held both consumption and investment to be substantially endogenous, in that they depend, via the accelerator, on the growth of income itself.[37] These two demand components can explain growth in manufacturing production only in particular circumstances.[38] Nor does autonomous demand from the public sector have a significant role to play in the long-term growth of the economy either, except in periods when there is a rapid increase in arms expenditure. It follows, therefore, that in peacetime conditions exports are the

[34] N. Kaldor, 'Economic Growth and the Verdoorn Law: A Comment on Mr Rowthorn's Article', *EJ* (Dec. 1975).

[35] Id., 'Causes of Growth and Stagnation in the World Economy', Mattioli lectures at the Università Boccori of Milan, 21–5 May 1984, lecture 4, p. 3.

[36] E. Denison, 'Why Growth Rates Differ: Postwar Experience in Nine Western Countries', *The Brooking Institution* (Washington, DC, 1967).

[37] The idea that, in the long run, the growth of output is governed by the growth of autonomous demand to which other components adjust via the 'super-multiplier' had been developed a number of years before by Hicks (see J. Hicks, *The Trade Cycle* (London, OUP, 1950)). On the use of the super-multiplier in the case of export growth, see J. S. L. McCombie, 'Economic Growth, the Harrod Foreign Trade Multiplier and the Hicks Super-Multiplier', *Applied Economics* (Feb. 1985).

[38] e.g. in the early stages of industrialization and in the presence of an agricultural revolution, the national income and the demand for products from the manufacturing sector may increase as a result of the development of the primary sector. For more detailed treatment see Ch. 9.3.

sole source of exogenous demand in an industrialized economy,[39] and that in every case the chief constraint on a country's growth is its trade balance. Kaldor used Harrod's multiplier principle[40] to show that the different dynamic of exports could explain the differences in the performances of countries. Harrod was the first economist to formulate the idea of the 'foreign-trade multiplier' as the cause of fluctuations in industrial output and as the mechanism that keeps the trade balance in equilibrium.[41] If exports X induce, through changes in income, expenditure on consumption and investment (induced by the accelerator) of an amount kY, after a certain time-lag one obtains the well-known formula for the multiplier:

(7.5) $Y = X(1/1 - k)$.

If the marginal propensity to import is m, and if M_a is autonomous imports, we have $M = M_a + mY$. For payments to balance we have $M = X$. Thus

(7.6) $Y = (X - M_a) \cdot 1/m$.

The two formulae (7.5) and (7.6) are equal if we assume that $m = 1 - k$: i.e. that income is wholly spent on domestic demand and imports. Given exogenous exports, as M increases, equation (7.6) tells us that income Y falls and that X/Y therefore increases. Kaldor first used this argument in a letter to *The Times*[42] in which he accused two economists[43] of having ignored this principle when claiming that the share of British exports had increased autonomously. For Kaldor the increase resulted from the greater penetration of imports on the British market which, by reducing income through the Harrod multiplier, had increased the share of exports in income. It was the autonomous increase in M/Y that had induced X/Y to increase.

As a matter of fact, the formula is an extremely limiting one. Among other things, it makes no allowance for other income leakages such as savings and taxes, nor for other autonomous demands like public expenditure; and it omits the import content of exports. Despite these limitations, however, an elaboration of equation (7.6) can develop it into an extremely powerful basis for explanation of international growth rate differences.[44]

Let us begin with a six-equation growth model, in which the roman letters all represent rates of growth and the Greek letters stand for parameters. The first is the export equation:

[39] An increase in domestic demand can come about in countries that have industrialized themselves through 'import substitution'. For Kaldor this was a process that was bound to fail, if it was anything more than purely temporary.

[40] N. Kaldor, 'The Role of Increasing Returns, Technical Progress and Cumulative Causation in the Theory of International Trade and Economic Growth' (1980), *EA* repr. in CP ix.

[41] R. Harrod, *International Economics* (Cambridge, Cambridge Economic Handbooks, 1933).

[42] N. Kaldor, *TT* (7 Sept. 1977).

[43] J. D. Wells and J. C. Imber, 'The Home and Export Performance of U.K. Industries', *Economic Trend* (Aug. 1977).

[44] For further details see R. J. Dixon and A. P. Thirlwall, 'A Model of Regional Growth Rate Differences on Kaldorian Lines', *OEP* (July 1975); C. Kennedy and A. P. Thirlwall, 'Import Penetration, Export Performance and Harrod's Trade Multiplier', *OEP* (July 1979).

(7.7) $$x = \pi(pi - pe - r) + \varepsilon z$$

where x is the rate of growth of exports, pi and pe the rate of growth of internal and external price levels, r the rate of growth of the exchange rate (if r is positive the country devalues its currency), and z the rate of growth of world income. The second is the import equation:

(7.8) $$m = \lambda(pe - pi + r) + \eta g$$

where m is the rate of growth of imports, and g of the GNP. The third equation is internal pricing, which, under the hypotheses of constant mark-up, constant wages, and zero import content of the national product, can be stated in growth terms as:

(7.9) $$pi = -pr$$

where pr is the rate of growth of productivity. The rate of growth of external price levels is taken exogenously. The fourth equation is a Kaldor–Verdoorn equation for the economy as a whole:

(7.10) $$pr = \alpha + \beta g.$$

The fifth equation is Hicks's super-multiplier:

(7.11) $$g = \delta a.$$

The last equation is the long-run equilibrium of the trade balance:

(7.12) $$pi + x = pe + m + r.$$

The model can be used for two purposes. If we leave the import equation (7.8) and the trade-balance constraint (7.12) out of consideration, and if we substitute (7.10) in (7.9), the result in (7.7) and the result in (7.11), we obtain:

(7.13) $$g = \delta[\varepsilon z - \pi(\alpha + pe + r)]/(1 + \delta\pi\beta).$$

The rate of growth of a country thus depends positively on the growth of world income (because $\pi < 0$), on autonomous growth of productivity, on the growth of foreign prices, and on the depreciation of the currency rate (it is assumed to affect neither wage rates, which are taken to be constant, nor, consequently, the rate of internal prices).

Having introduced equation (7.10) and the Kaldor–Verdoorn coefficient β, the model becomes 'circular' and reveals the likelihood of a virtuous circle of export-led growth. If two economies with different income elasticities of demand in world markets (ε) are compared, the exports of the economy with the higher elasticity will grow relatively faster than the other economy's exports. This gives rise to a higher rate of growth of output which, thanks to the positive value of the Kaldor–Verdoorn coefficient, leads in a cumulative process to higher productivity growth, lower domestic prices and higher export growth.[45]

---

[45] Whether the growth rates of different countries will tend to diverge or converge over time depends on the behaviour of the model out of equilibrium and on the stability of the parameters. See Dixon and Thirlwall, 'Model of Regional Growth Rate Differences on Kaldorian Lines'.

The model can serve a second purpose. If we assume that the real terms of trade are constant, i.e. if

$$pi - pe - r = 0$$

and if, consequently, we restrict ourselves to a reduced form of equations (7.7) and (7.8), and if we impose a reduced form of the trade-balance constraint of equation (7.12), the model becomes:

$$x = \varepsilon z, \quad m = \eta g, \quad x = m.$$

From this latter model we may deduce the following equation:

(7.14) $g = x/\eta$

which states that if the balance of payments is kept in equilibrium, the long-term rate of growth of income, g, is determined by the rate of growth of exports, x, divided by the elasticity of imports relative to income, η. This formula, which has been given the name either of the 'dynamic Harrod foreign-trade multiplier'[46] or of 'Thirlwall's law', can take the following alternative form:

(7.15) $g/z = \varepsilon/\eta.$

That is to say, the ratio between a country's rate of growth and that of the rest of the world is given by the ratio of the two elasticities of imports relative to income. Thirlwall has declared, that when formula (7.14) is verified empirically, it produces values that come extraordinarily close to the effective growth rates of a large number of countries over a long period of time.[47]

Thirlwall's law has aroused a great deal of controversy.[48] Formula (7.14) has been dismissed as a reduced formula with an empirical validity which constitutes no proof of the theoretical considerations on which it is based. Its empirical validity has been challenged as well, by McGregor and Swales,[49] and so too has its assumption of a constant long-run inflation differential among countries. Thirlwall has countered these objections by pointing out that the constant inflation differential is explainable by the coexistence in the

[46] In fact, (7.14) is deducible from (7.6) once–is the marginal propensity to import $m = \delta M/\delta Y$. If we go on to differentiate (7.6) in relation to time and divide the left member by Y and the right member by $X/(M/Y)$, which is also equal to Y, we obtain: $(dY/Y)(1/dt)$ $= [dX/X)/(\delta M/\delta Y)(Y/M)](1/dt)$ which is formula (7.14).
[47] A. P. Thirlwall, 'The Balance of Payments Constraint as an Explanation of International Growth Rate Differences', *BNLQR* (Mar. 1979). R. J. Dixon and A. P. Thirlwall, 'A Model of Export-Led Growth with a Balance of Payment Constraint', in J. Bowers (ed.), *Inflation, Development and Integration: Essays in Honour of A. J. Brown* (Leeds, University of Leeds Press, 1979). These models differ from the early export-led models of Beckerman and Lamfalussy in their explicit consideration of the constraint on growth given by the trade-balance long-run equilibrium.
[48] J. S. L. McCombie, 'Are International Growth Rates Constrained by the Balance of Payments? A Comment on Professor Thirlwall', *BNLQR* (1981). A. P. Thirlwall, 'A Reply to Mr McCombie', *BNLQR* (Dec. 1981).
[49] P. J. McGregor and J. K. Swales, 'Professor Thirlwall and Balance of Payments Constrained Growth', *Applied Economics*, 17: 1 (1985); A. P. Thirlwall, 'Balance of Payments Constrained Growth: A Reply to McGregor and Swales', *Applied Economics*, 18: 2 (1986); P. J. McGregor and J. K. Swales, 'Balance of Payments Constrained Growth: A Rejoinder to Professor Thirlwall', *Applied Economics*, 18: 2 (1986); J. Fagerberg, 'International Competitiveness' *EJ* (June 1988).

world market of different competitive regimes—competition and oligopoly—for different traded commodities. Further, the poor econometric results obtained by his critics when applying the formula arise from their use of cross-section regressions instead of more accurate time series, and because they have used incomplete samples in which deficits and surpluses do not sum to zero. Finally, recent empirical research testing the law expressed by formulae (7.13) and (7.14) for the period 1970–85—even though these years were regarded as least favourable for its validation—has produced largely corroborative results.[50] This outcome confirms both the validity of Harrod's theory that imports and exports adjust through variations in income (rather than through variations in exchange rates or relative prices), and also Kaldor's explanation of the differing performances by countries in terms of high export growth and low import penetration.

We thus come to the fourth law, which we may label 'the Kaldor–Thirlwall law' and summarize in five propositions: (1) economic growth is 'demand-induced' not 'resource constrained'; (2) the rate of growth of output of every area or 'region' is mainly led by the external demand for its products; (3) import variations are governed by real income variations rather than by price variations (real income varies with changes in the terms of trade and in output); (4) the growth of a country's exports must be seen—with world income remaining equal[51]—as the result of the efforts by producers to seek out potential markets and to adapt their productive structure to this purpose (I shall return to this point in the final section of the present chapter); (5) the main constraint on the economic growth of a country is given by its balance of payments.

7.7. Virtuous and Vicious Circles: A Reinterpretation of Great Britain's Low Rate of Growth

It is, therefore, international relationships that condition the rapidity of a country's growth. And the pure theory of international trade from Ricardo to Mill, from Marshall to Hecksher-Ohlin, has been unable to find a convincing explanation for this process.

If a country mostly produces goods subject to decreasing returns, where land and not labour is the limiting factor, and if another country produces mainly manufactured goods subject to increasing returns, the opening of international

---

[50] E. Bairam, 'Balance of Payments: The Harrod Foreign Trade Multiplier and Economic Growth: The European and North American Experience 1970–1985', *Applied Economics*, 20 (1988). E. Bairam, 'The Harrod Foreign Trade Multiplier Revisited', *Applied Economics*, 22: 6 (1990). The formula (7.14) is a rather good approximation of actual rates of growth in the countries considered: in all cases, imports and exports are not significantly affected by prices, but by income (with the partial exception of West Germany).

[51] If the world is treated as a whole, the system is a closed one and exports cannot stand as the exogenous component. In this case, for Kaldor the world sector producing raw materials is exogenous to the world industrial sector. See Ch. 8.

trade brings the price of manufactured goods in terms of agricultural products so low in the manufacturing country that such activity practically disappears in the other. If the workers thus 'freed' from manufacturing production can produce more agricultural products, the real income of the agricultural country will, the theory requires, be higher than before. But if land is in short supply this is impossible. Nor can more manufactured goods be produced by reducing wages, for there is a minimum wage in terms of agricultural products below which workers in the manufacturing sector cannot survive. The opening of international trade for the agricultural country results in increased exports of agricultural products but a lower national income, because the income earned from the greater quantity of agricultural exports cannot compensate for the loss of income resulting from the demise of the manufacturing sector. International trade makes the agricultural country poorer, with lower employment and a lower national product. This impoverishment of the agricultural country is matched by the enrichment of its manufacturing counterpart.

This outcome contradicts the classical and neo-classical pure theory of international trade, according to which free trade benefits every participant country by reallocating resources in such a way that every unit of labour can contribute more than previously to the national product. The reason for this is the classical and neo-classical assumption of constant returns in all activities and, for neo-classical theory, in the assumption that there exist production functions that are homogeneous for all commodities and equal for every country.[52] On the basis of these assumptions, and in the absence of mobility of factors, it is widely known that, according to Samuelson's factor-price-equalization theorem, trade in commodities equalizes the price of the factors. Therefore not only do all countries benefit from international trade, but the poor countries benefit even more than the rich ones.

However, the realities of world trade in the nineteenth and twentieth centuries have disproved this theoretical conclusion: the gap between the rich and poor countries has instead widened.[53] Since decreasing returns predominate in the poor agricultural countries, and increasing returns in the rich industrial ones, the effect of international trade has been to increase the gap in per-capita income between the two groups. Different returns and international trade are responsible for the process that Gunnar Myrdal called 'circular and cumulative causation';[54] and free trade in manufactured goods has led to the concentration of manufacturing production in certain areas[55] and to its inhibition in others.[56]

[52] As is well known, the neo-classical model differentiates countries only by their factor endowments, not by their production techniques.

[53] Neo-classical economists have recently seemed willing to accept some of Kaldor's more provocative arguments. See P. Krugman, 'Trade, Accumulation and Uneven Development', *Journal of Development Economics* (Apr. 1981).

[54] G. Myrdal, *Economic Theory and Underdeveloped Regions* (London, Duckworth, 1957).

[55] Following this line of reasoning—developed mainly in 'Role of Increasing Returns'—Kaldor analysed the problem of the polarization of regional development and suggested a number of policies for regional development: N. Kaldor, 'The Case for Regional Policies', *SJPE* (Nov. 1970); id., 'Why are Regional Policies Necessary?', in *Regionalpolitik und Agrarpolitik in Europa* (Berlin,

All this is summed up by the opening sentences of Kaldor's 'The Role of Increasing Returns, Technical Progress and Cumulative Causation in the Theory of International Trade and Economic Growth'. They constitute a sort of anti-*laissez-faire* manifesto:

Traditional theory, both classical and neo-classical, asserts that free trade in goods between different regions is always to the advantage of *each* trading country, and is therefore the best arrangment from the point of view of the welfare of the trading world as a whole, as well as of each part of the world taken separately. However, these propositions are only true under specific abstract assumptions which do not correspond to reality. Under more realistic assumptions unrestricted trade is likely to lead to a loss of welfare to particular regions or countries and even to the world as a whole—that is to say that the world will be worse off under free trade than it could be under *some* system of regulated trade.[57]

However, the diffusion of knowledge, the development of transport, and in part trade itself have led not only to the 'polarization process' described above, but also to the 'spread of industrialization'. It is this latter process (of the opposite sign to polarization) that Kaldor holds responsible for the long-term decline of the British economy.[58] The spread of industrialization, in fact, is successful to the extent that the newly industrialized country manages to implement a strategy based on exports; meaning, at least in some sectors, an increase in its share of the international market. At the same time, an older industrialized country sees a reduction in its share of the international market and often greater import penetration of its domestic market as well. According to the fourth of Kaldor's laws, a slow-down in growth and greater penetration by imports entail a decline in a country's growth of income and employment. These effects can be blunted if the older industrialized country counterbalances imports of mature goods with its own exports of more advanced technological goods to the newly industrialized country, which has a growing income. But there is no reason why these two contrasting factors—greater import penetration and an increase in the incomes of the countries traded with—should, in a system of multilateral exchanges, balance each other out in any particular country.

In the nineteenth century Great Britain benefited from the polarization process; in the twentieth century the country has suffered from the process of

Dunker & Humboldt, 1975); id., 'The Foundations of Free Trade Theory and their Implications for the Current World Recession', in E. Malinvaud and S. P. Fitoussi (eds.), *Unemployment in Western Countries* (London, Macmillan, 1980).

[56] British manufacturing received a major boost from the transport revolution and from the opening of markets in Europe, South America, India, and China. International trade 'specialized' many of these areas in the production of raw materials. Such activities could by their nature only occupy a minor proportion of the population. The dependence of many of these areas on activities with decreasing returns was, for Kaldor, the cause of their impoverishment.

[57] Kaldor, 'Role of Increasing Returns', 201.

[58] Ibid.; and esp. id., 'Capitalism and Industrial Development: Some Lessons from Britain's Experience', *CJE* (June 1977).

the diffusion of industrialization. Until 1870 the share of British exports on the world market had created primary products and then brought them to the United Kingdom, while international trade distributed British manufactured products throughout the world (destroying much local manufacturing in the process). Simultaneously, however, the countries of Europe and North America industrialized themselves by importing British capital goods, and then protected their own industries against competition from British finished goods.[59] There followed a period in which the United Kingdom maintained its share of the world market because it exported more technologically advanced products. This situation could not last, however; and soon, after the protectionist phase, the countries of second industrialization turned into exporters, first of goods produced by their light industry and then of heavy industrial goods. Britain's loss of markets was delayed for a further sixty to seventy years by the creation of new ones through British financial investments in the industrializing countries (the typical example being the railways of Latin America and India). But this protection was not enough: once the late comers—initially protected by tariff barriers—had become competitive, they increased their share of the international market and successfully challenged British industry.

As we saw in the previous section, a country's growth is higher compared with the rest of world, the greater its share of exports in world demand and the lower its share of imports in domestic GNP.[60] A country with an increasing share of the market attains a faster rate of growth of output than does a country with a diminishing share. Between the end of the Second World War and the early 1970s the world economy enjoyed an unexpected boom and, unlike the 1880–1940 period, a rate of growth of inter-industrial exchanges higher than the rate of growth of industrial production itself. This gave rise to the paradoxical situation where two countries, the United States and Great Britain, registered their highest ever domestic growth rates but the lowest growth rates among all industrialized economies. This was explained by two factors: the boom in world trade, which accounted for the maximum levels of development of the two countries; and Britain's and America's loss of their market shares to continental Europe and to Japan—the reason for their minimum rates of comparative development. Of the two countries, however, the privileged po-

---

[59] Newly created Germany protected first her light industry and then her heavy industry against British competition by means of the Bismarck tariffs of 1879. The USA followed Germany when the McKinley tariff made her isolationist. It was then the turn of Italy under Giolitti, with a tariff policy that was an expression of an alliance between the new and the old—the 'historical bloc' (to use Gramsci's term) comprising northern industrialists and absentee landowners in the South. Japan instead adopted a more courageous policy to achieve economic take-off via subsidies to exports financed by a land tax.

[60] This can be demonstrated as follows: in the general case where the marginal propensity to import varies, by differentiating equation (7.6) in relation to time, we obtain: $dY/dt = (1/m) (dX/dt) - (x/m^2)(dm/dt)$. Dividing by Y, under the constraint $X = M$, and subtracting from both sides of the equation the growth of world demand $(dY_w/Y_w)(1/dt)$, we obtain: $(dY/Y - dY/Y_w) (1/dt) = [(dX/X - dY_w/Y_w) - (dM/M - dY/Y)](1/dt)$.

sition of the dollar in the post-war international monetary system made the United States less prone to stop-go policies than Great Britain, and until very recently the growth of the United States has been less dependent on the balance-of-payments constraint.[61]

This section has outlined what we may take to be Kaldor's vision of the economic history of the capitalist countries over the last two centuries, with its emphasis on the factors that create divergences among countries. There is, however, a quite different view which takes the basic forces responsible for the rate of growth of countries to be those that induce the late-comer countries to 'catch up' with the first-comer country or countries. The idea that the follower countries seek to close the technological and economic gap between them and the leader has its roots in the work of Veblen and Gerschenkron.[62] So-called 'catching up' theory has recently been extended to embrace longer periods of time, and also to explain more recent trends in the economic growth of output and productivity in developed countries[63] (note, however, that the theory breaks down when applied to underdeveloped countries—a not negligible weakness). This theory of convergence among countries has also been specifically contrasted with Kaldor's theory of cumulative economic divergences among countries.[64]

---

[61] In my opinion, Thirlwall's formula (7.14) is a good approximation of the rate of growth of countries except for Japan and the USA. The formula overestimates Japan's growth, which is not limited by an external constraint, but most probably by internal ones (e.g. land); it underestimates American growth because the USA can overcome the external constraint given by the trade balance for longer periods than other countries on account of its peculiar position on world financial markets. For a partly critical assessment of Thirlwall's formula when applied to Japan and the USA during the 1980s, see F. Targetti, 'The Economic Instabilities of the Eighties', in J. Michie (ed.), *The Economics of Restructuring and Intervention* (London, Edward Elgar, 1991).

[62] T. Veblen, *Industrial Revolution and Imperial Germany* (1914; New York, Viking Press, 1939). A. Gerschenkron, *Economic Backwardness in Historical Perspective* (Cambridge, Mass., Harvard University Press, 1965).

[63] A. Maddison, *Phases of Capitalist Development* (Oxford, OUP, 1982); R. Marris, 'How Much of the Slow-Down was Catch-Up?', in R. C. O. Matthews (ed.), *Slower Growth in the Western World* (London, Heinemann, 1982); M. Abramovitz, 'Catching Up, Forging Ahead and Falling Behind', *Journal of Economic History*, 46: 2 (1986); S. Gomulka, 'Catching Up', in J. Eatwell *et al.* (eds.), *The New Palgrave: A Dictionary of Economics*, (London, Macmillan, 1987); S. Gomulka, 'The Gerschenkron Phenomenon and Systemic Factors in the Post-1975 Growth Slowdown', *European Economic Review*, 32 (1988); J. Fagerberg, 'A Technology Gap Approach to Why Growth Rates Differ', *Research Policy*, 16: 2–4 (1987); id., 'Why Growth Rates Differ', in G. Dosi *et al.* (eds.), *Technical Change and Economic Theory* (London, Frances Pinter, 1988); A. Maddison, *The World Economy in the 20th Century* (Paris, OECD, 1989). This recent intensification of empirical study stems from the work of I. Kravis, who has recalculated output and per-capita output of a large group of countries for long periods of time on the basis of purchasing power parity.

[64] S. Gomulka and M. E. Schaffer, 'Kaldor's Stylized Facts, and Systemic, and Diffusion Effects in Productivity Growth', in G. Fink *et al.* (eds.), *Economic Theory, Political Power and Social Justice* (Vienna, Springer, 1987).

7.8. The Debate on Kaldor's Laws

A weak link in Kaldor's argument is his explanation of why, in a process of polarization, an older industrialized country should lose its shares of the market to recently industrialized ones.[65] The successful diffusion of industrialization may mean that competitiveness does not arise *solely* from endogenous technical progress—an implication of Kaldor's theory which has led to wide-ranging controversies on the Kaldor–Verdoorn law, on the endogeneity of technical progress, and on cumulative processes.

The debate on Kaldor's laws has been part of a more generalized conflict between two competing explanations for the differing rates of growth of output among countries. The classical or neo-classical supply-oriented approach has stressed the role of factor inputs in limiting growth: excess public spending, which structurally displaces private investments;[66] differing trade-union attitudes in their opposition to innovations; the diverse social environments in which technical progress can take place.[67] The post-Keynesian or Kaldorian demand-oriented approach has instead emphasized the role of demand factors, combined with the balance-of-payments constraint, as the crucial element in explanation of why growth rates differ.

Important verification of Kaldor's first law is provided by a study of the European countries conducted by Boyer and Petit. The merits of this study are that it treated the relations linking growth, productivity, and employment together as medium-term phenomena, not as short-term fluctuations, and that its analysis extended to the 1970s. As regards Kaldor's first law, Boyer and Petit's findings support Kaldor's thesis that in the medium period it is industry that acts as the engine of the economy as a whole. In fact, the hierarchy of

[65] I asked Francis Cripps—who discussed the subject with Kaldor at length—how Kaldor would have answered the objection that if the 'polarization principle' was valid, it did not explain why GB had lost shares of the market to late-comer countries. According to Cripps, Kaldor's position was that in the 19th cent. GB *already* had a great world market and was a free-trader; the late-comer countries were protectionist, and under their protective umbrella they were able to *increase* their market. Since increasing returns are achieved as a result of the *growth* of the market and not as a result of its *size*, the late-comer countries entered a virtuous circle where output increase ––> productivity increase ––> market increase ––> output increase, to the detriment of the British markets. To the objection that, according to this line of reasoning, the protection of infant German or Japanese industry gave results different from those obtained by the imperial preferential tariffs, Kaldor replied that the Commonwealth was not a proper market comparable with those of Germany or Japan.

[66] R. Bacon and W. Eltis, *Britain's Economic Problems: Too Few Producers* (London, Macmillan, 1978).

[67] S. Gomulka, *Incentive Activity and the Stages of Economic Growth* (Aarhus Institute of Economics, 1971); A. Kilpatrick and T. Lawson, 'On the Nature of Industrial Decline in the U.K.', *CJE* 4 (1980); G. Hodgson, 'Theoretical and Policy Implications of Variable Productivity', *CJE* (Sept. 1983). For a critique of the Kaldorian cumulative process from a neo-Marxist standpoint, where greater weight is given to the social structure in constraining the process, see D. M. Gordon, 'Kaldor's Macro-System: Too Much Cumulation, Too Little Disaccumulation', paper presented to the conference at New school for Social Research and Bard College, New York, 29–31 Oct. 1987, proceedings pub. under the conference title: E. J. Nell and W. Semmler (eds.), *Nicholas Kaldor and Mainstream Economics: Confrontation or Convergence* (New York, St Martins Press, 1991).

productivity levels among the six European economies examined match those of their industries. Moreover the study shows that, in the medium period and even more so between 1973 and 1976, it was the growth of manufacturing output that induced the growth of the services and agricultural sectors and therefore of the overall economy. (Building and public works had a stimulating role during the 1950s and a passive one during the 1970s.)[68] However, a subsequent cross-country study referring to the three sub-periods of 1960–73, 1973–9, and 1979–84 shows that, in the most recent period, de-industrialization and 'tertiarization' have diminished the validity of Kaldor's first law.[69] As far as Britain is concerned, in fact, industry lost its role as the engine of growth as early as 1965.[70]

Kaldor's second law aroused fierce controversy. The first and most trenchant criticism of his use of the Verdoorn equation was Rowthorn's,[71] who took as his point of departure the relation between manufacturing output and manufacturing employment—which Kaldor used in 1966 and 1967 to verify his law, and which Cripps and Tarling[72] put again to the test in 1973.[73] From these relations—especially if one takes Cripps and Tarling's specification of them—one concludes that these authors believed that the growth of manufacturing output *depends* on the growth of employment in the sector itself.[74] This, as we know (see Chapter 7.5), is not consistent with the development of Kaldor's ideas after 1968. Rowthorn was probably unaware that Kaldor had changed his mind (it may have passed his notice because Cripps and Tarling—members of the 'Kaldorian' DAE at Cambridge—were still using the same specification). He therefore argued: (1) that Kaldor's and Cripps and Tarling's relation

---

[68] R. Boyer and P. Petit, 'Productivité dans l'industrie et croissance à moyen terme', *Cepremap*, 8102 (Paris, Dec. 1980). 'Progrès tecnique, croissance et emploi: un modèle d'inspiration Kaldorienne pour six industries europeénnes', *Revue Économique* (Nov. 1981).

[69] P. Petit, *Slow Growth and the Service Economy* (London, Frances Pinter, 1986).

[70] V. J. Stavrinos, 'The Intertemporal Stability of Kaldor's First and Second Growth Laws in the U.K.', *Applied Economics*, 19 (1987).

[71] R. Rowthorn, 'What Remains of Kaldor's Law?', *EJ* (Mar. 1975).

[72] T. F. Cripps and R. J. Tarling, *Growth in Advanced Capitalist Economies 1950–1970* (Cambridge, CUP, 1973).

[73] Since the rate of growth of manufacturing output (gm) is given by the sum of the growth rates of productivity (pm) and of employment (em), Kaldor–Verdoorn's relation can have four specifications: $pm = a + b \cdot gm$, $0 < b < 1$; $em = a + (1 - b)gm$, $gm = a/(1 - b) + [1/(1 - b)]em$, $pm = a/(1 - b) + [(b/(1 - b)]em$. The first specification was the one generally used. Kaldor used the first two in his lectures, Cripps and Tarling the third, Rowthorn the fourth. Rowthorn's criticism was that the second and third formulae constituted an indirect method of investigation when assessing the relation between the growth of productivity and the growth of employment, while the fourth was a direct method. Prof. Beckerman has told me that, as early as 1965, he had pointed out to Kaldor that his research findings (W. Beckerman, *The British Economy in 1975*, app. 7, p. 530) showed there was no correlation between productivity and employment, although there was between productivity and output.

[74] Before 1968 Kaldor did in fact believe that there was a correlation between productivity growth rates and the growth rates of manufacture labour input. Since there was no more labour to be squeezed out of agriculture, in order to increase the productivity growth rate of British industry, labour would have to be squeezed out of the tertiary sector. And for this purpose he advised the Labour government to introduce the SET—which it did in 1966 (see Ch. 10).

should be taken to mean that manufacturing output *depends* on the growth of
employment, which is the exogenous magnitude; (2) that the formula misrep-
resents Verdoorn's relation; (3) that although Kaldor's results, as well as those
of Cripps and Tarling, were mostly accurate for the 1951–65 period (but less
so for the following period), they depended on the inclusion of Japan among
their sample of countries. Had Japan not been included, the econometric
relation (correctly specified) would have been much poorer; (4) international
differences in productivity were better interpreted in the light of the notion of
the 'technological gap'.[75]

Kaldor objected that Rowthorn had both misunderstood and misrepresented
his theory.[76] He admonished him for failing to realize that the first law—
deduced from the close correlation between the growth of gross national
product and the growth of industrial output—was still valid even if the second
law (Kaldor–Verdoorn) on returns to scale did not apply: this was because of
the operation of his third law—namely, that the growth of manufacturing
production reduces employment in the sector with diminishing returns.[77]

In Kaldor's view, the weakness in Rowthorn's first criticism (point (1)) was
his mistaken interpretation of causal relationships: output must be taken to be
the exogenous variable and employment to be the endogenous one, not the
other way round as Rowthorn maintained.[78] Rowthorn's failure to give a
proper account of cause and effect was also responsible for the inadequacy of
his second criticism (point (2)). The existence of a significant relation between
the growth of employment and the growth of output was the best available test
for deciding whether the law had something concrete to say about reality, or
whether it was merely a statistical mirage. In Kaldor's specification, the law
held true for industry but not for agriculture and services; hence one could
legitimately claim that, behind the statistical relation, the law of increasing
returns was at work. This was a sufficient condition (if the coefficient was
significantly lower than one) for the law; whereas Rowthorn's specification
(used by Kaldor in the 1968 article, which Rowthorn had not referred to) was
a necessary one. Regarding Rowthorn's third criticism (point (3)), various
studies subsequent to the debate showed that the significance of the Kaldor–

---

[75] Gomulka, *Incentive Activity, Diffusion and the Stages of Economic Growth.*

[76] N. Kaldor, 'Economic Growth and the Verdoorn Law: A Comment on Mr. Rowthorn's
Article', (Dec. 1975).

[77] This had already been shown by Cripps and Tarling (*Growth in Advanced Capitalist Economies 1950–1970*), who used the following equations (not considered by Rowthorn) relative to
two 5-year periods to place the economy's overall productivity dynamic ($pGNP$) in direct relation
to the growth of industrial output (gi) and in inverse relation to the growth of industrial employment (eni): 1950–65: $pGNP = 1.172 + 0.543gi - 0.812eni$, $R^2 = 0.805$; 1965–70: $pGNP = 1.153
+ 0.642gi - 0.872eni$, $R^2 = 0.958$.

[78] Parikh used a model of simultaneous equations for the manufacturing sector (which tests both
Kaldor's and Rowthorn's specifications) where employment is a function of output growth and of
the growth of the work-force, and output growth is a function of employment growth, export
growth, and the share of investment in output. He finds that employment is endogenous, and that
it is output growth in manufacturing that determines and constrains employment, not the other way
round. A. Parikh, 'Differences in Growth Rates and Kaldor's Laws', *EC* (Feb. 1978).

Verdoorn relation did not depend on whether Japan was included or not, since the relation was significant even when it applied to the European countries alone.[79] Finally Kaldor's rejection of Rowthorn's primitive explanation of Great Britain's decline, which he saw in terms of insufficient labour supply to the manufacturing sector, led Kaldor to emphasize the role of exogenous demand and to warn against following in the footsteps of 'Rowthorn, Gomulka or the neo-classicals'. In particular, the argument that the higher rate of productivity growth of late-comer countries like Japan could be explained by the diffusion of technological knowledge (point (4)) failed to take account of the fact that the growth of productivity of the follower and imitator countries continued to be higher even after the productivity *level* of these countries had outstripped the level of the countries that had diffused the technology.[80]

Discussion of the Kaldor–Verdoorn law continued in numerous articles and papers,[81] many of them concentrating on the weight to be given to the capital factor and, more in general, on the use of the production function in making a presumably correct derivation of the law.[82] I shall not go into details of this discussion here: the reader is referred to Kaldor's critical remarks on the production function as briefly outlined in the first section of this chapter. I shall instead concentrate on more important issues.

7.9. Critical Remarks and an Extension of the Model

I wish to address my attention to three critical aspects of Kaldor's laws. The first concerns the degree of stability through time and among countries of the Kaldor–Verdoorn relation. The second concerns the extent to which technical progress is autonomous. The third concerns the weaknesses in an explanation of differences among growth rates that treats them solely in terms of demand.

---

[79] G. Vaciago ('Increasing Returns and Growth in Advanced Economies: A Revaluation', *OEP* (July 1975)) found the following relation for eighteen European countries in the period 1950–69 which confirmed the Kaldor–Verdoorn relation: $pm = 1.05 + 0.60gm$, $R^2 = 0.786$. Similarly, Boyer and Petit, 'Productivité dans l'industrie et croissance à moyen terme', provided confirmation of the validity of Kaldor's relation (and the baselessness of Rowthorn's objection) for the 6 major European countries (West Germany, France, Italy, UK, Holland, and Belgium)—both individually and taken together—for each period considered and *also* (but not *only*) when Japan, as well as the USA, Canada, Sweden, and Denmark, were included (pp. 17–20).

[80] In a later article ('A Note on Verdoorn Law', *EJ* (Mar. 1979)), Rowthorn stated that his ideas on the subject had changed since he had criticized Kaldor for his emphasis on dynamic economies. These he now regarded as of great practical importance.

[81] Many of these were collected in the *JPKE* 3 (1983), including a useful guide to the debate by A. P. Thirlwall ('A Plain Man's Guide to Kaldor's Growth Laws'). See esp. J. S. McCombie, 'Kaldor's Laws in Retrospect', and id., 'What Still Remains of Kaldor's Laws?', *EJ* (Mar. 1981). For a more recent survey article, see E. Bairam, 'The Verdoorn Law, Returns to Scale and Industrial Growth: A Review of the Literature', *Australian Economic Papers* (June 1987).

[82] Rowthorn, 'A Note on Verdoorn Law'; P. J. Verdoorn, 'Verdoorn's Law in Retrospect: A Comment', *EJ* (June 1980); Thirlwall, 'Rowthorn's Interpretation of Verdoorn's Law'; M. Chatterji and M. R. Wickens, 'Verdoorn's Law and Kaldor's Law: A Revisionist Interpretation?', *JPKE* 3 (1983).

In their analysis of six European countries, Boyer and Petit showed that the Kaldor–Verdoorn relation was valid not only before, but also during, the decade that followed the years that Kaldor examined (when the rate of growth of output accounted for more than two-thirds of the variation in productivity). However, for every country considered by Boyer and Petit, the significance of the law diminished with time—a temporal variable that blunts the law's explanatory power. In a more recent work Boyer and Ralle have compared EEC countries and subsectors before and after 1973 (1960–73 and 1973–84). They confirm that after 1973 the Kaldor–Verdoorn correlation coefficient between productivity and output dropped on average to one-third of its value before that date.[83] This failure is also reported by T. Michl, who has conducted a broad cross-country econometric analysis of the Kaldor–Verdoorn law for industrialized countries.[84] As regards Britain, the Kaldor–Verdoorn law in its classic specification breaks down at two points: 1973 and 1979 (oil and Thatcher?). Although returns to scale in the manufacturing sector were still significant in the period 1980–4, they gradually diminished with the passage of time.[85] A recent study[86] confirms that the 'breakdown' of the law for the period 1973–85 is deducible not only from a strong reduction in the Kaldor–Verdoorn coefficient, but also from the law's decreased significance. This, however, concerns only the OECD countries, since the law maintains its validity, and the Kaldor–Verdoorn parameter is high over the same period of years, for the Latin American countries. One may therefore argue that the law works in different ways under different Schumpeterian technological waves. The OECD countries during the twenty years after the Second World War, and the industrializing countries for the following twenty years, were affected by a technological wave in which dynamic and static returns to scale played a major role in introducing technical progress. By contrast, in the last twenty years the OECD countries have entered a new technological wave where increasing returns to scale have relinquished their importance to what we may call 'flexible automation' as a way of introducing technical progress. And this explains why, in recent years and in the most developed countries, the Kaldor–Verdoorn law has largely lost its explanatory power.[87]

[83] R. Boyer and P. Ralle, 'L'Insertion internationale conditionne-t-elle les formes nationales d'emploi?', *Économies et sociétés*, 29: 1 (1986).

[84] T. Michl, 'International Comparisons of Productivity Growth: Verdoorn's Law Revisited', *JPKE* (summer 1985). Michl tested two specifications of the law: a traditional one (where the rate of productivity growth is only a function of the rate of growth of output), and a second function 'augmented' by Kaldor's technical progress, where the rate of productivity growth depends not only on the rate of growth of output but also on that of capital accumulation. The estimate of the first specification reveals an increasing looseness of fit, explained by an asymmetrical working of the law—a reduction in the rate of growth of output is not governed by the same laws as an increase. The estimate of the second specification, by contrast, gives better results.

[85] Stavrinos, 'The Intertemporal Stability of Kaldor's First and Second Laws in the U.K.'.

[86] F. Targetti and A. Foti, 'Growth and Technical Progress: Convergence or Divergence among Countries', in G. Pegoretti (ed.), Research, Motivation and Economic Growth (Berlin, Dunker & Humboldt, forthcoming).

[87] G. Dosi ('La circolarità tra progresso tecnico e crescita: Alcune osservazioni sulla legge

The Kaldor–Verdoorn law has a further weakness. Its validity changes substantially from country to country (even among industrialized ones). Its validity is greater for economies like those of France and Italy, and lesser for more developed economies like Germany's, although it has a good degree of validity for a highly developed economy such as Japan's, where the ratio between productivity growth and output growth has been constant and regular over time. In the late 1960s Vaciago[88] too reached the conclusion that during the twenty-year span of the 1950s and 1960s returns to scale had influenced the performances of the European countries, albeit to a varying extent. In particular, he found that they counted for less in countries with high growth rates. However, the fact that in recent years the law holds strangely in the case of Japan seems to contradict the general validity of this finding.[89]

The law's greater or lesser adaptability to specific national cases raised the problem of the degree of endogeneity of technical progress, the record issue mentioned at the beginning of this section. If the residue of productivity change left 'unexplained' by the change of output differs from country to country, then technical progress flows into each economic system through different channels. This was a view common to the majority of neo-classical economists as well as to proponents of the 'catching up' approach.[90] Kaldor had already pointed out that more intense accumulation and a higher ratio between investment and output leads, the output dynamic remaining equal, to greater productivity growth. In his Cambridge inaugural lecture and during his course of lectures at Cornell, he noted that countries like Denmark—with an elasticity of productivity compared with growth of output better than that deducible from the average values of all the countries examined—were also the countries that had a higher proportion of invested income.[91] This therefore raised again the vexed question of whether the causal relation between output dynamic and productivity went, as Kaldor maintained, from the former to the latter, or whether it operated the other way round. Among the first to discuss the problem was Salter,[92] who preferred a relation of the latter kind: technical progress is introduced by the accumulation of capital, which increases labour

Verdoorn-Kaldor', *L'Industria* (Apr.–June 1982) puts forward the argument—also subscribed to by Clark, Freeman, and Soete—that there is a tendency for the value of income growth connected with unchanged employment to be an increasing one. This means, especially in recent years, that there has been a 'systematic trend toward rationalization and labour-saving in productive processes *also* independently of increases in the size of productive activities'. Dosi attributes this tendency to the introd. of micro-electronics in productive processes. For a recent analysis of the static and dynamic economies of scale in manufacturing sectors heavily influenced by micro-electronic innovations, see B. Coriat, *L'Atelier et le robot* (Paris, Bourgois, 1990).

[88] G. Vaciago, 'Rendimenti crescenti e "residuo" nello sviluppo europeo (1950–1970)', *Retribuzioni, produttività e prezzi*, ed. P. Alessandrini (Bologna, Il Mulino, 1978).

[89] For a result of opposite sign to Vaciago's in the 1980s, see Targetti, 'Economic Instabilities of the Eighties'.

[90] See n. 75 above.

[91] Kaldor, *Strategic Factors in Economic Development*.

[92] W. E. G. Salter, *Productivity and Technological Change* (Cambridge, CUP, 1960).

productivity and hence leads to lower prices and costs and therefore higher demand and production.

By contrast, it was an integral part of the more general Kaldorian view that the determining principle of the dynamics of output and productivity was to be found in demand factors. There is no escaping the fact, however, that 'supply' considerations are hard to ignore. These include: (1) the extent to which the economic system is penetrated by developing sectors with a high autonomous change of productivity; (2) a country's type of manufacturing specialization (a country specializing in chemicals, for instance, lends more validity to the Kaldor–Verdoorn law than one specializing in footwear); (3) the labour force's degree of rigidity (a fall in income in countries with more 'rigid' labour forces leads to a steeper decline in their productivity); (4) the availability of industrial policies and the percentage of expenditure on R & D; (5) a country's ability to imitate available international technologies.

Freeman and the neo-Schumpeterian school of the Science Policy Research Unit of Sussex University[93] have attempted to resolve the antithesis between demand-pull versus technology-push innovation theory. In doing so they have also offered an explanation for the temporal breakdown in the Kaldor–Verdoorn law. According to this approach, radical innovations ('changes in technological paradigms') occur just as frequently during periods of rapid economic growth as they do during periods of stagnation. These innovations lead to further, induced innovations, thus creating technological systems lasting for more than one decade and primarily based on one cheap fundamental resource ('cheap steam 1820–80, cheap steel 1880–1930, cheap oil 1930–80, cheap chips 1980–today'). Within the life-spans of such technological systems, there is ample room for incremental innovations: the dynamic economies of scale of Young, Arrow, and Kaldor. The dynamics of effective demand are crucial for the birth of these latter innovations, but not at all for the original, radical ones. It is via incremental innovations that radical innovations generate strong productivity growth rates. However, incremental innovations weaken with the passage of time, because the technological potentialities of the technological system engendered by the radical innovation eventually exhaust themselves. In Freeman's words: 'No matter how much a rayon plant was improved, you would never get nylon. Studies of incremental improvement must be complemented by studies of more radical discontinuities in the economy. A satisfactory theory of innovation must embrace learning-by-doing incrementalism and Schumpeterian entrepreneurship.'[94]

My final point concerns Kaldor's cumulative causation mechanism and his insistence on the demand factors governing the growth of output and productivity. In his reply to Rowthorn, he accepted that the output–productivity relation is biunivocal; but he stressed that the effect of the growth of produc-

---

[93] C. Freeman (ed.), *Long Waves in the World Economy* (London, Frances Pinter, 1984).

[94] Id., speech at the 'International Seminar on Science, Technology and Economic Growth', OECD (Paris, 1989).

tivity on the growth of output 'is far less regular and systematic than the first' (Kaldor–Verdoorn) relation, and that econometric techniques based on a single equation are therefore justified. This, however, conflicts with Kaldor's principle of cumulative causation, and with his fourth law stating that the growth rate is conditioned by external competitiveness. I therefore agree with Skott's criticism that 'cumulative causation . . . is only important when there is a strong feedback from productivity to demand, and a weak feedback is needed in order to justify single equations method'.[95] If (1) an increase in manufacturing productivity is induced by the growth of manufacturing output, which is in turn directly linked to external demand and indirectly governed by the penetration of imports; if (2) these latter factors depend on the competitiveness of manufactured commodities; and if (3), as Kaldor claimed, it is the productivity growth that determines the real rate of exchange and not vice versa[96] (which amounts to saying that it is useless to try to increase competitiveness by devaluing the exchange rate)—then we are caught up in a circular process (whether virtuous or vicious) where it is extremely difficult to decide what is cause and what is effect. In fact, if, on the one hand, it is correct to say that the rate of growth of output is constrained by export demand (equation (7.14)), on the other it also depends on the parameter η; not only this, but the rate of growth of exports (according to equation (7.5)) is also dependent on ε and the elasticities η and ε depend in turn on supply factors.

The fact is that the Kaldor–Verdoorn equation must be taken to be an equation in an interdependent system. Among the first to state the problem in these terms was J. Cornwall,[97] and recently the argument has been widely explored by the French 'regulation school'.[98] A model of cumulative causation must be based on the action of two forces: the first represented by the Kaldor–Verdoorn equation where productivity growth depends on output growth; the second by an equation operating in reverse and based on two explanations.[99] According to the first equation, effective demand can grow because of the growth of wages indexed to productivity growth (which is the French

[95] P. Skott, 'Kaldor's Growth Laws and the Theory of Cumulative Causation', memo 1988: 17, Institute of Economics, University of Aarhus, 1988.

[96] N. Kaldor, 'The Effect of Devaluations on Trade in Manufacture' (1977), pub. in CP vi.

[97] J. Cornwall *Modern Capitalism* (Norwich, Martin Robertson, 1977). For Cornwall, the missing link was the technological gap that divided an imitator country from an innovator country. Cornwall's variable is open to the same kind of criticism that Kaldor brought against the Rowthorn–Gomulka argument.

[98] R. Boyer, *Regulation Theory: A Critical Assessment* (New York, Columbia University Press, 1985).

[99] Id. and P. Petit, 'The Cumulative Growth Model Revisited' (Paris, Cepremap, 1987). The model is able to show the system's stability property: it is stable when the second function is steeper than the first in a Cartesian plane with output growth on the horizontal axis and productivity growth on the vertical one. P. Ralle ('Estimation d'un modèle en coupe internationale 1960–1987' in R. Boyer (ed.), *La Seconde Transformation* (Paris, Economica, forthcoming)) holds that in the 1960–73 period the growth of demand was independent of productivity growth—i.e. the second function was perpendicular—that is to say that Kaldor's single equation was a correct representation of a stable relation between output area productivity. However, after 1973 cumulative growth was unstable; in the 1980s the situation was undefined.

explanation for the 'Forcist' stage of growth). According to the second, effective demand grows because of the growth of exports induced by high competitiveness given by productivity growth (which is the cumulative model à la
Thirlwall).

Figure 7.1 sets out the complete system with the various forces at work and
their interconnections. From it one deduces that if, as has already been pointed
out, exchange-rate policy cannot determine medium–long-term competitiveness, then renewed emphasis must be placed on the causes of entrepreneurial
dynamism which fix the position of the technical-progress function; an aspect
that was neglected in Kaldor's work of the late 1960s. The position of the
technical-progress function determines both the rate of capital accumulation
and the rate of growth of productivity. The latter—if it is not transformed into
higher real wages—affects foreign competitiveness, which acts on the Harrod–Kaldor–Thirlwall dynamic multiplier in an open market and thus on the
rate of growth of demand for manufactures—which is also acted upon by
investment in the manufacturing sector induced by the position of the technical-progress function. The growth of manufacturing production affects, according to the Kaldor–Verdoorn law, the induced growth of productivity of
the sector. This latter has a retroactive positive effect on foreign competitiveness, and thus activates a cumulative process which, according to the first
Kaldor law, causes the entire economy to grow.

Figure 7.1 can be divided into two halves: sections A and B. Section A is
the engine of the cumulative process, the speed of which depends on the
parameters of Kaldor's laws. The process is more rapid the higher the Kaldor–Verdoorn coefficient, the greater the difference between the growth of
real wages and the growth of productivity, and the lower the import elasticity
to income. Section B represents the set of exogenous factors which, to varying
extents, activate the cumulative process.

Having clarified this distinction, as a final comment I wish to stress that the
Kaldor versus Gomulka–Rowthorn debate is, in my view, wrongly specified.
The process of cumulative causation set in motion by Kaldor's laws does not
conflict with the catching-up theory; indeed, the two models can and should
be integrated together. The catching-up theory is based on the idea that it is
much easier to imitate than to invent. If the world is divided between one
innovator country and several imitator countries, the theory states that the
dynamism of the leader country's innovations will be slower than that of the
follower countries, while the followers experience higher growth rates than
the leader's. Moreover, the narrower the gap between the productivity levels
of the two groups becomes, the closer the followers' productivity growth rates
will approach the leader's; they will, therefore, slow down. However, the
theory holds only for 'intermediate countries', for if the gap with the leader
is too wide the follower is unable to imitate.

I have argued above that Kaldor's growth laws alone (Figure 7.1, section
A) cannot constitute a satisfactory model of growth because something is

FIG. 7.1 Kaldor's laws of growth: exogenous and endogenous factors

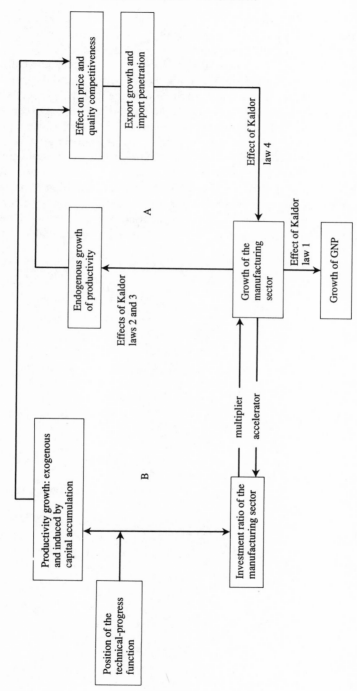

lacking outside the process of cumulative causation. Moreover, the evidence is in favour of greater convergence among industrialized countries than can be deduced from Kaldor's cumulative model of growth.

On the other hand, the catching-up theory on its own is also weak, since it is unable to explain why different countries (all belonging to the intermediate group of industrialized countries) catch up with the leader's productivity level at a speed which is often independent of the initial distance between follower country and leader. Integrating the two models[100] (Kaldor's laws represented in Figure 7.1, by section A and catching-up by section B) gives a powerful model of growth which provides an explanation for the different catching-up processes of industrialized countries in terms of the parameters of Kaldor's laws. Furthermore, incorporating Kaldor's laws into the model offers an explanation of long-run cumulative divergences between the rate of growth of OECD countries and that of several industrializing countries—for example those of Latin America—which catching-up theory alone is unable to provide.

---

[100] An example of a model which integrates Kaldor's cumulative growth and the theory of catching-up is given by Targetti and Foti, 'Growth and Technical Progress'.

Chapter 8

The 'Agriculture–Industry' Model and the Instability of the World Economy

Actions for the stabilization of commodity prices at remunerative levels should be undertaken as a matter of urgency.

North–South: A Programme for Survival

8.1. Some Open Questions

Although differences in the rate of growth of different countries derive, in the last analysis, from the different degrees of their foreign competitiveness, how can the growth of the world economy as a whole be explained? One may, similarly, ask: What determines the growth of a country closed to international trade?—a question that becomes extremely important when it refers to very large countries, or to countries in the early stages of industrialization. In general terms the issue is this: If the distinguishing feature of Keynesian growth is the exogeneity of a component of demand, in cases (a closed country or the world economy) where this distinguishing feature cannot be exports, which demand component takes over as the driving force of growth?

This is a first issue; but there is another. Kaldor's growth models of the 1950s were one-sector models of a closed economy with no government. Exogeneity was given by the technical-progress function. The models represented a mature industrialized economy, where full utilization of plant was matched by full utilization of the work-force; and its only sector was the manufacturing sector.

The passage from the Keynesian economy of the determination of short-term income to the post-Keynesian economy of the determination of the rate of growth of income in the medium–long period entailed moving from Keynes's autonomous investment function to the induced investment function. For Kaldor, a one-sector model with an investment function induced by the level or variation of income *had to* assume the full utilization of productive capacity, which in mature economies signified full employment. What happened in actual fact, however, was that economies grew for long periods with unemployment rates that varied greatly from country to country. Kaldor therefore became increasingly aware that his one-sector models failed to provide a satisfactory explanation for the phenomenon of growth attended, even in the industrialized countries, by unemployment.[1] In Kaldor's view, investigating growth with unemployment entailed abandoning the hypothesis of a one-sector economy.

Another weakness in these growth models was that they envisaged balanced growth in which the various sectors grow proportionately over time—even though this is never actually the case in the real world, in either the medium or long term. In the long term especially, the hypothesis has proved to be an extremely 'heroic' one, in view of the more conspicuous structural transformation that economies display in the growth process—namely, the varying contributions made by the three sectors of agriculture, industry, and services to the GDP.

Thus in the early 1970s Kaldor began to develop a theory of growth based on a model comprising the first two of these three sectors. This model remedied the defects of the earlier models—their consideration of only one sector and their assumption of full employment—and set out to answer the question asked at the beginning of this section (Kaldor abandoned analysis of income distribution).

8.2. The Dynamic Equilibrium of a Two-Sector Economic System[2]

The economy is divided into two sectors providing primary commodities and manufacturing goods. For simplicity's sake, the first sector is called agriculture and is assumed to produce corn and the second is called industry and is assumed to produce iron. Each of the two sectors depends on the other, and in two ways: as a market providing an outlet for its products and as a market where the means necessary for its productive activity can be purchased. Ag-

---

[1] Certain of the various 'ages' in Joan Robinson's theory of accumulation envisage growth with unemployment, but her analysis of the investment function lacks thoroughness. The problem of induced investment she solved with the loophole of 'animal spirits'—which Kaldor rejected. A richer theory is R. Goodwin's 'Marxian' model integrating the cycle and growth with the swelling and dwindling of the industrial reserve army ('A Growth Cycle', in *Socialism, Capitalism and Economic Growth*, essays in honour of M. Dobb, ed. C. H. Feinstein (Cambridge, CUP, 1969). The Cambridge Keynesians, however, criticized the model for its 'classical' slant: in the upswing phases of the cycle the profit rate tended to fall (and vice versa in the downward phases of the cycle), whereas for the Keynesian and Kaleckian tradition the reverse was the case—as a number of empirical research studies had shown (see Ch. 2 n. 9, above).

[2] This section is based on the following works by N. Kaldor, 'Equilibrium Theory and Growth Theory' (1973), pub. in M. Baskin (ed.), *Economics and Human Welfare—Essays in Honour of Tibor Scitovsky* (New York, Academic Press, 1979); 'What is Wrong with Economic Theory?' (1974), repr. in CP v; 'Inflation and Recession in the World Economy' (1976), repr. in CP v; 'Causes of Growth and Stagnation in the World Economy', Lectures at the Univerzità Bocconi of Milan 21–5 May, 1984 (forthcoming), 3rd Lecture. See also F. Targetti, 'Growth and the Terms of Trade: A Kaldorian Two Sector Model', *Metroeconomica* (Feb. 1985); and A. Thirlwall, 'A General Model of Growth and Development on Kaldorian Lines', *OEP* 38 (1986). An extension of the model with the introduction of financial markets can be found in T. Moutos and D. Vines, 'A Prototype Macroeconomic Model with Integrated Financial and Commodity Markets', *EN* 1 (1988).

riculture supplies industry with primary products and the principal wage goods; industry supplies agriculture with capital goods. Regarding the latter connection, the model emphasizes that, in the agricultural sector with technology remaining constant, the returns on capital[3] and labour decrease because of the fixity of land. In the course of time, however, agricultural output per hectare increases because of land-saving technical progress—which may be labour-saving technical progress as well—and this requires investment in capital goods. As a first approximation, capital accumulation and land-saving technical progress proceed at equal rates in this sector.

As regards employment, the model assumes that there is disguised unemployment in agriculture; that every worker has his livelihood guaranteed as a member of a household; and that he participates in the distribution of output. In industry, workers are wage-earners, and the supply of labour is unlimited as long as the purchasing power of wages in terms of corn is sufficiently high to induce the migration of labour that industry requires. The economy as a whole has a surplus of labour, in the sense given to the term in Chapter 7.5.

A further difference between the two sectors concerns their saving–investment ratios (and therefore the role played in them by finance). In agriculture, saving requires the deliberate non-consumption of a part of output, which is sold in exchange for capital goods incorporating new technology. The intensity of the accumulation process and the introduction of land-saving technical progress therefore depend on the share of saving and on the ratio at which corn is exchanged for iron.

In industry, the causal relationship operates the other way round: it is the decision to invest that, once taken, determines profits and the corresponding amount of saving. In aggregate, producers of iron accumulate capital by ploughing part of their output back into the sector and by selling the rest. If costs are given entirely by wages, if these are fixed in terms of corn, and if iron output per worker is given, once the share of reinvestment of net output in the sector has been decided, the mark-up on costs that follows[4] generates a profit flow that will finance the investment itself. Decisions on capital accumulation depend on expectations of variations in investment demand in both sectors.

The final difference between the behaviours of the two sectors lies in the relation between variation in the demand directed towards the sector and the

[3] Here again Kaldor does not bother to define 'capital' (physical goods or magnitudes in value) before enunciating its decreasing returns to scale in agriculture. His notion of decreasing returns is Ricardian. It can handle a single agricultural sector but raises the usual logical difficulties when applied to the manufacturing sector, or to the agricultural sector in a model which represents an economy producing more than one good and in which relative prices change because of a change in production techniques or distribution of income.

[4] Under these hypotheses the profit margin is given by the ratio between the share of net output reinvested in the sector divided by the residual share. e.g. if a quarter of the net output of the industrial sector is reinvested, the residual share is three-quarters. The ratio between the two fractions is one-third, which is the mark-up on wage costs that determines the price of the net output of the industrial sector.

variation in the monetary price set by the sector:[5] in the industrial sector a fall (rise) in demand leads to a fall (rise) in output; in the agricultural sector a fall (rise) in demand leads to a fall (rise) in the monetary price of agricultural output.[6]

The two sectors can be represented by two equations. Let Q stand for output, C for the consumption of agricultural products, I for the investment in capital goods produced by the industrial sector, P and W for profits and wages, S for savings, l for the amount of labour per unit of output, w for the wage rate and p for the (real) price of iron in terms of corn (which is the inverse of the ratio between the quantities exchanged). If we use the suffixes a and i to indicate the agricultural and industrial sectors, we obtain

(8.1]
$$\begin{cases} Q_a = S_a + C_a = pI_a + C_a \\ Q_i = I_i + wlQ_i 1/p = P_i + W_i = S_i + C_i 1/p. \end{cases}$$

The first expression states that the agricultural sector's net output (Q_a) is in part consumed (C_a) and the saved surplus (S_a) is exchanged (at price p) for goods from the industrial sector (I_a). In the industrial sector net output (Q_i) is in part held back to augment productive capacity (I_i) and in part exchanged (at price $1/p$), so that the totality of workers employed by this level of activity (lQ_i) receives agricultural consumption goods in exchange at rate given by their unitary wage (w) in real terms $1/p$. The industrial sector is activated by its own demand (I_i) and by demand from the agricultural sector (I_a); at equilibrium the quantity produced will satisfy these two demands and will be sold at a price such as to leave a profit (P_i) which, on the hypothesis that such profit is used entirely for self-financing (S_i), and on the hypothesis that wages in the sector (W_i) are wholly consumed ($C_i 1/p$), will equal investment. Profit in the industrial sector is given by the difference between the output of the sector and the goods that the sector exchanges with the other sector at the equilibrium

[5] One of the first economists to emphasize the different kinds of price formation in the two sectors was M. Kalecki, *Theory of Economic Dynamics* (London, Allen & Unwin, 1954). A similar idea was later elaborated by P. Sylos Labini, *Oligopoly and Technical Progress* (Cambridge, Mass., Harvard University Press, 1962). Sylos Labini has also developed an econometric model with different price formation in agriculture and in industry: *Sindacati, inflazione e produttività* (Bari, Laterza, 1972). Subsequently, Hicks has also divided the market into the 'flex price' and 'fix price' sectors, which roughly correspond to agricultural and manufacturing prices in Kaldor's model: see J. Hicks, *The Crisis in Keynesian Economics* (Oxford, Basil Blackwell, 1974).

[6] The explanation that follows clarifies the difference between real price and money price. The real price or term of trade between the two sectors is the inverse of the ratio between the quantities exchanged. There is only one real price because there are two sectors; therefore the variation in this price for one sector is equivalent to a variation of the opposite sign for the other. There is instead one money price for each sector, which is given by the inverse of the quantity of output of the sector purchased by a unit of money. The ratio between the two money prices gives the real price or the term of trade. However, as we shall see, a shock can push the system out of its equilibrium position, and two money processes come into operation to bring the system to another real equilibrium price, given by the ratio between the two money prices—which is different from the real equilibrium price that would obtain if only the forces leading to real equilibrium as described above were in operation.

price, so that workers can purchase consumption goods at the prevailing wage rate.

Moving to growth rates, the system can be expressed by the usual Harrod–Domar equation of dynamic equilibrium: the rate of growth of the equilibrium income is given by the ratio between the propensity to save and the marginal capital/output ratio. Thus we have for the two sectors:

(8.2)
$$\begin{cases} g_a = (S_a/Q_a)/(pI_a/\Delta Q_a) \\ g_i = [(Q_i - wlQ_i \cdot 1/p)/Q_i](\Delta Q_i/I_i). \end{cases}$$

Calling $(S_a/Q_a)(I_a/\Delta Q_a) = k$ and $\Delta Q_i/I_i = h$ gives us

(8.3)
$$\begin{cases} g_a = k(1/p) \\ g_i = h(1 - wl \cdot 1/p) \end{cases}$$

Plotting p on the vertical axis and g_a and g_i on the horizontal axis, we obtain Figure 8.1.

FIG. 8.1 The rate of growth of output of agriculture and industry and their terms of trade

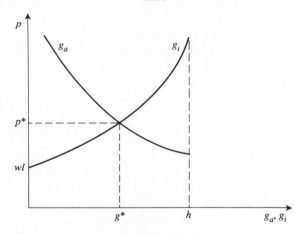

Given the share of agricultural surplus S_a/Q_a, and on the hypothesis that investment in agriculture will bring land-saving progress to counterbalance the decreasing returns from land, curve g_a is a hyperbola. Curve g_i has zero value when p is equal to the intercept wl on the vertical axis and a maximum value at h, which corresponds to a value of p tending to infinity: in the former case all output goes to the workers and there is no investment and no growth; in the latter case, the price of agricultural products is so low relative to industrial goods that the industrial output reinvestable in the sector tends to coincide with the whole of industrial output.

The value g^* represents the equilibrium growth rate of both sectors. If the system stands at this value, there will be no constraints on its growth on either the demand or the supply side.[7] This rate of growth is matched by a term of trade p^* between the two sectors which performs the following function: it obtains, for the agricultural sector in exchange for its surplus, the quantity of investment goods necessary for the growth g_a of the potential of agricultural production and, for the industrial sector in exchange for its investment goods, sufficient agricultural goods to satisfy the consumption demand of industrial workers. This term of trade also functions as the industrial sector price at which costs are marked up to yield the profit necessary to finance investment through the ploughing back of industrial output into the sector itself. In fact, the second equation (first equality) of the system (8.1) can be rewritten as

$$(8.4) \qquad\qquad p = (I_i/Q_i)p + wl$$

which is compatible with the price equation based on the mark-up π of costs

$$(8.5) \qquad\qquad p = (1 + \pi)wl$$

if $I_i = \pi(wl \cdot X_i \cdot 1/p)$, which follows from the hypothesis that profit is obtained by marking up costs, and that it is wholly invested.

The situation described by p^* and g^* results from fulfilment of equilibrium conditions. However, in a situation out of equilibrium, one must ascertain whether there are forces bringing the system back into equilibrium and, analogously, whether the system moves from one equilibrium situation to another, should phenomena arise which shift the curves. I shall first deal with the former case and then consider which important phenomena can be represented by shifting the curves.

8.3. Adjustment, Shocks, Stagnation, and Stagflation

Let us assume that the system comprises a price p^* lower than p_1; that at this exchange ratio, industrial output increases more slowly than the system's demand for iron; and that perception of this deficiency in productive capacity induces an increase in investment in the industrial sector. On the other hand, $p_1 < p^*$ signifies that the agricultural sector has an excess supply of agricultural

---

[7] The outcome that g^* is common to both sectors depends on the dual assumption that there is neither technical substitutability nor substitutability of tastes. In reality, the opposite is the case. Agricultural input to the industrial sector comprises not only wage goods but also raw materials, and technical progress replaces many of these with industrially manufactured products; hence the dependence of one sector on the other diminishes with time. The same applies to goods purchased out of wages. These, with the passage of time, are increasingly less agricultural goods and increasingly more industrial goods. If the change in the income elasticity of demand is exogenous, this can be shown by shifts of the curve. Not so, however, when it depends on the rate of growth itself. When e.g. changes in technology or taste are brought about by a change in the terms of trade (e.g. the reduction of the energy content in the manufacturing output of OECD countries consequent on the two oil shocks): in this case, a movement along the curve entails a movement of the curve—hence graphic analysis must give way to more complex treatment.

products which tends to drive down the monetary price of corn; and this—with the monetary price of iron remaining the same—signifies an increase in p (which, it will be remembered, is the price of iron per unit of corn). The mechanism works in reverse if p is higher than p^*. This adjustment mechanism induces the system to converge on equilibrium. Note that two different kinds of force are at work in the two sectors. In the industrial sector, disequilibrium is signalled by quantities, and re-equilibrium is accomplished through variations in quantities. In the agricultural sector, it is competition among producers that moves the price towards the equilibrium value at which the market 'clears'. The term 'equilibrium price' in this context also signifies the terms of trade at which the two sectors grow at the same rate.

The mechanism that I have described operates when movements away from the equilibrium position are minor—for example, when the curves shift slightly. One cause of a slight shift of g_i may be technical progress in the industrial sector. So far I have only considered one sort of technical progress: the land-saving technical progress in agriculture brought about by capital accumulation. In the industrial sector, by contrast, technical progress may occur in one of two ways: either through an autonomous reduction over time in the amount of labour per unit of output (from l_0 to l_1) which, *ceteris paribus*, shifts curve g_i nightwards (Figure 8.2); or through dynamic increasing returns to scale, so that the amount of labour per unit of output decreases as output increases and hence, *ceteris paribus*, curve g_i flattens (Figure 8.3).

FIG. 8.2 Autonomous technical progress in industry

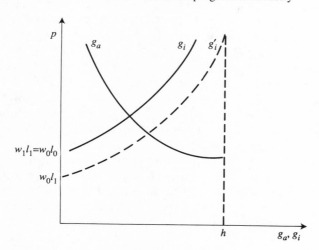

These two phenomena may appear together. The outcome is still an acceleration in balanced growth and an improvement of the terms of trade in agriculture. In fact, though, the qualification *ceteris paribus* is illegitimate, especially as regards wages. Wages in industrial countries have a long-term tendency to

FIG. 8.3 Dynamic increasing returns in industry

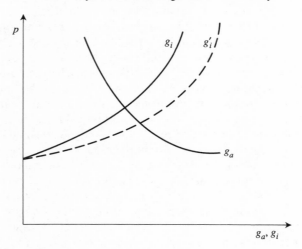

increase at the same rate as the amount of labour per unit of output decreases. This keeps the value of wl constant ($w_1 l_1$ is at the same level as $w_0 l_0$ in Figure 8.2) and leaves the position of curve g_i in the plane unchanged. (There may be intermediate situations in which there is a partial and limited shift given by the difference between the increase in productivity and the increase in wages.)

When the technical progress takes place in both sectors, but in the industrial one is offset by wage increase, the terms of trade go against the agricultural sector (Figure 8.4). This was the essence of the thesis held by Prebish and the United Nations in the 1940s.

Abrupt, major, and unpredictable shifts of a curve may also occur—most frequently in the case of phenomena relating to curve g_a. Exceptionally good or exceptionally bad harvests shift the curve rightwards and leftwards respectively. Shifts in the two directions may also result from the diffusion of a discovery in agronomy or the explosion of what is nowadays termed a 'green revolution' (curve g_a shifts rightwards). Or they may be induced by the formation of a cartel in order to exploit an exhaustible resource—as happened during the 1970s in the case of oil extraction—which keeps supply of the product lower than that potentially producible and raises its price to the point of the maximum present and foreseeable profit for the producers in the cartel[8] (curve g_a shifts to the left).

---

[8] There is a vast literature on the determinants of the price of oil, the behaviour of the oil cartel, and the history of oil production over the last 15 years. See esp. J. M. Griffin and D. J. Treece, *Opec Behaviour and World Oil Prices* (London, Allen & Unwin, 1982), and A. Roncaglia, *L'economia del petrolio* (Bari, Laterza, 1982). A forecasting econometric model of Kaldorian stamp incorporating the price of energy has been produced by the Cambridge DAE and by ISMERI-Europa of Rome and used in F. Targetti, 'Energia e crescita dell' economia mondiale', *Economia delle fonti di energia*, 26 (1985).

Although abrupt, these shifts may set off a process of gradual re-equilibrium, of the kind described at the beginning of this section. For example, an abrupt rightward shift in g_a signifies a major increase in the supply of corn. If there exist wholesalers or public bodies with enough 'finance' to purchase greater quantities at monetary and real prices which, although slightly lower, are such that the industrial sector can purchase more corn, there will be a shift from p_0 to p_1. Simultaneously, both the industrial rate of growth (shift along g_i) and the agricultural rate of growth (shift of g_a) will increase up to the new equilibrium point g_1, which will be greater than g_0 for both industry and agriculture.

If, instead, these conditions for the gradual absorption of the surplus of agricultural supply do not hold, and dealers reduce their purchases of corn because they expect a further drop in the monetary price, the shift in g_a may set off a process of disequilibrium culminating in the perverse effect of a balanced rate of growth g_2 which will be lower, rather than higher, than the initial value g_0 (Figure 8.5).

In fact, the drop in the monetary price of corn, with the monetary price of iron remaining the same, forces the term of trade down to p_2. Industry does not purchase larger quantities of corn, despite its lower price, because there is no increase in productive capacity and employment due to the fact that, in this case, there is no actual or foreseeable increase in demand for iron to stimulate industrialist entrepreneurs. Thus farmers see the value in iron terms of their sales to industry diminish, and they reduce their demand on the industrial sector accordingly. Industry will have to cope with a lack of effective demand, will sell less iron even though its productive capacity has not fallen, and will thus be induced to reduce the rate of increase in capacity itself. This process causes g_i to shift to the left. The new equilibrium position g_2 will be to the left of the initial position: the terms of trade will move abruptly against the agricultural sector, and both sectors will grow more slowly.

The outcome is pure stagnation (of the 1929–32 kind) with agricultural monetary prices in steep decline, industrial monetary prices dropping, but to a lesser extent, the terms of trade against the agricultural sector, and slow growth of the overall economy.

In the case where g_a shifts leftwards,[9] the industrial sector reacts differently. The effect of the reduction in the rate of growth of supply (or even in the level of supply) of corn not only forces g down (from g_0 to g_i), but also drives down the value of p through an initial increase in the monetary price of corn. However, the monetary price of iron is formed with a mark-up on wage costs (that is, on the monetary costs of corn). If wages in terms of corn remain the same, and if the mark-up also remains fixed, the change in the terms of trade will push up monetary prices in the industrial sector in order to restore the previous value of the terms of trade (equation (8.5)). For p to be able to perform, even in this new situation, its dual role of equilibrating the quantities

---

[9] Although treatment of this case is not to be found in Kaldor, it has been analysed in F. Targetti, 'Growth and the Terms of Trade: A Kaldorian Two Sector Model'.

FIG. 8.4 Technical progress in agriculture: fall in agriculture's terms of trade

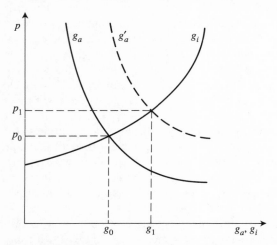

FIG. 8.5 A perverse effect of technical progress in agriculture: stagnation in the two sectors

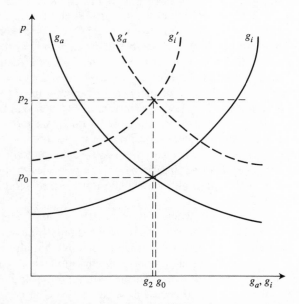

exchanged between the two sectors and of reflecting the ratio between the two monetary prices, the g_i curve must shift leftwards until the previous value of p_0 is reached. Now, however, the overall outcome is a drop in the balanced rate of growth between the two sectors to a value (g_2) even lower than the value (g_1) that would have been reached after the single initial shock had shifted g_a to the left (Figure 8.6).

In this case we have stagflation—that is, a fall in the rate of growth of the quantities iron and corn and inflation in the general level of monetary prices consequent on the fact that the monetary price of iron tries to catch up with the monetary price of corn.

FIG. 8.6. The effect of a reduction in agricultural output: stagflation

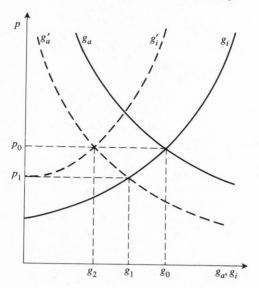

8.4. Limits on Growth

For Keynesian economists of the late 1950s and early 1960s, the limit to growth was full employment. This transpires from Harrod's concept of the 'natural growth rate' (which was taken up by numerous Keynesian growth models), from Joan Robinson's 'inflation barrier', and from the assumption of full employment in Kaldor's models. Kaldor, moreover, on various occasions during the 1960s (see Chapter 7.4) identified the exhaustion of the labour supply to manufacturing industry as the constraint on Britain's growth.

In the Bretton Woods period full employment was the effective barrier; since the 1970s, however, one may say, quoting Hicks, that:

the Keynesian identification of the limit to growth with Full Employment of Labour is called into question . . . full employment cannot now be reached since the supplies of primary products that would be needed to support it are not available.[10]

This was a point that had been repeatedly and forcefully made by Kaldor from 1974 onwards.[11] He insisted that the ultimate limit to growth was not the

[10] J. Hicks, *Economic Perspectives* (Oxford, Clarendon Press, 1977), 98–9, quoted in N. Kaldor, 'Limits on Growth' (1985), repr. in CP ix. 257.
[11] Id., 'What is Wrong with Economic Theory'.

scarcity of the labour supply but the rate of change of land-saving technical progress. He slightly changed his mind during the 1980s, however, as testified by one of his last lectures, delivered at Oxford in honour of Hicks, where he redefined land-saving technical progress as one of the 'potential limits' to growth, in the sense that other constraints 'bite' before the scarcity of primary and exhaustible resources makes itself felt.[12] He was entirely convinced of the baselessness of the view, expressed by many 'on both sides of the Atlantic', that the depression of the 1970s and before was the consequence of supply-side constraints, and that it would therefore have been aggravated by Keynesian economic policies. In actual fact, although he agreed that economic policies designed to revive (domestic) demand had proved to be impracticable, when undertaken by individual countries in a context of generally slow growth of demand, he was entirely convinced that 'it was the disproportionality between import and export propensities of individual countries under conditions of fully liberalised trade which was the major cause of the well-nigh universal state of recession'.[13]

But this was not the only cause of depression:[14] it operates in harness with the process that I analysed in the previous section. The two-sector model shows that variations in the terms of trade in any direction, if they are abrupt and wide, may, instead of balancing the growth of the two sectors, have the effect of setting in motion macro-economic disequilibria because of the different market behaviour in each sector. Moreover, one can hardly imagine the industrial sector returning to an eighteenth-century system with prices not 'administered' but determined by the market. Further, in such a fully competitive system the monetary fluctuations of prices within the two sectors would be much more marked. Following the 1950s failure of the proposal for the unilateral stabilization of raw-material prices by the producer countries (see Chapter 9.4), from 1964 onwards[15] Kaldor repeatedly proposed a scheme of 'buffer stocks' of raw materials; a scheme to be administered by a multinational body jointly with an international currency system. Kaldor was op-

[12] In 'Limits on Growth', Kaldor cautioned against the doom-laden prophesying of the early 1970s, e.g. by the Club of Rome, on the stagnatory effects that the exhaustion of non-renewable resources would bring in the medium period. He was instead of the opinion that in the future, as in the past, technical progress would compensate for natural shortages.

[13] Ibid. 258–9. See also 'The Foundations of Free Trade Theory and their Implications for the Current World Recession', in E. Malinvaud and J. P. Fitoussi (eds.), *Unemployment in Western Countries* (London, Macmillan, 1980). An attempt at integrating Kaldorian analysis, set out in this and the preceding chapter, as a tool for understanding the main features of international economic disequilibria in the 1980s can be found in F. Targetti, 'The Economic Instability of the Eighties', in J. Michie, *The Economics of Restructuring and Intervention* (London, Edward Elgar, 1991).

[14] In 1980 Kaldor divided the accumulated loss of world income between 1973 and 1980, calculated at 15%, between 3% due to changes in the terms of trade and 12% due to the deflationary policies of the industrialized countries ('What are the Threatening Economic Issues?', paper given to the *Financial Times* conference on 'European Banking', Amsterdam, Dec. 1980).

[15] N. Kaldor et al., 'The Case for an International Commodity Reserve Currency' (1963), pub. in CP iv.

timistic that land-saving technical progress could secure the growth of agricultural output that industrial progress required, provided that the buffer-stock scheme was created to stabilize primary commodity prices and to eliminate the bottlenecks between the primary and the industrial sectors. I shall give a detailed description of his proposed scheme in Chapter 13.2.

Chapter 9

Underdevelopment, Industrialization, and Policies for Development

> For unto every one that hath shall be given, and he shall have in abundance; but from him that hath not shall be taken away even that which he hath.
>
> Matthew, 25: 29

> Because of . . . circular causation a social process tends to become cumulative and often to gather speed at an accelerating rate.
>
> G. Myrdal, *Economic Theory and Underdeveloped Regions*

9.1. Stages of Industrialization

The principal problem faced by economically backward countries is how and when they can industrialize. Kaldor was fully aware that a theory of development must include elements of history, society, and culture in any explanation as to why certain regions of the globe have been unable to participate in the prolonged process of growth that has accompanied the rise of capitalism, and why in many parts of the world this process is still being obstructed. However, when analysis of the deficiencies of economic development narrows its compass to strictly economic investigation, research must necessarily concentrate on industrialization's fragility or even failure. As a colleague at Cambridge University said of him:

Nicholas Kaldor was an apostle of the rapid industrialization of the Third World since, in his view, this was the only means by which the developing countries could improve the standard of living of their people.[1]

Kaldor's analysis of underdevelopment hinged on two fundamental concepts:[2] the agriculture–industry relation and the internal market–external market relation. Put briefly, he believed that: (1) economic development requires industrialization; (2) that this in turn presupposes an 'agricultural revolution';

[1] A. Singh, 'Third World Competition and Deindustrialization in Advanced Countries', *CJE* (Mar. 1989).

[2] N. Kaldor, *Strategic Factors in Economic Development* (1966) (Ithaca, Cornell University Press, 1967); id., 'Capitalism and Industrial Development: Some Lessons from Britain's Experience' (1977; 1st pub. in Sp., 1972) repr. in CP vi.

(3) that it (economic development) requires a temporary stage of protection for newly established industry; and (4) that it needs a subsequent phase of export-led growth. I shall now examine each of these propositions in turn.

(1) Economic development depends on industrialization for two reasons. First, the proportion of income spent on agriculture diminishes (as a consequence of Engel's law). Second, in countries with high agricultural output per worker, only a small proportion of the population can be absorbed by the agricultural sector—as evidenced by the low percentages of the work-force employed in agriculture in Australia, Denmark, and New Zealand, countries with high levels of agricultural productivity.

(2) On the other hand, both the birth of industrialization and its continuing growth presuppose an 'agricultural revolution'. This, historically, has taken a variety of forms. In England it came about because the landowners expropriated the peasants; in France because the peasants expropriated the landlords; and in Japan because of the Meiji Revolution, or Restoration (1868) which imposed a fiscal system capable of raising large sums in direct taxes imposed on the agricultural sector. Those areas of the world that had not undergone a fully fledged agrarian revolution were seriously hampered in their industrial development, whether they were the overpopulated regions of South-East Asia or the underpopulated regions of Latin America.[3] In Sir Arthur Lewis's celebrated paper,[4] growth of productivity in the agricultural sector thwarted the process of industrialization because it gave rise to an increase in agricultural wages, thus raising the price of workers to industry, depressing the profit rate in the industrial sector, and consequently halting the accumulation process.

Kaldor, on the other hand, believed that an increase in agricultural productivity was a necessary condition for industrialization. He did so for two reasons. First because it created the extra wage goods for the growing urban population which, in Lewis's model, would have to be forcibly 'extorted' from farmers—for whom the diminishing percentage of the population in agriculture would have otherwise meant greater per-capita consumption. Second, because it created the conditions for autonomous demand in the manufacturing sector, conditions which were absent from Lewis's model. However, one notes that Lewis subsequently changed his mind. In his last writings on the subject, he took the agricultural revolution to be the necessary prerequisite for development.[5]

---

[3] Kaldor's thesis that the agricultural revolution is a general pre-condition for the economic 'take off' of a country partly contrasts with Gerschenkron's which gives a minor role to agriculture in the take off process of backward countries (A. Gerschenkron, *Economic Backwardness in Historical Perspective*, (Cambridge, Mass., Harvard University Press, 1965)).

[4] W. A. Lewis, 'Economic Development with Unlimited Supply of Labour', *Manchester school* (May 1954).

[5] Id., *The Evolution of the International Economic Order* (Princeton, NJ, Princeton University Press, 1978).

In Kaldor's view, agriculture and industry stand in a close relation, for the two reasons already discussed in Chapter 8. First, the growth of output in non-agricultural sectors is constrained by the excess of agricultural production over agricultural food consumption,[6] which does not depend on employment in the sector itself (given the constant presence of disguised unemployment), but on farming methods, on advances in agriculture, on the terms of trade, and on the rate of taxation. Second, although the development of agricultural production is 'led' by progress in agronomy and farming methods and by the accumulation of capital goods originating from industry, the development of industrial production needs a stimulus that is external to the sector. Although this stimulus comes from the rest of the world at stages of greater industrial maturity, in the early phases of industrialization it usually originates in agriculture.

Not only are the developments of agriculture and industry closely connected, there is an equally close link between economic development and the entrance of an economy on to the world market. Industrial development in Europe created a market which provided an outlet for the food and mining products of many developing countries; at the same time, investment opportunities for European capitalists were created in the agricultural and mining sectors of those countries. Only in a few cases, Kaldor argued, had this meant the creation in the backward countries of 'foreign enclaves' which contributed little to their development. Thus—and this should be stressed—Kaldor did not share the opinions of what we may call the 'conflict school'. In his review of Baran's *Political Economy of Growth*,[7] he agreed with the Marxist economist that the social basis of underdevelopment is the politico-social coalition of rich purchasers, powerful monopolists, and great landowners which defends the mercantile and feudal status quo and obstructs industrial capitalist development. But he refused to accept that coalitions of this kind are always the creation of Western countries, or that they are instrumental to their economic expansion. In fact, there were many underdeveloped countries, neither politically nor commercially dependent on the European countries, which had been unable to industrialize because of the hegemony of backward ruling classes impervious to foreign influence. Conversely, history provided examples of countries, such as Germany and Japan, which were late to "take off" but whose industrialization increased the economic well-being of their older industrialized counterparts like Great Britain and the United States instead of diminishing it. The earnings from exports by the primary sector of the developing countries became industrial demand in the countries with suitable socio-economic conditions, and therefore stimulated the creation of local industry.

(3) Generally speaking, this initial stage of 'openness' to the products of the primary sector was followed by a phase of 'closure' and of protective tariffs

[6] As he had already argued in 1954 in a paper trans. from the Italian as 'Characteristics of Economic Development', in CP ii.

[7] P. A. Baran, *Political Economy of Growth* (New York, Monthly Review Press, 1957).

on industrial products. Kaldor agreed with List that the countries that began their industrialization later had no chance of developing their industry without protective tariffs. The lower level of real wages per man-hour in industrializing countries was outweighed by the lower productivity of the labour employed in their newly established industries, with the result that their cost of labour per unit of output was relatively higher. Hence, apart from Great Britain, which was the first country to industrialize and which therefore found herself in a position of monopoly, all other countries had begun their industrialization by protecting their national manufacturing with tariffs.

During this 'protected' stage, on the demand side, industry received an external impetus (which is still internal to the country) from the growth of incomes in the agricultural sector; on the costs side, money-wages were kept low by widespread disguised unemployment in agriculture. However, the country quickly profited from increasing returns to scale and from the acquisition of know-how. This accounted for the success of those countries which began by developing industrial sectors requiring easily assimilable production techniques and which were able to create a sufficiently broad national market, even if per-capita incomes were low. The most typical example of this was the textiles industry.

Protection must therefore be temporary, and restricted to those industrial sectors that the country decided should be given first priority. If protection was applied generally and if it was prolonged, the process of industrialization became sluggish. Evidence of this was provided by the countries of Latin America, which had pursued a generalized policy of import-substitution for many years. I shall return to this topic later.

The only option for industrializing countries was to copy the model of development adopted by all the economically advanced countries. None of these—neither England, Western Europe, North America, nor Japan, perhaps with the sole exception of the United States—would have been able to develop without industrial export-led growth.

(4) In countries just beginning to industrialize, exports should increase at a rate no lower than the rate of growth of national production. Kaldor believed that such countries should never forget Bismarck's famous phrase: 'We must export or die'.[8]

However, from this latter point of view, the developing countries were in a more difficult position than the countries that had industrialized during the nineteenth century and were thus able to develop in an international context of free trade. Goods imported from developing countries now faced widespread discrimination, which stemmed from the fear of the developed countries that imported goods produced by low-paid labour would threaten the living standards of their own much higher-paid workers. This was certainly true in the short term, especially if unaccompanied by full-employment

---

[8] Kaldor, *Strategic Factors in Economic Development*, 61.

policies. But if economic activity was kept at the level necessary to reabsorb unemployed workers, the transfer of labour—from activities adversely affected by competing goods produced in developing countries to other activities—acted on the economic system in the same way as technical progress did: by saving labour and/or replacing old products with new ones.[9] This was to the benefit of the workers themselves if the cheaper imported goods were wage goods.[10] Nevertheless, while no country would want to obstruct the introduction of technical progress, many did in fact still oppose the removal of tariff barriers on goods from developing countries.[11] For Kaldor, it was precisely these restrictions that represented the major obstacle to the rapid economic progress of those regions of the world that had started out on the difficult road to industrialization.

Over the last three decades many of the Third World countries have undergone rapid industrialization; a number of them have achieved extremely rapid expansion in their manufacturing exports to the advanced countries; and some of them (like Taiwan and South Korea) actually have large and growing trade surpluses. The question now is whether these trends will lead to the 'de-industrialization' of the advanced countries—a problem that preoccupied Kaldor a great deal.[12] During the so-called Golden Age (1950–73), the rapid growth of manufacturing exports from the newly industrialized countries did not conflict with full employment in the advanced regions. In the world of the last two decades, however, with low rates of growth and high unemployment in many industrialized countries, such conflict is now indeed manifest, and has provoked strident calls for protection against products from the Third World, the newly industrialized countries, and Japan. One may conclude with Singh that

[9] The importing of textiles from Hong Kong had the same effect on the cotton industry as the invention of the synthetic fibres that had replaced cotton.

[10] The opposite conclusion has been reached by the theory of the equalization of factor prices based on the Stopler–Samuelson theorem. The theory's weakness lies in its assumption of a given amount of capital, so that if highly labour-intensive industries contract and highly capital-intensive industries expand, there will be a change in the capital/labour ratio in all industries until the point is reached at which the (given) amount of capital 'employs' the same amount of workers as before. Thus the marginal product of labour decreases and with it wages, although average labour output has increased. These conclusions are in fact fallacious because capital is not like land, and its quantity is not fixed irrespective of the distribution of output among various industries. The increase in the output of the highly capital-intensive industries is matched by an increase in the total amount of capital. The fact is that highly capital-intensive industries have high per-capita output. Their output therefore increases at the same rate as the accumulation of capital in these sectors increases.

[11] On the occasion of a lecture during which I defended Kaldor's position, Alain Liepitz raised the objection that the protective barriers imposed by the industrialized countries *can* be justified if wages are kept low in the developing countries by repressive and non-democratic governments. Willy Brandt, on the other hand, in a lecture given to the Fondazione Feltrinelli on 26 Nov. 1987 on North–South relations in the 1980s, argued that, as a general rule to which only a very few cases are the exception, the industrialized countries should not impose prejudicial policies on aid to, and free trade with, the industrializing countries.

[12] See N. Kaldor, 'What is De-Industrialization', in F. Blackby (ed.), *De-Industrialization* (London, Heinemann, 1979).

the resumption of the Golden Age growth path is the first best solution to the present problems of the world economy; if this is not feasible,[13] (Kaldor's proposal for) planned, co-ordinated trade is a second best solution, much to be preferred to the current unsatisfactory state of ad hoc protectionism which can easily degenerate into a negative sum game.[14]

9.2. Import-Substitution and Structural Inflation in Latin America

For a policy of import-substitution to be effective and to discourage inefficient local industries, Kaldor advocated protective measures that were modest, discriminatory, and temporary—as has already been said. The temporary nature of these measures is important. As the internal market broadens and as industry moves out of its 'infancy' stage, there should be a progressive relaxing of tariffs. Heavy industry (chemicals, steel, and engineering) should be established when light industry has begun to export a high proportion of its output. Latin American countries, however, had not followed this pattern. The initial impetus to their industrialization was not an explicitly industrial policy, but the necessity to save foreign currency created by a sudden change in the terms of trade during the 1930s.

In Latin America, restrictions on imports raised the prices of imported goods rapidly and by a large amount. As such, they were the equivalent of a protective measure that was sudden, drastic, and indiscriminate. Protection made production for the domestic market extremely profitable, at costs which were, in terms of food output, many times higher than international prices.

Under these conditions, protected national industry expanded—thereby accelerating the process of urbanization. This increase in industrial production led to an increase in profits and wages in both the industrial sector and in services. Most of the profits were spent on consumption goods,[15] mainly of foreign origin, and even those profits that were reinvested generated further imports of components and raw materials. On the other hand, the Latin American countries could not offset their imports by exporting manufactured goods, because their industry produced at costs, expressed in terms of domestic

[13] For examination of the reasons for believing that the world economy will continue to expand in the foreseeable future at the post-1973 rate, and that it will not resume its Golden Age growth path, see A. Glyn *et al.*, 'The Rise and Fall of the Golden Age', in S. A. Marglin (ed.), *The End of the Golden Age* (Oxford, OUP, forthcoming).

[14] Singh, 'Third World Competition', 119.

[15] In a study of Chile (N. Kaldor, essay trans. from the Spanish as 'Economic Problems of Chile', in CP iv) commissioned by the UN ECLA in 1956, Kaldor showed how the share of profits in the national income had been enormously increased in the period of industrialization by import-substitution, how it had taken up the entire average increase in per-capita output, and how it had reached levels much higher than in the Anglo-Saxon countries. However, in Chile, unlike the industrialized countries, this high share of profits was accompanied by a low average propensity to save due to the high propensity to spend on luxury goods. In 1964 Kaldor calculated that the cost of maintaining the idle rich was more burdensome on the Latin American economy than armaments on the US economy.

agricultural products, that were many times higher than the international costs of such products.

Trade deficits were accompanied, moreover, by inflation when the increase in wage costs—which meant increased demand in the agricultural sector—occurred in countries where agriculture was stagnant.[16] In this case, the increase in demand for wage goods led, in an upward spiral, to higher prices in the national currency of agricultural products, to a rise in nominal wages, and thence to a rise in the prices of non-agricultural prices.

This brings us to Kaldor's theory of Latin American inflation, which he had already outlined in his 1956 study of the Chilean economy.[17] For Kaldor and the economists of the 'structuralist school', a distinction must be drawn between the initial 'structural' cause of the upward pressure on prices and the 'propagation mechanism' by which the initial push generates an inflation spiral. Whereas for Kaldor the main cause of Latin American inflation was the inelastic supply of agricultural products, the structuralist school[18] held that inflation was not solely agricultural in origin, but was also caused by a number of bottle-necks. The initial cause of inflation was for Kaldor the disproportion between the growth of agriculture and manufacturing production, which led to an increase in the price of agricultural products. This increased wages, and the resultant wage-price spiral propagated the initial push into an inflationary process. Note that higher wages were not generated by a shortage of labour but by a 'shortage of land'. Nor were they due to trade-union pressure, since it was the entrepreneurs themselves who paid higher money-wages in order to improve their employees' diet, to raise their productivity and therefore to reduce the cost of labour per unit of output.

If this was the nature of the inflationary process in the countries of Latin America, it explains the following phenomena: (1) for more than twenty years (until the oil shock) the Latin American countries had inflation rates of 20–50 per cent; (2) for a long period of time this high level of inflation did not explode into the sort of hyperinflation that afflicted certain countries of Cen-

---

[16] The reasons for the stagnation of agriculture varied from country to country. In Argentina, where agriculture was more 'commercialized', the important factor was unfavourable changes in the terms of trade (especially during the years of the Peron regime). In Chile, the problem was due to absentee ownership, the lack of incentives, and the absence of land reform.

[17] Kaldor, 'Economic Problems of Chile'.

[18] A theory of inflation of this kind was first developed by Kalecki (M. Kalecki, 'What is Inflation?', *Bulletin of the Oxford University Institute of Statistics* (May 1941)), who also applied it to developing countries (id., 'The Problem of Financing Economic Development', *Trimestre Economic* (Oct.–Dec. 1954)). Subsequently, several economists, mainly Latin American, formed the so-called 'structuralist school' to pursue the Kalecki–Kaldorian line of thought. Ahumada, Sunkel, and Pinto were among its first members, Prebish and Seers among its best-known (R. Prebish, 'Economic Development or Monetary Stability: The False Dilemma', ECLA, *Economic Bulletin*, 1 (1961); D. Seers, 'A Theory of Inflation and Growth in Underdeveloped Economies Based on the Experiences of Latin America', *OEP* (June 1962)). Despite the structuralist school's use of Kaldor's approach, it criticized him for laying too much emphasis on inelastic agricultural supply as the primary cause of inflation, and adduced other, complementary reasons: distributional problems, lack of foreign currencies, adverse terms of trade, and rigidities in public finance.

tral Europe after the First and Second World Wars; (3) these countries experienced inflationary processes of varing intensities, none of which, however, appeared to have any connection with the rate of growth of national income; (4) inflation in these countries was instead generated by the rate of change in agricultural prices.[19]

Because of the specific nature of its causes,[20] structural inflation could only be cured by the introduction of measures designed to promote exports or to increase agricultural surplus. This latter remedy entailed land reform,[21] accompanied by appropriate taxation[22] or the liberalization of imports of agricultural products.[23] Restrictive monetary policies, however, were futile,[24] since, by cutting back non-agricultural output, they reduced affluence without addressing the root of the problem.

Just as ineffective as restrictive monetary policy in dealing with structural inflation was the policy of devaluation propounded by numerous economists and imposed by the IMF on the developing countries.[25] Devaluation was of little use in remedying the persistent trade deficit of these countries, in that the problem was not caused by the overvaluation of their domestic currencies.[26] In fact, their major exports were primary products, and most of these were goods for international markets (and not for domestic consumption). Competition therefore made the monetary cost in national currency of all agricultural products depend very closely on the prices, expressed in the same domestic currency, of the agricultural products that could be sold on international markets. In these circumstances the first effect of a fall in the exchange rate was an increase in the incomes, expressed in domestic currency, of exporters. Only if these higher incomes induced an increase in national production of such proportions as to expand the world supply of these products, would the fall in the exchange rate have the beneficial effect of lowering the

---

[19] N. Kaldor, 'The Role of Industrialization in Latin American Inflations' (1971), repr. in CP vi.

[20] There were certain countries, like the republics of Central America, which were able to cope with the fall in their exports in the 1930s by not pursuing a policy of import-substitution, partly because they were still colonies of European powers at the time. These countries were not affected by serious inflation until the 1960s.

[21] The distribution of land among numerous new owners after the revolution in Mexico gave a dynamism to the country's agriculture that enabled food supplies in excess of self-consumption to keep pace with the growth of urban demand.

[22] This was the policy that Kaldor recommended for Brazil in the early 1970s. See his speeches published in the conference proceedings, W. Baer and I. Kerstenetzky (eds.), *Inflation and Growth in Latin America* (Irwin, Ill., 1964).

[23] Venezuela's oil exports and Peru's exports of products from its fishing industry allowed them to liberalize food imports. This is why inflation in those countries was relatively low.

[24] N. Kaldor, 'The Role of Fiscal and Monetary Policies in Latin American Inflations', in *Interamerican Institute of Capital Markets* (Caracas, 1979).

[25] See T. Killick, 'The IMF Role in Developing Countries', *Finance and Development* (Sept. 1984).

[26] See N. Kaldor *et al.*, *Une politique monétaire pour l'Amérique Latine* (Paris, Institut Atlantique, 1966); N. Kaldor, 'Devaluation and Adjustment in Developing Countries' (1983), repr. in CP iv.

dollar prices of these products, with a consequent increase in international demand for them. Should this not happen, devaluation would not have the effects it was designed to achieve. Furthermore, with the opportunities provided by an increase in the dollar prices for export crops, farmers would tend to cut back on the supply of foodstuffs so that a certain proportion of agricultural land could be withdrawn from food production for local consumption and switched to the production of crops for export. Hence an increase in prices in international currency of export crops would, sooner or later, lead to a corresponding increase in the local prices of foodstuffs.

Since money-wages, especially in the developing countries, were closely linked with the prices of foodstuffs, it followed that an increase in earnings from the exports of agricultural products would tend to bring about a corresponding increase in the monetary costs of the industrial sector. This was why devaluations were generally followed by waves of inflation, which rapidly cancelled out the initial stimulus to export that the devaluation was designed to provide.

For these reasons Kaldor was convinced that in a developing country, unlike a developed country, there existed no *single* equilibrium exchange rate between national costs of production and international prices. Balance-of-payments equilibrium could therefore only be achieved by adjusting the cost structure (that is, reducing industrial costs relative to agricultural prices)—not by changing the general level of costs in terms of an international currency, which was, instead, the result of devaluation. The only remedy for the problem of trade deficit and structural inflation was, according to Kaldor, a system of dual exchange rates,[27] or a system of taxes and subsidies which produced the same effect.

9.3. Dual Exchange Rates, Taxes, Duties, and Trade Subsidies

A dual exchange rate would produce 'as good an approximation to the Pigouvian prescription of adjusting relative prices in accordance with marginal social costs as the more orthodox method involving a system of differential taxes and subsidies'.[28] Kaldor argued that there should be two exchange rates, one official and one free. The official rate would apply to exports of raw materials and to all essential imports, including those required by the government's policy of industrialization. The free rate (which should be floating) would govern the exchange of the foreign currency demanded by importers and supplied by the exporters of manufactured goods. The more demand for unnecessary imports and therefore for currency increases relative to export receipts, the higher the free rate will be relative to the official one. This would

[27] Id., 'Dual Exchange Rates and Economic Development' (1964), repr. CP iv.
[28] Ibid. 188.

make it more profitable to produce manufactured exports, would improve the trade balance and would bring the two exchange rates closer together.

Compared with a simple tariff system, the dual exchange-rate system has the advantage that the *ad valorem* import duty is counterbalanced by an *ad valorem* export subsidy. Moreover, adjustment of the balance through the exchange rate does not affect the prices in domestic currency of staple goods and therefore does not have inflationary consequences. Adjustment takes place instead through the promotion of national industry. The advantage of promoting national industry may therefore be added to the beneficial effects of free trade in terms of international specialization and division of labour. Each country is encouraged to concentrate its resources on the industrial sectors in which it enjoys relative advantages. By contrast, the alternative of promoting industrialization through differential taxes (which gives each industry the differential protection it needs to become profitable) tends to have the damaging consequence of excessive diversification and fragmentation.

Kaldor saw two possible alternatives to a policy of dual exchange rates. The first was combining currency devaluation with export duties on primary products so that the incomes in domestic currency of the producers of these goods remained the same. The proceeds from these export duties could then be used to subsidize essential imports, thus forestalling the inflationary effects of higher import prices on the cost of living. The other alternative was to leave the exchange rate unchanged and to levy a tax on the export of primary products, the proceeds from which could be used as subsidies on exports of manufactured goods.

Kaldor preferred his dual exchange-rate policy to these two alternatives. A policy of devaluation coupled with export duties on primary products has two drawbacks. First, if the measure is to be a successful one, the devaluation has to be large, and the duty on the export of primary products will therefore have to be high. It would be difficult for the government to levy high export duties on such a politically influential category as exporters. There would therefore be a tendency not to impose the duty to its fullest extent on export earnings, thus reducing the overall impact of the manœuvre. Second, devaluation would bring a major change in the internal price structure, which would be difficult to compensate for through subsidies on essential imports. The disadvantage of the second alternative, a policy of export taxes on primary products with subsidies on manufactured goods, is that it requires the co-operation of importing countries if subsidies are not to be regarded as a 'dumping' policy. Moreover, the developing countries in the scheme would have to agree to a progressive reduction in their participation as their levels of industrial development rose. Further, countries qualifying for the scheme would have to be carefully defined; and, finally, it is more difficult to draw a distinction between 'primary products' and 'manufactured goods' than it is between the goods exchanged at a fixed rate and/or a floating rate in a system of dual exchange rates.

Adoption of a dual exchange rate, however, does not rule out cases (even though limited) where a developing country has to resort to a general devaluation. This may happen, for instance, when the production cost of a country's staple export (cash crops, tropical or temperate foodstuffs, or mining products) differs greatly from the international price expressed in local currency at the prevailing rate of exchange. This overvaluation of the currency erodes the country's export of primary products should the real price obtained by farmers be so low that they no longer find it worthwhile to harvest the full crop.

A situation of this kind may arise when the official exchange rate has moved so far from what one might call 'purchasing power parity' (i.e. when domestic prices in the primary sector are much higher than world prices at the prevailing rate of exchange) that only a significant change in the exchange rate can align internal and external prices and increase the profits of the staple exporters.

However, in this case too, devaluation as a remedy for the trade-balance problems of the developing countries is less effective than one might think. When the devaluation is caused by a sudden and major change in the terms of trade (for example a bad harvest or an international increase in the price of oil), it may lead to losses of real wages so large as to be socially unacceptable: in which event the country should be allowed to adopt other measures, the limitation of non-essential imports, for example, instead of devaluing. The same applies to devaluation due to an exorbitant breakdown in purchasing power parity. In general, this situation is the outcome of an inflationary process generated by structural factors which devaluation does not eliminate. Moroever, it may happen (Kaldor cited the African countries of the southern Sahara) that the disequilibrium in the trade balance arising from the reduction by farmers of their agricultural production—because of low profits—is primarily due to their being forced to sell their crops to marketing boards or co-operatives at prices fixed at levels lower than those of the domestic market. Devaluation in this case increases the profitability of producers only if there is political consensus on changing the distribution of incomes.

Generally speaking, every devaluation in a country exporting primary products leads to an increase in domestic agricultural prices and thence to a redistribution of income from urban wage-earners to rural producers. The benefits of devaluation will persist only so long as it does not activate a process which re-establishes the previous distribution of incomes through an increase in urban wages. Kaldor therefore concluded that these considerations 'point to the fact that the basic requirement is political and social reform, involving the creation of a consensus on income distribution'.[29]

---

[29] Id., 'Devaluation and Adjustment in Developing Countries', 274. For an investigation of the importance of political aspects in economic-policy analysis and proposals for the developing countries, see the essay on inflation in Latin America by A. Hirshman, *Essays in Trespassing: Economics to Politics and Beyond* (Cambridge, CUP, 1981). For survey articles on devaluation in developing countries, see J. Williamson, 'A Survey of the Literature on the Optimal Peg', *Journal of Development Economics*, 11 (1981); P. Wickman, 'The Choice of Exchange Rate Regime in Developing Countries: A Survey of the Literature', *IMF Staff Papers*, 32 (1985).

9.4. Unilateral Stabilization of Commodity Prices

Another source of difficulty for the developing economies was that they sold their commodities on competitive markets and bought manufactured goods on oligopolistic markets. The instability of the terms of trade hit them hard. In 1952 Kaldor assisted, on behalf of the FAO, with the renewal of the International Wheat Agreement of 1949.[30] Although the agreement was formally renewed in 1953, it was never actually implemented because the major importing countries refused to participate by undertaking to pay minimum prices. After 1953 any regulation of fluctuations in commodity prices (with the exception of tin) by means of international agreements based on buffer-stocks systems ceased to exist. The only instances of this kind of agreement, covering sugar in 1953 and coffee in 1963, concerned individual commodities and involved only producers belonging to some sort of cartel (the coffee agreement also included the consumer countries).

Ten years after his report on the International Wheat Agreement, Kaldor was invited by Raul Prebisch, the executive secretary of the ECLA, to write a paper on the stabilizing of commodity prices. Kaldor was worried not only by the instability of the prices of primary products, but also by the deterioration of the terms of trade of primary commodities, a long-running trend.[31] His paper examined the framework within which a solidly based cartel of producers could be organized able to influence commodity prices via the regulation of supplies to the world market (similar to OPEC).

There were three conditions for the success of such price agreements. First, they should secure the full participation of a large number of producer countries. Second, they should comprise mechanisms that regulated not only trade, but also the production of commodities, otherwise accumulations of excess stocks might occur which the commodity-producing countries would find financially difficult to bear. Third, the agreements should provide for a gradual change in the export quotas of participating countries in favour of those producing at lower costs, otherwise these latter would have more to gain from breaking the agreement.

For the achievement of these objectives, Kaldor devised a mechanism for adjusting the level of production of each member country by means of a variable export levy. This was to be high for the more efficient countries and low for the less efficient ones. Every three years, however, the quotas of international trade of the countries participating in the scheme would be

---

[30] N. Kaldor, *A Reconsideration of the Economics of the International Wheat Agreement* (1952), repr. in CP iv. 25 years later Kaldor wrote to Charles Schultze, chairman of the Council of Economic Advisers in the USA, to propose a new policy for stabilizing the world price of wheat. Although he received a sympathetic reply, his effort was fruitless. (A. P. Thirlwall, 'Kaldor as Policy Adviser', *CJE* (Mar. 1989), 138).

[31] N. Kaldor, 'Stabilizing the Terms of Trade of Underdeveloped Countries' repr. in (1962), CP iv. The same argument was restated 20 years later in id., 'The Role of Commodity Prices in Economic Recovery' (1982), repr. in CP v.

modified by changing the structure of the export levies, but by no more than 5 per cent. The scheme would not apply to all commodities, only to those from tropical regions (coffee, sugar, etc.) and to commodities the bulk of which was exported.

Clearly, for the agreement to have any chance of success the degree of co-operation and self-discipline among producer countries would have to be extremely high; as high in fact as the far-sightedness that had been required of the importing countries for the International Wheat Agreement to be feasible.

Numerous discussions with economists of developing countries led Kaldor to the sad conclusion that the political conditions necessary for the functioning of his scheme did not exist. Henceforth, he would pin his hopes for the stabilization of commodity prices and the terms of trade[32] on reform of the international monetary system, along the lines described in Chapter 13.2.

9.5. The Choice of Techniques

Although Kaldor had argued that a country must first develop its light industry, this should not be taken to mean that he believed either that industrialization should be based on small decentralized units or that techniques with a low capital/labour ratio should be adopted. He did not agree with the policy of 'rural industry' pursued by India and China in order to delay the process of urbanization. The regional concentration of industries brought advantages that were not measurable in terms of economies of scale alone: what the developing countries really needed was know-how and skilled workers, and these were more easily found in urban centres. Geographical concentration also gave easier access to markets; though, on the other hand, the development of transport and availability of electricity had made industries much less dependent on local sources of energy.

As for the choice of technologies, Kaldor disagreed with the neo-classical thesis that, on account of the relative scarcity of factors, techniques with a low capital/labour ratio should be used; indeed he recommended the opposite.[33] A high capital/labour ratio did not imply a high capital/output ratio, as the example of the United States over the previous fifty years had demonstrated: here a rise in the capital/labour ratio had been matched by a fall in the capital/output ratio. Furthermore, India's policy of using old machinery to reduce the capital/labour ratio was misguided. Because of the need to replace unusable or worn-out parts, the policy had led to a rise in the capital/output ratio, because the working capital per unit of raw material and per unit of output was greater.

[32] See J. Spraos, 'Kaldor on Commodities', *CJE* (March 1989).
[33] N. Kaldor, 'The Choice of Technology in Less Developed Countries', *MLR* (Aug. 1969).

On the other hand, believing labour to be a free good was a mistake, for the simple reason that there was disguised unemployment in agriculture. In fact, if labour was employed in industry, it should receive wages higher than the agricultural subsistence level: industrial employment involved greater physical effort (and obliged every worker to feed his family, which could no longer rely on the subsistence provided by agricultural self-consumption); and because it was profitable for employers to pay higher wages if this led to a lower labour cost per unit of output.[34] Given wages, the best technique was one that maximized the rate of accumulation and therefore the ratio between output and necessary consumption.[35]

However, Kaldor did not overlook practical considerations—which worked partly in favour and partly against his view that more modern techniques with a high capital/labour ratio were the most appropriate. If, on the one hand, the scarcity of skilled manpower in the developing countries entailed the adoption of more modern techniques if this saved on skilled labour, on the other, it was preferable to adopt older, more labour-intensive techniques if more modern machinery was underutilized because nobody knew how to operate it, or if it stood idle because it was not properly maintained. Also, more than physical capital, what the developing countries lacked was organizational capacity; thus those who had to choose between old and new techniques should decide which technique required fewer skills of organization and management. The choice was therefore a complex one.

A last point needs stressing. Advanced technologies at an increasing capital/labour ratio often involve large-scale production (steel mills being the most typical example) and require markets much larger than those available in the countries moving through the early stages of industrialization. In these cases, so-called 'appropriate technology', such as the outcome of research into small-scale technologies for industries like chemicals and steel, might be most suitable.[36]

9.6. The Role of Taxation in Developing Countries

For reasons of space, I shall not go into details of Kaldor's numerous proposals as an official tax-adviser to India, Ceylon, Mexico, Ghana, Guiana, Turkey,

[34] Given that wages in agriculture are at subsistence level in the developing, but not the developed, economies, this explains why the difference in wages between agriculture and industry is higher, the less developed the country.

[35] In the well-known 1960s debate on this point, Maurice Dobb and Amartya Sen, who argued in favour of a view shared by Kaldor, were ranged against Michael Kalecki, followed by Joan Robinson, who proposed the maximization of employment and output. See A. K. Sen, *Choice of Techniques* (Oxford, Basil Blackwell, 1960); M. Dobb, *An Essay on Economic Growth and Planning* (London, Routledge & Kegan Paul, 1960); M. Kalecki, *Selected Essays on the Economic Growth of the Socialist and Mixed Economy* (Cambridge, CUP, 1972), ch. 10.

[36] With the diffusion of electronics, the idea that industrial development might not be synonymous with increasing returns from large-scale plant becomes more persuasive. See C. Sabel, 'Industrializzazione del terzo mondo e nuovi modelli produttivi', *Stato e Mercato* (Aug. 1986).

Iran, and Venezuela, in the twenty years between January 1956 and December 1976.[37] In general, he believed that taxation had two functions to perform in developing countries: providing incentives, and releasing the resources needed to finance education, health, communications, and infrastructures in general. This latter function, he believed, ought to be given first priority by the tax systems in these countries.[38] However, in some specific but important cases, taxation had a further function. We know from Chapter 5 that Kaldor held that, in a developed country, the adjustment of the ratio between investment and output which secures full-employment growth is performed by shifts in the share of profits in the national income. However, there were certain developing countries, an example being Chile (a case examined by Kaldor in 1956), where the propensity to consume of capitalists was too high ('British property owners appear to have saved 48% of their post-tax income and spent 52%, whereas the Chileans saved 26% and spent 74%'[39]) and the rate of investment too low (according to Kaldor's calculations, in the United Kingdom the proportion of after-tax profit ploughed back into investment was 60 per cent, in Chile 15 per cent). Here an increase in the share of profits would exacerbate the unequal distribution of income without raising the rate of investment. In circumstances where an increase in the share of profits in national income would have little or no effect in encouraging saving and investment, but would only lead to greater expenditure on luxury consumption, the most appropriate means to achieve a fast rate of growth and high levels of employment were government intervention through taxation on profits and an effective investment policy by the public sector.[40]

The aim of the tax system, Kaldor argued, should be to define the 'taxable surplus', i.e. the taxation potential given by the difference between the actual consumption and the minimum consumption of the population. Although minimum consumption was not easily measurable—since it was not just a matter of material conditions but also depended on historical and social factors—it should nevertheless be the sole criterion governing the system of taxation in

[37] Most of these case studies have been collected in CP viii. For a general appraisal of Kaldor's work as a tax-adviser to developing countries, see J. Toye, 'Nicholas Kaldor and Tax Reforms in Developing Countries', *CJE* (Mar. 1989). This provides a useful table with an outline description of Kaldor's advisory activities. See also A. P. Thirlwall, *Nicholas Kaldor* (Brighton, Wheatsheaf Books, 1987), ch. 5.

[38] N. Kaldor, 'The Role of Taxation in Economic Development' (1962), pub. in CP iii.

[39] Id., 'Economic Problems of Chile', 621. Kaldor did not discuss, however, the low propensity to save of the middle classes: he 'should have also asked why the middle class had such negligible savings, and not direct that question only at the property-owning class'. J. G. Palma and M. Marcel, 'Kaldor on the "Discreet Charm" of the Chilean Bourgeoisie', *CJE* (Mar. 1989), 253.

[40] Palma and Marcel have written: '[T]he realization that after thirty years most of his policy proposals are still on the agenda is rather depressing . . . [because] nothing [is] more resistant to change than a social formation in the South . . . However, even if Kaldor's 1956 article has not yet influenced Chilean economic policies in the way that it obviously should, it has at least had a significant influence on development literature, particularly by thoroughly destroying the case for worsening income distribution as a necessary condition for growth in developing countries.' Palma and Marcel, 'Kaldor on the Chilean Bourgeoisie', 265–6.

a developing country. Taxation potential depended not so much on the level of income as on the degree of inequality in the distribution of income and of wealth, on the structure of land ownership, on the pressure of population on land, and on the proportion of national income accruing to non-residents. Only if taxes were levied on this taxable surplus could inflation or the contraction of private accumulation be avoided.

Once this surplus was defined, reform of the tax system should seek to increase tax revenue in relation to income, a ratio that was relatively low in developing countries. At the beginning of the 1960s the average total tax revenue of the developing countries was 8 to 15 per cent of national income, while in the more advanced countries it was between 25 and 33 per cent.[41] In the developing countries the bulk of wealth derived from land ownership, yet most of these countries' tax revenues in the modern age[42] accrued from industry and commerce. Tax systems were therefore progressive in theory but regressive in practice: direct tax revenue was only between 10 and 20 per cent of overall income.

Because the growth of non-agricultural labour was governed by the growth of agricultural surplus, taxation on agriculture and the ensuing extraction of surplus from the sector had a critical role to play in the acceleration of economic development—as demonstrated by the 1870s land tax in Japan and by the compulsory selling of foodstuffs at low prices in Soviet Russia between the wars. In order to avoid the socially unacceptable consequences of agricultural taxation, and in order to turn it into a more effective incentive for production, Kaldor recommended a progressive agricultural tax with exemptions for small-sized farmholdings.

Agricultural taxation was only partially effective when fixed or if levied on goods purchased by the agricultural sector. Instead, the criterion for assessing taxation potential should be the 'potential relative fertility' (PRF) of the land. This was to be determined from values of average fertility deducible on the basis of various indicators such as rainfall, irrigation, the quality of the soil, the slope of the ground, and so forth. A progressive tax on PRF would act as an incentive to farmers, since the income after tax from an efficiently managed farm would be higher than the income to be earned from another farm with the same PRF. The tax encouraged a better system of land ownership because less efficient farmers would transfer their land to those who obtained—from land with the same PRF—a higher income after tax.

---

[41] N. Kaldor, 'Will Underdeveloped Countries Learn to Tax?' (1962), repr. in CP iii. 10 years later this ratio for developing countries was on average still around 15%. R. J. Chelliah *et al.*, (Mar. 1975). We remind the reader that this ratio today in the EEC countries is on average around 40%. 'Tax Ratios and Tax Efforts in Developing Countries, 1969–1971', *IMF Staff Papers*.

[42] Unlike today, in past centuries in Europe, Asia, the Middle East, India, and Japan the principal source of revenue was land tax; since the beginning of the 20th cent. tax erosion has reduced the incidence of land taxes in total taxation.

From the early 1960s onwards Kaldor coupled his land tax with a tax on trade (because of the incentive it gave to more efficient firms). This took the form of what is generally known in Europe today as value-added tax.

The great disparities among personal incomes in the developing countries required a reform of personal taxation that hinged on four essential conditions. Taxation should encompass all incomes; it should be levied on family income and not on individual income; it should, as far as possible, be deducted at source; the levy system should be simple and with moderate rates, but with no loopholes and incentives for evasion. There was, however, a futher require-ment which was absolutely vital if a personal tax was to become a stable and important fiscal instrument: that the secrecy and anonymity of property should no longer be regarded as a sacred and inviolable right.

This personal income tax would be flanked by two other taxes: one on personal wealth, with very low rates (from 0.5 to 2 per cent) and with exemp-tions for property of less than a certain amount; the other on the transfer of property, either gratuitously or through inheritance, and proportionate to the wealth of the recipient, not to the value of the transfer.

Two major problems for the developing countries were the tax treatment of the incomes of non-residents and the functioning of the government depart-ments responsible for tax administration. As regards the first problem, the country had to decide whether investments by foreign firms were intended to develop local industry or whether they were made simply in order to re-export the manufactured product. Only in the former case could tax concessions encouraging reinvested profits be justified, and only after careful examination of the book profits of the multinational companies—which, by means of transfer prices among subsidiaries, could easily shift their profits to tax-haven countries. It was therefore extremely important to co-ordinate the tax treat-ment of foreign companies among the developing countries, and also between them and the companies' home countries.

As regards the second problem, Kaldor pointed to corruption as one of the principal reasons for the low tax yield in developing countries. The battle against corruption should be conducted on two fronts: first, tax law should be simple and universally understood; second, tax officials should be carefully selected and offered high wages, status, and good career prospects. Imperial China had adopted this strategy when it established the corps of the finance inspectors of the Maritime Customs. The measure had eradicated the corrup-tion of the tax administration in a country where the evil was deeply ingrained in society.

9.7. Economic Development and Democratic Reformism

Kaldor may have generalized when he was examining the problem of econ-omic development, but he never dealt in abstractions. The first section of this chapter sought to give a summary of Kaldor's analysis conducted in his several papers, documents, and articles describing the progress of industrialization through its various stages. Although he frequently stressed *common* elements in the pre-conditions for industrialization (chief of these being the agricultural revolution) and in the limits to industrialization (low agricultural surplus and non-export-oriented industrial strategies), he never became entangled in the analytical rigidities of the Rostowian stages of economic development.[43]

Although he did not participate directly in the well-known debate between the proponents of balanced development à la Nurske[44] and unbalanced development à la Streeten and Rosenstein Rodan,[45] Kaldor's preferences were nevertheless for the latter: he believed that a country should specialize, and that its growth should be based on the exports from a limited number of light industries. At the same time, however, he advocated the balanced development of agriculture and industry to ensure that industrialization was not attended by structural inflation.

In his search for the causes of failed development, Kaldor laid little blame on colonialism; indeed one can argue that colonialism as such has no specific role to play in his analysis of underdevelopment. This is not to imply that he was unaware of the operation, at an international level, of the mechanisms of cumulative circular causation à la Myrdal[46] that make the rich countries even richer and drive the poor ones further into impoverishment. Nevertheless, the regions of the world were, or could become, economically complementary, and there was no necessary reason why the development of some should be in conflict with the development of the others.[47] This, however, does not mean that he saw the advanced countries as entirely without responsibility for the laggard industrialization of the developing countries: the imposition of customs barriers on the latters' exports had been one of the major reasons for their slow growth. *A fortiori* Kaldor was opposed to this policy, because if the industrialized countries pursued a full-employment policy, customs protection against the developing countries was also damaging to the developed countries themselves. The only escape from the spiral of increasing impoverishment was industrialization, and one of the necessary conditions for successful industrialization was the entrance of the developing countries on to the world market.

---

[43] W. W. Rostow, *The Stages of Economic Growth* (Cambridge, CUP, 1960). Rostow worked for Kaldor at the UN in Geneva, but only briefly. He soon transferred to the Economics Department headed by Gunnar Myrdal.

[44] R. Nurske, *Lectures on Economic Development* (Istanbul, 1958).

[45] P. Rosenstein Rodan, 'Notes on the Theory of the "Big Push" ', in H. Ellis (ed.), *Economic Development for Latin America* (London, Macmillan, 1961); P. Streeten, 'Unbalanced Growth', *OEP* (June 1959).

[46] G. Myrdal, *Economic Theory and Underdeveloped Regions* (London, Duckworth, 1957).

[47] Kaldor's ideas on growth and inflation in the developing countries resembled those of the ECLA economists and the Latin American structuralist school. However, the latter stressed 'external' factors, such as the international division of labour and the unequal distribution of gain from trade, while Kaldor emphasized 'internal' factors like the absence of a progressive entrepreneurial class. See Palma and Marcel, 'Kaldor on the Chilean Bourgeoisie', 246–7.

The nations of the First World were also blameworthy in their dealings with the Third World for their refusal to stabilize the terms of trade and therefore the revenues from exports of primary products.

Kaldor was certainly not a free-trader à la Viner[48] (we need only remind ourselves of the importance that he attached to the protection of infant industry and his criticism of the neo-classical theory of international trade for its staticity). Nevertheless he identified autarchic economic policies as the principal obstacles to the industrialization of Latin America. The chief reason for the state of economic backwardness of the many countries that had failed to profit from the benefits of industrialization was neither colonialism, nor capitalism as such, but the inability of their ruling classes to manage the process of industrialization. This governmental incapacity at times derived from errors in economic policy—for example the choice of an import-substitution policy[49]—but in the majority of cases it was the result of the short-sightedness of ruling classes unwilling to sacrifice their immediate interests for the future well-being of the community and of themselves. This was true of the failure to reform agriculture or the public administration—or to reform tax systems which, because of the inadequacy of the revenues they generated, could not finance the infrastructures necessary for industrialization and could not transfer agricultural surplus to the industrial sector.[50]

Kaldor's energy in the pursuit of suitable instruments for political and economic action was unflagging. His analyses of the problems of the developing countries generated all the various policies described in this chapter: the expenditure tax, his scheme for levying taxes on the exports of primary products in order to stabilize the terms of trade, the progressive land tax based on average fertility, dual exchange rates, and the combination of a tax on the exports of primary products with a subsidy on imports of essential goods or with a subsidy on the export of manufactured goods. Such enlightened faith in the real effectiveness of political and economic intervention was frequently criticized, even by his friends and colleagues. Robert Neild once told me of

---

[48] J. Viner, *International Economies* (Free Press, 1951).

[49] Kaldor never went into the socio-political reasons for this choice of economic policy; he only pointed out that such a policy had been made necessary in the 1930s by changes in the international terms of trade. For a deeper scrutiny of the political reasons leading to these measures in the Latin American countries see A. O. Hirschman, 'The Political Economy of Import-Substituting Industrialization in Latin America', *QJE* (Feb. 1968).

[50] M. Kuczynski from the University of Cambridge has argued against this. He contends that Kaldor's position, in 'Will Underdeveloped Countries Learn to Tax?', overlooks the fact that in the developing countries, whose economies have a dual structure, the advanced sector with a high productivity dynamic obliges these countries to learn to tax—while the backward sector with a low productivity dynamic requires that they should not learn to tax but instead keep the propensity to save at a high level. (M. Kuczynski, 'The Third World since the Thirties', in L. Marcolurgo *et al.* (eds.), *L'economia mondiale in trasformazione: contributi per una comparazione tra sistemi economici* (Milan, Franco Angeli, 1987). We know, however, that Kaldor would argue that in developing countries a higher disposable income of wealthy classes (and industrialists of backward sectors also belong to this class) does not entail a higher propensity to save and to invest (see above sect. 6).

Myrdal's verdict, which he himself seemed to share, that Kaldor placed excessive trust in his various contrivances of economic engineering whenever he was faced with a problem of economic policy. I do not believe that Kaldor was unaware of the socio-political implications of his economic-policy proposals, nor of the political conditions that were necessary for their success. Although he regarded fiscal reform, for example, as undoubtedly the most appropriate instrument for transforming the feudal or quasi-feudal regimes of many countries of the Third World into governments capable of leading them towards the economic development and mass ownership of Europe and North America—and although he thought that economists should make governments aware of the economic consequences of such reform—he nevertheless knew that whatever could be accomplished did not depend on the goodwill of ministers or on the competence of officials: it was 'predominantly a matter of political power'.[51]

Kaldor's activities as a tax-adviser aroused the fierce hostility of those who felt their interests threatened by his radical measures and of those that represented such interests—both in the developing countries and in Britain. Certain of the City columnists of the English newspapers seized on the results of Kaldor's work in the developing countries to discredit Callaghan's tax-adviser. For instance, James Macmillan of the *Daily Express* wrote in 1966: '(W)herever Kaldor has proferred advice from India to Ghana, from Turkey to Ceylon, it has been followed by revolution, inflation and toppling governments'.[52] But this was precisely because Kaldor's policies hit the interests of dominant or privileged groups (which in the developing countries may also include manufacturing workers), those who hold power and used it to preserve their advantages. In fact, this conflict was always fomented, inspired, or led by representatives of the classes whose privileges were under attack from the reforms. The social and political institutions that, in the West, mediated between conflicting interests were often ineffectual in the developing countries. Power was firmly in the hands of tightly knit oligarchies, regardless of whether the country was governed by a parliamentary system or by a dictatorship, or whether one party stayed in office or several parties took turns to govern.[53] Opposition to social reforms was 'ostensibly motivated by fear of Communism: in reality it serves to bring Communism nearer'.[54] The solution was educating the ruling classes into awareness of their long-term interests. Kaldor's sincere admiration for the United Kingdom suggested to him the

---

[51] Kaldor, 'Will Underdeveloped Countries Learn to Tax?', 264.

[52] *Daily Express* (26 May 1966), taken from Thirlwall, *Nicholas Kaldor*, 157.

[53] The political realities that set the limits to effective tax reforms such as the one suggested by Kaldor was listed in: (1) division of opinion within the central leadership of the government; (2) vested interest of groups having important positions in the cabinet; (3) peculiar class alliances; (4) fragile political institutions; (5) corruption. See J. Toye, 'Tax Reform in Developing Countries', *CJE* (Mar. 1989).

[54] Kaldor, 'Will Underdeveloped Countries Learn to Tax', 265.

example of nineteenth-century England: of a ruling class which voluntarily gave up some of its privileges for the sake of greater social stability.

Kaldor was not a revolutionary, but as a democrat he was sincerely and radically reformist: he believed that the dilemma faced by many developing countries was how to bring about the sort of change in the balance of power that results from revolution, but without having to resort to such revolution and without incurring the human and social suffering that revolution brings.

Chapter 10

Public-Finance Policy*

Unless savings are exempted from income tax, the contributors
are twice taxed on what they save and only once on what they
spend.

J. S. Mill, *Principles of Political Economy*

10.1. Introduction

Kaldor's contributions to the field of public finance are scattered over a very
large number of publications, many of which did not deal expressly with
problems of public finance. This makes it singularly difficult to assess his
work in this area as a whole and to isolate its main lines of argument.

Kaldor's interest in the problems of public finance certainly pre-dates his
appointment to the Royal Commission on the Taxation of Profits and Income
in 1950, for which he wrote his first major work on public finance: the
'Memorandum of Dissent to the Final Report of the Royal Commission on the
Taxation of Profits and Income'.[1] He had already addressed problems of public
finance in his paper 'The Income Burden of Capital Taxes', written in 1941–2,
and before that in 1935 in his study of tax-financed subsidies on wages as a
remedy for unemployment.[2] That Kaldor's interest in taxation problems was
more than transitory is evident from a footnote in his book *An Expenditure
Tax*,[3] where he traces his idea of an expenditure tax back to a meeting of the
Econometric Society in 1935.

Hence Kaldor was probably being unduly modest when he wrote in his
introduction to the first volume of *Reports on Taxation* that: '[A]ny "expertise"
that I could genuinely claim in this field was largely the result of the education
acquired during four years' work on the Royal Commission.'[4] Nevertheless,
it is probably true to say that Kaldor's major interest in the technical aspects
of the structure of fiscal systems began in the 1950s, as demonstrated by his
detailed discussion in the 'Memorandum of Dissent'.

---

* The author of this ch. is Aldo Chiancone.

[1] N. Kaldor *et al.*, 'Memorandum of Dissent to the Final Report of the Royal Commission on
the Taxation of Profits and Income', pub. with the *Final Report of the Royal Commission on the
Taxation of Profits and Income*, Cmd 9474, (HMSO, London, June 1955), 354–424, repr. in CP
vii. 1–14.

[2] Id., 'Wage Subsidies as a Remedy for Unemployment' *JPE* (1936), repr. in CP iii. 3–22.

[3] Id., *An Expenditure Tax* (London, Allen & Unwin, 1955), n. 2.

[4] Id., introd. to CP, vol. vii, p. vii.

I have already implicitly indicated the dual aspect of Kaldor's approach to problems of public finance: on the one hand, his use of fiscal instruments for achievement of the aims of general economic policy; on the other, his treatment of theoretical problems. Regarding the former, Kaldor's wide-ranging interest in the use of fiscal instruments, the abundance of his publications—articles, reports, and more or less official documents—on the subject (his published recommendations for tax reform in India, Ceylon, Mexico, British Guiana, Iran, and Venezuela alone fill an entire volume[5]), and the many and various proposals distributed throughout his work make even 'reasonably incomplete' study of his ideas impossible. I shall therefore only consider his contributions that deal specifically with public-finance instruments.

As regards Kaldor's second and theoretical area of study, he concentrated on the problem of what we may term 'the optimal tax base'—or, in slightly more general terms, the ways in which different comprehensive tax bases can be structured, and the problems they engender. Here there emerges a recurrent theme that is perhaps characteristic of Kaldor's work on public finance as a whole: his strong moral commitment to distributive justice. In the discussion that follows—which examines first Kaldor's studies of the theoretical problems of taxation, then his more 'policy-oriented' contributions, and finally his proposals for tax reform—we shall come across numerous examples of his fervent belief in fiscal equity.

10.2. Wealth Taxes

I shall begin by examining Kaldor's work in which theoretical and technical considerations predominate. His earliest article on tax problems, 'The Income Burden of Capital Taxes' published in 1942,[6] belongs to this first category. The paper deals mainly with specialized issues to do with the British war economy; nevertheless, it is of lasting interest for its distinction between taxes on income and taxes on capital:

the fundamental criterion for determining whether a particular tax falls on *capital* or on *income*, is not whether it is singular (a once-and-for-all-payment) or recurrent. Thus an annual tax on capital is merely a particular species of income tax; even though it is expressed as a percentage of capital value and not as a percentage of income; while an income tax which is only expected to remain in operation for a short period, . . . is really a levy on capital and not on income.[7]

This is not the place for a detailed critique of Kaldor's definition: I would only point out that, as a general rule, the time element is not sufficient to define a tax; indeed it leads to conclusions in Kaldor's paper that not many

[5] Id., CP viii.

[6] Id., 'The Income Burden of Capital Taxes' (1942), repr. in CP vii. 180–99.

[7] Ibid. 180, Kaldor's italics.

would share—namely, his assertion that an income tax, when enforced for a brief period of time, 'is really a levy on capital'. In fact, whether the tax falls on income or on capital depends not so much on whether it is recurrent or otherwise as on, amongst other things, the level of tax rates.

In this article Kaldor goes on to note that an income earned from capital is qualitatively different from an income of an equal amount earned from work, since capital owners are better able to cope with unforeseen events. However, if we admit to the possibility of capitalizing, within necessarily approximate limits, the annual flow of incomes or, vice versa,

the concept of the 'income burden' of inheritance taxes can be given a clear and definite meaning; it is the annual tax on income which gives the owners of the estates the same loss of satisfaction as the future liability for death duties.[8]

In concrete terms, according to Kaldor the problem then becomes one of finding an interest rate that can be used as a discount rate in this operation. However, he overlooks the fact that the interest rate is not the only element relevant to this calculation: there is also the time horizon, which certainly differs from person to person.

For reasons set out, amongst others, by Pigou—reasons which may be summarized in the datum that the individual has a shorter life and less predictive ability than the state—Kaldor rejected the market interest rate as an expression of individuals' intertemporal choice. If the market criterion is discarded, choice becomes to a certain extent arbitrary. And this Kaldor acknowledges when he suggests the adoption of an 'average yield of capital'— i.e. the rate arrived at by dividing the estate owner's 'statutory income' by the market value of his assets (as assessed for death-duty purposes).

10.3. Income Tax and Expenditure Tax

The works chiefly responsible for Kaldor's fame in the field of public finance are his essay 'Memorandum of Dissent', published in 1955, and his book *An Expenditure Tax*, also published in 1955.

Both were occasioned by Kaldor's appointment to the Royal Commission on the Taxation of Profits and Income in 1950. After the resignation of its first chairman, Sir Lionel Cohen, the commission was chaired by Lord Radcliffe. Notwithstanding the harmony in which its members had worked for four years, Kaldor could not bring himself to sign its final report. Instead, he wrote his 'Memorandum of Dissent' (which was signed by two other members of the commission, G. Woodcock and H. L. Bullock).

Aside from specific points, some of which are too technical and others too limited to the historical context for our purposes here, the main thrust of Kaldor's dissent from the commission's majority report was his dissatisfaction

[8] Ibid. 187.

with the concept of taxable base adopted in its recommendations. This, he believed, led to the consequence that

neither the public, nor the legislature, nor the Courts, are conscious of the extent to which the tax system, behind a facade of formal equity, metes out unequal treatment to different classes of the taxpaying community.[9]

And this ran counter to the purpose of progressive income taxation, which is 'to allocate the burden of tax fairly between different members of the community'.[10]

Kaldor's dissatisfaction with the outcome of the Royal Commission's work took two forms that were, in a certain sense, complementary to each other. On the one hand, in the 'Memorandum of Dissent' he abided by the majority decision and tried to find all those components which, in combination and without duplications or exclusions, could form the basis of a general income tax that was fairer than that in force. On the other, in *An Expenditure Tax*, he tried to lay the theoretical and practical foundations for a system with a different and more satisfactory tax base: expenditure.

From a conceptual, philosophical, and political point of view, Kaldor accepted the commission's majority principle that, in theory, income is the best base for a general tax:

In our view the taxable capacity of an individual consists in his power to satisfy his own material needs, i.e., to attain a particular living standard. We know of no alternative definition that is capable of satisfying society's prevailing sense of fairness and equity. Thus the ruling test to be applied in deciding whether any particular receipt should or should not be reckoned as taxable income is whether it contributes or not, or how far it contributes, to an individual's 'spending power' during a period.[11]

The definition of income that best reflects this point of view is Schanz and Simons's, for whom income is 'the sum of two separate elements, namely personal consumption and net capital accumulation', so that

income is the algebraic sum of (1) the market value of rights exercised in consumption, and (2) the change in the value of the store of property rights between the beginning and the end of the period in question.[12]

According to the report by the commission's majority, the practical application of this definition has three consequences. First, there is no income unless there has been an actual receipt. Hence any improvement (or deterioration) in the market value of an individual's property should not be considered until it is reflected (as in the long run it inevitably must be) in actual receipts and outlays. Second, it is best to ignore receipts (and outlays) of a kind that cannot be checked by an efficient tax administration. Third,

---

[9] Id., introd. to CP, vol. vii, p. viii.   [10] Id., 'Memorandum of Dissent', 1.
[11] Ibid. 2–3.   [12] Ibid. 3.

under a progressive system of taxation, recognition needs to be given to the fact that unique or non-recurrent receipts obtained in a particular period do not confer the same spending power on the recipient within that period as recurrent receipts of like amount.[13]

These three assertions are certainly not immune to criticism, apart from the objections that Kaldor would shortly raise against them. In my view, the third of them is not sufficiently demonstrated and is certainly not *wertfrei*: one can plausibly argue that 'non-recurrent', and hence probably 'non-earned' receipts, can be taxed more heavily than 'recurrent' and therefore 'earned' receipts.

Kaldor's argument was developed in rigorous relation to the concept of income that I have outlined above. He maintained that the critical area of an income-tax system is capital gains: these must be taxed, because they increase a person's taxable capacity by increasing his power to spend or save. In fact, he declared:

ignoring the exceptional periods following in the wake of great wars or great economic depressions—capital gains are not, to any important extent, the consequence of either rising prices or falling interest rates . . . In a modern industrial community such as ours a high proportion (four fifths if American experience can be taken as a guide) of all capital gains are derived from transactions in securities, and mainly in ordinary shares of business corporations.[14]

Under current conditions, capital gains could be foreseen and anticipated, and were

by far the most important part of (the normal reward of a successful enterprise), the expectation of which is a crucial factor in the supply of risk capital and business ability to new ventures.[15]

According to Kaldor, the importance of capital gains as a source of income is obvious when one considers that the majority of such gains do not depend at all on chance, but on the activity of the taxpayer and on the practice of certain firms who retain most of their profits instead of distributing them. All countries with developed markets and sophisticated investors hold out repeated opportunities for capital gains which privilege the wealthier classes.

It is only possible, in practice, to tax realized capital gains, since it is these alone that are brought to light by firms' accounting practices. In addition, over a longer period, a tax on non-realized capital gains tends to be tantamount to a tax on non-realized gains. In general, a tax on realized gains may entail the postponement of the moment when the gains are realized; with a progressive income-tax system, however, it would be to the advantage of the taxpayer to render the realization of his gains as uniform over time as possible.

---

[13] Ibid. 5.   [14] Ibid. 22.   [15] Ibid. 23.

Kaldor suggested instead that capital gains should be taxed with a proportional levy. If the tax were progressive, equity problems might arise when goods had to be sold in a single transaction, as in the case of death. Moreover, a progressive tax would reduce incentives for risk-taking.

Of course, although Kaldor did not dwell on the point, this solution, like many others in public finance, fails to achieve all aims satisfactorily: it does not adversely affect incentives; nor does it discriminate according to the moment when capital gains are realized nor according to their size; nor does it deal with the phenomenon, which Kaldor himself described, of the positive correlation between capital gains and wealth; nor, finally, does it remove the possibility of converting taxable income into less heavily taxed capital gains. These two latter shortcomings tend to restrict the progressive nature of the tax.

After arguing in favour of a capital-gains tax, Kaldor gives more precise specification of its features: there should be no distinction between long-term and short-term capital gains; capital losses should be taken into account; and capital gains on owner-occupied houses should not be taxed, so that personal mobility was not impaired.

The other controversial problem addressed by Kaldor in his 'Memorandum of Dissent' was corporate taxation and its relationship to personal income tax—a problem that he would return to in the future, as we shall see. He cut incisively through the tangle of controversy surrounding the issue by stating: 'the profits tax paid by companies is a different tax from the income tax paid by individuals'.[16] This principle has two consequences: first that 'the one can be levied at rates which are quite independent of the other';[17] secondly that

the principles of equity no more require us to offset the payment of the profits tax against the individual's liability to income tax than to call for such a tax credit in connection with the many other duties (such as local rates, the petrol duty or the stamp duty) the incidence of which directly or indirectly falls on the individual taxpayer.[18]

One has to admit that this argument of Kaldor's is somewhat forced: the logical principle entailing that consumption taxes are not deductible from income is, of course, that consumption and income are two wholly different tax bases. It is true, as we have seen, that Kaldor considered the income tax paid by companies to be a different tax from that paid by individuals; from this, however, it does not necessarily follow that the two tax bases differ from either a logical or a practical point of view.

Kaldor goes on to state that different forms of income tax cannot be evaluated according to whether they are more or less equitable with respect to different taxpayers, but only according to their general economic effects. Consequently there should exist only a tax on enterprises with a constant rate, and this should have the total profits of the firm as its base. Moreover,

---

[16] Ibid. 48.   [17] Ibid.   [18] Ibid.

the artificial encouragement of the retention of profits by companies is not necessarily an economic advantage. Beyond a certain point it does not in itself stimulate the rate of capital formation.[19]

Firms should also be subject to a capital-gains tax, net of losses.

However, as Kaldor declares at the beginning of *An Expenditure Tax*, despite all attempts to render income tax compatible with principles of equity, it is still unacceptable, and mainly because

a host of conceptual and measurement problems crop up as soon as the search begins for a tax base which both provides a definition capable of measurement and which satisfactorily assesses a man's capacity to spend independently of his actual spending.[20]

The book begins with a discussion of the principles of taxation according to the ability to pay; a progressive tax linked to means is desirable because it meets the political objective of promoting economic and social equality. Here, though, the concept of 'means' requires further clarification. Kaldor asserts that its most widely accepted meaning is 'spending power': 'the ability or power of an individual to satisfy his own personal needs, measured by some extraneous criterion that is independent of his actual spending'.[21] The term 'means' does not just refer to money, but

money in relation to certain objective needs, obligations, commitments . . . taking into account, and making allowance for, variations between individuals in the opportunity, in terms of living standards, which any given amount of money commands.[22]

Thus annual income is not an adequate measure of taxable capacity: capital wealth is in fact a separate component of taxable capacity.

Some of the problems inherent to income taxation can certainly be solved by imposing a separate tax on wealth. However, other problems are involved which stem from the fact that incomes do not accrue in a steady and continuous fashion. Clearly, Kaldor argues, those incomes that the recipient does not regard as constant do not give rise to the same spending power as those receipts that he expects to continue. They should therefore be taxed more lightly, although, under present progressive tax systems, the opposite is the case. Moreover, existing income-tax systems include some of these receipts in the tax base while others are omitted, according to mutually inconsistent principles and criteria.

Such problems would only be partially solved by defining income more closely in accordance with Haig-Simons; a definition that would bring all irregular receipts of any kind, as well as capital gains, within the scope of taxation. The difficulties arise from the inclusion of capital gains in the tax base—since these, as Kaldor had already shown in his 'Memorandum of Dissent' cover a multitude of situations.

[19] Ibid. 54.   [20] Id., *An Expenditure Tax*, 29.   [21] Ibid. 28.   [22] Ibid. 29.

There are in fact some capital gains which are simply a hidden form of interest or dividend payment; there are others which reflect a change in market expectations during the period in which the capital gain takes place; there are others, again, which reflect only an increase in the general price level and which go *pari passu* with it; and others, finally, which reflect a fall in interest rates, rather than the expectation of greater receipts.

And, as one easily deduces from these cases,

it is not that capital gains, *as such* provide less spending power than other forms of profit; there are some kinds of capital gains which represent the same kind of spending power as conventional income; other kinds which represent none at all; and yet others which are in-between; these types, moreover, shade into one another gradually and imperceptibly.[23]

These difficulties are created more by the limits on the concept itself of income than by defects in the tax laws; there therefore exists no ideal definition of income that would resolve them.

Kaldor had thus established the foundations of an expenditure tax:

[A]ccruals from the various sources cannot be reduced to a common unit of spending power on any objective criteria. But each individual performs this operation for himself when, in the light of all his present circumstances and future prospects, he decides on the scale of his personal living expenses. Thus a tax based on actual spending rates each individual's spending capacity according to the yardstick which he applies to himself.[24]

Having therefore solved all the problems that we have encountered so far, Kaldor now has to deal with possible criticisms of his expenditure tax. He examines four likely objections.

The first, that an expenditure tax is regressive with respect to income, he rejects on the ground that, if so desired, an expenditure tax can also be made progressive vis-à-vis income. The second, according to which those who customarily spend little pay less in tax than those who spend a lot, is a minor objection: tax systems cannot and should not be designed to take account of individual temperament. A third, similar objection—that higher expenditure may be determined not by special personal tastes, but, for example, by the costs involved in supporting a family—Kaldor meets by pointing out that, just as there is no difficulty in making deductions on income tax to take account of different personal situations, so an expenditure tax could be adjusted according to the individual's circumstances. There remains the fourth and most serious criticism: that consumption, like income, may be subject to fluctuations caused, for instance, by the purchase of certain durable goods or by certain needs such as grave illness. According to Kaldor, this problem could be solved by the use of appropriate averaging devices.

---

[23] Ibid. 45, Kaldor's italics.   [24] Ibid. 47.

What would be the effects of the expenditure tax on economic activity? I begin with the *locus classicus* of an expenditure tax, John Stuart Mill's classic dictum that a tax on income is 'not only impolitic, but unjust'[25] because those that spend all of their income are taxed only once, whereas those who save a part of their income are taxed twice, first on their income when it is received and then on the fruits of that part of income that is saved and invested.

The core of Mill's theorem is beyond dispute, of course. It has sometimes been objected, however, that exempting saving would aggravate the maldistribution of wealth by encouraging the accumulation of capital. Kaldor's obvious reply is that the problem should be solved not by taxing savings, but by taxing wealth.[26] Moreover, if the expenditure tax was given sufficiently progressive rates, it would reduce the savings of the wealthier classes.

Let us now follow Kaldor in his examination of an expenditure tax on investments with different degrees of risk. Compared with an income tax, an expenditure tax would have lower disincentive effects on both risk-taking and work effort. Kaldor's analysis becomes extremely complex at this point; and detailed exposition would be beyond our present scope. Suffice it to say, therefore, that in the case of risk-taking, an expenditure tax would have two constrasting effects: 'it is less discriminating against risk, in so far as a part of taxable income is saved; but it is also more discriminating in so far as part of capital gains is spent.'[27]

Kaldor solves this problem by considering the case of an investor who spends all his income: an income tax may induce him to rearrange his investments in favour of less risky assets. If, under an equivalent expenditure tax, he behaved in the same way and preferred less risky assets, he would discover that returning to his original combination of assets and yields provides him with a higher income, keeps his consumption constant, and also enables him to save more. As Kaldor observes,

this saving, unlike ordinary saving, is not at the cost of consumption: he could not consume it, because if he did, it would not be worth his while to incur the risks to get it . . . An expenditure tax may thus be said to discriminate not against the assumption of risks, but against the spending of income obtained through the assumption of risks.[28]

As regards an expenditure tax's effects on incentives to work, Kaldor points out that there are no a priori arguments in its favour. Here he takes an extremely innovative and interesting approach by arguing that

an individual's consumption . . . is not at all closely related to his short-period earnings—say his earnings in a particular week, or in a particular year—but to his average expected earnings over time, where his time-horizon is only limited by the

---

[25] J. S. Mill, *Principles of Political Economy* (1848), bk. 5, ch. 11, sect. 4.
[26] For Kaldor, therefore, wealth taxation is justified first—as we have seen—by the need to take into account individual differences in wealth (and therefore in spending capacity); second because it corrects the maldistribution of wealth.
[27] Kaldor, *Expenditure Tax*, 119.   [28] Ibid. 120.

increasing uncertainties of life as the expectations stretch out into the further future. In other words, the shorter the period taken into consideration, the less is the dependence of consumption on income.[29]

Discussion of this assertion would clearly go beyond my brief: I merely point out that as early as 1955 Kaldor had already given precise specification to the consumption function hypotheses that Friedman and Modigliani and Ando later developed.

If we assume that consumption is steadier than income, it follows that a progressive tax on consumption will have fewer disincentive effects on work effort than a progressive income tax. Further, the greatest part of saving is made in order to provide for expenditure after retirement—in a period, that is, when expenditure is relatively low—and would thus be liable to relatively low rates. On the other hand, most saving takes place in that period of the taxpayer's life when he earns the most; when, therefore, the marginal rate of income tax is highest and when, consequently, the disincentive effects on work are also highest.

A final point to consider concerns the problem of implementing an expenditure tax; a point all the more important because it later became a key component in many of Kaldor's proposals as tax-adviser to foreign governments. Kaldor's recommendation—which referred to the British context—was that an expenditure tax should replace not income tax, but surtax: in practice, of course, this meant that income would be subject to a proportional tax, and that the expenditure tax would not only take the place of all existing excise and consumption taxes, but would also serve to determine that degree of progressiveness in the tax system as a whole that had previously been determined by surtax.

However, acceptance of Kaldor's proposal entailed many other changes in the British tax system. First, as Kaldor pointed out, it would have to be made more comprehensive, so that capital gains and other non-recurrent incomes not 'in the nature of trade' could be brought into the tax net.

Moreover, income tax would be supplemented by a wealth tax (as discussed above), and by a gifts and inheritance tax. In Kaldor's view, gifts and inheritances should not be taxed according to their value, but according to the total amount of property owned by the beneficiary at the time of transfer. The logic behind this proposal becomes clear once the basic reason for advocating an expenditure tax is understood. Apart from practical reasons,[30] such as the need to combat some forms of tax avoidance (e.g. of inheritance taxes by means of gifts *inter vivos*), for Kaldor the basis of taxation must be the spending power of the individual: hence all those elements that constitute this spending capacity must be taxed, whatever their origin.

---

[29] Ibid. 136–7.
[30] These Kaldor repeatedly sets out in *An Expenditure Tax*, e.g. p. 204.

Having examined the logic of the overall system envisaged by Kaldor, we may turn to one of its major problems, namely the taxation of capital gains. Despite Kaldor's claims to the contrary, an expenditure tax does not appear, *by itself*, to be a complete solution to the problem of taxing capital gains. Since expenditure is calculated as

income (as at present) *adding* monies received from the sale of capital assets, depletion of bank balances, etc., and *deducting* sums spent on the purchase of capital assets and on 'non-personal' or 'non-chargeable' expenditure.[31]

under-reporting income (and capital gains) still seems to be worth the taxpayer's while: given the amounts spent on the purchase of capital assets, the lower the income, the lower the expenditure, and hence the lower the tax. The under-reporting of income can be counteracted by maintaining an income tax which, as far as possible, includes capital gains in its base. Those capital gains that cannot be identified as such, and which therefore cannot be subjected to income tax, would therefore be taxed either as a component of wealth or in the roundabout way provided by the expenditure tax.

However, the inclusion of capital gains in the income-tax base raises the problem of how to define and calculate them as accurately as possible as a component of income. Although this is, apparently, an important element in Kaldor's overall system, he devotes no discussion to it—either in his book on an expenditure tax or in the reports that he wrote as a tax-adviser to foreign governments (see Chapter 10.8).

Furthermore, as long as an income tax is kept in existence, John Stuart Mill's problem is left unresolved: in Kaldor's system it is still the case that whenever a part of income is saved and invested and its fruits then taxed again by income tax, that portion of the contributor's income is taxed twice.

Although Kaldor himself wrote at length on the practical application of the expenditure tax I shall dwell only shortly on this. He suggested that the liquid funds and savings held at the beginning of the tax year should be added to the income earned during the year. If the savings–investments made during the year—which the taxpayer must declare together with his income—are deducted from this amount, the value obtained is his consumption. (For simplicity, I shall not consider the problems raised by the contracting of debts and credits.) Exemptions could be applied to this tax basis for certain expenditures (for example, on education or medical treatment) and deductions made for the taxpayer's dependents. Moreover, an expenditure tax could be made progressive relative to both spending and income—as Table 10.1 shows, where Y is income, C consumption, t_c the tax-rate on consumption, T_c the yield on the consumption tax, and t_y the rate of the tax relative to income. The table shows clearly that not only does t_c increase with respect to income, but, if one inspects the ratio between the yield from the expenditure tax and the corresponding income, the tax is progressive.

[31] Ibid. 192.

Public-Finance Policy

TABLE 10.1

Y	C	t_c %	T_c	t_y %
10,000	10,000	10	1,000	10
15,000	13,000	15	1,950	13
20,000	15,000	20	3,000	15

As Kaldor pointed out, no developed country has ever implemented an expenditure tax. However, among developing countries, India and Ceylon both introduced an expenditure tax on Kaldor's recommendation during the 1950s. After its implementation in India in 1964, the tax was first temporarily suspended and then, after its reintroduction, definitively abolished, all in the same year. In Ceylon the measure was introduced in 1959, suspended in 1963, and reintroduced in 1976. The experience in both these countries was not a happy one. In both cases the tax was introduced to stimulate savings, especially by the wealthier classes. But when applied, it was severely restricted: in India less than 1 per cent of taxpayers subject to income tax were also subject to the expenditure tax. Problems also arose over its application, because consumption was in part calculated directly.

Although the tax has never been introduced in an industrialized country, it has always aroused lively theoretical interest. For instance, as early as 1958 a Danish government committee published a 'Report on Consumption Taxation' which recommended, amongst other things, the introduction of a progressive expenditure tax. In another Scandinavian country, Sweden, a government commission on taxation reported in 1977 that:

In three important respects, however, the properties of an expenditure tax seem to be superior to those of the present income tax. The effect of the expenditure tax in stimulating saving would facilitate the necessary supply of capital in the community; the expenditure tax would enable all income to be treated equally and would provide fewer opportunities of tax avoidance; and it would automatically take into account the changes in value due to inflation, with the result that no undue tax gains or tax losses need arise on account of inflation.[32]

In Anglo-Saxon countries, the US Advisory Commission on Intergovernmental Relations declared, in the conclusions to a report published in 1974, that the expenditure tax could be considered as an important supplement to income tax, an instrument for strengthening capital tax, and as an alternative to indirect taxes. From the administrative point of view, the tax was practicable, even if it would entail additional costs, both for the taxpayer and for the

[32] *Oversyn av Skattesystemet* (An Overview of the Tax System) (SOU, Stockholm, 1977), 91. The report was based on Sven-Olof Lodin's study published in 1976: *Progressivs Utgiftsskatt—Ett Alternativ* (SOU, Stockholm, 1976: 62). For an English trans. of this report, see S.-O. Lodin, *Progressive Expenditure Tax—An Alternative?* (Stockholm, Liber–Ferlag, 1973).

administration. At any rate, as regards control, an expenditure tax appeared to be simpler than an income tax and better able to control evasion.[33]

Internationally, however, the study of expenditure tax with greatest impact has been the Meade Report published in January 1978 under the title *The Structure and Reform of Direct Taxation.*[34] The Meade Committee examined the functioning of the English income-tax system together with proposals for its reform, and in its final report drew the following conclusions:

> There may be some degree of inevitable conflict between these two objectives of 'efficiency' and 'equality'. But the clash can be minimised by an appropriate choice of social, political and economic policies and institutions; and the structure of the tax system is one important element of the outcome. An appropriate structure for this purpose would be the combination of (i) 'new Beveridge' development of social welfare to remove poverty and to set an effective and satisfactory floor to standards of living, and (ii) arrangements for the taxation of wealth, in particular inherited wealth, which would effectively encourage a wider dispersion in the ownership of property with (iii) a basic reform of direct taxation which levied a charge on what people took out of the economic system in high levels of consumption rather than on what they put into the system through their savings and enterprise. This last ingredient is of the utmost importance. By shifting the tax base in this way all forms of enterprise—big or small, privately owned, State owned or labour-managed—would be able to plough back their own profits or to borrow the savings of others free of tax for all forms of economic development. But at the same time wealthy persons who were maintaining a high standard of living by dissaving from their capital wealth would be more heavily taxed than at present.[35]

10.4. Alternative Systems of Corporation Tax

I now turn to the group of Kaldor's publications devoted to study of public finance as an instrument of economic policy—beginning with his 1971 article 'The Economic Effects of Alternative Systems of Corporation Tax'.[36] This article in fact draws on theoretical principles that Kaldor had already set out in his 'Memorandum of Dissent'. Put briefly, it examines the problem of the autonomy of corporate income taxation relative to income taxation on shareholders and the evaluation of corporation income tax according to its economic consequences.

Kaldor concentrated mainly on specific issues relating to the British economy of the time. However, he made a number of more general and important

---

[33] *The Expenditure Tax: Concept, Administration and Possible Applications* (Information Report M-84; Washington, DC, Advisory Commission on Intergovernmental Relations, 1974).

[34] *The Structure and Reform of Direct Taxation: Report of a Committee Chaired by Professor J. E. Meade* (London, Allen & Unwin, 1978).

[35] Ibid. pp. xv–xvi.

[36] N. Kaldor, 'The Economic Effects of Alternative Systems of Corporation Tax' (1971), pub. in CP vii. 124–40.

points. First, the marginal rate of taxation must be as low as possible, because it is the marginal rate that is relevant to investment decisions. The tax must not induce firms to reduce the ploughback of their profits, since these are the main source of corporate growth (as testified by the ample literature on the topic, from which Kaldor quoted copiously). One notes that Kaldor had manifestly altered his opinion on the relevance of internal financial resources since writing his 'Memorandum of Dissent'—where he maintained (unsupported by the literature) that there was no conclusive evidence that the ploughing back of profits by firms is to the advantage of the economy. Kaldor made no mention of his change of mind in the 1971 article; we can only surmise, therefore, that it was the wide, largely statistics-based literature on the subject, published almost *in toto* after the 'Memorandum of Dissent', that had caused him to shift his position.

The article raised a third point: that distributed profits are for the most part consumed rather than invested in the purchase of shares, and that this too must encourage the ploughing back of profits. Finally, the purchase of new shares does not depend on the amount of dividends distributed, but on the expected increase in share values; and this, again, depends on the amount of self-financing.

All this induced Kaldor to favour a system of corporation taxes that encourages the retention of profits.

10.5. The Economic Foundations of a Selective Employment Tax

Much more relevant to income policy, and probably the most important of all Kaldor's proposals in practical terms, was his selective employment tax.[37] This, in fact, was his only tax recommendation ever to be effectively implemented: by the Labour Government under Callaghan in May 1966. It was levied on firms in the 'service trades' and building sectors as a lump-sum tax differentiated according to the sex and age of their employees. The tax was abolished when valued-added tax was introduced in 1973.

For the Government (advised by Kaldor) the purpose of the tax was to balance the tax burdens on the services sector and the manufacturing sector (the former was less heavily taxed), and to bring 'a beneficial longer-term effect by encouraging economy in the use of labour in the service trades, thereby making more labour available for the expansion of the manufacturing industry'.[38] With hindsight, however, Kaldor declared that the tax was introduced at an unfavourable moment when the long period of post-war full employment had given way to a period of unemployment: this obscured the effects of the tax.

---

[37] Id., 'The Economics of the Selective Employment Tax' (1980), repr. in CP vii. 200–29.
[38] Ibid. 205.

In proposing the tax, Kaldor maintained that a capitalist market economy tends towards excess manpower in services because of the way that the market operates, and therefore that the average productivity of labour in the economy will vary in inverse relation to the labour costs in the manufacturing sector relative to the services sector. Measures that increase the cost of labour in the services sector vis-à-vis the manufacturing sector will increase the economy's 'welfare'. *In a full-employment economy*, moreover, the growth of the manufacturing sector is constrained by the availability of labour for hire.

Kaldor's argument depends on a number of assumptions (which he had already developed in various fields of economic theory), including the existence of increasing returns to scale in the manufacturing sector and prevailing imperfect competition, combined with free entry, in the services sector.

Under conditions of imperfect competition, sellers are usually 'price-makers', i.e. they add a tax to the price that they charge to buyers. Under such conditions, in fact, price is the result of a twofold operation: first, prime costs are calculated (costs for labour and raw materials that would not have existed had the given quantity of the goods not been produced); a percentage mark-up is then added to account for all other costs (e.g. profits, depreciation). The amount of the mark-up depends on the degree of market imperfection, that is, on the elasticity of the demand faced by the seller.

Given the mark-up, the amount of labour absorbed in the services sector, relative to the manufacturing sector, will be higher, the lower the cost of labour in the services sector compared with the manufacturing sector. (Differences in the cost of labour may derive from differences in the degree of worker unionization.) If we consider behaviour over time, the services sector acts as a 'sponge' which absorbs labour from the manufacturing sector and releases it when demand increases in the manufacturing sector through consequential changes in relative wages.

Whereas taxes on those elements constituting prime costs are immediately shifted, taxes on other elements are not. Rather, they increase the amount of minimum turnover that enables the firm to earn a normal yield on capital. Taxes of this second kind therefore accelerate the exit of marginal firms from the market. Consequently, the amount of the tax on labour cost that will be shifted on to prices will vary depending on whether or not labour is included in prime costs. A typical feature of the services sector is that, in the great majority of cases, labour costs are not included in prime costs.

When the hypothesis of imperfect competition is abandoned and the case of oligopoly with price leadership considered instead, the aim of the price-leader is to achieve a surplus with respect to total costs, and not just to prime costs. Hence any increase in labour costs will tend to be shifted forwards in the form of higher prices.

However, according to Kaldor, in practice imperfect competition prevails in the services sector, so that 'it is true to say that a considerable part (perhaps one-half or more) of the tax was "paid out of" increased productivity rather than reduced profits per unit of sales or higher prices (in the form of increased gross margins)'.[39]

A government enquiry conducted by W. B. Reddaway[40] provides further analysis of the effects of an SET. Although hampered by political changes, so that its final report was conditioned by numerous tentative conclusions, Reddaway's enquiry found that, by and large, the SET probably led to increased efficiency and reduced profits in some sectors; the tax was therefore not wholly passed on in the form of increased prices. As regards productivity, the available data suggested that there were increases in physical productivity per worker over and above what would be expected in the absence of the tax. The tax's other effects—on the quality of services and on the labour-market as a whole—were, however, minor.

10.6. A Levy on the Advertising Revenue of Newspapers

This is one of Kaldor's relatively minor proposals. Nevertheless it demonstrates not only his gift for devising new forms of taxation to meet specific economic-policy objectives, but also his commitment to controlling oligopolistic market behaviour through taxes that would limit the size of firms.

Kaldor suggested the introduction of a tax on newspaper advertising revenue in 1962 to the Royal Commission on the Press[41] in order to counteract the progressive reduction in the numbers of quality newspapers in London and the provinces, and to stop the increasing concentration of their ownership.

In the brief essay describing the theoretical basis for his proposal, Kaldor showed that economies of scale typically lead to oligopoly: a market form where competition among sellers takes place through advertising or through trifling improvements in the product. As a consequence, there is constant growth in the value of the sales required to cover fixed and variable costs, and it becomes increasingly difficult both for old producers to stay in the industry and for new ones to enter it.

This phenomenon is particularly damaging in the case of newspapers. Popular newspapers with high circulations tend to push quality newspapers—with relatively low circulations, but whose survival is necessary for the functioning of a democratic system with a plurality of opinions—out of the market. The levy on newspaper advertising revenue would therefore take the form of a progressive tax on the numbers of copies sold, with rates adjusted so that no newspaper could gain an advantage from pushing its sales above a certain level. The yield from the tax would be used to pay subsidies—at a flat rate

---

[39] Ibid. 227.

[40] W. B. Reddaway, *Effects of the Selective Employment Tax: First Report—The Distributive Trades* (London, HMSO, 1970); id. *Effects of the Selective Employment Tax: Final Report* (Cambridge, CUP, 1973).

[41] N. Kaldor (with R. R. Neild), 'A Proposal for a Levy on the Advertising Revenue of Newspapers' (1962), pub. in CP vii. 115–23.

and in proportion to the number of copies sold—up to a certain predetermined maximum.

The Royal Commission rejected Kaldor's proposal on the ground that it would be intolerable 'to force the proprietors of the two newspapers primarily affected to have for decades a major objective of progressively reducing their circulation'.[42]

10.7. Tax-Reform Plans

The plans for tax reform that Kaldor produced in his capacity as tax-adviser to various governments adhere quite closely to the principles elaborated in his theoretical work. Since these have already been discussed, I shall avoid repetition by providing the briefest of outlines—using Kaldor's 1956 report on Indian tax reform[43] (the most important and the model for all his subsequent plans) as my basis.

Kaldor only dealt briefly with personal income tax, stating that it should be progressive in form:

[O]wing to the fact that the savings of a community are more unevenly distributed than income, there is an inevitable tendency . . . for the wealth of the largest property owners to grow at a faster rate than wealth in general.[44]

Traditionally, progressive income taxation has never been able to correct this increasingly inequal distribution of wealth among individuals. Kaldor gave the following reasons:

a) absence of a clear and comprehensive notion of what constitutes 'income' for tax purposes; and the consequent exclusion of numerous kinds of beneficial receipts (of which capital gains and capital profits of all kinds are the most important) . . . b) failure to recognize that the ownership of disposable assets confers a benefit to the owner over and above the income which the property yields; . . . c) the elastic definition of expenses as permissable deductions to be set against receipts in the calculation of trading profits; . . . d) failure to secure the true aggregation of a man's (or a family's) total property or income for tax purposes, due (in part) to defective provisions concerning the compulsory aggregation of family income; . . . e) failure to secure the full reporting of income or of property, due (1) to the absence of any automatic reporting systems for property income (2) to the failure to make tax reporting fully comprehensive and (3) self-checking.[45]

In Kaldor's view, an effective tax system required a combination of taxes levied on (1) income; (2) capital gains; (3) net worth; (4) personal expenditure; (5) gifts.

[42] Id., introd. to CP, Vol. vii, pp. xv–xvi.
[43] N. Kaldor, *Indian Tax Reform: Report of a Survey* (1956), repr. in CP viii. 31–189.
[44] Ibid. 43.   [45] Ibid. 44–5.

An annual tax on net wealth was justified—as Kaldor had already noted as far back as 1943 (see section 2, above)—by the principle that, since the ownership of property in the form of marketable assets gives the owner a taxable capacity over and above the money income yielded by the property, only a combination of income and property taxes can give an approximate practical application to the principle of taxation according to the ability to pay.

I have already examined the problem of the tax treatment of capital gains. In his design for a tax system, Kaldor reiterated the idea that capital gains should be treated as all other kinds of income. But, to avoid reducing economic incentives and increasing tax evasion or avoidance, these other kinds of income should be taxed at a proportional rate. To bring all capital gains into the tax net, transfers of assets of every kind (gifts or legacies, as well as sales, etc.) should be treated, without exception, as realization for tax purposes.

Progressive taxation acts principally through a personal-expenditure tax. Tax would be chargeable on the value of all goods and services received for personal consumption, irrespective of how and by whom these have been financed.

Company taxation raises the following question. Considering that distributed profits are taxed as personal income, and that undistributed profits are taxed by the tax on capital gains, is there any justification for levying a further tax on the undistributed income of companies? Kaldor's reply was that there are in fact two justifications for such a tax: first, a tax on capital gains is really an indirect tax on company savings paid after a long delay; second, the company savings actually invested in real assets do receive partial exemption in the form of capital expenditure allowances—in fact, the higher the discounted value of the capital allowances granted in any form, the greater and the more justified the effective rate of company taxation. Companies should, of course, be charged at a uniform rate.

In Kaldor's view, from the point of view of equity (as we have seen), 'it is only the savings of companies which justify a tax levied on corporations as such'.[46] However, in terms of economic expediency, we must bear in mind that

since the expanding companies are likely to plough back a larger part of their earnings than companies which are not expanding, the system which levies taxes on the whole profits treats expanding companies relatively more leniently and stagnant companies relatively more severely than a system which charges tax on the undistributed profit only.[47]

10.8. Taxation and Economic Development

In developing countries the general system of taxation would remain unchanged. Kaldor had, however, some specific additional suggestions to make. Here, the important point is that

---

[46] Ibid. 150.   [47] Ibid. 151.

the taxation of agriculture . . . has a critical role to play in the acceleration of economic development, since it is only the *imposition of compulsory levies on the agricultural sector itself* which enlarges the supply of 'savings' for economic development in the required sense.[48]

But a 'standard' income tax is a clumsy and inefficient instrument for taxing agriculture, even in advanced Western countries:

one of the fundamental difficulties seems to be that modern accounting techniques have never succeeded, in the case of agriculture, in separating current expenses from increases in capital . . . As a consequence, the farmer's accounts may show continuing losses even though both the production and the value of the farm is continually rising.[49]

An income tax on agriculture would have two main features:

it would be based on the average net product of agriculture, of each particular region and each particular type of land, as defined *for purposes of national accounting*, (and) it would be a progressive tax, taking into account the size of the landholding of the individual farmer.[50]

The tax would be on the potential output of the land, by which is meant

(the) output which the land would yield if it were managed with average efficiency. Thus the inefficient farmer whose production is less efficient than the average for the region and for the type of land concerned would be correspondingly encouraged . . . It would thus give the maximum incentive for efficient farmers to improve their land and expand their output; it should also greatly encourage the transfer of land ownership from inefficient to efficient hands, and thereby raise the average productivity of land nearer to that obtained in the best-managed farms.[51]

It may be of interest to point out that Kaldor's system corresponds quite closely to the Italian cadaster, the origins of which, in the form described here, go back to the second half of the eighteenth century. Under the cadastral system, the income from each particular piece of land is assessed as a mean of its product over a number of years—under normal conditions in each given year. The value thus calculated remains constant for a number of years. Italian economists (e.g. Einaudi[52]) have repeatedly stressed the incentive provided by the cadaster.

Kaldor continues by spelling out at length and in great detail how the tax would be organized. Specific points concerned compulsory saving and the taxation of multinational companies.

Some countries might require a scheme for compulsory saving in order to increase the flow of resources for economic development and to reduce undesirable pressures on demand. Kaldor's plan for compulsory saving[53] envisaged

---

[48] Id., 'Report on the Turkish Tax System' (1962), pub. in CP viii, Kaldor's emphasis.
[49] Ibid. 134.   [50] Ibid. 315–16, Kaldor's emphasis.   [51] Ibid. 316.
[52] See e.g. L. Einaudi, *La terra e l'imposta* (1942; Turin, Einaudi, 1974).
[53] N. Kaldor, 'Proposals for a Reform of Taxation in British Guiana' (1961), pub. in CP viii. 303-7, and id., 'Economic and Taxation Problems in Iran' (1966), pub. in CP viii. 336–44.

the deduction of some percentage of current pay at source. This would be credited to the employee and repaid with interest at some future date. Contributors would be given government bonds registered in their names, not transferable or negotiable, and redeemable with accrued interest at the end of a given time period.

Another potential or actual problem faced by developing countries (and not only by them) were the schemes devised by multinational enterprises for tax-avoidance purposes.

It is well known that foreign companies which are merely branches or subsidiaries of companies resident abroad can understate their true profits through the over-invoicing of imports or the under-invoicing of exports, in so far as their transactions are conducted with associated companies.[54]

Since it is difficult in most cases to know what approporiate prices should be, Kaldor's suggestion was that

the profits for the year of a company operating in a given country, which is a branch establishment, a subsidiary or an associated company of a non-resident company, shall be deemed to be no less than the proportion of the total consolidated profit of the whole group of associated companies . . . which the turnover of that company, as shown in its accounts, bears to the consolidated turnover of the whole group of associated companies.[55]

10.9. Equity in Kaldor's Thought

In the limited space available it is of course impossible to give an exhaustive account of Kaldor's massive contribution to public finance. Even if, as we have seen, Kaldor's argument might sometimes seem forced, his theory sometimes insufficiently justified and explained, his proposals sometimes over-concerned with what we might call economic engineering, these are shortcomings that, on balance are negligible when compared with the fertility, variety, and depth of his work as a whole.

We probably find best proof of the intellectual force of Kaldor's arguments in his proposals in favour of an expenditure tax. Here a theoretical argument, with a noble tradition but too often consigned to the footnotes of public-finance studies, was transformed by passionate, painstaking analysis into a viable instrument, one which may find concrete application in the not too distant future.

In conclusion, I wish to return to the significant feature of Kaldor's thinking on public finance mentioned at the outset: namely his insistence on fiscal equity. It was because of a deep-rooted sense of distributive justice that Kaldor considered it intolerable that income-tax systems failed to take account of capital gains—a failure that the majority of writers on public finance, even

---

[54] Id., 'Reform of Taxation in British Guiana', 276.   [55] Ibid.

such a lucid and meticulous analyst as Simons, tend either to overlook or to solve with *ad hoc* and largely futile expedients.

Kaldor's reasoning proceeded rigorously from its premisses. Capital gains cannot be excluded from the income-tax base. Although it is impossible to determine when they occur and in what amounts, it is certain that these amounts correlate with income. Therefore the only option for the legislator is to tax the spending power generated by capital gains and to trust the individual to make the relative calculations.

The fact that Kaldor subsequently concentrated mainly on problems of economic growth does not contradict my conclusion. It is well known that inequities tend to be significantly attenuated, if not eliminated, by economic growth. And as an economist always mindful of the practical side to his proposals, Kaldor came to regard growth as perhaps the best solution to distribution problems. Indeed, towards the end of his life Kaldor declared that, as the years passed, he became increasingly aware that economic growth and public social expenditure were more powerful instruments for the equitable distribution of income than taxes.

Chapter 11

The Interest Rate, Monetary Policy, and the Supply of Money

> The basic need, on which the whole of this financial
> development is based, is the need for widening the circle of
> credit-worthy borrowers.
>
> J. R. Hicks, *A Theory of Economic History*

11.1. A Monetary Determination of the Rate of Interest

Kaldor first dealt with monetary policy in his writings of 1939 on interest rates, speculation, and economic stability. As we saw in Chapter 2, sections 3 and 4, these articles had a manifold purpose: first they sought to define those hypotheses concerning speculation that, in a competitive market, were necessary in order to validate Keynes's principle of savings–investment re-equilibrium via changes in income rather than in the rate of interest; secondly, they sought to define the relations that held between the short-term rate of interest and the demand for money and between short- and long-term rates; finally, they sought to define the conditions that must apply if the rate of money interest is to represent the standard to which returns on other assets must conform, and the conditions that must be fulfilled for the rate of money interest to influence the level of activity. It was this latter aspect, the so-called 'transmission principle', that forms the link between these strictly analytical considerations and monetary policy. It is, therefore, a convenient point to start from before we move to analysis of what Kaldor held to be the determinants of the demand for and the supply of money.

Compared with Keynes's model, Kaldor's is a three-assets model, since, apart from 'money', he also includes two other kinds of asset: a 'short-term asset' and a 'long-term asset'. In principle, every asset brings benefits to its holder: namely, the interest rate $i > 0$, the 'convenience yield' $q > 0$ (which will be defined and exemplified later), the appreciation or depreciation of the asset in terms of money $a > 0$, and a carrying cost $c < 0$. The three above-mentioned assets all have $c = 0$, but they have different values as far as other yields are concerned. We can compare them using the suffixes 1, 2, and 3 to stand for the three assets. The first asset, money, is defined as Central Bank money in the hands of the public plus current deposits with the clearing banks (which is roughly the modern statistical definition of M_1). Money has a positive 'convenience yield', $q_1 > 0$, because it is the general instrument of payment for goods and services, for hiring production factors, for paying taxes, and for discharging a debt. However, money (M_1) does not yield interest (at that time; today it yields low interest), $i_1 = 0$, and since its value in terms of money cannot change, $a_1 = 0$ as a consequence. Short-term assets comprise savings deposits and short-term securities, which represent the closest substitute for money. Short-term assets cannot be used as payment, hence $q_2 = 0$, but they do yield interest $i_2 > 0$. They also have the property of being a virtual store of value, because the gain or loss incurred if they have to be unexpectedly converted into money is close to zero, $a_2 = 0$. Long-term assets also have a zero convenience yield $q_3 = 0$, a positive interest rate $i_3 > 0$, and an expected gain or loss a_3. Because of this risk, holders of these assets have to be compensated with a risk premium r_3.

An asset-holder will choose that portfolio combination which secures the highest total benefit. There are inverse relations between the amount of long-term assets held and the risk premium, and between the convenience yield of holding money q_1 and the quantity of money. These relations tend to equalize all benefits: $q_1 = i_2 = i_3 + a_3 - r_3$. Chapter 2.4 discussed the relation between the short (i_2) and long rate of interest (i_3), and how a change in the liquidity preference affects the yields of long-term assets. Here it is stressed that the same maximization process induces the asset-holder to hold money up to the point where $q_1 = i_2$. From this one deduces the demand for money: it depends directly on the level of income and inversely on the short-term rate of interest, but it is independent of the long-term rate of interest—i.e. of expected future rates of interest.

On the other hand, the supply of money is a function of the short-term rate of interest. In 1939 Kaldor wrote:

The elasticity of the money supply in a modern banking system is ensured partly by the open market operations of the central bank, partly by the commercial banks not holding to a strict reserve ratio in the face of fluctuation in the demand for loans, and partly it is a consequence of the fact that under present banking practices a switch-over from current deposits to savings deposits automatically reduces the amount of deposit money in existence, and vice versa.[1]

For a given income level, money demand and supply are represented by two curves (Figure 11.1), both depending on the short-term rate of interest. 'And since the elasticity of the supply of cash with respect to the short-term rate is usually much higher than the elasticity of demand',[2] this implies that 'in a modern community it is best to regard the short rate of interest (i_2) (rather than the quantity of money) as being fixed by the policies of the monetary authorities . . . and the quantity of currency in circulation as being determined by

---

[1] N. Kaldor, 'Speculation and Economic Stability' (1939), repr. in CP ii. 40.
[2] Ibid. 39.

FIG. 11.1 Kaldor's first representation of the endogenous money supply

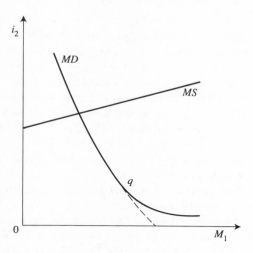

the demand for cash balances by the public'.[3] This constitutes a clear statement
of what Kaldor subsequently called the endogenous theory of money supply.[4]

Further investigation is required of the higher elasticity of money supply
with respect to the interest rate; and this brings us to Central-Bank policy.
Kaldor examined the case where the monetary authorities implement, for the
purposes of stabilization, an anticyclical policy such as those advocated by
various economists of the time—chiefly Hawtrey.[5]

From the beginning, Kaldor was opposed to a monetary policy of fine
tuning, mainly because there was a risk that it would turn out to be destabilizing rather than stabilizing. Monetary authorities are ignorant both of the
delays with which a change in the rate of interest will affect real magnitudes,
and of the extent of this effect. (This point would be made again in post-war
years by the monetarists in their polemic against the Keynesians of the neo-

---

[3] Id., 'Keynes' Theory of the Own-Rates of Interest' (1939), pub. in CP ii. 64.

[4] Some authors have claimed that Kaldor only introduced the notion of endogenous money
supply in 1970, in his critique of the Chicago school. See M. Lavoie, 'Endogenous Money, Kaldor,
Cambridge and Contemporaries', paper given at a conference at New school for Social Research
and Bard College, New York, 29–31 Oct. 1987, proceedings pub. under conference title: E. J. Nell
and W. Semmler (eds.), *Nicholas Kaldor and Mainstream Economics: Confrontation or Convergence?* (New York, St Martin's Press, 1991); M. Desai, 'The Scourge of Monetarists: Kaldor on
Monetarism and Money', *CJE* (Mar. 1989); B. J. Moore, 'A Simple Model of Bank Intermedia-
tion', *JPKE* 12: 1 (1989), 10–28. Others have demonstrated that Kaldor's work of the 1930s and
1940s links closely with his later polemic (of the 1970s and 1980s) against monetarism. See M.
Musella and C. Panico, 'Kaldor on Endogenous Money and Interest Rate', mimeo 1989. In the
Italian edn. of the present book I too held this latter view; the details provided by Musella and
Panico's paper have strengthened my opinion even further, which I hope now emerges unequivocally.

[5] R. G. Hawtrey, *Capital and Employment* (London, Longmans Green & Co., 1937).

classical synthesis.) But apart from these criticisms, Kaldor had others of a deeper nature.

The use of the monetary intrument may in fact be efficient in achieving a high level of income *or* in reducing the magnitude of the trade cycle; but it cannot perform both functions. Kaldor's proof of this rests on three premisses. First, the effect of a change in the short-term rate on the level of activity is a wholly temporary one. Once firms have adapted their stocks to the new level of the rate of interest, its effect peters out. A short rate at 6 per cent is no more deflationary than one at 4 per cent, as long as the latter operates for a relatively long period. A tendency in the market to continual reflation or deflation may be counteracted only by a *continual* raising or lowering of the rate of interest.

The second premiss concerns the asymmetry of monetary policy when the short-term interest rate is at 'normal' levels between 2 and 6 per cent. It is possible, in fact, to slow down the expansion of productive activity by repeatedly raising the interest rate, which has no upper limit. But it is not possible to provide constant stimulus to expansion by lowering the rate of interest, because there is a minimum below which it cannot be pushed by monetary policy (i.e. the point at which the demand for cash balances becomes infinitely elastic to the rate of interest). To eliminate this asymmetry, the short-term interest rate must be kept at very high average values so that it can be made to rise or fall in equal measure.

The third element in Kaldor's demonstration was that long-term interest rates—i.e. those that influence investment decisions and therefore economic activity—depend on the average of the short-term interest rates expected for a long period in the future. Thus, if the monetary authorities keep the levels of short-term rates high, the long-term interest rate will rise as well.

From these three premisses Kaldor drew the conclusion that if the monetary authorities wish to slow down an expansive cyclical phase, they must keep short rates at a very high average level. But this entails raising the long-term rate, which conflicts with the other aim of monetary policy: the maintenance of a satisfactory level of activity. For these reasons, Kaldor believed, there should be increasingly less use of the rate of interest as an instrument of monetary policy. Hence it follows that, 'the monetary authorities are not free to vary the short term rate as they like . . . the two main aims of monetary policy, to secure a satisfactory level of incomes, and to secure stability of incomes, may prove incompatible: the one may only be achieved by sacrificing the other'.[6] The conflict would be resolved in favour of the former policy objective with increasingly less use of the rate of interest as an instrument of monetary policy. 'Assuming that the monetary authorities regard the achievement of a satisfactory level of activity as the paramount consideration, we must expect the bank rate mechanism, as an instrument of economic policy, to become increasingly ineffectual.'[7]

---

[6] Kaldor, 'Speculation and Economic Stability', 57–8.   [7] Ibid. 58.

Consequently, should the monetary authorities choose to keep the rate of interest at a low level in order to stabilize it at that level, the assumption of the high elasticity of money supply (Figure 11.1) is appropriate.

11.2. The Radcliffe Report, the 'Whole Liquidity' Concept, and the Subordinate Role of Monetary Policy

With the Great Depression and Britain's abandonment of the Gold Standard in 1931, monetary policy lost its role as the central instrument for dampening the economic cycle. Within twenty-four hours the Bank Rate was reduced from 6 to 2 per cent; and after the outbreak of the Second World War, Great Britain persisted in this direction. The war was partly financed by enormous loans—not only short-, but also medium- and long-term, and at extremely low rates of interest. The Bank Rate remained fixed at around 2 per cent. Immediately after the war the principal policy instruments adopted by the Attlee government were rates of interest kept at a minimum and an active fiscal policy aimed at maintaining full employment. In 1951 the Conservatives returned to power, with Churchill as Prime Minister and Butler as Chancellor of the Exchequer, and the government once again began to put its faith in monetary policy as an instrument of economic control.

During the first two years of the new government, the inflationary tendencies of previous years were reversed and the balance of payments moved into surplus. However, it very soon became apparent that this disinflation was not internal but external in origin, and that it derived mainly from the fall in international prices after the speculative boom of the Korean War. When in 1955 inflation and crises in the balance of payments again broke out, monetary policy was resorted to with increasing severity, but to little effect. At about the time of the Suez Crisis (September 1956), the conviction grew that monetary measures operated in ways that were insufficiently understood. And it was for this reason that in May 1957 a committee was set up to examine the working of the British monetary and credit system, and to make recommendations to the government. Chaired by Lord Radcliffe, the committee consisted of two economists (A. K. Cairncross and R. S. Sayers), two bankers, two trade-unionists, and two businessmen. In its two years of work the committee collected evidence from over two hundred witnesses and examined more than one hundred and fifty written memoranda.

Kaldor expressed his admiration for both the political and intellectual qualities of Lord Radcliffe on more than one occasion. 'A conservative in the best English sense of that term,' he called him; one who 'had the rare quality of making one feel on the top of one's form in discussion with him'.[8] Although

---

[8] Id., 'A Personal Note on Lord Radcliffe', in id., *The Scourge of Monetarism* (Oxford, OUP, 1982).

Radcliffe was trained as a lawyer, Kaldor recalled, he soon absorbed the methods of reasoning of economists and knew how to distinguish between analysis and value-judgements. Under his chairmanship, the committee managed to produce a unanimous final report,[9] despite its heterodox arguments and despite its criticism of British monetary policy of the 1950s. Given the system of fixed exchange rates adopted since the war, the committee considered its task to be one of evaluating the effectiveness of monetary policy on aggregate expenditure. It sought, in other words, to assess the suitability of this instrument for the control of the trade cycle. The committee's findings gave no support whatsoever to those who advocated a return to monetary policy as the cornerstone of economic policy; on the contrary, its findings bore 'a certain family resemblance on critical issues'[10] to the arguments that Kaldor himself had put forward in his memorandum[11] prepared at the request of the committee.[12] The ideas on the money supply and monetary policy contained in this memorandum and in Kaldor's review of the work of the Radcliffe Committee were substantially the same as those expressed in his 1939 articles.

In the light of recent debates, one may say that the Radcliffe Report set out the most radically Keynesian arguments concerning monetary policy ever expressed by an official public body of any country. The theoretical premiss from which it drew its conclusions was that the velocity of money is variable. Kaldor dwelt at length on this premiss in his memorandum and complained[13] on several occasions that the committee had not gone deeply enough into a point that repudiated the entire basis of monetarist doctrine from Cantillon to the present day. Indeed, the variability of the velocity of circulation severs the direct relation between money in circulation and money spent. It may be high or low; but differences in velocity from one country to another depend on historical factors and have little to do with forms of payment. Moreover, the velocity of circulation can increase or decrease without limits: its variability does not depend on the rate of inflation but on monetary policy.

The velocity of circulation (the ratio between cash balances and the turnover of money payment per unit of time) depends not so much—as it did in Keynes—on the attitudes of speculators (choices affecting the demand for money) as on the attitudes of the monetary authorities (policies affecting the

---

[9] The first Radcliffe Commission on taxation produced two reports: a majority one, and a minority one written by Kaldor himself. The report of the second Radcliffe Committee on the working of the monetary system was unanimous. In his essay 'The Radcliffe Report' (1959), repr. in CP iii, Kaldor complained that the committee's desire for unanimity at all costs led to vagueness and contradictions in its final report.

[10] R. Harrod, review of CP iii in *EJ* (Dec. 1965), 796–7.

[11] N. Kaldor, repr. in 'Monetary Policy, Economic Stability and Growth' (1958), CP iii.

[12] Lord Kahn was another Cambridge economist whose clear and concise submission undoubtedly greatly influenced the committee. Other memoranda considered by Kaldor to be extremely interesting and still relevant in the 1980s were submitted by A. J. Brown, J. C. R. Dow, R. F. Harrod, I. M. D. Little, R. R. Neild, and R. Ross.

[13] Kaldor, 'Radcliffe Report', 163, and id., 'The Radcliffe Report and Monetary Policy', in id., *Scourge of Monetarism*, 9.

money supply). 'In countries where the authorities pursue a restrictive policy, the ratio tends to fall, and *viceversa*.'[14] For Kaldor, monetary policy has its first impact on the velocity of circulation of money; any variation in prices and incomes is neither immediate nor direct, but only works through the induced changes in interest rates.

Decisions to spend are influenced not so much by the quantity of money (notes and bank deposits) as by the 'whole liquidity position'. After the Radcliffe Report, this concept would become a standard feature of Keynesian monetary economics—even though, as Kaldor complained, the report had provided it with no clearcut definition. Kaldor defined as liquid assets 'all those assets that can be exchanged for money . . . at any time, at short notice and at a relatively small "transaction cost" '.[15] The more an asset is standardized, and hence the 'thicker' the market for that asset, the smaller the transaction cost from asset to money will tend to be.[16] As regards the private or public nature of the institution that issues the asset, Kaldor pointed out that private loan transactions increase the general liquidity only if the process of lending and borrowing does not come about directly, but through financial intermediaries. When it occurs, there are no differences among securities representative of a debt by the State (banknotes, Treasury Bills, short bonds, medium- and long-dated bonds) or by private financial intermediaries (paying deposit accounts in the clearing banks or deposits with building societies), because these are all held in their dual capacity as investments and as sources of liquidity which enable their holders rapidly to modify the disposition of their wealth. Moreover, there is no acceptable reason for drawing a sharp dividing line between bonds and the shares of major public companies, since these can be easily bought or sold in large amounts at very short notice.

Although the Radcliffe Committee did not dismiss the supply of money as an unimportant quantity, 'it is the *whole liquidity position* that is relevant to spending decisions, and our interest in the supply of money is due to its significance in the whole liquidity picture'.[17] However, it was pointless for the monetary authorities to exercise direct control over the whole liquidity position by increasing their control over intermediaries other than banks because— apart from the administrative costs involved—the situation would constantly get out of hand. A first conclusion was therefore that management by the monetary authorities of the quantity of money as an instrument for the control

[14] Id., 'Monetary Policy, Economic Stability and Growth', 129.

[15] Id., 'Radcliffe Report and Monetary Policy', 10.

[16] In his introd. to CP ii. (1st edn., 1960), 5, Kaldor tells us that 'the main point on which I have modified my views since 1939 concerns the demand function for cash balances (i.e. media of payments). I would not now regard the desire to hold cash balances as a single-valued function of the level of money-income (i.e. the volume of money transactions) and of the short-rate of interest (as implied by the demand curve of diagram (11.1)) but would say that, in addition, the desire to hold cash will vary with the amount of "money substitutes" available (e.g. bills, savings deposits of all kinds, and other forms of short-term paper).'

[17] Committee on the Working of the Monetary System, *Report*, Cmnd 827 (London, HMSO, Aug. 1959), para. 389, p. 132.

of spending and the trade cycle is doomed to failure, both because the velocity of circulation of money and therefore the ratio per unit of time between money and spending (turnover of money spending) is variable, and because decisions to spend are influenced by the whole liquidity position, which monetary authorities are unable to control quantitatively.

Having discarded the possibility that monetary policy could act effectively through the control of the money supply, in any strict or broad sense, Kaldor's memorandum argued that the cornerstone of monetary intervention should be the direct control of the level and structure of interest rates. And here, too, there was broad agreement between his opinions and those of the committee, which maintained that 'control of "the supply of money"—whatever that may be made to mean—is not by itself a reliable policy measure, and that the authorities must seek rather to influence the general liquidity situation by operating on rates of interest.'[18]

By arguing that the whole liquidity position is relevant to spending decisions, the committee had in mind not only that individuals are more willing to spend when their assets are liquid, but also that a large part of these assets are held by financial institutions—which means that the main effect of an interest-rate policy is on the behaviour of financial institutions rather than on that of private individuals. This was not to imply, however, that by acting on rates of interest, monetary policy would obtain an instrument for the effective control of the economy—even by restraining the expansive phases of the cycle. Although the Radcliffe Committee did concede that a restrictive monetary policy might reduce spending by making it difficult to grant loans, it nevertheless pointed out that during the 1950s the credit squeeze had not in fact affected aggregate spending; an outcome that, in Kaldor's view, was due to the fact that monetary policy was effective only if it was drastic.[19] An innovative finding by the committee—one that ran counter to an opinion that had been widespread and cogently argued in the past, mainly by Hawtrey—was that changes in inventories (which had usually been held responsible for many cyclical fluctuations) is influenced, not by short- but by long-term rates of interest. And in this it is no different from expenditure on fixed capital: that is, neither inventories nor fixed capital depend on short-term rates of interest. Moreover, Kaldor argued, if long-term rates change, they are not considered stable, and if they are moderate (not sufficient to close the gap with the rate of profit), they 'may have no appreciable effect on investment decisions'.[20] On the other hand, long-term interest rates react only sluggishly to changes in short-term rates.

---

[18] Ibid. para. 504, p. 179. On this point, the committee explicitly stated that it had 'follow[ed] Professor Kahn . . . in insisting upon the structure of interest rates, rather than some notion of "money supply" as the counterpiece of monetary action': para. 395, p. 134.

[19] In his memorandum Kaldor ruled out a monetary policy based on 'announcements' because the consequences would be entirely unpredictable.

[20] Kaldor, 'Monetary Policy, Economic Stability and Growth', 133.

It was for this reason that Kaldor wrote in his memorandum that if monetary policy is to deal effectively with spending on investment as a whole (in both fixed capital and in inventories), it must be draconian, because only 'drastic and spectacular changes in interest rates can be counted on to exert a marked effect on capital expenditure'.[21] This behaviour is in contradiction of the role traditionally attributed to monetary policy: 'that gentle hand on the steering wheel that keeps a well driven car in its right place on the road'.[22]

A policy of drastic variations in interest rates is inadvisable, however, because it interferes with the achievement of three other policy objectives: financing government debt; facilitating the smooth operation of financial markets; and keeping the long-run rate of economic growth high and stable.

As regards the first reason for the reluctance to make drastic changes in interests rates, Kaldor observed in his memorandum to the committee that: 'the existence of a massive short-term debt . . . and the constant need to refinance a large volume of bounded debt which matures each year . . . must undoubtedly reduce the relative attractiveness of the Bank Rate instrument as an economic regulator'.[23] Moreover, drastic changes in interest rates would also result in a high degree of instability in bond prices and capital markets. This is 'highly undesirable' because

[i]f bond prices were liable to vast and rapid fluctuations, the . . . capital market would become far more speculative, and would function much less efficiently as an instrument of allocative savings—new issues would be more difficult to launch, and long-run considerations of relative profitability would play a subordinate role in the allocations of funds. As Keynes said, when the capital investment of a country 'becomes a by-product of the activities of a casino, the job is likely to be ill-done'.[24]

Thirdly, drastic and rapid fluctuations in bond prices would make 'the average price that the investors would demand for parting with liquidity considerably higher'. This use of monetary policy 'can be bought at the cost of making the average long term interest rate higher than they would be if the interest rates were relatively stable'. If average interest rates are considerably higher, then the rate of profit also has to be higher to make investment attractive; but

to achieve this effect Government policies would have to aim at stimulating consumption at the same time as they restrain investment . . . and would thus gradually transform the economy into one of high consumption and low investment—with all its undesirable consequences on the long-run rates of economic growth.[25]

The implementation of a monetary policy would therefore lead to conflict between pursuit of control over the cycle, which required highly unstable rates of short-term interest, and pursuit of other highly desirable objectives requir-

---

[21] Ibid. 132.
[22] Committee on the Working of the Monetary System, *Report*, para. 472, p. 168.
[23] Kaldor, 'Monetary Policy, Economic Stability and Growth', 135–6.
[24] Ibid. 136.   [25] Ibid. 136–7.

ing stable rates of long-term interest. It is not surprising, therefore, that the Radcliffe Committee declared: 'we reject any suggestion that the rate of interest weapon should be made more effective by being used much more violently than hitherto'.[26]

As a corollary to this, whenever credit control is used as an instrument independently of budgetary policy, every energetic action by the monetary authorities reduces the efficiency of the instrument itself, because industry moves from commercial banks to other financial institutions.[27] The change in the financial structure of industry alters the velocity of circulation in terms of conventional money, but without significant effects on spending.[28]

Despite the many similarities between the findings of the committee and Kaldor's own position, he nevertheless objected to its final Report on a number of counts. In his view, the committee had not reached concrete conclusions either on the causes and effects of inflation, or on anti-inflationary measures (which Kaldor himself had examined in his memorandum); nor had the committee specified how the international cycle was to be controlled, nor how the economy was to be governed by direct manipulation of the components of effective demand. However, Kaldor did subscribe to the committee's overall philosophy: that control of the money supply should be seen as only one aspect, albeit an important one, of the management of the national debt, and more in general that 'the use of monetary measures (should) not in ordinary times play other than a subordinate part in guiding the development of the economy'[29] and that 'monetary measures can help, but that is all'.[30]

11.3. The Revival of the Quantity Theory of Money and the New Monetarism

At the end of the 1960s there began to emanate from Chicago, spreading first through the United States and then to Europe, a version of monetary policy— soon to be labelled 'New Monetarism'—that ran completely counter to the

[26] Committee on the Working of the Monetary System, *Report*, para. 491, p. 175.

[27] In terms of current Italian debate, one may say that the 'divorce' between the Treasury and the Bank of Italy has 'disintermediated' the banking system.

[28] In a private conversation with the present writer, R. Rowthorn criticized Kaldor's position as contradictory: either one argues that monetary policy has little effect on spending, or one argues that Thatcher's monetarist policies have been responsible for Britain's current productive crisis; but one cannot argue for both these positions. Rowthorn's criticism strikes me as mistaken. One can in fact argue that *monetary policy* does not affect spending under normal conditions, while a *monetarist policy* comprising restrictive monetary *and* fiscal policies combined with a revaluation of the exchange rate (which was relatively ineffective in the 1950s and 1960s) may have a profoundly depressive effect on industry. Not only this, but the policy followed by the Reagan administration until 1986 proved Kaldor right: a restrictive monetary policy did not reduce spending, because it was coupled with an expansive budget policy, but led to an explosion of financial intermediaries offering new debt-clearing instruments.

[29] Committee on the Working of the Monetary System, *Report*, para. 511, p. 182.

[30] Ibid. para. 514, p. 183.

philosophy of the Radcliffe Committee. In 1970 Kaldor was among the first critics of the Chicago school;[31] and both then and henceforth he would be its most radical adversary from both an analytical and political point of view. After ten years of monetarism, he expressed his opinions thus:

I consider 'monetarism' as a terrible curse, a visitation of evil spirits, with particularly unfortunate, one could almost say devastating, effects on our country, Britain. The biological process of natural selection should make for the development of favourable traits in human character . . . As we well know, this is not, unfortunately, either a smooth or a continuous process—it proceeds by fits and starts . . . Decadence, according to Nietzsche, is a state in which the individual intuitively goes for the bad solutions for getting out of difficult situations and fails to pick up the good ones.[32]

And four years later he wrote, in an analysis of the premises and failure of the doctrine,

The great revival of 'monetarism' during the 1970s, culminating in the adoption of the strict prescriptions of the monetarist creed by a number of Western Governments at the turn of the decade . . . will, I am sure, go down in history as one of the most curious episodes, comparable only to the periodic outbreaks of mass hysteria (such as the witch hunt) of the Middle Ages.[33]

Since modern monetarism is a direct descendant of the quantity theory of money, I shall follow Kaldor in setting out the theory's conditions of historical-institutional validity, its analytical formulation, the innovations brought to it by Keynes, and finally Friedman's critique of Keynesian theory and his proposals for monetary policy. The next section will examine Kaldor's counter-assault on monetarism and his own proposals for monetary policy.

David Hume and the classical economists developed the quantity theory in an age when money consisted only of precious metals such as gold and silver. These, as produced goods, had a production cost. For Ricardo it was the cost of the labour required to produce the gold that—the rate of profit in all sectors being equal—determined the value in gold of commodities in general. Hume's theory of the balance of payments guaranteed the optimal distribution of gold among countries. These propositions were extended to the case of an economy with paper money by the members of the currency school.[34]

---

[31] N. Kaldor, 'The New Monetarism', *LLBR* (July 1970).

[32] Id., 'Origins of the New Monetarism' (1980), repr. in CP v.

[33] Id., 'How Monetarism Failed' (1984), repr. in CP ix.

[34] Kaldor's exposition seems to imply that the invalidity of quantitative theory is limited only to its historical and institutional framework. The credit-based nature of a money economy can be conceived of as independent of the nature of the money-medium. Penetrating analyses of the endogeneity of metal money and on the indirect relation between money and prices can already be found in economists of the 19th cent., such as Thornton, the members of the banking school, and later Marx. Ricardo himself took an unorthodox position on international flows of gold (see C. Boffito, *La teoria della moneta* (Turin, Einaudi, 1973)) and before the *Principles* came very close to embracing the idea that gold money was governed by producer demand: gold in excess of money purposes would become goods (ornaments, jewellery, etc.). Wicksell explained this phenomenon by replacing private hoarding with hoarding by the Central Bank. According to De Cecco, it was the 19th-cent. Ricardians and the currency school who invented institutions on the

Following the debate between the currency school and the banking school provoked by the Bank Charter Act of 1844, and until the Cunliffe Committee and the Macmillan Committee of 1931, the quantity theory of money dominated British economic and political thought.[35]

The quantity theory can be expressed either in the version developed in America by Irving Fisher or in Europe by Marshall or Walras. In the European formulation the 'marginal utility of money' determines the value of money itself and hence its purchasing power. The value of money $(1/P)$ varies in inverse proportion to its quantity (M) and the parameter depends on the share of wealth held in the form of liquid balances (k). If V is the velocity of circulation of money, which is the inverse of k, the fraction of real wealth that individuals and businesses wish to keep in the form of money, and which can be kept constant, depending on the stable time intervals between payments established by institutions and custom, the two versions of the quantity theory of money can be written:

$$(11.1) \qquad p = (M/Q)V \qquad \text{or} \qquad p = (M/Q)(1/k)$$

where Q is annual output.

Before the Gold Standard was abolished, a transmission mechanism operated between the quantity of money and prices. If the quantity of gold in circulation increased (because of lower production costs, or the opening of new mines, or a greater inflow of metal from abroad), the actual balances held by individuals exceeded desired balances, and people increased their spending in order to shed excess gold. If the economy was at full employment, this increased spending pushed up prices. The situation was one in which: (1) it was the quantity of money that varied exogenously; (2) a variation in supply generated spending directly (via the increase in income due to the production of the money commodity) and indirectly (via the adjustment of actual to desired balances); (3) spending influenced prices not output.

In his 1923 *Tract on Monetary Reform* Keynes was still a proponent of quantity theory, although he favoured a managed currency rather than the Gold Standard to keep prices stable. It was only during the 1930s, first in *A Treatise on Money* and then in the *General Theory*, that he began to move in a different theoretical direction and to investigate the relation between prices and costs in the aggregate. His adherence to Marshallian theory, however, was still such that Pigou was able to amend the Keynesian 'model' with his equation expressing the price–cost relation:[36]

---

basis of the quantitative theory, and not vice versa (M. De Cecco, *Gold Coinage and Currency* (Fiesole, Università Europea, 1986)). I owe this observation to Dr Tamborini.

[35] It should not be forgotten, however, that, while official doctrine was one thing, the actual monetary policy of the Bank of England was quite another. Even in the 19th cent. the Bank of England adopted a monetary policy based on managing interest rates rather than the money supply. See W. Bagehot, *Lombard Street* (London, J. Murray, 1915).

[36] A. C. Pigou, 'The Theory of Unemployment', in R. G. Hawtrey (ed.), *Capital and Full Employment* (London, Longman Green & Co., 1937).

(11.2) $$p = (1 + \pi)(dl/dQ)\overline{w}$$

where π is the reciprocal of the elasticity of demand for the output of the representative firm (equal to zero in perfect competition), dl/dQ is the reciprocal of the marginal productivity of labour, and w is the exogenous money wage.

If the economy is close to full employment, the cost function is inelastic and (11.1) will determine p (quantity theory) and (11.2) will determine Q (production function), according to the neo-classical view. If the cost function is highly elastic, function (11.2) will determine p (which will come to depend on the level of money-wages), and (11.1) will determine Q (in terms of the monetary demand for goods and services MV). In intermediate situations, p and Q will be jointly determined by both equations. It is important to note that the Pigou 'amendment' admitted the possibility of permanent unemployment, as a consequence of excess money-wages with respect to the quantity of money.

In his *General Theory* Keynes tied the level of spending to effective demand, given by autonomous investment I via the multiplier $1/(1-c)$. However, this equation was incompatible with the $MV = Y$ equivalence (in which $Y = pQ$) if M and V are exogenous and the level of prices is given by the money-wage. It was, however, compatible with an equation where either M or V is endogenous. With the liquidity-preference function, Keynes chose V to be endogenous in terms of the rate of interest i. The system was thus completed by the following two equations:

(11.3) $$MV = (1/1-c)I;$$

(11.4) $$V = V(i) \quad \text{or} \quad k = k(i).$$

The system comprised four equations (11.1)–(11.4) which determine four unknowns, p (level of prices), Q (output), V (velocity of circulation of money) (or its inverse k) and i (rate of interest) with the aid of four exogenous variables, M (money supply), w (rate of money-wages), I (investment), and c (propensity to consume), as well as two behavioural functions: the production function $Q(l)$ and the liquidity-preference function $V(i)$ or $k(i)$.

These four equations laid the foundations of the neo-classical–Keynesian school of Pigou and Hicks in Great Britain and of MIT in the United States. Despite the fact that as early as 1937 Keynes had made clear in the *Economic Journal* that his ideas on liquidity preference were an outline sketch of a theory and nothing more,[37] the whole of subsequent Keynesian theory would in fact hinge on the money demand equation (11.4). The opponents of Keynes, from Pigou to Robertson, from Ohlin to Viner, immediately sought to refute his theory of involuntary unemployment, and would accept it only as a consequence of the extreme situation that Robertson called the 'liquidity trap'.

---

[37] J. M. Keynes, 'Alternative Theories of the Rate of Interest', *EJ* (June 1937).

More generally, Keynesian macro-economic theory seemed to entail that 'money does not matter': changes in expenditure could occur without changes in the quantity of money, since the adjustment of the money supply to demand took place through a speeding up of the velocity of circulation. The validity of the whole model therefore rested on the variability of V in response to changes in income and expenditure or—which is the same thing—on the absence of a relation between M and Y. In the United States in particular, the clash between 'classical' and Keynesian theorists narrowed its focus to empirical investigation of the elasticity of money demand with respect to income: both Keynesians, like Tobin, and anti-Keynesians, like Harry Johnson, agreed that this was the crucial test for the theory.

Keynes's formulation of the process of monetary equilibrium in terms of elastic money demand and exogenous money supply provoked the controversy from which the New Monetarism would spring.[38] Since the 1950s, in fact, Milton Friedman had been engaged in research for the National Bureau of Economic Research and had discovered a close correlation between changes in M and in Y. From this he deduced that the velocity of circulation V was stable and that its elasticity with respect to the interest rate was very low:[39] a finding that prompted his pronouncement that the Keynesian theory was wrong and that quantity theory should be revived.

According to the modern version of the quantity theory, the Central Bank determines the amount of cash (roughly the money base) to place in circulation; the non-banking public establishes in a stable manner the proportion of cash to keep in its pockets and the proportion to deposit in the banks. Deposited cash forms the basis of bank credit: in fact, banks do not increase their loans beyond a certain multiple of the cash held by them or deposited as legal reserve in the Central Bank. For the monetarists, therefore, the money supply can be regulated irrespective of the movement in interest rates by putting a fixed quantity of money base into circulation, sticking to that quantity and then ordering clearing banks to maintain a certain minimum proportion of reserve in proportion to their liabilities.

Given the observed regularity between the change in the money supply and money income, a policy of constant increase in the money supply entails a constant increase in money income. If the increase in real income is exogenous, the rate of inflation is under the complete control of the monetary authorities.

The money-to-prices transmission mechanism is analysed in much less detail by Friedman[40] than it was by pre-Keynesian economists. (Wicksell and the pupils of von Mises devoted much study to the effects of money production

[38] N. Kaldor, 'Keynesian Economics after Fifty Years', in D. Worswick and J. Trevithick (eds.), *Keynes and the Modern World* (Cambridge, CUP, 1983).

[39] M. Friedman and A. J. Schwartz, *A Monetary History of the United States 1867–1960* (National Bureau of Economic Research; Princeton, NJ, Princeton University Press, 1963).

[40] M. Friedman, 'A Theoretical Framework for Monetary Analysis', *JPE* (Mar.–Apr. 1970).

and exchange and hence on the level of prices.) However, according to the New Monetarists, there is no doubt that inflation must eventually be induced by the demand for goods, which may also take the form of excess demand on the labour market.[41] In both cases, an increase in output or a fall in unemployment below the 'natural rate' can only be temporary.[42]

11.4. The Critique of the New Monetarism based on the Endogeneity of the Money Supply

While in the United States the debate between monetarists and Keynesians concentrated on the empirical evidence for the stability of the *demand for money* with respect to income, Kaldor opened up new areas of debate over the endogeneity of the *supply of money*—an idea that he first began to develop during the 1930s and then expounded in detail from 1970 onwards. In the following passages Kaldor summarizes the evolution of his thinking on the subject:

I had already explained my ideas on the endogeneity of the money supply in 1939 . . . in 'Speculation and Economic Stability' and in the article 'Own Rates of Interest'.[43]

When in the early 1950s I first heard of Friedman's empirical findings, I received the news with some incredulity, until it suddenly dawned on me that Friedman's results must be read *in reverse*; the causation must run from Y to M, and not from M to Y. And the longer I thought about it, the more convinced I became that a theory of the value of money based on a commodity-money economy is not applicable to a credit money economy.[44]

As he retraced the various stages in the history of money, Kaldor pointed out that ever since money had been invented—as a means of exchange required by an economy that was increasingly socialized and based on the

---

[41] Id., *Inflation and Employment* (London, IEA, 1977). H. G. Johnson, 'What is Right with Monetarism', *LLBR* (Apr. 1976).

[42] The 'Mark II' monetarists claim instead that an even short-term deviation of employment and production from the equilibrium path must presuppose that expectations are formed irrationally. They hold, in fact, that it is in the interest of agents to establish a 'correct model' of the working of the economy, so that they can form 'rational expectations' which will restrain any divergence from the equilibrium path and nullify all attempts to bring unemployment below its 'natural' level, even in the short period. Inflation can be reduced if the authorities are able to convince the public of their determination to limit the money supply; the reaction will be a voluntary drop in price and wages, without the economy even temporarily having to suffer from the fall in income and employment. Kaldor agreed with Tobin (J. Tobin, 'The Monetary Counter-Revolution Today—An Appraisal', *EJ* (Mar. 1981)) that 'the dilemma of Mark II Monetarism is that it is compelled to regard inflation as quite harmless and as a great evil at the same time—two views which are not easy to reconcile with each other'. If all price increases are fully anticipated, the only cost of inflation is the higher cost of holding money and the inconvenience of holding less; a cost and an inconvenience that do very little to justify making the battle against inflation a government's overriding objective. (Kaldor, 'Radcliffe Report and Monetary Policy', 31–2.)

[43] Id., *Ricordi di un economista*, ed. M. C. Marcuzzo (Milan, Garzanti, 1986), 73.

[44] Id., 'Radcliffe Report and Monetary Policy', 22.

division of labour—demand for money has been an *effect* not a *cause* of the demand for commodities. In the long run, the value of commodity money was determined by production costs, and the more production expanded, the more economically convenient it became to increase the production of commodity-money as well.[45] However, some discrepancy between monetary and real production might arise, and it might come about that the supply of commodity money increased faster than the supply of other commodities (as happened when gold and silver were discovered in Spain's American colonies), and those who acquired commodity money grew rich and spent. If there was elasticity in the supply of commodities, the value of money compared with other goods dropped until the proportion of income that people wanted to hold in the form of liquid balances (the k in the Cambridge quantity equation (11.1)) returned to the desired level. The discrepancy, however, could also operate in reverse. If commodity money increased at a slower rate than the supply of other commodities, this would raise obstacles against the expansion of the economy, although these kinds of obstacle were, historically, always overcome a little at a time by money substitutes.

Thus an economy based on commodity money gradually developed into a credit money economy. In the early stages the certificates issued by gold-smiths for the gold deposited on their premisses were used as means of payment. The goldsmiths therefore became bankers, and the banking system 'created credit' through an increase in the supply of money.[46] The banks issued certificates backed by commodity-money deposited in their vaults. Since these certificates were promises to pay and functioned as currency, there was a long-standing debate over whether, by doing this, the banks were able to increase the overall supply of money in the system. In the chapter on money in the second book of the *Wealth of Nations*, Smith argued that the expansion of the banking system had been one of the most important inventions in the enrichment of Scotland. Kaldor gives a markedly Keynesian reading to Smith's argument: the birth of institutes that could create 'financial means' available to producers enabled them to make investments *before* the income was created from which the savings to balance investment were to be obtained.[47]

At a later stage in the evolution of the financial system, the right to issue such certificates was concentrated in the hands of a single institution: the

---

[45] For analytical convenience, Ricardo assumed constant production costs of gold so that money values and real values of goods could grow at the same rate.

[46] Not all economic historians agree with this widely held idea that the first credit money was created by goldsmiths. According to Postan, 14th-cent. English merchants issued means of payment which circulated as credit money (N. M. Postan, *Medieval Trade and Finance* (Cambridge, CUP, 1973)). Goldsmiths became bankers in the 17th cent. during the Tudor and Stuart period, but the idea of turning themselves into bankers also occurred to tradesmen, stockbrokers, tax collectors, and public notaries. These latter apparently started to accept deposits before goldsmiths did (cf. C. P. Kindleberger, *A Financial History of Western Europe* (London, Allen & Unwin, 1984)).

[47] Kaldor and Trevithick, 'A Keynesian Perspective on Money' *LLBR* 139 (Jan. 1981), 112.

Central Bank. Banknotes now became the basic form of money. However, just as coins had been replaced by banknotes, so these too were gradually replaced by cheques backed by deposits and issued by the commercial banks.

If in Europe the chief monetary innovations were introduced by private agents, in the English colonies of America they were created by local colonial governments. Strict monetary regulation by the English Crown and the inadequate growth of the gold and silver supply with respect to the growth of the North American market economy (i.e. the increase in the population, in per-capita output, and in the ratio between market economy and total economy) had since the seventeenth century induced the governments of the more rapidly developing colonies (like Massachusetts) to devise a new medium of exchange to meet the sharp rise in the demand for money.[48] Except in times of war, this supply of means of exchange was both rational and beneficial to economic growth: 'its primary purpose (was) to remove the constraints on real economic development that are implicit in an existing set of monetary arrangements and regulations'.[49]

This evolutionary process in the various forms assumed by money has been so profound and comprehensive that it is difficult to decide which specific asset may be denominated as such. If money is interpreted as a means for settling a debt–credit relation, then, as the Radcliffe Report pointed out, many assets possess this attribute and are therefore in some measure liquid. Money takes the form not only of banknotes in the hands of the public and the banks (monetary base) but also of deposits in current accounts (M_1). There are also disguised forms of money not included in the statistics: travellers cheques, unutilized lines of credit, banknotes in foreign currencies, banknotes in Euro-currency markets, and credit cards. In addition, money includes all savings deposits (in England these comprise, apart from interest-bearing deposits, also deposits in savings banks and building societies) which combine to form M_2. Then there are the various forms of short-term securities, mainly treasury bills, which, although they are not money in the strict sense of the term, are so readily convertible into cash that they are hard to distinguish from it. It is therefore obvious that no hard and fast distinction can be drawn between 'monetary' and 'non-monetary' assets: 'any broad definition of the money supply is therefore arbitrary since it is invariably surrounded by a spectrum of "liquid assets" which are not comprised in it but which are close substitutes to it'.[50]

Once a monetary system has transmuted itself into a credit money system, the discrepancy between the demand for and the supply of money has different

[48] Corn as legal tender in 1631, wampum as legal tender in 1643, and bills of credit in 1690 (which quickly evolved into a fiat-paper currency).

[49] See R. Sylla, 'Monetary Innovation and Crisis in American Economic History', in P. Wachtel (ed.), *Crisis in the Economic and Financial Structure* (Lexington Books, 1982) 25. Sylla also writes that: 'the innovations indicate that individuals and communities, like the federal government itself, would find ways to provide whatever money they needed in spite of specie standards and restrictive banking laws', ibid. 32.

[50] Kaldor, 'Monetary Policy in the United Kingdom', in id., *Scourge of Monetarism*, 72.

effects on the economic system. In a credit money system it is no longer possible to assert that when the money supply *exceeds* demand (at the prevailing level of income), the outcome will be an increase in spending and income sufficient to eliminate the excess of money. Kaldor believed that this mechanism of money adjustment only applies as long as the money system is based strictly on commodity money, since this, as a product of the mining industry, has to be in the hands of someone. Credit money, however, has sprung from borrowing by businesses, households, or public bodies from banks. If such borrowing brings more money into existence than the public wishes to hold, the 'excess of money' is eliminated by repayment of the loan. A credit money system therefore differs from a commodity-money system in that demand for goods and services can never increase as a result of a rise in the amount of bank money held by the public. Hence, in a credit money economy the causal link between money and incomes, or between money and prices, is the reverse of that presumed by the quantity theory of money: it is a rise in the level of spending that leads to an increase in the quantity of money and not vice versa.[51] The Chicago school's 'transmission principle' cannot work, therefore. In contrast with the monetarist assertion that an excess supply of money (which, in Friedman's example, supposedly comes about by money being thrown from helicopters) would result in higher inflation, Kaldor pointed out that: 'those who hold that an "excess supply" of money under these circumstances would *directly* increase spending forget that, barring helicopters etc., the "excess supply" could never materialize'.[52]

The money supply in a credit money economy is therefore *endogenous*,[53] since it varies according to the demand for cash and bank deposits and is thus not independent of this demand.[54] Kaldor's theory of the endogeneity of money can be regarded as a development of Keynes's ideas on finance set out in the *Treatise on Money*, where the finance motive was taken to be the principal source of the demand for money, and where the level of interest rates was set by the Central Banks rather than by the quantity of money supply. These ideas disappear, however, in the liquidity-preference function of the *General Theory*—where Keynes held the more orthodox view that the quantity of money was determined by the action of the Central Bank—and have been part neither of the neo-classical–Keynesian tradition nor of monetarist theory.

[51] As has already been pointed out (n. 34, above), one can argue, in terms even·more radical than Kaldor's, that the weakness of quantitative theory is conceptual, not historico-institutional.

[52] Id., 'New Monetarism', 11–12 n. 2.

[53] Kaldor first used this term in 1970 in 'New Monetarism'.

[54] J. R. Hicks had a similar position to Kaldor: J. R. Hicks, 'Monetary Experience and the Theory of Money', *Economic Perspectives* (Oxford, OUP, 1977). In the American literature, several writers hold similar views (although divergent in certain respects) on the endogeneity of money: H. P. Minsky, 'Central Banking and Money Market Changes', *QJE* (May 1957); P. Davidson, *Money and the Real World* (London, Macmillan 1972); P. Davidson and S. Weintraub, 'Money as Cause and Effects', *EJ* (1973); S. Weintraub, *Keynes, Keynesians and Monetarists* (Phil., University of Pennsylvania Press, 1978). A review of these positions can be found in V. Termini, *Motivo finanziario e saggi propri di interesse nella preferenza per la liquidità*, (Milan, Giuffrè, 1985).

If money is taken to be an endogenous variable, liquidity preference and the hypothesis that the demand for money is elastic with respect to the interest rate are no longer important, and no longer play that crucial role in verification of the Keynesian theory of money that the monetarists and the American Keynesians attributed to them.

The grounds for Friedman's first criticism of the Keynesian model were two observations of an essentially empirical nature: (1) a positive correlation between income and supply of money and therefore a stable velocity of circulation in terms of conventional money; (2) stable lags (although, in fact, not very stable[55]) between the peaks and troughs in the money supply and the peaks and troughs in money income (with the money supply in the lead).

The positive correlation between the supply of money—however defined— and the national income is of little significance: the same correlation can be found between the money supply and a large number of other macro-economic quantities like consumption, investment, wages, etc. Nor does the time-lag prove very much about causal relationships. Even in a perfectly Keynesian model—one where expenditure decisions determine incomes—if the money supply is endogenous (i.e. where credit is supplied freely for a given rate of interest) the turning-point in the money supply will precede that of the national income because the Keynesian multiplier takes time to show its effects on incomes, while the initial spending, for example on investment, requires a demand for credit as soon as it is undertaken.[56]

With regard to the constancy of the velocity of circulation, it should be remembered that changes in the money stock and in the velocity of circulation are two substitute forms of adjustment of supply. 'If the velocity of circulation *appears* stable this is only because the money stock is so *unstable.*'[57] Moreover, the supposed stability of the velocity of circulation (which is equivalent to the stability of the ratio between money and incomes) in time and space is anything but proven.[58]

---

[55] In the USA, before WWII the lag varied between 6 and 9 months; after the war it shortened to 3 months.

[56] This was the objection that Kaldor raised in 'New Monetarism'. However, because the idea of the time-lag was revived in the 1970s by various politicians like Lord Cockfield, Conservative Chancellors of the Exchequer, economists, and journalists, in 'Monetary Policy in the United Kingdom', paras. 79–83, Kaldor analysed ten countries in three different periods and concluded that 'the closest fit is shown when *no* time-lag is assumed' (p. 84).

[57] Id., 'Radcliffe Report and Monetary Policy', 29. Kaldor's historical example was the US and Canada during the Great Depression, 1929–32. The money GNP fell at an almost identical rate in the 2 countries. In Canada, however, the fall in the money supply was smaller because there were no bank failures, and the velocity of circulation was correspondingly higher.

[58] Considering 1958 and the period 1968–79, the only stability was that of M_3 during the period 1968–79 in the USA. This stability disappears if the dynamics of M_3 are considered in a set of countries cited by Friedman himself in reply to Kaldor's 1970 article (M. Friedman, 'The New Monetarism: A Comment', *LLBR* (July 1970)). What is more, if M_1 rather than M_3 is considered this stability is no longer to be found even in the USA (Kaldor, 'Radcliffe Report and Monetary Policy', 26–7.

Finally, one cannot fail to be surprised that ratios between money and incomes should vary so widely among countries.[59] Kaldor reported that it was precisely in the country with the lowest inflation rate (Switzerland) that the supply of money (M_3) showed a rate of growth persistently higher than money income, while the velocity of circulation of M_1 during the period between 1958 and 1978 was five times higher in Sweden than it was in Switzerland (and in Italy). The fact that the Swedes were satisfied with so much less money than the Swiss led, not to the conclusion that the Swiss were more prone to inflation, but to the conclusion that the phenomenon was a mere historical accident and that, above all, 'money, contrary to the fashionable view, is an "unimportant" quantity'.[60]

11.5. Kaldor and Monetary Policy: Its Instruments and Targets

Before the First World War controlling the money supply was a relatively simple matter in the United Kingdom. The Bank of England's intention was certainly not to control the money supply, but to protect its gold and currency reserves. Even small changes in short-term rates in London would create large changes in the liquidity of the banking system, and were sufficient to reverse the trend of movement in reserves. Subsequently, the aim of monetary supply was to keep the interest rate constant in order to ensure a stable market for funding the national debt. In the 1950s the Conservatives reintroduced an active interest-rate policy as an instrument to regulate credit. Under the Labour Government of the 1960s credit control was exercised through quantitative control of bank advances. The Conservative governments of the 1970s intermittently applied the 'corset' in order to limit the rate of expansion of bank credit.

In assessing English monetary policy of the past, Kaldor declared that 'the experience of using interest rates as the central instrument for the control of monetary aggregates has not been a happy one'.[61] In fact, monetary policy is effective, although only indirectly, when it works through changes in the demand for money brought about by variations in income induced by a change in the structure and level of interest rates. This change, in turn, stems from the policy of the Central Bank in its fixing of the short-term interest rate. However, a pure monetary policy is never the best instrument, whether the target is the level of income or whether it is the stability of the price level. The former target is best pursued through fiscal policy acting in harness with an

---

[59] The monetarists explain the occurrence of a high M/Y ratio in countries with low inflation by the fact that, if the growth of M falls, the growth of the price level slows down, and the velocity of circulation of money slackens (less money is economized if there is low inflation). M therefore grows more slowly than Y and their ratio is high (I owe this explanation to Prof. E. De Antoni). This may serve to explain a cumulative mechanism (fall in the M dynamic, therefore of p, therefore of V, etc.), but not a situation that lasted for 20 years.

[60] Kaldor, 'Monetary Policy in the United Kingdom', 83.   [61] Ibid. 106.

accommodating monetary policy, the latter by a structural incomes policy (see Chapter 12.6).

The policy propounded by the monetarists rests on very different foundations. They maintain that the monetary authorities should not focus their action on interest rates but directly on the quantity of money, and that the rate of growth in the money supply should be a pre-established target to be achieved through control of the monetary base.

Kaldor argued that these propositions are either unfounded or they are misleading. The policy of announcing the target of money growth—regardless of whether this target is achieved or not—influences the dynamic of prices and output only and to the extent that this objective is taken as a reference standard for wage negotiations. Even more trenchant was Kaldor's criticism that the Central Banks, in a credit money system, cannot set themselves a rate of growth in the money supply as a target, and for at least three reasons.

First, restriction of the monetary base and the raising of the interest rates that derive from it may induce the public to economize on its own money holdings and to deposit a larger proportion in the banks;[62] but this will increase the credit base. Thus a restriction of the monetary base can be accompanied by a stable or even increasing supply of money.

Secondly, the monetary authorities have only two instruments with which they can 'neutralize' the supply of credit induced by the change in demand so that the money supply can be kept constant.[63] The first of these instruments acts (mainly in the United States) through open-market operations (or through changes in the coefficient of legal reserves); the second (mainly in the United Kingdom) through variation in the Central Bank's discount rate governing the conditions under which financial institutions are willing to grant credit or to incur debt. However, there is a limit on both the extent to which the Central Bank can allow the short-term interest rate to rise and on the extent to which it can close the 'discount window'.[64] In fact, the Central Bank has to discharge its function as lender of last resort in order to keep the banking system liquid—in its capacity as the ultimate guarantor for its solvency. The fact that the money supply must be kept constant, despite the increase in demand, means that the chief financial institutions run the risk of failing to meet requests for cash made by deposit-holders. And this conflicts with the fact that

a monetary system based on credit money can function only so long as the central bank is willing to ensure that the credit pyramid remains in being, i.e., that the major financial institutions which provide the bulk of bank deposits are not exposed to the risk of being unable to pay cash to depositors owing to their illiquidity.[65]

---

[62] In the UK the monetary base in the hands of the public is ten times greater than that deposited in banks.

[63] Kaldor and Trevithick, 'Keynesian Perspective on Money', 110–11.

[64] This point was discussed by Kaldor from various perspectives in: 'Origins of the New Monetarism', 172; 'Keynesian Perspective on Money', 110; 'How Monetarism Failed', 190.

[65] Kaldor and Trevithick, 'Keynesian Perspective on Money', 110.

The third reason why the monetary authorities cannot set themselves the target of growth in the money supply—apart from the effects that this would have on interest rates—is that an increase in the latter determines the diffusion of new money surrogates. Some of these new credit instruments might be issued by the banks; others, however, would be paper issued by non-banking institutions; moreover, Kaldor added, private individuals and businesses can, with increasing ease, obtain loans on the Eurocurrency markets.[66] In many of these cases the Central Bank cannot remain indifferent to the process of disintermediation of the banking system.[67]

The financial innovations implemented in the United States during the 1970s lowered the transaction costs of assets purchases and sales, introduced new assets and liabilities, and enabled depository institutions to avoid reserve requirements and other requirements emanating from the Federal Reserve. All these factors altered the relation between the money base and the quantity of money, and between the latter and the rate of interest. Consequently, one cannot rely on a firm-policy multiplier, that is, a relation between the monetary policy instrument and its final targets—output, employment, and inflation. In an uncertain environment, where the curves of money supply and demand for money change their slope and position in a wholly unpredictable way, monetary policy becomes extremely difficult to manage. Furthermore, the rational expectations argument is of little help because the parameters of the functions are structurally unstable. The upshot in policy terms is that if financial innovations cause shifts and changes not only in the slope of the demand for money schedule, but in the banking multiplier as well, growth in the quantity of some monetary aggregates is a pointless target for monetary policy to set itself.

For these reasons the monetary authorities cannot maintain control over the supply of money—however the term may be defined and with the exception of its narrowest and least significant sense. '[The Central] Bank's power does not really extend beyond fixing interest rates on sterling loans, provided the rate chosen falls within some viable range of variation.'[68]

We are now in a position to summarize Kaldor's theory of the rate of interest in an economic system with endogenous money as follows: (1) both in a

[66] In the USA, the response to Volker's monetarist policy (formally announced on 6 Oct. 1979) was, apart from the introduction of new money substitutes like money market funds, a shift of activity towards banks that were not associated with the Federal Reserve System and towards branches of foreign banks. Although these loopholes in the system were closed by legislation, others soon opened up. As the Radcliffe Report predicted, the great wave of financial innovations of the 1980s in the USA nullified the country's policy based on quantitative targets. See W. L. Silber, 'The Process of Financial Innovation', *AER* Papers and Proceedings (May 1983); J. L. Pierce, 'Did Financial Innovation Hurt the Great Monetary Experiment?', *AER Papers and Proceedings* (May 1984); T. M. Podolski, *Financial Innovation and the Money Supply* (Oxford, Basil Blackwell, 1986).

[67] The process of financial innovation weakens the control of an economy based only on monetary policy. For the American case, see D. D. Hester, 'Innovations and Monetary Control', *Brookings Papers on Economic Activity*, 1 (1981); and Pierce, 'Did Financial Innovations Hurt the Great Monetarist Experiment?'

[68] Kaldor, 'Origins of the New Monetarism', 173.

system like the British one where the money supply is given by the commercial paper discount, and in a system like the American one where it is given by open market operations, the interest rate is the only effective instrument of the Central Bank's monetary policy; (2) a change in the interest rate acts by altering both the proportion of income that individuals wish to hold in the form of money and the level of money incomes; (3) however, since the influence of changes in interest rates on incomes is mostly indirect (in so far as it affects spending on building and on consumer durables) and of uncertain outcome, it is advisable in most cases for monetary policy to keep the interest rate constant and to allow fiscal policy and incomes policy to operate; (4) the use of the interest rate as an instrument to achieve quantitative control of the money supply is bound to fail; (5) the upper limit of variation within which the Central Bank can make the interest rate oscillate depends on its willingness to run the risk of rendering the banking system illiquid (in the English system in particular) and the risk of disintermediating it through the creation of new substitutes for money and/or new financial intermediaries: (6) if the Central Bank adopts a wholly accommodating policy, the interest rate may be regarded as fixed.

11.6. Central Bank, Commercial Banks, and Financial Institutions: On the Endogeneity of Money and the Horizontal Supply Curve

We now have sufficient material to clarify Kaldor's position on the endogeneity of money, both from the point of view of the development of his ideas and in terms of a graphic representation that he himself gave to the concept.

Let us briefly review the three basic propositions underlying Kaldor's idea of the endogenous money supply, all of which he developed many years before his assault on Milton Friedman's New Monetarism. The first proposition he stated as early as 1939 when he wrote: '(S)ince the elasticity of the supply of cash with respect to the short term rate is normally much larger than the elasticity of demand, the current short term rate can be treated simply as a datum, determined by the policy of the central bank.'[69] The second proposition dates to 1955, when Kaldor argued that 'the commercial banks . . . regulate the volume of borrowing not through interest variations, but through credit rationing'.[70] The third proposition Kaldor formulated in 1958 in his memorandum to the Radcliffe Committee:

The velocity of circulation of money . . . is not determined by factors that are independent either of the supply of money or the volume of money payments . . . In some communities the velocity is low, in others it is high, in some it is rising and in some it is falling . . . such differences can only be explained in terms of *historical develop-*

[69] Id., 'Speculation and Economic Stability', 39.
[70] Id., 'The Lessons of the British Experiment since the War: Full Employment and the Welfare State' (1955), pub. in CP iii. 106.

ments rather than psychological propensities or of institutional factors, while the movement in the ratio can only be accounted for by the varying incidence of the policies pursued by the monetary authorities.[71]

In the 1980s Kaldor used a diagram to illustrate the contrast between the concepts of endogeneity and exogeneity in the money supply. In the case of exogeneity, money is a given quantity and can be represented by a vertical line (Figure 11.2), while in the case of endogeneity, the money-supply curve is horizontal (Figure 11.3). With any rate of interest the money supply is infinitely elastic. This also means that monetary policy is represented, not by a given quantity of money, but by a given rate of interest. In short, the endogeneity of the money supply means that 'at any time, or at all times, the money stock will be determined by demand, and the rate of interest determined by the Central Bank'.[72]

However, representing the endogeneity of money supply as a curve infinitely elastic to the rate of interest might be misleading,[73] since the concept must comprise the three different causes of endogeneity expressed in the three sentences at the beginning of this section. In the short run it embraces the behaviour of the Central Bank and the behaviour of the banks; in the longer run it embraces the financial innovation process induced by Central Bank policy. The creation of new substitutes for money is a process which takes place over a longer period of time than that required by the other two processes.

---

[71] Id., 'Monetary Policy, Economic Stability and Growth', 129.

[72] Id., 'Radcliffe Report and Monetary Policy', 24. It was in this article, which comprises two lectures given at Warwick University in May 1981, that Kaldor first represented the endogeneity of money supply as a horizontal curve with respect to the interest rate, although in an article written with Trevithick published in Jan. of the same year, he had already described the diagram verbally ('Keynesian Perspective on Money', 109–10).

[73] There is, in post-Keynesian literature, broad agreement over the shortcomings of the monetarist notion of an exogenous money supply. However, according to Musella and Panico ('Kaldor on Money and Interest Rates', 3–5), with whom I agree, at the risk of drastic oversimplification it is possible to classify the various views on 'endogenous money' into two broad groups. The first group describes the money supply as an increasing function of the interest rate, the elasticity of which is high but not necessarily infinite. For the second group, the infinite elasticity of money supply is a logical necessity. Among economists belonging to the first group, apart from those cited in n. 54, above, see also S. C. Dow and P. E. Earl, *Money Matters: A Keynesian Approach to Monetary Economics* (Oxford, Martin Robertson, 1982); C. A. E. Goodhart, *Monetary Theory and Practice* (London, Macmillan, 1984); id., 'Has Moore become too Horizontal?', *EJ* (June 1989); S. C. Dow, 'Money Supply Endogeneity', *EA* 1 (1988) 19–39; V. Chick, 'The Evolution of Banking Systems and the Theory of Saving, Investment and Interest', *Économie et Société* (1986), 111–26; S. Rousseas, *Post Keynesian Monetary Economics* (London, Macmillan, 1986); P. Davidson, 'On the Endogeneity of Money Once More', *JPKE* (spring 1989); A. C. Dow and S. C. Dow, 'Endogenous Money Creation and Idle Balances', in J. Pheby (ed.), *New Directions in Post-Keynesian Economics* (Aldershot, Edward Elgar, 1989). Among those belonging to the second group, see esp. B. J. Moore, *Horizontalist and Verticalist: The Macroeconomics of Credit Money* (Cambridge, CUP, 1988); see also Moore's articles in several issues of *JPKE*: 2 (fall 1979); 5 (summer 1983); 10 (spring 1988); 11 (spring 1989); 12 (spring 1990). For an attempt to describe the features of a unified post-Keynesian perspective, see P. Arestis, 'Post Keynesian Theory of Money, Credit and Finance', in P. Arestis (ed.), *Post Keynesian Monetary Economics* (Aldershot, Edward Elgar, 1989).

FIG. 11.2 Kaldor's representation of the exogenous money supply

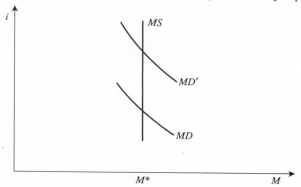

FIG. 11.3 Kaldor's extreme representation of the endogenous money supply

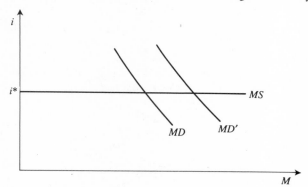

The point requires clarification. A fully *exogenous* money supply—that is, a money supply wholly in the hands of the monetary authorities, a change in which is the *cause* of a change in monetary income—entails that: (1) the money supply curve *must be* inelastic to the interest rate, *and* (2) the shifts in money supply *must not be* dependent on shifts in the demand curve. Conversely, to obtain an endogenous money supply, it is sufficient that: (1) the money supply *could be* elastic to the rate of interest (Figure 11.4), *or* (2) shifts in the money-supply curve *could be* dependent on shifts in the demand curve (Figure 11.5).[74]

The Kaldorian case is therefore the extreme one where the banks are willing and able to supply extra funds indefinitely at the same rate of interest (a rather implausible hypothesis)—i.e. a flat supply curve (Figure 11.3)—and/or where the Central Bank has a fully accommodating policy—i.e. a shift in the supply curve to the extent that it precludes any changes in the interest rate (Figure 11.6). However, what Kaldor had in mind was a more general case: when

---

[74] P. Davidson, 'On the Endogeneity of Money Once More'.

asked for clarification of the fixed interest rate at which the supply of money is infinitely elastic, he replied:

FIG. 11.4 A first case of endogenous money supply: a banking multiplier highly elastic to the rate of interest

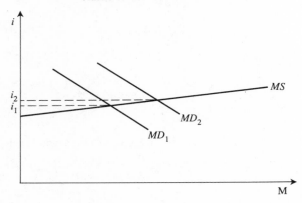

FIG. 11.5 A second case of endogenous money supply: an accommodating policy of the Central Bank

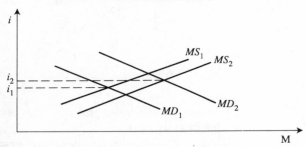

I do not want to claim that monetary policy is ineffective or that it does not have an influence on the interest rate: the diagram . . . only entails that for every rate of interest the money supply is infinitely elastic.[75]

This explanation strikes one as elliptical and not entirely convincing. Kaldor's diagram, though, was probably no more than a shorthand explanatory device: his concept of endogeneity was certainly much richer than the particular case represented by a flat supply curve.

My first step in demonstration of this latter contention is to show that Figure 11.4 represents Kaldor's second cause of endogeneity more accurately than does Figure 11.3. What Kaldor rejects is the notion that Central Banks control the money supply through the base-multiplier process. For a Central Bank to be able to do this, at least two parameters would have to be stable: (1) the

[75] N. Kaldor, letter written on 15 July 1985 to the author.

ratio between money held by the public and the money deposited in the banks; (2) the ratio between the monetary base and the supply of credit money by the banks.

FIG. 11.6 An extreme case of accommodating policy of the Central Bank

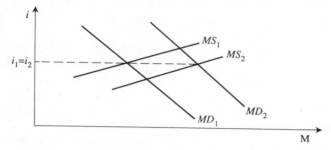

However, the first ratio is not independent of monetary policy. As we saw in the previous section, Kaldor held that a restriction of the monetary base and the raising of the interest rates that derive from it may induce the public to economize on its money holdings and to deposit a larger proportion of it in the banks. Since this increases the amount of credit that banks can lend, a restriction of the monetary base may be attended by a stable or even increasing supply of money—which comes about, however, not at the same but a *higher rate of interest.*

Nor is the second ratio—the multiplier—stable, since it is not wholly dependent on the legal reserves that the Central Bank requires banks to hold. It is, in fact, partly endogenous, because it also depends on the banks' voluntary reserves—which they are at liberty to change in response to pressure from their best customers. When trade prospects

are good or when the money value of the borrowers' assets (their collateral) rises as a result of a rise in prices, the demand for bank credit rises but, by the same token, the credit worthiness of potential borrowers also improves, so that both the demand and the supply of credit move simultaneously in the same direction.[76]

This means that the bank reserve ratios tend to vary during the trade cycle; but also that they vary, in an inverse relation, *with respect to the interest rate.*

Further, if a bank is short of reserves, it may borrow from other banks or from the discount window of the Central Bank. Even if the Central Bank regards discount window borrowing only as a last resort (as the Federal Reserve does), it cannot easily discriminate among the reasons that induce banks to apply for this form of discount. If the Central Bank wishes to dissuade banks from discount window borrowing and from lending to their customers, it can raise the discount rate and reduce the spread between it and the market rate. Since banks can pass on this higher 'cost' in the form of higher lending rates, the extent to which the Central Bank can reduce bank loans *depends on*

[76] Id., 'Fallacies of Monetarism', *Kredit und Kapital* (July 1981), 455.

the interest elasticity on the loans demanded by bank customers—which is not necessarily infinity. In all these cases infinite elasticity is a particular case.

The second step in my demonstration is to show that Figure 11.5 is more appropriate to the first and third of Kaldor's causes of endogeneity than Figure 11.6. We saw in the previous section that Kaldor considered the Central Bank's chief function to be the maintenance of 'sufficient liquidity in the banking system to prevent a collapse of the credit pyramid'.[77] This sets a further limit on the extent to which the Central Bank can allow the short-term interest rate to rise (first cause of endogeneity). However, 'the Central Bank function of "lender of last resort" . . . makes it impossible for the Central Bank to set *rigid limits* to the amount of cash which it is willing to put at the disposal of commercial banks through re-discounting. The "discount window" cannot be closed.'[78]

There is a further reason why the monetary authorities cannot set themselves the target of growth in the money supply: the increase in the interest rate due to a non-accommodating policy determines the diffusion of new money surrogates.[79] Some of these new credit instruments may be issued by the banks; others, however, will be paper issued by non-banking institutions. In many of these cases the Central Bank cannot remain indifferent to the process of disintermediation of the banking system (third cause of endogeneity). But the Central Bank's reaction to disintermediation is a process that unfolds in time—that is to say, *after* the increase in the interest rate takes place, because the Central Banks can adopt only partially accommodating policies even over the long period.[80]

For Kaldor, incomplete accommodation by the Central Bank entails an increase in the velocity of circulation. In fact 'changes in the stock of money and changes in velocity are substitutes for one another'.[81] However, the increase in velocity links with higher interest rates. If, therefore, endogeneity is the result of higher velocity of circulation, the money-supply curve cannot be perfectly elastic with respect to the rate of interest.

Moreover, the relation between changes in interest rates and the velocity of circulation has been shown to be unstable in time over the last twenty years,

---

[77] Id., 'Origins of the New Monetarism', 172.

[78] Id., 'Fallacies of Monetarism', 456 (my emphasis).

[79] I do not want to say that Kaldor held that *all* financial innovations were endogenous and induced by change in the rates of interest. In fact, Kaldor himself used the example of the British financial deregulation of the early 1980s to point out cases of exogenous increases in money supply created by the financial sector. However, for the American system between 1972 and 1980, Silber ('Process of Financial Innovation',) identified 7 causes acting jointly or individually on the 38, major innovations of the period. The vast majority of these latter were induced by the level and volatility of interest rates: indeed, these two factors were individually or jointly responsible for 23 financial innovations out of the 38. (The most important American financial innovations of the 1970s caused by high and variable interest rates were repurchase agreements, money market mutual funds (Mmmf), and interest-bearing transaction accounts.) Hence, although not all financial innovations are endogenously determined, the great majority of them are.

[80] In the letter to the author cited in n. 75, above, Kaldor agreed with this point.

[81] Kaldor, 'Radcliffe Report and Monetary Policy', 29.

both in the United Kingdom and in the United States. Interest rates have fluctuated, while the velocity of circulation of M_1 has increased regularly and constantly.[82] On the one hand, the constant increase in the velocity of M_1[83] is further confirmation of the baselessness of Friedman's contentions, and further proof of the accuracy of the Radcliffe Report's conclusion that there is no limit to the velocity of circulation of money. On the other hand, however, the lack of correlation between the velocity of circulation and the change in interest rates requires explanation. And this can be provided in terms of financial innovation. We may assume a curve of the velocity of circulation that correlates positively with the interest rate but which shifts over time because of the effect of financial innovations, which are in turn induced by the non-accommodating policies of the Central Bank.

A complete theory of the endogeneity of the money supply therefore requires a theory of the behaviour of the Central Bank and a theory of financial innovation as a response to a policy that is not wholly accommodating. It must also incorporate a change in the velocity of circulation of money defined in the narrow sense which, in the short term, is associated with changes in the interest rate.

Let *MD* define the demand for money as a function of the income level and the short-term rate of interest:

(11.5) $$MD = f(\overline{Y}, i).$$

The money supply *MS* is a function of the money base *BM* and the banking multiplier. But the money base *BM* is changed by the Central Bank (under non-monetarist regimes) to keep the interest rate within a narrow range of variation: that is, we can state *BM* as a function of the rate of interest. The legal and free reserve ratio, *b*, (which determines the banking multiplier) depends on *i* for the reasons given above. If the interest rate increases, the multiplier lessens and the money supply increases. We may therefore write:

(11.6) $$MS = [BM(i)][1/b(i)].$$

In graphic terms, the elasticity of the curve is represented by the multiplier $1/b(i)$, while *BM* is taken to be exogenously given in the very short run, and Central Bank policy is endogenized by inducing a rightward shift of the curve when the interest rate increases to an extent that reflects the degree of accommodation by the Central Bank.

Kaldor's figure 11.2 should therefore be redrawn as in Figure 11.7.

---

[82] Kaldor compared the GNP/M_1 ratio with the interest rates on Treasury Bills in the UK and the USA for the period 1963–78 (Kaldor, 'Monetary Policy in the United Kingdom', 76). S. Rousseas has compared the velocity of circulation of M_1 with the 3-monthly interest rates on US Treasury Bills in 1950–84 (S. Rousseas, *Post-Keynesian Monetary Economics* (London, Macmillan, 1986), 85–91.

[83] The steady increase in the velocity of money in the USA has puzzled economists for some years. See S. M. Goldfeld, 'The Case of the Missing Money', *Brookings Papers on Economic Activities*, 3 (1976).

FIG. 11.7 A general case of three sources of endogeneity of money supply

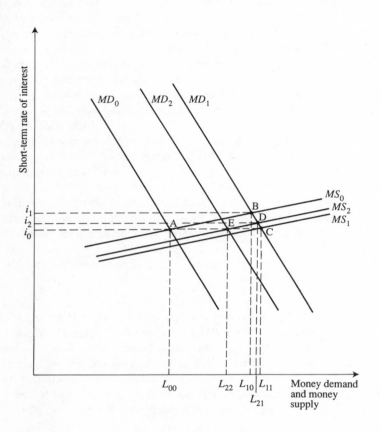

Let us suppose that we are at a point *A* along the money-supply curve MS_0 where the money demand MD_0, given the rate i_0 determined by the Central Bank, is equal to the money supply L_{00}. Let us assume that we have an autonomous rise in incomes and therefore in money demand at DM_1. The reaction of the banking system is to push the market rate of interest along the supply curve to i_1 at the new equilibrium point *B*. If this increase in the interest rate is higher than the one accepted by the Central Bank, the supply curve shifts to the right. If the Central Bank's policy is fully accommodating, the shift of *MS* will be large enough—to MS_1 to bring the interest rate down to the previous level at the equilibrium point *C*. If it is not fully accommodating, the supply curve shifts to MS_2, the equilibrium between money demand and supply lies at *D*, and the interest rate stays at an intermediate level, let us say i_2 with a money supply measured by L_1. The higher interest rate, however, will be matched by an increase in the velocity of circulation. In the longer term (which could only be graphically represented by a three-dimensional graph), the higher velocity of circulation may entail the introduction of money surrogates supplied either by the non-banking system or by the banking system, if it is allowed to omit these new forms of money from calculation of the legal reserve. As a result of this process, the same amount of money-M_1 can 'finance' a larger amount of income. That is to say, the demand for money-M_1 shifts to the left: plausibly, but not necessarily, MD_1 will only shift to MD_2, where the new equilibrium point E will be associated with an amount of money L_{22} and an interest rate at the previous level i_0. Should this happen, explanation is provided of both the weakness of the temporal link between M and Y and the instability over time of the velocity of the circulation of money.

This graphic representation of the endogeneity of money reflects the richness of Kaldor's analysis more clearly than his own. By using the devices of the movement along the supply curve, the shift of the supply curve, and the shift of the demand curve, it shows the three sources of Kaldor's endogeneity of money: the two short-term sources springing from the behaviour of the banks and the Central Bank, and the long-term one that stems from induced financial innovation.[84] Moreover, it is able to account for the different behaviours of these actors[85] and includes the effects of a fixed-interest rate as a particular case.

[84] F. Targetti, 'Kaldor's Endogeneity of Money and the Evidence of the Eighties', University of Trento, *Annali scientifici del dipartimentso di economia*, 3 (1990), a final version of a paper read at Kaldor's memorial lectures held in Budapest, 21–2 Sept. 1989, read at Messina University, 9 May 1990. Another solution is given in M. Musella and C. Panico, 'Kaldor on Endogenous Money and Interest Rate', 33–4, following the suggestions of M. Desai, 'Scourge of Monetarists', 176, 180–1, and S. C. Dow, 'Money Supply Endogeneity'. In Musella and Panico's solution, however, only the second Kaldor endogeneity is taken into account. Moreover, their model is a static equilibrium model, whereas the one I have presented here, even though not fully dynamic (the variables are not time-related), does introduce the dynamic element through the device of the curve shifts.

[85] The theory of endogenous money supply has been formulated in a macro-economic framework mainly in order to deal with problems of monetary policy. An attempt to build a bridge between this theory and the micro-economic theory of money can be found in R. Tamborini, 'The Endogeneity of Money: What Theoretical Foundations?' University of Trento, *Annali scientifici del dipartimento di economia*, 3 (1990), n. 3. Some economists in the neo-Walrasian school, notably Hahn, have suggested that money in the broad Hicksean sense (standard of value, currency, and store of value) (see J. Hicks, 'A Suggestion for Simplifying the Theory of Money' (1935), in id., *Critical Essays in Monetary Theory* London, OUP, 1967) cannot be fitted into an Arrow–Debreu model. Only a model of a sequential economy (R. Radner, 'Competitive Equilibrium under Uncertainty', *ETR* 36 (1968)) and imperfect information about the future can accommodate money as a store of value (F. Hahn, 'On Monetary Theory', *EJ* (Dec. 1988)). Outside the neo-Walrasian school, the so-called 'circuit approach', which derives from a merger between Keynes and Wicksell on money, has also proposed a model of sequential analysis with money as fully endogenous (A. Graziani, 'Introduzione', in *Moneta e produzione* (Turin, Einaudi, 1988)). In the 'circuit' model, however, the demand for and the supply of money are not distinguishable. It may therefore be citicized on the same grounds as the full horizontalists have been criticized here.

11.7. The Critique of a Monetarist Keynesianism

In the early 1980s Kaldor took strong issue with the new approach to monetary policy propounded by James Meade and David Vines[86] advocated. The two economists agreed with the government over the need for monetary control in order to curb inflationary pressure, but they believed that both the means used and the ends pursued were mistaken. The policy objective of the growth of money, they argued, should be replaced by one of growth in money national income.[87] This objective should be pursued by using the fiscal instrument of the public-sector borrowing requirement, while the monetary instrument of the short-term interest rate should act, through the exchange rate, on the rate of increase in exports. Finally, they called for reform of the system of pay settlements so that an increase in money income would not be 'dissipated' in higher wages and prices; the core of the reform therefore consisted in the taxing of wage increases exceeding the pre-established value of output growth.

In Kaldor's view, by advocating 'financial discipline to restrain the inflationary pressure of the economy' and 'the need to control the public sector borrowing requirement', Meade and Vines were trying to introduce Keynesian ideas into government policy by the back door. The flaw in their argument, he believed, was the fact that budget policy is an instrument of real, not money-demand management. A policy of this kind affects money income when it rises at the same rate as real income, but in this case it only presupposes the result that it sets out to achieve. With inflation, however, when the two magnitudes increase at different rates, it is just as difficult to control money income as it is to control M_3—the unattainable objective of the government. Inflation can be counteracted by means of monetary and fiscal measures only by reducing real income, employment and hence the growth of wages. However, the objective of growth in money income as such provides no guarantee that it will be real incomes and not prices that increase. If Meade was aware of this, in so far as he recommended the introduction of a wages reform, Kaldor could not see the point of disguising a Keynesian fiscal, exchange-rate, and incomes policy behind a façade of a target of growth in nominal income.

Kaldor's second criticism turned on the use of monetary policy and interest rates in order to obtain a desired rate of exchange, when this could be more easily achieved through direct intervention on the foreign exchange market. Such intervention (even though it would incur monetarist opposition because of the supposedly undesirable 'collateral effects' on the money supply) yields more easily predictable results.

[86] J. Meade *et al.*, 'A New Financial Strategy', *Financial Times* (8 Dec. 1981); J. Meade, 'A New Keynesian Approach to Full Employment' *LLBR* (Oct. 1983); D. Vines *et al.*, *Demand Management*, 2 vols. (London, Allen & Unwin, 1983); N. Kaldor, 'Lord Kaldor Replies to Professor Meade', *Financial Times* (Dec. 1981).

[87] As Samuel Brittan argued on numerous occasions in the *Financial Times*.

11.8. The Critique of Fiscal Monetarism

An off-shoot of monetarism is fiscal monetarism. In 1979 the British Treasury Minister declared that 'public expenditure is at the centre of the economic difficulties of Great Britain'. The explanation offered by the Financial Secretary of the Treasury, Mr Lawson, ran as follows:

Too high a PSBR (public sector borrowing requirement) requires either that the Government borrow heavily from the banks—which adds directly to the money supply; or, failing this, that it borrows from individuals and institutions, but at an ever increasing rate of interest, which places an unacceptable squeeze on the private sector.[88]

Thus an increase in the public-sector borrowing requirement, if financed by the Central Bank or by banks, increases the money supply; if it is financed by the non-banking public, it creates the phenomenon known as 'crowding out'.

Kaldor disputed both these propositions on empirical grounds.[89] He subjected the first to the simple econometric test of regressing the change of M_3: (1) on the 'unfunded' part of the public-sector borrowing requirement;[90] (2) on bank lending to the private sector; (3) on net overseas finance to the United Kingdom. The three regression equations show that

the role of the 'unfunded' PSBR was quite insignificant: it explains only 5% in the change in M_3 in the last fourteen years. As against that, bank lending in sterling to the UK private sector is the factor that was overwhelmingly responsible for the change in the money stock, as it explains 83% of the change.[91]

Kaldor applied a similar test to the second proposition and found that bank lending to the private sector was unaffected by the banks' absorption of public-sector debt. If one admits that the level of activity varies with effective demand, the savings available for private investments change in direct[92] and not inverse relation with the public-sector borrowing requirement.[93] For Kaldor, the 'squeeze' on the financial situation of industry was to be blamed, not on gilt-edged yields, but on the MLR (minimum lending rate) imposed by the monetary authorities.[94] In a speech to the House of Lords aimed at his customary adversary, Lord Cockfield, Kaldor declared that it could be proved

---

[88] Both quotations are taken from Kaldor, 'Monetary Policy in the United Kingdom', 86–7.

[89] In 1980 and 1981 Kaldor's speeches to the House of Lords insisted on the political 'suicide' of Mrs Thatcher's budget policy and reiterated the arguments illustrated here. See speeches of 5 Dec. 1979, 27 Nov. 1980, 18 Mar. 1981, 12 Nov. 1981, in N. Kaldor, *The Economic Consequences of Mrs Thatcher* (London, Duckworth, 1983).

[90] Which is equivalent to the indebtedness of the public sector to the banking system plus the issue of banknotes and cash.

[91] Ibid. 92.

[92] Kaldor's play on words was that this was 'crowding *in*' as opposed to 'crowding out', ibid. 99.

[93] However, the situation changes if the variation in the public-sector borrowing requirement caused by lower taxes and higher expenditure induces a variation in income spent abroad. On the relation between domestic and foreign deficit, see Ch. 13.4.

[94] When Britain went off the Gold Standard, there 'began the era of low interest rates which lasted for 30 years and enabled us to borrow our way through a Second World War . . . enormous

that there is no necessary connection whatever between the budget deficit and the interest rates; you can have high interest rates and no deficit, enormous borrowing and very low interest rates; you can have a 2 per cent war (as we had in the Second World War) or 6 per cent war (as we had in the First World War).[95]

In fact, the budget policy of the 1980s served the same purpose as an overvalued pound and anti-inflationary policy implemented through control of the money supply.

The important consequence of the strategy is to alter the balance of bargaining power, to weaken the trade unions through the intensification of unemployment and through the loss of jobs, through factory closures and bankruptcies and thereby to succeed in bringing wages settlements well below the rate of inflation; that is to say, to reduce real wages[96]

or, to use Hicks's expression, break 'real wage resistance'.[97] Kaldor denounced this 'true' aim of the Conservative government in a number of speeches in the House of Lords from 1979, i.e. the year that Mrs Thatcher moved into Downing Street.[98] The government's avowed purpose of weakening the bargaining power of the workers was pursued through the Employment Bill, which, in the words of the Chancellor of the Exchequer, sought 'to restore a broad balance of power in the framework for collective bargaining'.[99] In this sense, monetarist policy was an effective weapon: unemployment did indeed weaken the bargaining power of the labour force, and control of the money supply was merely a smoke-screen providing ideological justification for anti-social measures.[100]

11.8. The Failure of Monetarism: Kaldor's Vindication

Monetarism (as the imposition of monetary targets) was, in practice, first introduced by a Labour Chancellor of the Exchequer, Healey, in 1976, although it was only officially adopted in 1979—the same year as its adoption by the American Federal Reserve.

It was also in 1979 that Kaldor first foresaw the effects of such a policy on the English economy, in these premonitory words addressed to the House of Lords:

---

sums—a much greater proportion of the GDP than now—in medium- and long-term loans at 3 1/4 to 4 per cent'. *Economic Consequences of Mrs Thatcher*, 85 (speech made on 18 Mar. 1981).

[95] Ibid. 87–8 (speech made on 12 Nov. 1981).

[96] Ibid. 62 (speech made on 27 Nov. 1980)

[97] J. R. Hicks, 'What is Wrong with Monetarism', *LLBR* (Oct. 1975).

[98] Kaldor, *Economic Consequences of Mrs Thatcher*, esp. speeches of 5 Dec. 1979, 16 Apr. 1980, 27 Nov. 1980, 12 Nov. 1981, 3 Mar. 1982.

[99] Quoted by id., 'Monetary Policy in the United Kingdom', 57.   [100] Ibid. 58.

Winston Churchill once said that he was not willing to preside over the liquidation of the British Empire. I think that Her Majesty's present Ministers are quite willing to preside over the liquidation of Britain as an industrial power.[101]

Prior to the 1980s, apart from Kaldor and a handful of others, most economists and policy-makers—above all in the United States—were confident that the targeting of aggregate quantitative monetary measures was the correct monetary policy. There were those who thought that the money/income relation was highly stable even in the short run and were in favour of targeting money growth alone; there were others who were doubtful of this short-run stability and were in favour of targeting both money and other variables such as credit: 'few argued that money growth should not follow a narrowly specified trend over several years taken together'.[102]

The monetary events of the 1980s shook the foundations of these beliefs. The stability of the money-M_1/income relation disappeared even in the longer term. In the period 1960–80 the ratio of money to GNP in the United States oscillated in the short run; but these oscillations were around a distinct downward trend. In the 1980s not only did short-term fluctuations visibly widen, but, more importantly, the downward trend did not just disappear, it reversed direction. From this simple evidence (but also from more sophisticated data), 'it is difficult to escape the conclusion that not just for a year or a calendar quarter, but over an entire half-decade, money growth has simply been irrelevant to any outcome that matters for monetary policy'.[103]

Moreover, neither did the relationship between income or prices and other financial quantity variables show any improvement. Every narrow or broad measure of money, the monetary base or measures of credit had such wide fluctuations as to exclude any plausible connection with any quantitative target of monetary policy. 'As a result the entire role of such quantity variables in the monetary policy process . . . is now practically devoid of empirical support'.[104]

Two Central Banks conducted monetarist experiments in the 1979–82 period: the US Federal Reserve and the Bank of England. However, by 1982 monetarist policy in the strict sense of the term had been dropped in both countries. In the United Kingdom the primary target was control of M_3: 'this target (was) now abandoned'[105] and replaced by the overvaluation of the pound by means of high interest rates and a rigid wages policy in the public sector. Although the government had not forsworn its monetarist creed, as Kaldor pointed out, it tended to be 'increasingly forgetful about money and increasingly emphatic about the need to moderate the excessive rise in wages–which

---

[101] Id., *Economic Consequences of Mrs Thatcher*, 41 (speech of 5 Dec. 1979).

[102] B. M. Friedman, 'Monetary Policy without Quantity Variables', *AER Papers and Proceedings* (May 1988), 440.

[103] Ibid.   [104] Ibid.

[105] J. C. R. Dow, 'Incertezza e processo finanziario: le consequenze per il potere della banca centrale', *Moneta e credito* (Sept.–Dec. 1988), 452.

is quite contrary to Milton Friedman's philosophy'.[106] In the same year–according to statements made by H. Wallich, Governor Volker, and Vice-Governor Martin–the final targets of the Federal Reserve Bank increased in number, and the interest rate now became of prime importance.[107] Tobin reports[108] that the Federal Reserve reoriented its policy to fine tuning and its month-to-month decisions to macro-economic performance. But, since it received massive fiscal stimulus, it had to keep interest rates and the exchange value of the dollar much higher than would have been necessary if moderate pre-Reagan fiscal policies had remained in effect.

The experience of the two largest industrialized nations to have, for a certain period, officially professed their commitment to monetarist policy places Friedman and the monetarists in a highly embarrassing intellectual position. In 1984 Friedman declared that 'though the Federal Reserve System rhetoric was "monetarist", the actual policy that it followed was "anti-monetarist" because it was unable to achieve a steady and predictable rate of growth in whatever monetary aggregate was its target'.[109] Friedman also admitted that in England the money supply was *not* exogenously determined by the monetary authorities. And, first regarding the English and then the American cases, he has blamed this failure on the 'gross incompetence' of the two Central Banks. If two of the major Central Banks of the world are so incompetent that they are unable to control the money supply, Kaldor asked, how can we possibly expect the Central Banks of the highly inflationary countries of Latin America to be able to do so? And he finished his last work on money with this scornful dismissal of the monetarists: 'Surely we need a general theory of money and prices which is capable of embracing the cases of countries with 'incompetent' central banks, such as Britain and the United States.'[110]

Friedman had also predicted that, because of the abandonment of monetary targets and because of a two-year gap between money growth and inflation, 'the increased rate of monetary growth in the 1981–83 biennium suggests that . . . inflation will be decidedly higher from 1983 to 1985 than it was from 1981 to 1983'.[111] In fact, inflation proved to be lower not only during the period 1983–5 but also during 1985–7, despite continued high money growth between 1983 and 1985.

Final vindication of Kaldor's position is provided by the American Central Bank's behaviour in dealing with shocks from the financial sector. The Federal Reserve, as lender of last resort, in fact intervened five times during the 1980s. Despite Mr Volker's fame as a monetarist, therefore, he will be remembered

---

[106] Kaldor, 'How Monetarism Failed', 240.
[107] G. Gomel and R. Rinaldi, 'L'esperienza del "targeting" monetario negli Stati Uniti', *Contributi all'analisi economica della Banca d'Italia* (Dec. 1986).
[108] J. Tobin, 'Monetarism: An Ebbing Tide', *The Economist* (27 Apr. 1985).
[109] M. Friedman, 'Lessons from the 1979–1982 Monetary Policy Experiment', *AER* (May 1984).
[110] Kaldor, 'How Monetarism Failed', 197.
[111] Friedman, 'Lessons from the the 1979–1982 Monetary Policy Experiment'.

as the Central Banker who headed off financial crisis by sacrificing the stable growth of the money supply.[112] The same applies to his successor: just after the Wall Street crash of October 1987, 'the liquidity squeeze in the money and capital markets was immediately eased by open market operations under the new Chairman Alan Greenspan'.[113] And the same thing happened a year later during the second Wall Street crash.

---

[112] H. Minsky, 'Il capitalismo della "gestione monetaria" dop il crollo '87', *Politica ed Economia* (5 May 1988).

[113] C. Kindleberger, 'The Financial Crisis of the 1930s and the 1980s: Similarities and Differences', *Kyklos*, 41 (1988).

Chapter 12

Inflation and Anti-Inflationary Policies

Inflation is . . . a remarkable invention which enables a society
to live midway between the two extremes of social harmony and
civil war.

A. O. Hirschman, *Essays in Trespassing Economics: to Politics
and Beyond*

12.1. Kaldor's Early Interest in Inflation

In the summer of 1923 the Kaldor family spent the summer in the Bavarian
Alps. At the age of fifteen, the young Nicholas therefore had 'the rare opportunity to observe a state of on-going hyperinflation and the extraordinary
features of behaviour to which it gave rise'.[1] His curiosity was aroused by two
phenomena in particular. First, he noticed the speed at which the inflationary
process accelerated: shopkeepers revised their prices every week, then every
day, and then several times a day. Secondly, he observed that, in conditions
of accelerating inflation, the price level expressed in terms of a stable foreign
currency like the dollar was lower than abroad. This first-hand experience of
inflation made such an impression on the young Kaldor that he later said it
became one of the decisive factors in his decision to study economics when
he went to university.

Although inflation was never a central concern of Kaldor's research, he
nevertheless paid specific attention to it on a number of occasions. In the
1950s he examined creeping inflation; in the 1960s the structural inflation of
Latin America; in the 1970s and 1980s the inflation caused by different rates
of productivity between sectors and the inflation provoked by changes in the
terms of trade.

Kaldor's examination of the problem of inflation was a formative influence
on his theories on liquidity and the endogeneity of the money supply—which
he described in his articles of the 1930s on speculation and interest rates.

My thinking on these problems derives from observation of how inflation develops in
various countries. It used to be said that inflation was provoked by the behaviour of
the central banks in issuing too much money, something which seemed absolute
nonsense to me. In the great inflation of the 1920s in Germany it was not the increase
in the money supply that created inflation, but precisely the reverse: the increase in

[1] N. Kaldor, 'Recollections of an Economist' (1986), pub. in CP ix. 13.

the quantity of banknotes in circulation was an inevitable consequence of the increasing rise in the value of transactions.[2]

Two principal explanations were advanced for the hyperinflation that afflicted Germany during the 1920s: the first, the view propounded by German economists, held war reparations largely responsible for the fall of the mark and the inflation that followed; the second, the line taken by the economists of the victorious countries, blamed the State deficit and the excessive creation of money.[3]

Kaldor's explanation of the German hyperinflation turned on three interacting factors: excess demand, the open economy, and speculation. In post-war Germany a large amount of public expenditure had not been covered by taxes—which led to an extremely serious government deficit matched by an equally serious deficit in the balance of payments. Because there were no public or private international bodies able to finance this deficit, a supply of marks in excess of demand was created which had to be absorbed by the market. Those demanding marks could only be bullish speculators. But since the price of the mark (relative to other currencies) was falling, in order to turn bears into bulls the value of the mark had to be pushed down even further, so that a certain number of speculators would be induced to believe it was 'too' low: this was why in countries with accelerating inflation a gap opened up between domestic and foreign purchasing power.[4] A perverse mechanism was set in motion whereby the prices of imports rose faster than those of exports; and it was precisely the rise in the prices of foreign goods that triggered domestic inflation and governed its rate of growth.

---

[2] Id., *Ricordi di un economista*, ed. M. C. Macuzzo (Milan, Garzanti, 1986), 74.

[3] At the time, the leading German spokesman for the former view was C.-L. Holtferich. Among the foreign observers who agreed with him were J. W. Angell, *The Theory of International Prices: History, Criticism and Restatement* (Cambridge, Mass., Harvard University Press, 1926); and K. Laursen and J. Pedersen, *The German Inflation 1918–1923* (Amsterdam, North Holland Publishing Co., 1964). The best-known contemporary exponent of the quantitative view was C. Bresciani-Turroni, in his celebrated book *The Economics of Inflation: A Study of Currency Depreciation in Post-War Germany, 1914–1923* (London, Allen & Unwin, 1937), the extended English version of the essay *Le vicende del marco tedesco* (Milan, Giuffrè, 1931). Bresciani-Turroni's book was critically reviewed from the Cambridge school standpoint by Joan Robinson (J. Robinson, 'The Economics of Inflation', *EJ* (Sept. 1938). Two later restatements of Bresciani-Turroni's theory can be found in P. Cagan, 'The Monetary Dynamics of Hyperinflation', in M. Friedman (ed.), *Studies in Quantity Theory of Money* (Chicago, University of Chicago Press, 1956); and J. A. Frenke, 'The Forward Exchange Rate, Expectations and the Demand for Money: The German Hyperinflation', *AER* 67 (1977) 653–70. In Cagan's econometric model, expectations of inflation are formed on the basis of past prices; if they were formed on the basis of 'rational expectations', the money demand function would become unstable. See R. L. Jacobs, 'A Difficulty with the Monetarist Model of Hyperinflation', *Economic Inquiry*, 19, (1975) 337–60. Jacobs's remarks persuaded Cagan to abandon his primitive theoretical position and move closer to an explanation based on the balance of payments. See P. Gagan and G. Kincaid, 'Jacobs' Estimates of the Hyperinflation Model: Comment', *Economic Inquiry*, 14 (1977) 111–18.

[4] Kaldor's example was that in the summer of 1923 it was possible to live for a week in Berlin on 1 dollar, while in London or New York this was no more than the price of a meal. This example openly contradicted the monetarist theory of purchasing power parity. See N. Kaldor, 'Viaggi attraverso il mondo: 3. L'economia' (interview with F. Targetti), *MO*, (Aug. 1985), 119.

In Germany after the First World War, and in Hungary and Greece after the Second World War, hyperinflation displayed neither a constant rate of price increases nor a constant rate of acceleration of prices. Nevertheless, having accelerated at ever-increasing rates, when inflation came to an end it did so abruptly: it died away because the flight from money and from money contracts was total; contracts were drawn up only in foreign currencies.

12.2. Inflation and Growth

Once the immediate post-war period had passed, during the 1950s inflation no longer gave cause for serious concern in the OECD countries, although they still experienced 'creeping' inflation. Towards the end of the decade, however, interest in the phenomenon revived. 1958 saw publication of an article by Phillips which was destined to have an extraordinary impact on subsequent literature on the subject,[5] and in the following year Kaldor's article on inflation and wage increases appeared.[6]

What was the chief cause of the creeping inflation of those years? Was it seen as something that *invariably* had to be remedied? And if so, what should the remedy be? These were the questions raised by Kaldor; and they were questions to which he gave partly unconventional answers. The final section of this chapter sets out his answer to the last of the three questions: as regards the first two, Kaldor's analysis was closely bound up with the theory of growth that he was developing in those years.

The central proposition of the Keynesian economics of the late 1950s was that 'without a continued rise in money-wages inflation could not go on as a *process* in time'.[7] This was both because the growth of money-wages governed the growth of demand and of money incomes, and because it was unable to influence the share of wages: increasing money-wages generate increasing profits in money terms. First of all, therefore, one had to discover the causes of this increase in money-wages. The principal factors identified were demand in the goods market (under conditions approaching full employment) or supply on the labour market (i.e. wage negotiations conducted by the trade unions).

Kaldor did not agree with either of these two explanations. He was sceptical of the former because it required an unrealistic degree of perfection of the labour market. Moreover, the theory required wage inflation to be invariably attended by pressures in the labour market, although this was often contradicted by experience (Kaldor cited the case of Italy in the late 1950s. In that country wages increased in the industrial sector just as fast as they did in economies with full employment, despite the existence of a large reserve of

[5] A. W. Phillips, 'The Relation between Unemployment and the Rate of Change of Money Wage Rates in the United Kingdom 1861–1957', *EC* (Nov. 1958).

[6] N. Kaldor, 'Economic Growth and the Problem of Inflation' (1959), repr. in CP iii.

[7] Ibid. 137.

manpower). One also had to suppose that if there was a shortage of labour, an employer could increase his labour force, and therefore his output, by enticing workers away from other employers by offering them higher wages, but without increasing the pay of those already working for him. This kind of behaviour was well-nigh impossible in economies based on large-scale industries, where any deterioration in industrial relations was assiduously avoided. The second argument, according to which a rise in money-wages might simply be the consequence of an increase in the cost of living, also left Kaldor unconvinced.[8]

His own theory lay midway between the two positions. He maintained that money-wages rise as the bargaining power of labour increases, and that labour bargaining power grows with the prosperity of industry. It is this industrial prosperity that prompts trade unions to make higher wage claims and enables employers to grant them. When investment is high, production, productivity, and profits rise, and it is under these circumstances that the unemployment rate falls. When demand stagnates, however, employers are untroubled by the prospect of strikes and any consequent fall in production. Rather than a price-wage spiral, therefore, it is more correct to speak of a profit-wage spiral.

Phillips's correlation was therefore significant; but his 'demand-pull' explanation—according to which wage increases reflect the competitive bidding for labour by employers—was unsatisfactory.[9] Kaldor's theory was not contradicted by Phillips's evidence: indeed, if Phillips had correlated increases in money-wages with the increase in profits of the previous year rather than with the unemployment rate, his regression, Kaldor argued, would have been even more significant and would have held for the British economy in all the periods considered (pre-war, inter-war, and post-war)—perhaps with the exception of the years in which the Chancellor of the Exchequer, Sir Stafford Cripps, had introduced a policy of voluntary wage restraint by the trade unions.

If these were the causes of creeping inflation, what, according to Kaldor, were its effects? These should be judged in the light of his theory of growth, which states that given the propensity to save of profit-earners, the rate of growth of income determines the rate of profit. Steady growth is maintained, however, only as long as the profit rate does not drop below the level at which the capitalist will be dissuaded from investing because of 'the risk he runs in

---

[8] As we shall see, Kaldor would change his mind on this point in later years, arguing that, from the 1960s onwards, the increase in the cost of living had acted as one of the determinants of wage increases and had increased the acceleration of inflation. He was not the only economist at the time to have the wages dynamic depend on the cost of living. See esp. J. R. Hicks, *The Crisis in Keynesian Economics* (Oxford, Basil Blackwell, 1974).

[9] In his introd. to CP iii (1st edn., 1964), written 4 years after this article, Kaldor revised his position. He now accepted the 'demand-pull' theory of inflation, but only as long as it referred to certain brief periods of labour shortage; however, he did not change his opinion that an anti-inflationary policy that kept the economy at 'half-cock' was mistaken.

supplying his capital'.[10] Historical evidence[11] showed that this illiquidity risk (i.e. the risk of being unable to back out of a commitment once undertaken) amounted to 7 per cent—a margin which Kaldor assessed, for the years in which he was writing, at 5 per cent net of taxes or 10 per cent gross.

In addition to this minimum rate of return there was the percentage long-term rate of interest, which at the time stood at around 5 per cent. If, however, one allows for a sort of Keynesian liquidity trap (i.e. the minimum return on fixed-income securities) of around 2 per cent, the minimum rate of profit necessary to induce the capitalist-entrepreneur to invest was around 12 per cent. According to Kaldor's growth equation, continued accumulation of capital and growth of income was assured if the rate of growth stayed between one-half and one-third of 12 per cent—this presumably being the value of the saving propensity of profit-earners. Thus, only if income increased at a rate of between 4 and 5 per cent would accumulation be self-sustaining; at any lower rate of increase the economy proceeded in fits and starts, and the accumulation process and the growth of income was periodically interrupted.

It was at this point, according to Kaldor, that creeping inflation could become of crucial importance. The value of the minimum rate of profit depends on the Ricardian liquidity-risk premium and on the Keynesian minimum value of the interest rate: this latter value cannot be negative in money terms, although it can become negative in real terms under inflationary conditions.

Hence it follows that a rate of growth of money-wages some percentage points higher[12] than the rate of growth of productivity enables a sluggish economy to achieve steady growth, something which it cannot do in a regime of stable prices. Note that this conclusion was in marked contrast with the view generally held by neo-Keynesian economists who, by using the Phillips curve for normative ends, advocated setting a limit on the level of unemployment, and thus on the growth of output, in order to cure inflation. Kaldor instead favoured the policy of a 'gently rising price-level'[13] in a stagnant economy.[14] This was not to imply that an economy with slightly rising prices was the best of all possible worlds: a situation of stable or even falling prices was preferable if monetary stability was to be compatible with a steady growth

---

[10] Kaldor quotes here from Ricardo (D. Ricardo, *Principles*, in *Works and Correspondence of David Ricardo*, ed. P. Sraffa (Cambridge, CUP for the Royal Economic Society, 1951), 122), to whom he attributes the paternity of the 'liquidity-preference theory'.

[11] E. H. Phelps Brown and B. Weber, 'Accumulation, Productivity and Distribution in the British Economy, 1870–1938', *EJ* (June 1953).

[12] Kaldor estimated the rate at around 4% for the British economy at that time, slightly below the average post-war inflation rate of 7%.

[13] This expression was used by Sir Denis Robertson in *Money* (London, 1922), 122–5. In his early writings Robertson argued in favour of a slightly inflationary policy. At the end of his career, however, he became a convinced anti-inflationist.

[14] In Kaldor's view, Keynes had failed to realize that when money-wage rose faster than productivity, the moment when accumulation came to an end, because the marginal efficiency of capital met its lower limit in the liquidity preference, was infinitely delayed.

of output. Kaldor believed, however, that this happy state of affairs could only come about in very dynamic economies.

12.3. Wages, Productivity, and Inflation in a Dual Economy

For the rest of his life Kaldor never altered his opinion that demand for industrial goods has very little to do with the inflation of industrial prices. The central strut in his explanation of the causes of post-war inflation was modern forms of industrial collective bargaining. '(T)he inexorable rise in *industrial* prices in the post-war period was, in the main, cost-induced: it had virtually nothing to do with excess demand.'[15]

Although trade-union behaviour varies according to the time and the circumstances, Kaldor identified three overriding objectives for industrial collective bargaining this century (in Great Britain, it should be added):

a) the desire to preserve the status of their members in relation to other groups of workers; b) the desire to appropriate for their members what they regard as a 'fair' share of any significant increase in their companies' profits; c) to resist any encroachment on the attained standard of living of their members caused by unfavourable developments such as a rise in the price of energy or of imported raw material in terms of the price of manufactured goods.[16]

The first objective—defending wage differentials—had already been specified by Keynes, when he wrote that

Any individual or group of individals, who consent to a reduction of money-wages relatively to others, will suffer a *relative* reduction in real wages, which is a sufficient justification for them to resist it.[17]

The second behavioural hypothesis—one which we have already met in Kaldor's explanation of the wages dynamic described in the previous section—he now attributed only to the oligopolist sector, although this was the sector whose wage agreements set the standard for others. In the oligopolist sector, firms could afford to meet the wage claims made by their workers— because they wished to maintain good industrial relations and to attract the best workers, and because such wage increases were offset by a rise in productivity.

Economic systems do not grow at equal rates in all sectors. Let us suppose, for simplicity's sake, that there exist two sectors with different productivity

---

[15] N. Kaldor and J. Trevithick, 'A Keynesian Perspective on Money' (1981), repr. in CP ix. 121.

[16] Ibid. 121.

[17] J. M. Keynes, *The General Theory of Employment, Interest and Money* (London, Macmillan, 1936), 14. Similar behaviour in the labour-market has been described by J. Tobin, 'Inflation and Unemployment', *AER* (Mar. 1962), and Hicks, *Crisis in Keynesian Economics*, ch. 3.5 other causes of the downwards rigidity of money-wages in addition to this factor have been identified by R. M. Solow, 'On Theories of Unemployment', *AER* (Mar. 1980).

rates, and that the one with the highest rate is the oligopolist sector. An economy with two such sectors and subject to both kinds of worker behaviour as outlined above incorporates a slight degree of inflation. This is due to what has been called the 'leapfrog effect'. If wages in the oligopolist sector rise at the same rate as productivity, and if they do so in the other sector as well, the labour cost per unit of output of the second sector increases, and with it the money prices of the sector's output. Since the general level of prices is the weighted average of the prices of the two sectors, any rise in the prices of one sector's output will push up the overall price-level.[18]

This model explains price rises only as the effect of differing productivity rates. If, however, we add the third hypothesis of trade-union behaviour—that they 'resist any encroachment on the attained standard of living of their members'—an increase in the general price-level is followed by an increase in wages, and inflation is accelerated.

12.4. A Kaldorian Model of Creeping Inflation

The purpose of the following exercise is to show that an inflationary trend is associated with the growth of output in an economy with the following features: (1) it is divided between two sectors, with a leading sector in which productivity growth is induced by income growth; (2) in this sector, productivity increases at a rate r times higher than in the rest of the system; (3) workers seek to keep wage differentials in the two sectors the same (let us assume that wages are equal in the two sectors); (4) workers are guided in their wage claims by the leading sector, where money-wages grow in proportion to the sector's productivity growth (by hypothesis, they will grow at the same rate).

The two sectors are denoted by the suffixes 1 and 2; sector 1 is the one with the higher productivity growth. Per-capita output is denoted by y. The dot indicates that quantities are expressed in terms of variation by unit of time, p_1 and p_2 denote prices in the two sectors, and p the general price-level. Thus we may write the following equation:

$$(12.1(a)) \qquad \dot{p} = \alpha\dot{p}_1 + \beta\dot{p}_2.$$

---

[18] A number of authors have given interpretations of inflation similar to the one set out here. Among the first to do so was P. Streeten, 'Wages, Prices and Productivity', *Kyklos*, 15: 4 (1962). A variant is the Scandinavian model of a small, very open country in which the exposed sector is constrained by external price dynamics, wages are price indexed and absorb the increase in productivity, and the sheltered sector has the same rate of wage increases as the exposed sector. See G. Edgren, K.-O. Faxén, and C. E. Odhner, *Wage Formation and the Economy* (London, Allen & Unwin, 1973), and also O. Ankrust, 'Inflation in an Open Economy: A Norwegian Model', in L. B. Krause and W. S. Salant (eds.), *Worldwide Inflation* (Washington, Brooking Institution, 1975). This pure supply model of inflation has been extended to include demand determinants (Phillips curve) and tested against the Austrian case by H. Frisch, 'The Scandinavian Model of Inflation: A Generalization and Empirical Evidence', *Atlantic Economic Journal* (Dec. 1977).

If, despite the variation in the relative price, the national product remains the same, we have:

(12.1(*b*)) $\alpha + \beta = 1.$

The price variation in the two sectors is given by the variation in the labour cost per unit of output. Thus, using *w* to denote money-wages, we have:

(12.2(*a*)) $\dot{p}_1 = \dot{w}_1 - \dot{y}_1;$

(12.2(*b*)) $\dot{p}_2 = \dot{w}_2 - \dot{y}_2.$

By hypothesis (4) we have:

(12.3) $\dot{w}_1 = \dot{y}_1$

which introduced into (12.2(*a*)) means:

(12.4) $\dot{p}_1 = 0.$

By hypothesis (2) we have:

(12.5) $\dot{y}_1 = \gamma \dot{y}_2$ where $\gamma > 1.$

By hypothesis (3) we have:

(12.6) $\dot{w}_1 = \dot{w}_2.$

Inserting (12.5) and (12.6) in (12.2(*b*)) it follows, taking (12.3) into account, that:

(12.7) $\dot{p}_2 = [(\gamma - 1)/\gamma]\dot{y}_1.$

Inserting (12.7) in (12.1(*a*)), taking (12.4) and (12.1(*b*)) into account, we have:

(12.8) $\dot{p} = [(1 - \alpha)(\gamma - 1)/\gamma]\dot{y}_1.$

By hypothesis (1) we have

(12.9) $\dot{p} = [(1 - \alpha)(\gamma - 1)/\gamma]\delta g$

where δ is the parameter directly linking the productivity rate of the leading sector to the growth of income *g* according to a synthesis of the first two Kaldor laws (see Chapter 7, sections 2 and 3).

Expression (12.9) states a direct relation between the growth of the price level and the growth of income that depends inversely on parameters α and β and directly on parameter δ.

12.5. Inflation and Stagnation

Although the theory of the price dynamic elaborated in section 4, above can be used to interpret the creeping inflation of the first twenty years after the Second World War, the periods of inflation subsequent to those years require other explanations. For Kaldor, the wage explosion of the period 1968–1973 was an exogenous political phenomenon generated by the wage explosion of May 1968 in France, which spread throughout the world in much the same way as revolutions had swept through Europe a hundred years previously.[19] Kaldor's explanation of the inflation of the 1970s was based on his two-sector model,[20] of which a detailed description is given in Chapter 8. He also, on several occasions,[21] gave a 'historical' analysis of the functioning of his model.

Throughout the 1970s, despite a high and steady increase in demand for manufactured products, no inflationary boom ensued from changes in the terms of trade. This was both because of a growing supply of raw materials and agricultural commodities, which more than kept pace with demand, and because of the decision by government agencies to set aside stocks of commodities. When this accumulation of stocks became too burdensome, an attempt was made to subsidize consumption and to restrict production by subsidizing cutbacks in the use of agricultural land. In the latter half of the 1970s, these measures reduced the 'surplus' of commodities that had accumulated over previous years. When, at the end of the decade, the Soviet Union and China suffered from a series of failed harvests, stocks were exhausted and commodity prices began to rise.

Meanwhile, the suspension of the gold convertibility of the dollar by the Nixon administration in 1971 strengthened inflationary expectations and led to a sharp increase in commodity prices because of speculation. The industrialized economies were now also dependent on oil supplies from the Middle East, which formed a growing and disproportionate share of their overall energy requirements. This increasing dependence prompted the oil-producing countries to establish the OPEC cartel. The rise in commodity prices between 1968 and 1973 and the rise in the price of manufactures of the previous ten years had reduced the purchasing power of a barrel of oil. The OPEC members therefore decided from 1973 onwards to restrict production—thus pushing up the dollar price of oil and adjusting the terms of trade in their favour.

The inflation that followed can be explained as the combined effect of OPEC's determination to preserve their advantage in the terms of trade and

---

[19] Kaldor was never interested in long cycles, nor in political cycles. Nevertheless he was inclined to believe in the existence of forces which over the last 200 years had created quite regular cycles with time-spans between peaks and troughs of 25 years. The first cycle lasted from 1780 to 1815 (Napoleonic Wars), the second from the mid-1840s to 1873 (the Great Depression), the third from 1879 to the period between 1921 (pre-crisis) and 1929 (the Great Crash). The fourth period was an ascending phase between 1946 and 1973 but a descending phase thereafter. We are therefore now passing through the second half of the fourth Kondratieff cycle. As a possible explanation of this phenomenon Kaldor proposed the changes in preferences and ways of thinking that occur as one generation succeeds another, i.e. approximately every 25 years. However, since there is a generation *every* year, which is new with respect to the one 25 years previously but the same as the one of more recent years, this explanation can account for the length of the cycle but not its causes.

[20] See esp. N. Kaldor, 'Inflation and Recession in the World Economy' (1976), repr. in CP v.

[21] See 'Inflation: An Endemic Problem of Modern Economics', lecture at the University of Reykjavik, 8 June 1981; 'Economic Prospects of the '80s', lecture at the European University of Florence, pub. in *EN* (May 1982); 'The Failure of Monetarism, Chintaman Deshmukh Memorial Lecture, Bombay, 18 Jan. 1984; 'The Changing Situation of the World Economy: Possibilities and Limits of Adjustment', Cambridge, Mar. 1985, mimeo.

the reluctance of workers and firms in the industrial sector to accept any reduction in their real incomes.

There were repercussions not only on international prices but also on real produced income. The first oil-price explosion of 1973 had the same deflationary effect on world income as an additional tax not offset by public expenditure—due to the fact that the OPEC countries kept their balance of payments in surplus. The second oil shock of 1979 induced all the industrialized countries to adopt anti-inflationary policies designed to restrict demand, and these policies were largely responsible for the stagnation of the world economy during the early 1980s.

12.6. Anti-Inflationary Policies

Kaldor's conviction that the causes of inflation were multiple, and that the problem therefore required multiple remedies, is a further aspect that distances him from the Monetarists. Apart from the cases of structural inflation in the developing countries (see Chapter 9.2), and of inflation induced by changes in the terms of trade (see Chapter 8, sections 3 and 4), four possible inflationary 'pathologies', each requiring a specific kind of therapy, can be identified. We will therefore now examine, one by one, the policies that Kaldor recommended for dealing with inflations caused by: (1) deficit in the public sector and speculation on exchange rates; (2) misguided monetary and banking policy; (3) full employment; (4) the price-wage spiral.

(1) Kaldor cited the case of Brazil in the 1960s[22] as an example of inflation generated by the effects of the government deficit on the trade balance and, therefore, on the exchange rate. Inflation of this kind can be countered by increased taxation, although the problems created by such a policy, especially in the developing countries, make it difficult to implement (see Chapter 9.6). A public deficit even of large dimensions, however, does not have inflationary effects if it is accompanied by capital inflows and international loans, as evidenced by the United States during the early years of the Reagan administration. But if the deficit cannot be financed by international borrowing, ensuing speculation on exchange rates accelerates the inflationary process— an example being the German hyperinflation of the 1920s discussed in section 1 of this chapter.

(2) In certain cases of shortages of goods, expectations of future price increases lead to the conversion of liquid assets into real assets. When these expectations are encouraged by a misguided banking policy, shortages are exacerbated because goods are hoarded. Such hoarding is in fact profitable when the bank rate of interest is lower than the expected rise in the prices of

---

[22] N. Kaldor, various contributions in W. Baer and I. Kerstenetzky (eds.), *Inflation and Growth in Latin America* (Homewood, Irwin, Yale University Press, 1964).

goods. Under these circumstances, and only under these circumstances, an abrupt credit squeeze *might* be effective because it brings about a decumulation of stocks, reduces the actual—and therefore also the predicted—rise in prices, and thereby breaks the vicious circle generated by expectations. However, it cannot be taken for granted that this policy will act on prices and not on produced quantities, since a highly restrictive monetary policy leads to the breach of previously stipulated contracts, and there can be no guarantee that these contracts will only be those that concern speculative operations. As an example of an effective anti-inflationary monetary policy, Kaldor frequently cited the example of the measures introduced by Einaudi in Italy in 1947.[23] On the other hand, he also used to give the example of another university professor of economics, Salazar, who managed to achieve monetary stabilization in his country using the same methods. However, whereas in Italy the economy began to grow immediately after the credit squeeze, in Portugal it stagnated for thirty years.

(3) The problem of inflation in conditions of full employment not only worried the Keynesians; it also preoccupied Keynes himself, and even before peacetime demand policies created the conditions for extremely low unemployment rates in countries like Great Britain and the United States—a situation which lasted for a number of years. The problem spurred Keynesian economists to press for the replacement of free collective bargaining with permanent and institutionalized incomes policies. In 1950 Kaldor himself wrote a memorandum on the problem to the Chancellor of the Exchequer, Sir Stafford Cripps.[24]

In the early 1950s both wages and dividends were temporarily frozen, a measure which, in conditions of full employment, increased the 'inflationary potential', as well as incurring social pressure for the restraint to be lifted. The limitations of this kind of policy are its rigid and temporary nature, whereas 'the need for *some* restraint in both wages and profits is not a temporary need in a full employment economy, but a permanent need'.[25] Only by a flexible and long-lasting incomes policy, Kaldor argued, could the success of 'full employment in a free society' be ensured.

In Kaldor's scheme a wages policy should set itself two objectives: maintaining monetary stability and ensuring that changes in the wages structure were such that they led to the necessary adjustments being made to the structure of the economy. To achieve these objectives, the rate of increase in wages should keep pace with the average rate of increase in productivity, and those industries that managed to increase productivity the most should transfer

---

[23] Kaldor always greatly admired and liked Einaudi. Einaudi, economic professor at Turin University, became, after World War II, governor of the Bank of Italy, Chancellor of the Exchequer, and then the first Italian president of the Republic. Kaldor remembered with pleasure his trips to Italy, where he was a guest at the illustrious Italian economist's home in Dogliani.
[24] Id., 'A Positive Policy for Wages and Dividends' (1950), pub. in *CP* iii.
[25] Ibid. 113.

their productivity differentials to the community in the form of lower prices.[26] These two objectives were to be pursued by the establishment of a wages board, a body consisting of trade union representatives and government officials. The function of the board was to review wage agreements already reached in individual industries and to make sure that aggregate annual earnings did not exceed the targets set for that year. The powers of the board would consist of recommendations (which would not, however, be legally enforceable) for the postponement of excessive wage increases.

Kaldor was optimistic that voluntary wage restraints would succeed—despite the increased bargaining power enjoyed by the trade unions under the full employment conditions of those years, and despite their jealous protection of their bargaining freedoms. Workers, he argued, would understand that wage restraint was a price that they could afford to pay for maintenance of full employment, which was then regarded as the new, great social achievement.[27] This, however, was not going to be enough to give social justification for restrictive measures of this kind unless the wage-restraint policy was coupled with a policy for restraining dividends.

To render a policy of dividend limitation compatible with the reaping of the rewards of economic success (the *raison d'être* of the world of business), some connection between dividends and current earnings must be established.[28] This policy, too, would be 'voluntary' and presented to the public jointly with the wages policy. Kaldor believed that there would be no opposition to a policy of dividend limitation, because it was the *essential* complement of a policy of flexible and voluntary wage restraints.

Kaldor's proposals were not taken up. In 1951 the Labour Government was replaced by a Conservative Government which preferred to use monetary policies in dealing with inflation. When, ten years later, the Conservatives did decide to adopt an incomes policy, they limited it to wages control.

(4) There remains the fourth case of inflation in the form of a price-wage spiral occurring independently of conditions on the labour-market. When the spiral acquires a certain momentum, the different frequencies with which various prices are 'adjusted' by inflation make it extremely difficult to bring to a halt. There are those goods whose prices are adjusted at brief intervals, and others with prices adjusted at longer intervals. At any given moment, there is a backlog of prices that still have to be adjusted to past inflation, and every adjustment entails the future adjustment of other prices. As inflation accel-

---

[26] When commenting on this paper 10 years later, Kaldor still subscribed to its general philosophy, although he was less inclined to argue the case for complete wage stability in a slowly growing economy, for the reasons given in Ch. 12.2. See introd. to CP iii (1st edn., 1964).

[27] M. Kalecki was less optimistic. A few years previously he had forecast that the capitalist system would not tolerate full employment for very long, and would react with 'stop-go' policies and with a cyclical incomes trend. See M. Kalecki, 'Political Aspects of Full Employment, *Political Quarterly*, 4 (1943).

[28] Since the technical aspects of Kaldor's proposal are very dated, they are not discussed in any further detail here.

erates, the intervals between adjustments become shorter. When indexation is general and immediate, the backlog disappears and inflation suddenly vanishes. This, however, only comes about when inflation has reached such high levels that the economic system becomes unhinged. It is therefore obvious that measures have to be taken before these effects begin to appear.

If the initial inflationary shock is due to changes in the terms of trade, anti-inflationary measures can only be undertaken by international bodies (see Chapter 13.2). If, however, the price-wage dynamic is of the kind discussed in the previous section, an institutional framework must be created in which trade unions, employers, and government jointly set the target level for the aggregate growth rate of wages according to the expected increases in sectorial productivities.

When the pressure on wages is independent of the level of aggregate demand, for Kaldor, 'the question of the determination of money-wages can no longer be analysed in narrowly economic terms: it has become very much a *political* problem'.[29]

12.7. Incomes Policies and Consensus

Kaldor frequently cited Austria as a country with a successful wages policy. In his fifth speech to the House of Lords, he addressed those members of the Upper Chamber who spoke of the 'horrible effects of nationalization, of the horrors of social security and the effect of high social benefits on workers' willingness to work, or of the privilege enjoyed by trade unions', and advised them to study the Austrian example:

Austria has a very much greater public sector than our own. Far more basic industries have been nationalised in Austria. It has had a Socialist Government, either alone or in coalition, ever since the end of the last war. The rate of growth of the national product in Austria . . . has been much greater percentage wise than in any other industrial country except Japan . . . They have had no unemployment and no strikes, and at its maximum their rate of inflation is around 3 or 4 per cent a year.[30]

Austro-Keynesianism had many theoretical and practical points of contact with Kaldor's ideas (one might almost talk of an 'Austro-Hungarian Model'!). There were three areas in particular where the affinities were very close. Both Austro-Keynesianism and Kaldorian theory were grounded in the fundamental belief that capitalism was an unstable system which needed permanent institutions to control and, partly, to govern it. The actions of these institutions should extend over the long term, so that economic agents might have a secure framework within which to operate (note that this principle was considerably

---

[29] Kaldor and Trevithick, 'Keynesian Perspective on Money', 124.
[30] N. Kaldor, 'Industrial Recovery', in *House of Lords Official Report* (speech given on 17 Jan. 1979).

at variance with the doctrine of the neo-classical–Keynesian school—that when the system moves slightly away from natural equilibrium, it can be brought back to it by a 'fine tuning' policy). The second affinity between Kaldorian theory and Austro-Keynesianism was the idea that the chief obstacle to economic growth was the balance-of-payments constraint. Their third feature in common was a shared conviction that the causes of inflation in the industrialized countries were wage growth and exchange-rate variations.

Kaldor and Austro-Keynesianism also held very similar views on incomes policy. Kaldor never gave much thought to the purely political aspects of the neo-corporativist model;[31] but he had a clear idea of the features that any agreement among the social partners must possess to be effective and long-lasting. They were features that closely resembled those of the Austrian model of an incomes policy.

The first requirement was that agreements between trade unions, employers, and State should be trilateral. The presence of the State at the negotiating table was important: it gave greater permanence to the institutions responsible for implementing the incomes policy; it could provide compensation for groups and individuals who incurred losses as a result of the incomes policy; and it could offer organizational privileges that enhanced the prestige and the bargaining power of the trade-union leadership.

The second prerequisite for a successful incomes policy was that it should be administered by bodies that were centralized and officially recognized. Kaldor believed that the sectorial organization of the British trade unions had been responsible for Britain's failure to develop institutions able to devise a stable incomes policy. Centralized decision-making was necessary to ensure that negotiations began simultaneously, that wage adjustments were synchronized, and that the duration of agreements was standardized; and also to ensure that not only an average increase in wages, but also sectorial increases were fixed. In Great Britain, moreover, the trade unions still had not acquired the necessary official recognition. British trade unions had a complex and archaic structure, the result of many years of evolution and a long history of struggle. Their hard-won freedoms had not yet evolved into positive rights associated with specific obligations, but still took the form of immunities (like those granted to them by Disraeli and Campbell-Bannerman in 1906) to commit 'acts which under the common law are regarded as illegal and which are still so regarded by the courts'.[32]

---

[31] See A. Pizzorno, 'Political Exchange and Collective Identity in Industrial Conflict', in C. Crouch and A. Pizzorno (eds.), *The Resurgence of Class Conflict in Western Europe since 1968* (London, Macmillan, 1978). On the topic of neo-corporativism see S. Berger (ed.), *Organizing Interest in Western Europe* (Cambridge, CUP, 1981). M. Maraffi, *La società neocorporativa* (Bologna, Il Mulino, 1981). G. Lehmbruch and P. L. Schmitter, *La politica degli interessi nei paesi industrializzati* (Bologna, Il Mulino, 1984).

[32] N. Kaldor, *The Economic Consequences of Mrs Thatcher* (London, Duckworth, 1983), 59 (speech given on 20 May 1980).

Finally, an incomes policy should have a broad range of application. In Austria, labour organizations were part of the process of industrial decision-making in several areas, not just wage-bargaining. The people of Austria thus regarded their government's incomes policy as the outcome of general consensus among the social partners, and not as simply an instrument for curbing wage claims. In this latter part of the twentieth century, in which inflation

has become endemic to the capitalist system . . . and has now spread to communist countries as well [it] cannot be got rid of without a consensus policy on income distribution which allows effective and comprehensive controls over prices and wages.[33]

However, far from moving in the direction of the Austrian model, Great Britain had now forsaken consensus for conflict. Until the end of the 1970s the ideologies of the parties in government had been pragmatic in spirit: they all set themselves the task of achieving 'social cohesion'. This search for unity had been the common underlying aim of the policies of both Labour and Conservative prime ministers—an example being Harold Macmillan, later Lord Stockton, for whom Kaldor had words of high praise in his penultimate speech to the House of Lords, when he described him as 'one of our great national assets, although thankfully not for sale'.[34] In the years immediately after the war, both the Attlee government, the most radical Labour government of Britain's history, and the following Conservative Government under Churchill, pursued such similar economic policies that they were labelled 'Butskellism'—from the names of Gaitskell and Butler, the Chancellors of the Exchequer in the two governments.[35] As the years passed, however, it was not Great Britain but her neighbours Germany, Austria, France, Sweden, Denmark, and Norway—which Mrs Thatcher regarded as so much more successful—that had 'had a bigger dose of Keynes and Beveridge since the war, not a smaller one'.[36]

The turning-point came with the advent of Mrs Thatcher's Conservative Government: the country now began to move increasingly further away from the social and political ideals that Kaldor believed in. The ideology of the party in power became dogmatic and genuinely reactionary, in the sense used by Kaldor in his second speech to the House of Lords after Mrs Thatcher's first election victory.

[U]p to now Conservative Governments . . . were predominantly pragmatist . . . and their one consistent principle was that they were for the preservation of the country's existing institutions more than for their reform. But whether they alternated with

---

[33] Ibid. 97 (speech given on 11 July 1979).

[34] Id., 'Government Policy and New Technologies', *House of Lords Official Report* (speech given on 14 Nov. 1985). Macmillan died, aged well over 90, the year after this speech in 1986, which was the same year that Kaldor died.

[35] Id., 'Policies for Employment", *House of Lords Official Report* (speech given on 13 Nov. 1984).

[36] Id., *Economic Consequences of Mrs Thatcher*, 91 (speech given on 12 Nov. 1981).

Liberal Governments, as in the 19th century, or with Labour Governments, as in the present century, their policies could best be characterised as one of pause for consolidation and not one of the reversal of major long-term historical trends. This time it is different. This time we have a right-wing Government with a strong ideological commitment which is something new in this country[37]

This new philosophy was made plain in the Government's deliberate rejection of any policy of broad social consensus. In a subsequent address to the House of Lords, Kaldor quoted this passage from a speech by Mrs Thatcher: 'To me, consensus seems to be the process of abandoning all beliefs, principles, values and policies.' To which he replied: '[T]here was never a more far-reaching consensus in Britain than that attained by the war-time coalition Government of Winston Churchill, which certainly did not involve abandoning all beliefs, principles and values.'[38]

---

[37] Ibid. 12 (speech given on 13 June 1979).   [38] Ibid. 89 (speech given on 12 Nov. 1981).

Chapter 13

The International Monetary System, Managing an Economy in an Open Market, and the De-Industrialization of Britain

> The policies that each adopts react upon the others. The greater internal coherence of national policies makes international anarchy all the worse.
>
> Joan Robinson, *Economic Heresies*

13.1. On the International Monetary System

Kaldor's work on international monetary economics was deeply influenced by the need to find viable solutions for major problems. In his search for such solutions, his work ranged across a remarkably broad area of plans, proposals, and policies. The present chapter, addresses the following: his plan for reform of the international system and for managed devaluation; his proposals which acquired wide circulation through the work of the New Cambridge school; his recommendations for import controls and for reform of Common Market agricultural policy; and his criticisms of Thatcher's economic policies. All these contributions, despite their varied and sometimes irreconcilable natures, had at least two features in common. First, they demonstrated that political intervention at the national and international level is even more urgently needed in an open economy than it is in a closed one. Second, they provided further proof of Kaldor's skill in devising policies and schemes appropriate to economic systems that never stand still, but move in ways that are uniform neither over time nor—above all—among countries. Here too, Kaldor's reformism was addressed to the common good of the overall growth of the economies linked by international trade, and driven by the conviction that in recession and stagnation it is the poorest classes and nations that suffer the severest privations. Perhaps his most Utopian scheme in this area (one which I nevertheless believe will outlast the others) was his proposed reform of the international monetary system, which I have already mentioned on several occasions and describe in the next section.

The international monetary system based on the Bretton Woods Agreements—a system which lasted from 1946 until the American declaration of the non-convertibility of the dollar on 15 August 1971—was already beginning to show signs of collapse in the early 1960s. And on several occasions from 1964 onwards Kaldor put forward a proposal for its reform that had many points of similarity with Keynes's recommendations that went unheeded at Bretton Woods.[1]

Between 1914 and 1951 the world suffered from a severe shortage of gold and of dollars: indeed many economists of the time believed the dollar shortage to be a permanent feature of the capitalist world.[2] In the early 1950s the world economy began to move in a direction that no economist, apart perhaps from Keynes, had predicted. The reason for this shift in direction was that from 1951 onwards the American balance of 'basic transactions' (current account plus aid and foreign investment) was persistently in deficit. Now, instead of being scarce the dollar became plentiful—a development which brought two consequences. The dollar increasingly replaced gold as means of payment and as a reserve asset, and international purchasing power was now able to grow at a steady rate. This evolution towards a 'key-currency' system, however, suffered from an inherent contradiction known as the 'Triffin dilemma', a problem which Kaldor repeatedly raised during the 1950s and 1960s: '(the system) only provides international liquidity when the key currencies are weak, whereas the whole system presupposes that the currencies which serve as the reserve for others should be exceptionally strong'.[3]

Kaldor's explanation of the fragility and the unfeasibility of the Bretton Woods system was based, not on monetary and financial factors, but on examination of the differing evolutions of the world economies. A key feature of the international monetary system created at Bretton Woods was the stability of parities among currencies. A fixed parity system such as the one that had developed after World War II had the major shortcoming that the countries absorbing reserve currency (such as Germany, Japan, and Italy) were able to benefit from an 'export-led' growth that raised their rates of output and productivity. However, the primary and secondary reserve-currency countries (the United States as the former and Great Britain as the latter) had to pursue 'consumption-led' economic growth in order to provide international currency, and this entailed a reduced rate of growth of their productivity. Owing to their high growth rates of per-capita output, the reserve-currency-absorbing

[1] Keynes's plan presented at Bretton Woods gave great power to international bodies. Apart from creating liquidity, these were to impose exchange controls, not only on countries with deficits but also on those with surpluses. In the eyes of the Americans, such exchange controls were a weapon from the same armoury as the pre-war protectionism and imperial preferences that they had so fiercely fought against in the name of free trade. (Note that the OECD itself was born as an institution in defence of free trade.) The British position was much more in favour of protectionism, as witness the fact that after the war they rejected American aid rather than abandon the system of imperial preferences.

[2] See e.g. G. D. H. MacDougall, *The World Dollar Problem* (London, Macmillan, 1957).

[3] N. Kaldor, 'The Problem of International Liquidity' (1964), repr. in CP vi. 31.

countries could 'afford' rates of growth of their wage rates that were lower than their productivity growth rates. As a consequence, their exchange rates, compared with those of the reserve-currency countries, tended to fall in real terms 'not on account of deliberate acts of exchange devaluation, but simply because of the Verdoorn Law'.[4] The consequence of this progressive drop in the real exchange rates of the partner countries was that the industrial competitiveness of the reserve-currency countries also declined.[5]

The problem as it today affects the United States is widely debated. Kaldor had identified and denounced it, however, as early as 1971.

If continued long enough it would involve transforming a nation of creative producers into a community of *rentiers* increasingly living on others, seeking gratification in ever more useless consumption, with all the debilitating effects of the bread and circuses of Imperial Rome. In addition, the objectives on which successive American governments spent their freely printed money appeared either so useless or morally repellent—lunar flights or Vietnam wars—as to arouse increasingly universal hostility against the system.[6]

The widening gap among long-term productivity rates made a system of fixed exchange rates impossible to maintain. Nor could the reserve-currency countries resort to deflationary policies, since these would have further weakened the competitiveness of their manufacturing industries via the reverse operation of the Kaldor–Verdoorn law.

In 1945 the Americans regarded competitive devaluation as 'a major calamity to humanity, comparable to wars or pestilence'.[7] Kaldor, on the contrary, thought that devaluation of the dollar was absolutely necessary. 'Throughout the 1950s he believed the dollar to be overvalued and warned of the excessive increase in dollar liabilities. In 1960 he wrote to Walter Hebler, the chairman of the US Council of Economic Advisers, arguing for a devaluation of the dollar. In 1968 he issued the same advice to Arthur Okun occupying the same position.'[8] Viewed a quarter of a century later, the floating of the dollar was apparently the Americans' only option if they were to protect themselves against the forced undervaluation of the German mark and the Japanese yen. Nevertheless, for Kaldor writing in the 1970s, although fixed

---

[4] Id., 'Bretton Woods and After' (1971), repub. as 'The Dollar Crisis', in CP vi. 65. Kaldor had previously calculated that in the period 1953–61 alone the ratio between the cost of labour per unit of output in the USA and the UK and the cost of labour per unit of output in Germany, France, Belgium, Holland, Italy, and Japan had worsened by 20% ('Problem of International Liquidity', 38).

[5] Kaldor did not distinguish between the positions of the two reserve-currency countries as regards the structure of their balance of payments. Between 1950 and 1970 the USA showed a surplus in goods and a deficit in capital movement. Between 1880 and 1900 GB's position had been the reverse of that in which the USA now found herself. Real overvaluation and de-industrialization had been the long-term consequences for Britain, and these now seemed to be affecting the USA in equal measure. Kaldor's analysis of the USA, however, applied more to the actual situation than it did to that of the early 1970s. One can nevertheless say that in describing this phenomenon when he did, he showed exceptional foresight.

[6] Ibid. 64.   [7] Ibid.   [8] A. P. Thirlwall, 'Kaldor as a Policy Adviser', *CJE* (Mar. 1989).

parities could not work, neither could a system of 'fixed but adjustable' parities 'because it offers the maximum scope for anticipatory speculation',[9] as amply demonstrated by the frequent revaluations of the mark prior to the 1970s.

Nor was a universal system of freely floating exchange rates a viable solution, since individual exchange rates would tend to be determined by speculative forces, the effects of which were more destabilizing than stabilizing.[10] Above all, oscillations would be extremely wide because of the amount of non-official liquid funds held in the form of bank balances or short-term financial assets. These had accumulated in such vast proportions as to be unimaginable when the Bretton Woods system had been created and even more unimaginable at the time of the Gold Standard.[11]

Another alternative was flanking the dollar with three or four currency groups, each functioning as the reserve currency for a number of smaller countries. However, Kaldor believed that the operation of this system would constantly create international reserves. These would be difficult to control and—because the domestic inflationary pressures deriving from insufficient taxation or from an exaggerated expansion of credit would be politically more difficult to handle—would give an inflationary bias to the world economy.

Kaldor also objected to the proposal, advanced mainly by French economists and by de Gaulle during the 1960s, that gold should be used as a reserve asset. The return to gold was indeed a possibility and had the advantage of leaving each individual country free to decide on both monetary and credit matters, and on whether to adopt fixed or flexible exchange rates. But the scheme suffered from the major shortcoming that gold had great rigidity of supply. For this reason, its initial value would have to be at a level high enough[12] to ensure that its yearly production increased[13] at a rate sufficient to guarantee the full exploitation of the growth potential of the world economy; but this would have the undesirable political consequence of transferring the role of creator of the international reserve currency from the United States to South Africa or the Soviet Union. Kaldor advocated instead the creation of a *new* international commodity-reserve currency.

13.2. The Proposal of an International Commodity Currency

A reserve currency must satisfy two essential requirements: it must be easy to create and it must be readily acceptable to the market. A paper-based interna-

[9] N. Kaldor, 'Problems and Prospects of International Monetary Reform', (1973), repr. in CP vi. 80.

[10] Ibid. 81.   [11] Ibid. 88.

[12] When Kaldor was writing the value of gold was fixed at $35 per ounce of fine gold. Today (1990) it is nearly $390.

[13] Kaldor stressed on several occasions that an increase in the *production* of gold had a multiplier effect on income which could not be achieved by a simple increase in the *price* of gold.

tional currency—'a monetary bancor' like the Special Drawing Rights (SDR)—raised problems on both these counts. In fact, in the case of a national currency, the public's acceptance of a 'fiat money' would be determined by the political sovereignty of the State; whilst in the case of a group of sovereign states the willingness of each country to hold assets in a 'paper bancor' depended on its confidence that all the others would continue to accept it—and such confidence could be shaken by a variety of highly unstable factors such as prices and exchange rates. The creation of 'bancor' would face the further difficulty that the sovereign states would be obliged to delegate their powers to the officials of the IMF. Moreover, every paper-money system contains a fundamental injustice, 'because the powerful countries would, *de facto*, receive a different and more favourable treatment than the small ones'.[14]

A system tying additional money to a specific asset would also be extremely difficult to operate. Instead of issuing money against investments in the extraction of a commodity like gold that was of no social utility, an international 'paper gold' money could be issued against socially useful investments in the poor countries. However, this proposal—known as the 'link'—aroused the opposition of the rich countries, especially America and Germany, on the ground that 'charity demotivates'. Moreover, the system would have provoked endless wrangling over the criteria to apply in choosing the countries to benefit from the investments, and in selecting the socially useful projects against which the money would be issued.

The international monetary system, Kaldor argued, should instead be reorganized in order to provide an international money that was neither the currency of one particular country nor a paper money, but an international commodity reserve currency.[15] He first put forward a detailed scheme along these lines in a paper presented jointly with Hart and Tinbergen at a United Nations conference on 'Trade and Development' in 1963.[16] I shall first give a general outline of the scheme and its rationale, then describe the political and ideological criticisms brought against it and, finally, list the reasons why, despite these criticisms, the scheme was and is a feasible one.

---

[14] N. Kaldor, lecture (1974) trans. from the Italian as 'International Monetary Reform: The Need for a New Approach', in CP vi. 92. Kaldor gave the example of how much more the developed countries would have received, if this system had been in operation when they had had to deal with the rise in oil prices, compared with what the countries of the Third World would have obtained in the event of, say, the failure of their harvests.

[15] The idea of a commodity standard backing national currencies dates back to the 19th cent.; that of an international commodity reserve currency was first suggested by B. Graham, *World Commodities and World Currency* (New York, McGraw Hill, 1944).

[16] N. Kaldor *et al.*, 'The Case for an International Commodity Reserve Currency' (1963), pub. in CP iv. Kaldor had prepared a first draft of the paper in Apr. 1963, which Hart and Tinbergen read and agreed with. At the end of the year Kaldor and Hart worked on a new version to be presented to the conference. Tinbergen added his name when the few changes he suggested were accepted by the other two authors. See N. Kaldor, introd. to CP iv (1st edn., 1964). In 1965 a similar proposal to the one of Kaldor and associates was put forward by Jean de Largentaye (a top official of FMI who had translated Keynes's *General Theory* into French) and later published ('L'Étalon Marchandise', *EA* (Sept. 1967)).

The main features of Kaldor's scheme were the following: (1) The IMF would issue its own money—called 'bancor' in honour of Keynes—convertible into gold and a bundle of commodities (thirty commodities traded at the world level, with a high degree of standardization and durability). (2) The 'bancor' would be fully covered by gold and commodities; a fixed percentage of it could be a fiduciary issue. (3) Only the Central Banks of member countries would be entitled to hold 'bancor' balanced with the IMF, and 'bancor' would be used to settle claims by countries. (4) The recommended initial issue was 30 billion dollars, 5 billion of which would be covered by gold, 20 billion by commodities, and with 5 billion as the fiduciary issue.

The scheme required a fixed price of commodities irrespective of the exchange-rate variations of national currencies. If the primary commodity supply exceeded demand and its price tended to fall, the IMF would buy and stock the commodity. This would stabilize the price of primary commodities and the incomes of their producers, and increase international liquidity. If demand exceeded supply, the mechanism would operate in reverse.

Clearly the chief target of the proposal was the stabilization of primary commodity prices. In his previous work on this subject[17] Kaldor had not relied on buffer stocks as an instrument for stabilizing primary commodity prices. Now, however, they became central to his scheme. The 1963 paper laid less emphasis on the allocative properties of prices and accepted commodity stocks as alternative signallers, since these were better suited to the new macro-economic target: 'some allocative efficiency is traded-off against greater macro-economic stability or enhanced growth'.[18]

The scheme's rationale rested on Kaldor's two-sector model (see Chapter 8). Although he did not give this full development until ten years after he had first proposed his plan, he already had its rough outline in mind during the 1950s while he was working on Latin American development (see Chapter 9, sections 1–4).

Five reasons can be adduced in favour of his scheme, of which four relate to its ability to keep the prices of primary commodities stable. The first is that falling commodity prices depress industrial demand: the positive effect of higher real income in the industrial sector is more than offset by the fall in purchasing power in the primary producing sector, which entails reduced demand for manufactured goods and a fall in the scale of world investment in the primary sector.

These ideas are very similar to those of D. H. Robertson[19] and of Keynes. In 1942, in fact, Keynes had drawn up a plan for the flanking of the International Clearing Union (of which the IMF was a watered-down version) with

[17] N. Kaldor, *A Reconsideration of the Economics of the International Wheat Agreement* (1952), repr. in CP iv.

[18] J. Spraos, 'Kaldor on Commodities', *CJE* (Mar. 1989), 210.

[19] D. H. Robertson, 'The Terms of Trade', in id., *Utility and All That and Other Essays* (London, Allen & Unwin, 1952).

another agency, the International Commodity Control, responsible for financing the creation of buffer stocks of most raw materials through subsidiary agencies, all operating according to the same rules.[20]

However, Kaldor was unaware of Keynes's plan (which became public only thirty-five years after the war, when Keynes's complete works were published and security restrictions on government documents of the war years were lifted). By stabilizing the incomes of primary producers, the system of buffer stocks would replace the crude mechanism of rising and falling commodity prices—which had the damaging effect of setting off useless and perverse cycles in industrial activity and the production of commodities.

In the 1970s[21] and 1980s[22] Kaldor again and insistently proposed his scheme, although his 1983 version was slightly different from that of 1963. In the latter, commodities entered the bundle in fixed proportion; in the former, probably because of the influence of Keynes's paper, which had just been published, separate buffer stocks operated for various commodities. Kaldor simplified the scheme and related it to the existing system by proposing that the net expenditure of these buffer stocks should be funded by SDRs.

These papers of Kaldor's stress other arguments in favour of his stabilization plan for primary-commodity prices. And this brings us to the second reason for its introduction, which relates to the productivity-raising effect of price stabilization: of utmost importance, bearing in mind that, for Kaldor, land was the ultimate constraint on growth (see Chapter 8.4). Wide fluctuations in commodity prices engender uncertainty and discourage land-saving investment in agriculture; whilst the positive effect of price-stabilization schemes on raising productivity has been confirmed by the success of farm support programmes in the 1930s, agricultural marketing boards, and the Common Agricultural Policy (CAP).

A third argument in favour of a stabilization scheme is the cost entailed by wide price fluctuations and slow adjustment. The evidence had already been provided by Keynes in 1938,[23] and the problem became more severe after 1971.

In Kaldor's two-sector model, adjustment towards long-run intersectoral equilibrium through a change in the terms of trade is slow because it acts on

[20] J. M. Keynes, *The Collected Writings of John Maynard Keynes*, xxvii. *Activities 1940–1946: Shaping the Post-War Economy: Employment and Commodities*, ed. D. Moggridge (London, Macmillan, 1980). Keynes strongly recommended his proposal with the backing of Roy Harrod and Dennis Robertson, who believed it could act as a powerful mechanism for promoting world stability and prosperity after WWII. However, the plan was never given any serious consideration by the British government because of opposition by the Ministry of Agriculture and, above all, by the Bank of England, which regarded it as too interventionist.

[21] N. Kaldor 'Inflation and Recession in the World Economy' (1976), repr. in CP v.

[22] Id., 'The Role of Commodity Prices in Economic Recovery' (1982), pub. in *LLBR* (July 1983), 28.

[23] Keynes calculated the average annual difference over a 10-year period between the highest and the lowest prices of four commodities (rubber, cotton, wheat, and zinc) at 67%. J. M. Keynes, 'The Policy of government Storage of Foodstuffs and Raw Materials', *EJ* (Sept. 1938).

investment incentives and not through substitution in consumption. A slow-acting mechanism could increase the risk and effects of disequilibrating behaviour. Traders perform their equilibrating role properly if they have a notion of 'normal price' (see Chapter 2.3), otherwise their actions may lead it further away from equilibrium (see Chapter 8.3). Whether or not this notion exists in the same market depends on historical and institutional factors. In both the Gold-Standard and the Bretton Woods periods, prices were more stable because, as Kaldor argued in his 1976 paper,[24] the system was able to maintain the illusion that the dollar was a commodity-backed currency, and that commodities had a long-run normal price in dollars around which their market prices fluctuated. With the demonetization of the dollar and the elimination of any anchorage price, fluctuations increased enormously.[25] And the situation worsened with the passage of time, because after every round traders needed larger price movements before they believed that the movement would change direction.[26] In the scheme proposed by Kaldor, Hart, and Tinbergen, commodity prices would perform the role of the anchor for international currencies, and act as the link between the real and monetary spheres once provided by gold.

The fourth argument in support of Kaldor's scheme turns on the stagflationary effects of primary-commodity price changes (see Chapters 8.3 and 12.4). When the primary sector grows more slowly than the industrial sector, and if there are no stocks to be decumulated, the monetary price of primary commodities will rise. In the industrial sector fixed mark-ups and wage resistance will push the monetary price up to the point where the terms of trade are restored; but, since nothing has happened to remove the real causes of the supply shortage in the primary sector, there will be a further jump in primary sector prices and a new inflationary round will ensue.

Kaldor's system would guarantee an international money with a value that was stable with respect to the principal commodities. 'And this in itself would be a tremendous achievement—indeed it would largely deal with the problem of chronic world-wide inflation',[27] since this was caused by two interacting factors that would become inoperative if commodity prices were stable: (1) the inflation of costs induced by the rise in the commodity prices associated with indexed wages; (2) accelerating increases in commodity prices provoked by expectations of future increases whenever prices were pushed up even slightly by an increase in demand.[28]

---

[24] Kaldor, 'Inflation and Recession in the World Economy'.

[25] On several occasions Kaldor cited the study by P. Sylos-Labini, 'On the Instability of Commodity Prices and the Problem of Gold', (in A. Quadrio-Curzio (ed.), *The Gold Problem: Economic Perspectives* (Oxford, OUP, 1982)), in which the Italian economist showed how after 1971 the %age variation of the prices of raw materials in relation to changes in world industrial production had been three times greater than in the previous 15 years.

[26] Spraos, 'Kaldor on Commodities', 219.

[27] Kaldor, 'Role of Commodity Prices in Economic Recovery', 30.

[28] Kaldor was hostile to the idea that the volatility of commodity prices could be reduced if it became possible to spread risk through 'hedging': the use of larger facilities in buying and selling futures for every commodity and for a whole series of future periods. Although this would have

Inflation was not the only social cost that the scheme would eliminate. Industrialized countries seek to cure inflation, even a cost inflation, by means of deflationary policies that create industrial recession: they thus end up with simultaneous inflation and stagnation. In Kaldor's view (and this I would stress again) the rise and fall of commodity prices is an asymmetrical mechanism which creates stagnation in both directions.

The final factor in favour of his scheme is that when international reserves consist of assets with a stable value in terms of commodities, devaluation has the same real cost for a large country as it does for a small one.[29]

In conclusion, the introduction of an international monetary system based on an international commodity-reserve currency regulated by cumulation and decumulation of stocks of primary commodities and stabilizing prices and the incomes of primary producers would have given balanced growth to the world economic system without incurring the costs of inflation and recession that arise from changes in the terms of trade between the two sectors.

13.3. The Debate on Kaldor's Scheme and Why it was Not Accepted

As we have seen, the first argument in favour of Kaldor's scheme is that falling commodity prices do not lead to an expansion of manufacturing production, but depress manufacturing demand instead. For this to happen, certain conditions must hold.[30] Let us suppose a Keynesian equation for the industrial sector, where output Y is equal to expenditure E plus the trade balance B. Expenditure depends positively on industrial income Y and negatively on the prices of primary commodities in terms of manufactured goods p. The trade balance depends negatively on income (via imports), but it also depends on the prices of primary goods.

$$(13.1) \qquad\qquad Y = E(Y, p) + B(Y, p).$$

If we only consider the trade balance, a fall in income raises B via a fall in imports. But this effect is offset by a fall in B due to a fall in p, which is a rise in the relative price of manufactured goods. However, in order for this to occur, i.e. $\partial B/\partial p > 0$, the Marshall–Lerner conditions must hold. If they do

made spot prices on every market depend more closely on 'future' prices, there was no reason to suppose that future markets would be any less stable—indeed there was evidence that such volatility was less in the absence of future markets. The diffusion of the practice of hedging against risks increased the volume of speculative transactions, and this led to greater not smaller deviations from 'normal prices'. In support of this argument, Kaldor—Ibid. 31—cites N. Colchester, 'Protection from Chicago', *Financial Times* (4 Feb. 1983).

[29] The 1931 devaluation of the pound against the countries in the gold bloc and the devaluation of the dollar against the European countries 40 years later gave the two countries more competitiveness on the manufacturing side without worsening their terms of trade. This was because in 1931 the countries supplying primary commodities to the UK devalued to the same extent as the pound; similarly, 40 years later the countries supplying raw materials to the USA stayed tied to the dollar.

[30] For detailed treatment see Spraos, 'Kaldor on Commodities', 213–14.

not, a fall in p makes B progressively positive, which has a reflationary effect on the sector: the reverse of Kaldor's case. However, the Marshall–Lerner criterion, which in this context states that the sum of import elasticities of the two sectors must be greater than one, is satisfied by the assumption of Kaldor's two-sector model that there is no substitution effect between sectors as p changes, and that this constrains price elasticity to unity.

Moreover, even if we relax this assumption, Kaldor's predicted deflationary effect of a fall in primary prices could come about if $\partial E/\partial p \geqslant 0$. This holds in Kaldor's analysis because if p falls, income and saving in the primary sector fall, and this entails a fall in investment, which is expenditure on goods in the manufacturing sector. Hence careful inspection of the factors pushing in different directions justifies Kaldor's conclusion that 'allowing for these effects it seems quite likely that the *net* effect of a fall in the prices of primary products relative to manufactures is to depress rather than to stimulate, the level of activity in the manufacturing sector'.[31]

A second criticism of the counter-cyclical role of commodity-price stabilization is that demand management by fiscal and monetary policy would, in an industrial country, achieve the same macro-economic target as pursued by the commodity-price stabilization scheme and more efficiently.[32] This, however, is only true if, as a consequence of a price fall, the primary sector diverts some of the proceeds paid to it by the international agency in order to restore the *status quo ante* by buying financial assets instead of goods from the manufacturing sector: an unjustified hypothesis. Furthermore, in an integrated world, counter-cyclical policies cannot be undertaken by a single country; they require co-ordinated action—something that recent experience has shown to be extremely difficult to accomplish.[33]

A third ground for criticism is the cost of holding and managing the buffer stock. Hart, Kaldor, and Tinbergen were aware of this problem, estimating the gross cost at 3 to 3.5 per cent a year of the value of the stock. An opponent of the scheme, Grubel,[34] has put this at 6 per cent—and was criticized for doing so by Hart.[35] The cost could, however, be reduced if the buffer stock made a profit in its commodity transactions.[36] A more important point is that the existence of a stabilizing agency forces speculators to operate in a stabilizing manner, thus reducing the amount of stock that the agency has to accumulate.

[31] Kaldor *et al.*, 'International Commodity Reserve Currency', 163.

[32] H. G. Johnson, 'Economic Policies toward Less Developed Countries' (Washington, DC, Brooking Institution, 1967).

[33] Spraos, 'Kaldor on Commodities', 215–16.

[34] H. G. Grubel, 'The Case against an International Commodity Reserve Currency', *OEP* 17 (1965).

[35] A. G. Hart, 'The Case for and against an International Commodity Reserve Currency', *OEP* (July 1966).

[36] G. Bird, *International Financial Policy and Economic Development* (London, Macmillan, 1987).

A further objection has centred on the perverse reaction that might be set off by a commodity reserve currency if the bundle comprised a commodity like oil, the price of which could be pushed up by a cartel (like OPEC). In this case, the value of the currency would have to be kept constant relative to the price of such a commodity by means of sales from stock, thus reducing international liquidity precisely at the moment when the deflationary impact of the low absorption of the oil-exporting countries would require it to increase.[37] Although Kaldor's scheme is able to handle this eventuality, by expanding the fiduciary quota of the issue, it would be contrary to the fully automatic regime envisaged by Hart, Kaldor, and Tinbergen. This might therefore explain why Kaldor, in his 1983 paper, proposed buffer stocks for individual commodities and suggested that 'bancor' should be convertible into individual commodities rather than a basket of commodities. Nevertheless, he still maintained that stock acquisition must be financed by international money creation (which at the time he accepted should be SDRs) to prevent a possible crowding out effect of the acquisition itself.

One gathers from this debate that there were no serious technical objections to adoption of Kaldor's scheme. Nevertheless it was ignored, both when it was first proposed and in the 1980s when the world economy was afflicted by precisely the problems that its adoption would have eliminated: falling commodity prices and slow growth or declining GDP in many developing countries, with effects damaging to the exports and production of industrial economies. Thus

not only has Kaldor's scheme been rejected, but in the eighties even the spirit of counter-cyclical international financial measures to combat recession in developing countries, so eloquently defended by Kaldor, was also rejected, even though such measures could have been implemented with existing measures (by means of SDR issues). The cost of such a rejection has been dramatic, particularly in the developing world.[38]

Kaldor's scheme was rejected for several different reasons, all of which, however, share a common ideological denominator. It was opposed by those who were (and are) convinced that at every level, even internationally, the operation of market forces should not be interfered with, a particular example being the resistance to counter-cyclical measures at international level (between 1981 and 1988 there were no new issues of SDRs, mainly because of the intransigence of the United States). Another obstacle was the view that the cost of financing a commodity-price stabilization mechanism would fall on the industrialized countries, while the benefits would accrue to the developing countries. This, though, was directly contrary to the scheme's rationale.

[37] F. Stewart and A. Sengupta, *International Financial Cooperation* (London, Frances Pinter, 1982).
[38] S. Griffith-Jones, 'Kaldor's Analysis of International Monetary Reform', *CJE* 1 (Mar. 1989), 228.

A third reason for the rejection of the scheme was that in the 1980s the industrialized countries treated the battle against inflation as their first priority. As the slow-down in price increases of those years was largely due to a fall in commodity prices,[39] a stabilization scheme would have been counter-productive. However, had a commodity-price stabilization scheme been implemented when Kaldor first proposed it, the prime cause of commodity-price increases, supply bottle-necks, would have been largely eliminated by land-saving technical progress—which will come about in the primary sector as long as investment is not halted by a fall in income consequent on a fall in the prices of primary commodities.

The massive dependence of developing countries on primary commodity exports means that they are constantly preoccupied with prices; a matter of much less serious concern for industrial countries—mainly for ideological reasons, as we have seen. Nevertheless, the pressure of events and the weight of facts can change minds.

Kaldor would have considered himself vindicated had he lived a year longer to hear James Baker, then US Secretary of the Treasury, telling the 1987 annual meeting of the IMF/World Bank that, as part of the multilateral surveillance process, 'the United States is prepared to consider utilizing, as an additional indicator, . . . the relationship among our currencies and a basket of commodities including gold. This could be helpful as an early warning signal of potential price trends.'[40]

13.4. Export-Led Growth and Exchange-Rate Policy

For many years after the Second World War Keynes's teachings on active economic policy were heeded by successive British governments, which set themselves a broad range of quantitative economic targets in employment, the balance of payments, the rate of output growth, and the rate of wage increases.[41] In Kaldor's view, however, although Keynes's ideas had fallen on fertile ground, the same could not be said for the recommendations of Tinbergen and Meade[42] concerning the policy instruments needed to achieve these targets. In particular, his main criticism of Britain's post-war economic policies was that they 'treated the problem of full employment and (implicitly)

---

[39] W. Beckerman and T. Jenkinson, 'What Stopped Inflation: Unemployment or Commodity Prices', *EJ* (Mar. 1986).

[40] IMF, *Survey*, 19 Oct. 1987, taken from Spraos, 'Kaldor on Commodities', 221.

[41] A full-employment target was first announced by Chancellor of the Exchequer Gaitskell (Labour); a balance-of-payments target by Chancellor of the Exchequer Butler (Conservative); a growth target by Chancellor Maudling (Conservative) and then Callaghan (Labour); a wage-increase target by Chancellor Sir Stafford Cripps (Labour), Selwyn Lloyd (Conservative) and Maudling (Conservative), and also by legislation in 1966.

[42] J. G. Tinbergen, *On the Theory of Economic Policy* (Amsterdam, North Holland Publishing Co., 1952), chs. 4, 5; and J. E. Meade, *The Balance of Payments, Mathematical Supplement* (London, OUP, 1951).

of growth as one of internal demand management, and not one of exports and of international competitiveness'.[43] As Kaldor himself admitted, Britain had been making the mistake of treating its economy as a closed system ever since the 1944 Beveridge Report on Full Employment—which he himself had helped to write (see Chapter 4.3).

The policy of internal demand management pursued by post-war governments was better than no policy at all; but it was a 'second best' compared to a policy that had income change depend on export growth. In an open economy, growth led by 'internal consumption' is unstable because it is subject to the balance-of-payments constraint. Moreover, the incentive to long-term investment is weak and the investment/output ratio low because, in periods of fiscal expansion, consumption takes up a large share, while in periods of fiscal contraction the fall in consumption also weakens the incentive to invest. Finally, the productive structure of a developed economy is such that the percentage of expenditure on final consumption that becomes demand for goods from the manufacturing sector is much lower than the percentage of exports that becomes this kind of demand. For these reasons export-led growth generates a long-term rate of growth greater than that generated by consumption-led growth.

The chief factor governing external demand is international competitiveness, which—since it is given, as far as price competitiveness is concerned, by the ratio between the domestic cost of labour per unit of output and the external cost expressed in one particular currency—depends largely on productivity growth and the exchange rate. Thus, just as Keynes had done in the 1920s, during the 1960s Kaldor consistently advocated a policy for the 'management' of the exchange rate by the monetary authorities.[44] A change in the parity rate should not, however, occur once and for all through sudden devaluation, but should come about by frequent and limited adjustments of the exchange rate. This policy would speed up the otherwise slow process of adjustment in the structure of the manufacturing sector to the rate of growth of foreign demand, whereas a single act of devaluation—of whatever proportions—could not conceivably have a beneficial and permanent effect on long-term competitiveness. The British government had opted for the wrong policy when it had decided to resort to its two outright devaluations of 1949 and 1967.[45] In the former case, the devaluation had been too large and had been

---

[43] N. Kaldor, 'Conflicts in National Economic Objectives' (1970), repr. in CP v. 160.

[44] From the early 1920s onwards Keynes argued that the UK should go off the Gold Standard and opt for a 'managed currency' (*A Tract on Monetary Reform* (London, Macmillan, 1923), chs. 4, 5).

[45] From 1951 to 1966, in only 15 years, the share of British exports in total world trade shrank from 22.5 to 12.9%. This fall in market shares would have happened anyway, even if a different policy had been adopted—because of the industrialization of many emerging countries and the revival of the continental European economies—but it would not have happened so rapidly. According to Kaldor, sterling should have been devalued by 5% at various intervals—first in 1957, and then in 1962 and 1967 ('The Truth about the "Dynamic Effects" of the Common Market' (1971), repr. in CP v. 194).

implemented when the external constraint derived from high international prices and commodity shortages and not from a lack of competitiveness by British industry. In the latter case, the devaluation had been 'too late and too little': after three years its effect had already petered out.[46]

Until the mid-1970s Kaldor was convinced that a policy of managed exchange rates designed to secure a desirable growth of exports was more effective than a policy of straightforward devaluation—even though its implementation was more difficult because it required stable wages at home and foreign trading partners which did not follow suit by adopting their own policies of floating rates. Moreover, the monetary authorities had to be able to counteract whatever expectation happened to be dominant at the time so that the rate could be kept slightly undervalued.

This was not an easy task. Indeed,

the success of such a long-term strategy depends on the success of the monetary authorities in keeping the world 'guessing' both as to the country's true position and to its intentions, and in turn on the country's success in keeping its long-term intentions completely in the dark.[47]

The argument that an exchange-rate policy should be used to secure the desirable rate of growth of export did not mean, however, that fiscal policy had a purely 'neutral' role to play. On the contrary,

the instrument of fiscal policy would still be required to secure that fiscal balance (which may be positive or negative) which reconciles, over a run of years, the optimal rate of growth of exports and of the G.D.P. with the maintenance of a 'target surplus' in the current balance of payments.[48]

This idea encapsulates the analyses and the proposals of what came to be known as the New Cambridge school.

13.5. The New Cambridge school

Kaldor's proposals for flexible but managed exchange rates and his criticisms of government economic policies (as set out in the previous section) were taken up in the pages of *The Times*—in outline form in January 1973 and then in more detail a year later—by Wynne Godley and Francis Cripps, who

[46] On only one occasion, Kaldor believed, had the British government correctly adjusted currency parity: when the country left the Gold Standard (on 18 Sept. 1931) and for 3 years adopted a system of managed exchange rates. This though, was not a deliberate act of economic policy but a measure made necessary by large losses of reserves. So that the pound could maintain its role as medium of payment and reserve instrument in the sterling area even if it was now floating, the UK created a system for compensating official holders of sterling. The floating exchange rate, however, came to an end with the tripartite agreement of 1935.

[47] N. Kaldor, 'The Relative Merits of Fixed and Floating Exchange Rates' (1965), pub. in CP vi. 52.

[48] Id., 'Conflicts in National Economic Objectives', 167–8.

attacked the short-term nature of government measures and advocated a medium-term approach based on new principles.[49] Again in *The Times*, two other Cambridge economists, Michael Posner and Richard Kahn, joined the controversy to criticize Godley and Cripps and labelled them and those of their colleagues (also members of the Cambridge Economic Policy Group) who shared their opinions the 'New Cambridge school', or the 'New school' for short.[50] The school's prime mover was Kaldor,[51] although he never intervened directly in the argument. The debate first waged in the columns of a daily newspaper—which explains the disorderly way in which it was conducted and why there were clashes of opinion even within the school itself—then moved to a select committee of the House of Commons,[52] an environment more conducive to theoretical reflection;[53] but in the end it came to nothing. Although ten years later one cannot claim that very much is left of the New school, it would be a mistake to dismiss it entirely. As we shall see, its basic propositions were at variance, albeit not radically, with both the neo-Keynesian doctrine (à la Mundell-Flemming) of the 1960s and the monetarist doctrine of the balance of payments of the 1970s.

In the New school's early stages its members took up two distinct positions. The first, set out by Godley and Fetherston on the occasion of a well-known seminar at the LSE (15 May 1974), criticized the government's policy of fine tuning and declared that employment and the trade balance should be medium-term targets. This criticism of government policy therefore concerned its *temporal horizon*.

The most succinct statement of the school's other position was made by R. Neild in the following terms, which came to epitomize the New school's doctrine:

I do not repeat . . . the Keynesian orthodoxy that the Budget should be used to determine the level of employment and the exchange rate to regulate the foreign

---

[49] W. A. H. Godley and T. F. Cripps, 'Balance of Payments and Demand Management', *London and Cambridge Economic Bulletin* (Jan. 1973) (repr. from *TT* (8 and 9 Jan. 1973)). 'Budget Deficit and Demand Management', *London and Cambridge Economic Bulletin* (Jan. 1974) (repr. from *TT* (22 and 23 Jan. 1974)); ids., 'Budget Deficit and Balance of Payments', letter to *TT* (5 Feb. 1974).

[50] R. Kahn and M. Posner, 'Cambridge Economics and the Balance of Payments', *London and Cambridge Economic Bulletin* (July 1974) (repr. from *TT* (17 and 18 Apr. 1974)).

[51] Compare the passage from Kaldor quoted at the end of the previous section with the following from Godley and Cripps's article in *TT* (22 and 23 Jan. 1973), the article which sparked off the debate: "Fiscal policy should, with only small temporary exceptions, always be such as to ensure that total domestic expenditure is in line with national income, or different from it only to the extent required . . . (for) surpluses or deficits on current account. The budget deficit having been set in this way, success in achieving growth and full employment must then depend on (a country's) ability to gain access to foreign markets and on commercial policy." See also N. Kaldor, 'The Road to Recover', *NS* (Mar. 1974).

[52] T. F. Cripps *et al.*, 'Public Expenditure and the Management of the Economy', *Memorandum to the Select Committee of the House of Commons on Public Expenditure* (London, HMSO, 1974).

[53] R. P. Smith, 'Demand Management and the New school', *Applied Economics*, 8 (1976); D. Vines, 'Economic Policy for an Open Economy: Resolution of the New school's Elegant Paradoxes', *Australian Economic Papers* (Dec. 1976). F. Barca, 'Premesse analitiche e politica economica della nuova scuola di Cambridge', *Note economiche*, 5/6 (1977).

balance. I said the opposite: the Budget should be used to determine the foreign balance and the exchange rate to determine the level of activity.[54]

This criticism of government policies was aimed at their *assignment* of instruments to targets: the position attacked by Kahn and Posner, who took it upon themselves to defend the Keynesian orthodoxy of the 'Old school'.

The first hypothesis of the New school's normative model was that investment in the long run is endogenous and depends on income (a Kaldorian assumption); net private savings—which may be measured as the net acquisition of financial assets (NAFA)—are stable in the long period, hence changes in income are reflected in changes in expenditure. The clearest explanation as to why the private sector should show 'a small and stable surplus' was given by Neild,[55] who based his arguments on an idea initially propounded by Kaldor and then developed by A. Wood.[56] Profits derive from the mark-up that firms in aggregate apply to their costs in order to secure the cash flow they need for investments. If unexpected profits are created in the cycle, sooner or later they will be spent (on investments, dividends, wages, etc.); hence it is only in the short term that they take the form of a net acquisition of financial assets.

The New Cambridge school's second general hypothesis concerned taxation, which it regarded as exogenous and therefore as independent of income. This amounts to saying that the public deficit as a whole is an economic policy instrument. Such an assumption entails that the Treasury has perfect foresight of changes in income (and therefore of the induced tax revenues) which enables it to adjust both the tax rate and the amount of expenditure by the amount needed to achieve the desired ex-post fiscal deficit.

On the basis of these two behavioural hypotheses, the ex-post accounting identity:

(13.2)   Imports − Exports = (Investments−Savings)
                                    + (Public-Expenditure Taxes)

becomes the ex-ante equation:

(13.3)   Trade balance surplus = NAFA + Budget surplus.

Since, because of these behavioural hypotheses, a constant magnitude (NAFA) and an exogenous instrument of economic policy (national budget) stand on the right side of equation (13.3), the underlying causal relationship reads from right to left—i.e. budgetary policy determines the foreign-trade position.

These two hypotheses also provided the basis for the New school's further hypothesis that savings and taxation could be taken *not to be dependent* on

[54] R. Neild, letter to *TT* (26 Feb. 1974).

[55] Id., 'The Case for a Change in Fiscal Policy', *London and Cambridge Economic Bulletin* (July 1973).

[56] N. Kaldor, 'A Neo-Pasinetti Theorem', app. to 'Marginal Productivity and the Macro-Economic Theories of Distribution: Comment on Samuelson and Modigliani', *RES* (Oct. 1966); A. Wood, *A Theory of Profit* (Cambridge, CUP, 1975).

income, and that imports are the only leakage—whereas the orthodox Keynesian school held that, apart from imports, savings, and taxation are also income leakages. For this reason the New school's export multiplier was higher than that of the Old school; and so too, therefore, was the effect on income of a change in the exchange rate and in exports. On the other hand, the effect of devaluation on the trade balance was negligible: the positive effect brought about by a change in relative prices (given elasticities) is no greater than the negative effect of higher imports caused by an increase in income.

The hypotheses of the stability of the function of private-sector expenditure and of the negligible effect of devaluation on the trade balance provided the framework for the New school's 'assignment' of instruments to objectives.[57] To assess the validity of the school's arguments, these two hypotheses were tested empirically. However, as is well known, empirical results depend closely on the structure of the econometric model, on the time-lags that are incorporated into it, and on other factors that may render tests inconclusive. (One notes, though, that for many years the Cambridge Economic Policy Group made forecasts about the British economy, especially about the balance of payments, which were judged over-pessimistic at the time but which later turned out to be the most accurate.) Other critical avenues were therefore explored, and other objections were raised.

The first criticism came from strictly Keynesian economists, for whom it was inadmissable to lump consumption and investments together in one single function of aggregate expenditure, in that this removed what for Keynes had been the principal feature of the capitalist system: the instability of investment. A second objection arose when the model was given a dynamic configuration: which led to the conclusion that if the two instruments were used with suitable intensity, it was possible to achieve the joint internal and external target by manœuvring the instruments, independently of whether the old or the new assignment was followed—although the rapidity and the route by which equilibrium was reached might differ.[58] This, however, did not trivialize the assignment problem.

It was also objected that the New school proposed a policy of exchange rates managed for expansionist ends in such a way that one country would gain its advantage at the expense of others: a beggar-my-neighbour policy that would provoke the retaliation of other countries with similar policies, and nullify its effectiveness.[59]

Another drawback to the New school's model was its fiscal extremism: the monetary aspects of the problem were ignored, so too were different ways of financing the public deficit and the role of the interest rate and capital movements. However, despite this neglect of the role of money and of the interna-

---

[57] Under certain assumptions, it can be shown that in a static context the assignment made by the New school was more efficient than the orthodox assignment, when external leakages of income were greater than internal ones. See D. Vines, 'Economic Policies for an Open Economy'.

[58] G. Gandolfo, *Economia internazionale* (Turin, UTET), ii. 381–8.   [59] Ibid. 351.

tional flow of funds, some of the New school's hypotheses (such as the stability of the private sector and its emphasis on stable time-lags) and certain of its economic policy conclusions (such as the uselessness of devaluation as a remedy for the trade deficit, and its mistrust of short-term discretionary demand policy) were extraordinarily similar to those of the monetary approach to the balance of payments.[60]

But the model's two major limitations—as with the neo-Keynesian models of economic policy in an open economy developed in the 1960s—were its assumptions that wages were stable, that price levels did not depend on exchange-rate changes, and that, consequently, the effect of devaluation on exports could be predicted. Both Kaldor and the DAE at Cambridge soon realized that these assumptions were no longer acceptable—especially in the 1970s—and altered their position accordingly.

13.6. Devaluation, Protection, and Import Controls

The Smithsonian Agreement of December 1971 introduced a general readjustment of official par values. The agreement lasted little more than a year, however, because in early 1973 the new parities were abandoned because of the pressures generated by speculative movements of liquid capital invested at short term. From then onwards exchange rates were free to float without pre-established limits, although they were subject to discretionary official intervention (which varied in degree from country to country and from one period to another). Thereafter exchange rates among the leading industrialized countries underwent profound changes, not only nominally but also in real terms (i.e. after allowing for differences in the changes in labour costs per unit of output expressed in local currency). This situation should have constituted an acid test for the theory that changes in exchange rates equilibrate the balance of payments. But, as Kaldor was quick to point out, 'contrary to the general expectation (changes in the exchange rates) failed to bring about any large change in the relative position of 'surplus' and 'deficit' countries'.[61]

He analysed a period of twenty years (1956–76) to show that there was instead a 'perverse' relationship between changes in a country's 'competitiveness' (measured by the ratio between labour costs per unit of output) and changes in its export 'performance' (measured by the share of world exports of manufactures). Not only was this true up to 1970, it was even more so for the period 1970–6, in spite of the presumed re-equilibrating effect of changes in exchange rates. During this period the United States and the United Kingdom had reduced relative costs *and* had seen a decline in their shares of the

---

[60] J. McCallum and D. Vines, 'Cambridge and Chicago on the Balance of Payments', *EJ* (June 1981).
[61] N. Kaldor, 'The Effects of Devaluation on Trade in Manufactures' (1977), pub. in CP vi. 102.

market; Germany, Japan, and Italy had increased their relative costs *and* their market shares.[62]

These relations convinced Kaldor that

the changes in exchange rates and in 'competitiveness' as conventionally measured were not the cause, but the consequence of differing *trends* in the market share of different industrial countries, and the 'trends' themselves must then be due to factors that are not susceptible to measurement.[63]

Kaldor drew two conclusions from this evidence. First, measures of competitiveness based on export prices and labour costs are not adequate indicators of the competitive position of a country, since export prices are no more than unit values of exported goods. Thus higher prices might mean (and did in Germany, Switzerland, etc.) that goods of higher value added are exported, as goods for growing markets, and the same applies in reverse to lower priced exports. Relative labour costs per unit are also unreliable indicators: these are estimated for the manufacturing sector as a whole, but in the expanding export countries the rate of productivity growth in the export sector is higher than the average rate of productivity growth, whereas in the traditional exporting countries, like the United Kingdom, the rate of productivity growth of exporting industries tends to be equal to the average rate of the entire system.

Kaldor's second conclusion was that, although the instrument of exchange-rate adjustment reduces a country's wages level relative to its competitors, it acts on the *average* value of labour costs per unit of output. A fall in the exchange rate—at a given level of money-wages—has the same effect as a general reduction of real wages. Hence a policy designed to improve competitiveness through devaluation is limited by the extent to which wage-earners will accept a reduction in their real wages.

It should also be borne in mind that if, on the one hand, revaluation worsens a country's competitiveness in terms of relative labour costs, on the other it improves its terms of trade—that is, it makes imports of primary products cheaper, thus rendering the economy less prone to inflation and putting the country on the right road to regular and constant growth. These considerations provide a possible explanation as to why, despite changes in exchange rates, surplus countries tend to remain in surplus and deficit countries to remain in deficit.

From this it follows that

[s]o long as the world continues to be divided amongst sovereign states, each of which regards the interest of its own citizens as its first priority, universal free trade may not

---

[62] In the 20-year period examined by Kaldor the relative costs of the UK and the USA had fallen by 6% and 45% and their market shares had fallen from 19 to 9% and from 25 to 17% respectively. By contrast, the relative costs of Germany, Japan, and Italy had *risen* by 63, 36, and 8% and their market shares had *risen* from 16 to 21%, from 6 to 15%, and from 4 to 7% (ibid. 103). It should be pointed out, however, that Switzerland, Holland, and Canada had shown, albeit to a modest extent, a conventional inverse relation between increasing costs and market share.

[63] Ibid. 104.

be compatible with that objective in the long run any more than in the short run—
whether the world is under a régime of fixed rates or under a régime of floating rates.[64]

Balanced growth in a world of sovereign states therefore requires a system
which prevents the industrial countries that dominate world trade from maintaining a constant trade surplus in their manufacturing sectors and thus growing at the expense of other countries.[65]

The classical and neo-classical principle that free trade brings greater well-
being to all the countries that adopt it was based on two premises that did not
apply to industrial countries: (1) that they had full employment; (2) that
constant returns to scale prevailed in every sector. Failing these two conditions, the trade surplus of one group of industrialized countries entails a
deficit in their industrialized partners which prevents them from pursuing
full-employment policies and from fully exploiting their growth potential. The
positive relation that holds between trade surplus, growth of output and of
productivity is such that disequilibria tend to worsen and become chronic.[66]

Protectionism of the kind that existed before 1914 and between the wars
was not the answer either. On the one hand, there is little doubt that protectionism was much less damaging to certain countries than was generally
admitted—the United Kingdom being a case in point (see Chapter 13.8)—and
this induced Keynes gradually to alter his primitive orthodox position on free
trade.[67] On the other hand, uncontrolled trade restriction penalized small countries, which suffered cutbacks in beneficial trade that more than outweighed
the advantages accruing from the reduction of the trade that endangered their
industrial survival.

The solution proposed by Kaldor was a system that protected competitive
manufacture and guaranteed that

in the trade of manufactured goods between the highly industrialised countries, the
exports of any one country to other members of the group should be fully balanced by
the imports of manufactures of a corresponding value from the countries taken as a
group.[68]

Kaldor's idea of protection linked closely with his macro-economic dynamic
model. He envisaged a policy for an underemployed economy as follows.
Protection must be limited to competitive and not complementary imports of
manufactured goods. The intermediate target is reducing the *propensity to
import* competitive goods, not reducing the volume of such imports. The final

[64] Ibid. 113.

[65] Id., 'The Foundations of Free Trade and Their Implications for the Current World Recession'
(1978), pub. in E. Malinvaud and J. P. Firtoussi (eds.), *Unemployment in Western Countries*
(London, Macmillan, 1980).

[66] Id., 'The Case for Regional Policies' (1970), repr. in CP v; id., 'The Role of Increasing
Returns, Technical Progress and Cumulative Causation in the Theory of International Trade'
(1980), repr. in CP ix.

[67] Id., 'Keynes as an Economic Adviser' (1980), in A. P. Thirlwall (ed.), *Keynes as a Policy
Aviser* (London, Macmillan, 1982).

[68] Id., 'Effects of Devaluation on Trade', 114.

target is raising the rate of growth of the country that is constrained by the high import elasticity (see Chapter 7, sections 6 and 7). Because of the higher rate of growth of productivity and competitiveness entailed by a high rate of growth of output (see Chapter 7.3), the import restriction would act positively on the domestic traded-goods sector, not only by directly encouraging import substitutes, but also indirectly by enabling the manufacturing sector to expand.

Kaldor first gave a broad outline of the technical features that should be possessed by a plan of this kind if it was to function properly. His basic idea was that the manufacturing imports of every country participating in the international arrangement should, at regular intervals, be issued with a licence. These licences would be to a value that was greater (or smaller) than the value of exports of the previous period for the same amount of deficit (or surplus) in the primary products trade balance. If demand for the licences exceeded supply, they could be auctioned off, the price paid for them thus representing the equivalent of a uniform *ad valorem* duty on manufactured imports. The optimal result would be achieved by a subsidy on exports of an amount equal to this duty.

Like the idea that gave rise to the New Cambridge school, this proposal too was taken up and developed by Cambridge's DAE,[69] which very quickly acquired the reputation of being one of the few openly "protectionist" centres of the Western world.[70] Kaldor argued the case for import controls in a series of speeches to the House of Lords. In 1979 he declared:

If we want British industry to reverse its decline then we need a period of protection. It seems to me an absolutely inescapable conclusion, however unpalatable it is.[71]

He held this conviction until his death. In 1985, in fact, again in the House of Lords, he stated,

To get rid of unemployment, all you have to do is to restrict imports to the percentage which would be compatible with an equality of imports and exports at the full employment level.[72]

The supporters of a policy of import controls replied to the objection that it would provoke retaliatory measures from trading partners by pointing out that

[69] W. A. H. Godley and R. M. May, 'The Macroeconomic Implications of Devaluation and Import Restriction', *Economic Policy Review, Department of Applied Economics* (Cambridge, 1977); T. F. Cripps and W. A. H. Godley, 'Control of Imports as a Means to Full Employment and the Expansion of World Trade: The UK's Case', *CJE* (Sept. 1978).

[70] Even though the policy of import controls was designed primarily for countries with deficits in their manufacturing balances, e.g. the UK, and not for countries like Italy with a surplus in manufactures and a deficit in primary and energy products, it nevertheless found a number of supporters in Italy too. M. Pivetti, 'Il controllo delle importazioni nell 'impostazione del Cambridge Economic Policy Group', *Note economiche*, 4 (1978). G. de Vivo and M. Pivetti, 'International Integration and the Balance of Payments Constraint: The Case of Italy', *CJE* (Mar. 1980).

[71] N. Kaldor, *The Economic Consequences of Mrs Thatcher*, (London, Duckworth, 1983), 34 (speech given on 11 July 1979).

[72] Id., 'Social and Economic Policies', *House of Lords Official Report* (speech given on 23 Jan. 1985).

a deflationary policy pursued by a country to re-equilibrate its balance of payments would also reduce its partners' exports. A policy of import controls, therefore, should not be seen as a means to reduce the overall volume of international trade, but rather as an instrument for re-equilibrating the propensity to import of various countries which, once their external constraint has eased, would be in a position to pursue more vigorous growth policies and thereby contribute to a higher growth of world income and international trade. The proposal was put forward by the Cambridge DAE as either a plan for international trade or as a policy for the growth of an individual country.[73]

In either case, it was a policy that involved a high degree of State control and—in the increasingly *laissez-faire* climate of the 1970s and early 1980s— was given a lukewarm reception by international bodies and governments, and even by the reformist, socialist, and worker parties of the industrialized countries. In more recent years, however, the magnitude of the trade imbalance in the United States' manufacturing sector—with respect both to Europe and especially Japan—and the rapid de-industrialization of the American economy seem to have pushed major American political institutions much closer to protectionism than Kaldor could then have foreseen.

13.7. Opposition to the Common Market

The 1970 White Paper on *Britain and the European Communities* argued, in favour of Britain's membership of the Common Market, that the costs to the country of adopting the CAP would, with the opening of a market of more than 300 million people, be more than offset by its beneficial 'dynamic effects' on British industry. Kaldor believed exactly the opposite, and forcefully said so in numerous letters to *The Times*, in speeches, and in a series of articles in the *New Statesman*.[74]

In his view, membership of the Common Market would be doubly damaging to Britain: it would do away with the system of preferences enjoyed by British goods within the Commonwealth, EFTA, and the Republic of Ireland; and the abolition of customs duties on goods from the Common Market would expand the British market of European companies more than it would the European market of British companies.

These costs would be further increased by the CAP, which Kaldor regarded as fundamentally misconceived. He believed that industry should receive customs protection, but that such protection should be abolished in agriculture.

---

[73] In the early 1980s Kaldor was commissioned by the socialist French government to draw up a plan for economic revival. He based his proposals on a scheme similar to the one illustrated here. Id., 'A Plan for Securing Equilibrium in the Balance of Payments under a Policy of Economic Expansion', report to the French Minister of the Budget, 4 Oct. 1982.

[74] Id., 'Europe's Agricultural Disarray' (1970), 'The Dynamic Effects of the Common Market' (1971), 'The Common Market—A Final Assessment' (1971), all repr. in CP vi.

Entry to the Common Market would have produced precisely the reverse of this situation. The CAP has two objectives: guaranteeing self-sufficiency in food, and ensuring uniform prices for agricultural products—a system with enormous drawbacks, according to Kaldor. Barriers on imports of agricultural products set limits not only on the welfare of the countries producing primary products, but also on the welfare of European producers of manufactured goods, in so far as these are imported from Europe by the less developed countries (Kaldor forgot to point out, however, that the country deriving most benefit from the abolition of the CAP would have been the United States).

Moreover, a system where prices for agricultural products are relatively higher than those for manufactured goods has a doubly negative effect. It redistributes income to the disadvantage of poorer wage-earners, who spend a large percentage of their income on food, and it leads to higher labour costs in the manufacturing sector. Kaldor recalled (with obviously provocative intent) that a tariff system of the kind that operated in the Common Market had been first introduced in the United Kingdom, by the Corn Laws, after the Battle of Waterloo, and that it had lasted until 1846. It was precisely in order to persuade his fellow countrymen to abolish these laws that Ricardo had written his *Principles*, the book that was regarded as the fundamental text of modern political economy.

Not only was the CAP responsible for an undesirably high level of prices; it was also responsible for a structure of agricultural prices that militated against the best allocation of labour. Countries with different percentages of their national work-force employed in agriculture and with different labour-opportunity costs (compared with industry) should have different, not uniform, prices for their agricultural products.

The policy would be much more rational if the system of subsidies to agriculture did not consist of supporting agricultural prices by means of import levies, but, instead, consisted of free imports of agricultural products at international prices and with income support for farmers financed out of indirect taxation.[75] The system of income subsidies for farmers that the United Kingdom had used until she joined the Common Market brought long-term benefits to agriculture—if the subsidies were allocated according to a plan for the modernization of the sector's technology and land ownership structure.

In Kaldor's proposed scheme each country's contribution to the programme of transformation would be proportionate to its per-capita income, instead of being based on the absurd criterion of how much the country produced in excess of what could be absorbed by the EEC at its fixed prices. When Kaldor was writing—1970—the greatest burden of the CAP fell on the poorest country (Italy), and contributions were paid by all the member countries 'to ossify agriculture in its present pattern, not to modernize and to transform it'.[76]

---

[75] Higher taxes would not reduce the real income of consumers because they would be applied to the lower prices of foodstuffs.

[76] Kaldor, 'Europe's Agricultural Disarray', 185.

Francis Cripps has often argued that Kaldor was too deeply affected by his experience of the Second World War—waged by the dictatorships of Continental Europe against democratic Britain—to believe in a politically united Europe. This, however, is not the impression that one gains from his writings; nor does it chime with the many psychological, emotional and cultural links that he maintained with the Western European countries and with his native Hungary, or with his admiration for the Austro-German system of industrial relations.

It is true that in 1971 Kaldor opposed the fiscal 'harmonization' of the EEC because it would merely bring an increase in the weight of indirect taxation at the expense of direct taxation. It is also true that he argued that membership of the EEC would entail a loss of autonomy in exchange-rate policy without the benefits of a complete economic and monetary union.[77] Nevertheless, he also wrote:

Some day the nations of Europe may be ready to merge their national identities and create a new European nation—the United States of Europe . . . This will involve the creation of a full economic and monetary union.[78]

With a common government and parliament and a central system of taxation and public expenditure, one would expect the richer areas to help the weaker ones by means of regional and employment policies, but

it is a dangerous error to believe that monetary and economic union can *precede* a political union.[79]

The Common Market did not possess the political mechanisms that would enable it to become a single market of a single state or a real federation of states. Despite the proliferation of 'an enormous bureaucracy and a common parliament, with large expense accounts but with very limited powers',[80] Europe was not an effectively integrated economy; it was only a customs union, the effects of which, Kaldor believed, were damaging to Britain's industry.

13.8. The De-Industrialization of the United Kingdom and the Critique of the Thatcher Government

Ten years after Britain joined the Common Market, Kaldor repeated to the House of Lords the views he had expressed in 1971, the year when the country had joined the EEC.

---

[77] It should also be pointed out that in 1985, after the revaluation of sterling, he argued that the UK should join the EMS. Membership of the the EMS would have restricted the revaluation of the pound and forced the British monetary authorities to intervene directly on the exchange rate rather than on the money supply (N. Kaldor, 'Advantages of EMS Membership', mimeo, Cambridge, 1985).

[78] Id., 'Dynamic Effects of the Common Market', 206.   [79] Ibid.

[80] Id., 'The EEC Internal Market', *House of Lords Official Report* (speech given on 13 Dec. 1982).

Nothing which has happened since 1971 has made me change my mind. It was a disastrous decision from the point of view of the future of Britain . . . In manufacturing industry, the link with the EEC—aggravated no doubt by our own economic policies— has accelerated the de-industrialization of Britain . . . A study of the figures leaves one with no doubt that joining the EEC had negative dynamic effects on the British economy; it had dynamic effects but they were of the wrong kind.[81]

Free trade and misguided economic policies were therefore, he believed, responsible if not for the trend, at least for the acceleration of the country's decline[82] and de-industrialization.[83]

Free trade had been advantageous to the interests of British manufacturing industry when it had led to the abolition of the tariff barriers on corn midway through the nineteenth century. The country had benefited, even to an extra-ordinary extent, from free trade as long as British industry stood alone in the world. But from the 1870s onwards, Kaldor argued, with the protected indus-trialization of a number of European countries, and above all of Germany, Britain's commitment to free trade—which was total after Asquith's Liberal victory in 1906 and lasted until World War I—did grave damage to the economic interests of the country.[84] The decline of British manufacturing industry 'began in 1885. Since then our share of world trade has been dimin-ishing at a constant geometric rate.'[85]

Between the wars the trend went temporarily into reverse. In Kaldor's last work he argued that between 1932 and 1939 industrial output in the United Kingdom had increased more than at any other period (+ 50 per cent), not because wages dropped (there had been sharper downturns in other periods), nor because of the boom in the building industry (in so far as the really high growth was in the manufacturing sector), nor because of the devaluation of 1931 (which did no more than restore to the country the competitiveness it had lost by returning to the Gold Standard in the 1920s)—but because of import restrictions. Hence it followed that the propensity to import could be curtailed by allowing Harrod's multiplier to generate a sustained growth of income.[86]

[81] Ibid.

[82] M. Fetherston *et al.* (in *CJE* (Dec. 1979)) show that until 1971 the UK's manufacturing trade generally broke even with the 6 countries that originally formed the EEC and was in surplus against the rest of the world. After 1972 (the year the country joined the EEC) the trade balance of the manufacturing sector stayed in surplus against the rest of the world and went into deficit against the EEC (esp. against Germany)—and the deficit increased year by year.

[83] He once told me that he coined the term 'de-industrialization' in a lecture, and was astonished by its subsequent success. On de-industrialization see A. Singh, 'UK Industries and the World Economy: A Case of Deindustrialization?', *CJE* (June 1977); S. Brittan, 'De-Industrialization Revisited', *Financial Times* (26 Jan. 1977); F. Blackaby (ed.), *De-Industrialization* (London, Heinemann, 1979), in which see Kaldor, 'What is De-Industrialization?', and A. Cairncross, 'What is De-Industrialization'; and A. P. Thirlwall, 'De-Industrialization in United Kingdom', *LLBR* (Apr. 1982).

[84] N. Kaldor, 'The Nemesis of Free Trade' (1977), pub. in CP vi.

[85] Id., 'Causes of Unemployment', *House of Lords Official Report* (speech given on 12 Dec. 1984).

[86] Kaldor did not have time to publish this research (funded by ESRC), which he undertook

The matter has been debated from various points of view. Several economic historians have denied that tariffs had a positive impact on economic growth.[87] Others, rather than focus on the substitution effect of tariffs, have viewed them as a macro-economic policy instrument à la Kaldor and drawn the opposite conclusion.[88] An extremely convincing thesis has recently been put forward by Kitson and Solomou (the former of whom assisted Kaldor in his last research project). They show that tariffs were a major source of economic revival in the 1930s, although other factors were important. However,

they may have actually prevented the necessary structural change that could have benefited long term economic growth in the 1950-75 boom. Nevertheless in the unco-ordinated economic environment of the 1930s tariffs were successful in achieving a period of adjustment and pushing the British inter-war economy on to a higher long-term growth path.[89]

After the war Britain was in external equilibrium until 1954 because the deficit in food and raw materials was offset by the surplus in manufactured goods. After that date, however, as a result of the lifting of trade restrictions, the situation seriously deteriorated. In the thirty years between 1954 and 1984 imports of manufactured goods increased twelve times, although there was only a threefold increase in exports. Import penetration—that is, the share of imported goods in final domestic demand—rose from 5 per cent to 33 per cent (in 1983), while the world market share of English manufactures dropped from 20 per cent to 7 per cent. In the same period, other industrialized countries— France, Germany, Italy, and Japan (but not the United States)—increased their shares of world trade.

The decline of British industry was not only the responsibility of trade policy; it was also the fault of the City.

[The] existence of the City of London, the supremacy of financial capitalism . . . have had a deleterious effect on our industrial development. It has certainly increased the attractions and the facility of foreign investment against home investment.[90]

Nor should we ignore a further factor, which Kaldor repeatedly blamed for many of British industry's difficulties: the poor quality of the country's business leadership. Numerous British economic historians (Kaldor cited Aldcroft

with M. Kitson. It exists, however, as a mimeo entitled 'The Impact of Import Restrictions in the Interwar Period' in the Marshall library of the economics faculty at Cambridge.

[87] H. W. Richardson, *Economic Recovery in Britain, 1932–1939* (London, Weidenfeld and Nicolson, 1967); F. Capie, 'The British Tariffs and Industrial Protection in the 1930s', *Economic History Review*, 31 (1978).

[88] J. S. Foreman Peck, 'The British Tariffs and Industrial Protection in the 1930s: An Alternative Model', *Economic History Review*, 34 (1981); S. J. Eichengreen 'A Dynamic Model of Tariffs, Output and Employment under Flexible Exchange Rates', *Journal of International Economics*, (1981).

[89] M. Kitson and S. Solomou, 'The Macroeconomics of Protectionism: The Case of Britain in the 1930s', *CJE* (Mar. 1989), 167.

[90] Kaldor, *Economic Consequences of Mrs Thatcher*, 73 (speech given on 4 Feb. 1981).

and Gowing) have shown that since the 1880s the unsatisfactory performance of the British entrepreneur has been due to 'his prejudices against education, against anyone who had a university degree and against the introduction of new methods, new techniques, or entry into new fields'.[91] In Kaldor's view, even in the 1980s the system of management selection adopted by British business was still archaic, and greatly inferior to the practices of other countries—for example, Germany, where selection depends

entirely on criteria of efficiency and ability, and they (the members of the supervisory board) are people who are experts in the matter of selection. Professors of chemical engineering become heads of the biggest chemical concerns. That has always been the German tradition. In Britain the expert ends up as the best backroom boy. He is not in the administrative class, but only in the executive class, which is a rank below it.[92]

The decline in British industry had therefore been going on for over a hundred years and could be attributed to structural causes—although it had been accelerated in periods of free trade and by Britain's entry into the EEC. However, from 1979 onwards an added factor hastened its collapse: the economic policy of the Conservative Government. 'Clearly, Mrs Thatcher's Government cannot be held responsible for all this. She is responsible only for telescoping into a few years what otherwise might have taken some decades.'[93]

In its first two years the Government imposed a swingeing monetarist policy. Manufacturing output dropped by 17 per cent and unemployment rose by 1.3 million: the worst figures ever recorded by a nation with the sole exception of the United States in the two years after 1929.[94] Although after 1981 the government would quietly abandon its rigid monetarist position, in 1986 British industrial output was still 6 per cent lower than in 1979 and the economy grew at a yearly rate of 0.8 per cent: the lowest rate ever experienced in any seven-year period of the country's history. Nor was this offset by the greater per-capita output in manufacturing industry that had been so loudly acclaimed. During the five years of the first Thatcher government, productivity in the sector grew by 6 per cent—as compared to the 22 per cent in the five years before 1979.

Chiefly to blame for this accelerating de-industrialization was the government's restrictive monetary policy, combined with an artificially high value of sterling despite a growing surplus in the energy balance. 'It was a national misfortune that Mrs Thatcher and North Sea oil came on stream more or less at the same time.'[95] Although the process had in actual fact begun in October 1977, the overvaluation of the pound was accelerated by the government's monetary policy. During Thatcher's first two years in power the money

---

[91] Ibid. 32 (speech given on 11 July 1979).   [92] Ibid. 33.
[93] Ibid. (speech given on 10 Nov. 1982).
[94] Id., 'Economic Situation', *House of Lords Official Report*, (speech given on 19 Feb. 1986).
[95] Id., 'Oil and the Decline of Manufacturing', *House of Lords Official Report* (speech given on 29 June 1983).

squeeze and the revaluation of the exchange rate led to a 60 per cent overvaluation of the pound. It was for this reason that Kaldor confidently predicted
that 1980 'will be the first year in British history when Britain becomes a net
importer of manufactured goods'.[96]

Exploitation of the North Sea oilfields began in the 1970s. In 1980 Britain
became self-sufficient in her energy requirements; she subsequently became
a net exporter and in 1986 became the fifth largest oil-producing country in
the world. However, far from generating wealth, this good fortune provoked
further de-industrialization, via a mechanism that Holland had known ever
since she had become a net exporter of natural gas in 1965—a mechanism that
carried the name of the 'Dutch disease'.

As with petrol, the extraction of natural gas generates a negligible multiplier
of income and employment. Therefore, although it is the source of currency
earnings, it is not a stimulus to manufacturing production. The consequent
high trade surplus arises from the revaluation of the currency and from the
loss of competitiveness by the country's manufacturing industry. In the Dutch
case, the effects on industry were very serious indeed: in less than twenty years
the country suffered a 30 per cent drop in industrial employment.

But this has not been an inevitable consequence for every oil- and gas-pro-
ducing country. Norway, too, extracts oil from the North Sea, but as a country
run on Keynesian principles of macro-economic control and not on Thatcherian
principles of a free market, it has not been afflicted with the Dutch disease.
In fact

thanks to a devaluation of the kroner (which the Government carried out in the face
of a strong balance of payments . . .) and to its subsequent maintenance at a low level
in relation to costs through extensive market intervention by the Norwegian Central
Bank, in Norway manufacturing output and employment were maintained. Now Norway is the country with the lowest unemployment in Europe if not in the whole world
at 2 per cent.[97]

This, however, was not the policy of the British government, because the
country was led by a 'government of share-holders'. Kaldor concluded his last
speech to the House of Lords thus:

We should concentrate our efforts on reviving our manufacturing base . . . instead of
using the oil money for foreign investment of very dubious benefit to the country. We
now have 70 billions of foreign investment—50 millions more than before—but in
terms of remitted income, the benefit to the balance of payments is rather meagre. The
policy of Mrs Thatcher's Government meant that British industry derives *no* benefit
from the oil bonanza—the benefit such as it went to the big investors in the City.[98]

In actual fact, Kaldor believed, Thatcherism's disastrous effects on Britain's
economy and industry had been deliberately provoked. Their real purpose was
to redress the balance of power between workers and capitalists using mon-

---

[96] Id., *Economic Consequences of Mrs Thatcher*, 46–7 (speech given on 13 Feb. 1980).
[97] Ibid. 94–5 (speech given on 3 Feb. 1982).   [98] Id., 'Economic Situation'.

etary stability as an excuse. He was reminded of the words of Tacitus, who wrote of the Roman conquest of Britain, 'Ubi solitudinem faciunt pacem appellant.' This he translated as: 'They create a desert and call it stability.'[99]

[99] Id., *Economic Consequences of Mrs Thatcher*, 114 (speech given on 10 Nov. 1982).

Chapter 14

The Criticism of Equilibrium Theory and New Theoretical Hypotheses on Growth and the Distribution of Income

> The difficulty lies, not in the new ideas, but in escaping from
> the old ones, which ramify, for those brought up as most of us
> have been, into every corner of our minds.
>
> J. M. Keynes, *The General Theory*

14.1. The Criticism of Equilibrium Theory

In the 1970s Kaldor's thought came to the end of a long process of evolution that had begun in the 1930s with his membership—albeit only for a few years—of the Austrian school and his endorsement of the deductive method of neo-classical equilibrium. In his 'The Irrelevance of Equilibrium Economics',[1] Kaldor denounced neo-classical equilibrium theory as an intellectual exercise condemned to infinite regression because it was incapable of becoming a scientific theory—meaning by that term a set of theorems derived from observable phenomena. From Walras to Debreu the theory had been constantly reworked; but because the problem of its verification had been ignored, rather than remove the theory's scaffolding of unreal basic assumptions, this constant elaboration had only made it thicker and more impenetrable. And if abstract mathematical models were empirically barren, so too, Kaldor believed, was econometrics: sophisticated methods of statistical inference could not fill the void created by the absence of any theory on how the economy really works.

Walrasian equilibrium theory entailed hypotheses (like the 'convexity of sets') which, when related to the world of production, must be rejected. Very few productive processes occur at constant returns: in most cases they are at increasing returns in the manufacturing sector and decreasing returns in the primary sector. Then there are those of the theory's axioms which, although non-tautological, are not available to empirical verification; for example, the axiom that the action of all agents is guided solely by the principle of 'optimization'. Finally, equilibrium theory was based on the postulate that all prices are given parametrically to all agents and that prices are the sole source of

---

[1] Id., 'The Irrelevance of Equilibrium Economics' (1972), repr. in CP v.

information:[2] economic agents are price-takers and quantity-makers. The price signal is therefore prior to quantity adjustment; but how the process that leads to price equilibrium actually takes place had, for Kaldor, never been adequately explained.

Kaldor instead maintained that three other principles operate in industrial systems. First of all, there is a resources-allocation mechanism which works through variations in quantity rather than in prices. This principle, called 'the stock adjustment principle',[3] expresses the idea that supply adjusts to demand, not through price variations, but through changes in stock which act as the allocative signals of the market.[4] It is in the interest of producers to satisfy their customers and thereby satisfy demand. But in order to operate efficiently they have to keep their stocks at normal levels—except when stocks are subject to temporary oscillations—and they do this in the short term by stepping up production and in the medium term by increasing their investments. Neither of these adjustments is constrained by non-natural resources (capital and labour) because in the capitalist system demand for resources constantly falls short of their actual or potential availability.

Secondly, business does not take place in conditions of 'anonymity' with economic agents buying and selling in several markets at once, as equilibrium theory would have it. In the real world producers and consumers establish business connections (the 'goodwill' of a company), and it is these that constitute the true substance of business.

Finally, the major weakness of general equilibrium theory was its assumptions of constant returns to scale and perfect divisibility. These two postulates ignore Adam Smith's great discovery of co-operation among producers and the division of labour as the engine of capitalist systems. Kaldor continued a line of thought that had originated with Adam Smith and Allyn Young in arguing that, once increasing returns are introduced, the forces that produce change and development become endogenous—engendered from within the economic system. The division of labour is limited by the size of the market; but the size of the market is not a feature exogenous to the system of producers. This interrelation was, Kaldor believed, well illustrated by his technical-progress function and 'his' stylized fact that the capital/output ratio is stable in both dynamic and static economies and in both rich and poor countries. It is large-scale production (made possible by broader markets) that brings high profits, generates accumulation, and thus creates an increase in capital per worker which, by keeping pace with the increase in labour productivity, gives rise to the constancy of the capital/output ratio.

---

[2] Id., 'The Futility of General Equilibrium Theory', lecture given at Harvard, 28 Oct. 1983, mimeo.

[3] J. Kornai, *The Economics of Shortage* (Amsterdam, North Holland Publishing Co., 1981).

[4] See also N. Kaldor, *Economics without Equilibrium* (1983, pub. New York, M. E. Sharpe, 1985), chs. 1, 2.

Although the operation of increasing returns is restricted to the manufacturing sector of the economy, it entails the abandonment of such concepts as equilibrium or equilibrium path. 'There is no inherent tendency to anything that could be called equilibrium, or an equilibrium path. The state of the economy at any one point of time cannot be "predicted" except as a result of the sequence of events which led up to it':[5] every step was made possible by the step that preceded it. Equilibrium theory, by contrast, held that given exogenous variables were immutable in time and that the point of arrival of the movement of prices and production could only be deduced if these given quantities were known.

Two of Kaldor's above principles have radically affected the concept of what economic science is supposed to be. The first principle (which can be treated as deriving from a Younghian dynamization of Keynes) is a consequence of dynamic increasing returns to scale, and states that 'every reorganization of production activities creates the opportunity for further change *which would not have existed otherwise*'.[6] The second is that in an industrial economy where the main factor of production, capital goods, is itself produced, 'except in a purely short term sense, total output can never be *confined* by resources'[7] (as we saw in Chapter 8.4, natural resources are the only *potential* limit to growth). These principles represent the economy as an ever-expanding production set, from which it follows that 'the whole view of the economic process for the "allocation of scarce means between alternative uses" falls apart—except perhaps for the consideration of short-run problems'[8] where the endowment of resources and their distribution may be taken as given and as a legacy of the past, and where the effects of current decisions on future development are ignored.[9]

14.2. New Hypotheses for a Model of Growth and Distribution

After his growth models of the 1950s and 1960s (see Chapter 5) Kaldor's ideas continued to change and develop, though he never managed to arrange them into a fully coherent model. As he wrote shortly before his death:

---

[5] Id., 'Futility of General Equilibrium Theory', 15. Kaldor's argument closely resembles Joan Robinson's criticism of analysis in terms of equilibrium: that economic science could only progress by replacing analysis of logical time with analysis of historical time. J. V. Robinson, *Economic Heresies* (London, Macmillan, 1971); ead., *History versus Equilibrium* (London, Thames Polytechnic, 1974).

[6] Kaldor, 'Irrelevance of Equilibrium Economics', 187, Kaldor's emphasis.

[7] Ibid. 194, Kaldor's emphasis.   [8] Ibid. 187–8.

[9] On this trenchant criticism of economic science, one of Kaldor's most able adversaries, Frank Hahn, wrote: 'It is not surprising that these assertions have not found wide acceptance. Such a radical departure from traditional views requires a very great deal of argument and evidence. Kaldor produced neither, which, however does not mean that his vision was false in its essential.' F. Hahn, 'Kaldor on Growth', *CJE* (Mar. 1989), 49.

[T]he development of my theoretical ideas has by no means come to an end with the work on growth models. Since 1965 they have changed fairly drastically, though I have not been able to present the results (though perhaps I might still be able to do so in the future) in the comprehensive form of a 'model'.[10]

Kaldor's growth models of the 1950s and 1960s were grounded on three hypotheses—(1) the existence of only one sector (industry), which was treated as a homogeneous whole, (2) free competition, and (3) full employment—all three of which he subsequently abandoned as unrealistic.

Kaldor made four major changes to his theory so that it might more closely reflect the characteristics of a modern industrial system. First he introduced the hypothesis of firms of different technological structure within the same industry. Secondly he drew a distinction within this industry between leader-firms and follower-firms. Thirdly he introduced increasing returns to scale in the industrial sector. Fourthly he divided the economic system into two sectors, each with a different form of market and with different returns to scale. This last of Kaldor's modifications to his theory was analysed in Chapter 8; the other three will be examined below.

14.3. Firms with Different Technologies, the Differential Theory of Profit, and Okun's Law

Kaldor's first change to his model, then, concerned the internal technological structure of industry. He pointed out that within a particular industry there is always a large difference between per-capita output and the unit costs of individual firms.[11] Since the differences in the wages per worker paid by these firms are slight (they seldom amount to more than 10 per cent), it follows that there are considerable differences in their share of profits in value added[12]— because there is, roughly speaking, one single price within the industry. In fact, less efficient firms are willing to accept lower profit margins rather than lose the customers that they have made long-term investments to acquire.

The causes of this new 'stylized fact'—the permanence in time of firms with different productivity levels within the same industry—may be several. The first explanation of these differences was advanced by Hanns Joachim Rüs-

---

[10] N. Kaldor, 'Recollections of an Economist' (1986), repr. in CP ix. 31.

[11] Kaldor reported that an unpublished study by National Economic Development Office on British Industrial Structure, prepared by F. G. Brechling and R. G. Lipsey in 1963, showed that in 22 industrial groupings the average ratio between the 10% of firms with the highest value of output per worker and the 10% of firms with the lowest value was 4 to 1.

[12] On the basis of figures from the British Census of Production, Kaldor calculated that there was a 20 to 80% variation among 'establishments' (factory buildings with the same address) in the same branch of industry. The figures on firms (compiled by the Inland Revenue) showed that the top 10% of firms had margins of profit over value added amounting to 50%, while the bottom 10% had margins of 15%. *Economics without Equilibrium*, 43.

tow,[13] who attributed them to embodied technical progress and to the yearly renewal of only a part of capital stock. Kaldor rejected this explanation. A firm need only spread its investments over time in such a way that the average age of its equipment reflects the average age of the industry to be able to operate at average costs and with average profits. Leibenstein attributed the differences to managerial efficiency; an explanation that Kaldor dismissed as inadequate, because with differences of such magnitude less efficient managers would eventually lose their jobs.[14] Therefore either the phenomenon was the result of accidental factors or it still had not been explained properly.

Whatever the explanation, the fact remains that at every moment, in every industry, there are firms with different levels of efficiency. And this, according to Kaldor, was to be evaluated in terms of another stylized fact, generally known as Okun's law and according to which a 1 per cent increase in employment is associated with a 2 per cent increase in output. Average productivity is therefore an increasing function of employment. This, however, was at variance with Rüstow's differential theory of profit shares (see Chapter 5.3) which Kaldor largely agreed with. According to Rüstow, as demand and employment increase less efficient firms (plant?) are used. Hence average productivity is a decreasing function of employment.

Kaldor believed that the two positions could be reconciled only by discarding the assumption that the distribution of inputs takes place through the use of the best equipment available; and by assuming instead that under conditions of imperfect competition the market reacts differently to gradual or abrupt variations in demand. During the recession phase of a normal business cycle, *all* firms suffer from a drop in demand, and the reduction in capacity utilization is distributed more or less equally. During the recovery phase, however, productivity increases, because the rise in output and the fall in average unit cost is divided among all firms and is no longer concentrated among marginal firms. Okun's law therefore holds. But should there be a severe contraction of income, the least efficient establishments or firms are put permanently out of production. Here Rüstow's differential theory applies.

There still remains the difficulty, however, that acceptance of Rüstow's differential theory of profit shares entails the acceptance of a necessarily positive relation between demand and price levels. This necessity Kaldor rejected unless the relation was deducible from the behaviour of the leader-firm.

---

[13] H. J. Rüstow, 'The Development of the Share of Wages and Profits in an Industrial Society', *German Economic Review*, 5: 2 (1967).

[14] N. Kaldor, 'Gemeinsamkeiten und Unterschiede in den Theorien von Keynes, Kalecki und Rüstow' (1980), pub. in *IST* 29: 1 (1983). Further explanation of this phenomenon in terms of internal managerial economies or diseconomies of scale is given in R. Marris and D. C. Mueller, 'The Corporation, Competition and the Invisible Hand', *Journal of Economic Literature* (Mar. 1980), repr. in D. C. Mueller, *The Modern Corporation* (Brighton, Wheatsheaf Books, 1986), 271.

14.4. Price Formation and the Stability of Growth

In Kaldor's growth and stability models of the 1950s and 1960s the distribution mechanism performed the dual task of securing both the existence and the stability of the equilibrium growth rate. Bearing in mind the lengthy discussion of Chapter 5, two conditions must hold in Kaldor's steady-state equilibrium: productive capacity (fully utilized) must grow at the same rate as income ('knife-edge' stability), and it must grow at the same rate as labour supply ('natural growth'). Failure of the first condition will create (depending on the disequality) Keynesian unemployment or Keynesian inflation; failure of the second will create classical unemployment or Phillips's inflation (leaving aside the case of the constraint on the increase in domestic prices given by external competitiveness, where growth of capacity higher than growth of labour supply leads to an increase in the share of wages à la Marx–Goodwin).

In my view, Kaldor's distribution mechanism was unable to guarantee the stability of natural equilibrium. Let us suppose a steady-state growth equilibrium with capacity and labour fully utilized, and that at point t in time the growth of labour supply increases by x per cent. Although there will be disequilibrium in the labour-market, this does not induce, in a Keynesian model, any action by firms or a fall in the wage rate. On the other hand, the commodity market will remain in equilibrium. Of course, one can always *impose* that capacity will grow at the same rate as labour supply à la Pasinetti, but in this case (as Pasinetti has rightly pointed out on several occasions) the model represents a 'natural economy' from which the real economy may diverge.

Kaldor believed that his model was, by contrast, a behavioural model able to explain the stylized facts of Western capitalism. From this point of view, full employment was, as Kaldor later admitted, a 'silly assumption'.

Moreover, in Kaldor's model the distribution of income is the means by which capacity is kept fully utilized. As we know, this task is performed by prices and therefore profit margins—variations in response to a higher or lower rate of growth of demand in relation to the growth of capacity.

Flexibility of the price level in both directions in response to high or low pressure from aggregate demand entailed a firm operating on the commodity market like the Marshallian representative firm, and this is at variance with Kaldor's ideas on firms' behaviour in modern capitalist economies. In fact, over the twenty-four years that followed the publication of his last model of growth (1962) Kaldor changed his mind on the relation between price and aggregate demand. He proposed various elements of micro-economic theory which were closer to reality as far as firms' pricing behaviour was concerned, but he never provided a model in which this behaviour was made consistent with his distribution theory.

In oligopolistic economies, prices do not depend on demand, nor does demand depend on prices: demand depends on income and prices on costs.

However, Kaldor was aware that once this general frame of reference has been established, several questions concerning the functioning of the system still need answering. First, although firms operate in an imperfect market where customer relationships are extremely important, their freedom to fix their prices is restricted by the behaviour of the other firms in the same industry. It is true that it is the level of income and income per capita that determines aggregate expenditure and its distribution across macro-sectors (according to Engel's law); but it is equally true that within a particular sector demand tends to gravitate towards the firm that offers the lowest price.

Any statement that prices are determined by costs is an over-simplification. Although it may be meaningful as regards the *dynamics* of prices, it is meaningless as regards the *level* of the price that a firm may, at any particular moment, decide to establish by marking up its costs, because it does not indicate where the mark-up comes from. The device of the 'kinked' curve[15] can explain why prices and mark-ups are rigid, but it cannot explain why prices are at the level they are in relation to costs. To explain the price, and therefore the position of the kink, one must posit the existence of a firm (or a group of firms) that assumes the role of leader. This price-making 'representative firm' is not necessarily the most efficient or the least efficient one: it is simply the firm that, in collusion with the others or independently, 'sets the price' that they adopt.[16]

Setting the price means fixing the mark-up. Kaldor rejected Lerner and Kalecki's idea that this was given by $e/(e-1)$, where e stands for the point-elasticity of the (unkinked) demand curve. He did so for two reasons. First a firm is ignorant of its own demand curve, the existence of which presupposes that the prices of other firms are either given or identical with that of the price-making firm. Second the firm, under dynamic conditions, maximizes, not its current profit, but the rate of growth of its profits.

To maximize its growth rate (of output and therefore of profits), a firm must pursue two contrasting objectives. First, it must choose a mark-up that is sufficiently low for it to be able to maintain or expand its share of the market. If this is a leader-firm, it should be thought of as seeking to achieve the 'structure of market shares among firms' that it desires—which comes close to Sylos Labini's limit-pricing theory based on threat of entry.[17] The firm's second objective is deciding on a mark-up that is high enough to maximize the growth of its capital stock with as little recourse as possible to outside

[15] P. Sweezy 'Demand under Conditions of Oligopoly', *JPE* (1939), 563–73.

[16] Kaldor pointed out the existence over the last 50 years of a surprisingly uniform pattern—another 'stylized fact'—which was certainly connected with the idea of the leader-firm but which had not yet been given adequate explanation: the concentration into three large firms of the great majority of total sales (70 to 80% of the total), while the remainder was produced and sold by a large number, even 100s, of small firms. The pattern emerged in both large countries and small—irrespective, that is, of the absolute sizes of their markets. Kaldor, *Economics without Equilibrium*, 53.

[17] P. Sylos Labini, *Oligopoly and Technical Progress* (1956; Cambridge Mass., Harvard University Press, 1969).

Criticism of Equilibrium Theory

financing. Excessive use of external borrowing, in fact, weakens the financial structure of the firm and exposes it to the increasing risk of dependence on the financial decisions of banks (Kalecki and Minsky's notion of increasing risk) or to the risk of takeover bids. In Kaldor's view, this explained another British stylized fact: that firms tend to increase their dividends in line with earnings.

Therefore, the decisive factor in the leader-firm's mark-up decision is its desire to increase its stock of capital from internal sources without losing its share of the market. We saw in Chapter 6.4 that Kaldor used the oligopolist behaviour of firms to develop a distribution theory in which the profit rate depends on the propensity of firms to reinvest their profits, on their policy on equity issues, but also on the system's rate of growth. This latter was taken exogenously and not as an argument of the pricing-policy function of the firm itself. In subsequent development of his thought, the rate of growth and the rate of profit were two unknowns, simultaneously determined by an integrated system of two equations.[18]

However, even in this context, one may legitimately raise Harrod's instability problem. The price (and profit-margins) flexibility in Kaldor's 1950s model gave stability to the system—that is to say, it provided the adjustment mechanism which equalized the growth rate of demand to the growth rate of capacity. By rejecting the hypothesis of a free competitive market in favour of a non-competitive setting, Kaldor had to provide an alternative adjusting mechanism if his distribution theory was still to be valid. A possible solution (for the problem of having higher profit margins when capacity is over-utilized) could be that firms behave as a collusive oligopoly and that they tend to collude more in booms and less in slumps.[19] However, this behaviour cannot be assessed once and for all on a priori grounds, and the theory of co-operative games makes no direct predictions of this kind.[20] Moreover, in Kaldor's 1950s' models a rate of growth of demand higher than the growth rate of capacity induces a higher saving propensity, and this reduces the expansionist effects of the multiplier. In the non-competitive setting, an increase in collusion and in the price level relative to given wages increases profit margins; but, because higher profit margins cannot induce firms to increase their propensity to invest (in which case the model would be unstable), they must induce firms to reduce the issue of new equities to finance their capital accumulation. This, however, will increase the 'valuation ratio', and it is not clear how this outcome can reduce the multiplier and the growth of demand.

The theory of growth and distribution based on oligopolistic firm behaviour is still a fertile ground for further research.

[18] This approach has been developed in A. Wood, *A Theory of Profit* (Cambridge, CUP, 1975). The 2 equations are formalized in Ch. 3.4.

[19] This argument has been developed, in a different context, by J. Stiglitz, 'Price Rigidities and Market Structures', *AER Papers and Proceedings*, (1984).

[20] R. Marris, *Reconstructing Keynesian Economics with Imperfect Competition* (Aldershot, Elgar, 1991), 150.

14.5. Returns and Employment

The last alteration that Kaldor made to his models of the 1950s and 1960s was his controversial assumption of the full-employment hypothesis. Over the years he never changed his view that a model should refer to full employment if it comprises (1) one sector, (2) with constant returns to scale, (3) with induced investment. But in the last version of his economic-growth model the hypotheses of a single sector and of constant returns to scale were abandoned.

It is well known that Keynes formulated his theory of underemployment equilibrium in the decade that saw development of the theory of monopolistic competition. Only a handful of economists[21] have tried to reconcile these two theoretical constructs; mainstream theory has always kept them separate. In recent years M. L. Weitzman has revived an article written by Kaldor in 1935[22] (see Chapter 1.3) as part of a non-Keynesian interpretation of underemployment equilibrium, which was an area which Kaldor himself thought well worth investigating.

Weitzman writes that he cannot see why the existence of money savings investment and international trade should *per se* invalidate the basic proposition that the logical consequence of constant returns to scale and perfect competition is full employment.

With a sufficient divisibility of production . . . the unemployed are induced to create, on a level of scale proper to them, the exact replica of the economy in full employment from which they have been excluded.[23]

---

[21] One economist who made an attempt (subsequently abandoned) was R. Kahn. See R. Kahn, *L'economia del breve periodo* (Turin, Boringhieri, 1983), introd. by M. Dardi. Kalecki returned to the subject repeatedly and with great originality of insight throughout his scientific career. A seminal model though at an early stage of elaboration which connects the theory of market forms and the theory of activity level is to be found in his review of the General Theory. See F. Targetti and B. Kinda-Hass, 'Kalecki's Review of Keynes's *General Theory*', *Australian Economic Papers* (Dec. 1982). Kaldor wrote 'Kalecki's original model of unemployment equilibrium (read at the Leyden meeting of the Econometric Society in 1933 and published in *ECTR* in 1935) which takes monopolistic competition as its starting-point, is clearly superior to Keynes's. I heard Kalecki's exposition at Leyden but it was not until Keynes published his *General Theory* that I understood the notion of effective demand' ('Keynesian Economics after Fifty Years', in D. Worswick and J. Trevithick (eds.), *Keynes and the Modern World* ed. (Cambridge, CUP, 1983), 15 n., repr. in CP ix. 57 n. 27). A great deal has been written on the micro-foundation of macro-economics over the last 20 years. Several authors have tried to give a general equilibrium micro-foundation to a macro-economic model with Keynesian features—i.e. with stable unemployment. Some have based the macro-Keynesian model on imperfect competition foundations: outstandingly, Nikaido, Negishi, Ng, Benassy, Hart, Snower, Solow, Dixon, Blanchard, and Kiyotaki, as well as many others. The most recent attempt both to produce a (simulation) model and to re-examine much of the history of Keynesian economics in the light of imperfect competition is Marris, *Reconstructing Keynesian Economics* (Aldershot, Elgar, 1991).

[22] N. Kaldor, 'Market Imperfection and Excess Capacity' (1935), repr. in CP i.

[23] M. L. Weitzman, 'Increasing Returns of the Foundations of Unemployment Theory', *EJ* (Dec. 1982), 793.

The infinite divisibility of all the factors—Kaldor had argued in 1935—and their consequent constant returns to scale are a sufficient condition for the free play of economic forces to lead to perfect competition, and no degree of product differentiation can prevent this outcome. In the 1980s—perhaps flattered by the American resurrection of his 1935 article—Kaldor even went so far as to declare that he should have added that, under conditions of the infinite divisibility of all the factors,

the free play of economic forces will necessarily also establish (and maintain) a state of full employment. Unfortunately [the 1935 article] was published a year before the appearance of the *General Theory* and the notion of a macro-economic 'underemployment equilibrium' was unknown.[24]

It is in fact an exaggeration to claim that, in the case of constant returns to scale, the free play of market forces lead inevitably to full employment: even in these circumstances, a worsening in the Keynesian conditions of 'confidence' in the future may lead to a drop in demand, income and employment. This does not, however, rule out the possibility that the presence of increasing returns may be a cause of unemployment in addition to Keynes's and may be a valid explanation for the *persistence* of unemployment in a growing economy.

In Kaldor's view, for the system to be in underemployment equilibrium it is only necessary for *some* sectors of the economy to conform to increasing returns, with firms *making* the price while the others are price-takers with a production equilibrium at which price is equal to marginal cost. In this case, even if there are sectors at non-increasing returns, should demand for their products be determined by incomes earned in the rest of the economy, and should there be, in aggregate, sufficient pressure for a balanced and simultaneous expansion of all markets, the economy will behave as if increasing returns are in operation throughout the entire system.

This argument has an important corollary. In a system at increasing returns, the direct relation between real wages and employment tends to render the ordinary mechanism of wage adjustment ineffective and unstable. This serves to buttress Keynes's argument, which he restricted to money-wages.[25]

Kaldor's rejection of the inverse relation between the trend of real wages and employment (and income) is at odds with the explanation advanced for the stagflation of the 1970s and 1980s in terms of over-high real wages;[26] but

---

[24]   Kaldor, 'Keynesian Economics after Fifty Years' (1983), repr. in CP ix. 54.

[25]   It is well known that in the *General Theory* Keynes believed in the inverse relation between real wages and employment, and that his major work contains no reference to imperfect competition. However, Keynes himself (in 'Relative Movements of Real Wages and Output', *EJ* (Mar. 1939)) found, as he investigated the trend in real wages since 1886, that this relation operated in reverse; a phenomenon that he attributed—Kaldor told me that he seemed to remember that it was following discussions with Kalecki—to 'the operation of the laws of imperfect competition in the modern quasi-competitive system' in which the producer 'operates subject to decreasing average costs'.

[26]   M. Bruno and J. Sachs, *The Economics of Worldwide Stagflation* (Cambridge, Mass., Harvard University Press, 1984).

it is fully compatible with the theory that international stagflation was induced by changes in the terms of trade, as described by the Kaldor two-sector model (see Chapter 8).

Chapter 15

Method and Vision of the World

> But soon or late, it is ideas, not vested interests, which are dangerous for good or evil.
>
> J. M. Keynes, *The General Theory*

> What! Every citizen will be allowed to believe in his own reason alone, and to think whatever his reason, enlightened or benighted, suggests.
>
> Voltaire, *A Treatise upon Toleration*

> If one investigates exactly what the most part of all good consists of . . . one sees that it consists of these two chief objects: freedom and equality.
>
> J. J. Rousseau, *The Social Contract*

15.1. Economics and Economic Policy

Kaldor was neither a pure deductivist nor an extreme inductivist; neither an economist who dealt solely in grand abstractions nor simply an applied economist; neither a detached theoretician nor a mere 'counsellor to the prince'—he was, always, all of these things. But even though his interest in political matters and his appetite for facts may have sometimes prevailed over his concern for theoretical abstraction, especially towards the end of his life, he never neglected this latter dimension to his subject.

As the years passed, Kaldor became increasingly aware that theory must be grounded in 'stylized facts', and that economic theory should provide the basis for economic policy. This is not to imply, however, that he ever lost his passion for theoretical inquiry. He was convinced that the proper approach to a complex problem was to state it in clear and precise terms and then to provide a simple and elegant solution. Even so, there is much more to Kaldorian economics than a narrow conception of theory as a set of procedures for solving problems: his economic theories and policy proposals were always closely associated with a 'political philosophy', which I shall endeavour to describe.

At the beginning of his career, many of Kaldor's writings were on topics wholly 'internal' to the academic world (as evidenced by almost all of his work discussed in Chapter 1). But even then his views had tangible links with the great and real problems of the outside world: an example being his contribution to the 1937 debate on the theory of capital, which Kaldor saw as a search for the instruments with which to investigate the economic cycle and unemployment, the two salient economic phenomena of the inter-war years.

Kaldor's concern with practical matters was strengthened by his conversion to Keynesianism—as witness his writings in the latter years of the 1930s on wages, investment, and the cycle—and culminated during the war years, when his work as an economist was entirely devoted to problems of applied economics. This, however, was not a linear process. Kaldor, like Keynes, was aware that interpretations of concrete facts and proposals for action were of little value unless they were incorporated into a broadly based theoretical framework. And in the 1950s and 1960s it was his passion for pure theory that once again placed him at the centre of theoretical debate on growth and the distribution of income.

This phase was followed by another, lasting from the mid-1960s until his death, during which he felt impelled again to find political answers for practical problems: taxation, money, inflation, and the balance of payments. On each of these issues his 'applied' research provoked fierce controversy, but also a school of thought. On taxation his insistence on distributive equity aroused the hostility of a broad spectrum of conservative political opinion: his anti-conformist position made him the leading spokesman for an expenditure tax, the application of which is still subject to dispute in many countries. On monetary policy, in a period of increasing compliance with the doctrines of the New Monetarists, he was the most stubborn advocate of Keynesianism (in its English version of the Radcliffe Report) and the leading exponent of the theory of the endogeneity of money. On inflation and the balance of payments he made every effort to equip the economic system with stable and permanent institutions for correcting and directing the market. His ideas as expressed by the New Cambridge school aroused controversy; his recommendations for a policy of import controls created scandal; his proposals for reform of the international monetary system based on a commodity currency raised great interest. Most of these policy proposals were closely connected with his ceaseless research into the dynamics of the economic system.

15.2. His Changing Conception of Growth Equilibrium

Shackle has recently divided the great economists into two categories: those who search for general theories, and those who see theories as only flexible patterns of reasoning. Kaldor undoubtedly belongs to the latter category. One might say that he mastered the art of 'riding Ricardo's bicycle'—Joan Robinson's expression for what Marxist economists had, mistakenly, not been content to do in their quest for a holistic theory of economics, history, and the world.

Although there is a large degree of coherence in Kaldor's theories, especially after his conversion to Keynesianism, the flexibility of the patterns of his thought give rise to a certain number of (mainly temporal) inconsistencies, for which reason any search for a general Kaldorian theory would be fruitless.

Kaldor's principle change of mind is to be found in his treatment of growth equilibrium. In the 1930s he regarded the movement of the economic system as approximating more closely to a cycle than a stable 'trend' of growth: the road to full employment was an arduous 'steeplechase' with many obstacles in the way. He shifted ground in the 1950s, perhaps because of the altered political climate of those years and the interventionist leanings of Western governments: full employment now became a legitimate working hypothesis to account for the stylized facts emerging from the long-term evolution of the industrialized economies. There were, however, certain phenomena, like the introduction of technical progess or the distribution of income, which although explainable by Kaldorian theory under conditions of equilibrium growth, could not be accounted for under cyclical conditions. In this sense, therefore, there was a discrepancy between his theories on the cycle and on growth. When I asked him how the two theoretical components could be fitted together, he simply replied that they should be treated as different theories dealing with different historical periods.

The inconsistency in Kaldor's 1950s' models of stationary-state growth is also apparent in his later growth models: both the so-called Kaldor laws and the two-sector model. The main conclusion to draw from his laws, in fact, is the operation of cumulative mechanisms which openly contradict equilibrium analysis. The chief purpose of his two-sector model was to illustrate the stagflationary tendency of the world economy. In particular, the function of price flexibility in the models of the 1950s had been to equilibrate, through variations in the distribution of income, the savings and investment dynamic. In the agriculture–industry model, the function of the flexibility of the terms of trade was to give an account of stagnation and/or inflation rather than render the growths of the two sectors compatible. However, it should also be remembered that, during the 1950s, Kaldor frequently warned against an over-optimistic interpretation of his models and emphasized the numerous conditions that had to be fulfilled if economic growth was not to be hampered by inflation or deflation.

Kaldor's shifting emphasis vis-à-vis the stability of the capitalist system was basically the result of the contradictory nature of capitalism itself—which combines an inexhaustible impetus towards growth with manifold instability caused by various and mutable factors. I remember a Cambridge seminar during the early 1970s when a student asked Kaldor whether he believed capitalism was in crisis. He answered, 'Certainly it is, but the fact is it always has been.'[1] Nevertheless, this discontinuity in Kaldor's treatment of the sta-

---

[1] Today, after the final crisis of the Eastern European economies, capitalism seems not to be under challenge from other, rival systems. However, there is still no avoiding Scitovsky's question:

bility of the system is matched by a high degree of consistency in his method of investigation. The first constant element that I wish to illustrate concerns the connection between the growth and the exogeneity of the factors of demand.

15.3. Exogeneity, Growth, and History

Keynesian economists of the neo-classical synthesis use the framework of the static IS–LM model with given capacity and exogeneity of effective demand to define the short-term equilibrium of income. In analysis of the long-term 'dynamic' equilibrium of income, they employ the production function with exogenous technical progress and growth of the factors and endogenous effective demand. One of the principles of the Kaldorian method, though, is that demand is exogenous even in analysis of the economic growth. Supply factors, on the other hand, have a mostly passive role—that is, they are derived magnitudes endogenous to the model. This principle constantly recurs in Kaldor's work, at every stage of its development and in its most diverse areas of enquiry. In his 1950s theory of growth it was investment demand—the outcome of entrepreneurial activity as represented by the technical-progress function—that conveyed endogenous technical progress into the economic system. In his 1960s laws on growth rates, it was external demand that governed the endogenous growth of output and of productivity in the manufacturing sector. Likewise, it was labour demand which induced an endogenous labour supply via his so-called 'law of labour migration'. Finally, in Kaldor's 1970s debate with the Chicago school it was the growth of nominal income and therefore of money demand which determined the endogenous growth of the money supply. The examples proliferate.

The importance that Kaldor attributed to cumulative processes and structural changes reflects the influence of Adam Smith and Allyn Young: together with Keynes, his great masters. For Smith and Young increasing returns to scale can only be understood if they relate, not to the firm, but to the entire economy, or at least to the whole of the industrial sector. They are an essential ingredient in the cumulative process by which the division of labour is the outcome of the extension of the market, and the latter the outcome of the division of labour. Increasing returns to scale are made possible by the division of labour, which arises from the increase in the capital/labour ratio: hence, if the increase in the capital/labour ratio brings with it an increase in per-capita output, we have Kaldor's oft-stated conclusion that the capital/output ratio is stable even in systems that differ in their structures and in their economic growth.

'Can capitalism survive, given that it seems less able now than in the past to seize opportunities for development, to absorb shocks and to adapt to change?' (T. Scitovsky, 'Can Capitalism Survive? An Old Question in a New Setting', *AER Papers and Proceedings* (1980), 1–9).

The ideas of a cumulative process and of an exogenous variable are closely connected. Once the exogenous variable has been identified, the temptation arises to endogenize it and revert to an equilibrium process, perhaps with the inclusion of some sort of time-lag. To escape from this impasse one must select a method for identifying an appropriate exogenous variable for each *specific* stylized fact, to be analysed in terms of a cumulative process and the obstacles that stand in its way—obstacles which derive from the dynamic process itself.

The very nature of the dynamic process entails the passage of time: this is why changes occur in the parameters and in the structure of the functions that represent it. Consequently, any attempt to assert once-and-for-all general laws, or a general theory, is vacuous. Kaldor's method, above all when it deals with the theory of growth, is the building of an economic theory with its roots in history. It consists in the identification of processes and phenomena which develop over the long period, and with such regularity that they stand out from a myriad of contingent data to constitute stylized facts, thus acquiring economic and social, and therefore political, significance.

Changing phenomena require not only flexible hypotheses but also flexible patterns of thought. Kaldor's method therefore finds little favour with those who prefer the holistic method of basing all economic analysis on methodological individualism. Which brings us to Kaldor's selection of the appropriate level of disaggregation.

15.4. Degree of Disaggregation of Macro-Economics and Method

Adopting the method of methodological individualism requires the disaggregation of macro-economic models down to the elementary unit of the individual producer and consumer. Since, in this case, one has to renounce the principle of effective demand and identification of the *causal* priorities of the components of aggregate demand, this is not Kaldor's method.

For Kaldor, instead, the degree of disaggregation is an analytical tool: identification of the elementary unit is not an automatic operation, but a 'discretionary' one performed by the analyst according to the problem to be investigated. This is not to imply that he resorted to *ad hoc* hypotheses; rather, that he gave limited historical validity to the model and, within the historical limits thus established, focused his analysis on the actions of those subjects and institutions which, for the particular problem under examination, were taken to be fundamental and elementary. The behaviour of these elementary agents was hypothesized but not postulated—in the sense that such behaviour is open to empirical verification. This feature of Kaldor's method distinguishes it from the purely deductive method of the theoreticians of general equilibrium, who build their equilibrium (or disequilibrium) model on an extremely limited set of individual behavioural patterns postulated once and for all. It also sets it apart from the Friedmanite method of hypothesizing a pattern of behaviour by economic agents that is not directly available for verification, but accepted or rejected according to its congruence with the statistical evidence of the model's *results*.

I have already illustrated the various kinds of disaggregation that Kaldor employed according to the problem he was investigating. The reader is reminded of the disaggregation in Chapter 2 among speculative markets, each with its specific form of behaviour; of the disaggregation in Chapters 5 and 6 between social classes, each with its specific propensity to save; of the disaggregation in Chapter 14 among firms, each with its specific technology and with its specific behaviour as a price-maker or price-taker; and finally the disaggregation in Chapter 8 between sectors, each with its specific reaction to a variation in demand.

Dumping the ballast of the Walrasian micro-foundations of macro-economics opens up much broader horizons of enquiry. It enables macro-economic research to embark on a wide-ranging programme of micro-economic analysis. A research programme of this kind compels investigation of the types of rationality and of the limits on the rationality of economic agents.[2] Above all, it entails establishing an a priori connection between micro- and macro-economics enabling the investigation and explanation of phenomena, rather than the mere 'justification' of certain 'macro' laws by deducing them a posteriori from maximizing behaviour postulated at the individual level.

Any attempt to draw a distinction between theory and empirical analysis in Kaldor is a mistake. Endowed as he was with an extraordinary capacity for concentrating on the important facts, and with his refusal to defer to constituted authority, whether political or academic, Kaldor believed that scientific research in economics was hampered much more by old, unfortunately still fashionable, ideas than by any real complexity in its subject matter. Keynes's famous declaration in the preface to the *General Theory* that 'the difficulty lies, not in the new ideas, but in escaping from the old ones, which ramify, for those brought up as most of us have been, into every corner of our minds'[3] is echoed in these words taken from Kaldor's last book:

I am sure that empirical research of the right kind will, in time, considerably improve our knowledge of how modern market economies work . . . There is an enormous

---

[2] This does not entail surrendering to methodological individualism; rather, that research programmes must concern themselves with the processes of managerial decision making. These cannot be ignored in economic systems where the decisions of large-scale firms condition the market. In this sense, the post-Keynesian methodological approach enables macro-economic constraints to be integrated with research into individual and collective forms of behaviour, along the lines adopted both by the British managerial school and the American behaviourist school, See among the former, R. Marris, *The Economic Theory of Managerial Capitalism* (London, Macmillan, 1964); and among the latter, H. A. Simon, *Models of Bounded Rationality*, 2 vols. (Cambridge, Mass., MIT Press, 1982).

[3] J. M. Keynes, *The General Theory of Employment, Interest and Money* (London, Macmillan, 1936), p. viii.

amount of empirical research going on but it is stifled by operating within the framework of established theory.[4]

15.5. A Structuralist Political Economist

Kaldor's focus on the working of markets, on their dynamic potential, but also on their instability *and* inability to co-ordinate the decisions of their agents (in the sense given above, see note 2), sets him apart as a political economist from both the neo-classical Keynesian tradition and the monetarists and the new classical economists.

For neo-classical economists, market deficiencies must be blamed on economic policy: the market is, almost by definition, the best means of resources allocation (1) in terms of what is to be produced and at what relative price, and (2) in terms of how much is to be produced. Neo-classical–Keynesian tradition places less unquestioning faith in the market, judging it an inefficient allocator in sense (2) and advocating economic policy as the means to adjust the market, should it prove temporarily unable to utilize resources fully; nevertheless the market is still an excellent resources allocator in sense (1).

Kaldor's position was more radical. The lesson one learns from his work as a whole is that economic policy has a much more demanding task to perform. It must act not only on the degree of resources utilization, but also on the allocative and distributive mechanisms of the market.[5] Economic policy is not a set of fine tuning measures; it is the result of institutions created to correct the structural instability of capitalism.

Throughout this book I have discussed Kaldor's main—certainly not only—economic-policy proposals. On taxation, he produced an impressive number of recommendations designed to achieve efficiency and equitable targets, only the best-known of which have been described in Chapter 10. The various causes of inflation were illustrated in Chapter 12. In the majority of cases such causes can be identified in structural or distributive factors, regardless of whether explanation is based on the wage-profit spiral of Kaldor's growth models of the 1950s, on the wage-wage spiral of his dual-economy model of the 1960s, or on changes in the terms of trade in his agriculture–industry two-sector model of the world economy and of structural inflation in the Latin American countries. Economic policies vary according to the type of inflation, since they have to deal with different underlying structural or distributive factors. The range of anti-inflationary measures proposed by Kaldor therefore

---

[4] N. Kaldor, *Economics without Equilibrium* (1983) (pub. New York, Sharpe, 1985), 53–4.

[5] The idea that the modern disease of capitalism, stagflation, is the result of the allocative deficiency of the market in the above two senses and that economic policy must therefore be more wide-ranging than it has been in the past—not curtailed even further, as much contemporary economic thought has argued—is developed in P. Ciocca, *L'instabilità dell'economia* (Turin, Einaudi, 1987).

includes systems of buffer stocks, agricultural policies, or a stable wages policy involving not merely wage control, but action on the distributive mechanisms between wages and profits and among wages themselves; a variety of proposals that demonstrates Kaldor's belief that the distribution of income is not a process that can simply be left to the allocative capacities of the market. Chapter 9.3 gave detailed treatment of the dual exchange-rate policy. This Kaldor recommended on various occasions as a remedy for the inflation–devaluation spiral that afflicts economies with agriculture–industry structural disequilibrium when they pursue the external objective through simple money devaluation.

International economic policy faces an even more demanding task than its domestic counterpart. In his 1946 report to the United Nations Kaldor outlined a plan for full employment in the OECD countries which required the co-operation of every individual country if this objective was to be achieved at home, and a joint undertaking by the surplus countries to adjust both the level and the composition of income. As I argued in Chapter 4.7, the general lines and underlying philosophy of Kaldor's plan have not become obsolete, even though their implementation today would involve even greater co-operative effort—hampered, however, by the reluctance of countries to make it.

Finally, Kaldor's proposal for reform of the international monetary system was illustrated in Chapter 13.2. His recommendation for the creation of a commodity money—regulated by the world-wide excess supply of raw materials—was a continuation of his analysis examined in Chapter 8, sections 2 and 3 of the international stagflation consequent on the inability of markets to co-ordinate sectorial outputs by means of flexible terms of trade.

None of these measures would be part of the stock-in-trade of a monetarist or of many neo-Keynesians; they constitute instruments for structural changes in the allocative and distributive mechanisms of the market.

15.6 Industrialism

Another important linking theme in Kaldor's thought is his emphasis on industrialism, an emphasis which became more insistent the more Great Britain went into industrial decline. The road to the emancipation of the developing countries has been paved with high capital/labour ratio industries and production techniques. The economic policies of these countries should be designed first to protect 'infant' industries and then to subsidize manufacturing exports. In the industrialized countries, too, the chief agent of dynamism—in Kaldor's growth and technical-progress models of the 1950s—is the industrial entrepreneur, a figure who represents not only the Keynesian risk-taker, but also an innovator in the Marxian and Schumpeterian sense: one who discovers the most profitable combination of productive inputs. For more than ten years after his Cambridge inaugural lecture, the central concern of Kaldor's research was to demonstrate that the impetus to growth for the whole economy comes from the manufacturing sector. To counteract the situation in which the virtuous circle set in motion by the rapid growth of the manufacturing sector is broken by a shortage of labour, Kaldor devised the policy instrument of a selective tax on employment in the tertiary sector which finances employment subsidies in the industrial sector. As we saw in Chapter 7, the labour-supply constraint on industrial growth is only a temporary feature of Kaldor's analysis, while the limit set on industrial development by the external constraint is a constant in his thought.

His economic-policy writings on the trade balance range from the articles of 1932, his first year of writing on economics, to those of 1986, the year of his death. For forty years he argued in favour of flexible exchange rates and then for fifteen years in favour of import controls. It is surprising, however, that in defending both these policies he should resort to the concept of increasing returns: in the earlier period in order to stress the positive effect of the widening of the market, in the later one to warn against the policies that were accelerating Britain's de-industrialization.

The last ten years of Kaldor's career as an economic policy adviser and pamphleteer were devoted, as we saw in Chapter 13 and especially in its final two sections, to defence of British industry against the policies pursued during the 1980s by the Conservative government.

Thatcher's monetary and fiscal policy, combined with Britain's energy surplus when North Sea oil came on stream, had led to an overvaluation of the pound and afflicted the country with the so-called 'Dutch disease'. For Kaldor, the only remedy against the decline of British industry was a policy of import controls on manufactured goods and an industrial management policy along Japanese lines, using oil revenues to rejuvenate national industry instead of bringing benefits only to the City and to foreign financial investment.

Kaldor was more ready to accept the existence of an objective Keynesian conflict of interests between industry and finance than a Marxist struggle between industry and the working class. Marxian exploitation perpetrated by an increase in absolute and relative surplus value is ingrained in capitalism and works through technical progress and the distribution of income. Although Kaldor's thought apparently did not exclude Marxian conflict between workers and capitalist firms, it undoubtedly regarded such conflict as manageable, and therefore condemned the economic and social policies that exacerbate it as evil. Distributive conflict, in fact, only appears in stagnant economies, stifled by a lack of entrepreneurial dynamism or by misguided economic policies.

But in economies with high-powered manufacturing sectors and sustained growth, distributive conflict is blunted by dynamic returns to scale and the consequent increase in labour productivity leading to the growth of real wages. Moreover, accelerated growth leads to an increase in labour demand in excess of the labour supply created by the growth of labour productivity. In an expanding economy, therefore, the working class as a whole enjoys higher wage rates and higher employment, and employers a higher rate of profit. Further, the operation of increasing returns enabled Kaldor to reject Phillips's trade-off between higher growth of income and lower wage inflation—and in consequence also to reject economic policies which, on the basis of this trade-off, keep the economy at 'half-cock'—and to advocate instead an incomes policy that offsets the containment of money-wages with full employment and stable growth of real wages.

For Kaldor—one may argue—given his growth laws and the Cambridge equation, all that was needed for the elimination of the conflict between wage-earners and capitalist industry was a set of structural policies designed to lift the external constraint and a stable incomes policy. However, this optimistic view seems today at odds with the world economy of the last decade, which has laboured to emerge from a prolonged period of low growth; a period of technical progress made possible only by the violent restructuring of entire industrial sectors through the elimination of firms and the dumping of accumulated human capital.

15.7. His Social Philosophy

Kaldor was one of those rare thinkers who grow more radical with age. One could of course say, as he himself once did, that it is easier to be independent and iconoclastic as an old Lord than it is as a young immigrant. This, however, is not what usually happens: more often than not, privileges tame the rebellious and turn them into conformists. Kaldor cannot be criticized on this score, and one need only cite his last writings as evidence. Towards the end of his life he was violently critical of the Conservative government, not only for its 'errors' of economic policy, but also for its reactionary defence of class interests. Actually, there is a certain contradiction in Kaldor's interpretation of the motives behind Thatcher's conservative policies. He sometimes condemned them as a class-based strategy designed to set off violent conflict and with no concession to mediation and compromise; and sometimes as the fruit of what he saw as an era of decadence, which, because of ignorance and false beliefs, preferred the worst to the best. Generally, however, Kaldor's work reveals an evolutionary optimism in history and great faith in democratic-bourgeois institutions. In this he differed significantly from Michael Kalecki, whose analysis of capitalism otherwise has many points in common with Kaldor's. Kalecki's political philosophy was much more deeply rooted in Marxism, as evinced by his pessimism over the ability of democratic institutions, so long as they operated within a capitalist-bourgeois framework, to find a stable solution for even such a basic problem as the employment of labour. For Kalecki, in fact, a full-employment policy upset the balance of power among classes so radically that it would sooner or later lead to the overturning of the political system. Kaldor belonged instead to the great tradition of the Enlightenment, with its profound faith in human reason and its belief that, by correctly interpreting reality, the human spirit can influence events through appropriate action. And in this he was a master: his fertility in inventing schemes and devices in tax, trade, and other matters was legendary; it was said of him that he could produce from five to ten good ideas a day.

His faith in the ability of well-governed institutions to achieve the common good also extended to international institutions. As we have seen, his friend Sidney Dell of the United Nations said of Kaldor that he was always a 'U.N. man'. Here, too, Kaldor tirelessly invented plans of action representing a collective 'optimum', whatever their political pre-conditions might be. This is not to imply that an economist's task consists solely of outlining the technical features of a proposal regardless of its political feasibility. What it does mean is that too great a concern for immediate political considerations stunts the beneficial potential of a proposal. It is frequently the case that, although a good idea may not be practicable at the moment of its conception, it can be profitably revived when the problem has become more acute or when conflicting interests have attenuated—because those in power have altered their position or because they have become more far-sighted than before. In this area Kaldor's ideas (as discussed in Chapter 9.7) on the need for developing countries to adopt radical reforms (especially in taxation), as a guarantee for a democratic and progressive political system, are very persuasive.

Kaldor had more influence on policy-making than any other British political economist since Keynes. He was a friend to the intellectual leaders of the Labour Party, a tax-consultant to three Chancellors of the Exchequer, and the inspirer of Labour Party economic policy for many years. Shortly before he died he was still acting as adviser to Neil Kinnock, the most recent leader of the Party. Nevertheless, despite Kaldor's importance as a government consultant, one could never say of him that he was a subservient 'counsellor to the prince' or ready to compromise: he did not lend his intellectual support to government action at any cost and in every circumstance, but only so long as he was able to influence it according to his principles and provided he believed it was to the common good.

One might say of Kaldor's social philosophy that it lay halfway between unachievable Utopia and immobilizing hyper-realism. He received his political education from the English Fabian Movement, Keynes and Beveridge, and his political philosophy from the wholly Cantabrigian tradition of Sidgwick and the solidarist utilitarianism of Pigou (which perhaps explains why he always had great liking for the old Cambridge professor, despite the sometimes profound analytical differences between their economic theories). Although Kaldor was deeply read in Marx and respected him as an economist, Marxism had little influence on his political and social philosophy. Never blind to injustices and class conflicts, he was none the less reluctant to see class struggle as the engine of a dialectical process in which contradictions could be successfully overcome.

His political objective was the combining of political democracy with social justice. He had a deep admiration for his adopted country, which he believed had made great progress towards achieving this goal in the years between the Second World War and the advent of Thatcher's first Conservative Government. Thatcherism, in his view, had reversed the trend of the previous thirty years; years in which even Conservative Governments had striven to consolidate the social progress of the country rather than eradicate it. As Chapter 13.7 has shown, Kaldor believed that the great leaders of the Conservative Party from Churchill to Macmillan had, unlike Thatcher, sought to build national unity rather than provoke social conflict.

Just as the Keynesian revolution was an intellectual challenge to at least two generations of British economists, so the economic policies adopted during the Second World War, as Chapter 4 has tried to show, broke new ground in combining democracy with State planning. The war demonstrated the efficiency of public intervention in even the most delicate market mechanisms for the physical allocation of material and human productive inputs, and for the distribution of output among social classes and groups. The combining of the market with central planning by a democratic state found its most radical and authorative spokesman in Kaldor, and the reader is referred to the pages on the German war economy in Chapter 4.2 for his assessment of the greater planning capacity of democracy compared with that of dictatorship.

If we need a label for Kaldor we may call him a radical social democrat: his radicalism was evident in his egalitarian commitment to helping the weaker and more underprivileged sections of society. The reader is reminded in particular of Chapter 10, which describes his sense of justice in matters of public finance and his campaign for reform of the tax system, convinced as he was that tax evasion and erosion were much more readily exploitable by the wealthier classes. With time, however, he became increasingly convinced that greater social justice was more easily achieved by a welfare state, full employment, and the growth of output, than by improvements to the tax system. Today, however, with the world locked in a spiral of decreasing growth and with the tendency of public expenditure to increase in proportion to national income, wide-ranging projects for tax reform have moved back to centre stage.

Kaldor's policies for the developing countries is another area in which he repeatedly demonstrated his concern for the most vulnerable. In Willy Brandt's 1980 proposals for the provision of international aid by the North for the South, one finds not only the same political philosophy, but also the same policies as Kaldor had been advocating since the 1950s: abolition of the North's protectionism against manufactured goods from the developing countries, and the establishment of an international monetary system to boost the incomes of the countries producing primary products.

15.8. The Continuer of a Great Tradition

That Kaldor was a thinker in the great tradition of British political economy is demonstrated by the evident influence on his work by the classical economists. From Adam Smith he inherited his insistence on the link between the dynamics of the economic system and technical progress; from David Ricardo his interest in the distribution of income among classes and in the constraint on growth induced by diminishing returns to land. There are numerous similarities between his work and Marxist thought: suffice it to mention his view of technical progress as a necessary condition for the survival of the capitalist in a competitive market, his identification of the reasons for market deficiencies in economic growth, and his singling out of the cumulative processes that lead to unequal development. He also made a major contribution to the carrying forward of the Cambridge tradition of public intervention in the economic sphere. In the last century, Sidgwick endeavoured to demonstrate that, even when using a model based on the simplifying assumptions required by the deductive method, Adam Smith's system of 'natural freedoms' was unable, under all conditions, to achieve the maximum welfare of the community. Of the great economists of the marginalist tradition it was, of course, Marshall who most accurately identified the causes and effects of externalities: and in the presence of externalities individual decisions cannot guarantee the optimum that State intervention can instead help to achieve. At Cambridge again, and for many years at the beginning of this century, Pigou's doctrine of comparison among cardinal utilities made it possible to set optimizing targets for egalitarian public policies. Finally, Cambridge was the cradle of the Keynesian revolution: this century's outstanding doctrine on the instability of capitalism and on the need for national and international public intervention in the workings of the economic system.

Nicholas Kaldor was this tradition's last great standard-bearer. All these themes are to be found in his work, amplified and developed: from his critique of *laissez-faire* to his emphasis on returns to scale, from his redistributive policies to his Keynesian policies for intervention, whether cyclical or structural, national or international. The similarities with Keynes's theories are numerous. Although Kaldor has to be considered a 'Keynesian'—and he called himself one—he nevertheless developed and enriched Keynes's ideas without committing the error of forcing Keynes's new ideas into the old orthodox framework. The work of his maturity generated theories that, despite their Keynesian attribution, are to be more accurately labelled as 'Kaldorian' (John Kenneth Galbraith called him 'the last of the innovators in economics').

Kaldor's similarities with Keynes extend beyond economic theory. As Kaldor's greatest pupil has written,[6] the two thinkers shared both an originality

---

[6] L. L. Pasinetti, 'Nicholas Kaldor', *International Encyclopedia of the Social Sciences*, biographical suppl. (London, Macmillan, 1979).

of thought and a conviction that, although inherited economic orthodoxy should be revolutionized because of its weak logical and factual bases, what the institutions of a democratic society required is not revolution, but reform. Both Keynes and Kaldor were convinced of the effectiveness of market mechanisms; likewise, they were both convinced that the market was unjust in its distribution of income and that it should be equipped with institutions guaranteeing the stability of production and employment that, if left to itself, the economic system could not provide. Their love of Cambridge and of King's College, their habit of setting their ideas before the public in letters to *The Times*, their life peerages for scientific achievement—these, too, were common to both economists. And they also shared an exasperation with the mediocrity of a large number of eminent figures in politics and public life, and a confidence in intellectual prowess—especially their own.[7]

But what Kaldor and Keynes had most closely in common was the faith that inspired their economic-policy beliefs; a faith so vividly expressed by Max Weber when he wrote: 'The possible would never be achieved if there was nobody in the world who attempted the impossible.'

---

[7] Kaldor was proud of the analogies with Keynes. The walls of his study in the large house in Adams Road were lined with books from floor to ceiling, except for two pictures: one, put up after the death of Piero Sraffa, was a photograph of his late friend; the other a newspaper cartoon from the early 1960s showing a smiling Kaldor following an elegant and serious Keynes as they were leaving King's College, Cambridge, heading for London and Whitehall.

Appendix

Prime Ministers and Chancellors of the Exchequer in Britain 1945–1990

Party	Prime Minister		Chancellor of the Exchequer	
	Period	Name	Period	Name
Labour	1945–51	C. Attlee	1945–7	H. Dalton
			1947–50	Sir S. Cripps
			1950–1	H. T. M. Gaitskell
Conservative	1951–5	W. Churchill	1951–5	R. A. Butler
	1955–7	R. A. Eden	1955–7	M. H. Macmillan
	1957–64	M. H. Macmillan	1957–8	P. Thorneycroft
			1958–61	D. Heathcoat-Amory
			1961–2	Selwyn Lloyd
			1962–4	R. Maudling
	1964	A. Douglas-Home		
Labour	1964–70	H. Wilson	1964–7	L. J. Callaghan
			1967–70	R. H. Jenkins
Conservative	1970–4	E. Heath	1970	I. Macleod (d. 20.7.70)
			1970–4	A. P. L. Barber
Labour	1974–6	H. Wilson	1974–9	D. W. Healey
	1976–9	L. J. Callaghan		
Conservative	1979–90	M. Thatcher	1979–83	R. E. J. Howe
			1983–90	N. Lawson
			1990	J. Major

Bibliography of the Works of Nicholas Kaldor

NOT included in this bibliography are Kaldor's numerous letters to *The Times* (which over the thirty years between 1932 and 1986 numbered around 260), his articles for *The Economist*, the *Financial Times*, the *Guardian*, the *Manchester Guardian*, and many other newspapers, apart from those written for *The Times* and republished in his Collected Papers or in special booklets. Translations of Kaldor's books and articles into Italian, French, Spanish, and German are included, but not translations into other languages.

Works published over several years are listed under the first date of publication; published speeches and reports are listed according to the date when the speech or report was delivered.

Books and Articles

Collected Editions

Collected Papers (London, Duckworth, 1960–89), vols. i–ix:
- i. *Essays on Value and Distribution* (1960; 2nd edn., 1980);
- ii. *Essays on Economic Stability and Growth* (1960; 2nd edn., 1980);
- iii. *Essays on Economic Policy* (vol. i) (1964; 2nd edn., 1980);
- iv. *Essays on Economic Policy* (vol. ii) (1964; 2nd edn., 1980);
- v. *Further Essays on Economic Theory* (1978);
- vi. *Further Essays on Applied Economics* (1978);
- vii. *Reports on Taxation* (vol. i) (1980);
- viii. *Reports on Taxation* (vol. ii) (1980);
- ix. *Further Essays on Economic Policy and Theory* (1989).

An Italian edition of collected works has been edited by F. Targetti in two volumes:
- i. *Equilibrio, distribuzione e crescita* (Turin, Einaudi, 1984);
- ii. *Inflazione, moneta e tassazione* (Turin, Einaudi, 1986).

CP ii was translated into Italian as *Saggi sulla stabilità economica e lo sviluppo* ed. A. Chiancone (Turin, Einaudi, 1965) and I shall omit mention of the Italian translation of each article included therein.

1931

'The Paradox of Saving', trans. of F. von Hayek, *Gibt es einen Widersinn des Sparens*, EC (May).

1932

'A Case against Technical Progress', *EC* (May).
Review of C. Landauer, *Planwirtschaft und Verkehrswirtschaft*, *EJ* (June).
'The Economic Situation of Austria', *HBR* (Oct.).
Review of E. Lederer *Aufris de ökonomischen Theorie*, *EC* 12.

1933

Two letters to *NeN* (22 July and 5 Aug.), on Keynes's article 'National Self-Sufficiency', *NeN* (8 and 15 July 1933).
Monetary Theory and the Trade Cycle (London, Jonathan Cape, and New York, Kelley, 1966), trans. (with H. Croome) of F. Hayek, *Geldtheorie und Konjunkturtheorie* (Vienna, 1929).

1934

'A Classificatory Note on the Determinateness of Static Equilibrium', *RES* (Feb.); CP i; It. edn. i.
'The Equilibrium of the Firm', *EJ* (Mar.); CP i; It. trans. 'L'equilibrio dell'impresa', in G. Zanetti (ed.), *Contributi per un'analisi economica dell'impresa* (Naples, Liguori, 1980); It. edn. i.
'Mrs Robinson's Economics of Imperfect Competition', *EC* (Aug.); CP i.

1935

'Market Imperfection and Excess Capacity', *EC* (Feb.); repr. in *Readings in Price Theory: Selected by a Committee of American Economic Association* (Chicago, R. D. Irwin, 1952); CP i; Ger. trans. in *Wettbewerbtheorie* (Neue Wissenschaftliche Bibliothek, Wirtschafts-Wissenschaften, 77; Cologne, 1975); It. edn. i.
'Wages Subsidies as a Remedy for Unemployment', lecture to the Conference of the Econometric Society, New York, Dec.; pub. in *JPE* (Dec. 1936); CP iii.

1936

Review of E. Schneider, *Theorie der Produktion, EC* (Feb.).
Review of H. von Stackelberg, *Marktform und Gleichgewicht, EC* (May).
Review of O. Morgenstern, *Die Grenzen der Wirtschaftspolitik, EJ* (Dec.).

1937

'Limitational Factors and the Elasticity of Substitution', *RES* (Feb.).
'The Recent Controversy on the Theory of Capital', *ECTR* (July); CP i.
Exchange of letters between Keynes and Kaldor, 27 Sept.–1 Nov. (in preparation for the article cited immediately below), in *Collected Writings of John Maynard Keynes* (Macmillan for Royal Economic Society, London, 1973), xiv. 215–23, 240–50.
'Professor Pigou on Money Wages in Relation to Unemployment', *EJ* (Dec.); CP ii; It. edn. ii.

1938

'Addendum: A Rejoinder to Professor Knight', *ECTR* (Apr.); CP i.
'Professor Chamberlin on Monopolistic and Imperfect Competition', *QJE* (May); CP i.
'Mr Hawtrey on Short- and Long-Term Investment', *EC* (Nov.); CP ii.
'Stability and Full Employment', *EJ* (Dec.); CP ii; Ger. trans. in *Koniunktur und Beschäftigungstheorie* (Neue Wissenschaftliche Bibliotek, Wirtschafts-Wissenschaften, 14; Cologne, 1967).

1939

'Capital Intensity and the Trade Cycle', *EC* (Feb.); CP ii.

Review of A. H. Hansen, *Full Recovery or Stagnation*, *EJ* (Mar.).

'Money Wage Cuts in Relation to Unemployment: A Reply to Mr Somers', *RES* (June).

'Principles of Emergency Finance', *BK* (Aug.).

'Welfare Propositions in Economics and Interpersonal Comparison of Utility', *EJ* (Sept.); repr. in K. J. Arrow and T. Scitovsky (eds.), *Readings in Welfare Economics* (London, Allen & Unwin, 1969); CP i; It. edn. ii.

Review of W. Marget, *The Theory of Prices: An Examination of the Central Problem of Monetary Theory*, i, *EJ* (Sept.).

'Speculation and Economic Stability', *RES* (Oct.); CP ii; It. edn. ii.

'Keynes' Theory of the Own-Rates of Interest'; CP ii; It. edn. ii.

1940

'The Trade Cycle and Capital Intensity: A Reply', *EC* (Feb.).

'A Comment on a Rejoinder of H. M. Somers (on Kaldor's Money Wage Cuts in Relation to Unemployment)', *RES* (Feb.).

'A Model of the Trade Cycle', *EJ* (Mar.); CP ii; It. edn. i.

Review of M. Abramowitz, *An Approach to a Price Theory in a Changing Economy*, *EJ* (July–Sept.).

'A Note on the Theory of the Forward Market', *RES* (June).

'A Note on Tariffs and the Terms of Trade', *EC* (Nov.); repr. in A. M. Page (ed.), *Utility Theory: A Book of Reading* (New York, Wiley, 1968); CP i; It. edn. ii.

1941

'Rationing and the Cost of Living Index', *RES* (June).

'The White Paper on National Income and Expenditure', *EJ* (June–Sept.).

'Employment and Equilibrium—A Theoretical Discussion', *EJ* (Dec.); repr. in CP ii as 'Pigou on Employment and Equilibrium'.

1942

'The Income Burden of Capital Taxes', *RES* 9; 2 (June); pub. in part as 'The Estimation of the Burden of Death Duties' in G. F. Shirras and L. Rostas (eds.), *The Burden of British Taxation* (Cambridge, CUP, 1943), CP vii; It. edn. ii.

'The 1941 White Paper on National Income and Expenditure', *EJ* (June–Sept.).

'Models of Short Period Equilibrium', *EJ* (June-Sept.).

'Professor Hayek and the Concertina Effect', *EC* (Nov.); CP ii.

Economic Reconstruction after the War (with M. Joseph) (London, Association for Education in Citizenship).

1943

'Budgeting for Employment, National Income and State Finance, Closing the Deflationary Gap', in *Full Employment* (10 articles from TT (1942–3)); (London, The Times Publishing Company).

'The Beveridge Report—II. The Financial Burden', *EJ* (Apr.).

Review of A. H. Hansen, *Fiscal Policy and Business Cycles*, *EJ* (Apr.).

'Export Costs and Export Price Policy', *BK* (June).

'The 1943 White Paper on National Income and Expenditure' (with T. Barna), *EJ* (June–Sept.); Fr. trans. (Paris, Imprimerie de l'Agence France Press, 1946).

Planning for Abundance (with J. Robinson, A. A. Evans, E. F. Schumacher, and P. Lamartine Yatts), papers by the economists present at the meeting organized by the National Peace Council on 'Interrelation of National and International Reconstruction' held in Oxford; (London; Peace Aims Pamphlet, 21, National Peace Council).

'The Quantitative Aspects of the Full Employment Problem in Britain', memorandum submitted to Sir William Beveridge's Committee on Full Employment, pub. as appendix C to Sir W. Beveridge, *Full Employment in a Free Society* (Allen & Unwin, London); CP iii.

1945

The Effects of Strategic Bombing on the German War Economy, prepared by US Strategic Bombing Survey (Washington, DC).

'Obituary of Erwin Rothbarth' (with D. G. Champernowne), *EJ* (Apr.).

1946

'The German War Economy', speech to the Manchester Statistical Society, 22 May; pub. in *MS* (Sept.) and *RES* 13: 1 (1945–6); CP iv.

1947

'A Note on W. J. Baumol's Community Indifference', *RES* 14: 1 (1946–7).

'A Plan for the Financial Stabilization of France', report prepared for the Commissariat Général du Plan (Paris, Mar.–May); CP viii.

1948

'The Theory of Distribution', in *Chambers Encyclopedia*; It. trans. 'La teoria della distribuzione', in I. Musu (ed.), *I neokeynesiani* (Bologna, II Mulino, 1980).

'A Statistical Analysis of Advertising Expenditure and of the Revenue of the Press' (with R. Silverman) (NIESR Studies, 8; Cambridge, CUP).

'A Survey of the Economic Situation and Prospects of Europe: 1947', prepared by the Economic Committee for Europe, Research and Planning Division, under the direction of Kaldor (Geneva, UN).

1949

'A Survey of the Economic Situation and Prospects of Europe, 1948', prepared by the Economic Commitee for Europe, Research and Planning Division, under the direction of Kaldor (Geneva, UN).

National and International Measures for Full Employment (with J. M. Clark, A. Smithies, P. Uri, R. Walker) (New York, UN); It. trans., *Politiche della piena occupazione*, introd. by R. Tremelloni (Milan, Istituto per gli studi economici, 1950).

1950

'The Economic Aspects of Advertising', *RES* 18: 4 (1949–50).

'A Positive Policy for Wages and Dividends', memorandum submitted to the Chancellor of the Exchequer, 21 June; CP iii; It. trans., 'Per un'efficace politica dei salari e dei dividendi' (introd. added in 1964), in D. Cavalieri (ed.), *La politica dei redditi* (Milan, Franco Angeli, 1973); It. edn. ii.

'Employment Policies and the Problem of International Balance', paper given to the Conference of the International Economic Association, Monte Carlo, Sept.; pub. in *RES* 19: 1 (1950–1); CP iii.

Report on National and International Measures for Full Employment (with J. M. Clark, A. Smithies, P. Uri, and E. R. Walker) (Geneva, UN).

'A Survey of the Economic Situation and Prospects of Europe: 1950', prepared by the Economic Committee for Europe, Research and Planning Division, under the direction of Kaldor (Geneva, UN).

1951

'Mr Hicks on the Trade Cycle', *EJ* (Dec.); CP ii. *Report on Full Employment Objectives in Relation to the Problem of European Cooperation* (co-author) (Strasburg, European Council).

1952

'Beschäftigungspolitik und das Problem des Internationalen Gleichgewichtes', *ZN* (15 Jan.).

'The International Impact of Cyclical Movements', paper given to the Conference of the International Economic Association, Oxford, Sept.; pub. in E. Lundberg (ed.), *The Business Cycle in the Post War World* (London, Macmillan, 1955); CP iv.

'Foreign Trade and the Balance of Payments', written for the Fabian Society; pub. in CP iv.

A Reconsideration of the Economics of the International Wheat Agreement, report prepared for the UN FAO (Commodity Policy Studies, 1; Rome, FAO, Sept.); CP iv.

1953

'Relations entre la croissance économique et les fluctuations cycliques', lecture at the Institut de Sciences Économiques Appliqués, Paris 23 May; pub. in *EA* (Jan.–June 1954); repr. as 'The Relation of Economic Growth and Cyclical Fluctuations', *EJ* (Mar. 1954); Ger. trans. in *Konjunktur und Beschäftigungstheorie* (Neue Wissenschaftliche Bibliothek, Wirtschafts-Wissenschaften, 14; Cologne, 1967); CP ii.

'Caratteristiche dello sviluppo economico', paper given to the International Conference on Underdeveloped Areas, Milan, 10–15 Oct.; Engl. trans., 'Characteristics of Economic Development', in CP ii.

1955

'The Lessons of the British Experiment since the War: Full Employment and the Welfare State', paper given to the centennial meeting of the Société Royale d'Économie du Belgique, Brussels; CP iii.

'Professor Wright on Methodology: A Rejoinder', *EJ* (Mar.).

'The Economic Effects of Company Taxation', *Transactions of the Manchester Statistical Society*, 1954–5 (23rd Mar.).

'Memorandum of Dissent to the Final Report of the Royal Commission on the Taxation of Profits and Income' (with G. Woodcock and H. L. Bullock), pub. with *Final*

Report of the Royal Commission on the Taxation of Profit and Income Cmnd 9474 (London, HMSO, June); repr. as *Reforming the Tax System* (Fabian Research Series, 190; London, 1957); CP vii; partial trans. in It. edn. ii.

An Expenditure Tax (London, Unwin University Books, and New York, Macmillan, 1956); pub. in part as 'Taxation and Economic Progress' and 'Income Expenditure and Taxable Capacity' in H. Miffly (ed.), *Public Finance and Fiscal Policy Selected Readings* (Boston, 1966); Ger. trans., *Begründung einer Ausgabesteuer* (Cologne, 1969); It. trans., *Per un' imposta sulla spesa* (Turin, Boringhieri, 1962).

'Alternative Theories of Distribution', *RES* 23: 2 (1955–6); repr. in D. R. Kamerscher (ed.), *Readings in Microeconomics* (Cleveland, World Pub. Co., 1967); repr. in J. E. Stiglitz and H. Uzawa (eds.), *Readings in the Modern Theory of Economic Growth*, (Cambridge, Mass., MIT Press, 1969); repr. in I. Rima (ed.), *Readings in the History of Economic Theory* (New York, H. R. and W. Dryden, 1970); CP i; Span. edn., *RCE* 76 (1956–7); repr. in O. Braun (ed.), *Teoria del capital y la distribución* (Buenos Aires, Editorial Tiempo Contemporaneo, 1973); It. trans., 'Teorie alternative della distribuzione', in G. Lunghini (ed.), *Valore, prezzi ed equilibrio generale* (Bologna, Il Mulino, 1971); It. edn. i.

1956

'Capitalist Evolution in the Light of Keynesian Economics', lecture at the University of Peking, 11 May; pub. in *SAN* (May 1957) and *JES* (1957); CP ii; Fr. trans., *EA* (Apr.–Sept. 1957); Port. trans., *EB* 2 (1956) and *TE* (July–Sept. 1956); It. trans., *RPE* (Feb. 1958).

Indian Tax Reform: Report of a Survey, Dept. of Economic Affairs, Ministry of Finance (New Delhi, June); repr. in R. Bird and O. Oldman (eds.), *Readings on Taxation in Developing Countries* (Baltimore, Johns Hopkins Press, 1964); CP viii.

'Problemas Económicos del Chile', essay written for the UN ECLA, Santiago del Chile, July–Sept.; pub. in *TE* (Mexico, Apr.–June, 1959); Engl. trans., CP iv.

'Characteristics of Economic Development', *AS* (Nov.); It. trans., *IS* (May 1958).

1957

Four essays in *RBE* (Mar.): 'Caracteristicas do desenvolvimento económico: Crescimento equilibrado e disequilibrado'; 'O problema do crescimento acelerado'; 'Inflação e desenvolvimento económico'; 'Tributação e desenvolvimento económico'; It. trans. of 1st, 3rd, and 4th essays, *IS* (June, July, Aug. 1958).

'The Reform of Personal Taxation', paper given to the Conference of the Society of Chartered Accountants, London, 29 Oct.; pub. in *ACC* (12 Apr.); CP iii.

'La inflación chilena y la estructura de la producción' *PaE* (Nov.).

'A Model of Economic Growth', *EJ* (Dec.); Sp. trans., *TE* (Apr.–June 1958); Fr. trans., *EA* (Aug.–Sept.), CP ii; It. trans., 'Un modello dello sviluppo economico', in G. Nardozzi and V. Valli (eds.), *Teoria dello sviluppo economico* (Milan, Etas Kompass, 1971).

'Community Indifference, A Comment', *RES*, 14: 1.

1958

Review of P. Baran, *The Political Economy of Growth*, *AER* (Mar.).

Suggestions for a Comprehensive Reform of Direct Taxation in Ceylon (Colombo,

Ceylon Government Publications Bureau, 1960); CP viii.

'The Reform of Personal Taxation', *ACC* (12 Apr.).

'Observations on the Problem of Economic Development in Ceylon', essay written at the request of Prime Minister Mr S. R. W. Bandaranaike, 18 Apr.; pub. in *Papers by Visiting Economists* (Colombo, National Planning Council, Government Press, 1959); CP iv.

'Monetary Policy, Economic Stability and Growth', memorandum submitted to the Committee on the Working of the Monetary System, 23 June *Memoranda of Evidence*, PP 146–53, and *Minutes of Evidence*, PP 712–18, Cmnd 827 (London, HMSO); CP iii; It. edn. ii.

'Risk Bearing and Income Taxation', *RES* (June).

'Capital Accumulation and Economic Growth', paper given at the Conference of the International Economic Association, Corfu, Aug.; pub. in F. A. Lutz and P.C. Hague (eds.), *The Theory of Capital* (London, Macmillan, 1961); repr. in *AER* (June 1962); CP v; It. edn. i.

'Problems of the Indian Third Five Year Plan', memorandum written for the Secretariat of the Plan Bureau, New Delhi, Sept.; CP iv.

'Comment on a Note on Kaldor's Speculation and Economic Stability', *RES* (Oct.).

'Tax Reform in India', essay submitted to the Indian Parliamentary Committee, 16 Dec.; pub. in *EWA* (Jan. 1959); repr. in Bird and Oldman (eds.), *Readings on Taxation in Developing Countries*; CP iii.

'The Growing Disparity between Rich and Poor Countries', in *Problems of United States Economic Development*, (New York, Committee for Economic Development).

1959

'Economic Growth and the Problem of Inflation', lectures given at the LSE, 3 and 13 Feb.; pub. in *EC* (Aug. and Nov.); CP iii; Sp. trans., *TE* 28 (1961); Fr. trans., ed. Institut pour le développement économique de la Banque Internationale pour la Reconstruction et le Développement (Paris, 1963); It. edn. ii.

'The Radcliffe Report'; pub. in *REST* (Feb. 1960); CP iii; It. edn. ii.

'El concepto de ingreso en la teoria económica', *TE* (July–Sept.).

1960

'A Rejoinder to Mr Atsumi and Professor Tobin', *RES* (Feb.).

'Economic Growth and Distributive Shares: A Rejoinder to Mr Findlay', *RES* (June).

'Le Rôle de l'instrument monétaire en matière de croissance et de stabilité économique', *BID* (Aug.).

'Report on Mexican Tax Reform', essay written for the Finance Ministry of Mexico, Sept.; CP viii.

Introduction to CP i.

Introduction to CP ii.

1961

'Increasing Returns and Technical Progress: A Comment on Professor Hicks's Article', *OEP* (Feb.).

Ensayos sobre el desarrollo económico, written for CEMLA (Mexico, July; 2nd edn.,

Nov. 1964).

'Proposals for a Reform of Taxation in British Guiana', written for the Ministry of Finance of British Guiana, (Georgetown, 30 Dec.); CP viii.

1962

'A Proposal for a Levy on the Advertising Revenue of Newspapers', (with R. R. Neild) written for the Royal Commission on the Press, Feb.; CP vii; It. edn. ii.

'A New Model of Economic Growth' (with J. Mirrlees), *RES* (June); CP v; Ger. trans. in *Sonderdruck aus Heinz Köning, Wachstum und Entwicklung der Wirtschaft*; It. trans., 'Un nuovo modello di sviluppo economico', in M. G. Mueller (ed.), *Problemi di macroeconomia* (Milan, Etas Kompass, 1966); It. edn. i.

'Report on the Turkish Tax System', written for the State Planning Organization of the Turkish Government, Ankara, Apr.; CP viii.

'Symposium on Production Functions and Economic Growth: Comment', *RES* (June).

The Choice of Taxes in Developing Countries, paper given to the Nyasaland Economic Symposium on 'Economic Development in Africa', Blantyre, 18–28 July (Oxford, Basil Blackwell, 1965).

'Overdeterminateness in Kaldor's Growth Model: A Comment', *EJ* (Sept.).

'The Role of Taxation in Economic Development', paper for the Conference of the International Economic Association on 'Fiscal Policy and Organization of American States', (Santiago, Chile, Dec.); CP iii.

'Will Underdeveloped Countries Learn to Tax?'; pub. in *FA* (Council of Foreign Relations) (Jan. 1963); repr. in Bird and Oldman (eds.), *Readings on Taxation in Developing Countries* (3rd edn. 1975); CP iii.

'Stabilizing the Terms of Trade of Underdeveloped Countries', written for the UN ECLA; pub. in Eng. and Sp. in *EBLA* (Mar. 1963); It. trans., *MA* (Apr. 1964) CP iv.

1963

'Comment on I. Svennilson's Paper on "Economic Growth and Technical Progress"', OECD conference on 'Residual Factors and Economic Growth', (Château de la Muette, Paris, 20–2 May).

'A Memorandum on the Value Added Tax', memorandum submitted to the Committee on Turnover Taxation, July; CP iii; It. edn. ii.

'Taxation for Economic Development', *JMAS* (Mar.); repr. in H. E. Smith (ed.), *Readings on Economic Development and Administration in Tanzania* (Nairobi; Institute of Public Administration, University College, Dar-es-Salaam, Tanzania, 1966).

'El papel de la imposición en el desarrollo económico', *IE*, 67–96.

'The Case for an International Commodity Reserve Currency' (with A. G. Hart and J. Tinbergen), submitted to the UN Conference on 'Trade and Development', Geneva, Mar.–June 1964; CP iv.

'Prospects of a Wages Policy for Australia', essay written as Consultant Economist to the Australian Central Bank; pub. in *ER* (June 1964); CP iv.

1964

'Las reformas del sistema fiscal en México', *CEX* (Apr.).

'The Problem of International Liquidity', *BOIES* (Aug.); CP vi.

'Dual Exchange Rates and Economic Development', *EBLA* (Sept.), in Eng. and Sp. CP iv.

'International Trade and Economic Development', in 'Problems of Foreign Aid', papers for the conference on 'Public Policy' held in Dar-es-Salaam, Tanzania, Nov.; pub. in *JMAS* (Dec.).

Kaldor's speech at the conference pub. in W. Baer and I. Kerstenetzky (eds.), *Inflation and Growth in Latin America* (Homewood, Irwin, The Economic Growth Center, Yale University).

Introduction to CP iii.

Introduction to CP iv.

1965

'The Relative Merits of Fixed and Floating Exchange Rates'; pub. in CP vi.

'Les Prélèvements fiscaux dans les pays en voie de développement', paper for the Réhovoth Conference, 18 Aug.; pub. in *Les Problèmes fiscaux et monétaires dans les pays en voie de développement* (Paris, 1967).

1966

'Marginal Productivity and the Macro-Economic Theories of Distribution: Comment on Samuelson and Modigliani', *RES* (Oct.); CP v; It. edn. i.

'Economic and Taxation Problems in Iran', written for the Prime Minister of Iran, Tehran, June; CP viii.

Causes of the Slow Rate of Economic Growth in the United Kingdom, inaugural lecture at the University of Cambridge (Cambridge, CUP); Fr. trans., *EA* (Mar. 1967); Russ. trans., *Mirovaja Ekonomika i Mezdunarodnye Otnösenija* (Moscow, Institut Mirovoj Ekonomiki, 1968); CP v; It. edn. i.

Strategic Factors in Economic Development, Frank Pierce Memorial Lecture at Cornell University, Oct. (Ithaca, Cornell University Press, 1967); It. partial trans., 'Problemi di industrializzazione nei paesi in via di sviluppo', in B. Jossa (ed.), *Economia del sottosviluppo* (Bologna, Il Mulino, 1973).

Une politique monétaire pour l'Amérique Latine (with P. Uri, R. Ruggles, and R. Triffin) (Paris, Institut Atlantique); Sp. trans. for CEMLA (1966); Engl. trans., *A Monetary Policy for Latin America* (New York, Praeger, 1968).

1968

'Productivity and Growth in Manufacturing Industry: A Reply', *EC* (Nov.).

1969

'The Role of Modern Technology in Raising the Economic Standards of Less Developed Countries', paper given to the conference held in Jerusalem, 14–18 Apr.; proceedings pub. under the conference title: W. L. Hodges and N. A. Kelley (eds.), *Technological Change and Human Development* (Ithaca, New York State School of Industrial and Labour Relations, Cornell University, 1970).

'The Choice of Technology in Less Developed Countries', *MLR* (Aug.).

1970

'Some Fallacies in the Interpretation of Kaldor', *RES* (Jan.).

'Europe's Agricultural Disarray', lecture given to the International Press Institute, Paris, 13 Jan., as pub. 'Europe's Agricultural Disarray—ECC Farm Policy is Fundamentally Misconceived', *NS* (3 Apr.); CP vi; It. trans., 'La politica agricola della Cee è forse fondamentalmente sbagliata?', in T. Joshing and R. Pasca (eds.), *Analisi economica e politica agraria* (Bologna, Il Mulino, 1981).

'The Case for Regional Policies', lecture given at Aberdeen University as the 5th Annual Scottish Economic Society Lecture (Feb.); pub. in *SJPE* (Nov.); CP v.

'The New Monetarism', lecture given at University College London, 12 Mar.; pub. in *LLBR* (July 1970); CP vi; Ger. trans., *IST* 16: 1–2 (1970); It. trans., 'Il nuovo monetarismo', in G. Bellone (ed.), *Il dibattito sulla moneta* (Bologna, Il Mulino, 1972); It. edn. ii.

'Conflicts in National Economic Objectives', Presidential Address to Section F of the British Association for the Advancement of Science, Durkheim, Sept.; pub. in *Conflicts in Policy Objectives* (Oxford, Basil Blackwell, 1971); repr. in *EJ* (Mar. 1971); CP v; It. edn. i.

'A Rejoinder to Professor Friedman', *LLBR* (Oct.).

Un avenir pour l'Europe agricole (co-author), ed. P. Uri (Paris, L'Institut Atlantique); It. trans., *Un futuro per l'agricoltura europea*, introd. by G. La Malfa (Milan, Franco Angeli, 1971).

1971

'The Existence and Persistence of Cycles in a Non-Linear Model: Kaldor's 1940 Model Re-Examined: A Comment', *RES* (Jan.).

'The Role of Industrialization in Latin American Inflations', paper given to the conference on Latin America (Gainesville, Fla., Feb.); pub. in D. T. Geithman (ed.), *Fiscal Policy for Industrialization and Development in Latin America* (Gainesville, Fla., University of Florida Press, 1974; repr. Cambridge, CUP, 1976); CP vi.

'The Truth about the "Dynamic Effects" of the Common Market', *NS* (12 Mar.); repr. in *Destiny or Delusion? Britain and the Common Market* (London, 1971); CP vi.

'Le Professeur Kaldor relance le débat sur le coût de l'entrée de la Grande Bretagne dans le Marché Commun', *PE* (May).

'The Money Crisis: Britain's Chance', *NS* (14 May).

'The Distortions of the 1971 White Paper', *NS* (16 July); CP vi.

'The Economic Effects of Alternative Systems of Corporation Tax', memorandum submitted to the Select Committee of the House of Commons on the Corporation Tax; CP vii; It. edn. ii.

'Bretton Woods and After', *TT* (6, 7, 8 Sept.); repr. as 'The Dollar Crisis', in CP vi.

'The Common Market—A Final Assessment', *NS* (22 Oct.); CP vi.

'Functioning and Economic Perspectives of the EEC', seminar on 'The Trade Unions and the European Economic Community', Julsminde, Denmark, 31 Oct.–6 Nov.

1972

'Advanced Technology in a Strategy of Development: Some Lessons from Britain's Experience'; Eng. repr. in *Automation and Developing Countries* (Geneva, ILO); Sp. trans. in D. Alejandro (ed.), *Política económica en centro y periferia (Ensayos en honor a Felipe Pazos)* (Mexico, Jeritel & Tokman, Fondo de Cultura Económica, 1976); repr. as 'Capitalism and Industrial Development: Some Lessons from Britain's Experience', *CJE* 1 (1977); CP vi.

'Notes on a Talk to VAT Conference', *Financial Times* conference, London, 25 Apr..

'Mr Heath's New Socialism', *ST* (8 Oct.).

'The Irrelevance of Equilibrium Economics', lecture at the University of York as the Goodricke Lecture, 10 May; pub. in *EJ* (Dec.); CP v; Sp. trans., *ICE* (1975); It. trans., 'L'irrilevanza della teoria dell'equilibrio economico', in M. D'Antonio (ed.), *La crisi post-keynesiana* (Turin, Boringhieri, 1975); It. edn. i.

The Common Market: Its Economic Perspective (Trade Union against the Common Market and NATSOPA).

'Money and Gold', *Acta Oeconomica*, 9: 2.

1973

'Teoria del equilibrio y teoria del crecimiento', lecture at the University of Barcelona, Apr.; pub. in *CE* 2 (May–Aug. 1974); pub. in Eng. as 'Equilibrium Theory and Growth Theory', in M. Baskin (ed.), *Economics and Human Welfare—Essays in Honour of Tibor Scitovski* (New York, Academic Press, 1979); It. trans., in G. Caravale (ed.), *La crisi delle teorie economiche* (Milan, Franco Angeli, 1983); It. edn. i.

'La estrategia del desarrollo industrial en los países menos avanzados', in 'La financiación del desarrollo en los países en proceso de crecimiento', 3rd Semana Económica Internacional, organized by Mondo, Documento Económico 7, Barcelona.

'Problems and Prospects of International Monetary Reform', *BK* (Sept.); CP vi.

'Tax Credits: A Critique of the Green Paper's Proposals', essay submitted to the Select Committee of the House of Commons on Tax Credit; CP vii.

'Per una riforma monetaria internazionale: necessità di un nuovo indirizzo', lecture held at the Banca d'Italia, 12 Dec.; pub. in *BAN* (Mar. 1974); Eng. trans., CP vi.

1974

'Mr Heath's Road to Ruin', *NS* (22 Feb.); repr. (Cambridge, DAE reprint series no. 396).

'The Road to Recovery', *NS* (Mar.), repr. (Cambridge, DAE reprint series no. 396).

'Managing the Economy: The British Experience', the David Kinley Lecture given at the University of Illinois, 18 Apr.; pub. in *QREB* 3.

'What is Wrong with Economic Theory', a Political Economy Lecture given at Harvard University, 29 Apr.; pub. in *QJE* (Aug. 1975; repr. Cambridge, CUP, 1976); CP v; Sp. trans., *TE* (Apr.–June 1976); It. edn. i.

'The Case for Nationalizing Land' (with J. Brockebank, J. Maynard, R. Neild, and O. Sutchbury) (Campaign for Nationalizing Land, London).

1975

'Economic Growth and the Verdoorn Law: A Comment on Mr Rowthorn's Article', *EJ* (Dec.).

'Why are Regional Policies Necessary?', paper given at the conference organized by the Deutscher Wirtschaftswissenschaftlicher Forschungsinstitut, Bonn, 15–16 May; pub. in *Regionalpolitik und Agrarpolitik in Europa* (Berlin, Dunker & Humboldt).

1976

'Inflation and Recession in the World Economy', Presidential Address to the Royal

Economic Society, 22 July; pub. in *EJ* (Dec.); CP v; Fr. trans., *PE* (1977); It. trans., 'Inflazione e recessione nell'economia mondiale', in *Rassegna sulla letteratura dei cicli economici*, 3, (Istituto per la Congiuntura, 1977) and in *REA* (1977); It. edn. ii.

'The Economic Outlook', European Banking Conference, Stockholm, 2–3 Nov.

'Observations on Fiscal Reform in Venezuela', written for the Ministry of Economic and Planning Coordination (Caracas, Dec.); CP viii.

1977

'The Nemesis of Free Trade', lecture given at the University of Leeds, 21 Mar.; CP vi.

'The Effects of Devaluation on Trade in Manufacture', CP vi.

'Is Capital Shortage a Cause of Mass Employment?', paper for the Kiel Symposium; pub. in H. Giersch (ed.), *Capital Shortage and Unemployment in the World Economy* (Institut für Weltwirtschaft an der Universität Kiel, Tübingen, 1978).

Comment on 'Capital Requirements for Full Employment and Economic Growth in Developed Countries', paper given to the Kiel Symposium by K. Wernerschatz; pub. in Giersch (ed.), *Capital Shortage and Unemployment in the World Economy*.

1978

'A New Look at the Expenditure Tax', paper given to the Brooking Institution conference on 'Income versus Expenditure Taxes', Washington, DC, Oct.; CP vii; It. edn. ii.

'Uzroci svetske inflacije i posledice na zemlje u razvoju' (The Effects of International Inflation on the Economies of Developing Countries), paper given to the Conference of the International Organization of Bank Sciences held at Dubrovnik, 31 Oct.–5 Nov.; proceedings pub. under the conference title: *Medunarodno finansiranje ekonomskovo razvoja* (International Financing to Economic Development) (Beograd).

'Public or Private Enterprise: The Issues to be Considered', lecture in Mexico City (Jan.); pub. in W. G. Baumol (ed.), *Public and Private Enterprise in a Mixed Economy* (London, Macmillan, 1980).

'The Foundations of Free Trade Theory and their Implications for the Current World Recession', paper given to the Conference of the International Economic Association held at Bischenberg, France; proceedings pub. under the conference title: E. Malinvaud and S. P. Fitoussi (eds.), *Unemployment in Western Countries* (London, Macmillan, 1980); repr. in J. Los *et al.*, (eds.), *Studies in Economic Theory and Practice*, essays in honour of E. Lipinski (Amsterdam, North Holland Publishing Co., 1981); CP ix.

'Structural Causes of the World Economic Recession', in *Mondes en développement* (Centre Nationale de la Recherche Scientifique, 22; Paris).

Introduction to CP v.

Introduction to CP vi.

1979

'Inflation: an Endemic Problem of Modern Capitalism', mimeo (Cambridge); repr. in *WG* 8: 2 (1982).

'Economic Policy Dimension for Restructuring Industrial Economies', paper given to the Varenna conference, Sept..

'An Introduction to "A Note on the General Theory" by J. de Largentaye', *JPKE* 1.

'The Role of Fiscal and Monetary Policies in Latin American Inflations', in *Intera-merican Institute of Capital Markets* (Caracas).
'What is De-Industrialization?', comment on the article by Sir Alec Caincross, in F. Blackby (ed.), *De-Industrialization* (London, Heinemann).
Collected Economic Essays (New York, Holmes & Mayer).

1980

'The Role of Increasing Returns, Technical Progress and Cumulative Causation in the Theory of International Trade', lecture, Paris, Feb.; pub. in *EA* 34: 4 (1981); CP ix.
'Le difficili vie dello sviluppo', interview given to F. Targetti, *RI* (6 June).
'Memorandum of Evidence on Monetary Policy' (17 July) (London, HMSO).
'The World Economic Outlook', paper given to the 6th World Congress of the International Economic Association, Mexico City, Aug.; pub. in *Human Resources, Employment and Development* (London, Macmillan, 1983).
'Problems of Energy Self Sufficient Countries', lecture given in Oaxaca, Mexico, Sept.
'Gemeinsamkeiten und Unterschiede in den Theorien von Keynes, Kalecki und Rüstow', lecture given in Starnberg, Bavaria, 16 Oct.; pub. in *IST* 29: 1 (1983).
'Keynes as an Economic Adviser', lecture given at Canterbury, Nov.; pub. in A. P. Thirlwall (ed.), *Keynes as a Policy Adviser* (London, Macmillan, 1982); It. trans., *PEE* 4 (1983).
'Monetarism and United Kingdom Monetary Policy', *CJE* (Dec.).
'Origins of the New Monetarism', Page Fund Lecture, Cardiff, 3 Dec.; (Cardiff, University College Cardiff Press, 1981); It. edn. ii; CP ix.
'What are the Threatening Economic Issues?', paper given to the *Financial Times* conference on 'European Banking', Amsterdam, Dec.
General Introduction to CP i (2nd edn.).
Introduction to CP vii.
Introduction to CP viii.
'I guasti del monetarismo', *MO* 12 (Dec.).
'The Economics of the Selective Employment Tax', memorandum to the NIESR; pub. in F. Shirras and L. Rostas (eds.), *The Burden of Taxation* (London, NIESR); CP vii; It. edn. ii.

1981

'Discussion of "Verdoorn's Law, the Externalities Hypothesis, Kaldor's Proposition and Economic Growth in the U. K." by M. Chatterji and M. Wickens', in D. Currie *et al.* (eds.), *Macroeconomic Analysis* (London, Croom Helm).
'A Keynesian Perspective on Money' (with J. Trevithick), *LLBR* 139 (Jan.); It. edn. ii; CP ix.
'Fallacies of Monetarism', lecture given in Basel, 16 Feb.; pub. in W. Ehrlicher and H.-J. Krümmel (eds.), *Kredit und Kapital* (Berlin, Dunker & Humboldt).
'Theoretische Grundlagen der europäischen Wohlfahrstaaten', paper given to the conference on 'Systemkrisen in Ost und West' at the Creditanstalt Bankverein of Vienna, 22–4 Apr.
'The Radcliffe Report in the Light of Subsequent Developments in Monetary Theory', two Radcliffe Lectures given at the University of Warwick, 18–19 May; repr. in

Scourge of Monetarism. CP ix.

'Inflation: An Endemic Problem of Modern Capitalism', lecture at the University of
Reykjavik, 8 June; pub. as *Verdbólgan—Prálát vandamál, nútíma efnahagslífs*
(Reykjavik, Isafoldarpentsmidja HF, 1982); and in *WG* 2.

'La dama di ferro: una frana—Mitterrand: un modello', *EL* (28 Nov. and 5 Dec.); repr.
in *Incontri* (Radiotelevisione della Svizzera italiana, 1982).

1982

The Scourge of Monetarism (Oxford, OUP); Fr. trans. with introd. (Paris, Economica,
1984); Jap. trans. with introd. (Tokyo) (Nihon Keizai Hyron Sha Ltd., 1984); It.
trans. with the same Fr. introd., *Il flagello del monetarismo* (Turin, Loescher, 1984).

'The Role of Devaluation in the Adjustment of Balance of Payment Deficit', UNCTAD
(Apr.).

'Limitations of the General Theory', Keynes Lecture in Economics, British Academy,
London, 12 May; pub. in *British Academy Acta*, 68 (1982).

'Economic Prospects of the '80s', lecture at the European University of Florence,
Fresole, 11 Sept.; pub. in *EN* (May).

'La rivoluzione keynesiana e i suoi limiti', *MO* (May).

'Conclusion of Today Discussion', lecture at the Centre d'Études Perspectives et
d'Informations Sociales, Paris, 17 May.

Inflation: An Endemic Problem of the Twentieth Century, lecture at the Johann Wolfgang Goethe University, Frankfurt, 23 June, on the occasion of receiving his honorary degree (Johann Wolfgang Goethe University, Frankfurt-on-Main).

Grenzen der 'General Theory', two Merton Lectures given at the Johann Wolfgang
Goethe University, Frankfurt, June (Berlin, Springer, 1983).

'A Plan for Securing Equilibrium in the Balance of Payments under a Policy of
Economic Expansion', report to the French Ministry of Budget (4 Oct.).

'The Role of Commodity Prices in Economic Recovery', lecture in Brussels, Nov.;
pub. in *LLBR* (July 1983) and in *World Development* (June–July 1987); CP ix; It.
trans. in *ENR* 3 (1984).

1983

The Economic Consequences of Mrs Thatcher (Fabian Tract, 486; Jan.; repr. London,
Duckworth).

Review of *The Collected Writings of John Maynard Keynes*, xxvii. *Activities 1940–
1946: Shaping the Post-War World: Employment and Commodities*, *EJ* (Mar.).

'Keynesianism in the '80s', lecture at the Creditanstalt Bankverein, Vienna, Apr.

'Devaluation and Adjustment in Developing Countries', report to the Group of 24,
IMF; pub. in *FeD* (June); CP ix.

'The End of the Keynesian Era', *G* (8 June).

'Keynesian Economics after Fifty Years', lecture at the Keynesian Centennial, Cambridge, July; pub. in D. Worswick and J. Trevithick (eds.), *Keynes and the Modern
World* (Cambridge, CUP, 1983); CP ix.

'Le occasioni mancate dell'economia inglese', *MO* (July–Aug.).

'The Role of Effective Demand in the Short Run and in the Long Run', lecture on
Keynes, Paris, Sept.; CP ix.

'The Futility of General Equilibrium Theory', lecture at Harvard University, 28 Oct., mimeo.

Economics without Equilibrium, three Okun Lectures given at Yale University, Nov. (Armonk, New York, M. E. Sharpe Inc., 1985); It. trans., *Economia senza equilibrio* (Bologna, Il Mulino, 1988).

'Obituary of Piero Sraffa', address at Trinity College, Cambridge, 19 Nov.; pub. in *CR* (July 1984).

'The Changing Situation of the World Economy: Possibilities and Limits of Adjustment', lecture, Rome, Nov.

1984

'The Failure of Monetarism', Chintaman Deshmukh Memorial Lecture, Reserve Bank of India, Bombay, 18 Jan.

'Causes of Growth and Stagnation of the World Economy', four Mattioli Lectures at the Università Bocconi of Milan, 21–5 May (forthcoming).

Paper at the conference 'Un intellettuale europeo del XX secolo: Piero Sraffa, 1898–1983', held at Istituto Gramsci, Turin, May; It. trans., 'Sraffa come critico della teoria economica', in R. Bellofiore (ed.), *Tra teoria economica e grande cultura europea: Piero Sraffa* (Milan, Franco Angeli, 1986).

'Joan Robinson Obituary', *KCAR* (July).

'An Exchange Rate Policy for India', *EPW* (14 July).

'Lessons of the Monetarist Experiment', lecture at the conference 'Monetary Eruditions for Economic Recovery', held at University of Amsterdam, 14–16 Nov.; pub. as 'How Monetarism Failed', *CH* (May–June 1985); repr. in C. Van Ewijk and J. J. Klant (eds.), *Monetary Conditions for Economic Recovery* (Dordrecht, Martinus Nijkoff Publishers); CP ix; It. edn. ii.

'I Tories nell'era Thatcher: da conservatori a reazionari', *PEE* (Dec.).

'Se il dollaro cade: L'economia della instabilità', Kaldor's intervention at a Round Table, pub. in *RI* (22 Dec.).

1985

Review of P. Sylos-Labini, *The Forces of Economic Growth and Decline*, *EJ* (Dec.).

'The Changing Situation of the World Economy: Possibilities and Limits of Adjustment', Cambridge, Mar., mimeo.

Paper given to the Symposium 'In Search of Ways to Eliminate Economic Frictions' for the 50th anniversary of the Asahi Shinbun, Nagoya, Japan, 19 May.

'Viaggio attraverso il mondo: 3. L'economia', interview given to F. Targetti for *MO* (Aug.).

'John von Neumann (1903–1957)', (Cambridge, July); pub. in CP ix.

'Piero Sraffa (1898–1983)', *Proceedings of British Academy*, 81 (1985); It. trans., *BNLMC* (Sept. 1986); CP ix.

'Advantages of EMS Membership', mimeo, (Cambridge).

'Limits on Growth', Hicks Lecture given in Oxford, 28 Nov.; pub. in *OEP* 38 (1986); CP ix.

1986

Ricordi di un economista, ed. M. C. Marcuzzo (Milan, Garzanti).

'Recollections of an Economist', *BNLQR* (Mar.); It. trans., 'Reminiscenze di un economista', *BNLMC* (June), repr. in *Il mestiere di economista* (Turin, Einaudi, 1988); CP ix.

'The Impact of Import Restrictions in the Interwar Period', (with M. Kitson), mimeo (Cambridge, June).

'The Rise and Decline of Monetarism', (Labour Institute for Economic Research, Discussion Paper, 46; Helsinke).

Speeches to the House of Lords

Debate on the Address, 25 Nov. 1976.

The Economic Situation, 20 July. 1977.

Debate on North Sea Oil, 22 May 1978.

Debate on the Economic Situation, 2 Nov. 1978.

Industrial Recovery, 17 Jan. 1979.

Economic and Social Policies: Industrial Strategy, 13 June 1979.

Debate on the Budget, 19 June 1979.

Debate on the Oil Crisis, 4 July 1979.

Economic Policy, 11 July 1979.

Debate on the Government's Policies, 7 Nov. 1979.

Inflation and Employment: Policies, 4 Dec. 1979.

Gas and Electricity Price Increase, 30 Jan. 1980.

Economic Policy, 13 Feb. 1980.

Domestic Economic Strategy, 16 Apr. 1980.

BSC: Appointment of Chairman, 14 May 1980.

Employment Bill: Second Reading Debate, 20 May 1980.

Monetary Policy, 11 June 1980.

Employment Bill: Third Reading Debate, 14 July 1980.

Debate on the Address: Economic Affairs, 27 Nov. 1980.

Industry: The Public Sector, 4 Feb. 1981.

Motion: Unemployment, 4 Mar. 1981.

Debate on Cuts in Education, 18 Mar. 1981.

Debate on Defence, 21 July 1981.

Debate on the Address, 12 Nov. 1981.

The Arms Race and the Economy, 16 Dec. 1981.

European Monetary System, 27 Jan. 1982.

The Economic Situation and National Recovery, 3 Feb. 1982.

Unemployment and Industrial Recovery, 17 Mar. 1982.

Debate on the Address, 10 Nov. 1982.

Causes of Unemployment, 16 Nov. 1982.

The ECC Internal Market, 13 Dec. 1982.

The Policy on Deterrence, 16 Feb. 1983.

World Economy and Currency Stability, 23 Mar. 1983.

Oil and the Decline of Manufacturing, 29 June 1983.

Comment on ACARD/ABRC Report (decline of industry), 10 Feb. 1984.

Debate on Redeployment of Resources, 22 Feb. 1984.

Future Financing of the Community, 15 Mar. 1984.

Unemployment, 9 May 1984.

Policies for Employment, 13 Nov. 1984.
Causes of Unemployment, 12 Dec. 1984.
Social and Economic Policies, 23 Jan. 1985.
Government Policy and New Technology, 14 Nov. 1985.
Overseas Trade: Select Committee Report, 3 Dec. 1985.
Economic Situation, 19 Feb. 1986.

Author Index

Subject Index

CRISES, DE-INDUSTRIALIZATION, AND STAGNATION

DATE DUE

			Printed in USA